BODIES AND BIASES

Hispanic Issues

HISPANIC ISSUES
VOLUME 13

BODIES AND BIASES

SEXUALITIES IN HISPANIC CULTURES AND LITERATURE

DAVID WILLIAM FOSTER AND ROBERTO REIS

◆

EDITORS

UNIVERSITY OF MINNESOTA PRESS
MINNEAPOLIS   LONDON

Published by the University of Minnesota Press
111 Third Avenue South, Suite 290, Minneapolis, MN 55401-2520
Printed in the United States of America on acid-free paper

Library of Congress Cataloging-in-Publication Data

Bodies and biases : sexualities in Hispanic cultures and literatures /
    David William Foster and Roberto Reis, editors.
        p.   cm. — (Hispanic issues ; v. 13)
    Includes bibliographical references and index.
    ISBN 0-8166-2770-3 (hc.) — ISBN 0-8166-2771-1 (pbk.)
    1. Latin American literature—History and criticism.   2. Spanish
literature—History and criticism.   3. Literature and society—Latin
America.   4. Literature and society—Spain.   5. Sex in literature.
I. Foster, David William.   II. Reis, Roberto.   III. Series: Hispanic
issues ; 13.
PQ7081.A1B63   1996
860.9'3538—dc20   95-48961

The University of Minnesota is an equal-opportunity educator and employer.

Contents

Esto no es una despedida

Jenaro Talens

Querido Roberto:

La noticia de tu muerte me ha sorprendido en esta fría mañana de diciembre. Nick, el bueno de Nick, no sabía cómo decírmelo. La muerte es tan absurda y quedaban tantas cosas por hacer... Me pidió que pergeñara unas palabras para tu funeral y he decidido enviarte esta carta. Al salir de Minneapolis hace un mes prometí escribirte. Perdóname por hacerlo demasiado tarde.

Cuando te conocí, lo que más me sorprendió fue tu talante campechano y el trato antiengolado, algo que hasta entonces había percibido pocas veces en el mundo académico. Me pareciste alguien con la lucidez suficiente para estar poseído por la pasión de la inteligencia y la escritura, pero demasiado escéptico como para creerte los afeites que acompañan a la función pública del intelectual. En una tradición latina, donde abunda la soberbia y la vanidad, me desconcertó que alguien se negara a asumir el papel del maestro y representara con la mayor naturalidad el único papel que, de verdad, nos corresponde: el de eterno aprendiz. Esa sensación de respeto al pensamiento del otro y tu carácter dialogante no ocultaban la solidez de tus convicciones ni la capacidad de mantenerlas donde fuera menester, pero me dieron la sensación de que, en el trato con tus colegas y con tus estudiantes, la diferencia de lengua, de edad y de sabiduría no eran un obstáculo, sino un puente para el entendimiento.

Me gustaba tu rigor, la ilusión con que hablabas de tus proyectos y de tu trabajo, el orgullo mal disimulado con que te referías a tus hijos, y sobre todo, tu amor por la vida, esa lenta pasión que no termina. Dicen que la música amansa a las fieras. Nunca he podido escribir sin oir música y en los meses y los años que compartimos en Folwell Hall me apetecía acercarme a tu despacho para escuchar siquiera fuese por unos momentos la sonata de Bach o la pieza de Villalobos que en ese momento inundara la habitación. Nunca te lo dije, pero me reconocía en una idéntica necesidad de aplacar la angustia de la página en blanco. Para algunos, la literatura es un oficio; para otros es algo más doloroso: es nuestra forma de estar solos. Me ilusiona pensar que fueron esas pequeñas cosas no dichas, pero percibidas en la materialidad de la piel, las que tejieron una amistad que la muerte no tenía derecho de interrumpir.

Hay dos formas de entender la muerte. Una es la muerte propia, la de la persona (a máscara) que vamos creando día a día con nuestros actos, nuestros aciertos y nuestros errores. Nadie puede morir esa muerte ajena que testimonia nuestra irreductible soledad. La otra muerte no es propia: es la manera que la naturaleza tiene de estar viva. La muerte de cada uno es el reflejo del nacimiento de los otros. Es difícil convivir con cualquiera de las dos. Sin embargo, en esta fría mañana de diciembre, prefiero entender la tuya en su segunda posibilidad. No hay más eternidad que memoria de los otros. Hoy te ofrezco la mía, en testimonio de amistad.

Desde mi ventana veo al cielo azul. Sé que no es cielo ni es azul, pero ayuda a soportar el dolor de sabernos frágiles e indefensos.

Até sempre, Roberto; foi um grande prazer te conhecer.

◆ Acknowledgments

We wish to express our gratitude to Nicholas Spadaccini for his exemplary support to this project, and to Naomi Lindstrom, for her collaboration.

◆ Introduction

The Age of Suspicion: Mapping Sexualities in Hispanic Literary and Cultural Texts

Dário Borim Jr. and Roberto Reis

According to *Webster's New World Dictionary,* the word *introduction,* in strict usage, refers to the preliminary section of a book (often written by someone other than the author) that explains and leads into the subject proper. *Intro* derives from *intero,* which, akin to *inter,* denotes "inwardly." *Duce,* coming from *ducere,* implies "to lead," which, not surprisingly, will later become *duke* or *prince,* one who rules an independent duchy. Bearing in mind the etymology of the two terms that compose the word *introduction* itself, we suspect it is not exactly our role to introduce *Bodies and Biases: Sexualities in Hispanic Cultures and Literatures.* We wish not to lead the readers into the complexities of the following essays, but rather to present a speculative panorama that ideally would show how the studies may very well catch the reader's interest. Our hope is thus to draw a horizon of expectations (to use an optical metaphor, without boundaries) in terms of which or against which readers will find their own paths and their own destinations.

We shall begin by asking what is, after all, sexuality? Can we actually say confidently? What seems to be clear is that people have been trying to describe it. It is even likely that people of all races and times have thought about sexual behaviors and attempted to explain them, writes William DuBay, but it was left to nearly our own age to contrive a scientific explanation (30). Maybe a major step took place when the rise of the modern nation-state required new codes of law extending the power of the state into the realm of families and private lives of its citizens: "A whole new definition of sex and the family was forming, one that would support the industrial and military ambitions of the new rulers" (DuBay 6). It has likewise been believed that the emergence of the bourgeois and Christian notion of family in the Western cultures in the modern era confined sexuality to the goal of procreation. All other possible forms of sex would be proscribed as anomalies, an understanding that directed the scientific discussions on the issue to take place within the fields of medicine and psychology (and, later, psychoanalysis).

It is hard to contest the proposition that the move toward building the nation-state entailed the move toward the exclusion of behaviors potentially counterproductive to the execution of the national project. We may echo Peter Fry when he writes that the majority of individuals desire what is socially desirable (11). We desire what is socially desirable because our desire, to a large extent, is also molded by cultural and social constraints. In other words, we may say that the "authoritarian" discourse introduced by modernity intervenes in our desires and sexualities. In this regard, it is worth quoting Nelly Richards's synthesis:

> It is well known that modernity (historical, philosophical, political, economic and cultural) generates its principles from a threefold wish for unity. The enlightenment ideals on which it is founded define modernity in terms of rationalization, as an "advance" in cognitive and instrumental reason. This produces particular categories and systems through which historical development and social evolution are conceptualized, based on the notion of progress as the guideline of a universalist project. It also assumes the objective consciousness of an absolute meta-subject. The principles of modernity generate specific representations of society by means of bureaucratic and technological networks which incorporate institutional practises into an overall scheme. The spread of a "civilizing" modernity is linked to a model of industrial progress and in this way it is part and parcel of the expansion of

multinational capitalism and its control of economic exchanges. (6)

According to Richards, this threefold foundation of modernity's universalism shows a link between the totalizing tendencies of a hegemonic culture and the process of producing and reproducing consensus around the models of truth and consumption that modernity proposes. This concept of modernity, the author adds, "represents an effort to synthesize its progressive and emancipatory ideals into a globalizing, integrative vision of the individual's place in history and society." In other words, it rests "on the assumption that there exists a legitimate centre—a unique and superior position from which to establish control and to determine hierarchies" (6).

Richards goes further by saying that, traditionally, that unique and superior position has been the privilege of Western patriarchal culture, "whose representational apparatus has been the source of those homogenizing categories which apply to both language and identity" (6). His conclusion is that what we are calling the "authoritarian discourse of modernity" (for the sake of summarizing a discussion that would take this "introduction" too far) suppresses any notion of "difference" that might challenge the dominant model of subjectivity. All the extensions of the idea of modernity work toward confirming the position of privilege, and to this end they negate any particular or localized expression that could possibly interfere with the fiction of universality (6).

We may then write that such "authoritarian" discourse tends to hinder the emergence of difference and to repress sexual practices that go against what has been established as the "norm" or the "rule." The movement toward the building of the nation-state generates a complex spectrum of disciplinary forces that are designed to silence any dissidence and to reinforce the universalist and homogenizing project, particularly undertaken within Western cultures—madness was therefore confined to hospitals, homosexuality considered a disease or a sin, Blacks and Indians viewed as inferior primitives, women exclusively assigned to housekeeping and childcare. Michel Foucault, therefore, contends that discourses function as disciplinary forces in the social realm, and sexuality, undoubtedly, is one of these discourses. He isolates, in this respect, a very meaningful shift in the Western policing of sex that took place in the eighteenth century: such policing became much less determined by the rigor of a taboo than by "the necessity of regulating sex through useful and public discourses" (25).

Aware of the problematic origins of this "public" concept of sexuality, the basics of which still ring true in several cultural enclaves (such as traditional religions), we should, perhaps, refrain from taking heterosexuality as the only natural and normal sexual behavior; or procreation as the primary consequence of sexuality. An important sign of our times is certainly the recognition that a variety of sexual preferences are legitimate and that sexual pleasure is indeed an important component in humans' self-fulfillment.

Furthermore, we are beginning to apprehend sexuality according to socially, historically, and culturally constructed categories, at a time when the commercial circuit of arts and entertainment bombards society with sex and fitness images. Surrounded by notions of ideal looks and ideal practitioners,

> we have arrived at the point where we expect our intelligibility to come from what was for many centuries thought of as madness; the plenitude of our body from what was long considered its stigma and likened to a wound; our identity from what was perceived as an obscure and nameless urge. Hence the importance we ascribe to it, the reverential fear with which we surround it, the care we take to know it. Hence the fact that for centuries it has become more important than our soul, more important almost than our life; and so it is that all the world's enigmas appear frivolous to us compared to this secret, minuscule in each of us, but of a density that makes it more serious than any other. (Foucault 156)

Foucault is clearly speaking of a discourse that claims "the truth and sovereignty of sex," something so important to one's sense of self that it seems worth dying for. Sexuality as an enticing narrative that oppresses rather than liberates (with nearly unlimited impact on individuals) causes him to realize that "by saying yes to sex one does not say no to power" (157).

This is not the entire picture, however. Another compelling force tugs individuals further away from a plausibly or elusively comfortable sense of sexual identity: the fear of AIDS. Some of

Herbert Daniel's and Richard G. Parker's studies address that which has been called "the third epidemic," the stage of AIDS history in which fear, ignorance, and other social ailments threaten to be more devastating than the virus itself. Daniel urges us to watch out for the ideological manipulation of medical facts and knowledge, for example, which breeds panic and prejudice mainly against homosexualities. He argues that, ironically, "those who feed the fire of panic are willing to do away with Evil, and for that reason they appreciate AIDS, which, according to them, substantiates Goodness" (AIDS 120).

Paradoxically, we should also point out that not all messages taken as counterdiscourses on sexuality are necessarily "revolutionary" per se. A discourse that sounds "perverted" at first glance may end up being a conservative one. Gustavo Barbosa, in a study on restroom graffiti, reminds us that, in the Brazilian context, the lexicon of sexuality is linked to notions of power: often the penis is tied to force, power, prestige, pleasure (115) and associated with pistols and other guns. The bathroom being a "marginal" place in which manifestations forbidden in other settings are permitted, we might expect to find on its walls a liberating discourse. Nevertheless, we are confronted with prejudices against sex, defecation, and all social aspects of the human body. The corpus that Barbosa analyzed presents the stigmatization of the sexual "passive" (woman or homosexual), the phallocratic praise of manhood, the linkages woman/feeling and man/power/reason, the taboos of incest and virginity, racism, and social inequalities (194).

Indeed, the very fact that we speak about sexuality does not place us on the verge of subverting the disciplinary power of an "authoritarian" discourse. Daniel calls our attention to the notion that part of the oppression of gays has to do with instilling in them a belief that they are "something special," a type of human being predestined to be marginal. One of his contentions addresses the language of intimate extortion through which people expect to make gays and lesbians come out, "confess," or "bear witness" (*Jacarés* 26).

We may contend that sexuality, in regard to power, is now among other fascinating targets in the age of suspicion. Tying sexuality to microstructures of power and oppression, Foucault charges that "it is in discourse that power and knowledge are joined together" (100). He then suggests posing many questions, such as the following, if we wish to understand sexual discourses:

> In a specific type of discourse on sex, in a specific form of extortion of truth, appearing historically and in specific places (around the child's body, apropos of women's sex, in connection with practices restricting births, and so on), what were the most immediate, the most local power relations at work? How did they make possible these kinds of discourses, and conversely, how were these discourses used to support power relations? (97)

Postmodern times indeed spread skepticism upon all "great narratives" that attempt to impose the truth as a dominant and authoritarian force. The notion of wholesome and unitarian selfhood is one such narrative. Sexuality, indeed, seems to contribute far less to selfhood than what tradition and/or scientific knowledge has made the average individual believe. Several authors have developed remarkable insight on this issue. The self exists "as an arbitrary cultural fact," not a "delusion," Candace Lang explains (9), and "because language is molded by the politics and ideology of a community, it influences — in turn — the way a given community comes to think of the world," charges Françoise Lionnet (12). The images people build of themselves as sexual men or women actually have more to do with their perception of pleasure, desire, and propriety than with inflexible identity. This concept seems to follow Sidonie Smith's realization regarding the fictions of an autobiographer, which are "always mediated by a historic identity with specific intentions, if not pretensions, of interpreting the meaning of one's experience" (46). The self, therefore, can be taken as a construct undergoing continuous mutation both symbolically (through our understanding) and empirically (through all human deeds).

Today's new awareness urges individuals to come to grips with the understanding that they are much more than sexual beings, and the sexual beings they imagine themselves to be are far less deterministic and irrevocable constructs. Our selves would simply not exist in isolation, since (such) awareness appears to be mysteriously dialogic, the result of a dialogue constantly running between our perceived selves and the voices that, in our minds, seem to speak in the name of the Other, in the outer world, or of society (or power arena), where people imagine and press to be themselves in sexual terms. In our age we also have become more aware about issues of representation and interpretation: there appears to be no reason to enthrone the alphabet as a parameter to evaluate a culture's level of sophistication, or to draw world maps with the West in the center, or to think of mathematics as a universal language and the white and civilized Aryan as the ultimate masterpiece of the human race. Reason and rationality are receiving checkmates; ethnocentrism, logocentrism, phallocentrism, eurocentrism, liberalism, and humanism are likewise under siege. The same could be said about sexuality: feminism, the lesbian/gay movements, and the sexual revolution of the past decades, in general, have questioned the primacy and superiority of heterosexuality.

We hope that our discussion thus far has sufficiently implied that there are undebatable links between issues of sexuality and other cultural and ideological values. We now would like to elaborate on this premise while suggesting how certain ideological values are often expressed by certain types of discourse and texts, as well as why sexuality is an alluring and key element in the postmodern and poststructuralist 1990s.

The literary canon comes immediately to mind, since literature, as Terry Eagleton and many other authors have pointed out, has been closely attached to power. The works of literature that praise the mainstream values of the white male and Western civilization are the ones that often constitute the canon studied in academia or reviewed by literary newspaper sections. They are also the ones cited elsewhere as the pinnacles of human excellence and artistic achievement.

Perhaps Sigmund Freud was one of the first contributors to the scrutiny of texts from a sexual perspective. Yet, Freudian criticism (or even Jungian approaches) has fallen into the traps of symbolism. To put it roughly, everything could be read as the unconscious: the vagina, a repressed trauma, or a neurosis from early childhood. Because of these limitations, possible sexual approaches to literature are not exhausted at all. Fredric Jameson usefully explains that subjective or psychological phenomena are now increasingly seen as having epistemological and even practical functions. Fantasy is no longer felt to be a private and compensatory reaction against public situations, but rather "a way of reading those situations, of thinking and mapping them, of intervening in them, albeit in a very different form from the abstract reflections of traditional philosophy or politics" (171).

One of the alternative approaches to literature may be inferred by two of the words that name this volume: *sexualities* (the term is in plural form for a reason) and *Hispanic*[1] (no matter how debatable the category is). In other words, sexual issues and an imagined community[2] as intertwined, overlapped, parallel, complementary, or antagonistic constructs are certainly inquiries worth pursuing. Along these lines, and in light of our previous points on selfhood, we contend that some of the important reasons for the study of sexuality in cultural discourses have to do with the possibility of increasing awareness about the interplay between sexual behavior and collective identity, such as gender and ethnicity. Seldom a game of isolated pleasure (as suggested by Foucault), sexuality becomes, on the personal level, a relational category inseparable from self-esteem and self-indulgence, pride and power. As a collective phenomenon, sexuality can hardly be ignored as an integral component in the separation of individuals into imagined communities of gender and ethnicity. The way, for instance, in which people speak/write about the sexuality of other people may say more about the individuals communicating than about their subject. In this respect, the narratives of today and bygone years are bound to expose not only an author's view on specific sociohistorical features of sexual assumptions, but also the collective and often galvanized values of a human group regarding sexual issues.

While examining some of the purposes to which sexuality has been incorporated in speech and symbolic representations, we can easily pinpoint five possible (and somewhat distinct) modes. The first mode of representation concerns surviving religious voices that claim that sex is meant solely for procreation. Deriving from that understanding is the second mode, by which certain dominant groups use sexuality to disseminate racist ideals, like the whitening of society. Whether it runs consciously or unconsciously, the third mode is individual self-assertion and political propaganda. This is the case in some forms of gay activism, for instance, that glorify the gay lifestyle as the ultimate expression of openmindness. They may bash macho men in some meaningful ways but do very little for collective awareness of social injustice beyond some specific gay dilemma. Class and race prejudices are sometimes overwhelming in such discourses.[3]

A fourth potential discursive use of sexuality has to do with the advocacy of guiltfree pleasure in and of itself. Taking it as a biological necessity like the eating or sleeping of every human being, some gay writers — Herbert Daniel (1946–1992), Leila Míccolis, Manuel Puig (1932–1990) — are both critical of the ideology that locks homosexuals in a special category (with special rights and powers), and supportive of sexual freedom for all individuals. Rather than push for uniformity of opinion, they urge society as a whole, including the liberated gay community, to examine its own skeletons in the closet. The fifth mode of representation deals with some of the most recurrent interpersonal dynamics associated with sexuality: dominance and aggression. Adopting a version of male-centered ideology, sociologist Gilberto Freyre (1900–1987), for instance, blames a slave woman for her alleged African lasciviousness and not the white master who rapes her. Another version grants men, but denies women, the right to premarital sex and adultery.

When it comes to cultural manifestations, the debate over the role of sexuality should benefit from a cross-temporal approach. Take the almost commonplace case of sexist and ethnocentric contours of literature produced before the rise of feminist consciousness, which, in certain parts of the world, took place a little less than one hundred years ago, and, in others, is a phenomenon that has yet to occur. On the other hand, if the categories of gender and ethnicity are presently being questioned (or at least redefined by contemporary discourse), there has also been a backlash, the growing tendency to underscore (mis)conceptions of maleness and femaleness, or us and them, that resist the passing of the millennia.

Given the universality of such considerations, the study of Hispanic cultural discourses has obviously much to gain from investigating the issue of sexuality as a discursive category in the broadest sense (including pop culture, the media, and so on). As we continue our travel through time, we may encounter, for instance, the nineteenth-century emphasis on sexual conquest as a literary metaphor for nation building in Brazil, Peru, or Argentina.

Likewise, one may be stunned by the pervasive appeal to sexy women on television footage made in Mexico, Brazil, or Hispanic United States. There might be more elements in common among such cultural manifestations than we Latin Americans, Hispanics, or Latinos are ready to accept.

By the same token, the oral tradition of androcentric Amerindian cultures,[4] as well as the dreams and testimonials shared by the European colonizers in regard to lesbians and gay men residing in the Caribbean Gardens of Eden, may have had a bearing on the astronomical distance gays have to go before achieving full rights to citizenship. By examining the intricacies between sex and race in such various cultural manifestations, one is likely to discover images that are not very clear at first glance. As diverse and/or mestizo peoples, we differentiate and, not very subtly, establish the hierarchies of gender and race, while shaping our wildest sexual imaginations.

Furthermore, Hispanic cultures are generally considered to be male centered, *machista,* and patriarchal. Myths like the sensual Latin lover, the seductive tropics, and Mediterranean glamour (Rudolph Valentino and Carmen Miranda come to mind), from which the sensuality of the Brazilian carnival or flamenco dancing derive, are still very present in our everyday lives, cultivated all over the world by Hollywood and the tourism industry. Within this framework, it is worth emphasizing the pertinence of this volume for a broader understanding of Hispanic cultures.

Throughout this volume sexuality is understood in a broad sense that may include some of its corollaries, as in its appropriation by the cultural industry or family relations. Nevertheless, a representative sample of forms of sexuality is portrayed in the essays to follow: heterosexuality, homoeroticism, lesbianism, pornography. Most, if not all, of the essays discuss gender issues and different representations of sexuality *stricto sensu* in cultural artifacts. Regarding the authorship of the seventeen essays in *Bodies and Biases,* eleven are signed by men and six by women (as well as the afterword). Roughly speaking, the volume is organized by thematic affinities: transgression, social/gender relations, homoeroticism, lesbianism, pornography, and representations of sexuality.

Perhaps some of the most meaningful contributions from this collection are related to the critique of various forms of counter-discourse that challenges problematic dynamics between sexuality and power through different eras, places, and modes of representation. Apart from brief digressions retrieving historical processes present in nearly all seventeen essays, the greatest emphasis is on twentieth-century works, followed by those on literature from the nineteenth century, and others on works from the seventeenth and the eighteenth centuries. While a few texts combine nineteenth- and twentieth-century issues (Geirola, Reis), Borim's text is the only one devoted to a panorama of approximately five centuries (1492 to present). Geographically, Borim's scope is again divergent from the others: he aims at tying the Americas to the Iberian Peninsula, while the other essays deal with issues within single national boundaries. The countries featured are Spain (six essays), Mexico and Brazil (three each), Cuba and Argentina (three each), and Colombia (one).

The preference for a multigenre approach is overwhelming (fifteen), the only exceptions being Maydeu's essay on the theater alone and Gossy's on the novel. Methodologically, some essays depart from a general hypothesis and, from there, focus on particular texts while elaborating on the questions raised by the discussion therein. These contributions tend to deal with "long duration structures." They inscribe themselves in the field of cultural studies, and their goal is to describe, primarily, discursive patterns. One may say that the inconvenience of such an approach is that the argument may fall into dangerous generalizations. Nonetheless, it has the advantage of delineating a framework, a discursive horizon from which the particular cases can be scrutinized in depth.

Other contributions seem to adopt an opposite posture: starting from a case study, they carefully risk one or two hypotheses that encompass a broader corpus. Exploring texts in their singularity, they suggest that what is said about the cases in question may apply to other texts. Finally, there are essays in this volume that, grounded on issues of sexuality, privilege an isolated text or author, suggesting their (overdue) inscription into the current debate or shedding new light on canonical works. Another overall comment is that some studies are interested in cultural discourses, whereas others are more specifically concerned with literature. In the latter case, they have a historical focus, or they offer a fresh interpretation of a particular work, or they attempt to question the canonization process.

Nevertheless, our previous remarks are not meant to conceal a relative homogeneity of methodological approach. While all essays adopt multiple analytic stances, a quarter of them deal with semiotic, stylistic, or aesthetic traits, plus linguistic or anthropological inquiries. A great number of studies also regard cultural and ethnic issues at large, and establish a dialogue with literary historians and other critics. And if other studies approach philosophical, psychological, or economic interpretations, nearly all texts regard sexual symbolism in relation to gender issues, sociopolitics, and ideologies, which is certainly the prevailing feature of the collection. We must add that an important contribution of this volume is to be found in the theorization of both textual poetics and poetics of readership linked to sexuality and its corollaries.

We may unfold another rich perspective on this selection by cross-examining the topics or subtopics the various essayists have associated with issues of sexualities. They undoubtedly intersect one another and most often revolve around two thematic poles: gender identity, a concern of every essay, and homosexuality, at work in practically all analyses. The thematic veins that make up both overriding topics are so numerous that the limited scope of this introduction does not allow for a thorough listing. Yet, they seem to be so meaningful to any attempts at rewriting, and so provocative to the urge of changing the course of traditional literary historiography and cultural critique, that we have decided to highlight a somewhat representative sample of them.

Epps, for a start, elaborates on an unprecedented discussion of the AIDS metaphors. While addressing Carlos Fuentes's and José Ortega's critique of Goytisolo, he denounces the textual inscription of the disease as a troubling site for academic inquiry, especially among Hispanists. The "revision of literary tradition is inseparable from the vision of homosexual pleasure and pain," Epps contends. Such a vision is dangerous, "indeed dangerously double-edged, because even as it confronts them with the immorality of homophobia, it comes close to reifying this desire as dangerous in and of itself."

More light on blind reading comes from Geirola, who invites the public to reconsider the critical denial of homoeroticism in José Hernández, "a symbol of [Argentine] national affirmation and machismo." The "fundamental paradox of *Martín Fierro*" lies in the fact that the choice of the homoerotic object, as an instance of narcissism, has as its source the aggressiveness derived by this same specular construct: sexual discrimination, machismo, racism, and xenophobia have as a given and a cause not the difference of the Other, but his sameness, his similarity.

Chichester provides a third indictment of critical neglect toward pieces that address homosexuality. Examining the vanguard contours of his writing, she argues that Virgilio Piñera's poetry speaks of his suffering because of the official persecution of gays under Fidel Castro. It is implied how this fact may be related to Piñera's absence in traditional criticism. By addressing the author's life story, Chichester contributes to the circulation of much less revolutionary aspects of Cuban social history. After being incarcerated in 1961, when the Castro police targeted the three P's—prostitutes, pimps, and pederasts (i.e., homosexuals)—Piñera never recuperated from the fear, shame, and depression instilled in him by homophobia. Chichester also investigates his fictional use of grotesque imagery to represent bodily functions of the homosexual desire repressed throughout an individual's life. His desire becomes "the degrading illness that will eventually consume him."

The transgressive contribution of Bermúdez and Foster is to look into pornographic material, which places them at the forefront of contemporary cultural critique. The breakthrough, however, is not a mere question of subject matter, but, most importantly, a question of perspective. Their focus opens critical ground toward investigating sexuality without preconceived notions. Basically, one of these previous notions comes from a religious standpoint that faces pornography as something plainly "dirty"; and the other, from a certain trend of feminism, which faces pornography as debasing to women's condition.

Both authors contradict these established readings of pornography by emphasizing its fantasy component (Bermúdez) or the possibility of seeing it as a kind of "erotic revisionism" (Foster). In this sense, we may say that in their contributions, pornography assumes the status of a counterideological discourse that explores the possibilities of human (sexual and cultural) transgression.

Bermúdez points out how *Las edades de Lulú*, by Almudena Grandes, "expands and liberates the geographies of both 'women's literature' and 'women's sexuality' from any closed stereotypical representations assigned to them." The critic captures the taboo-breaking nature of sexual fantasies in cinematographic form within the novel, thus allowing her to question and reevaluate a priori notions of 'good' and 'bad' in terms of sexual pleasures for women. Thus, her analysis renders a paradigm that "blurs the already complex and unresolved boundaries of the pornographic and the erotic."

This questioning is also a major concern in Foster's essay. Focusing on pornography as a narrative production, Foster puts the emphasis on "an erotic imagination that reterritorializes the body in order to escape the genital privileging of patriarchal sexuality." This is exactly the first of two points that signal feminist consciousness in Alicia Steimberg's novel. The second is the displacement of the Other's body via the "recodification of masturbation." In this post-AIDS era, masturbation becomes a component of sexual pleasure, redefined as a legitimate practice among sexual partners, instead of being conceived as "unmanly" and substitutive. It is in the "writerly nature" of Hilda Hilst's texts, however, that Foster finds the most complex depictions of erotic revisionism in Latin America. According to Foster, Hilst's texts, through the humorous and the grotesque,

> undermine the profound meanings attached to the sexual
> by most of the Judeo-Christian tradition (not to mention
> others), and in this sense they resound of the post-modernist
> repudiation of depth psychology and master narratives.

Charnon-Deutsch's contribution endorses a more traditional (without any pejorative connotation on our part) understanding of the topic. In an implied dialogue with the editors of the *Sem* collection (eighty-nine watercolors signed by the Bécquer brothers), the critic argues that the watercolors fit into several quoted definitions of pornography. The Bécquer watercolors were a political commentary as much as a "handy pretext for producing and enjoying pornography." Charnon-Deutsch claims for pornography not its force as a possibility, but its connections with power; pornography is treated as symbolic violence, in which "sexual and political dimensions intersect in meaningful ways."

Strictly discussing lesbianism, Gossy's article attempts to theorize butch-femme readership and poetics, as well as to assess the symbolic and psychological character of lesbian sexuality at large. Cristina Peri-Rossi's *Solitario de amor* is not, at first sight, an explicitly lesbian novel, since the narrator applies masculine gender-marked deictics. Despite these textual features, the critic raises the suspicion that the narrative entails a lesbian representation and allows for a lesbian reading. Gossy states that the passion between the protagonists could be seen as basically lesbian. Besides, behind this apparently nonlesbian voice lies a lesbian subject. The essay then describes the process of decodification of this narrative structure, from buying the book up to the *jouissance* of reading, as encompassed by the "psychic space" of her "desiring reading." Gossy mentions a personal interview with the novelist in which the latter confesses her identification with the narrator and the autobiographical character of her work. This is an important element in Gossy's proposed reading strategy, inasmuch as

> the knowledge that the author is a man or a woman, straight or gay *does* change things for the lesbian reader, as it does in other contexts for other readers who find themselves oppressed and excluded from dominant discourses of race, class, or sex.

The trouble behind the rejection of gender and sexual identities is at stake in Brant, who investigates Denevi's novel *Rosaura a las diez*. Somewhat like Chichester's reading of fear and self-destruction that split one's personality, Brant studies the story of a gay man who constructs his own closet and lives a life of depression and dishonesty. To Brant, it serves to denounce society's brutal power to instill shame, as well as the enormous risk of self-destruction involved in marriage as a cover-up for unassumed homosexuality.

Ter Horst's focus shifts direction away from the negative by aiming at liberating possibilities, presenting an argument in favor of Cervantes's pursuit of gender equality in *Don Quixote*. Ter Horst compares Cervantes to Garcilaso in order to suggest that Garcilaso constructed an Amazonian reversal of gender just to make woman eroticize a heterosexual relation before going back to a position of submission to another of "unwilling subjection" and "voluntary degradation." On the other hand, desire in Cervantes's fiction (like nowhere else in the Golden Age) is the desire for equality. "Instead of a masculine religion of oppression, Cervantes appears to offer a new faith, clothed in the vestments of the old, of sexual equality, a new prose for an outworn poetics of dominance and submission."

Reis's study also verges on both the authoritarian and complex mechanisms of gender fabrication, even though his object of inquiry is not limited to literary discourse: it ranges from mass culture magazines, to architecture, to high literature. He underscores the need to understand gender, class, and racial systems by examining symbolic objects and discourses seldom considered as cultural products. In this sense, the critic is eager to suggest an unconscious gap between social behavior and cultural representation, especially those cultural products that attempt to bestow upon Brazil/Brazilians an image of modernization/progressiveness. Comparing and contrasting contemporary mass culture magazines, he observes that some discourses on sexuality, "which often try to show off a post-sexual revolution profile, are full of traditional and reactionary elements. The modernization of social habits is, subsequently, nothing but a façade hiding a nonprogressive society still stigmatized by its slave-dependent and patriarchal past."

The world of television and culture for mass consumption becomes, indeed, one of the issues between two of few dissenting voices in this collection. Whereas Oropesa equates television-dominated popular culture, culture of the people, and democratic culture, and defends populism as a form of democracy in Mexico, Schaefer is highly suspicious of the country's official effort to create and exhibit a holistic conception of national unity made incomplete by institutionalized modernity. Schaefer is concerned with television shows and other displays of Mexican modernity that mask the countryside and the misery behind the many-splendored transition to democracy. Oropesa, in turn, argues that

Mexican television as an industry "has become a model to be followed by other economic sectors of the nation."

If Schaefer seems disturbed by the discourse of democratic pluralism, since it runs parallel to the passing of strict legislation on the broad category of "delitos sexuales," Oropesa apparently believes Mexico is going on the right track with its soaps either telling about society's need to assimilate new realities (like women's new roles already "lived by a sector of Mexican women"), or "making livable periods of crisis, like Francoism or Cardenism to provide cosmopolitan models or tell truths." To Oropesa, the equalization of men and women, an "important feminist issue," is achieved, for instance, by portrayals of taboos (such as homosexuality), of women acquiring violent social habits (like sadistic pleasure), and of male politicians both in the public realm, where they exert power, and in the domestic sphere, where they are seen making love or doing less inspiring deeds, like "farting."

If to Oropesa Mexico's "democratic literature" is rewriting texts developed by television inasmuch as it mixes high culture and popular culture and continues "as an original and dissenting rupture of conservative morality," Schaefer equates such modernity with "cultural voyeurism," or the Americanization of Mexican society. For her, recent bestsellers, such as *Como agua para chocolate* (Like Water for Chocolate; 1989) and *Dos mujeres* (Two Mujeres; 1990), are "suffused with a strong sense of the media and its gendered images." Exploring the theme of homosexuality, such books, especially *Arráncame la vida* (Mexican Bolero; 1985), to which Oropesa dedicates much of his essay, are "part of a small dose of progressiveness to build up a capacity of resistance." Again the contrast in point of view is astounding, since Oropesa affirms that *Mexican Bolero* "is bourgeois literature that is proud of this adjective." The novel, after all, "sells well," and, as a "high quality Mexican product," it enacts the rediscovery of good parts of capitalism."

Schaefer, on the other hand, utilizes a metaphor of illness prevention, in the sense that the free circulation of cultural products featuring "tolerance" among the more affluent and educated Mexicans functions as immunization against "a subsequent (pathogenic) attack by collective organisms." One outstanding aspect of Schaefer's discussion has to do with the history of the gay movement in Mexico. Public acceptance of homosexuality has been eroded since the march for gay pride on October 2, 1978. In the late 1970s the López Portillo administration "encourage[d] solidarity for gays and their political participation in order to solidify the official institutions." Yet the 1982 oil crisis was accompanied by the deterioration of human rights, including those of gays and lesbians, who are problematically included in the ideological package for modernization and pluralistic society "communicated through the images of an erotic economy as well."

The history of gayness, mainly Brazilian, is actually the focus of Borim's text. Taking the ban on gays by the Left as a starting point, he utilizes anthropological research in order to explore the origins (European and Amerindian) and ideological developments of what is today a nonaggressive campaign (though often diluted by traditional party politics). Drawing parallels between the North American berdaches and African-Brazilian *candomblé*, Borim highlights a history of repression as well as of myths and realities in the genesis of alleged homosexual supernatural powers.

With a focus on Mexico, Pérez de Mendiola also addresses the history of homosexuality and the gay movement. While debunking the basis on which the literary canon is erected, she not only scrutinizes the complex poetics in *José Toledo's Diary*, but also expands, like Schaefer, on the links between discourses of Mexican identity and issues of sexuality. For Pérez (and Jean Franco), Mexico and very many other societies have blamed women for their falls and ignonimity. If, equating Malinche with national misfortune, Mexican sons are ashamed of their mother's rape, Christians at large have historically held a grudge toward women because of Eve's sin. Thus, it is no surprise that to be a male homosexual means to be feminine and tarnished, whereas to be a man has even become "the essence of Mexicanness, thereby implicitly denying women the right to Mexican national identity," argues Pérez.

Topics such as AIDS metaphors, homophobia, blind readings of the canon, social history of sexual violence, dangers of repressing sexualities, homosocial relations, strategies of liberation, gay and lesbian discourses, rape, pornography, authoritarian discourses on and myths around sexualities, traditional gender typification, nontraditional symbolic manifestations, patriarchy in modern packaging, family and marriage representations, national identity implying sexuality, poetics of sexuality, and the history and genesis of gay movements are among the numerous themes touched by the following essays. As we do not intend to "direct" the reading of this volume, we are about to conclude an introduction of which the only intent is to map some of the problems involving sexualities in the Hispanic cultures. Once we are culturally and historically traversed as writers, our task is to place the mapping within this postmodernist moment — an age of suspicion.

Notes

1. Considering chiefly the social dynamics in the United States, Juan Flores and George Yúdice emphasize the term *Latino,* since "unlike 'Hispanic,' it is not an identity label imposed by the politicized statistics of The Census Bureau and the market who seek to target particular constituencies for political and economic manipulations" (80). Their work attempts to critique the alleged shortcomings of their label: "Historical discrimination against Mexican-Americans and Puerto Ricans is an experience which cannot be permitted to disappear by projecting Latinos as an overcharging group. Such discrimination involves a complex of racial, class, and other 'otherness' factors which often make middle-class sectors of other Latino groups anxious" (80). As a result, Flores and Yúdice add, Latinos "seek to dissociate themselves," but "the fact that discrimination has been directed at all Latino groups contributes to a pan-Latino rejection of discrimination aimed at any particular group" (80). Another issue, though, that plays a part in our particular usage of *Hispanic* (beyond the scope of the Census or prejudice) is the inclusion of the Spanish and the Portuguese components.

2. Nation, gender, and ethnicity can be understood as artifacts of two forms of thought process: a "fabrication," on the one hand, but also, and most thoroughly, as a "grouping" of individuals who do share concrete and symbolic experience. Unlike Benedict Anderson's concept of the imagined community he names the "nation" (15–16), our notion of community applies whether or not the individuals imagine a "horizontal comradeship."

3. Graffiti at a Paris twenty-four-hour sauna teaches Daniel that one can barely expect a human group to be simply either oppressed or oppressor. Most clients were rich gay men, "who were not any less gay, but were members of the dominant class anyway" (*Passagem* 162). Besides the sauna users' disdain for old age, poverty, and what they considered bad looks, they tended to be violent toward one another and wrote racist remarks against Arabs and Blacks on the walls. Among other predicaments, like the capitalist interest in promoting gay ghettos (173), Daniel learned he was different from that group of so-called "homosexuals" (163). He starts to think of gays in terms of "homosexualities," plural.

4. Chicana author Gloria Anzaldúa informs us that the male-dominated Azteca-Mexica culture "drove the powerful female deities underground by giving them monstrous attributes and by substituting male deities in their place" (27). They split Coatlapeuh, who "possessed both upper (light) and underworld (dark) as-

pects," into two groups of goddesses: in one, Coatlicue, the Serpent; in the other, Tlazolteotl and Cihuacoatl, with more sinister aspects (27). The Spaniards, who conquered the Aztecs, soon exacerbated the polarities good and evil; they actually "made all Indian deities and religious practices the work of the devil" (28).

Works Cited

Anderson, Benedict. *Imagined Communities: Reflections on the Origin and Spread of Nationalism*. London: Verso, 1986.

Anzaldúa, Gloria. *Borderlands/La Frontera: the New Mestiza*. San Francisco: Aunt Lute, 1987.

Barbosa, Gustavo. *Grafitos de banheiro*. Rio de Janeiro: Anima, 1986.

Daniel, Herbert. *Passagem para o próximo sonho: um possível romance autocrítico*. Rio de Janeiro: Codecri, 1982.

Daniel, Herbert, and Leila Míccolis. *Jacarés e lobisomes: dois ensaios sobre a homossexualidade*. Rio de Janeiro: Achiamé, 1983.

Daniel, Herbert, and Richard G. Parker. *AIDS, a terceira epidemia: ensaios e tentativas*. São Paulo: Iglu, 1991.

DuBay, William H. *Gay Identity*. Jefferson: McFarland, 1987.

Flores, Juan, and George Yúdice. "Living Borders/Buscando America." *Social Text: Theory/Culture/Ideology* 24 (1990): 58–84.

Foucault, Michel. *The History of Sexuality*, vol. 1, *An Introduction*. New York: Vantage, 1990.

Fry, Peter. Prefácio. Néstor Osvaldo Perlongher, *O negócio do michê*. São Paulo: Brasiliense, 1987. 11–15.

Jameson, Fredric. "On the Negt and Kluge." *October* 46 (Fall 1988): n.p. (Cited in Flores 69.)

Lang, Candace. "Autobiography in the Aftermath of Romanticism." *Diacritics* 12 (1982): 2–16.

Lionnet, Françoise. *Autobiographical Voices: Race, Gender, Self-Portraiture*. Ithaca: Cornell University Press, 1991.

Richards, Nelly. "Postmodernism and Periphery." *Third Text* 2 (1987–88): 5–12.

Smith, Sidonie. *A Poetics of Women's Autobiography: Marginality and the Fictions of Self-Representation*. Bloomington: Indiana University Press, 1987.

Chapter 1

The Sexual Economy of Miguel de Cervantes

Robert ter Horst

To Diana de Armas Wilson for her splendid
Allegories of Love

Chapter XXII of Part I of *Don Quijote,* the episode in which the knight unwisely sets twelve galley slaves free, is justly celebrated for its indeterminacy. On the practical level, there seems to be no problem, for each condemned person more or less confirms his guilt, and once all are liberated they, taking their lead from Ginés de Pasamonte, refuse to reconstitute themselves as a small new society or state of freedmen that would obey Don Quijote's injunction to seek out the city of Toboso and there present themselves collectively before Dulcinea. Instead, in fear of the Santa Hermandad, the highway patrol created by the Catholic monarchs,[1] they disperse as individuals, but not before stoning down Don Quijote, Sancho, and their mounts. Nonetheless, on the theoretical level, this same chapter raises some truly troubling issues in connection with power. The word *fuerza,* throughout a whole diapason of acceptations, is the leitmotiv of the episode as it addresses the strengths of monarchy, the state, the criminal justice system, the police, individuals, and human sexuality. The central philosophic issue appears to be compulsion—not its reality, for in the chain gang and in the Santa Hermandad that is manifest, but its licitness and its efficacy.

By misunderstanding Sancho straight off, Don Quijote questions royal use of power. Sancho describes the chained men as a "cadena de galeotes, gente forzada del rey, que va a las galeras" (I.258).[2] Don Quijote interprets Sancho's *forzada* in the sense of *hacer fuerza,* to attack, to violate, to abrogate the legal recourses of another.[3] And so, as a believer in a just monarchy and judicial system, he inquires of Sancho "¿Es posible que el rey haga fuerza a ninguna gente?" (I.248).[4] Sancho at once understands how he has been misunderstood and most lucidly amplifies his original statement, explaining that these men are "gente que por sus delitos va condenada a servir al rey en las galeras de por fuerza" (I.248).[5] One must admire Sancho's legal precision in the choice of his terms: *delitos, condenada, de por fuerza.* But it is unavailing as Don Quijote insists upon framing the situation on the basis of an opposition between free will and constraint, without allowing for occasions when it is just to deprive a person of her or his freedom, a possibility of which Sancho is well aware: "Advierta vuestra merced ... que la justicia, que es el mesmo rey, no hace fuerza ni agravio a semejante gente, sino que los castiga en pena de sus delitos" (I.260).[6]

There is, moreover, a strong sexual undercurrent in the flow of the chapter. *Fuerza* itself is in Spanish a word of art that in a legal context denotes rape, *stuprum.*[7] But here sexuality emerges jocosely when the first prisoner examined by Quijote declares that love has brought him to his present condition of servitude, "por enamorado iba de aquella manera" (I.260).[8] However, the object of the prisoner's affection was no lady; rather it was a basket of household linens that he embraced so steadfastly that it required the police to make him turn it loose: "quise tanto a una canasta de colar atestada de ropa blanca, que la abracé conmigo tan fuertemente que, a no quitármela la justicia por fuerza, aún hasta agora no la hubiera dejado de mi voluntad" (I.260). The sly humor of the statement beautifully includes a periodic rhetoric that opposes compulsion (*por fuerza*) to the free expression of desire (*de mi voluntad*). That opposition produces the binary structure of the episode and also goes to the roots of its sexuality, in which Don Quijote comes to be included through his seeming misapprehension of the prisoner's use of the term *enamorado,* for in the courtly sense, he himself is such a one, and if being a courtly lover is grounds for being sent to the galleys, then Don Quijote allows that he has been a candidate for quite some time: "pues si por enamorado echan a galeras, días ha que pudiera yo estar bogando en ellas" (I.260). Yet, rhetorically speaking, this is no misunderstanding at all, for in poetry lovers are indeed sent to the galleys. The prime example is Mario Galeota, whom Garcilaso, in his *Canción quinta* (Fifth Canzone), punning on the name of the friend for whom he ostensibly intercedes, so condemns:

> Hablo de aquel cativo
> de quien tener se debe más cuidado,
> que está muriendo vivo,
> al remo condenado,
> en la concha de Venus amarrado. (31–35)[9]

This amusing conceit cannot extenuate the fact the *Canción quinta* derives from a dismaying reality. It is brute strength that governs sexual relations. *Fuerza* originally resides in the male and permits him to dominate other males and females as well. Here, however, Garcilaso's muse is transformational, a rhetorical metamorphosis in which he would modulate from the modes of masculinity to those of femininity. Thus, in the figure of *praeteritio* he appears to renounce crude subjugation even though he dwells upon it at some length as epic yields to lyric:

> no pienses que cantado
> sería de mí, hermosa flor de Gnido,
> el fiero Marte airado [...]
> ni aquellos capitanes
> en las sublimes ruedas colocados
> por quien los alemanes,
> el fiero cuello ata dos,
> y los franceses van domesticados. (11–20)[10]

The vanquished foes of the emperor are feminized, "van domesticados." And so is Mario Galeota, who has abandoned virile pursuits for plaintive music and rivers of tears. Commensurately, Violante Sanseverino has hardened. For the transformation, she has drawn strength from one of the few powers reserved to women in traditional society, that of refusal. Her denial of Mario Galeota's suit has put her in possession of his martial qualities so that what Garcilaso will indite to this Amazon will solely be

> aquella
> fuerza de tu beldad...
>   y alguna vez con ella
>   también sería notada
> el aspereza de que estás armada (21–25)[11]

Thus the Orphic mode in which the *Canción quinta* begins is, as its subjunctive mood so accurately indicates, a feint, a condition contrary to fact by means of which the poet, appearing to wish to placate and to soften the hardness of the lady with respect to his friend, in fact toughens and masculinizes her with a view to transforming her into a worthy foe he can undertake to subdue with the weapons that one man in warfare, and indeed in peace, deploys against another. The first and greater of these is fear: "Hágate temerosa / el caso de Anajárete, y cobarde" (66–68).[12] "Temerosa...y cobarde" — these are the terms of domination; and, just in case they should fail to be produced, a weapon is at hand. True, it is wielded by a goddess, Nemesis; but she is a wonderful choice.

Robert Graves interprets Zeus's pursuit and rape of her as a patriarchal reversal of her matriarchal pursuit and subjection of him. This is exactly the Amazonian impasse that lies at the heart of the Garcilasan dilemma. When the male softens, the female hardens, so that neither of them is ever of the same quality, as, despite every metamorphosis, *aspereza* ceaselessly and uncommunicatively confronts *terneza*. Nemesis is a female so injured by the male as to be made as pitiless as any male. It is her arrows that threaten Violante Sanseverino: "No quieras tú, señora, / de Nímesis airada las saetas / probar, por Dios, agora" (101–103).[13] And so it is that the very instrument of peace and love, the lyre of Orpheus and Apollo, is converted into a weapon of war, the bow and the arrow, aimed at a reluctant Neapolitan lady. War, conducted exclusively among men, divides them into the two classes of victors and vanquished; and the vanquished are chained and humiliated and sent to the galleys to row the engines of war against their will. This "domestication" feminizes and eroticizes them.

Garcilaso's genius in the *Canción quinta* consists in an Amazonian reversal of gender role that puts the female in the cruelly dominant, the male in a painfully passive, role. At the same time, he translates the sadomasochistic homoerotics of warfare into an inverted sadomasochistic heterosexuality of courtly address. And the goal of the poem, relentlessly pursued by means of every available tactic, is to reverse one last time the posture of the female with respect to the male, to put him in permanent power over her and to make her a willing partner in her subjection. The central process here is what eroticizes the relationship of dominance to submission and so converts an unwilling subjection into an acquiescent, voluntary degradation. The poem transmutes, or would transmute, *fuerza* into *grado,* the latter substantive used only in adverbial phrases in Spanish — i.e., *de grado* — its very modality thus suggesting that it is the product of force. Thus, the yield from Garcilaso's poem is gratification, one that, were it not so general, might be called perverse. Góngora, ever dependent upon and ever competitive with his most formidable rival, draws aesthetic pleasure from the pain of his poetic protagonists in the *romance artístico* "Amarrado al duro banco / de una galera turquesca" (*Obras completas* 60–61; chained to the hard bench of a Turkish galley). The allusion to the *Canción quinta* in that first line is unmistakable. But, predictably, Góngora intensifies the male lover's plight by portraying him as married and separated from his spouse for ten years and apprehensive of her death. The cruelest stroke comes at the end when six ships of the Knights of St. John are sighted and the slave master, the *cómitre,* compels the *galeote* to use all his strength to pull away from them: "y el cómitre mandó usar / al forzado de su fuerza" (39–40).[14]

Thus, both in Garcilaso's poem, which establishes the theme of the *galeote* for all Golden Age discourse, and in Góngora's masterful variation on it, the brute male power that divides persons of the same or of different gender into dominators and dominated is the tonic note. And since women make up the vast majority of the class of the dominated, *fuerza* as a harmonic, as a set of phenomena, inescapably involves an erotics; but males who find themselves oppressed as defeated enemies, rejected lovers, or condemned criminals also come into the system. Indeed, to the extent that warfare is primary, and Garcilaso's rhetoric certainly presents it as such, the first erotic of *fuerza* is a homoerotics, and the second a heterosexual expression. Sexuality is at all events an essential component of the *galeote* situation, and as Cervantes develops it as a product of the interplay between the adverbial modes of *de por fuerza* and *de grado,* in his own recension, he, like Góngora, shows himself to be a great and brilliant reader and redeployer of the Garcilasan *Urtext.*

In the burlesque version of Chapter XXII, Cervantes releases an even greater degree of sexual energy than does Góngora, one that floods into forbidden zones, as is the case with the prisoner questioned by Quijote just before he confronts Ginés de Pasamonte. This individual, who may be identical with the fifth *galeote,* the one who intervenes in Don Quijote's interrogation of the elderly man, explains: "Yo voy aquí porque me burlé demasiadamente con dos primas hermanas mías, y con otras dos hermanas mías que no lo eran mías; finalmente, tanto me burlé con todas, que resultó de la burla crecer la parentela tan intricadamente, que no hay diablo que la declare" (I.263).[15]

Cervantes achieves pronounced comic effect here with the anaphora of the forms of *burlar,* to mock, to trick, to deceive, but above all for a man to take advantage of his superior position in society in order to induce a woman to have sex with him on the basis of false assurances, usually a pledge to marry her. This *burlador* boastfully avows sexual relations and illegitimate offspring, both with his cousins and with several nuns (*hermanas*). He seems to have established an incestuous extended family in which all the bloodlines are hopelessly blurred. The situation is reminiscent of the passel of brats among whom Guzmán de Alfarache was reared: "Estábamos en casa cantidad de sobrinos" (Alemán 37; we were raised as a bunch of nieces and nephews). And indeed in Cervantes's own *La fuerza de la sangre,* Leocadia's illegitimate son Luisico is passed off by the family as a nephew, *sobrino.* That we may be in the presence of Cervantes's own humorous evocation of Guzmán himself[16] is suggested by his observation that "Este iba en hábito de estudiante, y dijo una de las guardas que era muy grande hablador y muy gentil latino" (I.263).[17] One recalls Alemán's description of "nuestro Guzmán, un muy buen estudiante latino, retórico y griego" (466).[18] In addition, Cervantes's student has been sentenced to six years in the galleys. That was the period of Guzmán's original punishment "las galeras por seis años" (872), until he occasioned its conversion into a lifetime sentence by an armed attempt to escape dressed as a woman. Whether or not the allusion is to Alemán's *pícaro*, with this brief inquiry Cervantes further extends the range of the sexual motif that is rhetorically inherent in the subject of the chapter.

It is, however, in the interview with the fourth prisoner[19] that Cervantes introduces radically new material. All the conversations that surround this one are with individuals who are wise guys, *socarrones*; but the exchange with the elderly man shows no signs of the complex of ironies that so infect the episode, except in the mouth of the fifth *galeote*, who, at first, speaks for his companion. The older man is sympathetically described by Cervantes as having a "venerable rostro, con una barba blanca que le pasaba del pecho" (I.262).[20] His interpreter explains that his crime is to have been both a pimp and a black magician, *alcahuete* and *hechicero*. But as a typically Cervantine *socarrón*, the fifth prisoner cannot resist having his bit of a joke, so that he first characterizes the fourth *galeote* as sentenced for having been a "corredor de oreja y aun de todo el cuerpo."[21]

In the realm of commerce, a *corredor de oreja* is a middleman who brings buyer and seller together in the credit market and is, according to the *Diccionario de autoridades*, synonymous with the *corredor de cambios*, who "solicita letras para otras partes, o dinero prestado para hombres de negócios, y también sus seguridades y resguardos."[22] I would guess that this kind of agent is designated *de oreja* because he scurries from client to client speaking confidentially in the ear of each. Moreover, this kind of brokerage is completely contaminated with the sexual, from the more or less acceptable activities of the *corredor de matrimonios*, or matchmaker, to the work of the pimp. Thus, the fifth prisoner's amusing synecdoche, ear representing the whole body. In addition, the casting of spells has left its mark on the older *galeote*, who has his "puntas

y collar de hechicero," "puntas y collar de" being, in the definition of the Diccionario de la lengua española a colloquialism that
suggests that a person has "asomos de un vicio o maldad."[23]

Everything in this chapter is binary and so is Don Quijote's
reaction to these dual activities. He lauds the work of the pimp
but denounces the efforts of the caster of spells. Indeed, one wonders how his eulogy of the pimp's profession, which I read as altogether unironic, though embedded in a maze of ironies, got past
the censor: *Dormitabat bonus censor.* In an eloquent little speech,
Quijote, whom one thinks of as retired from the sexual arena himself, links commerce to sex through semantics, but also adds to
the mixture an unexpected dose of politics and power, for he declares that one who is simply a pimp, "por solamente el alcahuete
limpio" (I.262—the *limpio,* I must confess, is not without ironic
reverberation) hardly deserves a sentence as one of the oarsmen
in the galleys, but rather should be sent to command and be admiral over them. Quijote exalts this profession, commonly held to
be vile, saying that it is vital to a well-constituted state ("república
bien ordenada"; I.262) and that only savvy people ("discretos";
I.262) should practice it. He adds that it should be regulated like
any other branch of commerce, but be open only to a good class
of persons ("gente bien nacida"; I.262) who would have their designated inspectors and examiners, just as stockbrokers ("corre-
dores de lonja"; I.262) do.

Regulation of the business of sex would, the knight asserts,
remedy many of the ills that stem from its being in the hands of
young, stupid, and inexperienced males who freeze when they
are confronted with a crisis. His concluding remarks cause one
to realize that this is an *arbitrio,* at least as wild as the one he proposes at the beginning of Part II, but here made somewhat firmer
by the actual existence of the activity and of persons who profess
it. Nor is Don Quijote able to leave the matter without rehearsing
Cervantes's familiar *dicta,* so well exemplified in *El licenciado Vidri-
era* and in *Persiles,* as to the inefficacy of love potions, "siendo...
cosa imposible forzar la voluntad" (I.263).[24] Just such a presumed
impossibility is of course the enterprise of the *Canción quinta.* In
Chapter XXII Cervantes restructures a poetic undertaking bipolar-
ized on the lines of *por fuerza* as against *de grado* in terms of a man
who conducts his sex business as both a consensual and a com-

pulsory commerce. The *alcahuete* arranges transactions between willing partners, whereas the *hechicero* undertakes to constrain the unwilling person to yield to the desire of the willing lover. As well as the wonderful degradation of Garcilaso, a wealth of subtexts is now manifest, *Celestina* in male attire, *Guzmán de Alfarache*, *Lazarillo de Tormes* as identified by Ginés de Pasamonte.[25]

But Cervantes takes his most significant and original cue from Mateo Alemán, that great commodifier of desire, whose Guzmán characterizes Seville as "bien acomodada para cualquier grangería y tanto se lleve a vender como se compra, porque hay mercantes para todo" (145).[26] Precioso's *abuela* in *La gitanilla* approaches Madrid with her ward in exactly the same sense, "pensando en la Corte vender su mercadería, donde todo se compra y todo se vende" (I.63).[27] Mahamut of *El amante liberal* uses the same phrase with respect to Islam when he describes how Arab government is altogether venal: "no se dan allí los cargos y oficios por merecimientos, sino por dineros: todo se vende y todo se compra" (I.141).[28]

One of Cervantes's greatest discoveries as a novelist, perhaps his greatest, is his revelation and exploitation of the sexual marketplace, surely a fundamental factor in all human systems of value and exchange, but one so far left unexplored even in this age of economics. In the examination of the condemned *alcahuete* in Chapter XXII of Part I of *Don Quijote,* we catch a sort of Smithian glimpse of how untrammeled transactions in the field of desire might operate. The major premise here is, I think, Alemán's: for the proper price, any desire can be gratified, "tanto se lleve a vender como se compra, porque hay mercantes para todo" (145). Regulation, especially Cervantes's, would be introduced not to impede exchange but to assure efficient functioning of the whole sexual economy. No manner of purchase or sale is privileged. All expressions of want and every move to satisfy it are equal, and the regulators are umpires who guarantee the fairness of the game by preventing fraud and deceit and all artificial advantages, such as those of gender. The mode of the system is egalitarian and adverbial. It works voluntarily, *de grado.*

This ideally meretricious vision of a state of absolute gratification needs to be seen in terms of an antecedent poetic economy that the sexual market displaces. In verse such as that of

Garcilaso de la Vega and Fray Luis de León, the goal is to develop so great a persuasive power that the beloved object, human or divine, will remain securely and lastingly in the possession of the lover, "sin miedo y sobresalto de perderte" (134) as Garcilaso puts it in a line that will echo, literally and figuratively, throughout Cervantes's fiction. For that desideratum is cruelly threatened by disdain, forgetfulness, absence, and death in the relationship between human lovers and by defects that undermine mortal address to God, especially material and sexual desire, *codicia*. The poetry from which Cervantes takes his departure is ardently economic in its obsessive desire to possess but antieconomic in its striving to remove the object of desire from the marketplace. Its fatal and wonderful flaw is, however, that it is essentially a poetry of anxious desire that cannot rid itself of the yearning by which it is constituted. Such verse, accordingly, is construed on paradox, a passion to possess countered by a sense of the impossibility of possession. Much as he would have liked to, Cervantes was unable to continue in this line of inquiry. Thus, he changes the direction of his succeeding enterprise. He replaces poetry's impulse to retreat from the marketplace with an irresistible tendency for poetry to contend with economic forces. Lyric verse like Garcilaso's is a kind of protectionism. It allows to pass its borders only enough libidinal energy for the system to be fueled, so that the doses of desire are always gauged and limited and measured. But Cervantes's tendency is, like Alemán's search for an overall norm of human misconduct, to dare to construe sexuality as an unlimited and inexhaustible universal. Accordingly, in his fiction after *La Galatea,* his first heroic move is to put desire's lyric hoard — the beautiful virgin female — into circulation, often in violent ways as women are torn from their frames: Isabel of *La española inglesa,* Leocadia of *La fuerza de la sangre,* and Constanza of *La gitanilla* all were abducted, for example.

But what impedes the free play of market forces is power, *fuerza,* especially in the male. Often the female is introduced into the field of desire only to be imprisoned in a tiny lyric segment of it, as Leocadia returns to sequestration in her father's house, or Isabel is immured in Clotaldo's establishment, or Leonora passes from her father's control to purdah under Carrizales. Dispossession in Cervantes frequently leads to repossession, but such in-fractions of sexuality's drive to achieve gratification through level-ing help define the arena of struggle as might defends its privilege against free exchange, Carrizales in combat with Loaysa.

Cervantes's address to power is various. There is a temptation to avoid the issue in his versions of pastoral. Libidinally speak-ing, pastoral is an expansion of lyric, an extension of the frame to include a larger population than could fit into lyric. Both forms, however, severely ration desire. Lyric is an instrument of the pa-triarchal, prehensile in its essential mode of apostrophe, one de-signed to hold the virgin female fast until she can be transferred to the nuptial couch. It is an anticipation of possession and so an expression of power, presently deferred. Spanish pastoral, be-ginning with *La Diana*, disengages itself from power by deferral as well. At the same time, the erotic suffuses the whole of pas-toral space, for love is its datum, that point from which all per-sonages take their measure, most of them by being in love, but others averse to or exempt from it. Yet, as a general rule, this is a Foucauldian erotic of verbal analysis purchased at the price of the prohibition of genital activity. By and large, in pastoral, peo-ple talk about sex, but do not engage in it. This relative absence of intercourse creates the illusion of an unrestricted market by diminishing the role of male strength, but at the same time dena-tures sexuality by ruling out transactions in it. Thus, even though pastoral moves in the direction of equality by restraining the male so that women can emerge, it is unsatisfactory because it end-lessly defers gratification; and narrative demands gratification, just as many people do.

In pastoral, power is in abeyance, but because its values derive from a cultivated upper-class existence it is indissolubly linked to privilege. Pastoral is a travesty of power, Marie Antoinette churn-ing milk at Le Hameau in maid's attire, and even though it may not do so in its own confines, it is destined to return to those scenes of force and inequality from which it derives, just as Horace's "Beatus ille" returns to the Rome of moneylenders and Maecenas. No one can be "solutus omni faenore" (*Odes and Epodes* 120).[29]

But perhaps there is a paradoxical freedom in oppression. Com-bining unhappy personal experience with poetic and literary mod-els, Cervantes extensively explores the realm of what one might call the vanquished. The most condensed expression of this situation is to be found in the galley slave, as is the case with Chapter XXII; but owing to the inevitable link between the Mediterranean galley and the Ottoman Empire, the Islam of Cervantes is a very great extension of the conditions of powerlessness that obtain among the captured or condemned rowers. Of course, as we have seen in Garcilaso, the sexuality of warfare is a sexuality of inequality, of victors over vanquished. Greek pederasty, with its insistence on rigid definition of role, erastés, the senior partner, dominating erómenos, the junior male beloved, surely is the product of a culture designed for triumph in battle, whether domestic or foreign. Indeed, in their subjection boys and women are alike, for erastés indifferently designates the male possessor of both (Dover 16). And the very few references in Cervantes to overt male homosexuality occur in the context of warfare at sea in galleys.

In the *Historia del cautivo* Ruy Pérez de Biedma describes the career of his master Tiñoso in positive terms, explaining how he came to be bey of Algiers "sin subir por los torpes medios y caminos que los más privados del Gran Turco suben" (I.161).[30] But sex was precisely the means of advancement for Biedma's next owner, the monstrously cruel Azán Agá, whom "el Uchalí cautivó, y le quiso tanto, que fue uno de los más regalados garzones suyos" (I.462).[31] Toward the end of Part I of the *Quijote*, in Barcelona, Ana Félix recounts, in her wonderfully implausible tale, how the bey of Algiers, upon her arrival there, learned of her remarkable beauty, as well as of that of her faithful lover, Gaspar Gregorio, who had accompanied her into exile. In the bey's presence she hears Gaspar described as "uno de los más gallardos y hermosos mancebos que se podía imaginar" (II.511).[32] In Golden Age Spanish the adjectives *hermoso* and *gallardo* apply to either gender. Ana Félix herself describes the youth's desirability as a "belleza que se deja atrás las mayores que encarecer se pueden" (II.511);[33] and she is terribly worried, for "entre aquellos bárbaros turcos en más se tiene y estima un muchacho o mancebo hermoso que una mujer, por bellísima que sea" (II.511–12).[34] So, to save her lover from a fate as pathic, Ana dresses him as a Moorish female. She herself is captured in male dress and is about to be executed as a man when her gender is discovered. Thus, the Ana Félix episode rehearses early events in *Persiles*, when Periandro in female clothing finds Auristela in male garb, about to be executed (I.23).

Both cases of transvestism occur under extreme coercion, so that the theorist of the sexual marketplace after the fashion of the *alcahuete* in Chapter XXII should be surprised to find so much fluidity in gender boundaries as well as, in homosexuality, a certain freedom of sexual expression. But Cervantes, in his investigations of Turkish and of vaguely barbarous northern polity, anticipates, I think, the Montesquieu of both *De l'Esprit des lois* and of the *Lettres persanes*. The Ottoman Empire is a radical form of government that concentrates all power in one individual, sultan or, more usually, the sultan's favorite. Any power exercised by subordinate individuals is purely vicarious. Thus, under despotism, all subjects are de jure powerless; all are equal, and their equality is a translation to the political arena of that abdication of power that is the enabling act of the pastoral Arcadia, its vacuum tantamount to the plenitude of the despotic. As Montesquieu points out (*Esprit* I.30),[35] whereas monarchical states thrive on rank and distinction, despotic ones efface differences, including those of gender and sexual orientation.

The Don Quijote of Chapter XXII ever so cunningly represents Philip III, that *roi fainéant*, as a despot ("¿Es posible que el rey haga fuerza a ninguna gente?" [I.258]), with the result that his tyranny erases the distinctions that come from lesser allowed degrees of might, especially that of man over woman. And even though Cervantes represents Turkish pederastic homosexuality in particular and Turkish sexuality in general as alien and uncouth, one of his great strokes of genius in fiction, in anticipation of *Lettres persanes*, is at once to expatriate the domestic and to repatriate the foreign. Just as Quijote can base a theory of sexual economy on the despised figure of the *alcahuete*, so Cervantes can found a novelistics of cultural exchange on the renegade, the Mahamut, who moves with shameless ease between Islam and Christianity. Expatriation is the first move, as an individual, usually but not always female, comes on the sexual market by being torn from home and family and cast into a seemingly strange environment where power and money alone determine gratification. But this is the cruel pleasure of the overlord in which the person, male or female, who is possessed endures violation of his or her young and comely flesh in the hope of replacing the oppressor one day, the history in short of Azán Agá, a sadomasochistic process in which the masochist ultimately comes to replace the sadist. S-M is Cervantes's macroeconomics since its reversible hierarchy encompasses all sexual orientations. Yet, his outlook also involves an ineradicable domestic ideal of sexual equality and intersubjectivity[36] that derives from pastoral, where denial and passivity create a fragile equality, but also a potent vision, for such an ideal haunts Cervantes from the beginning of his career until its end and validates his claim, unique, I think, among male Golden Age authors, to be something of a feminist. His fiction's desire to be a fiction of equality is greater than any other desire in his writings. However, since this goal is shared by only a very few beautifully obsessed individuals, it works as a microeconomics.

Departing from pastoral and the assumption of powerlessness by its poetry, Cervantes denatures his source of inspiration by causing it, usually involuntarily, to engage power through capture, abduction, rape, warfare, pilgrimage. Preciosa is cast among the gypsies, for whom plunder is the overriding rule. Yet, she shines in their society by outward conformity and tenacious inward adhesion to a higher law of desire. Once she acquires a lover who submits not to her, but to the principle of intersubjectivity, the couple constitute a small but strong economy of two within the rapacious gypsy world. Sexual egalitarians are everywhere an alien presence, whether in Christendom or Islam or England. By showing how it is possible for two lovers to be at ease between themselves in an utterly strange environment, Cervantes richly complicates the antithesis of "native" and "foreign." Home in his fiction is the pastoral and its recumbent androgyny, the effeminate Cornelio of *El amante liberal* in his Edenic garden by the sea.

But real fiction is created by the application of power to this dream of passivity. Thus, the Barbary pirates seize and carry off both Ricardo and Leonisa. Yet, in him as a male representative of his society they carry off one of their own, for jealousy has made him, in respect of Leonisa, as rapacious as any gypsy or Arab trader. Jealousy is the supreme expression of Cervantine macroeconomics and macrosexuality. It is at home everywhere as a hierarchical sadomasochistic system. Intersubjectivity is the supreme expression of Cervantine microeconomics and microsexuality. In all parts it is foreign, but wherever in its name there is constituted a society of two equal lovers it contends not unsuccessfully with the other system, and that strife is depicted by Cervantes both at home and abroad. But contact with sadomasochism as an alien phenomenon perhaps best leads to its recognition as a domestic problem. This is, I believe, Ricardo's experience in *El amante liberal.* Slavery enables him to realize that this in fact is his own jealous hierarchy of mind. Indeed, when Ricardo enters the *cadí*'s household as a slave and must deal as a powerless person with the unwelcome sexual advances of Halima, the *cadí*'s wife, his male history comes to duplicate Leonisa's story as a female, since both of them are objects of desire. Thus, Ricardo makes the connection, but is able to act upon it only when he and Leonisa have ostensibly regained their freedom, while they in fact have returned to sexual slavery in Trapana. There, in the tale's all-validating anagnorisis, he liberates himself from jealousy and so sets both himself and Leonisa free to love as equals, which they do with implausible promptitude.

In the *Quijote,* by contrast, I see Cervantes taking on the *alcahuete*'s role as regulator of the sexual economy with relatively little success, or mixed success. The great difficulty is that novel's poetic and parodic aversion to power, to the test of confrontation with it. It is a poem of and to the powerless that is nonetheless drawn to the seats of power. So Don Quijote and Sancho prudently but also somewhat cravenly turn off the high road, fearing the arrows of the Santa Hermandad once it is discovered that they have released the chain gang. In the Sierra Morena they paradoxically encounter the very same configurations of sexuality and coercion that they have fled. For the idyll of equal love as experienced between Luscinda and Cardenio is violated by the invasions of might, first that of the prohibition of Luscinda's father, and then the greater intrusion upon them of Fernando, second son of Duke Ricardo. Here the formula is duke = might, "un grande de España, que tiene su estado en lo mejor desta Andalucía" (I.283).[37] The reference surely is to Medina Sidonia, whose prestige, estates, and rent-roll far exceeded those of the dukes of Alcalá, Arcos, and Medinaceli.[38] And even though twice removed from direct power, Fernando is a sexual predator who moves in on Luscinda and besieges and seduces and abandons Dorotea.

In the end Fernando is prevailed upon to release Luscinda, literally brought as a prisoner to the inn, and to marry Dorotea, thus allowing Cardenio to reunite with Luscinda. But with Cardenio a half-mad fugitive and Luscinda also a fugitive as well as a captive, this solution is achieved in the macroeconomic, hierarchical context, as Dorotea's humble supplication of her seducer eloquently attests. The secret of the power and endurance of the sadomasochistic system lies in its ability to provide the manipulator of it with gratification through reversal. The complaisant victim sees herself or himself, potentially, in the overlord. Dorotea, de facto overseer of her father's estates and clandestine reader of the romances of chivalry, is a woman of dominant and calculating mind. She triumphs over Fernando by submitting to him, twice. In the light of this power play, the union of Luscinda with Cardenio seems pale. And, similarly, at the country place of the duke and duchess in Part II, where the great apparent issue is the love of Don Quijote for Dulcinea, we witness in chapter after chapter a theater of sexual cruelty that, for all the playful confidence of its might, draws its essential strength from the iconic idea of a woman — Dulcinea — under endless constraint from which it proves impossible to release her. The rhythm of *Don Quijote* is a manic-depressive one in which its protagonist's mind, freed at last by the intoxication produced as a consequence of deep chivalric draughts, engages, in fantasy, the simulacra of power, while that mind's aging body lives under an oppression that creates equality under despotism. And for all its exaltations, his mad mind is never able to lift the ceiling of oppression. The end of the cycle, the depressive phase, is the end of the story.

Los trabajos de Persiles y Sigismunda reverses the rhythm of *Don Quijote de la Mancha*, and for that and many other reasons it is becoming increasingly clear that critics and readers need to credit Cervantes's claim that his last is his greatest work. Of course in Cervantes all systems interlock, so that no single composition can safely be studied in isolation. One dare not read *La novela del curioso impertinente* without keeping *La historia del cautivo* in mind or, as Diana de Armas Wilson cautions (*Allegories of Love* xi), *Persiles* unaccompanied by *Quijote*. However, *Los trabajos* differs from its predecessors and undertakes to validate its claim to preeminence by taking a single poetic subtext, among a multitude of subtexts, as its point of departure. The seemingly major subtext is of course Heliodorus's *Historia aethiopica*, which occasioned many opinions as to its excellence because its prose was judged superior, poetic. In the usual understanding, this poetic prose differs from discursive prose by being heavily ornamented and not easily understood. In Lope's *La dama boba* the bluestocking Nise beautifully contrasts the clarity of ordinary prose with the challenge presented by Heliodoran prose, saying "la poética es hermosa / varia, culta, licenciosa, / y escura aun a ingenios raros: / tiene mil exornaciones y retóricas figuras" (Lope 38).[39]

However, for Cervantes in the *Persiles* the concept of poetic prose is, I think, considerably more organic. There, he systematically engages the corpus of Garcilaso's verse so as to complete in ultimate prose the process of *imitatio* with a loving though inevitably not unironic *superatio*. As I have tried to show on several occasions, Cervantes is obsessed with and haunted by Garcilaso; but in the *Persiles* the novelist would exorcise the poet by surpassing him. That his ghost is very much in residence in the novelist's house is shown by the tribute paid him by Periandro as he approaches Toledo and above all the Tagus River "por aver mostradole a la luz del mundo aquellos dias las famosas obras del jamas alabado como se deve poeta Garcilaso de la Vega, a averlas el visto, leydo mirado y admirado" (II.78).[40] Periandro then proceeds to quote and feels free to emend the *Egloga primera*, no small liberty, even though taken in reverence and awe.

Los trabajos, then, takes liberties with Garcilaso. Versions of his verse nearly circumscribe the novel. His most famous sonnet, the most often imitated and parodied of them, sonnet X, first emerges on page 24 of Part I when Periandro in female attire embraces Auristela in male attire and expresses his joy at finding her with the apostrophe "—¡O querida mitad de mi alma, o firme coluna de mis esperanças, o prenda, que no se si diga por mi bien o por mi mal hallada, aunque no será sino por mi bien, pues de tu vista no puede proceder mal ninguno" (I.24).[41] In his dream vision related toward the end of Part I Persiles imagines himself in Rome at last and in undisturbed possession of Auristela. His ecstatic apostrophe to such an anticipation dissipates the spell: "¡O unicas consoladoras de mi alma; o ricas prendas, por mi bien halladas, dulces y alegres en este y en otro qualquier tiempo" (I.278).[42]

In this line of discourse woman is an object (*prenda*) to be lost and found, to be bought and sold, in short a commodity to be garnered by the rich and powerful, although elusive of absolute possession. Woman's elusiveness, her sense of self and of ownership of that self, unsettles the man striving to possess her beauty absolutely, so that he constantly lives with the "miedo y sobresalto de perderte." In *Los trabajos* the greatest collector of female objets d'art is Arnaldo, so that his competition with Periandro for Auristela causes Periandro to be uninterruptedly "sobresaltado con la compañía de Arnaldo" (I.110).[43]

Possessiveness is not limited to the male, as Auristela's bout of jealousy over Policarpa, and Hipólita's rage to seduce Periandro, demonstrate; but it is far more frequent and far more intense in the male than in the female. With Arnaldo, heir apparent to the kingdom of Denmark, young, presumably comely Cervantes achieves not an original new personality but a strikingly fresh reformulation of an old obsession, that jealous proprietorship exhibited by Carrizales and Cañizares. Yet, these elderly husbands have, despite their wealth, the great disadvantage of age. Economically strong, they are physically impotent. With Arnaldo, Cervantes for the first time altogether abandons the artistic luxury of weakness in the form of pastoral and parody and directly confronts the problem of *fuerza*, of power. It and sexual love are, in the *Persiles*, equal: "el amor de Arnaldo igualaba a su poder" (I.105).[44] He, then, is the despot of the piece under whose tyranny Auristela and Periandro are equal potential objects of his plunder, though his taste decidedly runs in the direction of the female sibling of the pair.

The Ptolemaic couple composed by Auristela and Periandro are themselves far closer to the seats of the mighty than is elsewhere the case in the fiction of Cervantes, for she is heir to a crown and he is the younger brother to a crown prince. Thus in the *Trabajos* poetry addresses power. The result is two kinds of poetry. The first is modeled on Garcilaso and the male lover's fanatical urge to possess the female beloved that remorselessly objectifies her. It takes as its text the "O dulces prendas" sonnet, as well as the *Egloga primera* and, less obviously but all the more potently for that, the great and tragic Daphne sonnet (XIII). This is a lyric of failed metamorphosis in which Apollo's sexual pursuit of Daphne compels her to elude him by her transformation into a laurel tree, an object, a *prenda* that is completely beyond the pale of human reciprocity. The result is total frustration for his intended victim: "¡Oh miserable estado, oh mal tamaño, / que con llorarla crezca cada día / la causa y la razón por que lloraba" (*Poesías* 49).[45]

Similarly, Arnaldo's relentless pursuit of Auristela results in a reification of her. Jealousy transforms her into the portrait over which Arnaldo and the duke of Nemurs contend. The process culminates in their being dispossessed of her, the paradox of that poem, of a lust to own that yields only enduring loss. Arnaldo's Garcilasan career is the poetry of power, of a failure of that consciousness called male imaginatively to occupy the space of that consciousness called female, and, theoretically, the contrary, although Garcilaso's emphasis is very much on the male. Cervantes, on the other hand, seeks equality and balance between the genders, so that when Arnaldo rejoins Auristela and Periandro on the Island of the Great Mountain both Auristela and Periandro feel equally upset. Yet, when Cervantes has recourse to a free adaptation of several lines from sonnet XIII to express Auristela's dismay, he uses her affrighted immobility as the basis of a feminine point of view: "Auristela no se movio del lugar donde primero puso pie, y aun quisiera que allí se le hincaran en el suelo y se volvieran en torzidas rayces, como se volvieron los de la hija de Peneo quando el ligero corredor Apolo la seguía" (I.100).[46] The basal text is lines 7 and 8 of sonnet XIII: "los blandos pies en tierra se hincaban y en torcidas raíces se volvían" (*Poesías* 49).[47] And, ever fair-minded, Cervantes presents the situation in reverse when, on the Isle of Snow, Rosamunda unsuccessfully solicits Antonio with this echo: "Ves aquí, ¡o nuevo caçador, mas hermoso que Apolo!, otra nueva Dafne, que no te huye, sino que te sigue" (I.128).[48] In either case, the result is the same: frustration, dispossession, deprivation.

To this primal poetry of power and constraint, Cervantes opposes a secondary prose poetics of mutuality and reciprocity. As with Garcilaso, metamorphosis is the vehicle of the enterprise but Cervantes's succeeds where Garcilaso's fails because it amounts to a total spiritual transvestism. In the pages of the *Persiles* Auristela and Periandro first appear together when she is clothed as a man and he as a woman. These guises symbolize their translatability into each other, their vision of the self as other and of the other as self, although each retains the native idiom of original gender. Indeed, once Periandro is tricked out as a female, Cervantes describes the process as "hecho el metamorfosis de Periandro" (I.15).[49] The difference between the sense of subjectivity that unites this pair and its antecedent correlatives in pastoral and parody is that Auristela and Periandro, although scarcely better off for much of the novel than are the enslaved Leonisa and Ricardo of *El amante liberal*, are not cut off from power and its hierarchical dispensations. As royal persons they have access to the fount of the sadomasochistic system, even as it oppresses them in the present Arnaldo and absent Magsimino.

Accordingly, their notion of equality infiltrates governance based on male dominance and rape. Transila revolts against a society based on the sexual exploitation of women and is seconded by her husband and her father. And when it comes to be ruled by his and his daughter's lust, Policarpo's elective monarchy goes up in flames. Among those vague northern lands and seas, states are far less stable than on Iberian, French, and Italian *tierra firme*, where our equal lovers both find cognates of themselves and rise in the established scale. One great idea of Rome in the context of this novel as a pilgrimage to it is that of ultimate male hierarchy and physical and spiritual dominance. That its two sexual, though chastely sexual, lovers succeed in consummating their psychological union almost on the steps of the Church of St. Paul, who did allow that it is better to marry than to burn, seems to me to be describable only as subversion of male hierarchy and its celibate priesthood. Instead of a masculine religion of oppression, Cervantes appears to offer a new faith, clothed in the vestments of the old, of sexual equality, a new prose for an outworn poetics of dominance and submission.

Notes

1. "The crimes, reserved for its jurisdiction, were all violence or theft committed on the highways or in the open country." *Ferdinand and Isabella*, Prescott, I. 267.

2. a chain gang of galley slaves, men convicted by the king, who are going to the galleys.

3. Autoridades: "violéncia que se hace à alguno," "el acto torpe que se executa contra la voluntad de la mugér," "el agravio que el Juez hace à la parte en conocer de su causa, ò no otorgarle la apelación."

4. How could the king violate the rights of anyone?

5. persons who because of their crimes have been sentenced to serve the king in his galleys under compulsion.

6. Please remember that the law, which is sovereign, neither offends nor injures these people, but rather punishes them for their crimes.

7. Autoridades, *forzar*: "conocer à alguna mugér contra su voluntad *lat vim inferre, Stuprare.*"

8. When no translation is immediately provided, it is to be understood that the English text preceding the Spanish quote is a gloss or paraphrase of the latter.

9. I speak of that caitiff who should cause you the greatest concern, for he is experiencing a living death, condemned to the oar and in shackles on the vessel of Venus.

10. Don't imagine that I will sing of Mars in all his cruelty and wrath . . . nor of those generals triumphant on towering chariots because of whom the Germans and French, chains humbling their once proud necks, are tamed.

11. your beauty's might and together with it some mention of the invulnerability in which you are encased.

12. the example of Anaxarete should make you cowardly and fearful.

13. Lady, for the love of God, do not now draw down upon yourself the arrows of vengeful Nemesis.

14. And the slavemaster compelled the galley slave to exhaust his strength.

15. I'm here because I fooled too much with a couple of the daughters of my sisters, and also with a couple of sisters who were no sisters of mine. It came to the point where I'd fooled around so much with all of them that blood relations got so complicated that not even a devil could have straightened them out.

16. Germán Bleiberg, in a richly documented study in the *Revista de Occidente*, details Alemán's special mission of inspection of the quicksilver mine in Almadén in 1593. *Galeotes* worked it, and Alemán interrogated them one by one. Two had committed sexual crimes. Antonio Peláez was condemned as a pimp, while maestre Romano had been sentenced for the *pecado nefando* (nefarious sin), homosexual sodomy. In addition, a *fraile* was serving time in the mine as the murderer of the husband of the woman with whom he had committed adultery. Cervantes's prisoners are bound for the galleys, not the mines, but it is hard not to see some connection between Chapter XXII and Alemán's *Información secreta,* his transcription of the prisoners' interrogation, although the means by which Cervantes might have read the contents of that document is indeed a puzzle.

17. He was dressed as a student and one of the guards called him a very big talker and fluent Latinist.

18. our own Guzmán, an excellent student of Latin, rhetoric, and Greek.

19. Otis Green, in his "Alcahuete" article, rightly stresses the seriousness of the fourth *galeote*'s tone, but reads his speech as a justification for legalized prostitution, ignoring the presence in it of the idea of a regulated sexual marketplace.

20. a venerable countenance with a beard flowing over his chest.

21. a broker of the ear and even of the whole body.

22. arranges letters of credit for other areas, or loans for businessmen, and sets applicable exchange and interest rates, as well as conditions and collateral.

23. signs of some illness or vice.

24. for love cannot be compelled or commanded.

25. "Es tan bueno," says Ginés in shameless praise of his incomplete autobiography, "que mal año para *Lazarillo de Tormes* y para todos cuantos de aquel género se han escrito o escribieren" (GLASS; I.265).

26. very favorable to every kind of capital accumulation, since anything put on sale finds a buyer, because there are traffickers in everything.

27. planning to dispose of her merchandise in the capital, where anything can be bought or sold.

28. government jobs are not filled on the basis of merit but for money; everything is bought and sold.

29. completely free of debt.

30. without recourse to the self-prostitution that most of the favorites of the Grand Turk resort to in order to get ahead.

31. captured and so greatly loved by the Uchalí that [this cabin-boy] became one of his most cherished mignons.

32. one of the bravest [in the Shakespearean sense] and most beautiful of youths imaginable.

33. beauty that outstrips the greatest that may be extolled.

34. among those barbarian Turks a beautiful boy or lad is much more highly esteemed than any woman, no matter how beautiful.

35. "Ce n'est point l'*honneur* qui est le principe des États despotiques: les hommes y étant tous égaux, on n'y peut se préférer aux autres' les hommes y étant tous esclaves, on n'y peut se préférer à rien."

36. I have borrowed this term from Jessica Benjamin's *The Bonds of Love,* to which I am in general indebted for considerable assistance in trying to arrange my thoughts for this essay.

37. A Spanish grandee whose seat is Andalucia's choicest.

38. There is a profound but not yet fully elucidated connection between Cervantes and the commander of the Armada, whose extensive holdings are impressively mapped by Pierson, *Commander of the Armada* 2.

39. poetic prose is lovely, various, learned, and innovative, as well as difficult for even the keenest mind; it is replete with ornament and figures of speech.

40. because at that time the celebrated works of the poet Garcilaso de la Vega, to whom no praise can do justice, had been published and because [Periandro] had seen, read, studied, and admired them (all).

41. Oh beloved moiety of mine own soul, oh unshakable support for my hope, oh token, I hardly know whether found for my weal or woe though it can be for my weal alone, since no woe can emanate from the sight of you.

42. Oh sole consolers of my soul, oh sumptuous tokens found for my weal, welcome and warming at this and any other moment.

43. alarmed by Arnaldo's presence.

44. Arnaldo's love was equal to his power.

45. Oh wretchedness and monstrous woe, in which the lover's daily lamentation of her swells the causality of his tears.

46. Auristela did not move from the spot where she had first set foot and she would even have wished for her feet to go thrusting into the ground and to be changed into twisted roots, as did those of Peneus's daughter when fleet-footed Apollo was pursuing her.

47. her delicate feet went thrusting down into the ground and turned into twists of root.

48. Behold, oh modern huntsman comelier than Apollo, a second modern Daphne who flees you not, but rather pursues.

49. Once Periandro's metamorphosis had been accomplished.

Works Cited

Alemán, Mateo. *Guzmán de Alfarache*. Ed. Francisco Rico. Barcelona: Planeta, 1983.

Benjamin, Jessica. *The Bonds of Love: Psychoanalysis, Feminism and the Problem of Domination*. New York: Pantheon, 1988.

Bleiberg, Germán. "Mateo Alemán y los galeotes." *Revista de Occidente* 39 (1966): 330–63.

Cervantes, Miguel de. *Don Quijote de la Mancha*. 2 vols. Ed. John J. Allen. Madrid: Cátedra, 1977.

———. *Novelas ejemplares*. 2 vols. Ed. Harry Sieber. Madrid: Cátedra, 1981.

———. *Los trabajos de Persiles y Sigismunda*. 2 vols. Ed. Rodolfo Schevill and Adolfo Bonílla, Madrid: Rodríguez, 1914.

Diccionario de Autoridades de la Real Academia Española. Edición Facsímil. Madrid: Gredos, 1969.

Dover, Kenneth. *Greek Homosexuality*. Cambridge: Harvard University Press, 1978.

Góngora, Luis de. *Obras completas*. Madrid: Aguilar, 1961.

Graves, Robert. *The Greek Myths*. 2 vols. Baltimore: Penguin, 1955.

Green, Otis H. "Don Quijote and the *Alcahuete*." In *Estudios dedicados a James Homer Herriott*. Madison: University of Wisconsin Press, 1966, 109–16.

Horace. *Odes and Epodes*. Facsimile Reprint. Pittsburgh: Pittsburgh University Press, 1960.

Montesquieu, Charles-Louis de. *De l'Esprit des lois*. 2 vols. Paris: Garnier, n.d.

———. *Lettres persanes*. Paris: Garnier, 1960.

Pierson, Peter. *Commander of the Armada: The Seventh Duke of Medina Sidonia*. New Haven: Yale University Press, 1989.

Prescott, William H. *History of the Reign of Ferdinand and Isabella I* (Philadelphia: McKay, n.d.).

Real Academia Española. *Diccionario de la lengua española*. 18a ed. Madrid: Espasa-Calpe, 1956.

Vega, Lope de. *La dama boba*. Madrid: Ebro, 1960.

Wilson, Diana de Armas. *Allegories of Love: Cervantes' "Persiles and Sigismunda."* Princeton: Princeton University Press, 1991.

Chapter 2

The Sinful Scene: Transgression in Seventeenth-Century Spanish Drama (1625–1685)

Javier Aparicio Maydeu

(translated by Melissa A. Lockhart)

This essay will be limited to the period of time between the years 1625 and 1685. During this time, moralists frequently attest to the presence of constant erotic transgressions on the baroque stage. In the distorted mirror of the merchants of morality of the seventeenth century, it seemed not only that Spanish theater of that period did not comply with the orthodoxy of decorum, but that it took pleasure in deviating from it.

The priest Juan de Mariana, in his celebrated *De spectaculis* (1609), anticipates the decades of concern here with a valuable reference to the topic of the "woman dressed as a man," unavoidable when pointing out the dramatic resources that facilitate transgressive discourse:

> Síguese otra perversidad . . . ; mujeres de excelente hermosura, de singular gracia, de meneos y posturas, salen en el teatro a representar diversos personajes en forma y traje y hábito de mujeres y aun de hombres, cosa que grandemente despierta a la lujuria y tiene muy gran fuerza para corromper los hombres. (Cotarelo y Mori 431)

What is involved here is a commonplace (Bravo Villasante, Mac-Kendrick) that takes on special interest in a dramatic setting in which, as we shall see, sexual allusions are restricted to the areas of action and gesture, making use of the spoken word only in the burlesque model or in the carnavalesque circles of the *gracioso* (jester). The actress who lightens her clothing by putting on men's tights amply satiates the spectator's thirst for sensuality, while at the same time satisfying the voyeur by presenting to him an image of the feminine body that could not be contemplated in real life, since "the complicated clothing of the seventeenth-century woman could not permit erotic luxuries" (Díez Borque 47).[1] The stage topic of the "manly woman" did not distinguish genres throughout the 1600s, forming part of the dramatic resources of hagiographic comedies as orthodox as Calderón's *El Joseph de las mugeres* (Joseph of the Women; date unknown), illustrating once again the fact that generic conventions and the pragmatics of the plays followed courses that did not always converge. Doctor Jerónimo de Alcalá Yáñez y Ribera also spoke of this matter in *El donado hablador* (The Talkative Lay Cleric; 1624), recalling that the inappropriateness that this dramatic resource finally reached resulted in a prohibition on women acting:

> Por evitar algunos inconvenientes y por mayor honestidad en las comedias, se quitó el representar las mujeres, por parecer que el verlas vestidas curiosamente, ya de su traje ya de varón, cuando se ofrecía, incitaba a torpes y deshonestos deseos. . . . Mandando a las mujeres, cuando se hubiesen de vestir de hombre, fuese el vestido de modo que cubriese la rodilla, guardando en todas sus acciones honestidad y compostura. (Cotarelo y Mori 51)[2]

Father Ignacio de Camargo, in his *Discurso theologico sobre los theatros y comedias de este siglo* (Theological Discourse on the Theaters and Comedies of This Century; 1689), mischievously begins to imagine himself as this same woman dressed as a handsome young man dancing on the stage or interpreting one of these short plays that, in his judgment, have as their sole purpose devaluing the high morality of the stage:

> ¿Qué cosa más torpe y provocativa que ver a una mujer de esta calidad que estaba ahora en el tablado, dama hermosa afeitada y afectada, salir dentro de un instante vestida de galán airoso, ofreciendo al registro de los ojos de tantos hombres todo el cuerpo que la naturaleza misma quiso que

estuviese siempre casi todo retirado de la vista? ¿Pues qué
sería si en ese traje danzase como lo hace muchas veces?
¿Cuál estarán los corazones de muchos infelices que las
miraron antes y con cuidado en su traje de mujeres? . . .
Todo esto con la torpe fealdad de los entremeses y otros
sainetes impuros, con el inmodesto desgarro de las
mujeres vestidas de hombres, y con las demás indecencias
que dijimos y otras muchas que no se pueden decir.
(Cotarelo y Mori 124)

Fray Juan Márquez mentioned a few years later another pri-
mordial question regarding the treatment of erotic material on
the Spanish baroque stage. In *El governador christiano, deducido de
las vidas de Moysen y Josue, Príncipes del Pueblo de Dios* (Christian
Government, Based on the Lives of Moses and Joshua, Princes of
the People of God; 1612), republished six times until the middle
of the century, he points out that "ha de estar muy ciego el que no
echare de ver el peligro de irritar la sangre lozana con los sainetes
de los bailes y tonos lascivos que cada día se inventan para despertar la sensualidad" (Cotarelo y Mori 437).

It would not be worthwhile here to go back over the contro-
versy that was raised regarding the relationship between the main
text and the shorter theatrical pieces that accompanied the show
in its entirety. There is little doubt, however, that *jácaras* (the comic
ballads of low life) and *mojigangas* (farces) constitute a great part
of the so-called lewd intentions that would annoy censors and
baroque moralists (Huerta Calvo, Rodríguez and Tordera, Torres).
Also, Fray Juan de Santa María would argue against the dances
and the shorter theatrical pieces in his *República y policia christiana para reyes y principes, y para los que nel gobierno tienen su lugar* (Republic and Police for Kings and Princes, and for Those in
Government; 1624 [Cotarelo y Mori 540]).[3] Likewise the testimony
of Alfonso de Andrade, in his *Itinerario historial que debe guardar
el hombre para caminar al cielo* (Narrative Itinerary to Be Followed
by Individuals in Order to Attain Heaven; 1648) is very useful as
a reference concerning the ideas of the transgressional explorers
in seventeenth-century Spanish theater:

Los despertadores de este vicio y como los fuelles que
encienden el fuego de los apetitos sensuales son las
músicas y bailes lascivos y las representaciones

deshonestas con que las mujeres afeitadas y libres incitan a los hombres y despiertan los apetitos. (Cotarelo y Mori 58)

In light of the words of the Jesuit Andrade and other moralists after 1625, one can grasp how the Spanish theater was the reserve in which transgression was tolerated within the rigid and hopeless social order that prevailed during the years of Felipe III and even his son Felipe IV, a protector of the stage arts like no other monarch from the House of Austria. In this way, contemporaries of Alfonso de Andrade blame the theater for giving a forum to moral failings that in other circumstances the moralists would be willing to ignore, and they turn the theater into an accomplice of the array of transgressions that the majority of the time, while not exactly far removed from it, at least are in the realm of secondary theatricality. For D. Francisco de Araujo all that can be censored in the theater is also to be found in the surrounding society, and his *Variae et selectae decissiones morales ad statum Ecclesiasticum et Civiles pertinentes* (1664) is nothing more than a false treatise against the theatrical act/deed and an inflammatory reproach of the behavior of actresses, by way of which, once again, the question of transgressive or excessive sexuality mistakenly is judged a property of theater itself. Among those involved in this sort of criticism are Cristóbal Crespí de Valdaura and his *Observationes illustratae decissionibus, editio secunda* (Observations Illustrated by Decisions, Second Edition; 1667), and also Juan Bautista Fragoso in *Regimen reipublicae Christianae, ex sacra Theologia, et ex utroque iure ad utrumque tam internum quam externum coalescens, in tres partes divisum* (Guidance of the Christian Republic according to Sacred Theology and according to Both Laws Regarding Each One Both Internal and External, Divided into Three Parts; 1641), a treatise in which Fragoso, blinded by his strict moralist condition, does not even allude to any of the evidence of the transgression that could have been found among the verses of the comedia:

En las comedias . . . se mezclan muchas cosas impúdicas y obscenas, porque se introducen mujeres de no mucha edad a danzar y bailar, las cuales con su garbo y movimiento y con la desenvoltura de su semblante introducen en los que las ven y oyen el amor torpe. (Fragoso 45)

To the licentiousness unchained in dance movements, Father Pedro de Guzmán adds the meticulousness with which the actors looked after their appearances, altering their physical appearance in order to win over the lascivious desires of the public. In his *Bienes de el honesto trabajo y daños de la ociosidad en ocho discursos* (Good Things from Honest Work and Harmful Things from Leisure in Eight Discussions; 1614), which must surely be one of the most interesting treatises for glimpsing the varieties of pleasure among the people in the first decades of the seventeenth century, Guzmán points out:

> ¡Qué de centellas saltarán en los corazones de los oyentes, que muchos estarán, como yesca, dispuestos para este fuego! Las palabras lascivas echan centellas o ellas lo son; la voz, la música, los afectos, los afeites, la hermosura, el buen cuerpo, la gracia, el talle, el donaire, el cabello, el rizo, el copete, el vestido, el meneo, que aunque parece hecho al descuido, lleva estudiada su malicia y deshonestidad. Todo esto, entrando por los ojos y por los oídos, es fuego, es ponzoña, es secreto veneno. (Cotarelo y Mori 349)[4]

One need not insist on the importance of the sense of sight in baroque poetics. The *concupiscencia de los ojos* (concupiscence of the eyes) is produced each time the visual models to be found operating in the consciousness of each individual are knowingly altered. The first transgression would be the alteration of the images that the spectator carries with himself or herself as typified; the example of *la mujer vestida de hombre* (the woman dressed as a man) can illustrate this question. *La mujer vestida de hombre* breaks with the image of the woman's usual dress and confuses it with what typifies the man: light clothing, characterized by tights. It transgresses the moral code by altering the preestablished forms of dress, which produces a game of role exchanges that ends by inciting lasciviousness. In certain plays, although not frequently, the spectator's sexual appetite may be whetted by the contemplation of scenes in which someone appears practically nude, as Father Ignacio de Camargo found it imperative to point out in his *Discurso theologico* of 1689:

> Allí se ve una mujer hermosa mostrarse perdida de amores por su galán, y al galán no menos loco y apasionado por ella: significarse su afecto con cariñosas y ternísimas

palabras, hacerse amorosas caricias, darse las manos y aun los brazos muchas veces . . . , salir las mujeres a un jardín en guardapiés y justillo si la comedia lo manda. . . . Salen también muchas veces mal vestidas, por no decir mal desnudas. (Cotarelo y Mori 122)[5]

The festive nature of baroque theater hides, in its forest of sentiment, the trees of licentiousness and obscenity. The testimonies that we have been pointing out accentuate the idea that the presence of sexuality and transgression in the dramaturgy of the seventeenth century comes into being fundamentally by way of burlesque dances and performances typical of the whole of baroque theatrical spectacle, and not so much in the dramatic text of the comedia. When faced with the lewd exhibit of the zarabanda dance, the seminaked manly costume and the provocation of jácaras, mojigangas, and other lesser theatrical pieces of the general theatrical scene that we could term "explicitly sexual" and that revolve around the terms "provoke-unveil/reveal," there exist references and sexual games in the comedia's text, a network of formulas that by way of opposition we may refer to as "implicitly sexual" and that may be referred to by the terms "suggest-allude/elude."

With respect to the presence of sexual manifestations in the Spanish baroque comedia, there are two important matters that cannot be overlooked:

1. The scarcity of such manifestations results from the nature of the dramatic genre:
    (a) Its simultaneous and collective consumption;
    (b) The fact that it was directed to a massified public; and
    (c) The nature of its visual and oral transmission.

The greater the number of recipients of the message, the less the official permissiveness of the censors and authorities, and thus the greater the need for self-censorship on the part of the dramatists.[6] The space of erotic transgression must be reduced in the dramatic text, for which

2. the dramatist hides transgressive and erotic allusions by making use of a series of procedures that we will limit to three:

(a) limitation of direct sexual references to the world of the gracioso and the burlesque/carnavalesque modality and a reduction of erotic transgression in the court environment of ladies and courtiers. When the transgression appears it always does so following the characteristic rhetorical canons;

(b) the *preterición* or long passages of verses that serve to dilute the sexual references. See the example in Calderón's *El purgatorio de San Patricio* (The Purgatory of San Patricio; 1640); the sinner delays with digressive verses the final confession of rape and abuse of his cousin the nun:

> me atreví. . . . Turbada aquí
> —si desto, señor, me acuerdo—
> muda fallece la voz
> triste desmaya el acento,
> el corazón a pedazos
> se quiere salir del pecho,
> y, como entre obscuras sombras,
> se erizan barba y cabellos,
> y yo, confuso y dudoso,
> triste y absorto, no tengo
> ánimo para decirlo, si le tuve para hacerlo.
> Tal es mi delito, en fin,
> de destestable, de feo,
> de sacrílego y profano
> —harto ansí te lo encarezco—
> que, de haberle cometido,
> alguna vez me arrepiento.
> En fin, me atreví una noche. (Calderón de la
> Barca 87–89)[7]

(c) "metaphorization," a rhetorical limit of the term *allusion/elusion.* The woman must avoid direct sexual reference and so she adorns her words with the decorum of metaphor when she narrates how she loses her virginity in the conjugal bed. The following are verses from *La traición busca el castigo* (The False Friend; 1702), by Francisco Rojas Zorrilla:

Con amor así indignado,
Con iras mi esposo así,
Por esta flor de mi honor
Rompió el cerrado jardín;
Ya en campaña del lecho
Con lágrimas advertí
Que esta fuerza de diamantes
Se averiguaba rubís. (Rojas Zorrilla 276a)[8]

We must take note of a second example of the intermingling of sexual metaphor, one that corresponds to the comedia *El acierto en el engaño y robador de su honra* (The Success in Deceit and the Honor's Thief; date unknown) by Luis de Belmonte. Clara alludes to the incident of her violation with the following verses:

A las almenas de nacar
del hermoso Rosicler
bruto omenaje de aristas
guarnece porque haya en el
si labios para alauar
espinas para ofender
el pico dulce del que
pulido abril de el clavel
que facistol de sus fugas
por tantas auroras fue
organillo de la selba
desde su hermosa niñez
Pua es y no muy vil
taladro sutil con que
afilado nacar mudo
esgrime contra la red
pues con Revoltoso orgullo
con colerico desden
montantes hace las plumas
y de pared en pared
Roboloteando quiere

> toda la prisión Romper
> porque y Racional belleça
> alla a su bruto entender
> dice entre coleras mudas
> que las oye quien las ve....
> Al mar tormentos en llantos
> al fuego en yras poder
> y a la tierra que teatro
> de mi onor trajico fue
> Rajo a rajo en escarceos
> talar procuro y Romper
> sin que mi honor me detenga
> como Remora sin que
> el Recato prisión noble
> de vna principal mujer
> enfrene el ynpulso mio
> que a despeñarse esta vez
> bruto desbocado corre
> pues quando muere de sed
> el cordon de seda causa
> mas gemidos al lebrel

In the third segment, Clara refers once more to her violation, avoiding any direct reference:

> que ay tal calidad de ofensas
> y tal linaje de agrauios
> que para ser entendidos
> no es menester pronunciados. (Belmonte, fols
>   29r-30v and 56r-v).[9]

These last words of Doña Clara help to understand the repression that the dramatists placed upon themselves at the time regarding the mention of sexual matters. They avoided the topic whenever they could, justifying the idea that "in the Baroque theater . . . the most authentic and profound erotic scene is the one that does not exist, the one that is situated just beyond, the one that the word evokes by denying it" (Profeti 73–74).

Recall the now classic article by Everett W. Hesse about sexual transgressions in the Golden Age comedia, with examples that guarantee the presence of infidelity and adultery, divorce, prostitution, incest, and homosexuality in the verses of the comedias written throughout the seventeenth century. One must agree with him when he concludes that "the *Comedia*, like the Bible, at times expresses contradictory ideas and attitudes regarding sexual questions.... Some may argue that the *Comedia* reflects the moral decay of seventeenth century culture. Others might counter that at other times it points to a direction away from a stern theological ethic toward a more humanizing view of man's condition" (37).[10]

It is well known that the Spanish comedia of the seventeenth century distances itself frequently from any sort of erotic material,[11] but this forced prudence in the dramatic text occasionally slips, like Icarus, into carnal temptation.

Notes

1. We agree with the author when on the same page he states that "the greatest erotic pleasure that was given to the spectator was the woman dressed as a man."

2. The restraint that always had to be maintained with regard to women's costumes ended by dressing the women in layers upon layers of clothing, which is probably the reason that a fetish evolved around the feminine foot as a sexual object (Kossoff 381–86). It is clear that covering up a woman's knees in the hope of diminishing the perversion, as Jerónimo de Alcalá recalls, was far from a definitive solution.

3. Fray Juan de Santa María notes that "muy ciego está el que no echa de ver el peligro que hay en irritar la sangre lozana con tan lascivos sainetes, poderosos para despertar el apetito de la sensualidad." Note that the harmful discourses of some of the moralists multiply according to textual models that are repeated time and time again. The examples of treatises against licentiousness in the theater that are the hobbyhorses of denigration are those of dance and other paratheatrical forms of festivities brought to the stage are innumerable. The works of Fray Jerónimo de la Cruz and Juan Ferrer are especially revealing about the criteria with which the moralists of the second half of the seventeenth century purified the moral pulchritude of the theater, forgetting the direct reference to the comedia text and focusing on the criticisms leveled against the general artistic context in which it was inserted: the brief theatrical pieces, by way of their parody and insolence, corresponded to the texts of *introito*; the dances, due to

their exhibitionism of the body and the sexual symbolism of some of the movements; the negative disposition of the public in the playhouse who, as it is well known, from their entry into the playhouse were seated according to sex; and finally to the inappropriate morality of some of the actors and actresses. Concerning this last aspect Lupercio Leonardo de Argensola wrote to King Felipe II his *Memorias sobre la representación de las comedias* (Memoirs on the Representation of Comedies; 1598) and can be traced to the bad reputation of the baroque comedia in the Consulta al Consejo de Castilla in 1644, 1648, and 1666, from which may have been born the idea that the transgression is not in the theater itself, but rather in those who degrade it by dishonest behavior. It is easy to warn, nonetheless, that such an idea would require quite a few notes in order to accommodate the available testimonies. Concerning this, see Fomperosa y Quintana.

4. Concerning the bad press allocated to the actresses, and the dissolute life of the fraternity of the actors of the comedias in the beginning of the seventeenth century, as well as the presence of eroticism in the Spanish baroque stage, see Valdecasas. She states, "These behaviors gave way, in part, to continuous attacks by the Church for the dissolute lives that some of the actors led" (371). Also see Ferrer, in which he states that "obviously adulterous and infamous women, are those generally known to choose this profession" (64). Also see Hermenegildo.

5. We would be guilty of falsifying reality if we were to lead the reader to believe that these scenes that Camargo describes were frequent in the Spanish baroque drama; the moralist's opinion is obviously biased and, to this end, filled with prejudice. We can't forget, nonetheless, that around the middle of the seventeenth century the preoccupation that sight could awaken lewdity had already had a long history, as the various writers of treatises were to remember opportunely. Dávila points out in a chapter entitled "External sense, particularly sound and sight as catalysts and inciters to lustfulness," "Porque, aunque los ojos sólo ven y no son los que desean, manifiéstase tanto en ellos esta tan desordenada concupiscencia que, como si en los mismos ojos fuera su propio lugar, así los hace codiciosos, inquietos y desordenados con este deseo" (78). The Jesuit Luis de la Puente points out the importance of what San Juan Evangelista referred to as *concupiscencia de los ojos* by stating: "Primeramente, *con los ojos he pecado* gustando de ver cosas hermosas, vanas, curiosas y dañosas por sola vanidad o curiosidad, o sensualidad, con inmodestia y libertad de carne y desedificación de otros, de suerte que muchas veces peco en las cosas que veo, o en la intención con que las miro, o en el modo de mirarlas" (252).

6. Enrique Gacto states that, "while offering a certain benevolence or a relative tolerance towards the novel, the Inquisition demonstrates its uneasiness (in the only way in which it was able to demonstrate it, which is to say, by repression) concerning theater and poetry, two literary manifestations with a much greater social resonance, as genres capable of the sensorial transmission of the message, in which the public participates only as a passive recipient" (158).

7. Because of the dense linguistic nature of the dramatic poetry quotations, involving extensive word play, no attempt has been made to provide an English translation.

8. José María Micó has reminded me of the epithalamium verses with which Marino precedes Rojas: "Quando vedesse al fin l'armi deporre / la bella coppia essangue / de la prima ferita il primo sangue" (109).

9. "Que lo que as de decir calles / y lo que as de callar digas" (Calderón de la Barca, *La desdicha de la voz*, 5 vs 95–96).

10. See also Hesse's "Obstáculos" and Wade's "Love *Comedia* Style."

11. Spanish literature from the Golden Age "could not or did not openly accept sensual love as a rightful theme" according to Parker (62). Regarding the theme also see Siles's article on eroticism.

Works Cited

Alcalá Yáñez y Ribera, Jerónimo. *El Donado Hablador*. 1624.

Andrade, Alfonso de. *Itinerario historial que debe guardar el hombre para caminar al cielo*. Madrid: Francisco García, 1648.

Araujo, D. Francisco de. *Variae et selectae decissiones morales ad statum Ecclesiasticum et Civiles pertinentes*. Lugduni: Philippum Borde et socios, 1664.

Bravo-Villasante, Carmen. *La mujer vestida de hombre en el teatro español (siglos XVI–XVII)*. Madrid: Revista de Occidente, 1955.

Bautista Fragoso, Juan. *Regimen reipublicae Christianae, ex sacra Theologia, et ex utroque iure ad utrumque tam internum quam externum coalescens, in tres partes divisum*. Lugduni: Haered. Gabr. Boissat & Laurentii Anisson, 1641.

Belmonte, Luis de. *El acierto en el engaño y robador de su honra*. 1641. Biblioteca Nacional de Madrid, MS 15.009, fols. 29r-30v and 56r-v.

Calderón de la Barca, Pedro. *La desdicha de la voz*. 1639. Valencia: Castalia, 1963.

———. *El purgatorio de San Patricio*. Ed. José M. Ruano de la Haza. Liverpool: Liverpool University Press, 1988.

Camargo, Ignacio de. *Discurso theologico sobre los theatros y comedias de este siglo*. Salamanca: Lucas Pérez, 1689.

Cotarelo y Mori, Emilio. *Bibliografía de las controversias sobre la licitud del teatro en España*. Madrid: Revista de Archivos, Bibliotecas y Museos.

Crespí de Valdaura, Cristóbal. *Observationes illustratae decissionibus, editio secunda*. Antuerpiae: Typis Petri Belleri, 1667.

Cruz, Fray Jerónimo de la. *Iob evangelico stoyco ilustrado*. Zaragoza, 1638.

Dávila, Sancho. *De la veneración que se debe a los cuerpos de los santos y a sus reliquias, y de la singular con que se ha de adorar el cuerpo de Jesucristo Nuestro Señor en el Santísimo Sacramento*. 1609.

Díez Borque, José María. *Sociología de la comedia española del siglo XVII*. Madrid: Cátedra, 1976.

Ferrer, Juan. *Tratado de las comedias en el cual se declara si son lícitas*. Barcelona: Gerónimo Margarit, 1618.

Fomperosa y Quintana, Pedro. *El buen zelo*. Valencia: Sebastián de Cormellas, 1683.

Gacto, Enrique. "Inquisición y censura en el Barroco." In *Sexo barroco y otras transgresiones premodernas*. Madrid: Alianza, 1990, 152–64.

García Valdecasas, Amelia. "Los actores en el reinado de Felipe III." In *Comedias y comediantes. Estudios sobre el teatro clásico español*. Ed. Manuel V. Diago and Teresa Ferrer. Valencia: Universidad de Valencia, 1991, 369–85.

Grazia Profeti, Maria. *La escena erótica de los símbolos áureos: poesía, novela, teatro*. Madrid: Ediciones Tuero, 1992.

Guzmán, Pedro de. *Bienes de el honesto trabajo y daños de la ociosidad, en ocho discursos*. Madrid: Imprenta Real, 1614.

Hermenegildo, Alfredo. "Norma moral y conveniencia política. La controversia sobre la licitud de la comedia." *Revista de literatura* 93.47 (1985): 5–21.

Hesse, Everett W. "Obstáculos al amor erótico y al matrimonio en la comedia de Calderón." In *Estudios sobre Calderón y el teatro de la Edad de Oro. Homenaje a Kurt y Roswitha Reichenberger.* Barcelona: Promociones y Publicaciones Universitarias, 1989, 63–80.

———. "Theology, Sex and the *Comedia.*" In *Theology, Sex and the Comedia and Other Essays.* Madrid: José Porrúa Turanzas, 1982, 12–46.

Huerta Calvo, Javier. "Cómico y femenil bureo (Del amor y las mujeres en los entremeses del Siglo de Oro)." *Criticón* 24 (1983): 5–68.

———. "Risa y eros. Del erotismo en los entremeses." *Edad de Oro* IX: 113–23.

Kossoff, A. D. "El pie desnudo: Cervantes y Lope." *Homenaje a W. L. Fichter.* Madrid: Castalia, 1971, 381–86.

Leavitt, S. E. "Strip-tease in Golden Age Drama." *Homenaje a Rodríguez Moñino.* Madrid: Castalia, 1966. 1.305–310.

MacKendrick, Malveena. *Woman and Society in the Spanish Drama of the Golden Age (A Study of the "mujer varonil").* Cambridge: Cambridge University Press, 1974.

Mariana, Juan de. *De spectaculis.* Colonia: Antonio Hierato, 1609.

Marino, Gambattista. *Epithalami.* Milano, 1619.

Márquez, Fray Juan. *El governador christiano, deducido de las vidas de Moysen y Josue, príncipes del pueblo de dios.* Salamanca: Francisco de Lea Tesa, 1612.

Parker, Alexander A. *Philosophy of Love in Spanish Literature, 1480–1680.* Edinburgh: Edinburgh University Press, 1985.

Puente, Luis de la. *Meditaciones de los Misterios de Nuestra Santa Fe con la práctica de la oración mental sobre ellos.* 1612. Madrid: Editorial Testimonio, 1988.

Rodríguez, Evangelina, and Antonio Tordera. "Intención y morfología de la mojiganga en Calderón." *Actas del Congreso Internacional sobre Calderón.* Vol. 2. Madrid: Consejo Superior de Investigaciones Científicas, 1981, 817–24.

Rojas Zorrilla, Francisco. *"La traición busca el castigo."* In *Biblioteca de autores españoles.* Madrid, 1943, 54: 224–376.

Santa María, Fray Juan de. *República y policia christiana para reyes y principes, y para los que nel gobierno tienen su lugar.* Nápoles: Domingo Macarana, 1624.

Siles, Jaime. "Erotismo y Barroco: singularidad de un mundo culto de ficción." In *Diversificaciones.* Valencia: Fernando Torres Editor, 1982, 45–62.

Torres, Milagros. "Algunos aspectos del erotismo en el primer teatro de Lope." *Edad de Oro* 9 (1990): 323–33.

Wade, Gerald E. "Love *Comedia* Style." *Kentucky Romance Quarterly* 3 (1982): 47–60.

◆ Chapter 3

Desire and Decorum in the Twentieth-Century Colombian Novel

J. Eduardo Jaramillo Zuluaga

To Randolph D. Pope

(translated by Eric W. Vogt)

There is one incessant history: the history of the body, the history of its adventures and misadventures. Throughout the life of their country, Colombian writers have narrated the history of the body, invoking different words and thus weaving this history in quite diverse ways. We propose here to narrate the history of these words, a more modest history, as are all those written in modern times.[1] This would have been impossible were it not for the extraordinary and sad atmosphere that has enveloped Colombia for many years. In fact, to attribute the debut of the body as an erotic object to the influence of European literature on Colombian writers would be to offer only a partially correct history. When the social phenomenon of *La violencia* (The Violence), as the political turmoil of the 1950s is known, is first documented in the pages of Colombian literature, the body appears explicitly for the first time, and the restrictions of decorum are at last weakened.[2] Until then, the dictates of decorum had silenced such expressions completely, but at that moment, writers of quite different social or aesthetic backgrounds found themselves obliged to seek words to elucidate the experiences of the body, recognizing its exposed and fragile state. This violent period is the historical context shared by works of diverse mastery such as *Viento seco* (Harsh Wind; 1954), by Daniel Caicedo (1912), the premier and naturalist novel of La Violencia, and *Amantes* (Lovers; 1959), a collection of sophisticated and erotic love poems by Jorge Gaitán Durán.

A System of Nature Metaphors

Until these works appeared, erotic scenes in Colombian literature were, above all, episodes left to the reader's imagination. The principle of decorum ruled the imagination of traditional writers with a tenacity contemporary readers often consider naive or even irritating; thus, when they had occasion to describe lovers' bodies, their style becomes rarified and equivocal. Where we expect to find flesh, we find flowers, gardens, and resplendent goddesses. One of the achievements of *María* (1867) by Jorge Isaacs (1837–1895)[3] — one of its more exasperating qualities — is the way nature takes the place of the young woman's body, stealing her away and forever removing her from our view. In order to uncover her body, one must betray the code that masks it, just as the narrator, Efraín, is about to do when he enters the ciphered landscape of the Dagua River: to find María, one must travel back on this road of ciphers, penetrate the jungle in search of María, become inebriated at the sight of Nature now revealing her darker, mistier side wherein love and death become one, where one hears the clucking of hens and witnesses the sacrifice of a pair of vipers on the banks of the river (141).

From the time of its publication in 1867 and for more than half a century thereafter, *María* served as a narrative model in Colombia. It was a difficult model to overcome or surpass. In that period of Colombia's literary history, page upon page fell under its sway, attempting to imitate Isaacs's powerful description of the Dagua, in its luxuriant setting, or the idyllic image of María sitting on the banks of a stream one warm July afternoon, weeping with sorrow after hearing a poem by Chateaubriand (19). At the turn of the century, writers like Lorenzo Marroquín (1856–1918), José María Rivas Groot (1863–1923), and Emilio Cuervo Márquez (1873–1937) could not escape *María*'s spell. The influence of Isaacs is obvious in the enthusiasm with which Marroquín and Rivas Groot described the heroine of *Pax* (1907), a novel they wrote together; their haste to transform Dolores into an emblem of youth as well as the evening landscape that serves as a backdrop, immediately reveal the function of Isaacs's heroine as a model:

> ¡Qué hermosa estaba Dolores esa tarde! Era la juventud misma, la juventud en flor. En las orillas del río, recordando su niñez, había arrancado gajos de flores silvestres, de esas flores sin nombre que alegran las soledades y, sin espejo, sin reminiscencia de la moda, las había enredado en su cabellera abundantísima. Con su atavío sencillo, en ese tocado extraño y libre, su hermosura armonizaba deliciosamente con la hermosura de la naturaleza. (98)[4]

Only through excessive hermeneutic analysis could the principles of decorum that govern descriptions of this type be fully revealed; only a perverse emphasis upon certain marginal elements ("her flowing hair", "a delicious harmony") dismantles the sense of unity and coherence that these elements mask. The flowers surrounding the girl lack names because without them, they seem all the more natural; likewise, because it seems all the more natural, Dolores's hairstyle is unprecedented by fashion. Besides strictly identifying nature and the girl as one, little can be said: ironically, the words themselves are superfluous; even the gestures and details that could imbue her form with life seem unnecessary or inappropriate. The principle of decorum works as a curse: the body of a woman evaporates as she beholds herself in a flower as though she were gazing into a mirror, and she is converted into an emblem, a symbol, an unreachable ideal, intangible and eternal: among the flowers, she is youth in bloom.

Other Strategies of Decorum

In addition to using a system of nature metaphors to allude to the body as an erotic object, traditional writers employed other narrative devices to avoid speaking the unspeakable. An inventory of their devices attests to the existence of a discreet rhetoric or decorum.

Ever since Gabriel García Márquez (1928), in *Cien años de soledad* (*One Hundred Years of Solitude*; 1967) assembled euphemisms, periphrases, and suggestive scenes by which Fernanda del Carpio communicated with "the invisible doctors," the decorum of traditional writers holds a place of diminished glory in Colombian literature.[5] The following example comes from *Lilí*, a novel by Cuervo Márquez written in 1923. It relates the tale of a girl's love through the eyes of a mature writer suffering from the *mal de siècle*. The writer departs for Europe, where he eventually dies, and Lilí marries a young man her age from the same social class. After the wedding, Lilí and her husband take a long journey to the hacienda where they are to spend their honeymoon. In the course of the trip, between two adverbs (a *still* and a *now*) something important happens:

> su marido, su novio *todavía*, la había conducido, después de hacerla cambiar su blanco traje de novia por sencillo traje sastre, al cupé que esperaba en la puerta. Luego había seguido una carrera vertiginosa en el compartimiento reservado de un vagón de ferrocarril, al través de los campos. Después, amazona en un hermoso alazán, escoltada por su marido — ¡es decir que la ingenua y traviesa Lilí tenía *ya* un marido! — por el pintoresco camino . . . había llegado a la quinta . . . (4; emphasis added)[6]

Nowadays, it is difficult to imagine the stylistic dignity that an ellipsis once enjoyed on the printed page. Traditional writers used them to suggest or indicate censored text, or to mutilate a phrase or to complete a word: "Damn nig . . . , son of a b . . ." (94; *Las estrellas son negras* [Black are the Stars; 1949] by Arnaldo Palacios [1924]). The lines below come from *Phinées* (1903), another novel by Cuervo Márquez; the protagonist suggests to his friend Saulo the pleasures that the beautiful Cornelia bestowed on him the night before. Phinées tells him:

> De pronto una sombra de mujer cruzó la oscura alameda y llegó a mi lado: ¡Era Cornelia! ¿Qué pasó después? . . . No sabría decirlo. No se recuerdan los detalles de un sueño feliz. ¡Sólo sé que la amo!
> —¿Y ella? . . .
> —Ella . . . (16)[7]

Writers at the turn of the century often postponed descriptions of erotic scenes or the physical union of lovers. Whenever their union seemed imminent, they often introduced auditory or visual images that were out of place. In 1901 and 1903 respectively, Jacinto Albarracín published two novels, *Almíbar* (Syrup) and *Castidad*...? (Chastity...?). The first tells of the sad fate of Elvia Eterna, the daughter of a Bogotá aristocrat who decides to marry her to a millionaire named Loreto in order to recover his fortune. The second novel shows Elvia Eterna determined to preserve her virginity; she must resist a triple siege from her husband, the young seducer Carlos Pérgamo, and a sculptor and painter named Nacianceno. In the following scene, Loreto mistakenly enters the room where Elvia Eterna is changing clothes. In spite of what every reader anticipates, the narrator refuses to "focus" on the body of the girl, but instead directs the reader's attention to the eyes of unfortunate Loreto, who until then has not been able to go to bed with his new wife. In the novel, Albarracín declares:

> aquel remolinear de faldas, encajes y englobadó rodó sobre la fina y gruesa alfombra, y Loreto, embobado casi, con la boca abierta que ni le permitía una sonrisa de dichoso, cumplido su deseo tanto tiempo esperado, con los ojos agrandados por ver tras el ropaje que la ceñía, todavía por muchas telas el cuerpo [de] su esposa ... (8)[8]

In *Inocencia* (Innocence; 1903), Francisco de Paula Rendón (1854–1917) tells of how the widow Jacinta ends up marrying Angel, the young man whom her daughter Inocencia had loved in secret, but without the hope of her love being reciprocated. The episode below shows Angel and Jacinta, who have gone to the fields of the hacienda El Querido to harvest the corn:

> [Ángel] desprende la mazorca que persigue, mordiéndose los labios y cerrando los ojos, se vuelve ligero para tirarla a la jícara que Jacinta le presenta desde abajo, echando atrás aquel busto de *Ceres* encendida y agitada, anhelante la respiración y fulgosa la pupila ... Tiembla Angel ... Pierde el equilibrio ...
> . . . .
> . . . .
> . . . .
>   Recoge Jacinta la mazorca que rodó por allá y regresan a la casa; ella como Lycenta, satisfecha; él, como Dafnis, encantado. (81)[9]

This comparison of Jacinta with Lycenta and Angel with Dafnis does not exalt the lovers' bodies; on the contrary, the classical allusion only serves to obscure their corporeality. Just like the nature metaphors, euphemisms, and other elements that validate the rhetoric of decorum, these mythological allusions are not innocent ornaments of style; they are proof positive of self-censored language.

The Wandering Jews of Language

For a long time, there was no way of discovering that something was lurking beneath the surface of the Colombian narrative. In the twenties, the principle of decorum still managed to hold tenaciously to the conviction of its own invisibility. This conviction may be described as the belief that what was said was not at odds with the speakable and that the system of restrictions on which it rested was part of a normal way of behavior or written expression. Any works that could possibly contradict this opinion, such as *De sobremesa* (Table Talk; 1887–96) by José Asunción Silva (1865–96) or the novels of José María Vargas Vila (1860–1933), were relegated to the margins of the literary canon with the argument that such works could only please readers of poor taste or only interest literary historians.[10] In the thirties, however, discussions about words that could be spoken (or written) came to be more frequent. The principles of decorum eventually wound up revealing the system of restrictions (albeit ambiguously and awkwardly).

These restrictions were driven by extraliterary circumstances. As the city grew, Bogotá's upper class lost the control it had exercised over the language from the middle of the previous century (Marco Palacios 133).[11] In less than twenty years, between 1918 and 1938, Bogotá's population increased by 246 percent, while cities such as Cali, Medellín, and Barranquilla grew by 222 percent (Gilbert 89). Unable to prevent it, Bogotá's solid citizens witnessed the streets of the city swell with people coming from all corners of the country. This population of newcomers cared little or nothing for proper form, and for the first time in their lives, they came to know the privileges and the miseries of anonymity and license. To no avail, Father José María Campoamor, S.J., organized welcome brigades to save recently arrived peasants from perversion

(Casas 22ff.). At the same time, Eduardo Zalamea Borda (1907–63), bereft of the avant-garde spirit, proclaimed Bogotá as the city of 100,000 women and 1,500 cars (17).

In 1929, Dionisio Arango Vélez (1895–1943) published *El inocente* (The Innocent), a novel that warned Bogota's youth of the dangers awaiting them in the streets of the city. In telling his edifying tale, Arango Vélez was attracted to the very thing he was attacking and ended up composing some of the most uniquely comic scenes of a brothel ever written in Colombia: just after the police burst in, they join with the women, break into a dance and listen to an Italian friar reciting (in Italian) the scandalous strophes: "Cagnolino é quella cosa / che puó avere un gran valore, / specie poi per le signore, / perché é vispo e lecca i platti" (154; accent marks incorrect in text).[12] But Arango Vélez cannot bring himself to express such unbridled glee in his native Spanish; instead, compelled by decorum, he cites these scabrous expressions in the original Italian. When describing one character, he says:

> Era este el tipo del vividero, el tipo del... No nos atrevemos a estampar ese vocablo, pues es de aquellos que llevan en sí como una perenne maldición. *Son los judíos errantes del vocabulario,* obligados siempre a peregrinar de labio en labio, sin encontrar jamás un pedazo de papel en donde dormir y reposar de la fatiga. Esos vocablos, nacidos entre el fango, viven por la tradición, gracias a la potencia con que expresan un concepto o conjunto de conceptos; pero la vulgaridad y la grosería que los acompaña, impide que se escriban. (92; emphasis added)[13]

When Efraín enthusiastically recalls "las mujeres hermosas de Bogotá y pondera intencionalmente las gracias y el ingenio de P..." (16)[14] or when Arturo Cova, the protagonist of *La vorágine* (*The Vortex*; 1924), by José Eustasio Rivera (1888–1924), confines his comments to saying that, after being embraced by Zoraida Ayram, "lo demás fue de cuenta [suya] (252),"[15] there is not one word more to call attention to that which is silenced. Thus, one cannot assert that the act of speaking or not speaking is a dilemma for the writer. However, by the time Arango Vélez wrote his novel, this situation had changed completely: the author calls so much attention to his own artifice of silence that it no longer can be considered a mere discreet silence. Quite the contrary, for the emphasis it places on his words results in drawing more attention to that which he purportedly wishes to silence. In his prologue, he declares: "Es menester conocer el peligro que resulta o puede resultar de ciertos actos. Pero no basta: es menester que ese sentimiento sea intensamente sentido..." (13).[16] However, it still seems fit to ask if the "intensity" of which Arango Vélez speaks is appropriate for an edifying novel and, moreover, whether a work can qualify as edifying in which the protagonist—the innocent—ends up substituting his mother with a *cocota* from Bogotá. At any rate, the principle of decorum ceased being an assumed value, unquestionable and shared by all, and became a matter impossible to defend in a clear-cut manner. The writers of this era did not know how to silence words that referred to sexuality, nor how to encourage silence without creating a scandal, nor much less how to shield the body, enclose it and protect it from the strangers who were invading the city.

And among all those strangers were hundreds of women. According to Dora Orlansky and Silvia Dubrovsky, a high percentage of the Latin American population that migrated from the provinces to the cities was composed of women, the great majority of whom were single, young, and undereducated, usually employed in industry or in domestic service (15–16). Though Orlansky and Dubrovsky do not say so, certainly many found themselves obliged to engage in prostitution. In 1889 Dr. Manuel S. Algandona published *Profilaxis de la sífilis* (Prophylaxis of Syphilis), in which he lamented "que la República de Colombia, desde que nació centro planetario de las ideas, teniendo en su seno astros de vivificante luz en todos los ramos del saber, haya dejado tomar cuerpo a este mal [la prostitución]" (10).[17] Of Bogotá's 100,000 inhabitants at that time, 3,000 were registered prostitutes; 600, according to estimates of Algandona himself, worked clandestinely as prostitutes under the guise of being in "el negocio de hoteleras, mientras conquistaban a sus clientes, como yo mismo podría poner ejemplos" (23).[18] By the 1950s, when, according to Alan Gilbert, the city had a population of 715,250, some 40,000 were registered prostitutes (Sepúlveda 14).[19]

The scandal implicated by these figures explains the timid allusions to prostitution and to syphilis one finds in the novels of the first half of this century. In Cuervo Márquez's work published in 1903, Phinées one day discovers a red blotch on his lower lip (91). In *La marquesa de Yolombó* (The Marchioness of Yolombó; 1928) by Tomás Carrasquilla (1858–1940), published twenty-five years later, the proper, young Barbara Caballero still feels compelled to ask her future husband: "¿Me jura que no tiene ninguna enfermedad que pueda contagiar o afrentar a una mujer?" (3.190)[20] Only in 1935, when José Antonio Osorio Lizarazo (1900–64) published *El criminal* (The Criminal), are we able to find a Colombian work that develops the topic in a more or less direct manner (Osorio Lizarazo preserves a modest language, but employs an emphatic tone and a pseudoscientific jargon). The novel tells of the sufferings of Higinio González, a journalist who can feel "dentro de sí los efectos de la taberdorso-lumbar, claramente manifestados" (54).[21] He ends his days in jail after murdering the woman who was carrying his son. González's history, narrated in keeping with the precepts of the naturalist school (fatality, trompe l'oeil, scientific jargon), is cruder than the history of *El inocente*, but its purpose is equally edifying. Both works share the same attitude, the conviction that one should avoid physical contact with strangers and eschew writing those words that pass from mouth to mouth, mumbling about anatomy and the pleasures of the body.

In the 1930s, Colombian literature began to abandon the central position it occupied in the general framework of the politics of culture and timidly challenged the principle of decorum that had regulated it until then. It was a slow movement, incipient and unclear in direction. This new approach is apparent in works such as *4 años abordo de mí mismo* (4 Years aboard Myself; 1934), a novel by Eduardo Zalamea Borda; it also reveals itself in a law thesis presented before the faculty of the University of Cartagena in 1930, written by a student named Alfonso Romero Aguirre, whose writing still preserves the flavor of a manifesto. He declared:

> Hemos de iniciar la muerte definitiva del miedo a las palabras; aceptaríamos el remilgo, a cambio de borrar del idioma las palabras aludidas; de destruir en la anatomía humana las cosas por ellas entrañadas que son fundamentales de la misma ... Rompamos la conspiración

de silencio que se quiere hacer a las relaciones sexuales, y sobre la psicología de ellas, pronunciemos el *Fiat Luz*, o el grito de Goethe en su agonía: "es deber del siglo." (29)[22]

Where One Can Speak of the Body

Not everything about Romero Aguirre's proposal was difficult to achieve; it did not consist solely of breaking the silence and writing a scandalous word for the first time. Among all the narrative situations that made up the rhetoric of decorum, some already permitted suggestions of erotic scenes.

When a female character appears, the narrator describes her clothes in detail; but such descriptions are not innocent—they function metonymically, displacing the narrative observation (focus) away from the clothing and toward that which the clothing permits one to see. There are countless examples:

> mal trajeada, con el vestido de remiendos, desarmado y roto, cuyo amplio corpiño dejaba al desnudo las paletas, los brazos afelpados y el blanco pecho. (*Inocencia* 40)[23]

> [Orpha estaba] vestida con ligera túnica que le ceñía el apretado seno y que resbalando por las líneas de las caderas le caía hasta los tobillos, dejando ver los pies finos y pequeños. (*Phinées* 7)[24]

> Al empinarse [Elvira] y levantar los brazos hacia la jaula, su falda, inocentemente alzada, mostraba arriba de las rodillas la iniciación de la suave línea de sus formas. (Antonio Alvarez Lleras [1892–1956], *Ayer nada más...* [Only Yesterday; 1930] 110)[25]

The description of a dance or dancing is not merely an obligatory scene in novels of mores. Just as costuming, dance can be considered a form of metonymic displacement: it alludes to the body, appealing obliquely to its desires through the movements of dance. Such is the case in *Rizaralda* (1935), a novel by Bernardo Arias y Trujillo (1905–39):

> Juancho comienza a mover todo el cuerpo como un medium en trance y Rita lo hace con más sensualidad aún, como si estuviera gozando la sensación del orgasmo. Mueve las caderas con un ritmo de más porque el baile es costanero, y se va acercando, acercando, con los pies

resbalados contra el suelo, ceñidas las caderas y todo el
cuerpo en movimiento. Ella se menea como ofreciéndose
en goce, como urgiendo ávidamente la posesión. El, a su
turno, trémulo de apetito, se mueve con ese moverse
alebestrado del macho cabrío que no da espera. Al fin se
ayuntan; se besan, se aprietan, se huelen, se anudan, se
entrepiernan voluptuosamente, fingiendo el rito del
entrevero sexual. (*Rizaralda* 53)[26]

The boldness of Arias Trujillo in the preceding lines is autho-
rized not only by the honored place dance occupies in the system of decorum, but also because the dancers are blacks, living
in the midst of the jungle:

El amor libre era de muy buen recibo entre los habitantes
risaraldinos de Sopinga. Las negras tenían un natural
modoso y sumiso, pero era un misterio saber si en realidad
amaban a sus hombres. Obedecían ciegamente a los
varones y estos las trataban con rudeza silvestre. (27)[27]

The first bodies explicitly presented in an erotic manner in
Colombian literature are those of female slaves, Indians, peasants, or women from the servant classes. It was easy to relax the
principle of decorum in their case, because they had no honor to
defend: they were anonymous bodies with which men were free
to seek their own pleasures while setting aside for a moment the
duties of continuing a name or a dynasty. In *Almíbar*, the over-
indulged young lady, Elvia Eterna, preserves her virginity, while
one night, her servant Paulina loses "lo ido sin remedio de tornar"
(118).[28] In *Caín* (1969), by Eduardo Caballero Calderón (1910–1993),
the protagonist Martín has to imagine Margarita clothed, since
he cannot bring himself to visualize her naked: after all, she is
nothing remotely similar to "esas a las que tumbaba en un sem-
brado de trigo recién segado..., [esas que] no eran verdaderas
mujeres" (43).[29] And even as late as 1980, the protagonist of *Años
de fuga* (Years of Evasion), by Plinio Apuleyo Mendoza (1932), exposes the social discrimination operative among his generation
when examining loves and sexual attraction: "Sexo y pecado nos
los vendieron en el mismo paquete. Amamos con amor puro ciertas mujeres, preferiblemente de signo virgo, tipo Ingrid Bergman,
Audrey Hepburn, Greta Garbo. Sexualmente nos atraen las mujeres tipo novia de teniente" (33).[30]

The Writer's Privileges

An examination of the typology of Colombian writers yields two images. Both originated in the nineteenth century and endure until the middle of the twentieth century: one, that of the writer associated with political power; the other, the writer surrounded by the trappings of a bohemian. These are not fundamentally contradictory images: both enjoy a certain amount of license in society due to the idea that one who makes the law and he who breaks it share the same space. It is a neutral zone begrudgingly granted them by decorum.[31] Of these two images of the writer or the artist, the one important here is the second. The bohemian assumes a symbolist attitude toward life and art, and his precursor is the author of *De sobremesa,* José Asunción Silva.

De sobremesa is the first Colombian heterodox novel to clearly unfurl the fundamental devices of erotic expression: pretext, digression, verbosity, and a more skillful articulation of action and description. The novel chronicles the wanderings of José Fernández, a rich and sensitive poet who follows to Europe a girl named Helena, with whom he is deeply in love. But the novel consists of considerably less than the history of his wanderings; it is the history of an evening in which Fernández entertains his friends by reading his diary; the novel, then, is this reading of this writing (of a journal), of the manner in which his sensitivity has known to choose words to best express his experiences. It reveals that "eterna manía de convertir [las propias] impresiones en obra literaria" (229).[32]

Fernández's narration of his search for his ideal Helena permits him to give a detailed account of his amorous adventures (Lelia Orloff, Lady Vivian, Nini Rousset, Fanny Green, Constanza Landser) and lace them with tidbits about his interests, state of health, business enterprises, and political aspirations. The events do not follow one another in strict order; on the contrary, they are juxtaposed somewhat arbitrarily and illustrate that double principle of the symbolist aesthetics—a penchant for lists of miscellanea and morbid delight—that consists of presenting a series of heterogeneous objects to show the refined sensitivity of the protagonist. In his diary entry for April 19, Fernández records his tryst with Nelly, the beautiful wife of an American entrepreneur.

The description of the girl is governed by desire and by the anxiety that words are inadequate to describe her precisely. Consequently, the description extends itself in accumulating details, using similes and meticulous metaphors:

> Ahí estaba [yo] en la tienda de Bassot, cuando, frente, en la puerta, se detuvo el coche de elegante y sencillo aspecto. Con movimientos ágiles y miradas de inquietud, como de venada sorprendida, bajó de él, caminó diez pasos, en que a través del vestido de opaca seda negra, ornamentada de azabaches, adiviné las curvas deliciosas del seno, de los torneados brazos y de las piernas largas y finas, como las de Diana Cazadora de Juan Goujon, y vino a detenerse junto al mostrador donde estaban las joyas. Mi olfato aguzado percibió, fundidos en uno, un olor delicioso de pan fresco que emanaba de toda ella, de salud y de vida y el del ramo de claveles rosados que llevaba en el corpiño. Husmeé el olor como un perro de cacería lanzado sobre la pista, y antes de que pronunciara la primera palabra, ya la habían desnudado mis miradas y le habían besado con los ojos la nuca llena de vello de oro, los espesos y crespos cabellos oscuros de visos rojizos, recogidos bajo el gran sombrero de fieltro, ornamentado de plumas negras, los grandes ojos grises, las naricitas finas y la boca, roja como un pimiento, donde le asomaba la sangre. (257)[33]

With less good fortune than Silva and in a less accomplished way, many writers of the first half of the twentieth century developed a few features of the symbolist poet in their novels. They repeatly denounced people's lack of understanding of the artist's work, and raised him to the rank of a hero and martyr, enthusiastically defending their own right to be sensitive. At times, writers and artists were described as collectors of experiences, as souls whirling dizzily through life, exhausting all the possibilities it could offer. Phinées, for example, had a palace in Italy and a villa in Jerusalem and as soon would have devoted himself to studying an ancient manuscript or contemplating an Assyrian vase as to pursuing the love of "un raro ejemplar de mujer" (38).[34] On other occasions, less sophisticated perhaps, the writer, presenting himself as a moral soul, descended into the underworld of prostitution, exposing himself to a complex of feelings that were carrying him from temptation to guilt, and from guilt to compassion. In a novel of the mid-twentieth century as late as *Una mujer de 4 en conducta* (A Woman with a B- in Behavior; 1948), by Jaime Sanín Echeverri (1922), a group of poets purify a house of prostitution with their literary conversations: "Hablaban largas horas en el lupanar, al calor de la cerveza, sobre cosas que ella (Helena, la prostituta) nunca había oído allí: San Juan de la Cruz, Santa Teresa, el Padre Isla, Fray Luis de León, Fray Luis de Granada..." (162).[35] At any rate, whether they opted for hedonism or moralism, the great majority of these novels repressed erotic expressions. The body seemed something so recent that it lacked a name, and in order to indicate it, one had to point. Such was the task that Eduardo Zalamea Borda proposed to himself in 1934.

4 años a bordo de mí mismo is the second heterodox Colombian novel. Its protagonist, a young writer from Bogotá, tells of fleeing the city, the train trip to the Atlantic coast, his memories of Meme and the sensuous love of the Guajira Indians, of Anashka and Kuhmare. The novel bears the subtitle *Diario de los 5 sentidos* (Journal of the Five Senses), and, like the diary by José Fernández, it is a travel novel. Its pages express the desire (and the anxiety) of precisely naming various sensual experiences and indicating them using a numerical and geometric deixis in a present moment without correspondence to the historical account, but rather in response to a lyrical telling.[36] In the following lines, the narrator describes Meme, the woman he meets on the boat that takes him to Guajira:

> Meme duerme sobre la cubierta, está acostada a la altura de mis ojos. La veo, larga, extensa, como un puente para atravesar océanos. 2 inminencias lejanas—que si ella fuera ese puente quedarían en Oslo y en Riga—redondean la longitud máxima como 2 auroras boreales. Senos de Meme, redondos y frescos; senos de Meme besados y estrujados; senos de Meme, redondos como 2 auroras boreales... (44)[37]

Zalamea Borda's work provoked bitter disputes regarding what could be said (or written). In 1934, in a review of the novel, T. Galvis declared: "Poco ha ganado nuestra literatura con esta obra que apenas contribuirá a enriquecer con un ejemplar más las bibliotecas pornográficas" (10).[38] In August 1936, Zalamea Borda published a chapter of his unpublished novel *Cuarta batería* (Fourth

Battery) in the *Revista de las Indias,* in which he associated religion and eroticism; the publication of a second chapter in *Revista pan* compelled the editor, Enrique Uribe White, to write this prefatory note: "Recuérdese la agria discusión causada por la aparición en *Revista de las Indias* de uno de los capítulos de esta novela—y léase este sin temor" (34).[39] In self-defense, Zalamea Borda translated and published an article by Henri de Montherland in which the French author proposed that the primary task of the novel is expressing life in spite of moral restrictions and censorship (11). Yet, in 1948, in an interview that Zalamea Borda granted the newpaper *El Tiempo* at the time of the reprinting of his novel, he asserted:

> En cuanto a la forma y al lenguaje, no soy partidario de eufemismos, de pudibundences literarias. El hombre y la mujer en trance amoroso-sexual deben hablar en la novela como hablan en la vida . . . Desde luego: no hay que confundir con la pornografía, que es una forma despreciable. Pero la alta obscenidad, desde antes de Ovidio, ha sido un género mayor de la literatura. (12)[40]

Zalamea Borda's opinion is a synthesis of two quite distinct ideas: first, the old ethical argument (that literature must reflect life) by which realism and testimonial novels tended to justify their more daring scenes;[41] second, an aesthetic principle that would be reiterated many times in the following decades, namely, the affirmation of a constant erotics (not a pornographic one) in universal literature.[42] In such a brief interview, Zalamea Borda was unable to develop these ideas. Its principal purpose, after all, was to announce to the reading public the republication of his work in Buenos Aires in 1948. In the same city, five years earlier, the Colombian writer Jaime Ardila Casamijtana (1919) had published *Babel* (Babel; 1943), the third of Colombia's heterodox novels. It was a novel that proposed to take inventory of forgettable things and today forms a part, perhaps without deserving it, of that same inventory.

Ardila Casamijtana might have been able to write as provocative a work as that of Silva or Zalamea Borda if he had not yielded to his own scruples or resorted to some of the stratagems of decorum we have mentioned above. His novel was written after a disquieting reading of Marcel Proust; this is perhaps its best quality and its greatest contribution to the literary history of Colombia. Unlike Silva's or Zalamea Borda's heroes, Ardila Casamijtana's— Santiago—does not have a great adventure to tell; he is neither a rich poet who travels to Europe nor a youth who plunges into the sensuous world of the Guajira. Nothing has occurred to him beyond writing. Life is happening far from the pages over which he pours out his desires (and anxieties) about living someday:

> Se hace literatura a costa de sufrimientos. Un ser satisfecho calla. Los atormentados escribimos. Escribimos lo que queremos y no podemos hacer. Un pecado solitario, semejante a . . . Y de ahí que a veces se diga eso cuando se está escribiendo. "¿Con qué placer hubiera dejado de escribir lo que sé, con tal de ver realizarse una parte de lo que sé!" Lasalle. Cambio todas las obras de arte [. . .] por un puñado de mujeres. (162)[43]

Certainly, an old scruple has substituted the word *masturbation* with the ellipses in this passage; nevertheless, throughout the novel, the narrator adopts an attitude that never before had been taken rationally in Colombian literature. This attitude consists in conceiving narrative discourse itself as a syntax of erotic desire. Many scenes in the novel have no other object than to add a few more pages to the narration, and, in so doing, they prolong desire. The narrator is comparable to a voyeur, translating what he sees into words, making his words govern the actions of his characters as if they were puppets. One of Santiago's friends speaks the following lines as they play chess; the indirect style is less a concession to modesty than a verbal emphasis, a verbal strategem designed to reflect the erotic choreography of the girl's movements:

> Dicen que, luego de adobar a su hija con perfumes y cremas y despeinarla artísticamente para que diera la impresión de estar presa de indescriptibles espasmos, acentuábala los labios de rojo intenso, reteñíale las ojeras hasta el violeta oscuro, pintábale las uñas de los pies de color solferino, como de sangre detenida por una circulación presa de extraños paroxismos, y así dispuesta tendíala en el lecho, con la cabeza hacia atrás, doblando la nuca en arco de perfecta blancura, las piernas ligeramente abiertas, los brazos cual gajos tronchados, abiertos, como

para recibir, sin ánimo casi; los ojos entornados y vagos y
la pieza sometida a una estúpida penumbra que retocara
las facciones de ese cuerpo desnudo de mujer. (62)[44]

Unlike the voyeurism found in *De sobremesa,* in which José Fernández surprises one of his lovers with another woman (171), the voyeurism of *Babel* is not incidental; nor is it similar to that found in *4 años a bordo de mí mismo,* when the protagonist spies two lovers in the open night (96); similarly, nor can it be the possibility that he has yielded to the temptations of oratory as happens in the novels of Jacinto Albarracín or José María Vargas Vila.[45] The voyeurism of *Babel* is, rather, conscious of its verbal nature. Thus, for example, when Santiago remembers a time when he met one of his impossible loves, he says: "oí que adentro, en el interior de aquella casa, una niña estaba aprendiendo las primeras letras. A, e, i, o, u. De la voz que llegaba, adelgazada por la distancia, construí el cuerpo de aquella muchachita" (24).[46] In light of the serious events of those years leading to La Violencia, a dream of someone articulating a syntax of his own desire seems banal. Nor does anything seem more necessary. Although the era of La Violencia dismantled the imposing monolith of decorum constructed of metaphors, euphemisms, mythological references, and those scarce narrative spaces in which it was possible to suggest an erotic gesture, whenever the body appears in the testimonial novels of the era, it is decomposed, precarious, a body of horrors thrust upon us part by part.

A New Verisimilitude

A rather somber path led Colombian literature to modernity. To literary circles in Colombia, the years of La Violencia signified the beginning of a double distrust, the moment when words overflowed the riverbeds assigned to them by decorum at the same time when those very words were overcharged and overburdened by the tediousness of a terrifying and incommunicable reality.[47] In that no-man's-land, located somewhere between reality and decorum, the roads split in two. Some writers opted for making their convictions known in old, naturalistic terms, while others sought the strategies of a new verisimilitude. In any event, whether their works were considered independent or examples of naturalism or whether they would be consigned to the cultural enterprise recorded in the magazine *Mito* (Myth; edited by Jorge Gaitán Durán) or amid the legendary literary gatherings of the La Cueva group (Gabriel García Márquez, Alvaro Cepeda Samudio [1927–72], Félix Fuenmayor [1885–1966]), every page published in that era was written to conjure incredulity.

But how does one demonstrate that what one says is true? In the 1950s and 1960s, when Colombia had to endure La Violencia, every realm of social discourse had exhausted its capacity for persuasion: newspapers vacillated between journalistic ethics, political banter, and obedience to censorship committees; sociology and history lack authorities who could enable them to understand such recent events, and literary discourse was pressed to abandon detailed accounts of violent deaths. As late as 1983, Gustavo Alvarez Gardeazábal proclaimed that in Colombia, history is written by the winners, and novels by the losers; in a less pathetic way, it could be said that truth is something disputed by and among the various types of social discourse. Whether it be the press, history, or literature, when all is said and done, persuasion consists of having an arsenal of rhetoric strategies designed to score points with the reader's convictions by citing documents, describing details, presenting testimony, or, better yet, being able to dismantle all those strategies of "truth" with a hyperbolic guffaw: "Esta es, incrédulos del mundo entero, la verídica historia de la Mamá Grande" (García Márquez, *Los funerales de la Mamá Grande* 131 [*Big Mama's Funeral*; 1958]).[48]

Consequently, the theory of the novel of La Violencia could be formulated in terms of an economy of truth or, to employ an expression quite familiar to literary criticism, in terms of a "poetics of representation." In a way more vehement than ever, writers of this era faced two alternatives that were not always complementary: either they reinforced the identity the overwhelming majority of their predecessors had established between "author" and "narrator" that served as alter egos in their novels (Isaacs and Efraín in *María*, Silva and José Fernández in *De sobremesa*, Rivera and Cova in *La vorágine*), or, taking the contrary position, writers dissolved that identity, introduced atypical narrators, multiplied narrative voices, and, consequently, provoked a widening of the "framework of truth" of their fictions, a presentation of the various versions that exist about the same event. This is the function of the monologues in García Márquez's *La hojarasca* (*Leaf Storm*; 1955), of the posters in his *La mala hora* (*In Evil Hour*; 1962), of the voices that rumble through *La casa grande* (*The Big House*; 1962) by Alvaro Cepeda Samudio, of the documents intercalated in *El cadáver del Cid* (The Cid's Corpse; 1965) by Arturo Echeverri Mejía (1919–64), or of the muffled mischievousness of the narrator in the latter's *Bajo Cauca* (The Lower Cauca River; 1964).

In most cases, writers who opted for a testimonial form or an autobiographical account produced sensationalist narrations in which meticulous descriptions of violence were abundant. Many pages of Daniel Caicedo's *Viento seco* seem to have been written less from indignation than from a desire to obtain some obscure pleasure. The death of one of his characters, Jorge López, is illustrative: "le [cortan] los dedos de la mano y de los pies, le [mutilan] la nariz y las orejas, le [extraen] la lengua, le [enuclean] los ojos, y a tiras, en lonchas de grasa, músculos y nervios, le [quitan] la piel" (60–61).[49] Luis Iván Bedoya and Augusto Escobar have classified nine sorts of sexual and violent acts that appear in the novel: emasculation, fellatio, rape of women, rape of children, collective rape and murder of girls, multiple rape of women and girls, rape and murder of pregnant women and of the fetus, and "target practice" (39ff.). This pornography of La Violencia has given rise to many polemics. While some reiterate realism's old ethical argument, according to which literature must reflect real life, others have criticized the dramatic effectiveness of these catalogs of horror.[50]

Unlike Daniel Caicedo, authors such as Alvaro Cepeda Samudio and Arturo Echeverri Mejía opted for a sober style and a greater care in the design of dramatic effects. In *La casa grande*, the erotic encounter of Sister and Father is narrated in a contained and imperturbable manner; the movements of the Sister are precise and proceed like a mechanical dance: "La muchacha, con las dos manos, se levanta el lado izquierdo de la combinación descubriendo toda la pierna hasta la cintura y sin mirar, con dedos hábiles y seguros, comienza a desatar el nudo de tira que le sujeta la jareta de los pantalones también de percal rosado" (76).[51] *Marea de ratas* (A Tide of Rats; 1960), a novel of Echeverri Mejía, tells of the arrival of a captain in a peaceful town upon which he immediately imposes a reign of terror. In order to get him to have mercy on the town, the people beg the beautiful Nelly to satisfy all the captain's desires. Nelly accepts, and when, finally, she tells the captain of her intentions, he whispers in her ear his own secret. The lines that follow are filled with confusing suggestions. The last scene shows Nelly awaiting the arrival of the captain, while in the bedroom, lying resignedly under clean sheets, is Nelly's brother, Pedro.

The City of Mirrors or Mirages

Bajo Cauca is Echeverri Mejía's last work, and it is also one of the climactic novels of La Violencia. The novel's narrator is a peasant who arrives in Barranquilla seeking refuge, but declaring his resolve to return down river to rescue his wife and son from violence. The story is told with a classic sauciness and with a sense of uncomplicated humor. When the narrator recalls the first night he spent with his wife, he describes the shyness both of them felt in the loft, lying side by side, so still that they got cramps, while in the adjacent room, his father anxiously awaited the noises of lovemaking. Then comes the supreme and decisive moment, when they began to stir, making unavoidable sounds:

> Estábamos en esas, saboreando lo más bueno de la vida, cuando oí a alguien renegar y lanzar injurias. Era mi padre. El viejo estaba hecho un demonio, me gritó que dejara esa maldita joda, que no le diera tan duro porque iba a derribar la casa, a romper el zarzo, aplastarle las nalgas a la pobre muchacha. Naturalmente, continué moviéndome . . . ¿Qué más podía hacer? (437)[52]

The second erotic scene of the novel occurs in a brothel in Barranquilla where the narrator has been taken by a friend. The peasant is openmouthed with amazement. Everything he sees seems artificial and prearranged according to rules he does not understand. A girl named Guiomar leads him to a room where they quickly copulate. When they finish, Guiomar puts on some black silk panties and stands in front of a mirror:

> —Bésame aquí—me dijo, señalándome un lugar justo debajo de la oreja.

Me incliné y la besé. Parecía ser feliz viéndose besada a través del espejo. Mientras la besaba comenzó a mover las caderas y a frotarse contra mí. Parecía una gata. Yo, sin embargo, continuaba preocupado. Tenía remordimientos y pensaba en las venéreas...

—No te preocupes—me dijo. Mira qué bien nos vemos. (468–69)[53]

While providing us a view of the initiation of the narrator into urban life, the contrast between these two scenes also indicates a change in the poetics of representation that governs the novel of La Violencia. In fact, in a more elemental way than in *Cien años de soledad*, *La mansión de Araucaima* (The Mansion of Araucaima; 1973) by Alvaro Mutis (1922), or some passages in Jorge Gaitán Durán, the work of Echeverri Mejía illustrates that now classic moment when Colombian literature finally overtakes decorum, in order to display the naked body, but, more significantly, discovering that that nudity is desirable, provided it is sought in its own image as in a mirror. In the instant that the body is depicted in a more lucid manner, the realism of the novels of La Violencia is subverted: it is no longer sufficient to explore the alternatives of some new verisimilitude or to represent the nudity of lovers, "simply, without words."[54] Furthermore, it now becomes necessary to prolong erotic passages, yield to the inexhaustible whispers of desire, dissolve the transparency of words amid the opaqueness of language. Echeverri Mejía's novel thus may serve as symbolic of the change that then was wrought: the lovers who obeyed their instincts in the loft are succeeded by the bodies of those who sought to pursue their images into depths of the looking glass.

Thus, the search for an ultimate verisimilitude ends, if it ends, in aporia and a return to the infinite: it ends that day when the body is lost within its own image and the writer apprehends the joke that is hidden within the verbal condition of the narration itself. The writer (as also the critical reader) discovers that the words (and only the words) are an artistic medium, and that the truth, the one truth they can communicate is limited to the moment in which they are written or read. What is left, the true fullness of the body in all its corporeal joy and everything else he attempts to capture by marshaling myriad devices of the rhetoric of verisimilitude,

comes to resemble the torments of Tantalus or the arrow of
Zenon that never strikes its mark: any attempt to truly capture
corporeal ecstasy by means of language remains just out of
reach, so far—and yet so near—the words. That day is recorded
in the diary of Jorge Gaitán Durán. In the lines below, written in
May 1959, the poet gathers his notes of his journey, organizing
thoughts he had copied from Bataille and two or three recollections of Betina:

> Sólo puede uno saber la intensidad de tales meteoros *si ha*
> *tenido la experiencia*; sólo puede uno aducir su propio
> combate contra la soledad y las Parcas. Recurro
> entonces—no por exhibicionismo, sino por un cuidado de
> verdad, sin cuyos rigores mi exploración cesaría
> brutalmente—a la noche que pasé en Madrid, en el Hotel
> Emperador, con Betina, al cabo de la cual—al cabo de
> cinco orgasmos—ella susurraba: *Nunca nadie me ha hecho*
> *sentir tanto*. Habíamos vivido un instante único, hurtado a
> dioses implacables.
>
> El valor de la afirmación erótica reside en nuestra
> personal historia; pero ¿cómo insertar ahora, cuando
> escribo, *aquella irreductible experiencia* . . . ? (291)[55]

In his essays, poems, and notes of his journeys, the thing that
obsesses Gaitán Durán is that irreducible experience, the impossibility of fusing body and words into one mass, all at once. On
October 12, 1959, aboard Jaime II, he recalls the days he has shared
with Betina in Ibiza; he records: "Soy mientras sienta contra mí
este caliente cuerpo dorado" (307).[56] And while he writes? His
most lucid poems and paragraphs consist of a poetics of eroticism
that is at once resigned and enthusiastic. It is sustained by the conviction that words are a "luna inútil" (139),[57] a vantage point from
which the poet, a paralyzed voyeur, screams or mutters his unending
desires: "La literatura puede ser mirada erótica. Si su palabra llamea
nos otorga el privilegio de *vernos mientras hacemos el amor*. La
desnudez revela los cuerpos impenetrables y desaparece cuando
estos se anudan y retuercen. Durante el coito no nos vemos; somos el amor, somos el sol que nos deslumbra" (293).[58]

The notion of eroticism as an irreducible experience also pervades the depiction of the astonishing lovers in *Cien años de sole-*

dad. Its audacious poetics is founded on the desire of rendering the words transparent, making them stand out, and thus showing the bodies at the instant when pleasure makes them shudder. The secret of its verisimilitude consists in the innocent mention of unexpected details. The reader can forget those details, but it is precisely their status as forgettable objects that imbues all the erotic scenes with verisimilitude. For this reason, the reader believes in the amorous paroxysms of José Arcadio Buendía and Ursula Iguarán at that very moment when a fresh June breeze blows through the lovers' room. Likewise, readers accept the unspeakable pleasures that shook José Arcadio only at that moment when he smelled ammonia replacing the smoky odor, characteristic of Pilar Ternera; simply because of the unexpected revelation that it was Thursday, the reader also believes in the stupor of the young gypsy girl who surrenders herself to him at the fair. It also seems credible to readers when they behold Aureliano Buendía entering the room where a poor girl lies because sixty-three men had preceded him that same night, and we only see him take refuge in the arms of Pilar Ternera, when she caresses his head with the tips of her fingers. The cyclonic power of José Arcadio, the inconceivable pleasure, the intolerable pain and the supernatural effort of Rebeca when she embraces him, are empty hyperboles until the instant it is announced that "la hamaca que absorbió como un papel secante la explosión de su sangre" (145).[59] The unforseeable love games of Gastón and Amaranta Ursula become real for the reader when they tumble onto the muriatic acid; likewise, the body of Nigromanta is tangible only when Aureliano notices on her waist "un cintillo que parecía hecho con una cuerda de violoncelo, pero que era duro como el acero y carecía de remate, porque había nacido y crecido con ella" (419).[60]

But if the verisimilitude ascribed to such bigger-than-life lovers is based on the mention of some innocent detail, the brilliance of the erotic representation in *Cien años de soledad* is clear upon recognizing that, finally, the representation per se is a mirage constructed of words whose task is to extend incessantly the illusion of the bodily contact those words describe. In order to indicate the incessant nature of desire in *Cien años de soledad*, three rhetorical devices are employed. The first, and most basic of the three, is enumeration. The best examples are found in the love verses Aureliano devotes to Remedios and writes all over the house: "Remedios en el aire soporífero de las dos de la tarde, Remedios en la callada respiración de las rosas, Remedios en todas partes y Remedios para siempre" (119).[61] The second device consists of substituting the face of one's lover with that of another, for example, searching for one's lover through the bodies of others. The first Aureliano, embracing Pilar Ternera, thinks of Remedios, just as the last Aureliano, embracing Nigromanta, contemplates Amaranta Ursula. The third device pervades the fabric of the entire text of *Cien años de soledad*, and consists of the manner in which the saga of the Buendías doubles back on itself at the moment when the reader discovers that it has been "escrita por Melquíades hasta en sus detalles más triviales" (446).[62] The use of this device results in an elaboration more complex than the aporia that stifled Gaitán Durán. In fact, when the reader discovers the history of the Buendías has been written by Melquíades, he will conclude that events of the novel are "made flesh" as Aureliano deciphers the manuscripts. Consequently, the numerous encounters of all these extraordinary lovers occur precisely when the reader-voyeur reads them. Aporia, however, never resolves the verbal/corporeal dilemma, and the verbal arrow continues its endless flight, never hitting its mark, without the words on the page ever managing to reach the body of an Aureliano-reader. The words remain trapped within the verbal looking glass (Melquíades's manuscripts) that tell the reader he is reading the words that tell him that he is reading.

A Skin of Words

It will always be possible to carry the dizziness of aporia one step further and suppose for an instant that the words touch the body they seek. Ever since the sixties, Colombian novels have conjured or conjectured the possibility in quite diverse ways. When asked about the body and the words used to describe it, contemporary writers at times have formulated an ethics of eroticism, a scrupulous attention to the minutiae of sensory experience, a personal notion about language and a place for literature in the widest cultural milieu of our times.

The same year he died, 1962, Jorge Gaitán Durán finished an essay that encompasses his obsessions, entitled "El libertino y la revolución" (The Libertine and Revolution). Three years later, the poet Alvaro Mutis presented two conferences on "La desesperanza" (Despair) at the Universidad Nacional Autónoma de México, where he presented a rational explication of his own poetic thought. Both texts describe an archetypal man and how that man views life and his relationship to others. In addition, both texts postulate a world without absolutes, pierced by the erratic discourse of desire. Thus, for example, if a libertine understands that "las leyes son relativas y las virtudes convencionales" (399),[63] an individual without hope "está evidentemente fuera de la ley" (Malraux, cited by Mutis 295).[64] And again, if the libertine conceives of eroticism as "la prueba real de que estamos en el mundo" (405)[65] then the person without hope experiences "la confirmación, a través del cuerpo, de un cierto existir inapelable" (296).[66] While the libertine finds in literature the language of his sovereignty (409), the hopeless modifies the relationship that exists among things, "de la misma manera como el poeta substituye la relación de las palabras entre sí, por una nueva relación" (Malraux, cited by Mutis 295).[67] The lawlessness, absurdity, and brilliance of eroticism form the thesis of Mutis's *La mansión de Araucaima* (The Mansion of Araucaima; 1973).

Whisked away to the edge of the world, the mansion hosts most unusual beings: a soldier who speaks five languages, a homosexual who masturbates with menthol soap, a nervous and frigid aviator, a friar with a magnificent physique, a gigantic and sweet butler from Haiti, and a sensuous matron (named Machiche), in whose body all the erotic desires of the others are balanced. According to one interpretation, the mansion's felicity would have lasted forever if a girl, an intruder, had not altered that fragile balance of desires. Another interpretation suggests the possibility that the girl could be the cause, as a scapegoat, who raises the desires of the other inhabitants to a level of perfection.[68] The girl is initiated in the erotic rituals of the mansion; at the beginning, an acute self-consciousness hampers her pleasures. The narrator reports that "se sentía extraña y ajena a sí misma en el momento de gozar y, en ciertas ocasiones, llegaba a desdoblarse en forma tan completa que se observaba gimiendo en los estertores del placer y sentía por ese ser convulso una cansada y total indiferencia" (145).[69] In another instance, brought into the mansion by the custodian and made the brief lover of the pilot and friar, the girl pays a visit to the servant, in whose arms she "no logró desdoblarse como era su costumbre [y] se lanzó de lleno al torbellino de los sentidos satisfechos" (148).[70] Finally, seduced by Machiche, she feels herself become "presa de un inagotable deseo siempre presente y sugerido por cada objeto, por cada incidente de su vida cotidiana" (156).[71]

The girl's suicide, the mysterious death of the pilot and Machiche, and the scattering of the other inhabitants of the mansion could be understood as an exemplary punishment for their excesses, except that the novel resists so closed an interpretation. The series of uncertainties it is composed of—the hints, paradoxes, and abundance of its blind motifs—present any attempt at a hermeneutics of *La mansión de Araucaima* as an erratic and incessant task. Thus, comparable to the erotic events it narrates, Mutis's novel overburdens the critical attempts to understand it and demonstrates that resigned conviction of Gaitán Durán, which states that literature is a "lenguaje del deseo que hasta la eternidad sigue siendo deseo" (405).[72]

Rejecting the glee with which other writers declare the brilliance of eroticism, Héctor Rojas Herazo (1922) chooses to relate the daily life of the body. It is a history prior to time, a dream periodically renewed by keeping a diary of the five senses, by documenting sensations in rigorous detail or recording intuitions as yet unorganized into a narrative and lacking direction. From *Respirando el verano* (Inhaling Summer; 1962) to *Celia se pudre* (Celia Is Rotting Away; 1986), his pages evoke details, brief messages, little tidbits, all such minutiae of wisdom plucked from flighty epiphanies that never manage to form a coherent or a self-contained doctrine. His joyous scatology (beyond body and heaven) frees him from the suspicion, announced by Gaitán Durán, that the language of desire also could be the expression of a devalued solipsism, akin to the language of a prisoner or an onanist (Gaitán Durán 406). Toward the end of his last novel, the eyes (of the character) are turned toward a pile of magazines resting on a dusty staircase. On the cover of one he sees the figure of a girl, with her lips slightly parted, whom he imagines to be surrendering herself to a crowd of men, and who afterward:

> sería conducida ante el gran chulo, ante el imponente cabrón-madre del multicirculante falo de llamas. Dejaría que él se introdujera, absolutamente todo él, por su envaselinado firibitilo hasta sentir que, saliéndole por la boca, le dejaba un sabor a noche estrellada con glándulas de vinagre y almíbar, a profusa cabellera de niña asustada entre las faramallas de un ropero, a ceniza de hormigas arropando unos comidos talones y unas agrietadas pantorrillas que olvidaron la lluvia y la ventana donde han derramado polvo de polvo y ella misma polvo, furioso polvo [. . .] Pero y yo, entonces, ¿yo qué saco de esta movida? Pues nada, grandísimo pelotudo. Simplemente te quedarás sin nada, concibiendo puras corrientísimas y ridículas necedades, pues ni siquiera tienes buenos sesos para estas imaginomasturbotonterías.(791)[73]

Unlike Rojas Herazo, the work of R. H. Moreno-Durán (1946) has expressed the erotic body in ways that owe more to culture than to sensuousness. Thus, for example, a character in *Juego de damas* (Checkers; 1978), when explaining her sexual prowess, relates:

> Decía que en aquella época de impericia hacía el amor como si fuera la novela que definen las más intransigentes preceptivas, esto es: a) con exposición, b) con apretado nudo y c) con lento desenlace. Pero en Suiza todo esto quedó atrás y el acto de amor, rápidamente conquistó deliciosos parámetros de complejidad creciente. (95)[74]

In *El toque de Diana* (Reveille; 1981) the lovers are joined by following a grammatical process, beginning with the Conditional, then the Concessive, and finally, "como está mandado, [con] las Copulativas" (19).[75] Lastly, in *Metropolitanas* (Metropolitan Ladies; 1986), a woman professor of literature discovers that, in the arms of her lover, she is transformed into "una página donde la escritura es un goce" (91).[76]

These passages are characteristic of Moreno-Durán's reflexive, intelligent, and solitary humor; they also are redolent of that ancient Western dream that proposes to identify word with flesh, book with world, an *ars poetica* with an *ars erotica*. But Moreno-Durán's work pursues this dream with a skeptical enthusiasm. Just as Gaitán Durán understands poetry as a "useless looking glass," the position Moreno-Durán has adopted consists of a resigned irony before the "uselessness" of words. In his works, language tells of and desires bodies that language itself cannot possess and laughs at its own desire.

In recent years, while reality (those events of history, this erotic body) is understood as impossible for language that tells of it and dreams of it, the writer's voice adopts a most modest attitude. The writer no longer proposes a moral lesson for preserving the cohesion of a group in a city that others are taking over, nor does he proclaim his dominion over the real truth about events. In *Transplante a Nueva York* (Immigration to New York; 1983) by Alvaro Pineda Botero (1942), *Las puertas del infierno* (Inferno's Doors; 1985) by José Luis Díaz Granados (1946), the works by Moreno-Durán, as well as in *El río del tiempo* (The River of Time; 1985–88) a collection by Fernando Vallejo (1942), the image of the writer is one of a vain demiurge, a vagrant lord of words who stumbles upon every page by blind luck of literary invention and finally composes what almost always is a random novel composed of countless, confused voices. In *Sin remedio* (Without Hope; 1984), Antonio Caballero (1945) relates the nonsensical vicissitudes of Escobar, a poet from Bogotá "acorralado por la literatura" (43).[77] Much of the novel's humor and disrespect rests on Caballero's ability to stage various intonations of language. Thus, for example, when Escobar lies impotent at the side of a prostitute, he decides to dedicate a sonnet to her because "en fin de cuentas, (un soneto) es una expresión de amor tan válida como una erección" (53).[78]

Parody is not the only way by which language is staged. Works as different as *¡Que viva la música!* (Long Live the Music!; 1977) by Andrés Caicedo (1951–77), *La tejedora de coronas* (Lady Weaver of Crowns; 1982) by Germán Espinosa (1938), *Metropolitanas* (Metropolitan Women; 1986) by Moreno-Durán, and *Un pasado para Micaela* (A Past for Micaela; 1988) by Rodrigo Parra Sandoval (1937) are all narrated by female characters, and, consequently, they oblige the implicit author to assume a certain distance with respect to language, adopting certain modulations of expression not his own. On many occasions, some of these female narrators have not been considered entirely true to life, possessing androgynous attitudes or a refined and obscure language. The effect of verisimilitude, however, is not of the highest priority in these works; on the contrary, in these works, the feminine voice is a source of intertextuality, a condition capable of invoking texts of diverse origins on their pages (song lyrics, quotes from encyclopedias, allusions to the opera). It is also one of the clearest forms by which language shows the desire of that other who provokes this desire, and thus puts words into the mouth of that other (the woman) that make her more desirable. "Soy rubia, rubísima,"[79] the protagonist declares in the first line of ¡Que viva la música!

But language of desire is not always directed toward the voice and the body of another. At times, it also can turn toward the speaker's own body, less to take inventory of his or her sensory perceptions than to claim the place that belongs to him or her in the culture of sexuality. When Guiomar in *Bajo Cauca* looks at herself in the mirror, she confirms with her own eyes the look with which she is desired by men and thus establishes a continuum of the desire flowing from her to her own image. And contrarily, when Ana González, a character in *Cola de zorro* (Fox Tail; 1970) by Fanny Buitrago (1943), examines herself meticulously in front of a mirror, she resignedly proves to her own eyes that she looks like "una mala portada de Vogue" (67).[80] This disarticulation of the language of desire is a recurring feature in works of women writers. In *Misiá señora* (*Ma'am*; 1982) by Albalucía Angel (1939), for example, the protagonist recalls her wedding night as a siege: "pero él que no, que ésta es labor del novio, volviendo hilangos las enaguas, rompiendo los botones, te adoro, estás muy linda, frotándose, mordiéndola, y ella quería decir espera un poco, pero no se atrevía porque esperar a qué" (136).[81] A lovers' embrace doesn't always symbolize that union the language of desire longs for; it can also be occasion for exposing psychological distance between lovers. In any event, whether a voice dreams of a body that it describes with more desirable words or whether this voice articulates the speaker's right to a bit more space for his or her own body, only at the moment when Colombian literature moves toward a marginal position in the national culture does it finally overcome the aporia that stifled

Gaitán Durán. Literature can be understood as a language in which we tell of our desires, but it is also a space for discovering the nature of others' desires.

Conclusion

The history of the words with which the Colombian writers have spoken of the erotic body is riddled with discontinuities. During the long years in which histories of Colombian novels have entertained their readers with colorful catalogs about groups, schools, movements, and generations, the vast system of decorum has circumscribed the possibilities of erotic expression. Its persistence is founded upon a certain dose of flexibility, upon its capacity to toy with censorship along with some narrative spaces wherein it is possible to suggest the erotic body. It is a question of playing with elementary strategies: the system of nature metaphors, matters left to the imagination, use of ellipses, abrupt changes of "focus," and mythological allusions that occur together with those momentary deviations from the narrative glance that rushes to speak of the body by means of clothing, a dance, or a nameless girl.

The most important concession of decorum is that curious sensory privilege granted to the writer. Thanks to this privilege, some Colombian heterodox works are written. In fact, the reserved nonconformity of *De sobremesa*, only published when those who might have been scandalized by it had died, the iconoclastic attitude of *4 años a bordo de mí mismo*, and the introversion of *Babel* contrast against a background silenced by discretion, as a consequence of which, undoubtedly, they are upheld. Only in the mid-twentieth century, at the beginning of the bloody era of La Violencia, does the hegemony of decorum break down dramatically. It is not important, then, whether there are authors who rely on the precepts of the naturalist school or assimilate certain literary novelties from abroad. What is fundamental is that their works disengage from the demands of decorum and that they introduce the complexities of representation and the concept of literature as a language of desire. Due to circumstances and a certain urgency, Colombian literature always has conceived of the erotic body in the context of a threatened society. In the fifties, Jorge Gaitán Durán was one of the Colombian writers who meditated more explicitly on eroticism and literature. Some of the ideas in his essay "El libertino y la revolución" serve as a basis for engaging the problems of eroticism (not merely a typology) appearing in the novels of the following decades: the ethics of the erotic body, the diary of sensory experiences, the utopia that enjoins body and word. Since only a few years ago, when it was noted that the novel is made of language inhabited by countless voices, has it come to be viewed as an understanding of eroticism that Gaitán Durán could not have suspected: a polyphony of desires, crisscrossing on every path, interweaving in all directions and on every level of textuality, leaving fleeting marks on the skin of words dissolving before our eyes.

Notes

1. The scope of this essay is even more modest. Most of what I deal with here comes from literary works that are not unfamiliar to the specialist. If, as I suggest in the last pages, contemporary novels express more often than ever sexual desires different from the dominant masculine and heterosexual ideology, the same tendency is followed by literary criticism and its intention to rewrite Colombian literary history. Studies like *¿Y las mujeres?* (And Women?; 1991) by María Mercedes Jaramillo, Angela Inés Robledo, and Flor María Rodríguez Arena, with an extensive bibliography of literary works written by women since the beginning of Colombian history, are certainly at the avant-garde of this new trend. Whereas this is true about the feminist perspective, Colombia still lacks a study of representation of homosexual desire in literature. Recent works like *Gay and Lesbian Themes in Latin American Writing* (1991) by David William Foster may encourage more detailed research on this matter in Colombia.

2. The use of the term "rhetoric of decorum" enables us to describe a system of liberties and limitations, prohibitions and permissions; it is a rhetoric of what is "appropriate" by which is established, in the words of Gerald Else, "the kind of things a certain kind of person is likely to do or say according to probability or necessity" (28).

3. *María* (1867), written by Jorge Isaacs, is the most important romantic novel in Latin America. It tells the love story of a beautiful girl and a young man, Efraín, who, after leaving her, goes to London. From London, he writes her love letters, and in her answers learns she is suffering from a terminal illness. He returns to Colombia, sails up the Dagua River, and on horseback continues his journey to see her. When he arrives, he runs and leaps up the stairs, but not in time to see her on her deathbed. The hacienda where most of the story takes place is today a national monument. Coincidentally, it is called Hacienda El Paraíso (Paradise Hacienda).

4. How beautiful Dolores was that afternoon! She was the very embodiment of youth, youth in bloom. On the banks of the river, recalling her childhood, she

had plucked a handful of wildflowers, that kind without a name that cheer the lonely hours, and, without a mirror, unguided by the dictates of any fashion, she had woven them through her flowing hair. With her simple adornment, in this strange and free style, her beauty deliciously harmonized with Nature's. (Unless otherwise noted, all English versions of the texts are Eric Vogt's.)

5. In this novel, Fernanda del Carpio represents the solemn people of the Andes (specifically solemn and ceremonious when compared to the joyful and festive people of the Caribbean). Suffering from a mysterious disease, Fernanda decides to invoke a group of spirits known as "the invisible doctors." These doctors ask her questions in order to suggest some treatment, but the answers become confusing because of "her twisted habit of not calling things by their names [that] made her put first things last and use 'expelled' for 'gave birth' and 'burning' for 'flow'" (294; trans. G. Rabassa).

6. her husband, *still* really her groom, had taken her to the coach awaiting them at the front door, after having her change from her white wedding dress to a simple tailored one. They then took a dizzying ride in a reserved compartment of a rail car, through the countryside. Afterward, she looked like an Amazon on her cinnamon steed, led by her husband through the picturesque fields to the ranch — which is to say that *now*, the naive and mischievous Lilí had a husband!

7. Suddenly, a woman's shadow crossed the grove and came up next to me: It was Cornelia! What happened next? . . . I wouldn't know how to express it. You just can't remember the details of a pleasant dream. I only know that I love her!

—And she? . . .

—She. . . .

8. all that waving mass of her skirt, of lace and hoop skirt slid down onto the fine thick carpet, and Loreto, nearly stupefied, stood there with his mouth open, unable to even smile at his good fortune, at the fulfillment of his long awaited desire, his eyes wide open trying to peer beneath the fabric of the garments that still held his wife's body. . . .

9. [Ángel] broke off the ear of corn he was grasping for, biting his lips and closing his eyes. He turned slightly to toss it into the basket Jacinta was holding out for him below, tossing aside her *Ceres*-like bust, aglow and agitated, breathless with desire and her glance darting away. . . . Angel trembled. . . . He lost his balance. . . .

. . . .

. . . .

. . . .

Jacinta picked up the ear that was rolling away and they returned to the house; she like Lycenta, satisfied; he, like Daphnis, bewitched.

10. The position of *De sobremesa* in Colombian literature is yet to be defined precisely. The novel was not published until 1925, more than thirty years after it was written. When it was published, Jorge Zalamea declared: "How should contemporary criticism treat the work, so long delayed in publication, that appears today, with an aggressive gesture, reminding us of the spirit that encouraged artists during the past quarter of a century? In response to the rationalist imperative that commands the critic to situate himself in the milieu of the period in which the work was produced in order to judge its value . . ." (428).

11. Traditionally, people from Bogotá thought of themselves as the best speakers of the Spanish language in the Americas. They considered their city to be the Athens of South America and praised their philosophers and poets. Most of these intellectuals were successful politicians: José Manuel Marroquín, the founder of the Academy of Language, was president of Colombia from 1900 to 1904; Miguel Antonio Caro, author of a Latin grammar, was president from 1896–98; and Marco Fidel Suárez, author of numerous essays on linguistics, was president from 1918–21. These three figures are known in handbooks of history as the "grammar presidents." An excellent essay on this topic is *Del poder y la gramática* (1993) by Malcolm Deas.

12. A puppy dog is something / that can have a great value / especially for ladies / because it is lively and it licks the plates.

13. He was that type of hard-living individual, a regular.... We don't dare print that word, since it's one of those that bear their own eternal damnation. *They are the wandering Jews of our lexicon,* obliged to forever journey from the lips of one to another, without ever finding so much as a piece of paper on which to rest from their exhaustion. Those words, born amid the mud, live on by tradition, thanks to their power to express a concept or group of concepts; but their vulgarity and the grossness that accompanies them, prevent their being written (emphasis added).

14. the beautiful women of Bogotá and praises of the graces and wit of P—

15. the rest [was his] own story (264).

16. One must realize the dangers that lie in committing certain acts or that can result from them. But that is not enough: that sentiment must be intensely felt....

17. that the Republic of Colombia, since its foundation a world center of ideas, home to brilliant intellectuals in all fields of knowledge, has allowed this social ill [prostitution] to spread.

18. "the hotel business, all the while seducing their customers, as I myself could provide examples." Algandona notes that of the 619 cases of syphilis treated in 1889 in the Hospital San Juan de Dios, 269 patients were maids, 67 seamstresses, and 47 prostitutes (20–21). In 1909, Dr. Aparicio Perea reported to the Argentine physician Emilio R. Coni that in Colombian military hospitals 22 percent of the cases treated were syphilis and other venereal diseases. In Colombia, the bibliography on syphilis begins quite early. In 1881, García Pharmacy, in Cartagena, had the text of Eduardo Langbert translated for their bulletin: *Aphorisms on Venereal Diseases Including a Master Formula for Their Treatment.* In 1893, the thesis of Manuel S. López, a physician from Bogotá, appeared: *Syphilis and Its Relation to Marriage.* In 1899, *Microphitosis,* a fanciful work by Manuel de Jesus appeared, and in 1935, the study by Ricardo Bonilla, et al., *The Twelve Greatest Plagues.* Besides these treatises, the writings of Fournier also were in circulation: *The Anti-Syphilis League, Syphilis, The Social Danger, For Our Daughters When They Turn 18, For Our Daughters When Their Mothers Deem These Counsels Necessary* (Coni 397).

19. In Medellín's case, these figures are even more scandalous. According to Kristina Bohman, "Between 1933 and 1946, the population of the city increased by 75% and the number of prostitutes by 200%. In the later years there existed 4,260 registered prostitutes in Medellín or 'one prostitute for every 30 males of all ages'" (Parsons 1949; 108 [English original 64]).

20. Can you swear to me that you don't have any disease that could contaminate or be an affront to your wife?

21. within him the effects of taverno-lumbarditis, clearly manifested.

22. We must begin pronouncing a death sentence on the fear of words; we would accept prudery, in exchange for erasing from the language all allusive words; in exchange for destroying in human anatomy itself those things which are fundamental to it.... Let us break the conspiracy of silence that seeks to obscure sexual relations, and the psychology of sexuality, let us pronounce *Fiat luz*, or the cry of Goethe on his deathbed: "It is the duty of our time."

23. The poorly dressed young girl, her clothes made of gaping and torn patches sewn together, whose ample corset easily revealed her shoulder blades, her velvety arms and white breasts.

24. [Orpha was] wearing a light tunic that pressed in her bosom and that, gliding along the line of her hips, reached to her ankles, revealing her fine, small feet.

25. When [Elvira] stood on her tiptoes, lifting her arms toward the cage, her skirt, raised innocently, revealed the beginning of the soft outline of her figure above her knees.

26. Juancho began to move his entire body like a medium in a trance and Rita moved with even-measured sensuality, as if she were enjoying the sensation of an orgasm. She moved her hips with that extra rhythm because the dance was a coastal one, and she moved closer, closer, her feet sliding along the floor, her hips and whole body pulsing in one sensuous motion. She shivered as if offering herself in ecstacy, as if she were urgently inviting him to take her. For his part, he trembled with appetite, moving like a billygoat that can't wait. Finally, they come together, kissing, squeezing each other, sniffing each other, entangling legs and arms like a knot, voluptuously, imitating the rhythm of a sexual union.

27. Free love was well received among the *rizaraldinos*, the inhabitants of Sopinga. The negresses were of a submissive temperament and well-behaved, but it was a mystery to figure out if they truly loved their men. They blindly obeyed them and in return were treated with a jungle-like rudeness.

28. that which is irreparably lost.

29. those women whom he used to have his way with in a recently cut wheat field . . . [who] weren't women in the true sense of the word.

30. Sex and sin were sold to us in the same package of goods. We love purely certain classes of women, preferably Virgos, the Ingrid Bergman, Audrey Hepburn, Greta Garbo types. Sexually, we are more attracted by the lieutenant's-wife type.

31. In an essay published originally in *Mito* in 1961, Jorge Eliécer Ruiz takes up these two images in his consideration of the freedom of writers, both in the aesthetic sense (freedom to create) as well as in a political sense (to change the state of things to seek greater freedom) (28).

32. eternal mania of seeking to turn one's impressions into a work of literature.

33. There [I] was in Bassot's shop, when, right in front of the door, this carriage, a simple and elegant model, stopped. With agile movements and looks of inquietude, like a frightened fawn, she climbed out, walked ten feet, during which I visually felt out, through her opaque black dress adorned with sequins, those delicious curves of her breasts, of her sinuous arms and long, fine legs, like Juan

Goujon's The Huntress Diana, and she came over and stopped next to the counter where the jewelry was. My keen sense of smell made out a single delicious scent of fresh baked bread, emanating from all around her, a scent of health and of life and of a bunch of rose-colored carnations she had in her bodice. I inhaled the scent like a hunting dog on the trail of game, and before she could speak the first word, I had already stripped her naked with my looks and kissed her golden-laced neck with my eyes, as well as her full and wavy dark hair with just a hint of red, which she gathered under her big felt hat with its black feathers, her big grayish eyes, fine nose and that mouth, red like a pepper, where her blood was rushing.

34. a rare specimen of a woman.

35. They would speak for hours in the whorehouse, fueled by beer, about things she [Helena, the prostitute] had never heard there: San Juan de la Cruz, Santa Teresa, Fr. Isla, Fr. Luis de León, Fr. Luis de Granada.... Regarding the meaning of the brothel in modern Latin American literature, see the article of Kessel Schwartz, "The Whorehouse and the Whore in Spanish American Fiction of the 1960s."

36. Linguists designate as $\delta\ \epsilon\iota\kappa\tau\ \acute{o}\zeta$ those particles of language that point out something concrete: this, here, over there, you. There are several varieties of $\delta\ \epsilon\iota\kappa\tau\ \acute{o}\zeta$; the one used most frequently in literature is called $\delta\ \epsilon\iota\kappa\tau\ \acute{o}\zeta\ \alpha\ \phi\acute{a}\nu\tau\alpha\sigma\ \alpha$ (phantom $\delta\ \epsilon\iota\kappa\tau\ \acute{o}\zeta$) and occurs "when a narrator whisks the listener off to the realm of that which is absent, but memorable, or to the realm of constructive fantasy" (Lázaro Carreter 130). Regarding the poetics of sensuality in the novel of Eduardo Zalamea Borda, see J. Eduardo Jaramillo Zuluaga, "La poesía en *4 años a bordo de mí mismo*."

37. Meme is sleeping on deck. She is lying at my eye level. I see her, long, extended, like a bridge that could cross oceans. 2 distant hills—so that if she were that bridge, they would be in Oslo and in Riga—round out the most distant longitude like 2 aurorae boreales. Meme's breasts, round and fresh; Meme's breasts kissed and squeezed; Meme's breasts, round like 2 aurorae boreales.... (44)

38. "Our literature has gained so little from this work that its one volume will barely enrich pornographic collections." These collections tend be designated as "Hells." There are catalogs of "Hells" such as the one in the Vatican Library and another by Antonio Villalonga y Pérez, *Infierno de la Biblioteca Villalonga* (Palma de Mallorca: F. Soler y París, 1923); perhaps the most famous catalog of these pornographic collections is the one possibly composed by Guillaume Apollinaire with Fernand Fleuret, and Louis Perceau, *L'Enfer de la Bibliotéque Nationale* (Paris: Mercure de France, 1913). Among the Spanish books Apollinaire includes in his catalog are *Vida de la mujer del deleite o de las veinticinco posturas que usó* (London 1892), and *Travesuras de amor. Galería del deleite. Colección de todo lo más sabroso y lechoso que se ha esgrito (sic) sobre el coño é islas indecentes. Recopilado por un aficionado* (London 1870). Other references about pornographic libraries can be found in the superb book by Walter Kendrick, *The Secret Museum: Pornography in Modern Culture.*

39. Recall the bitter disputes caused by the publication in *Revista de las Indias* of one of the chapters from this novel—and read this without fear.

40. Inasmuch as form and language are concerned, I am not partial to euphemisms, nor to literary pruderies. [In a work of literature, a] man and a woman,

caught up in an amorous-sexual encounter, ought to speak as they speak in real life. . . . Therefore: it is not to be confused with pornography, which is a despicable form. But high obscenity, since before Ovid, has been a major literary genre.

41. Lorenzo Marroquín repeats the same argument in his foreword to *Pax*: "The writer of mores, just as leguminous plants, absorbs the atmosphere surrounding him and is nourished by it, whether it is pure or sullied; perhaps all the more nourishing and fertile when it is more pestilent" (xv).

42. Former discussions about the thin line distinguishing pornography from eroticism still have a contemporary ring. In 1850, Germán C. O. Muller put the word ποξνογξάφοξ into circulation "in reference to the authors of the sensuous frescos of Pompey." Muller took the term from Ateneos, a chronicler of the second century A.D. The word "eroticism" was employed by American and European writers between the two world wars to defend the aesthetic intentions of their more sensuous scenes in their works. The term is wrongly derived from the ancient Greek word έξωτικόξ, which referred to one of the sexual practices of youths. In this regard, see the work of Joan Hoff, "Why Is There No History of Pornography?"

43. Literature is written at the cost of suffering. A satisfied being is quiet. It is we, the tormented, who write. We write of what we desire and what we can't do. It's a solitary sin, similar to. . . . So that's why at times one says this when he's writing: "With what relish I would have stopped writing what I know, if only I could have seen the smallest part of what I know come to pass!" Lasalle. I'd trade in all the works of art . . . for a handful of women.

44. They say that [the mother], after spicing her daughter with perfumes and creams and undoing her hair artistically so as to give the impression that she was rapt with indescribable spasms, made her lips up intensely red, even applying a deep violet shadow around her eyes and painting her toenails a sulphur color, like that of blood whose circulation has been blocked by some strange paroxysms. Thus disposed, she would stretch her daughter out on the bed, her head back, arching her milk-white neck, her legs slightly spread, her arms crooked like broken branches, open, as if to receive, almost listlessly; her eyes rolled back and with a vacant look and the whole room plunged into torpid shadows in order to make her naked womanly features stand out all the more.

45. The weakness of these two authors is due not only to their inability to control the oratorical pace they establish in their texts, but also to their inability even to mention one realistic, natural detail in their more erotic passages. We offer here two examples. In the following scene from *Castidad . . . ?*, Albarracín describes how Nacianceno, the artist, asked Elvia Eterna to pose for him, and to assume increasingly daring postures, until "blind, insensitive, crazed, unbuttoning her top more, he deposited on her white, exceedingly white flesh, on her firm breast, a biting kiss that surely penetrated her to the bone with love" (153). The case of Vargas Vila is very well known in Latin America. The fame of some of his pages can be attributed to the way he exaggerated—to the point of incredulity—some of the very devices of the rhetoric of decorum. In the following lines from *Flor de fango*, the protagonist exhibits all her mythological nudity to the reader: "As a white deer, abandoning the lukewarm bed of weeds and moss where it had lain sleeping, at the break of dawn, Luisa tossed the coverlets to her feet, and lightly sprang from her bed.

Standing on the carpet, she let the inconvenient slip drop, gliding to her ankles, covering her feet completely. And thus she seemed as if she were emerging from the immaculate foam, or from snowy polar ice; as if she were standing on a seashell; thus then, she resembled Febea, standing erect on the fleece of a cloud, charting the course for the chariot of the moon toward distant Latmos.

And there she remained nude, chaste, grand" (84).

46. I heard that inside, in that house, a girl was learning her letters. A, E, I, O, U. Judging from the sound of the voice that reached me, attenuated by the distance, I reconstructed the body of that little girl.

47. The exercise of an "aesthetics of modernity" in Colombia could have its origins in Silva's *De sobremesa* or Eduardo Zalamea Borda's works of the 1930s. However, novels faced the problems presented by this aesthetic (the problem of representation) in a more systematic manner than they did during the era of La Violencia. In the fields of history and sociology, other authors also have suggested the connection between the phenomenon of La Violencia and the culture of modernity in Colombia. In his book *Colombia: The Political Dimensions of Change,* Robert H. Dix has said that La Violencia was the manifestation of a modern crisis, that is, the result of the policies by which the dominant class opposed the urgent needs of a pluralistic society in Colombia (7). For his part, Camilo Torres asserts that "our rural society, affected by La Violencia, began its urbanization in the sociological sense, in the sense that it began to acquire urban behaviors. . . . In a word, we can say that in a society affected by La Violencia, we have urban attitudes without the tools of a urban society" (70–71). Torres is of the same opinion as Dix, who stated that La Violencia was the result of a lack of mechanisms for social mobility. In a conference he gave in 1989, Francisco de Roux supported the same thesis and proposed the establishment of systems of secularization as a solution for Colombia.

48. This is, for all the world's unbelievers, the true account of Big Mama (trans. J. S. Bernstein).

49. [they cut off] his fingers and toes, [they mutilate] his nose and ears, [they cut out] his tongue, [they gouge out] his eye sockets, and in strips, in slabs of fat, muscle and nerves [they peel away] his skin.

50. Bedoya and Escobar note that the success of *Viento seco* consists in its "relating events and news that official censors wanted to relegate to oblivion" (105). As far as Alberto Aguirre is concerned, as he notes in the prologue to Arturo Echeverri Mejía's collected novels, the writer "steps back in order to understand the matter: just as he avoids the *tremendismo* that characterizes much of horror, and allows facts to indicate cruelty, he also avoids indignant sermons, the proclamations of protest and yelling accusations; *tremendismo* refers to a Spanish literary trend of the 1940s, led by Camilo José Cela and identified by its explicit treatment of violent material. The author does not insert himself into his book (as character) in order to condemn: he is not omniscient in any sense, neither as narrator nor creator. In the purest style of a realist, he permits circumstance to bespeak the world of violence, purified of elements of baroque abstractions" (30).

51. The girl, with her two hands, raises the left side of the slip, revealing her whole leg up to her waist and without looking, with nimble and steady fingers, starts to untie the knot of the string that holds up her drawers, also made of pink percale (trans. Seymour Menton).

52. We were smack in th' middle of it, enjoying the best part of life, when I heard someone swearing and hollerin' insults. It was my father. Th' old man was acting like th' devil. He yelled at me to stop 'at goddam bangin', not to go at 'er so hard 'cause I's gonna bring th' house down, break th' bedframe and smash th' poor girl's ass. 'Course, I kept agoin' . . . . What else could I do?

53. "Kiss me here," she said, showing me a place just below her ear.

I leaned over and I kissed her. She seemed happy seeing herself being kissed in the mirror. While I was kissing her, she began to move her hips and rub herself against me. She seemed like a cat. But I was still nervous. I was feeling guilty and was afraid of catching something. . . .

"Don't worry," she said. "See how nice we look?"

54. In an interview given in the 1960s, Echeverri Mejía affirmed that his novel, *Marea de ratas*, was "escrita con sencillez; sin palabras" (Aguirre 13). As for *Bajo Cauca*, a similar observation cannot be made, since the protagonist knows there is a verbal dimension to his life, for his stated intention to recover his wife and son, "something that can happen in two or three months" (502), is, first and foremost, a desire cast in words.

55. One can only know the intensity of such meteors *if he has had the experience*; only then can one adduce one's own combat against loneliness and the Parcae. I then recall—not out of exhibitionism, but out of a carefulness with truth, without whose rigors my exploration would brutally come to an end—that night I spent in Madrid, in the Hotel Emperador, with Betina, after which—after five orgasms—she whispered: *Nobody has ever made me feel so much.* We had lived a unique moment, stolen from the implacable gods.

The value of erotic affirmation lies in our personal history; but: how can I insert now, as I write, *that irreducible experience? . . .*

56. I am, as long as I feel that warm golden body next to me.

57. a useless looking glass.

58. Literature can be seen as an erotic window. If its words inflame us, it offers us the privilege of *watching ourselves make love.* Nudity reveals the impenetrable bodies and disappears when they embrace and entwine. During lovemaking, we don't see ourselves; we are love, we are the sun that blinds us.

59. the hammock . . . absorbed the explosion of blood like a blotter (trans. G. Rabassa).

60. a small belt that seemed to be made out of a cello string, but which was hard as steel and had no end, as if it had been born and grown with her (trans. G. Rabassa).

61. Remedios in the soporific air of two in the afternoon, Remedios in the soft breath of the roses, Remedios in the water-clock secrets of the moths, Remedios in the steaming morning bread, Remedios everywhere and Remedios forever (trans. G. Rabassa).

62. written by Melquíades down to the most trivial details.

63. laws are all relative and virtues all conventional.

64. is obviously outside the law.

65. the only proof positive that we are in the world.

66. the confirmation, via the body, of existing without appeal.

67. in the same manner that poets substitute one relationship among words with a new one.

68. For a comparison of these two interpretations, see the works of Carolina Salazar Mora, "Transgresión e interdicto en *La mansión de Araucaima*," and R. H. Moreno-Durán, "El falansterio violado."

69. she felt foreign and strange to herself at the moment of orgasm and, at certain times, came to detach herself so much so that she could observe herself whining and shuddering with pleasure, and felt, in this convulsive state, a tired and total indifference.

70. did not manage to detach herself as was her custom [and] gave herself up to the whirlwind of satisfied sensations.

71. captivated by an unquenchable, constant desire, suggested by every object around her, by every event in her daily life.

72. language of desire that into eternity continues to be desire.

73. would be escorted into the presence of the great pimp, before the imposing figure of the mother-cuckold of the multicirculating flaming phallus. She would let him, all of him, into her vaselined bisulcafundibula, until she could feel him coming out her mouth, leaving her with the flavor of a star-studded night with glands of vinegar and syrup, her hair tousled like a little girl's, startled at the cajolery of a clothier, smelling of the ashes of ants mixing eaten claws and boiled wine and of cracked shins that forgot about the rain and the window where they have spilled dust of dust and she herself dust, furious dust. . . . But then I, what do I get out of all this jazz? Well, nothing, a big-balled nothing. You'll just stay right there with nothing, conjuring up pure, free-flowing and ridiculous foolishness, 'cause you ain't even got the brains to handle these imaginomasturbatory-dildoneries.

74. She said that in that age of inexpertness she used to make love as if it were the novel defined by the narrowest of precepts, that is: a) with an exposition, b) with rising tension and c) with a slow denouement. But in Switzerland all that was cast aside and the act of love rapidly conquered delicious territories of increasing complexity.

75. "as it should be, [with] the Copulatives." The titles of *Juego de damas* and *El toque de Diana* are puns, whose playfulness is lost in translation. Literally, the first can mean as well "ladies' game" and the second can be rendered as "the touch or caress of Diana."

76. a page on which writing is a pleasure.

77. hemmed in by literature.

78. in the final analysis, [a sonnet] is just as valid an expression of love as an erection.

79. I'm blond, oh, so blond.

80. a bad front cover of *Vogue*.

81. but not him, no, that's the man's job, tearing her petticoats into shreds, breaking buttons, I adore you, you're gorgeous, rubbing himself, biting her, and she the whole time wanting to say wait just a minute, but didn't dare because wait for what.

Works Cited

Albarracín, Jacinto. *Almíbar*. Bogotá: La Luz, 1901.
———. *Castidad . . . ?* Bogotá: El Ciclón, 1903.

Algandona, Manuel S. *Profilaxis de la sífilis*. Bogotá: Imprenta de Zalamea Hermanos, 1889.

Alvarez Gardeazábal, Gustavo. Conference presented at Washington University, St. Louis, Missouri, Spring 1983.

Alvarez Lleras, Antonio. *Ayer nada más...* París: Le Livre Libre, 1930.

Angel, Albalucía. *Misiá señora*. Barcelona: Argos Vergara, 1982.

Apuleyo Mendoza, Plinio. *Años de fuga*. Bogotá: Plaza y Janés, 1985.

Arango Vélez, Dionisio. *El inocente*. Bogotá: Minerva, 1929.

Ardila Casamijtana, Jaime. *Babel*. Buenos Aires: Calomino, 1943.

Arias Trujillo, Bernardo. *Rizaralda*. Medellín: Bedout, 1963.

Bedoya, Luis Iván and Augusto Escobar. *La novela de la violencia en Colombia: "Viento seco" de Daniel Caicedo—una lectura crítica—*. Medellín: Ediciones Hombre Nuevo, 1980.

Bohman, Kristina. *Women of the Barrio: Class and Gender in a Colombian City*. Stockholm: Stockholm Studies in Socio-Anthropology, 1984.

Buitrago, Fanny. *Cola de zorro*. Bogotá: Tercer Mundo, 1970.

Caballero, Antonio. *Sin remedio*. Bogotá: Oveja Negra, 1986.

Caballero Calderón, Eduardo. *Caín*. Barcelona: Destino, 1969.

Caicedo, Andrés. *¡Que viva la música!* Bogotá: Colcultura, 1977.

Caicedo, Daniel. *Viento seco*. Buenos Aires: Nuestra América, 1954.

Carrasquilla, Tomás. *Obras completas*. Medellín: Bedout, 1958.

Casas, María. *El R. P. José María Campoamor y su obra "El círculo de obreros."* Bogotá: Santa Fe, 1953.

Cepeda Samudio, Alvaro. *La casa grande* (1962). Buenos Aires: Jorge Alvarez, 1967. *La casa grande*. Trans. Seymour Menton. Austin: University of Texas Press, 1991.

Coni, Emilio R. "Frecuencia y profilaxis de las enfermedades venéreas en la América Latina." In *Ciencias médicas e higiene*. Ed. Germán Greve. Santiago, Chile: Imprenta Barcelona, 1909, 393–433.

Cuervo Márquez, Emilio. *Phinées*. Bogotá: Luz, 1909.

———. *La selva oscura* (*Lilí, La ráfaga, La selva oscura*). Bogotá: Cromos, 1924.

Deas, Malcolm. *Del poder y la gramática, y otros ensayos sobre historia, política y literatura colombianas*. Bogotá: Tercer Mundo, 1993.

Dix, Robert H. *Colombia: the Political Dimensions of Change*. New Haven and London: Yale University Press, 1967.

Echeverri Mejía, Arturo. *Novelas*. Prólogo de Alberto Aguirre. Bogotá: Colcultura, 1981.

Else, Gerald. *Plato and Aristotle on Poetry*. Chapel Hill: University of North Carolina Press, 1986.

Gaitán Durán, Jorge. *Obra literaria*. Bogotá: Colcultura, 1975.

Galvis, T. "Eduardo Zalamea Borda. *Cuatro años a bordo de mí mismo.*" *Revista Javeriana* 2.6 (July 1934): 10.

García Márquez, Gabriel. *Cien años de soledad*. Barcelona: Austral, 1985. Orig. 1967. English version as *One Hundred Years of Solitude*. Trans. Gregory Rabassa. New York: Avon Books, 1971.

———. *Los funerales de la Mamá Grande*. Bogotá: Oveja Negra, 1982. Orig. 1958. English version as *No One Writes to the Colonel and Other Stories*. Trans. J. S. Bernstein. New York: Harper and Row, 1968. Includes "Big Mama's Funeral."

Gilbert, Alan. "Bogotá: Politics, Planning, and the Crisis of Lost Opportunities." In *Metropolitan Latin America: The Challenge and the Response*. Ed. Wayne A. Cornelius and Robert V. Kemper. Beverly Hills: Sage, 1978, 87–126.

Guzmán Campos, Germán, et al. *La violencia en Colombia*. Vol. 1. Bogotá: Tercer Mundo, 1963.

Hoff, Joan. "Why Is There No History of Pornography?" In *The Dilemma of Violent Pornography: For Adult Users Only*. Ed. Susan Gubar and Joan Hoff. Bloomington: Indiana University Press, 1989, 16–46.

Isaacs, Jorge. *María*. México, D.F.: Porrúa, 1978. Orig. 1867.

Jaramillo Zuluaga, J. Eduardo. "La poesía en *4 años a bordo de mí mismo*." *Revista Casa Silva* 1 (enero 1988): 29–42.

Kendrick, Walter. *The Secret Museum: Pornography in Modern Culture*. New York: Penguin, 1987.

Lázaro Carreter, Fernando. *Diccionario de términos filológicos*. Madrid: Gredós, 1962.

Marroquín, Lorenzo, and José María Rivas Groot. *Pax*. Bogotá: Ministerio de Educación Nacional, 1946. Orig. 1907.

Moreno-Durán, R. H. "El falansterio violado." In *Tras las rutas de Margral el Gaviero*. Ed. Santiago Mutis Durán. Bogotá: Gradiva, 1988, 77–85.

———. *Juego de damas*. Barcelona: Seix Barral, 1977.

———. *Metropolitanas*. Barcelona: Montesinos, 1986.

———. *El toque de Diana*. Barcelona: Montesinos, 1988.

Mutis, Alvaro. *Poesía y prosa*. Bogotá: Colcultura, 1981.

Orlansky, Dora, and Silvia Dubrovsky. *The Effects of Rural-Urban Migration on Women's Role and Status in Latin America*. Paris: UNESCO, 1978.

Osorio Lizarazo, José Antonio. *El criminal*. Bogotá: Renacimiento, 1935.

Palacios, Arnoldo. *Las estrellas son negras*. Bogotá: Iquemia, 1949.

Palacios, Marco. "La clase más ruidosa: a propósito de los reportes británicos sobre el siglo XX colombiano." *Eco* 254 (diciembre 1982): 113–56.

Rendón, Francisco de Paula. *Inocencia*. Bogotá: Minerva, 1935. Orig. 1903.

Rivas Groot, José María. *Resurrección*. In *Novelas y cuentos*. Bogotá: Ministerio de Educación Nacional, 1951, 43–103.

Rivera, José Eustasio. *La vorágine*. Bogotá: Círculo de Lectores, 1984. Orig. 1924. English version as *The Vortex*. Trans. Earle K. James. New York: Putnam's, 1935.

Rojas Herazo, Héctor. *Celia se pudre*. Madrid: Alfaguara, 1986.

Romero Aguirre, Alfonso. *El sexo en la legislación colombiana*. Thesis presented to the Universidad de Cartagena, Bogotá, August 1930.

Roux, Francisco de. "Lección inaugural." Conference given at the Universidad Javeriana, Bogotá, August 1989.

Ruiz, Jorge Eliécer. "Situación del escritor en Colombia." In *Sociedad y cultura*. Bogotá: Instituto Caro y Cuervo, 1987, 19–39.

Salazar Mora, Carolina. "Transgresión e interdicto en *La mansión de Araicauma*." Unedited monograph, Pontificia Universidad Javeriana, 1988.

Sanín Echeverri, Jaime. *Una mujer de 4 en conducta o la quebrada de Santa Helena*. Medellín: Bedout, 1981.

Schwartz, Kessel. "The Whorehouse and the Whore in Spanish American Fiction of the 1960s." *Journal of Interamerican Studies and World Affairs* 15.4 (November 1973): 472–87.

Sepúlveda Niño, Saturnino. *La prostitución en Colombia: una quiebra de las estructuras sociales.* Bogotá: Andes, 1970.

Silva, José Asunción. *De sobremesa.* In *Poesía y prosa.* Ed. Juan Gustavo Cobo Borda and Santiago Mutis Durán. Bogotá: Colcultura, 1979, 139–291. Orig. 1887–96.

Torres, Camilo. "*La Violencia* y los cambios socio-culturales en las áreas rurales colombianas." In *Camilo, el cura guerrillero; antología.* Buenos Aires: Cristianismo y Revolución, 1968, 60–128.

Vargas Vila, José María. *Flor de fango.* Paris: Librería de la Vda. de C. Bouret, 1908.

Zalamea Borda, Eduardo. "*4a batería* (Capítulo de una novela inédita)." *Revista Pan* 13 (marzo-abril 1937): 34–48.

———. *4 años a bordo de mí mismo* (1934). Lima: Editora Latinoamericana, 1958, 34–48.

———. Interview. *El Tiempo,* 23 mayo 1948, 2a sección, p. 3.

———. Translator, "Reflectores sobre la vida," by Henri Montherland. *Revista Pan* 17 (noviembre 1937): 44–54.

Zalamea Borda, Jorge. "Una novela de José Asunción Silva." In *Poesía y prosa.* Ed. Juan Gustavo Cobo Borda and Santiago Mutis Durán. Bogotá: Colcultura, 1979, 428–32.

Chapter 4

Representations of Family and Sexuality in Brazilian Cultural Discourse

Roberto Reis

(translated from the Portuguese by Dário Borim and Ann Fifield-Borim)

A família não é apenas instituição social, mas também política. Ora, como através dela o Estado regula a sexualidade, o sexo é, também, uma questão política.

(Marilena Chauí, *Repressão sexual: essa nossa (des)conhecida* 141).[1]

Unconscious Messages

During Carnaval, half-dressed women show their tanned bodies to the beat of the samba rhythm. In Ipanema, girls in their tiny bikinis parade their gracefulness down the southern beaches of Rio. The most exotic images associated with Brazilian culture are highly charged with eroticism, perpetuating the myth of sexual permissiveness. Anything is possible south of the equator.

Such images are not to be found only in the foreign imagination; they are fostered by the ideas Brazilians hold of themselves. According to a survey on Brazilians' sexual behavior, a sort of *Hite Report*, some individuals claimed to sustain an enviable performance rate of up to sixty-two acts of intercourse per month. Brazilians, indeed, regard themselves as "hot" and adroit in bed. There is, therefore, the myth of superb sexual prowess of Brazilian men and women, especially the *mulatas*. Granted that every myth tries to mask reality, one may ask: to what extent can we envision Brazilian society beyond the representations it fabricates of itself through sexuality? If sexual roles are socially forged (as Fry and MacRae point out), and if ideas and practices associated with sex

"são produzidas *historicamente* no interior de sociedades concre-
tas [e, sendo assim, estão] intimamente relacionadas com o todo
destas sociedades" (10–11),[2] the study of sexual representations
leads us to the questioning of society at its core, where such representations have been engendered.

I would like to establish a distinction between deliberate speech
acts and those that are not voluntary. I am mainly interested
throughout this study in the second kind. Although we may read
the unconscious dimension of any text, there are other discourses
that tell us about meanings that are not explicit regarding their
communicative willingness.[3]

I once witnessed a Brazilian middle-class woman during a visit
to the United States who became angry over the fact that there
was no bag boy available to carry her groceries out for her. This
anecdote suggests the lingering echoes of slavery in contemporary Brazil. When a tropical society builds bedrooms without win-
dows or any ventilation for domestic servants — clearly violating
city ordinances — it is concealing how hierarchical and authoritarian it really is and how it discriminates in terms of gender, sex,
race, and class against the servants, generally women of color and
low income. This is an unconscious message that results in an
involuntary act of communication, and the ideology of the archi-
tects betrays them. In the floor plan for the apartments, they underscore their indelible class-biased discourse. By the same token,
the representations of sexuality in Brazilian cultural discourse say
much about this society and its culture.

The point is, therefore, to understand the universe of socially
produced representations within which social actors operate. The
visions that social agents construct in regard to sexuality end up
producing clusters of meaning that ought to be unscrambled, inasmuch as such visions dramatize the Brazilian social and cultural
unconscious. Sexuality, like the Balinese cockfight (cf. Geertz), will
also offer us a reading of Brazilian society, the subject of this essay.
It is on the excess or fringes of discourse, on the crisscrossing of
different versions and formulations about sexuality — and other
unconscious messages — that we shall read. Through the images
of the family and the woman, as well as the configurations of sexuality in literature and mass culture, Brazilian society allows itself to be read.

Through this essay, I will seek out the insidious presence of the patriarchal family as an ideological construct of the Brazilian collective imagination. I will also examine the sanitary and disciplinary endeavors of hygienist doctors, the survival of myths inherited from patriarchy, and the literary reverberations of prescriptive sexual and familial behavior. Next, leaving the colonial past and the nineteenth century behind, I will explore the Brazilian transition and try to show how Brazilian fiction published in the 1930s, which is thematically linked to the period of modernization, deals with sexuality in terms of power. The last segment of this essay approaches the contemporary era by examining the effort of culture industry in perpetuating old images in "modern" clothing. Reviewing recent sociological data, we realize how low-income groups seem to have internalized patriarchal and *machista* patterns. Inspired by anthropological research, we reencounter, within homosexual relationships (this time in a transparent manner), the binomial sexuality/power that permeates a significant portion of erotic discourse in Brazilian culture. The reader will find that the last section contains several questions raised by this essay.

The Plantation-House Veranda

Sérgio Buarque de Holanda wrote that the family was a mandatory model of every social composition in Brazil (106). Such a statement should take into consideration Dante Moreira Leite's warning: the concept of patriarchal family is applicable to a small portion of society and should be seen as a unit of power (282) and not as an explanation of social organization as a whole — a mistake made by master ideologues such as Gilberto Freyre, whose work is "escrita e interpretada do ponto de vista da classe dominante" (Leite 281).[4]

In addition to Leite, various scholars have questioned Freyre's plantation-house approach (Mota, *Ideologia*; Bastos). Furthermore, various works that recast the concept of patriarchal family as capable of explaining Brazilian society as a whole have appeared recently. They show the importance of women's roles within less privileged families, in which the nuclear unit prevailed over the extended one. These works have also shown how, in areas where the main economic activity was not the plantation, patriarchy had a harder time establishing itself (Samara, Corrêa). It is the case here neither to review those points nor to map out the different directions of today's discussions. Yet, it is worth stressing one or two aspects concerning this study.

Marisa Corrêa, for instance, summarizes current research findings on the Brazilian family:

> a história das formas de organização familiar no Brasil tem-se contentado em ser a história de um determinado tipo de organização familiar e doméstica — a "família patriarcal" —, um tipo fixo onde os personagens, uma vez definidos, apenas se substituem no decorrer das gerações, nada ameaçando sua hegemonia, e um tronco de onde brotam todas as outras relações sociais. Ela se instala nas regiões onde foram implantadas as grandes unidades agrárias de produção — engenhos de açúcar, fazendas de criação ou de plantação de café —, mantém-se através da incorporação de novos membros, de preferência parentes, legítimos ou ilegítimos, a extensos "clãs" que asseguram a indivisibilidade de seu poder, e sua transformação dá-se por decadência, com o advento da industrialização e a ruína das grandes propriedades rurais, sendo então substituídas pela "família conjugal moderna." Esta é o ponto de chegada onde aquela é o ponto de partida, e seu oposto: típico produto da urbanização, reduzida ao casal e seus filhos, a finalidade do casamento não é mais principalmente a manutenção de uma propriedade comum ou dos interesses políticos de um grupo, mas sim a satisfação de impulsos sexuais e afetivos que na família patriarcal eram satisfeitos fora de seu círculo imediato. (Corrêa 13–14)[5]

This synthesis leads the author to some dissenting points: given the wide range of possibilities that existed in colonial Brazil, very slowly occupied and organized, Brazil cannot be reduced to a history in which personages changed but discourse remained the same. Despite the new rhetoric of every generation, the meaning persisted, as if an integral, homogeneous line marked the development of our history. Contrary to the images of a "bloodless" itinerary inscribed by traditional historiography, this dominant scheme imposed itself through dirty and violent struggles. Such images disregard the multitude of social agents who participated in numberless conflicts that rocked colonial society (Corrêa 15). The author then approaches Freyre's sociological theory and Antonio Candido's famous 1951 essay to stress that, in both authors, one finds a contrast between a multifaceted and dispersed society and the attempt to accommodate it within the narrow limits of the sugar plantation or other large farms, which are taken as the birthplace of the Brazilian society as a whole. Corrêa contends that Freyre and Candido adopt the eyes and the vantage point of the white masters and their families, while retreating to the core of a dominant institution at a certain moment in Brazilian colonial history (22).

Freyre espouses a dualistic view of society: the plantation house and the slave quarters, the master and the slave. Pieces of a system contradictorily integrated, their encounter takes place in bed and in the kitchen, the subunits of the plantation house that lie in the center of Freyre's sociological analyses (Corrêa 22). Candido, in turn, underscores the terms that designate the "stabilizing nucleus" of patriarchy ("supporting axis," "anchor," "stabilizing force"), as against those terms that name the subsidiary and dispossessed "periphery" ("amorphous and anonymous social stratum," "vagabond and disorderly individuals," "sexual chaos") (Corrêa 27–28). The patriarchal family may have had an extremely important role, but it neither existed in isolation nor oriented the total process of development in Brazil (Corrêa 25). Can one take the patriarchal family as both the center of the order and thus the focus of analysis, even if it existed in the midst of such a large and disorderly milieu in which unlawful unions were the dominant order (Corrêa 26)?

I have no doubt that Corrêa's excellent work can be related to a series of others that have been reevaluating Brazilian society and reformulating the interpretations drawn by social scientists between the 1930s and the 1950s. The new works command an approach highly influenced by the French history of mentalities — a new form of knowledge that attempts to give voice to minorities and to question the dominant-class biases bequeathed by sociologists and historians of yesterday. The new theoretical framework tries to examine day-to-day life by analyzing the mediation and resistance undertaken by the oppressed. Its interest focuses on praxis of individuals as social agents rather than on great facts and deeds. Such works reexamining the family are mainly based on the study of demographic data and documentation such as the census. They show that there were many families run by women, which raises questions about women's subordination to men, and many families composed of a few members, which raises questions about stereotypically large ones.

Ronaldo Vainfas writes that, even though recent works enrich our understanding of colonial Brazil, they are not always fair to Freyre's and Candido's points. No exclusive nature is granted to the colonial patriarchal family in Freyre and Candido (and Caio Prado Jr., he adds). No emphasis is given to the number of dwellers in each residence either. The only aspect stressed is the structure of power that oriented social life in the colony while historically connected with slavery, seignorial prepotency, and the cultural traditions of Iberian cultures (Vainfas 110).

One could approach the issue of the patriarchal family through two other angles. The first one, suggested at the opening of this segment, has to do with the power structure, unquestioned by recent works. Apart from the contributions of recent historiography, it is clear that the notion of power structure is particularly circumscribed within dominant groups. Furthermore, if this notion is broadened to the level of discourse and ideology (the second angle), that power structure would have been used to reinforce and impose the hegemony of these very same dominant groups.

Angela M. de Almeida, one of the revisionist essayists, seems to insist on this aspect: the patriarchal family was not quite like a social reality that extended itself over all Brazilian society, but a representation, instead, mainly related to the dominant sectors. It was an ethic that permeated all social spheres (156). In this sense, Mota argues that slavery penetrated all institutions very deeply, and, above all, their "mentalities" ("Cultura" 19). The patriarchal family is, thus, the starting point. The rural patriarchal family is based on the kind of economic activity that prevailed during colonial times: production for export and slavery. This is a slaveholding patriarchal family, a polygamous one whose ethics make all sexual relations possible and desirable for the white man, while premarital chastity and marital fidelity are reserved for the white woman (Almeida 55).

It was Holanda who said that the word *família* derives from *famulus*, whose etymology implies the idea of servitude (49). The patriarchal family was ultimately a form of hierarchically structured power organization, the model of which could be portrayed as a series of concentric circles. In the middle is the almighty landed master (the prevalence of a seignorial order) who combines the role of father (the prevalence of a patriarchal order) and that of man (prevalence of a male order). Within the plantation house, directly controlled by the master, were the wife and the children. The further away from the power nucleus, the less prestige a person's social standing had, which in part explains why everyone wanted to be sheltered by the patriarch at the center. The presence of an individual in this center is fundamental for the definition of the other social stations. In the most outward of the circles, the base of the social pyramid is the slave (prevalence[6] of a slave-owning order).

As suggested before, the patriarchal order had slavery as its counterpart in the economic sphere. Slavery actually caused an extreme polarity in the social stratification of Brazil, which was established according to the relation master–slave. Roaming around this organized sector of society are the so-called "free men." While attached to this sector, they are indeed dependent on some power individual with whom they interact on a mechanism of favor exchanges. What the new historiography has tried to do is shift the focus of analysis onto these marginal sectors.

Such a configuration of this Brazilian seignorial establishment endures through at least the outset of the 1930 revolution. After the abolition of slavery, the patriarch — absolute owner of his estate, family, and serfs — becomes the *coronel* and the political boss that decides local matters with an eye on his personal preferences, family ties, and circle of friendships (Leite 283). As Brazil becomes more urbanized, the "rural aristocracy" starts to assume new social positions in which they perpetuate the family mentality. The seignorial structure became enfeebled and the patriarchal family fell away. The 1930 revolution shows the weakening of a social structure, forcing landowners and exporters of products such as coffee to share power with the new and upcoming bourgeois sectors. Yet the relevance of the family takes root in the social unconscious and fosters phenomena like paternalism and nepotism, which, still widely practiced, are detrimental to political relations.

It is important to keep in mind that the notion of the patriarchal family constitutes one of the pillars upon which social power in Brazil is based. (The patriarchal family here refers mainly to the social structure of the ruling elites, which is, after all, a structure of power transformed into ideological discourse.) That notion of the patriarchal family will be replaced by the idea of the bourgeois nuclear family that emerges in Brazil in the nineteenth century. That was also the time when liberalism and the advances of the industrial revolution arrived, along with historical changes incubated within a different socioeconomic reality transplated into the new soil of Brazil. Brazilian reality, then, was one without a strong rising urban bourgeois class (either an industrial or a commercial one). On the contrary, it was the same colonial society, now formally independent and based on exporting latifundism, the essential feature of which was still slavery. The rural family transplanted to the cities of the nineteenth century had undergone superficial changes. Yet, the mentality based upon patriarchy continued to be the dominant one. The imported idea of a bourgeois nuclear family, therefore, does not rest on a *tabula rasa*. People try to acclimate it to Brazil—the activities of hygienists and doctors will be one of the strategies—but the local reality resists and attempts to take hold of the esoteric idea and put it into service by framing it according to the kernel of the previous model (Almeida 57–58). The match between the mentality of the bourgeois nuclear family and the reappropriation and adaptation of this notion by the patriarchal family mentality is what one needs to explore, according to Almeida (63): part of this task is undertaken by the hygienist doctors.

The Mother's Children

The model of the Brazilian social organization—structured within the circle of dominant elites and based on the family as a unit—needs to be interfaced with the issue of gender, even if this issue is limited to the domain of the plantation. In general, the upper-class woman was submissive to her husband. Yet, inside the home she developed intense activities. While indolence and passivity on her part were rare, according to Maria Isaura Pereira de Queiroz, she always gave orders to the slaves who actually did the hard domestic chores (193). Studying the family as an institution, Candido shows how the woman was in charge of an active function that differed from that of the man: she supervised the slaves' work, the making of clothes and food, and the rearing of her children (296). The father's authority over his children was indisputable. It remained unchallenged until the power of the priest, and the power of the family doctor, later, were able to play a part. Obedience to the husband was an extension of obedience to the father. The management of the house, with all household chores and slave supervision under her responsibility, was the white plantation woman's prevailing role, even though authors often label her life idle (Maria Inacia d'Avila Neto 47). The socialization of woman was, therefore, directed toward the thorough acceptance of male supremacy.

The fact that woman stayed at home performed an economic function as well, since she was supposed to look after her husband's domestic patrimony.[7] Her confinement and exclusion from socialization with guests and visitors stood as a distinctive mark of her social status, since the "street," or the world out of the house from which such people came, was considered the domain of vagabonds, prostitutes, and nameless individuals (Costa 119). In colonial Brazil, the opportunities for socialization were otherwise restricted to attending church or religious celebrations, occasions in which chaise longues, sedan chairs, and the palanquins distinguished social hierarchy (Costa 105). At the same time, within that system where skin color instantly differentiated the master from the slave, the woman's white skin acquired a social meaning as relevant as land ownership (Costa 118).

The arrival of the imperial family in 1808 initiates a variegated process of transformation in colonial Brazil. When the administrative institutions shift from the Portuguese to the Brazilian court, the colony becomes practically separate from the metropolis. The presence of the nobles will not only bring about improvement in Rio de Janeiro, the capital, but also influence the seignorial elites' way of life. The urge to meet the standards of Dom João VI's court leads women to wear corsets that hamper their breathing or hoop skirts that encumber their movements—the discomfort was the index of their belonging in a privileged and idle social class. Men, in turn, start to wear waistcoats, use walking sticks, and smoke cigars — true class insignia (Souza) that are the precursors of the fountain pen, the "doctor" title, and the graduation ring.

Furthermore, the capital's population increases, which creates serious health problems. Among the improvements, however, is the establishment of higher education institutions such as the School of Medicine. The Rio de Janeiro Medical-Surgical Academy was opened in 1813 and became the College of Medicine in 1832. At the College of Medicine, medical students presented theses upon graduation. A great many of such works focused on public health, which caused the doctors to be identified as hygienists. Mainly after the country's independence, especially when the agricultural elites had embraced the process of nation building during the Second Empire, the hygienist doctors exerted a considerable influence over the Brazilian family.

Jurandir Freire Costa charges that in colonial Brazil the family became the synonym of plantation familial order, inasmuch as the slave family was destroyed by physical violence and the free men's family by corruption, favoritism, and clientele vices. A family, even if dispossessed, will organize itself according to the seignorial frame. This is particularly true for the middle segments of society, such as small merchants, the military, and liberal professionals. In these families, he contends, the father's attitudes toward his sons, as well as those of husband toward wife and adults in general toward children, will repeat, in almost the same terms, the familial ties of the old master (Costa 47).

Outlining the analytical tendency that sees the patriarchal family as the social motor of Brazil in colonial times, Costa reiterates that the family founded its cohesion upon a pyramidal system. Its top was occupied by the male in his multiple functions as father, husband, enterprise boss, and troop commander. The father represented the principles of unity for the estate — morality, authority, hierarchy — and, at last, all values that sustained the family's tradition and status quo. The only interest pursued, he adds, was "that of the group and its properties, as always stated by the father" (Costa 95).

In light of this, the family functioned exclusively for the benefit of the clan, which rendered it harmful to the interests of the state, since it produced family members rather than citizens. The hygienists came to realize that those individuals' participation in society was restricted to the defense of their group and that the whole familial system inherited from colonial times had been assembled in order to satisfy the demands of private property. Therefore, adds Costa, the Brazilian state "always saw in the family one of its greatest obstacles to its consolidation" (30). With the conviction that the state was more important than the family group, "the medical order will introduce a family norm capable of forming individual citizens who were domesticated and made available for the city, the state, and the nation" (48). The doctors' endeavor operated in strict agreement with the ongoing urban development and solidification of the national and agrarian state. This state needed a few bosses to run it and a great many "fathers" to serve it. Fathers and sons, therefore, will put their careers to the service of the nation. The society idealized by hygienists would comprise stern but pliant men who, having been closely watched by medical professionals since childhood, would be able to offer their lives to their country as adults (Costa 170–79).

The private lives of individuals were consequently attached to the political destiny of a certain social class, the bourgeoisie, says Costa (13). The male, adds the author, relieved of his land, other goods, and slaves through the hygiene campaign, became a sire for the state. He was granted, in return, the right to concentrate on the woman alone all the dominion that he used to exert on all other individuals depending on his estate. The wife has become his only private property (Costa 252). This man no longer exploits the slaves or *agregados* (indentured servants), but millions of people who had begun to consume his products (250).

If the colonial patriarch's honor and power once rested on the family's name and possessions, now that doctors started intervening, power and honor mainly depended on his wife as property and on her sexual respectability (Costa 252). Among the greatest targets of the hygienists were women and children, who were freed from the despotism of their fathers. The woman is subdued by her husband instead, and she assumes the control of her children. Bound to serve their husbands in the past, women were also elevated to the position of mediators between children and the state (Costa 73). Rather than the "father's children," they are now the "mother's children," being educated to become the "nation's children" in the future.

The hygienist discourse is aimed at families of elitist background. The goal of the state was not to change the familial order of slaves, who should continue to abide by punitive rules as usual. In the course of the Second Empire, social medicine is directed toward the urban "bourgeois" family. That medicine is supposed to alter their physical, intellectual, moral, sexual, and social behaviors, while keeping an eye on their expected adaptation to a new economic and political system (Costa 33). That discourse had a guaranteed set of addressees: the intellectual elite, who could educate their children as well as join the state (Costa 69).

Like Woman, Like Literature

Patriarchy bequeathed us certain myths that still reside in the Brazilian social imagination, which is the case of the virility complex (or machismo) among men and the virginity one among women. Madonnaism, or the exaltation of the virgin woman, observes d'Avila Neto, is reflected in the reverence to the Virgin Mary, with whom Brazilians have always had strong identification. Contrasting the image of virtue, in which women should stay virgins while single and faithful as wives, men were supposed to act differently. It was up to the men, even while married, to meet other women and to have lovers as a proof of their masculinity, which installs the sexual double standard to be discussed further on in this essay. The black woman was exclusively reserved for the needs of the master, sexual ones included. While the white woman was literally hidden in the plantation house, myths were woven about the sexual prowess of the mestizos (d'Avila Neto 47–49).

A relevant point is the gap between what supposedly was women's reality, on the one hand, and women's ambiguous representation in the Brazilian cultural discourse, on the other. Women are, thus, said to be submissive to men; at the same time, there is the myth of immaculate women, who deserve spiritualized love if they belong to the upper classes. The opposite token is men's attraction to the woman of color. Extolled for her sexuality, she invariably belongs to the less privileged classes. These aspects can be discerned in literary texts through various recurrent images. In one of them, the white lady instills desire in the white man, yet he will repress it and transfer it to another object of desire. As regards the black or mulatto woman—either a slave or a member of the lower class—the white male's desire is not repressed, and it will be her destiny to be possessed by the master. This split image of the Brazilian woman remains not only as a real phenomenon in society, but also as a literary theme even in contemporary authors such as Carlos Drummond de Andrade.

Elsewhere (*A permanência do círculo* and "Muita serventia"), I have analyzed *Lucíola*, José de Alencar's 1862 novel, where narrative point of view is doubly male-oriented: Paulo's and that of his society as a whole. Men are allowed to fulfill their desires (as long as they avail themselves of courtesans), and innocent women are reserved for the "holy pleasures" of matrimonial love. In the meantime, Lúcia, the courtesan-protagonist, is not allowed to change roles, because if she did, it would subvert the prospects of marriage. Thus, a moral double standard occurs. While endorsing the young man's amorous exploits, society tends to discriminate against women more often than it seems: "basta estarem desacompanhadas para não serem olhadas como 'senhoras'" (30).[8]

Carnal desire and pleasure are, therefore, tolerated within the male realm as long as men are interested in courtesans, since the familial space must remain chaste. For the female characters socially installed in the center of the concentric circles (the social model explained above), the role is to revere idealized and spiritual love heavily charged with religious connotations. Not surprisingly, in *Lucíola* there are two objects of repression: sex and women. Women are forced to decide where to stand: within the family, the space of ladies and innocent girls, or within the pleasure zone, the space of courtesans, women of color, and women of low social strata. Social mobility and ambiguity between the two spaces are not granted to women. For the men, however, circulation from one side to the other is permissible, since the social organization, as it is displayed in the text, is constructed so that the male order is benefited.

This sketch of *Lucíola* points out the hierarchical, repressive, and authoritarian character of the society at issue here. According to Priore, who specializes in the history of Brazilian women, the colonial woman was more closely a daughter of Eve than of the Virgin Mary (20). Alencar's novel somehow elaborates an ideal panorama: it extols the family and places the courtesan "in her place," while keeping her away from the seigniorage. It is as if the novel purified the daily sexual behavior of the Brazilian 1800s but, at the same time, revealed society's true face behind the narrative's contrived mask.

It is important to highlight that the hygienists' operation (described earlier) has its counterpart in the literary field. Indeed, Brazilian literature was not lavish in terms of readership in the nineteenth century. The reading public basically included women, students, and a few enlightened men. An enormous contingent of people, though, were illiterate, which suggests that literature was circumscribed within the narrow seignorial circles. The same process of domination taken by the doctors will be carried out by authors like Alencar: we may say that their purpose was to domesticate and make chaste the elites toward a certain kind of social, familial, and sexual behavior under the rules of patriarchy. The preservation of patriarchy and male order was required to ensure its dominion and hegemony.

The reading of a play, also by Alencar, *O demônio familiar* (The Family Demon; 1857) leaves us questioning whether the patriarchal society and the male order were on the wane. This suspicion would explain the text's tendency to reiterate the strength of fractured family values. The play seems to be indoctrinating the characters and the audience. While using the slave as a scapegoat and reinstalling order and tranquillity, Alencar's play seems to relocate the confused characters in their due place, reinstating the patriarchal order. I'm not suggesting that the reality of the Brazilian family was such: as aseptic and distilled as suggested by the nineteenth-century texts, placing the patriarch back on his throne. Alencar and a number of Brazilian nineteenth-century intellectuals left us with the suspicion that they intended to put an end to what must have been an enormous sexual permissiveness (without any Puritan connotation on my part). In this sense, literature was domesticating the chaos of social practices. These intellectuals also intended to direct their elitist project toward the construction of the agrarian and monarchic state first and later the oligarchic republic.

The insightful study by Flora Süssekind in which she sketches the cyclical return to naturalist aesthetics in Brazil reinforces my thesis. Süssekind deals with the concurrence of three projects: the familial (like father, like son), the literary (like author, like text), and the national (like Brazil, like literature). These projects strengthen various identities: patriarchal, within the family; authorial, as part of the literary tradition; and national, at the core of Brazilian society (*Tal Brasil* 42). In other words, these three traditions are inextricably bound together. During the country's transition to modernity, which occurred at the turn of the century, the crisis of Brazilian modernization takes hold. The social patterns inherited from a "feudal" past mingle with modern trends, shuffling together the nuclear bourgeois family and the seignorial and patriarchal one, while compounding versions of the new woman with myths such as Madonnaism.

Much Servitude

The period between approximately 1850 and 1950 may be considered of capital importance. The first date refers to the second and most effective measure prohibiting slave traffic, the Eusébio de Queirós law. The second refers to the establishment of the automobile industry in Brazil, which marks the outset of a period in which the most dramatic economic development takes place. The second half of the twentieth century brings import substitution — to a large extent, the policy that entailed an efficacious yet contradictory and uneven modernization.

That one-hundred year period reveals a crucial process of transition, in which agriculture-based economy will gradually be replaced by industrial production. Simultaneously, three phenomena occur. First, the southeast becomes the country's sustaining source of revenues (a trend begun in the eighteenth century). Second, the middle classes will assume political roles that are increasingly more powerful. Third, an urban proletariat emerges, which hastens Getúlio Vargas's populist policies toward work legislation by the mid-1930s.

Due to readjustments undertaken by international capitalism when it enters the phase of expansion toward a world consumer market, Brazil is somewhat forced to modernize itself. There are internal pressures, inasmuch as revenues resulting from the extinction of slavery and from the economic success of western São Paulo coffee growers have been invested in the industrial sector and have brought about the appearance of the urban bourgeoisie. Even though it basically has origins in the rural oligarchies, the bourgeoisie now begins to claim its own space within the country's hermetic power bloc. There are foreign pressures as well, since Brazil, the old-fashioned sleeping giant, would become an unwanted enclave for the expansion of a new world economy launched by developed countries. During the first decades of this century, Brazil is still a nation attached to its colonial and peripheral heritage, where capitalism is such a late manifestation that authors have argued that the nineteenth century did not end until 1930.

Florestan Fernandes and Raymundo Faoro have insisted on showing how the bourgeoisie was implemented in Brazil in an autocratic form, even before the traditional structures of a patriarchal society had been surpassed. The ultimate consequence is the coexistence of the contractual order of capitalism and the colonial order of solidarity, which restricts the competitive system to a small fraction of the population. This fraction is the one taking part in the market but also having to share it with a bigger fraction, one still attached to the oligarchical scheme (Ventura 153).

In the northeast, phenomena of social protest like *messianismo* (messianic cults) and *cangaço* (social banditry) underscore the decline of the old patriarchal order and local despotism. Such a decline does not necessarily prompt a new order to replace the old one. *Coronelismo* (a system based on the local political power of landed patriarchs) would become another symptom of this phase of historical vacuum, when the private sphere overwhelms the public order. At the same time, *Coronelismo* signals the weakening of northeastern oligarchies and, at the same time, their lingering power, which is proven by their role in the advent of the 1930 pact (an alliance between the new sectors of industry and the old landowners) and in the new political model it inaugurated.

Far from a real rupture, the so-called 1930 revolution consisted of an event that would represent best the whole transition process. Mainly induced by the dissident oligarchies of the old republic, the revolution will reach its full purpose during the *Estado Novo* (New State, which came to be synonymous with fascist dictatorship) starting in 1937. The purpose was to adjust Brazil to the new economic order without causing great commotion in the social stratification or changing the political order to any extent. This is the origin of the urge to resort to authoritarianism. Dictatorship is thus applied. While mostly maintaining the status quo, it places Brazil in a more modernized context: it now provides raw material, substitutes imports, establishes an industrial complex, and opens its doors to foreign capital. All these changes are supported by a nationalist discourse that endorses a variety of initiatives, from the massive campaign known as "The Oil Is Ours" to popular radio programming selling Vargas's image as "Father of the Poor."

A great many 1930s intellectuals came from patriarchal families that migrated to the south while experiencing rampant social and economic decadence. Due to their families' bankruptcy, these writers resort to producing symbolic assets, the only ones within reach. The literary field turned out to be, for writers, their chance to regain the social prestige they held in the past when patriarchy and seigniorage reigned. In such texts, a notable recurrence is the tale of a large family's downfall, portrayed in the resentful spirit of impotence and nostalgia. À la Marcel Proust, writers seek their own past as if they were driving and, yet, could not keep their eyes off the rearview mirror. Silviano Santiago's metaphor (*Vale* 28) explains their condition in relation to Brazil as a whole. What lies ahead for these "drivers"/writers is progress, while they are, at the same time, looking toward the past. Still sharing power (though much less than they wished), the authors relive the good old plantation times, while justifying their present political participation. The undisguiseable debilitation of their power as a social class, as the country's male and patriarchal order wanes, will also have its literary reverberations in the domain of sexuality.

Indeed, I am struck by the level of impotence and apathy among characters in the texts of the transition period in general and the 1930s in particular. The incapacity to honor the male and patriarchal order they have inherited ends up turning into a display of virility and the overbearing need to subdue women sexually. Therefore, sexuality in Brazilian literature is dislocated from the erotic field to a different motif, usually related to a question of power. This phenomenon arises rather clearly in João Alphonsus.

Totônio Pacheco (1935) narrates the life of a *coronel* who lost his wife and farm and moves to the big city in order to live with his son Fernando, a lawyer. The city functions like a strange agent of transformation that has been traumatizing the rural world. Due to the transition affecting Brazil as a whole, urbanization means modernization, and Pacheco, the father, falls victim to this process. His son's family and household, located in the middle of the city, perhaps signaled the beginning of a "new tradition whose starting point would be his own death" (Alphonsus 209).

In this new scenario, Pacheco feels like a displaced good-for-nothing. He thinks it strange how his grandson grows up and how people can live in a place where they don't know and don't care about one another. His son, in turn, wants to change his father's ways, such as his dress and eating habits. His failure to adapt to a new environment at approximately seventy years of age has thrown him out of the center of power around which people and nature seemed to have revered him. This is "the center of a vast, ideal circle encompassing men, beasts, water, and plants that lived for him, energy that converged toward the center, where he was" (Alphonsus 88).

Pacheco then tries to regain his past via machismo, the notion of sexual prowess typically held by the old farmers. He believes it is his son's duty to repeat his father's sexual glories, which perpetuated those of the grandfather, which in turn repeated those of his great-grandfather. Totônio himself is the old kind of father who imposes respect by being harsh and distant and often resorting to yelling. This is a patriarch, likewise, who thinks that "a man is worth the value of his sins and a woman, her virtues" (Alphonsus 121).

Two kinds of representation testify to the downfall of the male lineage. One portrays male characters who do not fulfill the social expectations of patriarchies; the other, women characters (usually masculinized) who eventually manage farms and sugar mills. Both could be related to some kind of "seignorial mentality." The first group is illustrated by Bentinho in Machado de Assis's *Dom Casmurro* (1899); Belmiro Borba in Cyro dos Anjos's *O amanuense*

Belmiro (1943); Coronel Lula in José Lins do Rego's *Fogo Morto* (1943); and the Meneses brothers in Lúcio Cardoso's *Crônica da casa assassinada* (1959). The second group is demonstrated not only by Fernando's mother as the manager of the farm in *Totônio Pacheco*, but also by the "virgin warriors" in Domingos Olímpio's *Luzia-Homem* (1903); Bibiana, Ana Terra, and Maria Valéria in Érico Veríssimo's *O tempo e o vento* (1949–61); and Rosalina in Autran Dourado's *Ópera dos mortos* (1967).

The prevailing image of woman in Brazilian literature is not that of a boss, nevertheless. It is rather that of an object of dual love: spiritual love for the white maiden, sexual desire for the women of color or socially inferior, when they are portrayed in the text. This is a trend that may be found in poems by the romantic Álvares de Azevedo (1831–52). If in "Sonhando" (Dreaming) no one but the sea can touch the damsel, in "É ela! É ela! É ela! É ela!" (It's her...) a laundress, after being compared to famous literary mistresses, may be touched. The male persona approaches her, even if he is "a tremer de devaneio" (60).[9] It is fair to say that such an image of woman still remains strong today. Suffice it to mention authors like Jorge Amado, who, through one of his characters, writes that "mulher tem muita serventia, o senhor nem imagina. Ajuda até na política. Dá filhos pra gente, impõe respeito. Pro resto, tem as raparigas..." (173).[10]

The sexual possession of the female may turn into grand metaphors of national scope as well. Santiago shows how the conquest of Brazil is illustrated by a sexual subjugation in *Iracema* (1865). In "Brazil," a poem by Olavo Bilac (1865–1918), the conquest of the land is also equated with taking the land in sexual terms. Metaphorization linking land conquest and sexuality will lead to the erotic submission of women of color — or to the exaggerated and pathological sexual profiles in naturalist works such as those by Júlio Ribeiro.

In a number of fiction works closely associated with the 1930s, however, the effort to subdue woman through lasciviousness reflects the desperate need to make the male order prevail over a changing universe. This is the universe in which women are rapidly gaining power and the patriarchy is being questioned. Sexuality, therefore, ceases being sexuality alone and becomes a metonymy for the greed for power. Since this intricate relationship between sexuality and power emerges in so many other discourses, I will argue that it suggests itself as an important trait (in psychoanalytic terms) of the Brazilian collective unconscious.

Power relations portrayed in terms of sexuality within the family strikes a major key in Nelson Rodrigues, who commands more fiery images of this institution in crisis than any other Brazilian author. As suggested by Süssekind, his plays question the family as an agency that restricts and prescribes gender roles and relationship rules. Rodrigues, among other points, maintains that the Brazilian family structure prevents its members from getting too close to one another (Nelson 21). Maria José Carneiro, in turn, explores the hypertrophy of family roles in his theater. The family becomes very tight knit in order to defend itself from the dangers of a society on the move, especially from the incongruity between institutionalized roles and new values emerging outside the family (72–73).

City and state have begun to assume social functions that, in the past, were delegated to the family. This is a process that started much earlier in other societies, ever since the industrial revolution. Rodrigues's characters try to assume traditional positions — those established by patriarchy — but cannot succeed. Their failure induces the use of violence, usually undertaken by sexual means, according to Maria José Carneiro (76). Yet, this violence does not manage to restore the good old order in that it is neither capable of restraining transgression of the order nor apt to make it tougher. Violence thus becomes an empty enterprise. As Carneiro contends, it is precisely due to his characters' incapacity to fulfill the roles imposed on them by society that Rodrigues is a tragic playwright (77).

Cinderella and Don Juan

Philippe Ariès's works trace the history of the family up to its bourgeois configuration in modern times. The modern family, formed by affectionate ties, is self-centered. It constitutes its own private and intimate domain. It is anchored to internal relations rather than to links that bring several families together, such as marriages with the specific purpose of maintaining or joining properties and/or ensuring lines of genealogy (Castro and Araújo

152). Modernization will drastically jeopardize the old familial structure: the capitalist oligopolist model and the generation and administration of capital no longer depend on the passing and retaining of bourgeois family assets (Chauí, *Repressão* 137).

The contradictory process of modernization in Brazil arises much more intensively from external overdeterminations and the political failures of the colonial system than from a ripening internal evolution of the country's capitalist market (Fernandes 7). Indeed, such anteriority of peripheral capitalism causes its implementation to take place without the necessary socioeconomic infrastructure to support it. As a result, Brazilian modernization does not necessarily entail the rise of modernity. Furthermore, regional and social inequalities prevent the modernization of lifestyles and ideas from becoming uniform and homogeneous. In today's Brazil, the latest technology operates side by side with the most traditional mentalities of small towns that interact with, but also resist, the changes suggested by television.

It was not until the 1970s that modernization materialized, despite all its unevenness and maladjustment, when capitalism effectively entered the country. The consolidation of an industrial base meant to attend to the demands of the internal market will contribute to the concomitant expansion of an industry specifically oriented toward a growing market for culture merchandise. Inaugurated in the previous decades with radio, the culture industry will settle in for good with the incentives provided by the military government. The generals, while interested in promoting uniformity in the circulation of news and information, not only spread their "nationalistic" ideology, based on the Doctrine of National Security, but also ensure the implementation of a sophisticated telecommunications system. This state-supported system will allow for nationwide television broadcasting as well as the establishment of powerful private networks like Globo.

A significant part of masscult production is aimed at middle and upper sectors of the population living in urban centers, those with easier access to expenditure and closer contact with fashion, progressive behavior, and the latest fads coming in from abroad. A series of new sexual images is then elaborated by the industry of symbolic goods in order to reach those segments of society. Alluding to masscult magazines, Chauí synthesizes the typical prescription from each publication. *Cláudia,* a monthly magazine marketed for the modern housewife, teaches "how to keep your man" by being the perfect wife-lover-mother—that is to say, staying clean, smelling good, cooking well, listening to the daily news, as well as remaining forever discreet, youthful, and jovial. *Nova* (New), in turn, enlightens the professional woman on how to be intelligent and seductive without startling the male. The woman ought to like herself just like she is, which of course can be enhanced with a little help from facial creams, massages, gymnastics, and plastic surgeries. As for *Carícia* (Caress), oriented toward adolescents, the tips are on becoming fancy-free, although within certain boundaries. The ideal young woman must always respect the man's freedom, which scientific studies endorse.

Indeed, the general idea concerning sexuality in such publications, adds Chauí, is to improve sex by means of easy and effective techniques so that some will salvage their marriage; others will improve their capability for seduction and caressing. For all of them, the important point is the maternal ideal, the natural purpose of femininity (Chauí, *Repressão* 204–5).

Chauí's analysis is fundamentally confirmed by other research, like that of Dulcília Buitoni on the woman-oriented press and Denise Alves on *Nova* and *Ele/Ela* (a male-targeted magazine). Alves shows how the man–woman relationship remains hierarchical, with significant remnants of the patriarchal order when it comes to the man's authority over the woman and their children. She stresses that the double standard prevails: men are allowed to have premarital and extraconjugal sex, while women are requested to remain virgins before marriage and then faithful to their husbands afterward. Alves adds: "Embora predominantes, estes valores convivem com tendências liberalizantes e concepções de modernidade sobre as relações familiares, o papel da mulher e a educação dos filhos" (15).[11]

According to Alves, both magazines revitalize ancient myths. *Nova* updates Cinderella and the myth of eternal and symbiotic love typical of Western civilization. *Nova* reconciles the myth with the modern woman who is both emancipated and seductive. This modern woman is still seen as a Cinderella that wears a crystal shoe and establishes a fragile contact with the ground and with reality. Next to a man, this fragile woman is nullified. She then hangs on to him, and he protects and supports her. *Ele/Ela* reconfirms the Christian myth that ascribes impurity to sex while denying it to women and granting it to men out of wedlock. The male in this magazine is Don Juan, the inveterate and glorious gallant (Alves 130).

The result, the author contends, is that the "new" woman ought to be beautiful, sensuous, seductive, maternal, intelligent, independent, and professionally successful; the "new" man, strong, protective, companiable, sensitive, sensuous, open to dialogue. While the male–female mismatch is pathetic, "Os novos padrões questionam a dependência feminina e o machismo, mas não os eliminam, atualizando-os sob novas modalidades," Alves explains (122).[12] If nostalgia and the desires of a modern macho prevail in *Ele/Ela*, *Nova* still treats the woman as an object commodified by articles of consumption and uniformed by the mandates of fashion (151). While the ideal reader of *Ele/Ela* misses the good old days when a woman asked no more than to be revered and possessed, the ideal reader of *Nova* seeks, through consumerism, both a prince and her independence at the same time (158). If *Ele/Ela* hopes every man will have one woman at home who is a submissive wife/mother and another one outside the home who is the happy prey, that man may come across the *Nova* woman, who wants to eroticize her marriage (160). It seems inevitable to realize that the new/old woman in *Nova* and the modern macho in *Ele/Ela* reduplicate—despite their modernist façade—some anachronistic images that continue to inhabit the Brazilian collective imagination.

If it is important to reiterate that these "modern" ideas of the culture industry circulate mostly among middle and upper social strata, it is also meaningful to investigate sexuality among other groups. For Chauí, machismo within lower-income groups is the rule. Peasants and workers, for instance, often reply that their husbands are good because they don't beat them. For the middle classes, pornographic magazines and movies, as well as visits to a no-tell motel, turn out to be new sexual possibilities. Needless to say, the female bodies idealized have little to do with those of their partners. Women of all classes, except for those from the intellectual urban middle classes, condemn masturbation, homosexuality, and excessive female employment (Chauí 220–21).

In brief, the ideal family—as in *Lucíola*—becomes the point of reference for the appreciation and condemnation of the real family.

One of the conclusions to draw from Chauí's observations is that a large portion of lower income families has assimilated the patriarchal ideology. The cultural model prevailing in Brazil establishes the husband/father as the head of the domestic group, which results from taking biological sex as the governing principle. Dominance and authority, in turn, derive from the male's role as bread earner and as status bestower. The concept of husband/father as the head of the family or as the head of the couple has indeed a juridical basis,[13] "o modelo dominante é um modelo ideal" (Woortmann, *A família* 65).[14]

Several authors have stressed how the public and the private orders in Brazil are articulated in conjunction with other antinomies like "house" and "street" (studied by Roberto DaMatta) or "man" and "woman." Man is granted the public universe and woman, the cozy home space. What is often happening, however, is confusion between the two instances, and one ends up invading the other, which results in the contradictory profile of Brazilian society.

In her research on a small community in Rocinha (the largest shantytown in Rio de Janeiro), Tania Salem argues that "a família emerge como a esfera prioritária de identificação feminina, isto é, o *locus* no qual sua identidade é gerada, construída e referida."[15] Such a phenomenon is actually revealed "no fato de a mulher só conseguir se definir na ou através da família—seja como filha, esposa ou mãe" (60).[16] Within the images the *faveladas* (women slum dwellers) draw of man, there is an individual who is more fancy-free, the agent of his own existence and possessed of free will. The world of woman, though, is that of bondage, and she sees herself as the target of other people's will (Salem 61). The emotional and financial stability, in particular, are cosubstantiated in and delegated to the male figure, who assumes undisputed prominence in the family hierarchy. In other words "a inserção da mulher no mundo está sempre intermediada por figuras familiares—pai, marido ou filhos" (Salem 62).[17] According to what the *faveladas* think of themselves, it is the male's role to direct the female's existence, since it is through him that she envisions the possibility of a better order to her own life. In this sense, the recurrent displacement of supporting male figures, to the extent that they present a true possibility of problem solving and sheltering, exposes the woman's delay in finding "vida mais tranqüila" (92–93).[18] The self-portrait she provides is, consequently, built upon and sustained through fragility, passivity, and impotence. While internalizing the preconcepts of patriarchy, the woman cosigns and accepts the title of a status that someone else ascribes to her (93–94).

From data collected among peasants in the northeast of Brazil, Klaas Woortmann describes their typical home as a real palimpsest of the hierarchical, patriarchal, male-dominated structure of such a social environment.[19] The father is always served first, followed by the male children. Women and children, though, won't sit before the father is done eating; then they will eat whatever is left over. The anthropologist adds that eating leftovers does not mean they eat badly, but it definitely conveys a hierarchical assertion that each individual takes his rightful place. Every meal, therefore, feeds not only the people's bodies, but also their symbolic standings (Woortmann, "A comida" 114).

In his study on *favela* (slum) families on the outskirts of Salvador, Woortmann affirms that the husband is head of the domestic group and/or of the family, but it is the woman who performs the dominant role. Even though such males may deserve "respect," they do not hold authority. It is the woman who

> é o "principal" dominante, pois é ela que mantém relações rotineiras diárias com as crianças e que gerencia o orçamento doméstico, além de feqüentemente contribuir para ele. É ela que exerce autoridade imediata sobre os filhos, que decide sobre questões de escolaridade ou com quem podem ou não brincar; é ela que determina a alocação dos recursos do grupo doméstico para sua reprodução e deve ser consultada na eventualidade de se planejar dispor de dinheiro para fins de "acumulação" (aquisição de bens de consumo duráveis, reforma ou ampliação da casa, etc.). [. . .] Em todas essa famílias estáveis, os homens aceitavam a dominância da mulher na organização do grupo doméstico: "assunto de família é assunto de mulher"; "assunto de casa quem resolve é a mulher". De fato, o pai tem pouco relacionamento com os filhos e pouco a dizer sobre a organização da casa, assunto

que, de resto, pouco lhe interessa. O que ocorre nessas
famílias é que o homem tem um status de "respeito" e
uma autoridade teórica, enquanto a mulher exerce
autoridade concreta e gerencia. (*A família* 139–40)[20]

The home, continues Woortmann, is the place for woman, or the
place that belongs to her. The street is the place for men, whereas,
the family is women's domain, where men don't have much to
say or do. The "street" is a conception that men share as part of
their self-images as machos. Married or single, men supposedly
spend their free time at the bars, pool saloons, and other spots
considered "male territory," from which women are banned. This
is the territory for entertainment, "while the home is the place
for eating, sleeping, and serious sex." To "hang out" there is part
of an image of independence, but it also reflects men's uneasiness at home. Machismo, in this case, doesn't necessarily entail
men's dominance, argues Woortmann:

De fato, quanto menos autoridade o homem tem, tanto
mais ele "fica por aí". É exatamente quando perdem seus
empregos, e com eles seu "respeito", que eles gastam mais
tempo nos botequins, "posando de macho" (no dizer de
algumas mulheres) a fim de compensar subjetivamente a
perda de status dentro do grupo doméstico. [. . .] Não sei o
que ocorreria caso as mulheres tentassem fazer com que
seus maridos participassem das tarefas domésticas.
Presumivelmente, eles "dariam no pé" mais cedo do que
de costume, pois seguramente sentiriam sua "macheza"
ameaçada; seguramente, pareceriam ridículos do ponto de
vista da ideologia tradicional brasileira. (Woortmann, *A
família* 104–5)[21]

Woortmann also takes the liberty of guessing why men wouldn't
help with the domestic chores instead. If women tried to have
them work in the home, men would probably run out, feeling that
their maleness was in jeopardy: "seguramente, pareceriam ridículos do ponto de vista da ideologia tradicional brasileira" (105).[22]

The poor sectors of society invert the dominant familial model,
which stresses matrimonial stability and turns marriage into a
male-dominated institution of high political, economic, and social
prestige. Among the elite groups, says Woortmann, marriage used
to transfer to men some of women's properties: her reproductive

capability (while sexual services could be provided by a concubine), her dowry, and herself (as a legally dependent individual, upon which male power descended from father to husband). Woortmann also recalls that, until recently, woman did not have a juridical identity. Among the poor, however, conjugal instability is related to the reduced importance of this lack of identity and to the dominant role of women within the kinship system, with an emphasis on mother-daughter binding. The conjugal instability also expresses an ideology of gender roles that are somewhat inverted, especially if compared to those of middle or elite classes. The subjacent reason for it is men's shortcomings and women's participation in the job market (Woortmann, *A família* 115, 292).

In view of this, the truth is that the exception confirms the rule. Even if the low-income woman is the lead character in a familial model that differs from what we find among the elite, we are still dealing with a relation between unequal beings: this is still a relation in which the will to power is implicit. The examples taken from studies on low-income groups show that representations of sexuality related to issues of power are not exclusive to the dominant groups. They are indeed extended throughout Brazilian society. The very language habitually employed to name sexual elements, which is discussed next, tends to corroborate this hypothesis.

"Amorous Cannibalism"

Brazilians conceive of [hetero]sexuality, writes DaMatta, not as the encountering of opposite and equal individuals (a man and a woman who can be their own persons), but as a way for one to absorb the other, which does away with a sense of equality symbolically consented to by society. Sexual acts, therefore, establish a difference and a radical heterogeneity by just changing the individual into either the "eater" or the "eaten," Portuguese metaphors that, as we have seen, resemble the English duality top/bottom (*O que faz o Brasil, Brasil?* 60).

I have yet to come across a convincing explanation for the widespread semantic use of "to eat" when the issue is sex. I suspect it may have something to do with one individual's assimilation and destruction of the other during sexual contact, since aspects of sexuality and power are intimately intersected in the Brazilian case. Yet, I have no supporting evidence for this suspicion. It is interesting to point out, however, that according to the patriarchal and male-oriented values still held in the Brazilian imagination to date, the woman must "give herself" and be "eaten," but not the man. The man who is "eaten" is thought of as effeminate (if not queer), which contradicts the manly image he is supposed to put forth.

Up to the nineteenth century, sexuality had little effect on the stability of the patriarchal family. Between married couples, sex was basically restricted to intercourse for procreation. For the male's pleasure, there were slaves and prostitutes. In just about every Brazilian town, brothels were as important as the mother church, the public school, or the local political boss. Thus, the virginity of young women, including brides, was ensured. There was also an outlet for the young men's libido as well as for the husbands who were raised not to confuse their saintly consorts with their voluptuous and shameless lovers (Chauí, *Repressão* 80). In the meantime, the Catholic Church condemned sex if not had for procreation, and society not only disdained homosexuality, but also jeered and often punished practitioners (Costa 246).

Still today, the centuries-old hierarchy suggested by linguistic terms continues to dictate that men are "eaters" and women are "eaten." Whereas *dar* (to give) implies weakness, such as in "give in," the verb *comer* (to eat), apart from referring to "eating food," denotes a notion of defeating an opponent in a game, such as when a checkers piece takes another. As Fry and MacRae argue, "o ato sexual é percebido também em termos hierárquicos, pois a idéia é que quem penetra é de certa forma o vencedor de quem é penetrado" (48).[23] Men are, thus, raised thinking that "os homens são criados para pensar que sua própria masculinidade está sempre a ser provada pelo desempenho sexual tanto potente quanto freqüente" (49).[24] It should not be surprising that the terms used for the male genitalia are based on the semantic field of power:

> They place emphasis on the potentially active quality of
> the phallus — on its aggressive quality, on its potency not
> merely as a sexual organ, but, in the language of metaphor,

as a tool to be wielded, as a kind of weapon intimately
linked to both violence and violation. . . . In the play of
words, the phallus becomes, figuratively if not literally, an
arma — a weapon, an instrument of metaphoric
aggression, . . . of symbolic violence. . . . In the symbol of the
phallus the diverse meanings associated with masculinity
in Brazilian culture merge and intertwine. It links notions
of virility and potency to notions of force, power, and
violence in varying degrees of conscious and unconscious
understanding. (Parker 36–38)

Active/passive, dominance/submission, violence/inferiority —
the heterosexual world seems dual-party, opposing the world of
men, who "eat" while penetrating their partners, to that of women,
who passively offer themselves to be penetrated and possessed
(Parker 43). By extension, these images perpetuate themselves in
the homosexual world: the active male penetrates, and the queer
(or *viado*, terms used here without any pejorative intent) is pene-
trated/eaten, in a putatively passive position, "as if he were a
woman." So-called activity and passivity acquire the sense of
dominance and submission. Furthermore, the relation between
men and queers is analogous to that between men and women. In
homosexual relations, homosexuals are considered as such only if
they are eaten. The men doing the eating, according to this cultural
system, may have sexual intercourse with people of the same sex
(this being homosexual relations) without losing their male status
(Fry and MacRae 90). The representations of sexual relations between men and queers and men and women, consequently, speak
of dominance and submission, rather than of sexuality per se.

What is considered deviant is not the homosexual relation in,
say, physiological terms, but the infringement of the sexual code regarding the partners' social roles (Fry and MacRae 45). The Brazilian concept of sexuality is one that says more about masculinity
versus femininity, activity versus passivity, and top versus bottom than it does about heterosexuality versus homosexuality (Fry
and MacRae 49). The main concern seems to be the success or failure of stereotypical roles. As Parker puts it, "The crucial point is
not simply that neither the *viado* nor the *corno* [the betrayed husband, who also 'fails' to be masculine] is a 'true' man, but that both

figures function . . . as negative alternatives in building up a positive image of what the true man in fact should be: the *homem* [man], the *machão* [stud], the *pai* [father]" (45).

It is useful to relate such sense of failure to the discoveries made by masscult magazines. While reporting on men's fears in regard to women, feminine *Nova* cited, among the most common ones, those of being betrayed, challenged at work, and outsmarted by sexually experienced women (Alves 105). Masculine *Ele/Ela*, in turn, explains the men's crises and problems in the age that follows the sexual "revolution." Women's liberation makes him anguished. Both at home and at work, he no longer feels unvanquishable and omnipotent, which causes him to lose interest in work itself. He is even forced to admit he will have to share the household chores. He not only has to face the decline of the old, gender-biased double standard, but also hide his chauvinistic manner in order to seduce liberated women. On both sides of his social life, he struggles with the fear of impotence (Alves 56).

What we see is that the discourse on sexuality doesn't refer to an exchange between equals, but inscribes itself within the dynamics of a power struggle. The loss of the old omnipotence that the patriarch/father/master/macho had over his family, land, and political scene is underscored by the dialectics of power on the level of sexuality. As Michel Debrun suggests, there is a political form of conciliation that, far from linking individuals by mutual tolerance, reestablishes ties between the weak and the strong by virtue of constraining co-optation (46). Indeed, the sexual discourse seems to corroborate a pervasive social logic that says "the deal is to take advantage, no matter how." It is not by chance that, in Brazilian penitentiaries, the veteran male inmates compete for "marrying" the young and beautiful, a pattern of dominance that reproduces itself via sexuality by linking sexual supposed passivity to social weakness (Fry and MacRae 52–53).

Eros and Thanatos

My purpose is not to confine the far-reaching considerations of this work to conclusions that put an end to the question of representation of family and sexuality in Brazilian cultural discourse. I hope, however, to have suggested, by means of the scholarship of various different disciplines, that in Brazil's case the representation of family and sexuality is, on one hand, associated with power, and, on the other, intertwined with the ideology of hegemony in a modern sort of packaging. The social component is the one that prevails in Brazilians' mental images of sexuality. Such images — indeed our machista and patriarchal heritage — have spread not only to low-income strata but also to various other population groups.

I also have attempted to show that, despite Brazilian modernization, certain myths and patriarchal legacies still impregnate the social imagination in regard to sexuality, which makes me wonder to what extent the country has really been modernized and to what extent the contradictions of such changes have prevented the thorough emergence of modernity. Perhaps no process of modernization can come true without many paradoxes, but this is not the point here. My goal is to question the "modernizing" discourse of a large group of Brazilian intellectuals who take modernization for granted. They speak about the country's postmodern condition before casting any doubt on whether we have reached the modern stage. The discourse on sexuality, which often tries to show off a post–sexual revolution profile, is full of traditional and reactionary elements. The modernization of social habits is, subsequently, nothing but a facade hiding a nonprogressive society still stigmatized by its slave-dependent and patriarchal past. Furthermore, a substantial part of the Brazilian discourse — whether it is official or hegemonic — has been disciplinary, serving the interests of the dominant groups and the inflating nation-state, the institution that absorbs several functions held by the father within the patriarchal order. The 1900s literati, the hygienists, and the culture industry (from Vargas to TV and "modern people" magazines) have carried over the old prescriptive attitude that sustains the traditional foundations of the family and its sexual mores, in spite of their modernizing touch-ups.

Sexuality in itself, I believe, is a relationship between equals, between human subjects. To some extent, it arises between people regardless of their histories, individual concerns, class, gender, ethnicity, or sexual orientation. Taken as a social construct and mediated by its role in a certain society, within a specific historical framework, sexuality activates systems of differentiation that compartmentalize people into cultural categories. Rendered "natural" by powerful ideologies, sexuality fosters notions such as masculine/feminine, active/passive, heterosexual/homosexual. This is the context in which the study of representations of sexuality in Brazil's cultural discourse allows us to read that society by carefully attending to unconscious messages, assessing the sexual, familial, and power symbolism they (messages) give off.

It is undoubtedly possible to approach sexuality from various perspectives: the psychological, anthropological, philosophical, ethical, legal, or religious ones, for instance. My aim is not to explore the human realms where sexuality plays a part. I am not looking for empirical profiles, either, since discursive representations of sexuality are the focus of this essay. Such representations arise from, and ultimately say much more about, power relations and debatable modernization than about sex itself.

In the case of Brazil, I am tempted to believe that discourse on sexuality is, above all, a mask that hides the struggle for power. We are undoubtedly dealing with a very authoritarian society. As Chauí puts it, "as diferenças e assimetrias sociais são logo transformadas em desigualdades, e estas em relações de hierarquia, mando e obediência" (*Conformismo* 54).[25] Whether one thinks of the family or interpersonal relations in general, the nation-state or various other public and private institutions, she adds, all such relations "take the shape of dependency, tutelage, concession, authority and favoritism" (54). Symbolic violence becomes "a regra da vida social e cultural" (54).[26] Violence is enhanced even further by its invisibility, "sob o paternalismo e o clientelismo, considerados naturais e, por vezes, exaltados como qualidades positivas do 'caráter nacional'" (54).[27]

Human sexuality, in the Brazilian context, is not simply sexuality, which has also been suggested by Fry and MacRae (78). One may suspect, therefore, that the celebrated Brazilian sensuality and sexual permissiveness in the tropics are nothing but myths camouflaging a society actually unequal, hierarchical, violent, paternalist, and reactionary. This is a society that, while averse to changes, deals with conflicts either by appealing to conciliation or by "taking advantage," the common denominator always being one individual's cannibalistic abuse of the other. It is my duty to ask if everything is truly permissible south of the equator, or if, in that tropical paradise of suntanned bodies on the beaches (on display almost like in shopwindows), there is room for difference, common experience, solidarity, dialogue, and eroticism.

Notes

1. The family is not merely a social institution, but also a political one. In other words, as the state controls sexuality through the family, sex becomes also a political question.

2. are produced historically within concrete societies (and, therefore) "intimately related to the whole body of each society".

3. I am inspired here by Clifford Geertz's understanding of culture as a juncture of texts. In his famous essay on cockfighting, he shows how Balinese culture "implies something" and allows itself to be "read" by means of two cocks tearing each other apart in a ring. Societies, as he puts it, uphold their own interpretations that are shaped within a set of recollections they draw of themselves (Geertz 321).

4. written and interpreted from the vantage point of the dominant class.

5. The history of various forms of familial organization of Brazil has been limited to that of a specific domestic type — the "patriarchal family." This is a rigid order in which the characters, once defined, will merely substitute for one another generation after generation. Its hegemony is not threatened, as it is a power line from which all other social relations derive. It establishes itself where large agricultural units are based: sugar mills, ranches, and coffee farms. It sustains itself through the attachment of new members, preferably relatives (legitimate or illegitimate), to the extended "clans," which ensures the indivisibility of power. Its decadence occurs with the advent of industrialization and the downfall of the large rural properties. It is then replaced by "the modern matrimonial family," which is the final outcome (whereas the other one is the starting point). By contrast to patriarchal unity, the matrimonial family is a typical byproduct of urbanization. Reduced to its children, marriage no longer has as its chief purpose the maintenance of a large property shared by an extended family or the political interests held by a single group. The purpose is the fulfillment of sexual and affectionate impulses, which in the patriarchal system were fulfilled outside the immediate family.

6. In using the term "prevalence," I do not mean to imply that I advocate the absolute existence of this model — either in social or in geographic terms. As a semblance, however, the term will embody the discourse of the hegemonic sectors, and, as long as it is internalized by the dominant groups, it will be present in their views on life.

7. Queiroz observes that alliances and social ascent through marriage reflected the woman's standing within the family. The image of the woman lying in a hammock and eating sweets while submitting to her husband's brutality is a legend created by writers. The author argues that the Brazilian upper-class woman was submissive to her husband as a general rule; within the home, her role was to complement and cooperate with him, most often by developing intense activities. Indolence and passivity tended to be rare. When the husband was an outlaw or a member of lower social strata — two cases in which he moved up the

ladder through matrimony—the woman held greater advantages; she some-times even commanded the estate, since she kept the inherited fortunes for her-self (193).

8. all it takes is to see them unattended for them not to be regarded as "ladies."

9. shaking deliriously.

10. women provide much servitude—it's incredible. They are useful even in politics. They give us children, impose respect. For all the rest, there are joy girls.

11. Even though they actually prevail, such values are sustained together with liberating tendencies and modern concepts regarding familial relations, the wo-man's role, and child raising.

12. the new patterns question female dependency and machismo but cannot eliminate them.

13. Leila L. Barsted informs us that the "family, whose structure is defined by the Brazilian legislation, isn't simply the reflection of how members relate to one another, according to different social groups. It is, instead, the codification of the dominant elite's point of view, the sector of society concerned about the legiti-macy of family ties, in legal terms, which implies the establishment of marital and paternal power for men." Another characteristic of this family structure hi-erarchy is that "the legal family has a male head, to whom the wife and children are subordinated." It is his role to mediate the relations of the family group with society at large. Another element of this model is monogamy, and adultery is considered a crime (104–5).

14. a dominant model that is taken as the ideal by the poor.

15. the family emerges as the primary sphere of identification for the woman; that is, it is the locus in which her identity is generated, developed, and fixed.

16. by the fact that the woman manages to define herself either in/through the family as a daughter, wife, or mother.

17. woman's participation in society is always intermediated by family fig-ures—father, husband, or children.

18. an easier life.

19. "The *living room* (the male's domain) and the *kitchen* (the female's do-main) are located at opposite poles (front and rear), while the *dining room* is lo-cated in an intermediary position, like the couple's bedroom." Man and woman get together every day in such intermediary spots, the dining room during the day, the bedroom at night. These two spaces are those of family reproduction—nutritionally and sexually speaking—and are set on the same plane within the total space of the house. The spatial configuration also suggests the relationship between eating and "eating" [the different connotations of *comer,* a verb that most commonly refers to the "active" role in sexual intercourse] ("A comida" 114).

20. maintains routine interaction with the children and who manages the do-mestic budget, besides contributing to it frequently. It is she who exerts immedi-ate authority over her children by deciding on school matters or on whom they should or should not play with. It is she who determines the allocation of the do-mestic group's resources for living expenses, and she must be consulted if there is any planning for investing money with the purpose of "accumulation" (the acquisition of durable goods, or the remodeling or enlargement of their house, etc.). In all stable family units, men accepted the women's dominance over the organi-zation of the domestic group: "family matters are women's matters" or "home

issues are taken care of by women," they say. Indeed, the father has little interaction with the children and very little to say about domestic organization, a topic that doesn't interest him much. What happens is that the man has a "respectful" status and a theoretical authority, while the woman exerts true authority and management.

21. In fact, the lesser his authority at home, the more he hangs out there. It is precisely when they lose their jobs, and their "respect" with them, that they waste more time at the watering holes, "posing as machos" (as some women put it) in order to compensate subjectively for their loss of status within the domestic group.

22. they would certainly feel ridiculed in compliance with the traditional ideologies of Brazil.

23. the idea is that the one who penetrates defeats the other.

24. their own masculinity is always to be proven by their sexual performances: the more frequent the sexual relations, the more potent the individuals.

25. social differences and asymmetries are quickly transformed into inequalities, which turn into relations of hierarchy, dominance, and obedience.

26. the golden rule of the country's social and cultural life.

27. which functions as a cover-up for paternalism and patronage, features often considered "natural" and occasionally exalted as positive qualities of the "national character."

Works Cited

Alencar, José de. "O demônio familiar." In *Obra completa*. Rio de Janeiro: Aguilar, 1960, 4.79–136.

———. *Lucíola*. Rio de Janeiro: Ouro, s/d.

Almeida, Angela Mendes de. "Notas sobre a família no Brasil." *Pensando a família no Brasil,* q.v. 53–66.

Alphonsus, João. *Totônio Pacheco*. 3a ed. Rio de Janeiro: Imago, 1976.

Alves, Denise. *O desencontro marcado*. Petrópolis: Vozes, 1985.

Amado, Jorge. *Gabriela, cravo e canela*. 51a ed. Rio de Janeiro: Record, 1975.

Ariès, Philippe. *L'Enfant et la vie familiale sous l'Ancien Régime*. Paris: Plon, 1960.

Azevedo, Alvares de. *Poesia*. 3a ed. Rio de Janeiro: Agir, 1969.

Barsted, Leila Linhares. "Permanência ou mudança? O discurso legal sobre a família." *Pensando a família no Brasil,* q.v., 103–13.

Bastos, Elide Rugai. "Gilberto Freyre e a questão nacional." In *Inteligência brasileira*. Ed. Reginaldo Moraes et al. São Paulo: Brasiliense, 1986, 43–76.

Buitoni, Dulcília Helena Schroeder. *Mulher de papel*. São Paulo: Loyola, 1981.

Candido, Antonio. "The Brazilian Family." In *Brazil, Portrait of Half a Continent*. Ed. T. Lynn Smith. Westport, Conn.: Greenwood Press, 1972, 201–312.

Carneiro, Maria José. "A desagradável família de Nelson Rodrigues." In *Uma nova família?* Ed. Sérvulo A. Figueira. Rio de Janeiro: Jorge Zahar, 1987, 69–82.

Castro, Eduardo Viveiros de, and Ricardo B. de Araújo. "Romeu e Julieta e a origem do Estado." In *Arte e sociedade*. Ed. Gilberto Velho. Rio de Janeiro: Zahar, 1977, 130–69.

Chauí, Marilena. *Conformismo e resistência*. São Paulo: Brasiliense, 1986.

———. *Repressão sexual: essa nossa (des)conhecida*. 11a ed. São Paulo: Brasiliense, 1988.

Corrêa, Marisa. "Repensando a família patriarcal brasileira." In *Colcha de retalhos; estudos sobre a família no Brasil*. Ed. Maria Suely Kofes de Almeida et al. São Paulo: Brasiliense, 1982, 13–38.

Costa, Jurandir Freire. *Ordem médica e norma familiar*. 2a ed. Rio de Janeiro: Graal, 1983.

DaMatta, Roberto. *A casa e a rua*. São Paulo: Brasiliense, 1985.

———. *O que faz o brasil, Brasil?* Rio de Janeiro: Rocco, 1984.

d'Avila Neto, Maria Inacia. *O autoritarismo e a mulher*. Rio de Janeiro: Achiamé, 1980.

Debrun, Michel. "A identidade nacional brasileira." *Estudos avançados* 4.8 (1990): 39–49.

Fernandes, Florestan. *A revolução burguesa no Brasil*. 2a ed. Rio de Janeiro: Zahar, 1976.

Freyre, Gilberto. *Casa-grande e senzala*. 19a ed. Rio de Janeiro: José Olympio, 1978.

Fry, Peter. *Para inglês ver*. Rio de Janeiro: Zahar, 1982.

——— and Edward MacRae. *O que é homossexualidade*. São Paulo: Brasiliense, 1983.

Geertz, Clifford. *A interpretação das culturas*. Trans. Fanny Wrobel. Rio de Janeiro: Zahar, 1978. (Translation of *The Interpretation of Cultures*.)

Holanda, Sérgio Buarque de. *Raízes do Brasil*. 12a ed. Rio de Janeiro: José Olympio, 1978.

Leite, Dante Moreira. *O caráter nacional brasileiro*. 2a ed. São Paulo: Pioneira, 1969.

Mota, Carlos Guilherme. "Cultura brasileira ou cultura republicana?" *Estudos avançados* 4.8 (1990): 19–38.

———. *Ideologia da cultura brasileira (1933–1974)*. 4a ed. São Paulo: Ática, 1980.

Parker, Richard. *Bodies, Pleasures, and Passions*. Boston: Beacon Press, 1991.

Pensando a família no Brasil; da colônia à modernidade. Ángela Mendes de Almeida, org. Rio de Janeiro: Espaço e Tempo/Editora da UFRRJ, 1987.

Priore, Mary del. *A mulher na história do Brasil*. São Paulo: Contexto, 1988.

Queiroz, Maria Isaura Pereira de. *O mandonismo local na vida política brasileira*. São Paulo: Alfa-Omega, 1976.

Reis, Roberto. "Muita serventia." *Literature and Human Rights* 4 (1989): 567–80.

———. *The Pearl Necklace*. Gainesville: University of Florida Press, 1992.

———. *A permanência do círculo*. Niterói: Editora da Universidad Federal Fluminense, 1987.

Salem, Tania. "Mulheres faveladas: 'com a venda nos olhos.'" *Perspectivas antropológicas da mulher* 1 (1981): 50–99.

Samara, Eni de Mesquita. *A família brasileira*. São Paulo: Brasiliense, 1983.

Santiago, Silviano. *Iracema (Edição comentada)*. Rio de Janeiro: Francisco Alves, 1975.

———. *Vale quanto pesa*. Rio de Janeiro: Paz e Terra, 1982.

Souza, Gilda de Mello e. *O espírito das roupas*. São Paulo: Cia. das Letras, 1987.

Süssekind, Flora. "Nelson Rodrigues e o fundo falso." In *I Concurso Nacional de Monografias-1976*. Brasília: Serviço Nacional de Teatro, 1977, 5–42.

———. *Tal Brasil, qual romance?* Rio de Janeiro: Achiamé, 1984.

Vainfas, Ronaldo. *Trópico dos pecados*. Rio de Janeiro: Campus, 1989.

Ventura, Roberto. *Estilo tropical*. São Paulo: Cia. das Letras, 1991.

Woortmann, Klaas. "A comida, a família e a construção do gênero feminino." *Revista de ciências sociais* 29.1 (1986): 103–30.

———. *A família das mulheres*. Rio de Janeiro: Tempo Brasileiro, 1987.

◆ **Chapter 5**

The Body in Context: Don Quixote and Don Juan

James A. Parr

Must not all things at last
be swallowed up in death?
　　Plato, *Phaedo* 72

Death alone reveals how small are
men's poor bodies.
　　Juvenal, *Satires,* No. 10

I

In an initial approximation, there could hardly be two more disparate works or two more dissimilar protagonists than Don Quixote and Don Juan. The differences in age, social class, self-assigned mission, attitudes toward women, and the Apollonian versus Dionysian worldview would seem to mitigate against any similarities of consequence. It will be my purpose, nevertheless, to seek out those similarities and to suggest that difference assumes a secondary role—one that could be equated with surface structure—in comparison to the commonalities of the deeper structure made manifest in the characters' final disposition at the hands of their authors, but also in their anal-sadistic interactions with other characters and with society at large on the way to that common end.

While each of these texts might be viewed as a case history in its own right, I shall try to demonstrate that, in the aggregate, those histories are more complementary than disparate. My approach will be different from—but, I trust, complementary to—the other studies included here, for I view the body and its functions, particularly the sexual and scatological, within the context of, and as anticipations of, death and disintegration. Although we may not rejoice in the prospect, these are the destiny of the body. Not for nothing, surely, is the sexual climax associated with death: "la petite mort."

Initially at issue is a methodological consideration. Françoise Meltzer cautions in a recent essay titled "Unconscious" that it is a misuse of the medium to read texts as symptoms of authors' psychological states (153) and, moreover, that it is a "particularly useless undertaking" (154) to attempt to psychoanalyze fictional characters. My own conviction that fictional personages are not real persons, and cannot be analyzed as such, is a matter of record, as is the complementary stricture about "ingenious extratextual speculation" passing for literary criticism (*Anatomy* 85–86). Is there a methodologically respectable way out of this impasse? If we take to heart Freud's modest disclaimer that the poets and philosophers preceding him were the real discoverers of the unconscious (see Brown 62, 311), then it may not be amiss to read them in precisely that vein. That is to say, the poet presents a symbolic action, consciously or unconsciously, that we may decipher in terms of insights that came to be systematized much later, by Freud and others. The "poet" is here a flexible generic construct that stands for the author, while the "poem" is the work or text.

But a further refinement is called for. This poet is not the historical author of flesh and blood but rather the authorial presence a competent consumer infers upon completion of the reading. It is not an implied but an inferred author. Authors do not go about "implying" themselves, as Wayne Booth's term would suggest (74); readers infer them by assembling the bits and pieces that go together to make the text a coherent (or incoherent) whole. When one sorts through point of view, characterization, the generic medium employed, the narrative masks assumed, and so forth, there emerges a presence that we can call the inferred author. This is the poetic presence that interests me.

So it is not my purpose to psychoanalyze the authors or the characters per se, but, instead, to see what glimmers of insight into human nature are latent in them, insights of the sort that are later consolidated and systematized into a theory of culture and of the individual psyche's formation by and relation to its environment, as adumbrated by Freud in particular. The more philosophical notion that ontogeny (the development of the individual) recapitulates phylogeny (the development of the race) will be a crucial consideration in discussing Don Quixote.

With the preceding as a guiding principle—that is, looking back in order to look forward, while attempting, as Malcolm Read puts it, to "explore a textual unconscious" (vii)—it should be possible to eschew Meltzer's "useless undertaking," while at the same time recognizing, with Freud, that poets in all times and places have demonstrated intuitive but profound insights into the human condition. Unlike Freud's, however, my authorial presence is an extrapolation from the text, made by a late-twentieth-century reader, and should not be mistaken for the historical Gabriel Téllez or Miguel de Cervantes. By the same token, the quest for insights into a supposedly universal condition of Western man, made manifest through a character who exists only on the page (or the stage), should not be mistaken for a misguided attempt to psychoanalyze the character per se. The guiding assumption is that characters are metaphoric constructs, while the *mimesis* that sets them in motion is likewise "displaced" action that may, therefore, be read symbolically.

This will be a methodologically self-conscious exploration, then, but I should make clear at the outset that I am not a Freudian. I am not trained in psychoanalysis, or even in psychology. My approach, therefore, is to draw upon two distinguished interpreters of Freud, Norman O. Brown and Herbert Marcuse, each of whom has used the master's ideas to advance his own views of culture. Since my own perspective coincides closely with theirs, my reliance on these two stalwarts is perhaps understandable and, I hope, justified. Having read sparingly in the *Collected Papers*, it strikes me, frankly, that Freud is much more engaging and suggestive when he abandons the couch for culture, that is, when his analysis becomes collective rather than individual, leading him to grapple with Western illusions and delusions on a grand scale, as occurs in *Moses and Monotheism, The Future of an Illusion*, and, for present purposes, *Beyond the Pleasure Principle*.

It is primarily Freud the amateur philosopher and speculative culture critic who interests me here, and my concern is less with

Eros per se, or with manifestations of the erotic in the two texts under scrutiny, than it is with the central paradox that this life-affirming principle, sometimes referred to as the pleasure principle, has its downside, or dark side, or backside, for it seems to lead inexorably beyond itself, beyond the search for pleasure, or even self-realization, toward disintegration and death. Some of the best evidence in support of this assertion derives from the attention paid, in both works under consideration, to what Mikhail Bakhtin called "the material bodily lower stratum." The excremental vision encountered in both texts — along with a diffuse emphasis on anality and sadism, in varied manifestations — calls attention to the backside of reality, complementing the inverted quests of the two personages, while foreshadowing their calm or calamitous ends, as the case may be.

II

The explanations of Carlos Blanco-Aguinaga and Claudio Guillén to the effect that *Don Quixote* is properly viewed as a response, or countergenre, to the first person narrative of the picaresque, with its attempt to sketch a "life" from the beginning, continue to persuade. Clearly, the *Quixote* does not tell its story in first person, nor does it offer any systematic presentation of the life of the main character as a biological entity — there are only hints — prior to the age of fifty or so. Not only is the "talking cure" therefore inapplicable, partly because we cannot place him on a couch to get at the dynamics of repression, but, even more important, because nothing is revealed of his childhood. It would be much easier to psychoanalyze Lázaro de Tormes — if that were a legitimate undertaking for the literary critic — since we know at least something about his childhood and fictional formation.

Should we attempt to reconstruct those formative years for Alonso Quijano? Hardly. It is nonetheless safe to say that there is another absent presence somewhere in that background, in a sense anticipating the ethereal Dulcinea, and that is a mother figure. If she appears, it is in disguise (like Dulcinea), but she is not assigned a Christian name (unlike Dulcinea). How does she appear? If the mad Knight is a child of his naive reading of romance, and is sustained by those fictions throughout his career, then a symbolic displacement has occurred: he is born, nurtured, guided, and set on his way by books. Indeed, he is not weaned from them until the very end. The Logos he has figuratively devoured becomes his substitute father, the reading his mother—and the dramatized author's distancing of himself in the 1605 prologue (his claim to be only the stepfather of the character) assumes a meaning that may not have been noticed heretofore (see my "Plato..."). In a very real, yet symbolic, sense we are given a *vida* in its entirety, from birth to death, or, to take another perspective, from inspiration to expiration. Don Quixote's "fictional" formation is firmly fixed in fiction itself. In that regard, it is not unlike the type of narrative it can be seen to counter, the picaresque. It is superior to the picaresque in one important aspect, its ability to recount the final hours of the life of its protagonist, but its slice of life technique, beginning somewhat past *medias res*, may leave one equally perplexed and dissatisfied.

Now there is evidently more to the character's involvement with art—albeit a somewhat degraded form of art—than the preceding comments capture. Freud's notion of art is that it is a substitute-gratification (i.e., a replacement for sex), an illusion in contrast to reality, and, as one commentator explains, "An escape into an unreal world of fantasy [is] indistinguishable from a full-blown neurosis, both art and neurosis having the basic dynamic of a flight from reality" (Brown 56). We are presented with a character who not only takes refuge in art—which might be construed as an attempt to return to the womb, or to Nirvana—but this naive reader then takes on the self-imposed mission of changing reality to bring it into conformity with his equally naive notion of a Golden Age. Those who refuse to be guided by the reality principle, who would instead impose their will upon their surroundings to make them conform to some delusional notion, exhibit an exaggerated form of neurosis that is more properly termed psychosis (Iriarte, following Huarte, would say "constitucionalmente prepsicótico" [constitutionally prepsychotic; see Green "El 'ingenioso' hidalgo" 185]). Freud distinguishes between the two concepts as follows:

> Neurosis does not deny the existence of reality, it merely tries to ignore it; psychosis denies it and tries to substitute something else for it. (*Collected Papers* 2.279–80)

Cervantes's creation can thus be said to anticipate the extreme neurosis that would much later come to be called psychosis (Johnson 45 et passim). But the situation presented by Cervantes and later described by Freud is considerably more complex. The passage just cited goes on to maintain that

> a reaction which combines features of both of these [neurosis and psychosis] is the one we call normal or "healthy"; it denies reality as little as neurosis, but then, like psychosis, is concerned with effecting a change in it. This expedient normal attitude leads naturally to some achievement in the outer world and is not content, like a psychosis, with establishing the alteration within itself; it is no longer *auto-plastic* but *allo-plastic*. (*Collected Papers* 2.279–80)

While these comments might suggest that Don Quixote is normal and healthy, that is clearly not the case, because his efforts lead to no achievement in the outer world — indeed, great pains are taken to show that they are invariably counterproductive — and his concept of an idyllic past is demonstrably delusional. He is not configured as passively psychotic but as actively deranged, meddlesome, and downright dangerous — both to himself and others — on numerous occasions.

It is not my purpose to press the distinction between psychosis and neurosis, however. It will be sufficient to say that the character is presented as someone who participates, at a bare minimum, in the universal neurosis of mankind. In that sense, he is a kind of Everyman who, moreover, reflects the "Dulcineated World" of his society, as Arthur Efron maintained several years ago in a book that can only be appreciated more as time goes by.

Neurosis and sublimation go hand in hand, of course. They are complementary but not synonymous. Culture and "Dulcineism" require sublimation, however, and *are* essentially synonymous with it:

> In a cultural formation [i.e., via sublimation] the activity, though sexual in origin, is desexualized, socialized, and directed at reality in the form of work; in a neurosis the activity is resexualized, withdrawn from the social, and involves a flight from reality. (Brown 143)

Or, as Róheim put it so succinctly, "A neurosis isolates; a sublimation unites" (Marcuse 209). There can be no doubt that Cervantes's arrant Knight anticipates both possibilities. As Alonso Quijano, he might be said to sublimate by channeling sexual energy into hunting, reading, and, occasionally, administering his estate—all socially acceptable and seemingly innocuous activities. He does not engage in work as such—certainly not in alienated labor—for he is a man of modest means, a member of the landed gentry, and his quest, during those days of his prehistory, is to find ways to fill up "los ratos que estaba ocioso—que eran los más del año" [the times when he was idle—which was most of the year] (71).

When his brain overheats and dries up—when obsessional neurosis takes over, in today's terms—he will continue to sublimate (and repress) in conformity with the demands of society, as Efron has shown, but there is decidedly a transformation, and the emblem of that reconfiguration is surely Dulcinea. Through this parody of the *belle dame sans merci* (see Close), with its corollaries of courtly service and suffering, the woman distanced and unattainable—figuratively on a pedestal—we witness a transfiguring of sexuality into a more diffuse and abstract Eros, a withdrawal from the social in order to pursue a private agenda, and the obvious flight from reality.

Repressed sexuality finds its symbolic expression in the antics of Rocinante, when he feels the urge to dally with the Yangüesan mares in I.15, with fairly predictable consequences. In some of his earlier writings, Freud compared the relation of the ego to the id with that of a rider to his horse, a metaphor that harks back to Plato's *Phaedrus*. When the rider fails to control his steed, as in this misadventure, the situation is tantamount to the unconscious pleasure principle erupting into consciousness, much to the chagrin of the reality principle and its personification in the ego.

Another suggestive anticipation of Freud can be found in the assertion that "repression weighs more heavily on anality than on genitality" (Brown 180). Our mock hero is quick to suppress the *-ano* of his last name in favor of a slightly more savory suffix, the equally witty but also pejorative *-ote* (see Baras). This could be construed as an attempt to put anality behind him, so to speak.

The *quixote* is the piece of armor that protects the thigh, thus serving to shift the focus from back to front, from the anal to the genital, since the thigh is more closely associated with the latter area. It might also be taken to reflect castration anxiety, which is to say, "a fear of losing the instrument for reuniting with a mother-substitute in the act of copulation" (Brown 114).

The character's disdain for money is likewise significant in terms of anality, if we assume the virtual synonymity of filthy lucre and feces (see chapter on "Filthy Lucre" in Brown). It is again a question of repressing that stage of sexual development within the id. A final instance of lower body features and functions intruding upon the idealized fantasy world in which the character has taken refuge would be Sancho's failure to show proper respect when Nature calls during the fulling-mills episode (I.20). While the Knight sits erect astride Rocinante, his sensitive nostrils provide confirming evidence of what his ears had led him to suspect, as the heady vapors ascend in the Stygian darkness.

While it is curious that I.20 should so emphasize the auditory and olfactory senses, it is even more remarkable that I.21 should complement these foci by stressing the visual (in discerning Mambrino's helmet in the distance). Is this clustering a chance happening or does it represent the sort of intuition Freud readily vouchsafed to poets?

> Abstraction, as a mode of keeping life at a distance, is supported by that negation of the "lower" infantile sexual organizations which effects a general "displacement from below upwards" of organ eroticism to the head, especially to the eyes: *Os homini sublime dedit caelumque videre jussit.* The audiovisual sphere is preferred by sublimation because it preserves distance. (Brown 173)

Indeed, Cervantes's text ups the ante by showing that the olfactory supplements the audiovisual. What we have in this witty supplement is an insinuation of the identity between what is highest and what is lowest in human nature—Don Quixote with his patrician nose pointed toward the heavens and Sancho with his plebeian buttocks aimed at the earth—and, by extrapolation, the further insinuation is that, as Jonathan Swift put it bluntly in a late poem: "No wonder how I lost my Wits; / Oh! *Caelia, Caelia, Caelia* shits."

The flight from the feminine, exemplified in the transformation of the smelly Aldonza into the disembodied Dulcinea, can be seen upon further consideration to be a flight not just from the prosaic but from the bottom side of the prosaic, from all that is remindful of the an(im)al nature we have in common. It is a matter of keeping dirt out of the dream. Recognition and acceptance of that animal nature, symbolized in the antics of Rocinante and in the excremental vision just sketched, would, of course, negate and render untenable the illusory world within which the quest for a fantastical ideal takes place.

In Don Quixote we have a fictional personage who prefigures poetically — even as he strives valiantly to deny both his and his beloved's bodies — an anal-sadistic stage of arrested development. The "obsessional commitment to transform passivity into activity is aggressiveness" (Brown 117). The passive Alonso Quijano becomes the active Don Quixote, whose aggressiveness toward Sancho and others becomes a hallmark in Part I.

According to Freud, "Aggressiveness represents a fusion of the life instinct with the death instinct" (Brown 101). His final position seems to be that there is a "primary masochism directed against the self and that sadism [is] an extroversion of this primary masochism ... identified with the death instinct" (Brown 88). While there are two other ingredients associated with Thanatos, namely the Nirvana principle and the repetition-compulsion, "it is only the third element in Freud's death instinct, the sado-masochistic complex, which introduces death in the real and literal sense into the death instinct," since "the repetition-compulsion and the Nirvana-principle appear to be two interconnected aspects of the instinctual demand for complete satisfaction and the abolition of repression" (Brown 97).

The characterization of Don Quixote is one that surely invites the label of masochist, on one hand — think only of his predilection for placing himself in harm's way, along with his abstinence from both food and sex — and sadism, on the other (cf. Combet 265–68). His violence toward Sancho has been mentioned, but there is also the more subtle struggle to obliterate the Other — more specifically, the memory of the Other — by eclipsing the great deeds of such as David, Joshua, Caesar, Roland, King Arthur, Charlemagne, and any number of illustrious precursors (I. 5: 106). In existential terms, the essence of sadism is just that: the negation of the Other.

The characterization of Don Quixote anticipates many features of the sort of tension between life and death instincts that Freud describes in *Beyond the Pleasure Principle.* If "the past continues to claim the future," as Marcuse suggests, in that "it generates the wish that the paradise [experienced in earlier stages of development] be re-created" (18), what Cervantes's text figures forth is an attempt to recapture through fantasy the personal paradise about which we are not told—but which would need to be assumed if Freud's topographic, hydraulic model were to play any role in further deliberations—in other words, to return to a state that prevailed before the reality principle reared its ugly head. This state of grace is one in which Eros reigns supreme within the little world of the id, manifesting itself through a body that is polymorphously perverse, prior to the development of the ego or the superego. This ontogenic Eden has its counterpart, of course, in the phylogenic Golden Age. It is surely no coincidence that the character's search for self-realization has as its counterpart the quest to restore that paradisiacal idyll when Saturn taught men agriculture and the useful and liberal arts.

But now we come to the disillusioning paradox. It is precisely this quest to revert to an earlier state, real or conjectured, that anticipates the complementary desire to return to the "quiescence of the inorganic world" (*Beyond* 108) that is at the heart of the death instinct. Elsewhere in the same essay we find:

> The upshot of our enquiry so far has been the drawing of a
> sharp distinction between the "ego instincts" and the
> sexual instincts, and the view that the former exercise
> pressure towards death and the latter towards a
> prolongation of life. . . . On our hypothesis the ego instincts
> arise from the coming to life of inanimate matter and seek
> to restore the inanimate state. (78)

As Cervantes presents the paradigm, a man makes a conscious decision to evade reality by taking refuge in a more gratifying fantasy world. This escape into fantasy can be seen as a regression to childhood, a stage of development repressed by the text. This metaphorical return to a time of innocence and diffuse sexuality finds its complement in the urge to substitute a golden age for the "iron age" of reality. The pleasure principle associated with the id asserts itself in both cases. The paradox lies, however, in the fact that this search for "pleasure," pushed to its logical extreme, leads to the dissolution of the individual in the figure of the mother, and of civilization, discontents and all, in a prelapsarian Eden antedating the primal horde. That is to say, the regression leads ultimately to disintegration and, therefore, death.

Within the *Quixote*, one of the key episodes to present symbolically the affinity between Eros and Thanatos is the Cave of Montesinos. John G. Weiger comments perceptively that "the reader may readily expect the climax of this adventure: Dulcinea is also in the Cave—where else would she be, if the adventure includes among its variegated aspects the perhaps hidden hope on the part of our timid hero that here he may at last experience a sexual union?" (61).

Although Meltzer would consider that such treatment of a fictional character illustrates "a particularly useless undertaking" (154), the linking of Dulcinea and Eros is the insight that interests me. Marcuse's remarks on the images of Orpheus and Narcissus may provide the rest of the equation: "The Orphic-Narcissistic images . . . are committed to the underworld and to death. . . . They do not teach any 'message'—except perhaps the negative one that one cannot defeat death or forget and reject the call of life in the admiration of beauty" (165).

The Cave connotes femininity (Cirlot 161), a degraded Dulcinea finds her way into this feminine space, reminiscences of the reading that brought Don Quixote forth into the world are ubiquitous, but, at the same time, the underworld suggests death. Thus, the episode brings together suggestively three feminine presences within its own symbolically feminine space: the reading that gave birth to the character, then Dulcinea, then this imaginative underworld, which is unmistakably a scene of death, or Thanatos. That feminine constellation is more readily and effectively communicated in Spanish: *la lectura → la mujer idealizada → la muerte*.

Dulcinea, the text's ironic icon of pulchritude and displaced Eros, leads only uncertainly to Glory (cf. Madariaga 118), but unerringly to the arms of another woman, the second maternal presence the character will know within his stepfather's text: *Pallida*

Mors. The individual's progressive regression to an inanimate state — anticipated frequently throughout Part II — finds fulfillment in the final chapter. But the return of society to a pristine Nirvana, or Golden Age, is necessarily left in abeyance, for it is a Utopian fantasy. While ontogeny may in fact mimic phylogeny in their respective developments, it would be less than realistic — an impossible dream — to expect those processes to synchronize in reverse. The time differential is decisive. Don Quixote dies blissfully unaware that phylogeny is not undone in a day, or even a lifetime.

Furthermore, and finally, the absence of a childhood — to pursue the analogy between ontogeny and phylogeny a step further — intimates that there is likewise no idyll to which the race may return — or to which it may aspire, for that matter. This paradoxical variant on the Freudian parallel, this less-than-Utopian perspective encoded in what we may take to be the unconscious of the text is, nonetheless, suggestively Freudian in its own way, for he had no illusions about the perfectibility of human nature. It would follow from this implicit rejection of both preterit and future idylls that Cervantes's text likewise anticipates, but in order to question *avant la lettre,* a Utopian mythography that is still with us.

III

While we are told nothing of Don Juan's childhood either, Tirso is somewhat more forthcoming than Cervantes about his character's pretextual history. Two decisive details bear mention, for, emanating from the unconscious of this particular text, they assume the role of foreshadowing events within the represented action. Together they allow us to conjure up a preliminary notion of the character and, more important, the characterization process.

At the beginning of the play, Don Juan is in Naples, in enforced exile for having deceived and dishonored a young woman of Seville. This pretextual treachery takes on the coloring of an archetypal *burla,* and, indeed, we need not wait long to find it replicated in the very first scene. Viewed retrospectively, the "seduction" in Seville serves to establish a pattern, even before the curtain rises, and it is one that will be copied not only with Isabela but also with Tisbea, Ana, and Aminta.

A second aspect of the prehistory has to do with the *perros muertos* perpetrated on the Portuguese prostitutes of his hometown. The *burla*, or trick, in these instances is to beat a hasty retreat without paying for services rendered. Again a pattern can be seen to emerge. These relations with social inferiors, and the power they confer upon the client, would necessarily contribute to the formation of a negative attitude toward women generally and to the feeling that women are objects and playthings, whether as sex objects or as objects to be tricked and toyed with.

It is surely significant also that these women are Portuguese. Foreigners are considered in all cultures to be somewhat mysterious and also to be more proficient sexually than domestic partners (Young 319–29). This overvaluing of the foreign, accompanied by a pervasive disrespect toward women, immediately manifests itself in the play. It is reasonable to assume that Isabela is not Spanish, but Italian. It may be that the seductions of Tisbea and Aminta respond to a variation on the theme, not because they are ethnically different, but because they are of a social class foreign to the nobility, and are thus exotic and therefore erotic.

The text makes clear that Don Juan was accustomed to visiting the prostitutes of Seville's "little Lisbon" in the company of his friend, the Marqués de la Mota. Catalinón was also included in the noctural forays, to judge by his account of the *horas menguadas*, that time of night when people emptied chamberpots out the window, sometimes with the warning of *¡Agua va!*:

> Ir de noche no quisiera
> por esa calle crüel,
> pues lo que de día es miel
> entonces lo dan en cera.
>   Una noche, por mi mal,
> la vi sobre mí ven[id]a,
> y hallé que era corrompida
> la cera de Portugal. (1516–23)[1]

The excremental vision rears its indecorous derrière once again. *Comedia* lackeys are notorious for dwelling on the seamy side, of course. But more interesting is the reminder that with honey comes wax, that appetite has as its end product excretion, that beauty has a backside — or, as Swift put it so succinctly in his admonition to lovers who would glorify the female form, "*Caelia* shits." As will become clear in retrospect, at the end of the play Don Juan's desire is turned to ashes, as Eros metamorphoses into Thanatos, in much the same way that honey is transformed here into "wax."

The business about the *perros muertos* (vv. 1250–54; 1524–26) shared with Mota and, more especially, the mention of a sexual adventure involving the two of them, for which Don Juan has laid the groundwork ("cierto nido que dejé / en güevos para los dos" [1256–57; a little situation I left on hold, just for the two of us]), raises the specter of homoeroticism. Shared adventures of this sort may be only the expression of a frivolous and playful sexuality, but they can also strengthen the bond between the two males involved. In such cases, the woman is the means for them to express sexuality in the presence of the other, while also observing the other *in flagrante* and thereby satisfying a natural curiosity about how another performs the primal act. It is interesting indeed that when Don Juan is absent, Mota shares this sort of activity with another male friend, Pedro de Esquivel (v. 1251). What becomes apparent is that, underlying these sexual adventures with women, there is the imperative of male bonding at the very least, with latent homosexuality a definite possibility. While such intimations are certainly not shocking in themselves, they do serve to undermine the image of the original Don Juan, raising doubts about his status as archetypal Latin lover.

The text further highlights the omnivorous sexuality of the protagonist in this curious passage, once again expressed by the *gracioso*, in what Bakhtin has described as chaotic "coq-à-l'âne" style, coupled with the ambiguous "blazon," which combines both praise and abuse (422–34):

> (¡Fuerza al turco, fuerza al scita,
> al persa y al caramanto,
> al gallego, al troglodita,
> al alemán y al japón,
> al sastre con la agujita

> de oro en la mano, imitando
> contino a la blanca niña!) (1983–89)[2]

This is an aside to the audience just before leaving the stage. His master either does not hear or ignores what he hears. Discounting the hyperbole and the chaotic enumeration of "partners," the comment serves to suggest, at the very least, the bisexuality of the protagonist. Turks were much given to sodomy, according to common opinion (Herrero García 544). Perhaps for that reason, the Turk occupies the place of privilege. The tailor with his sewing and the young girl with her embroidery serve to tie up any loose ends. The sense of the "golden needle" is probably obvious, while the movements associated with sewing typify a distinctive rhythm of the sexual act in northern Africa, called in Arabic *el-khiyati,* distinguished by inserting and withdrawing the penis with rapid strokes, but not deeply, imitating the act of sewing (Edwardes and Masters 190–91).

The image of the innocent young girl tranquilly embroidering in the background contrasts markedly with the activities alluded to in the preceding lines. Yet it is she who serves as the model for those actions, according to Catalinón. It is a brilliant and insightful touch, this juxtaposition of innocence and perversion, as is also the intimation that the one is an image of the other. There is, in other words, an insinuation among the interstices of the text that the two activities may be more similar than dissimilar, that it is merely customs and mores that set them apart.

Would the historical author have suggested such a thing? Not likely. Nor do I want to say that the inferred author offers a pre-Sadean perspective. The point is that this nonchalant juxtaposition of innocent assiduity and equal-opportunity anality serves to highlight the main character's dedication to the pleasure principle, his rejection of the "repressive order of procreative sexuality" (Marcuse 171), and the concomitant rejection of the reality principle. Don Juan is presented in this play as someone who is governed almost entirely by the id, with little ego awareness (beyond the quest to enhance his infamy), and absolutely no hint of a superego.

I take the id to be a function of the unconscious and to be closely allied with the pleasure principle; the ego is conscious and is associated with the reality principle; the superego partakes of both consciousness and the unconscious and is linked to inhibitions, conscience, and self-denial. Don Juan personifies the id, with a dash of ego, while Don Quixote—a considerably more complex characterization—prefigures what Freud will call the superego, striving to recover an id that apparently never had a chance to develop, again with a trace of ego. Despite their common quest to augment their reputations, which is certainly ego-centered, there is little in either one to suggest sensitivity to the reality principle that should accompany ego-centeredness. Both evade the awareness that would bring them into line with "normality."

Elsewhere I have discussed the relations between master and servant in the *Burlador,* the implications of the name "Catalinón" (cf. "catamite") and, going beyond homoeroticism, the intimations of bestiality, which the unknown author of *Tan largo me lo fiáis* picked up on and developed further by referring to Don Juan as "el garañón de España" (II.686). A *garañón* is an ass or horse used to service mares or female donkeys. What is underscored in both primitive versions of the Don Juan myth, *El burlador* and *Tan largo,* is not just the character's abuse of the opposite sex, but also a potential for homosexuality and even bestiality (see my "Erotismo..."). These added dimensions function, of course, to underscore his rebelliousness and monstrosity.

In the article just mentioned, there is also a discussion of the relationship between food and sex, two spheres of activity that find a semantic nexus in the word "appetite." It is not surprising to find that the Portuguese prostitutes of Seville are classed in descending order, according to how appetizing they are, as either trout, frogs, or codfish (vv. 1232–36). In a similar vein, Tisbea compares her hymen to a juicy fruit (vv. 423–26). And the wedding feast in Dos Hermanas (the Aminta episode), when Don Juan pushes aside Batricio's hand each time the groom tries to serve himself (vv. 1814–17), foreshadows what will occur momentarily in the sexual arena.

The banquet in Dos Hermanas likewise anticipates the aborted wedding feast of Don Juan, and, equally important, the two dinners of the double invitation. His last supper, in the Comendador's chapel, is the inversion of a wedding feast, but also of the mass for the dead. It might be called a satanic mass, due to the darkness, the filthy table (a substitute altar), and the acolytes dressed in mourning. The fingernails, serpents, and spiders substitute for the host, here the devil's body, while the bile and vinegar represent his blood.

So it is that the sexual inversions of Don Juan find their final counterpart in the inverted wedding feast. In point of fact, he does figuratively marry a feminine presence he can be seen to have courted for some time: La Muerte. The chapel menu serves also to call attention to the hedonistic paradox, namely, that a life dedicated to the self-indulgent pursuit of pleasure leaves one with a bitter taste in the mouth, at a bare minimum.

The metaphorical metamorphosis within the scatological (honey to "wax") likewise finds its counterpart in the realization of a lengthy series of foreshadowings in the denouement, when the fire of desire is reduced to ashes. As some wit once put it, Don Juan makes an ash of himself. Catalinón's erotic-scatological metaphor, linking food and sex (honey → wax), is the first part of yet another "fearful symmetry" within the play (cf. Rogers), serving as it does to foreshadow the precipitous erotic-eschatological trajectory (Eros → Thanatos) of the protagonist.

Now James Mandrell has recently advanced the thesis that Tirso's Don Juan serves a "patriarchal" social function in two senses: (1) "he unifies society against him and assumes a collective burden of guilt"; (2) "he engenders the conditions by which desire is directed toward matrimony in socially productive ways" (82). These are debatable assertions, and my impression is that Mandrell is reading back into Tirso's text a posture made explicit by Unamuno's *hermano Juan* and, indeed, cited on this same page of the study. First, there is little "unity" in the clamoring for self-centered redress; second, Don Juan may be many things but he is hardly a scapegoat who assumes a collective burden of guilt; third, while he contributes to the humbling and humanizing of Tisbea, which allows her to see Anfriso in a new light, both Isabela and Aminta are already more than slightly inclined toward marriage, as is Batricio, and Octavio is ready to exchange vows with Isabela, Ana, or apparently anyone else, as the sovereign at hand may dictate. So Mandrell's inference that Don Juan is a demonic force in the world, "like his forebear, Eros, or Cupid" (82), who may therefore be identified with Freud's Eros or life instinct, is only partially accurate. It is the king who restores order at the end, reclaiming comic integration from tragic isolation, and while Don Juan has precipitated this gathering of aggrieved parties, he can scarcely be credited with expiating the sins of society.

I have argued instead that Don Juan's trajectory illustrates a disregard for the reality principle — evidenced in his failure to heed his uncle, his father, and, particularly, Catalinón — and that it leads inexorably to his demise, thus "acting out" the death instinct that Freud will explain in the fullness of time.

IV

To avoid abstracting these characters and their literary worlds from sociohistorical context, it should be mentioned that each is traditionally taken to reflect certain tenets of Christianity in general and Roman Catholicism in particular. One dimension of Tirso's play clearly has to do with free will and with the need for good works in order to secure eternal salvation (over against the Protestant claim that faith alone can suffice). Don Juan has free will, which he abuses, and his good works are nonexistent, so it is generally understood that he is isolated and exiled from "polite society" to the maximum extent imaginable, by being dragged down into hell.

As for Don Quixote, Otis Green speaks of the *Sic et Non* of his truancy and recantation (*Spain and the Western Tradition* I.15), while also offering a more secular interpretation based on Huarte de San Juan's typological psychology, encompassing "an exciting cause, a resolving crisis, a diminution of cerebral heat, three times repeated and all eventually joined together in a greater unity as the initial adust humor [taken to be choler] yields to its enemy, the ultimate cold of death" ("El 'ingenioso' hidalgo" 189–90).

So we move, with time, from Huarte's typology to Freud's topography, but the end result in each instance is remarkably similar as far as the character is concerned. The melancholy and "infinite sadness" adduced by Green ("El . . . hidalgo" 188) may represent an earlier, less well-defined conception of whatever it is that impels one beyond the pleasure principle. Lawrence Babb observes that "melancholy is the humor most inimical to life" (11–12).

What, then, are the commonalities between the two characters that would constitute a unifying deep structure? First, both are shown to be in flight from the feminine through "practices that exclude or prevent procreation" (Marcuse 49). Don Quixote's fabrication of Dulcinea makes it unnecessary for him to have meaningful contact with the Aldonzas of this world, while Don Juan's polymorphous perversity and his immediate abandonment of the victims he has tricked into submission likewise renders impossible a sustained heterosexual relationship. Marcuse contends that "the societal organization of the sex instinct taboos as *perversions* practically all its manifestations which do not serve or prepare for the procreative function" (49). By this logic, both are characterized as being sexually "perverted," whether they indulge the body or deny it.

Second, each is characterized as a compulsive, and this is one of the three factors (along with sadomasochism and the Nirvana principle) that come together to configure Freud's death instinct. The course followed by both indicates not only a compulsion to repeat but also differing degrees of sadomasochism. The rejection of the reality principle, along with the relatively weak ego structure depicted in each case, suggests an unsuspected affinity with the drive toward self-annihilation. The fact that both are successful in this unstated quest tends to confirm the assumption.

Although the Don Juan is shown to be dominated by id, and Don Quixote by superego (the books of chivalry and their models of behavior symbolically replace the more usual forms of "parental" influence that make up this tier of the topographic model), each in his own way manifests anal-sadistic tendencies and an instinctive attraction to activities that would be interdicted by the reality principle in more rational beings. Catalinón and Sancho obviously speak for the reality principle within their respective worlds. As Bakhtin recognized long ago, the classic example of "images in pairs, which represent top and bottom, front and back, life and death" is Don Quixote and Sancho (434). Clearly, Don Juan and Catalinón are a similar and complementary pair.

The dramatic irony evidenced in both works centers on the fact that neither quest is what the main character assumes it to be; the apparently life-affirming trajectory of each of them turns out, over time, to be life-denying. Both Don Juan and Don Quixote are shown to be directed, in other words, by a force that transcends the pleasure principle, and that drive is what Freud terms the death instinct. Eros, whether sublimated or exploited, is shown to lead inexorably, and paradoxically, to Thanatos. Freud's pessimistic secular perspective is thus foreshadowed by the Christian pessimism toward the things of this world articulated in both *Don Quijote* and *El burlador de Sevilla*.

Finally, I return to the matter of method. If I have occasionally lapsed into speaking of these characters as facsimiles of real people, it is merely a form of shorthand in order to avoid lengthy and verbose qualification or tedious restatement of the guiding principles set out at the beginning. They are characters, not real people, but through their *characterization*—a more important concept for the literary critic than *character*—we can glimpse unsystematic foreshadowings of what the father of psychoanalysis will subsequently codify into a system and a philosophy. Freud's philosophical and cultural extrapolations from his psychological insights are among his more interesting and provocative contributions, as I suggested at the outset. It is unfortunate, as Marcuse maintains in his epilogue, that the negative, pessimistic, and other unpleasant aspects of both his psychology and his critique of culture have been glossed over or set aside by the neo-Freudian feelgood schools (e.g., "I'm OK, you're OK").

Notes

1. Spare me any [more] nocturnal visits to that dreadful place [la Calle de la Sierpe], for it is then they give you the wax [read "excrement"] that during daylight passes for honey; one night, poor devil that I am, they dumped a generous portion of it on me, and I discovered that Portuguese "wax" is pretty rotten stuff. (My translation.)

2. He takes the Turk, he has the Scythian, the Persian and the Libyan, the Galician, the Troglodyte, the German and the Japanese, the tailor with the golden needle in his hand, taking his cue throughout from *la blanca niña* [a character in a ballad who worked diligently at her embroidery frame]!

Works Cited

Babb, Lawrence. *The Elizabethan Malady: A Study of Melancholia in English Literature from 1570 to 1642*. East Lansing: Michigan State University Press, 1951.

Bakhtin, Mikhail. *Rabelais and His World*. Trans. Hélène Iswolsky. Bloomington: Indiana University Press, 1984.

Baras Escolá, Alfredo. "Una lectura erótica del *Quijote*." *Cervantes* 12.2 (fall 1992): 79–89.

Blanco-Aguinaga, Carlos. "Cervantes y la picaresca: notas sobre dos tipos de realismo." *Nueva revista de filología hispánica* 11 (1957): 313–42.

Booth, Wayne C. *The Rhetoric of Fiction*. Chicago: University of Chicago Press, 1961.

Brown, Norman O. *Life against Death: The Psychoanalytical Meaning of History*. Middletown, Conn.: Wesleyan University Press, 1959.

Cervantes, Miguel de. *El ingenioso hidalgo don Quijote de la Mancha*. Ed. L. A. Murillo. 2 vols. Madrid: Castalia, 1984.

Cirlot, Juan-Eduardo. "Cueva." *Diccionario de símbolos*. Barcelona: Labor, 1988, 161–62.

Close, Anthony J. "Don Quixote's Love for Dulcinea: A Study of Cervantine Irony." *Bulletin of Hispanic Studies* 50 (1973): 237–55.

Combet, Louis. *Cervantès ou les incertitudes du désir*. Lyon: Presses Universitaires, 1980.

Edwardes, Allen, and R. E. L. Masters. *The Cradle of Erotica: A Study of Afro-Asian Sexual Expression and an Analysis of Erotic Freedom in Social Relationships*. New York: Julian P. (Bell), 1962.

Efron, Arthur. *Don Quixote and the Dulcineated World*. Austin: University of Texas Press, 1971.

Freud, Sigmund. *Beyond the Pleasure Principle*. 1920. Trans. James Strachey. New York: Bantam, 1959.

———. *Collected Papers*. Ed. Joan Riviere and James Strachey. Vol. 2. New York: International Psychoanalytic Press, 1924–50. 5 vols.

Green, Otis H. "El 'ingenioso' hidalgo." *Hispanic Review* 25 (1957): 175–93.

———. *Spain and the Western Tradition: The Castilian Mind in Literature from El Cid to Calderón*. Vol. 1. Madison: University of Wisconsin Press, 1963–66. 4 vols.

Guillén, Claudio. "Luis Sánchez, Ginés de Pasamonte y el descubrimiento del género picaresco." *El primer siglo de oro: estudios sobre géneros y modelos*. Barcelona: Crítica, 1988. 197–211.

Herrero García, Miguel. *Ideas de los españoles del siglo XVII*. Madrid: Gredos, 1966.

Johnson, Carroll B. *Don Quixote: The Quest for Modern Fiction*. Boston: Twayne, 1990.

Madariaga, Salvador. *Guía del lector del Quijote*. 1926. Madrid: Austral, 1976.

Mandrell, James. *Don Juan and the Point of Honor: Seduction, Patriarchal Society, and Literary Tradition*. University Park: Pennsylvania State University Press, 1992.

Marcuse, Herbert. *Eros and Civilization: A Philosophical Inquiry into Freud*. London: Routledge, 1956.

Meltzer, Françoise. "Unconscious." *Critical Terms for Literary Study*. Ed. Frank Lentricchia and Thomas McLaughlin. Chicago: University of Chicago Press, 1990, 147–62.

Parr, James A. Don Quixote: *An Anatomy of Subversive Discourse.* Newark, Del.: Juan de la Cuesta, 1988.

———. "Erotismo y alimentación en *El burlador de Sevilla:* reflejos del mundo al revés." *Edad de Oro* 9 (1990): 231–39.

———. "Plato, Cervantes, Derrida: Framing Speaking and Writing in *Don Quixote.*" In *On Cervantes: Essays for L. A. Murillo.* Ed. James A. Parr. Newark, Del.: Juan de la Cuesta, 1991, 163–87.

Read, Malcolm K. *Visions in Exile: The Body in Spanish Literature and Linguistics: 1500–1800.* Amsterdam/Philadelphia: John Benjamins/PUMRL, 1990.

Rogers, Daniel. " 'Fearful Symmetry': The Ending of *El burlador de Sevilla.*" *Bulletin of Hispanic Studies* 42 (1964): 141–59.

Tan largo me lo fiáis. Ed. Xavier A. Fernández. Madrid: Revista *Estudios,* 1967.

Téllez, Gabriel (pseud. Tirso de Molina). *El burlador de Sevilla y convidado de piedra.* Ed. James A. Parr. Binghamton, N.Y.: Medieval and Renaissance Texts and Studies, 1994.

Weiger, John. *The Individuated Self: Cervantes and the Emergence of the Individual.* Athens: Ohio University Press, 1979.

Young, Wayland. *Eros Denied: Sex in Western Society.* New York: Grove, 1964.

◆ Chapter 6

Popular Culture and Gender/Genre Construction in *Mexican Bolero* by Angeles Mastretta

Salvador A. Oropesa

I believe life is melodramatic. Why can't movies imitate life? Those who are afraid of melodrama are melodramatic, those who are afraid of tackiness are the tackiest.

Agustín Lara[1]

Mexico, a Country of Television, a Country on Television

My hypothesis (Monsiváis 1992, Rebeil), in order to define the meaning of the term *Mexican* in the 1980s and 1990s (during the administrations of Miguel de la Madrid, 1982–88, and Carlos Salinas de Gortari, 1988–94), is that television[2] has to be considered as the chronotope where the term *Mexican* is being redefined. Television in Mexico is synonymous with Televisa[3] (Provenemex is its editorial house). Televisa ("Televisión") is a private company, almost a monopoly, that makes money through publicity by appealing to the demands of the Mexican population. At the same time, it has to comply with the duties imposed by the State due to Televisa's clientele situation, since only the State has the power to grant the quasimonopolistic status Televisa enjoys.

Mine is not an apocalyptic approach as defined by Eco, but certainly without considering the importance of television in Mexico, it is impossible to study the contemporary culture of this country. Lance Morrow said about the United States: "A central truth: what is occurring today is a war of American myths, a struggle of contending stories. And pop culture, often television, is the arena in which it is being fought" (50).

Or in the words of the Catalonian writer Terenci Moix:

> Por primera vez en la historia de la humanidad, puede hablarse de mitos que no son de origen divino (todas las religiones) ni humanos (mitología renacentista) ni tampoco ideológicos (gestas) sino que son realidades objetales que el estructuralismo—no siempre correctamente—ha sabido ver como lenguaje. (262–63)[4]

Television is dominated by popular culture: the culture that defines itself as dominant in society. If popular means "of the people," we are talking about a democratic culture, or a culture that perceives itself as democratic (populism is a form of democracy). This is the reason for the parallels between most Mexican popular culture and the system of government that the country has. It is in this context that a more truly democratic literature is working, rewriting the texts developed by television, especially pop and camp texts. Democratic literature goes beyond the best-seller phenomenon. It wants to join big sales and the pleasure associated with best-seller literature and the political values commonly associated with realism (liberalism, socialism). It usually employs the new mythology created by popular culture (television, movies, soap operas, sports arenas), because this is the culture shared by the writer and the readers. When Angeles Mastretta (1949) rewrites a Mexican canonical text like *La muerte de Artemio Cruz* (*The Death of Artemio Cruz*; 1962) by Carlos Fuentes (1928), she can appeal to Agustín Lara (1897–1970), a cultural icon shared by all Mexicans and by Latin American people in general. Lara's popular music represents the realm of sentiments, the importance of feelings, putting into words the belief that the common people have the need for pleasure and its complement, the healing of their sorrows. Mastretta cannot use, for instance, André Gide (1869–1951) like the avant-garde Contemporáneos did. Gide represents an elitist literature and the individual values of a minority bourgeoisie, while Mastretta is interested in a far broader audience.

This is not a new phenomenon. Let us remember *Allá en el Rancho Grande* (Down on the Big Ranch; 1936), a movie that in one year produced more than twenty imitations (Mistron 47) and several feminine and melodramatic sentimental novels (cf. Coll). Mexicans and the rest of Latin America recognized themselves in the charro costumes and in the description of putatively native customs. At a moment of radical change, like that experienced during the presidency of Lázaro Cárdenas (1934–40), the recreation of an artificial stability made bearable the social changes of the moment.

Melodrama will provide the focus as the dominant technique in *Arráncame la vida* (*Mexican Bolero*; 1985) by Mastretta, because melodrama dominates fiction in Mexican television. In 1983 Carlos Monsiváis said:

> En el melodrama, el suspenso equivale a una promesa: Jovencita, serás idéntica a tu madre, aprenderás la realidad en los embarazos y en las privaciones y en la incomprensión de lo que te rodea y en el deseo de que los sueños prefabricados te compensen por lo no vivido. ¡Ah!, y si quieres identidad, acude al nacionalismo, en el caso de que por nación se entienda un cúmulo de canciones, de chismes de columnistas, de programas y series, de tramas donde la pobreza accede al amor del rico y no por eso pierde su bondad o su pobreza. (*Escenas* 146)[5]

Popular culture has become quintessential in a postmodern world where it is very difficult to define a center, even in a country experiencing late capitalism like Mexico. It can be argued that the center of the country is the president, but in a country dominated by the *mentira oficial* (the official lie), where the president is not the Orwellian Big Brother but the Big Liar, the accumulation of lies and the overlapping of them create a far-fetched official discourse in which it is impossible to find a center or coherent axis around which to develop discourses. These lies create both a cynical reader/listener and a believing reader/listener who reproduce these lies. Popular cultural myths try to put some order to this pandemonium.

High culture and popular culture are becoming more and more difficult to distinguish. And at the same time, popular culture has not surrendered its marginality as dissident discourse and rupture with a conservative morality (for instance, melodramatic situations without a moral; cf. Franco 1986). It is in this context, at a moment of ideological and epistemological indeterminacy, that melodrama can be the vehicle of new cultural commodities. And the key term here is *commodity*: what is not sold, revealed, or reproduced is not democratic, cannot belong to the people, does not exist. This does not mean a total denial of artistic avant-gardes or necessary artistic experimentation, but these stages are part of the process of reification (necessary to circulate the commodity), a process that attempts to lead the *res* to where the artistic appetite of (an important sector of) the public is or to create a new need that educates the public. This is the case with seminal novels such as *Cien años de soledad* (*One Hundred Years of Solitude*; 1967) by Gabriel García Márquez (1928) and with the potato chips brand *Sabritas* (Tasties).

Because television is the most important mass medium, it tends to affect the rest of the fictive arts. In this medium melodrama and comedy are the most popular ways of telling stories devoured in the hundreds by the viewers. In the Mexican situation it is even more significant because Mexico is one of the most important countries in the production of soap operas. In this area of capitalism Mexico is a first-world country, and this idea is repeated again and again to Mexican viewers in the self-publicity produced by Televisa. Also, in a very nationalist country like Mexico, with few triumphs in the global economy, soap operas become a synecdoche of the national effort to *develop* the country, and this industry becomes a model that has to be followed by other economic sectors of the nation. What is more, soap operas are encouraged by the State and the party in power, the Partido Revolucionario Institucional (PRI, Institutional Revolutionary Party), because of the economic success and ideological control that can be imposed upon the nation through them. Political correction and censorship are the norm in soap operas. Predecessors of the soap opera have been, among others, romances by Corín Tellado (Catalina, the protagonist of *Mexican Bolero*, learns to read and write literature reading the Spanish sentimental novels of Rafael Pérez y Pérez [1891–1984]), and in music, boleros.

In melodramas women develop a technology of love that has evolved with time and that has allowed women to perform different roles.[6] Melodrama has evolved to make the succession of social ruptures bearable to readers and viewers. For instance, in the eighties we find that soap operas parody themselves or that they address issues that have been taboo; in "Encadenados" (Tattered) by Ernesto Alonso (1987) we find the villainess (the actress Julieta Rossen) feeling sadistic pleasure when her foreman (Sergio Jiménez) explains to her how her men have tortured the man she loves (the star Umberto Zurita). She is inside the barn where he has been tortured. In the same soap opera, Zurita's mother (Raquel Olmedo), a gypsy queen and entrepreneurial woman, is the owner of a chain of hotels in Cancún. Even if these examples are far-fetched, they tell about the need felt by society to assimilate new realities, to make normal at the level of television what is already becoming normal at street level. According to Mastretta, 40 percent of Mexican households are run exclusively by women (Pfeiffer 121).

Mexico, a Melodramatic Country

Arráncame la vida (*Mexican Bolero*) by Mastretta, who is from Puebla, manipulates traditional[7] Mexican cultural patrimony — the Victorian period, in the Mexican case the Porfiriato (1876–1910) — to unfold a new ideological and formal feminine program (cf. Oropesa) concerning the new reality lived by a sector of Mexican women.

Canonical literary criticism does not like melodrama; it has been considered an inferior form of doing literature. But since the sixties authors and literary critics (cf. Jameson 1988) have been rewriting the canon, and consecrated authors like the Spaniard Carmen Martín Gaite (1925; *El cuarto de atrás* [*The Back Room*; 1978] and *Nubosidad variable* [Variable Cloudiness; 1992]) or the Mexican Rosario Castellanos (1925–74) find positive values and a feminine language that has to be recovered. There is more in melodrama than the reactionary message of not allowing women to find answers beyond the husband or home. There are positive functions like making livable periods of crisis such as Francoism (1936–75) or Cardenism (1934–40) — to provide cosmopolitan models or tell truths, like "everyone cannot be happy at the same time" or the hope that "the good must be rewarded and the wicked punished" (Modleski 90). This is particularly important in a period when this basic Christian message has been obliterated by

(Victorian) mainstream religions. If civil (or religious) justice is not possible (the inequalities women endure), a woman can have at least the consolation of poetic justice.

The next step is to study how the norm of modernity is being subverted. Following Castellanos we are going to relate melodrama to the logical pair superficiality/depth (cf. Castillo 140–42), which produces the subsequent aporia: what is really important in a woman is the depth you can find in her. This is where her real values are, in what is hidden in her interior, in what is under the surface. But at the same time surface has other values, because in our society beauty also means power. As Rosario Castellanos said:

> Latin American women novelists seem to have discovered long before Robbe-Grillet and the theoreticians of the *nouveau roman* that the universe is surface. And if it is surface, let us polish it, so that it leaves no roughness to the touch, no shock to the gaze. So that it shines, so that it sparkles, so that it makes us forget that desire, that need, that mania, for seeking out what is beyond, or the other side of the veil, behind the curtain. (Quoted by Castillo 51)

For instance, there is the issue of makeup, to pursue an example brought up by Castellanos. We live in a society where women are supposed to follow fashion and its changing definition of beauty. But the worship of surface is against the implied deep values of the eternal feminine. An excess in the importance of surface can disqualify someone as a woman. But a woman without makeup is a menace to society. Let us remember Andrea, the protagonist of *Nada* (*Nothing*; 1944) by Carmen Laforet (1921). According to Martín Gaite, *Nada* is a frontal attack on the sentimental novel (*novela rosa*) written by the Falangist writer Carmen de Icaza (1899–1979; *Desde la ventana* 89–110). And Andrea's lack of makeup semiotizes her rupture with the canonical feminine characters of the sentimental novels of the early stages of Francoism. The opposite example is Modesty Blaise, the comic character. In the movie version directed by Joseph Losey Modesty Blaise hides her concealed weapons in her beauty supplies (Moix 264–65).

The dichotomy depth/surface generates a situation that always puts women in an atopia (in the best of circumstances, in the margins). By the end of *Mexican Bolero*, Catalina is getting ready to attend her husband's funeral: "I put very little make-up on, mascara on my eyelashes and cream on my lips, no rouge. My hair was scraped back in a bun. Andrés would have said I was a splendid widow" (264).

Makeup is a perfect example to illustrate the dichotomy of depth/superficiality. Makeup responds literally to the term surface, and the text of makeup is generally read as a frivolous feminine detail. This quotation expounds on the semiotic reading of Catalina's makeup by a masculine "reader," in this case, General Ascencio, who throughout the novel represents Man par excellence in Mexico's male culture. Once the masculine reading is given, the aporia (a built-in deconstruction) is "revealed." In this case there is an explanation of not just what makeup Catalina has on, but what makeup she doesn't. Catalina, the implied author, stresses that this is a complex code, that there are different options, and that women can learn how to manipulate the code. Makeup may be an imposition of the patriarchal society, but as a semiotic code it can be handled by the person who knows how to control it. It can be a weapon like Modesty Blaise's or its absence can be subversive like Andrea's *Nada*. For a female reader the reading of the paragraph is more obvious and reminds her of the possibility of empowerment when a person knows how to use cultural codes. The depth/surface logical pair must also be related to the lie/truth pair. I already mentioned Mexico as a country of official lies. I agree that it is an epistemological error to think that we have to dig for the truth. This novel exemplifies very well the futility of this way of reading. I think it is an error to say that this novel has three different readings, a frivolous one, a sanitized one, and an engaged reading as a political novel.

The characters, especially the powerful masculine Mexican politicians, are presented in different contexts: giving an official discourse, making love, farting, killing, buying real estate, talking, getting drunk. There is no distinction between the public and the private image/person, the exterior and the interior. This is an important issue in a feminist novel, because it gives equal treatment to masculine and feminine bodies. It gives no more importance to the public life of the masculine characters, to their public domain, as is the case in a patriarchal society. This is of particular importance in a novel full of houses like *Mexican Bolero*.

Women are always vulnerable to attack by men or other women in this regard. Let us analyze one of the attacks against Mastretta's novel. *Mexican Bolero* has two main axes: melodrama and popular songs, the boleros. These boleros are melodramatic in themselves: "Arráncame la vida" (Tear My Life Apart) is a bolero by Agustín Lara. When Ann Wright translated the novel into English, she made a very accurate free translation of the title: *Mexican Bolero*, as I have already said. When Alisson Carb Sussman reviewed this novel in the *New York Times* (August 26, 1990), she defined it as a "spare, seamlessly translated book." But let's look closely at this intriguing commentary: "Unfortunately, Ms. Mastretta sometimes seems to forget her own obligations to her readers; too often, for example, she states rather than shows the reasons for the townspeople's ignorance and apathy." Written by a woman, the novel is "seamless"; as a woman she should sew better. Besides this she "states" but does not "show"; we only have depth, the novel lacks the first two dimensions, it is just the surface of showing.

Of course, Mastretta's novel takes for granted the apathy of the townspeople: the memory of the civil wars was still there; the memory of the Porfirian dictatorship or the Praetorian revolutionary generals was present. Mastretta could also suppose that the readers of her novel had also read Fuentes's *Death of Artemio Cruz,* the masculine version of Mastretta's story, for there is an obvious intertextuality between the two novels. It is a situation similar to the intertextuality between *One Hundred Years of Solitude* and the reading of *La casa de los espíritus* (*The House of the Spirits*; 1982) by the Chilean Isabel Allende (1942) as a feminist response to García Márquez's novel. It is entirely legitimate to read Mastretta's novel as a feminist response to Fuentes's novel. Both novels deal with similar situations, the lives of two successful generals of the Mexican Revolution. Sussman doesn't consider the possibility that Mastretta is deconstructing the dichotomy between high modern literature (the novels of the so-called boom) and a popular culture that is consumed by millions of Mexicans, a culture present in their political and artistic unconscious (Jameson 141).

Based on this departure from the modernist writing of the boom, Mastretta can develop a heroine as rich as Catalina Guzmán. Catalina uses the first person to relate the novel in the tradition of the Spanish picaresque (one recalls that Edward Friedman includes Jesusa Palancares, the protagonist of *Hasta no verte Jesús Mío* [*Here's Looking at You, Jesus*; 1969] by Elena Poniatowska [1933] in his book on the feminine picaresque). Some critics (Behar) have noted that female biographies receive less attention than male ones. These women have to use the "I" form because, as in the picaresque novel, there is no omniscient masculine narrator willing to tell the story of a secondary character of contemporary Mexican history like the wife of General Ascencio, Governor of Puebla, Compadre[8] of the President of the United States of Mexico, and aspirant to *tapado* (official candidate to the presidency who remains *tapado* [hidden] until his candidacy is announced by the outgoing president). The model in reality is Maximino Avila Camacho.[9] Carlos Fuentes in the *Death of Artemio Cruz* develops a very sophisticated technique to tell the story of General Cruz, a character parallel to Ascencio. In Fuentes's novel there is a masculine logic. Three voices—the I, You, and He—follow a strict order of alternation. The novel is a rotation of male monologues instead of a dialogue. Mastretta chooses the "I" form of the autobiographical novel (in fact the technique followed by Mastretta to document Catalina's life was to interview people who knew her). The "I" is more than enough to give full body to a character like Catalina, and, at the same time, it reaffirms the present-day situation that women are the only ones who can give voice to themselves. For instance, as a counterexample, there is *Aura* (1962) by Fuentes, in which the male narrator is afraid of Aura, who has a monstrous side (Franco 1989, 176–77). Although the main difference between *The Death of Artemio Cruz* and *Mexican Bolero* is the pleasure felt reading Mastretta, while Fuentes is an exercise in linguistics. And the difference between Mastretta's novel and *Aura* is the difference between the voice of an individual woman and women in general seen as monsters.

According to Maravall, the Baroque invents the picaresque genre because of the appearance of a new ideologeme: society promises the possibility of social advancement. This is what is happening nowadays with women: they have the possibility of advancing socially. Lazarillo (the eponymous sixteenth-century pícaro) thinks his good fortune is holding an unimportant position on the bureaucratic ladder, but the rest of the pícaros want to be millionaires with palaces and servants. Catalina has a similar attitude. What is more, there are other characteristics of the picaresque novel that fit her: the life of a character from childhood to adulthood (no old age as in most bildungsromans), the passage from illiteracy to a lettered person (her literary formation is the sentimental novel, as I have already said). She tells her own story, and she really does an outstanding job. Both *Lazarillo de Tormes* (1554) and *Mexican Bolero* share these characteristics (cf. Hutcheon 89). Catalina wants everything: power, money, lovers, language. That's why her image evokes the women of soap operas: they share the same aspirations in life and undergo a similar literary formation. Catalina wants mansions, fine restaurants, and handsome men to sleep with. But she is in charge of making her own choices.

A couple of quotes can help to understand how melodrama works in this novel. First, when Bibí, Catalina's friend, needs help, she states:

> —No. Necesito conmoverlo, notarme triste. Pero ando tan contenta que no me sale nada dramático. Por eso te vine a ver, tú eres experta en dramas, no me salgas con lo que lo único que puedes hacer son recados como los míos. (197–98)[10]

Second, it is the very end of the novel and Catalina has to cry, because she is the widow and this is the traditional role assigned to widows in funerals:

> Cuando los enterradores iban a palear la tierra sobre su padre les dije que tomaran un puño y lo echaran antes.
> Me agaché hasta el suelo al mismo tiempo que ellos. Tomé la tierra y la tiré contra la caja que ya estaba en el fondo de un hoyo oscuro. Los demás hijos hicieron lo mismo que nosotros. Yo quise recordar la cara de Andrés. No pude. Quise sentir la pena de no ir a verlo nunca más. No pude. Me sentí libre. Tuve miedo.... Pensé en Carlos, en que fui a su entierro con las lágrimas guardadas a la fuerza. A él sí podía recordarlo: exactas su sonrisa y sus manos arrancadas de golpe.
> Entonces, como era correcto en una viuda, lloré más que mis hijos. (226)[11]

Catalina dominates the cultural codes of her gender and the genres associated with femininity. She knows how to textualize her behavior, and how to map her body in order to get the effects she pursues. As Ascencio says: "[Catalina], you're the best woman and the best man" (250). Catalina, according to Ascencio—and readers can agree with this assertion—is "bloody clever, like a man, that's why I forgive you your loose morals. I fucked *with* you better than anyone."[12] (250) Ascencio's machismo makes him understand Catalina's behavior (i.e., adultery) because she won equality with man thanks to her "masculine" attribute of cleverness. It is in the theoretical field of the famous dichotomy developed by Octavio Paz in *The Labyrinth of Solitude* (1950), *chingón/chingada* (fucker [male]/fucked [female]), that Ascencio textualizes his life with Catalina. "I fucked WITH you" in the translation and reading of Ann Wright, or "me chingué" (you fucked me), as the original in Spanish says. Both played an active role in their sexual encounters, which were understood as a synecdoche of their marriage, and the textualization of the power displayed in their relationship. How far we are from the nineteenth-century adultery interpreted as the empty tedium of the newly liberated married woman, liberated in the sense of having plenty of leisure time but without having yet developed activities to fulfill her life.

Analysis of the Climax of the Novel

In her study on camp Susan Sontag says, "The whole point of Camp is to dethrone the serious. Camp is playful, anti-serious. More precisely, Camp involves a new, more complex relation to 'the serious.' One can be serious about the frivolous, frivolous about the serious" (288).

The climax comes in chapter 16, a private party at the Ascencios'. The entertainer is Toña la Negra, the famous singer of Lara's boleros. Carlos Vives is playing the piano. Vives is a famous conductor and political enemy of Ascencio. Vives represents a more truly revolutionary fashion within the PRM party (the PRM, Partido Revolucionario Mexicano [Revolutionary Mexican Party] was replaced by the PRI in 1946). And what is more important, Vives is Catalina's lover. We can establish several levels: Toña represents popular music, the cinema of the Mexican Golden Age, urban and rural taste, the proletariat and the peasant, servility, an indigenous skin. She is *la Negra,* the one with dark skin. She is also a Latin American star. But that specific night her pianist is the conductor of the national philharmonic. Carlos Vives represents synecdochically the attempt of the revolutionary administrations to bring high culture (European culture) to Mexico. It was Vasconcelos who created the OSM (Symphony Orchestra of Mexico), and Carlos Chávez (1899–1978), the nationalist composer, was its conductor during the 1940s and 1950s.

Because Vives and Chávez share the same name, Carlos, it can be assumed that a reader who knows Mexican music can create a parallelism between the well-known musician and the fictional character. Vives/Chávez represents high culture, the bourgeoisie, the creole community, a cosmopolitan society, democracy, Mexico City, part of the establishment, and old money. General Ascencio represents upward mobility, the new money of the Revolution, the nouveaux riches, the provinces, parochialism, the other part of the establishment, fascism, and, above all, *caudillismo* (bossism). Toña belongs to the same generation as the general, Vives and Catalina to a younger generation that did not fight in the Revolution. When the general tells Toña to sing "Temor" (Fear) she answers:

¿"Temor," general? Lo malo es que no traigo pianista, así que como salga.
— ¿Cómo ha de salir Toñita con su voz? — dijo Andrés.
— ¿Quiere pianista? — preguntó Carlos sentado frente al piano.
— ¿No me diga que usted sabe de estas músicas? — le dijo Toña.
Carlos le respondió tocando los primeros acordes de "Temor." (140)[13]

What is important here is that Vives — who represents high culture and (paradoxically) the interests of the proletariat — can share the same code of popular culture as Ascencio, although in an active way he can play music; because Ascencio is a modern consumer of popular culture, he can only listen to the music. At the same time, Vives can read different cultural codes, like the

European, that Ascencio cannot decode. In the novel the caudillo Ascencio solves the problem by assassinating Vives (the civilization versus barbarism dichotomy: Ascencio, a man of the nineteenth century, can be read as part of the "people" and American nature; Indians, mestizos, gauchos, the "people" in general were considered barbarian, while civilization—culture as opposed to nature—should be in charge of changing the barbaric elements of the continent in order to Europeanize and whiten America). Vives did not read the Mexican political codes well when he did not perceive that he could be assassinated. In real life we know that Chávez outlived Maximino Avila Camacho, and Chávez represents the success of the attempt by someone like José Vasconcelos (1881–1959), an influential minister of culture in the post-1910 Revolution government, to bring high culture to Mexico.

But there is also a relationship between Maximino Avila Camacho and Vasconcelos. Don Maximino was in charge of part of the bloody repression and murder against Vasconcelistas during the 1929 electoral campaign that Vasconcelos lost. What is really outstanding in this chapter is that with an economy of means (four characters, a piano, and a couple of melodramatic effects), Mastretta brings together all the class, gender, political, and artistic conflicts of the moment in Mexico, and most of them are far from being solved. Three points (among others) can be studied: the meaning of the attack on caudillismo, Mexico as a country of lies, and the construction of gender in Mexican art.

José Joaquín Blanco in his book *Se llamaba Vasconcelos* (His Name Was Vasconcelos; 1977) says the attack on *caudillismo* is the attack on the only mystique[14] present in Mexico, because Mexico is not a democratic or a nationalist country. Mastretta's feminist attack on the caudillo system voids the only (irrational) truth left in Mexican ideology. The gap has to be filled, according to Blanco, with Maderismo:

> Madero significaba realizar una mística y una vida republicana. Hacer posible el liberalismo que la dictadura impedía. Un estado democrático, representativo y federal; una Ley vigente, por encima de caudillos; un libre juego para potencialidades individuales; una vida institucional ajena a la arbitrariedad, a la crueldad y el despotismo;

libertades: expresión, pensamiento, reunión; libertad de
empresa; una nación capitalista moderna, una sociedad de
ciudadanos con espacio real para los individuos fuertes,
dinámicos y ambiciosos.

Madero meant to accomplish a mystic and a Republican
life, toward making possible the liberalism the [Porfirian]
dictatorship prevented. A democratic, representative and
federal State; a Law over caudillos; a free game to develop
the potential of individuals; an institutional life alien to
arbitrariness, cruelty, and despotism; freedoms:
expression, thought, assembly; freedom of economy; a
modern capitalist society, a society of citizens with real
room for strong, dynamic and ambitious individuals. (59)

This rhetoric is familiar to the contemporary official Mexican lie.
These are the words repeated again and again but never fulfilled.
If the Porfirian dictatorship did not allow the fulfillment of Madero's ideas, the same happened with the Revolution, with the
difference that the Revolution after Manuel Avila Camacho (compadre Rodolfo in the novel) appropriated these words but without any content. The words uttered by the leaders of the Revolution are just sounds, mumbo jumbo. The official rhetoric of Mexico
stresses the arbitrariness between signifier and signified, because
there is a displacement between the dictionary meaning of the
words and the reality of the country. The extralinguistic status of
the referent in the Saussurean sign is a reality in Mexico, where
the referent has hardly been uttered. It is in Mastretta's novel
and other texts with a political purpose that Mexican reality is
being put into words.

When Mastretta empties the space of mystique (to follow
Blanco's terminology), when she denounces the caudillo system,
the gap may be filled by the old modernist mystique or by a new
one. The effect is that the old words acquire a new meaning: their
true meaning. A word like *democracy* is a subversive word in Mexico. It is basic to the political agenda to democratize Mexico to
go to the roots where the problems are and at the same time to
find the old democratic roots.

The 1930s to 1940s period is the moment when an intense debate between virile and feminine art took place in Mexico. The
painter Diego Rivera (1886–1957), among others, denounced the

feminization of Mexican art and proclaimed the virile values of the Revolution. Boleros represent a twist in this debate, to the extent they are feminine. Although boleros do not challenge the virility of the revolutionary system, by singing or listening to boleros men can give freedom to their "feminine," sentimental side. Agustín Lara is at the same time feminine and a virile Don Juan, and he represents the deep and agonizing crisis of the patriarchal system (Amorós 141). This is important because virility is what gives legitimacy to the institutional, revolutionary, and patriarchal government. The nonvirile, if not antivirile, literature of the gay avant-garde Contemporáneos had already challenged the virility of the Revolution, and what was more important, its legitimacy. When the Contemporáneos bring to the parochial Mexico City of the early twenties the literature of Spain, France, and the United States, they show at a symbolic level the lack of modernity as it is generated in the developed countries of the Western world, where important advances in democratic values brought more and more so-called feminine values to the definition of these societies. Or, in other words, the crisis of gender borders did not affect the distinctness of these countries. The right of women to vote can be the more obvious example (a topic that Ascencio manipulates), and the rise of fascism as the paradigm of political virility the counterexample.

José de Vasconcelos (Maximino Avila Camacho was his enemy, as I already mentioned) supported the Contemporáneos: the celebration of the centenary of the independence in 1910 included Vasconcelos's secretary, Jaime Torres Bodet,[15] a nineteen-year-old poet who read "El alma de los jardines" (The Soul of Gardens) in front of President Alvaro Obregón while receiving the natural flower from the hands of the queen Titina Calles (the daughter of President Plutarco Calles [1924–28], who was secretary of war at that time). *Mexican Bolero* won the Mazatlán Award for literature in 1985, and the competition is still called Juegos Florales (Flower Games) as in Romanticism, and this term implies a feminine sensitivity. In a bizarre article about this novel, Janet N. Gold tries to explain how a female writer won the award; she talks about "the gossip this text inspired" (36). A much easier explanation is that Elena Poniatowska was part of the jury, and she truly liked the novel:

> Se trata de una novela muy vital y divertida, que por primera vez nos presenta a una mujer que no sabe lo que es la autocompasión ni la lamentación sobre sí misma; sigue la vida sin pensar que tiene que sufrir, resolviendo por sí misma todas las instancias de su vida.
>   No se había dado en la literatura mexicana femenina un personaje como Catalina Ascencio. En general se presentaba a la mujer como alguien complaciente y dócil cuyo destino dependía del hombre. Mientras que Catalina toma decisiones y sabe moverse en un mundo tan atroz como lo es el de la política.... [Es] una mula bien hecha.[16]

Virility is felt as a need by the Revolution to balance the lack of democratic values. Subsequently, a term like *democracy* is feminized when masculine fascist values arise. Let us not forget that General Ascencio belongs to the right wing of the Revolutionary Party. It is in this context that the political debate between Vives and Catalina, who sympathizes with Vives, and Ascencio, can symbolically be fought in the bolero[17] chronotope. When Catalina sings, Ascencio tells her: "Catalina, no jodas" (141).[18] Catalina becomes a male aggressor when she makes clear that the content of the songs she is singing with Toña is addressed to her lover, Carlos, instead of her husband. This circumstance labels Catalina as a fucker, as a man. She is not a *chingada* (fucked woman) but a *chingona* (female fucker). Mastretta is rewriting Paz's epistemological tool. What is more, once the party is over, Catalina has "to put [her] trousers on" (166) to go ride with her son Checo. She literally and metaphorically puts her trousers on, because she has to cover up Vives's clandestine political activities. Once she returns to the house, she has to go by Ascencio's bed, with her trousers[19] on, and lie about Vives's conversation with a Union leader. Because of the stress of these political and loving activities,[20] she has to put herself together and calm down, and then she takes a bubble bath, a feminine activity. Catalina undermines the superiority of Andrés's maleness when she can move from one gender to the other, something that Andrés cannot do. He is constrained by his maleness (and the hangover and the constipation produced by the party).

After this episode, we have chapter 17, a brief but interesting one. We find Catalina at a massage studio with her friend Andrea

Palma. Notice that Andrea is the feminine of Andrés, the first name of General Ascencio. Andrea, by chance, has found out that Catalina is cheating on General Ascencio, and she is amazed at Catalina's courage. What is important from a literary point of view is that this is not like the adultery portrayed in the novels of the nineteenth century such as Tolstoy's *Anna Karenina* (1877). In the present case there is a political value attached to Catalina's adultery, and it is a question of life or death in the literal sense of the expression. Catalina's adultery is not a feminine escapade of the new tedium of an upper-middle-class wife of the Victorian period, but the political statement of a liberated woman or a woman in the process of liberating herself or, at least, a woman conscious of the crisis of the gender system. In the middle of her conversation with Andrea, the masseuse says that Ascencio has killed a young woman in Morelos because she refused him. Catalina says to Andrea:

> —Pero, ¿cómo va a ser verdad Andrea? Es una pendejada. Mi marido mata por negocios, no va por ahí matando mujeres que no se dejan coger.
> —Vaya, así te oyes mucho más inteligente. ¿Pero por qué no iba a hacer las dos cosas?
> —Porque no.
> —Muy razonable, porque no. Porque tú no quieres. Pues entonces no y ya.
> —Pues sí. No y ya —le dije.
> —Como quieras —me contestó con su media risa maligna—. ¿Sigues a dieta? (194)[21]

It seems that Andrea's information is accurate, that Ascencio killed a woman that did not obey him, refusing to allow him to satisfy his role as an aggressive fucker. With this murder and the frivolity the author connects to it, readers are shocked by Ascencio's machismo, and at the same time Ascencio's definition of the feminine. Following Celia Amorós in her article "La ideología del amor y el problema de los universales" (Ideology of Love and the Problem of Universals), she explains how Hegel in his *Phenomenology of the Spirit* put in words what many men had previously thought, that "the woman is not an individual but generic essence" (179). In order to be an individual you need an autoconsciousness that according to Hegel women don't have: "Feminine individuality is a mere accident of the carrying essence" (Amorós 180). This is Amorós's explanation to Hegel's (and patriarchal ideology's) process of thinking (?):

> This [masculine] ideology maybe responds to a reaction by men to the fear produced by their own competition in sexual matters, real or imaginary. This ideology gives women an indifference in desire, and at the same time men constitute themselves as addressers of feminine desire. They, until a certain point, neutralize or ward off women's competition/competence. Men prefer to guarantee themselves the minimal advantages of belonging to the group exercising domination, instead of risking not being chosen by the dominated. (183)

The presence of this murdered woman without a name, the essence of the feminine, represents a first stage in the process of women gaining consciousness of their own individuality. This woman challenges Ascencio's machismo and patriarchal ideology, and she has to pay with her life. Because she is unimportant Ascencio can dispose of her. Catalina's acquired consciousness during her life with Ascencio illustrates the crisis of the system, at least in the upper classes, where women have more power because of their position in society and their money. Note how the conversation becomes dangerous and both women realize the importance of the reach of the knowledge they possess. Andrea uses, as a way to end the conversation, the return to the symbolic "safety" of the feminine world: "How's your diet doing?" (Ascencio is always eating or drinking good food, and he takes showers instead of bubble baths.) These upper-class women learn gender codes little by little and how to use them to their advantage. They can play a masculine role when they please or think it is necessary (Catalina as a fucker according to Ascencio), or return to the feminine realm when they want to reevaluate a situation.

The title of the novel, *Arráncame la vida,* is a bolero by Lara. This puts the novel in the tradition of Mexican cinema. Feature films named after a Lara bolero are: *Santa* (Saint [female]; 1931), *Novillero* (Young Bullfighter; 1936), *Adiós Nicanor* (Goodbye, Nicanor; 1937), *Noche de ronda* (Night on the Town; 1942), *Santa* (1943; a remake), *Palabras de mujer* (Woman's Words; 1945), *Pervertida* (Perverted Woman; 1945), *Humo en los ojos* (Smoke in Your Eyes; 1946), *Carita de cielo* (Heaven's Little Face; 1946), *Mujer* (Woman; 1946), *Pecadora* (Sinner Woman; 1947), *Señora tentación* (Lady Temptation; 1947), *Revancha* (Revenge; 1948), *Aventurera* (Adventuress; 1949), *Sólamente una vez* (Only Once; 1953), *¿Por qué ya no me quieres?* (Why Don't You Love Me Anymore?; 1953), *Nacida para amar* (She Was Born to Love; 1958), and, one more time, *Santa* (1968). This is extremely important, because Mastretta's novel does not want to place itself in the tradition of an aristocratic literature like Paz's poetry or Fuentes's macronovels, but in the popular realm. What is more, the novel evokes the singers of that period: Lucha Reyes, Jorge Negrete, Tito Guízar, which is also a class attitude. Even if the singers were millionaires, they always adopted a very humble public attitude like that of the people who heard their songs. The critic Federico Arana compared these singers with the folk singers of the 1980s: "Los folcloroides *out* no abren la boca más que para cantar o para anunciar que 'el siguiente número va dedicado con todo cariño y respeto para la señorita Malena' o para 'nuestro querido amigo el licenciado Fulánez'" (83).[22] Mastretta's novel is more like the humble singers of the 1940s, in the sense that her novel is not an open attack on the system, but a subtle novel following the old Horatian apothegm *prodesse et delectare,* or, as popular culture rewrote it, "with a spoonful of sugar, the medicine goes down." In the list of movies based on songs by Lara, women dominate the titles. This is the case of Mastretta's, an engaged novel of the feminist cause (even if Mastretta both likes and dislikes the term; in different interviews she has taken contradictory positions), but admirably combining the pleasure of knowing how to tell a love story and the political and social content of the novel. For instance, one of the problems with the novels of social realism used to be the presence of schematic, flat characters. This is not the case in this novel, where the characters are perfectly rounded, and there is a difference between the first time they appear in the novel and the last time, once they have evolved with the circumstances told in the novel.

I disagree with Claudia Schaefer when she says:

> Curiously similar to the codified postrevolutionary
> political system and its personalization of power, the
> Mexican romantic *bolero* refuses innovation and adaptation
> in favor of solidifying (institutionalizing) its success with

trite sentimentalism over and against changing economic and social conditions. (93)

My hypothesis is the opposite: Mastretta chose the bolero because of its flexibility. It is this versatility, the use of the different valences of the bolero that gives this form the malleability the writer needs. First, the bolero is a mestizo Cuban import that in Mexico ended — thanks to Lara — the supremacy of tango, also a foreign product. It is in the mid-fifties, with the apparition of the bolero-ranchera, that this song was totally Mexicanized, and in the seventies in the era of rock-and-roll, it influenced the ballad. The bolero is a living form that has adapted itself to different moments, and at the same time certain elements remain the same (like sentimentalism). What Schaefer reads as immobility can also be read, in an ecological view, as use, in the best sense of the term. Lara's best boleros are heard by new generations, meaning that in a society dominated by consumerism, certain elements are recycled again and again. Martín Gaite noticed in *The Back Room* that during the 1940s in Spain, people used to enjoy songs for long periods of time, because rationing included all kinds of goods.

The climactic scene leads to Vives's assassination by Ascencio's gunmen. The novel denounces this violence, and Vives's murder is contrasted with the memory all readers have of the love songs he has been playing. Jean Franco, in her studies of Mexican popular culture, has noticed how the *novela semanal*, the weekly novel (Franco 1986, 134) denounces violence, and how women are in charge of breaking the spiral of violence (Castellanos, *Juicios* 270). Women, who own love, will be in charge of feminizing Mexican culture in order to stop masculine violence. The pacifist position of the novel already has its match in popular culture. The supposedly reactionary songs by Lara (according to high culture) are reevaluated in Mastretta's novel and are given a new political meaning, that of pacifism. The *cursi*, once reevaluated within the field of the camp, has a subversive meaning.

Conclusion

What is the difference between the archetypical protagonist of sentimental literature and a character like Catalina Guzmán? According to Debra Castillo,

> The *novela rosa* does not challenge the sort of
> conventional assumptions about male-female relations
> which Castellanos outlines in "The Liberation of Love";
> rather, it manipulates them in the service of a fantasy
> gratification that asserts the power of love to create a
> psychological space for a woman's victory over a man. It is
> a kind of cosmetic solution to a difficult and intricate
> problem of gender relationships. (52–53)

It is true that in Mastretta's novel we have the "fantasy gratifica-tion" of the victory, because at the end Ascencio dies. What is different here is the presence of the political reality of Mexico. The novel is situated in the recent past (the root of the current system), but the problems of corruption and abuse are still part of the present, and far from being solved. Even if nostalgia is an important part of the novel, in this case nostalgia is the bait to remind us of the political problems of the supposedly golden pe-riod being nostalgized. Mastretta has learned well the failure of social realism to denounce failed political realities. Mastretta's literature is a bourgeois literature that is proud of this adjective. It is a novel that generates revenues, that brings hard currency to the country. It is a Mexican product that sells well at home and abroad. It is a high-quality Mexican product. The novel belongs to the new understanding that to share we have to produce first. It is in this rediscovery of the good parts of capitalism that the old dichotomy of popular/high culture can be challenged, as the pop movement already did. It is fascinating to notice that novels like this one or *Como agua para chocolate* (*Like Water for Chocolate*) by Laura Esquivel (1950; Oropesa) have two different kinds of en-emies, the reactionary sectors of the obsolete Mexican political system and those who think that they own Mexican Culture (with capital letters), artists and literary critics who cannot see art in anything that is not produced by their own minoritarian and elit-ist monopoly. And what is worse, they cannot find any artistic values in popular culture, unable see the need for and the plea-sure of pleasure.

Moreover, Rosario Castellanos, in her article "Corín Tellado; un caso típico," included in her *Mujer que sabe latín* (Corín Tellado was at that moment the second author in the world in sales), says that in Tellado's novels, the protagonist's virginity is never threatened (143), and in *Mexican Bolero* Catalina's development and education is postvirginal. At the same time, Catalina is not redeemed by maternity, although she is a mother several times and adopts her husband's illegitimate children. Marianism is an absence in the novel. Maternity as a dominant ideologeme to define womanhood in Mexico does not play a role in this novel.

In the sentimental novel we have a displacement of the moment of love, and the novel concludes as soon as the victory of the woman is achieved (Castillo 53). In Catalina's situation the question is more complicated. She starts from love. In the beginning she loves her General Ascencio, but it is a love that later she loses; her second important love is assassinated for political and sentimental reasons. The novel ends with the death of Ascencio and the opening to a promising future for Catalina. As the popular saying asserts: widowhood is the perfect state for women. She has the respect of a married woman and more freedom than a single woman if she knows how to do things properly and read correctly the cultural codes of her society:

> Checo [su hijo] seguía tomado de mi mano, Verania [su hija] me hizo un cariño, empezó a llover. Así era Zacatlán, siempre llovía. Pero a mí ya no me importó que lloviera en ese pueblo, era mi última visita. Lo pensé llorando todavía y pensándolo dejé de llorar. Cuántas cosas ya no tendría que hacer. Estaba sola, nadie me mandaba. Cuántas cosas haría, pensé bajo la lluvia a carcajadas. Sentada en el suelo, jugando con la tierra húmeda que rodeaba la tumba de Andrés. Divertida con mi futuro, casi feliz. (226)[23]

Happiness or quasi happiness comes with a widowhood complete with *palancas* (influences) and money. Catalina goes from love to cynicism in her relationship with Ascencio. Of course, Catalina's morality can be questioned. But what is interesting here is the change effected: happiness lies not in marriage with a rich man, but in being a rich man's widow.

The novel tries to explain the everyday reality of high politics in the Mexico of the 1930s and 1940s. This is a historical novel, the traditional genre to "scratch the surface" behind the big battles, the opportunity to see the heroes wearing slippers. In recent years we have been overwhelmed by such novels: *Vigilia del almirante* (The Vigil of the Admiral; 1992) by the Paraguayan writer

Augusto Roa Bastos (1917), *Noticias del imperio* (News from the Empire; 1987) by the Mexican Fernando del Paso (1935), *Maluco* (1989) by the Uruguayan Napoleón Baccino Ponce de León (1947), *El general en su laberinto* (*The General in His Labyrinth*; 1989) by the Colombian García Márquez (1928). But the difference with Mastretta's novel is that in her case she is interested in the feminine side; she really makes true the term "first lady" when she gives voice to the woman. It is not Ascencio who tells (hi)story like Cruz did.

In the second half of the twentieth century, the new rich Mexican widow, like her Spanish grandmothers and widows (*Pepita Jiménez* [1874] by Juan Valera [1824–1905] or *Doña Perfecta* [1876] by Benito Pérez Galdós [1843–1920]), enjoys an impeccable reputation and (within certain limits) she does what she wants. The open ending of *Mexican Bolero* means that Catalina is going to have more opportunities. This is (poetic) justice, and this is the revenge of María (the protagonist of the novel *María* [1867] by the Colombian Jorge Isaacs [1837–95]). María, the epitome of the Latin American sentimental heroine, like Cinderella, is a passive character; she doesn't make decisions. This is the revenge of Ana Ozores, the protagonist of *La Regenta* (1885) by Leopoldo Alas (1852–1901), a representative of the attempt to commit adultery in the Hispanic society of the nineteenth century: Catalina's adultery is her own decision. Efraín, a virtuous aristocrat, is María's fiancé. Ascencio dies because he had broken the link between virtue and wealth typically found in the sentimental novel (Modleski 50–51; Rodríguez 141). The unhappy ending of *María* was necessary because María's truth could not be unveiled: the symbol of aristocratic culture and the spiritual values of the new bourgeois. Catalina's happy ending is possible because her truth is that she only has the remains of Culture (as the opposite of Nature), and nobody remembers where the spiritual values of the bourgeois are.

Notes

1. "La vida es melodramática, creo yo. ¿Por qué el cine no debe de imitar a la vida? Los que tienen miedo al melodrama son melodramáticos, como los que tienen miedo a lo cursi son los más cursis" (Taibo 66).

2. Since 1985 Television reaches the whole national territory thanks to a modern satellite. Also, Angeles Mastretta said in an interview: "Estudié la carrera de

Comunicación en la UNAM pensando en dedicarme a la televisión. Porque la televisión es glamorosa y bien pagada, histérica y enervante como uno piensa que deben ser los trabajos cuando uno tiene veinte años" (I studied Journalism at the UNAM to work on TV. Because television is glamorous and well paid, hysterical and enervating. This is how you think work should be when you are twenty) (Pfeiffer 116).

3. There is an intertextuality between the novel and Televisa. In the novel Lilia, Ascencio's daughter, marries Emilio Alatriste, the son of the owner of XEW, the famous radio station of the Azcárraga family, actual owners of Televisa. One of the funniest moments of the novel happens when Agustín Lara and Pedro Vargas give a piano serenade to Lilia.

4. For the first time in the history of humankind, we can talk of myths that are neither divine (all the religions) nor human (the mythology of the Renaissance), nor even ideological (gestes), but objects of the reality that structuralism—not always correctly—has seen as language.

5. In melodrama, suspense equals a promise: Young lady, you will be like your mother, you will learn reality in pregnancy and in material need, and in the incomprehension of that which surrounds you, and in the desire that your dreams (made by others) will balance what you are not going to live. And if you want an identity, look for it in nationalism. *If by nation we mean an accumulation of songs, gossip, columnists, programs and serials, plots where the poor woman gets the love of the rich man without losing her goodness or poorness* (my emphasis). In a similar context and about the United States Lance Morrow said in *Time*: "But in a bizarre way, television's storytelling has become a form of representational democracy—or symbolic democracy, anyway" (51).

6. A good example is in the novel *El cuarto de atrás* (1978; *The Back Room* by Carmen Martín Gaite [1978]), where she contrasts Elizabeth Mulder and Carmen de Icaza's sentimental novels as a liberating artistic and oppressive form respectively.

7. I understand traditional values as Victorian values: nuclear family, the appearance of being a moral person, individualism, denial/cult of the body, denial/cult of sex. It is the petit bourgeois period, and we are still in it.

8. *Compadre* (feminine *comadre*): in this case, a religious sponsorship that creates family-like ties among parents, "co-parents," and their godchildren.

9. Maximino Avila Camacho (1891–1945), governor of Puebla (1937–41), whose wealth was estimated at two to three million pesos, brother of President Manuel Avila Camacho (1940–46) and Rafael Avila Camacho, governor of Puebla (1951–57), divisionary general, was in charge of the prison where Vasconcelistas were murdered, leader of the right wing of the National Revolutionary Party (Camp 22; Vasconcelos was candidate for the presidency in 1929, opposing the official canidate, Ordiz Rubio, who was elected and served 1929–32). It is also interesting to note that Lanin Gyurko demonstrated the intertextuality between *Citizen Kane* and *Death of Artemio Cruz*, and Salvador Novo, commenting on the death of Maximino Avila Camacho tells that he always saw a parallel between Kane (Hearst) and Maximino Avila Camacho (*La vida en México* 335).

10. No, I need to move him [Bibí's husband], make him see I'm sad. But I'm so happy I can't think of anything dramatic. That's why I came to you, *you're an expert in dramas.* (232, my emphasis)

11. When the grave-diggers were about to shovel the earth in over their father I told the children to get a handful of earth and throw it in. I bent down at the same time and threw the earth against the coffin at the bottom of a dark pit. The children did the same. I wanted to remember Andrés's face. I couldn't. I wanted to feel the grief of never seeing him again. I couldn't. I felt free. I was afraid . . .

I thought of Carlos, whose funeral I went to forcibly holding back my tears. I could remember him. I remembered his exact smile and hands, taken away so suddenly. At that point, as was fitting for a widow, I began to cry more than my children. (267)

12. The original in Spanish reads: "No me equivoqué contigo, eres lista como tú sola, pareces hombre, por eso te perdono que andes de libertina. Contigo sí me chingué. Eres mi mejor vieja, y mi mejor viejo, cabrona" (211).

13. "*Fear*, General? The problem is, I didn't bring a pianist, so I don't know what it'll be like."

"Could it be anything but wonderful with your voice, Toña?" said Andrés.

"Want a pianist?" asked Carlos, sitting at the piano.

"Don't tell me you know that sort of song?" said Toña.

Carlos replied by playing the first bars of *Fear*. (163)

14. Mystique in the sense of irrational truth.

15. Jaime Torres Bodet (1902–74) became secretary of Education during the presidency of Manuel Avila Camacho, identified as Rodolfo the compadre in the novel. Part of the evolution of the revolutionary system was the assimilation of the members of the Contemporáneos Group to the institutionalized Revolution.

16. It is a very vital and funny novel. For the first time we have a woman who doesn't know the meaning of self-pity, nor does she have regrets about herself: she lives her life without thinking she has to suffer. She resolves by herself all instances of life.

We had not had in Mexican literature a character like Catalina Ascencio. In general terms we represent women as complacent and docile, with a destiny dependent on men. But Catalina is a decision maker and knows how to conduct herself in the atrocious world of politics. . . . She is a well-made mule. (Quoted in Vega)

17. The *ranchera* (ranch song), the other song associated with the Revolution, can also have gender ambiguity: it can be sung by women "with masculine strength and authority" (Geijerstam 125). This is the case of Lucha Reyes, Amalia Mendoza, or Lola Beltrán.

18. Catalina, stop fucking around (164).

19. Two other different moments of the novel can be related to this one in order to construct the semiotic paradigm: first, when Catalina is undressed by Andrés the first time, her panties are removed by him because she is only an object of desire, and second, the moment when she closes her legs and denies Andrés carnal access to her.

20. In romantic novels, political conflicts are solved through love. Love is used to symbolically resolve conflicts that the romantic man does not know how to deal with. Sandra C. Messinger has studied effectively how Ireneo Paz (Octavio

Paz's grandfather), a famous romantic writer, used love to "solve" the conflict between the Creole and the Indian Mexican identity in novels like *Doña Marina* (1883). Love was used to hide the political conflict. In Mastretta's novel, love stresses the political conflict.

21. "My husband kills for his business interests, he doesn't go around killing women who won't fuck him."

"You see, that's much more intelligent. But why he wouldn't do both?"

"Because he wouldn't."

"Very reasonable. Because he wouldn't. Because you don't want it. He wouldn't and that's it."

"Yes. He wouldn't and that's it," I said.

"As you wish," she replied with her mischievous half-smile.

"How's your diet going?" (173)

22. The *out* folcloroids only open their mouths to sing and to announce that "the next song is dedicated with all our love and respect to Señorita Malena" or to "our beloved friend licenciado Fulánez." (83)

23. Checo kept clutching my hand, Verania tried to comfort me, it started to rain. That was Zacatlán for you, always raining. But I didn't care what happened to that town, I wasn't ever coming back. I stopped crying at the thought. There were so many things I would never have to do again. I was myself, nobody could order me about. So many things I could do, I thought laughing to myself in the pouring rain. Sitting on the ground, playing with the wet earth around Andrés's grave. Delighted with my future, almost happy. (267–68)

Works Cited

Amorós, Celia. *Hacia una crítica de la razón patriarcal.* 2a ed. Barcelona: Anthropos, 1991.

Anderson, Danny J. "Displacement: Strategies of Transformation in *Arráncame la vida,* by Angeles Mastretta." *Journal of the Midwest Modern Language Association* 21 (1988): 15–27.

Arana, Federico. *Roqueros y folcloroides.* Mexico: Joaquín Mortiz, 1988.

Blanco, José Joaquín. *Se llamaba Vasconcelos: Una evocación crítica.* Mexico: Fondo de Cultura Económica, 1977.

Camp, Roderic A. *Mexican Political Bibliographies 1935–1981.* 2nd ed. Tucson: The University of Arizona Press, 1982.

Carmona, Gloria. Jacket notes. Eduardo Mata, cond. *The Six Symphonies of Carlos Chávez.* By Carlos Chávez. Vox Cum Laude 3D-VCL 9032, 1983. 2–6.

Castellanos, Rosario. *Juicios sumarios: Ensayos.* Xalapa: Universidad Veracruzana, 1966.

———. *Mujer que sabe latín. . .* Mexico: Fondo de Cultura Económica, 1984.

Castillo, Debra. *Talking Back: Toward a Latin American Feminist Literary Criticism.* Cornell: Cornell University Press, 1992.

Coll, Edna. *Injerto de temas en las novelistas mexicanas contemporáneas.* San Juan: Juan Ponce de León, 1964.

Cypess, Sandra Messinger. *La Malinche in Mexican Literature: From History to Myth.* Austin: University of Texas Press, 1991.

De León, Fidel. Res. de *Arráncame la vida,* de Dolores Mastretta [sic]. *Chasqui* 15 (1986): 96–97.

Franco, Jean. "The Incorporation of Women: A Comparison of North American and Mexican Popular Narrative." In *Studies in Entertainment: Critical Approaches to Mass Culture.* Ed. Tania Modleski. Bloomington: Indiana University Press, 1986.

—. *Plotting Women: Gender and Representation in Mexico.* New York: Columbia University Press, 1989.

Friedman, Edward H. *The Antiheroine's Voice: Narrative Discourse and Transformations of the Picaresque.* Columbia: University of Missouri Press, 1987.

Geijerstam, Claes af. *Popular Music in Mexico.* Albuquerque: University of New Mexico Press, 1976.

Gold, Janet N. "*Arráncame la vida*: Textual Complicity and the Boundaries of Rebellion." *Chasqui* 17.2 (1988): 35–40.

Gomís, Anamari. Res. de *Arráncame la vida* por Angeles Mastretta. *Nexos* 8.91 (julio 1985): 51–52.

Gyurko, Lanin A. "*La muerte de Artemio Cruz* and *Citizen Kane*: A Comparative Analysis." In *Carlos Fuentes: A Critical View.* Ed. Robert Brody and Charles Rossman. Austin: University of Texas Press, 1982, 64–94.

Hutcheon, Linda. *A Poetics of Postmodernism: History, Theory, Fiction.* New York: Routledge, 1988.

Jameson, Fredric. "Periodizing the 60's." In *The Ideologies of Theory: Essays, 1971–1986.* Vol. 2. Minneapolis: University of Minnesota Press, 1988, 133–47.

—. *The Political Unconscious: Narrative as a Socially Symbolic Act.* Cornell: Cornell University Press, 1981.

Maravall, José Antonio. *La literatura picaresca desde la historia social (siglos XVI y XVII).* Madrid: Taurus, 1986.

Martín Gaite, Carmen. *El cuarto de atrás.* Barcelona: Destino, 1988. *The Back Room.* Trans. Helen R. Lane. New York: Columbia University Press, 1983.

—. *Desde la ventana: Enfoque femenino de la literatura española.* Madrid: Espasa-Calpe, 1987.

Mastretta, Angeles. *Arráncame la vida.* Mexico: Cal y Arena, 1990. *Mexican Bolero.* Trans. Ann Wright. London: Viking, 1989.

—. Interview. With Braulio Peralta. *La jornada,* junio 11, 1985.

—. "Las mujeres somos especialistas en fantasear." In *EntreVistas: Diez escritoras mexicanas desde bastidores.* With Erna Pfeiffer. Frankfurt am Main: Vervuert, 1992, 113–22.

Mistron, Deborah E. "A Hybrid Subgenre: The Revolutionary Melodrama in the Mexican Cinema." *Studies in Latin American Popular Culture* 3 (1984): 47–56.

Modleski, Tania. *Loving with a Vengeance: Mass-Produced Fantasies for Women.* Hamden, Conn.: Archon, 1982.

Moix, Ramon-Terenci. *Los "comics": Arte para el consumo y formas "pop."* Barcelona: Llibres de Sinera, 1968.

Monsiváis, Carlos. *Amor perdido.* Mexico: Era, 1988.

—. *Escenas de pudor y liviandad.* Mexico: Grijalbo, 1988.

—. Mesa redonda. Latinos and the Los Angeles Uprising. Latin American Studies Association, International Congress. Los Angeles, September 26, 1992.

Morrow, Lance. "Folklore in a Box." *Time,* September 21, 1992, 50–51.

Oropesa, Salvador A. "*Como agua para chocolate* de Laura Esquivel como lectura del *Manual de urbanidad y buenas costumbres* de Manuel Antonio Carreño." *Monographic Review/Revista Monográfica* 8 (1992): 252–60.

Paz, Octavio. *El laberinto de la soledad.* Mexico: Fondo de Cultura Económica, 1950. *The Labyrinth of Solitude: Life and Thought in Mexico.* Trans. Lysander Kemp. New York: Grove Press, 1962.

Rebeil Corella, M. Antonieta. "What Mexican Youth Learn From Commercial Television." *Studies in Latin American Popular Culture* 4 (1985): 188–99.

Rodríguez, Juan Carlos, and Alvaro Salvador. "La estructura melodramática. La *María* de Isaacs y la novela sentimental hispanoamericana." In *Introducción al estudio de la literatura hispanoamericana.* Madrid: Akal, 1987, 128–48.

Schaefer, Claudia. "Popular Music as the Nexus of History, Memory, and Desire in Angeles Mastretta's *Arráncame la vida.*" In *Textured Lives: Women, Art, and Representation in Modern Mexico.* Tucson: The University of Arizona Press, 1992, 88–110.

Sontag, Susan. "Notes on 'Camp.'" In *Against Interpretation and Other Essays.* New York: Farrar, Straus and Giroux, 1966, 275–92.

Sussman, Alison Carb. Rev. of *Mexican Bolero* by Angeles Mastretta. *New York Times,* August 26, 1990.

Taibo I, Paco I. *La música de Agustín Lara en el cine.* Mexico: Filmoteca de la Universidad Nacional Autónoma de México, 1984.

"Television in Mexico. Changing Channels." *The Economist,* May 1–7, 1993, 76–77.

Vega, Patricia. "Angeles Mastretta, Premio Mazatlán de literatura 1985, por su novela." *La jornada,* 1 jun. 1986.

Chapter 7

Sexing the Bildungsroman: *Las edades de Lulú*, Pornography, and the Pleasure Principle

Silvia Bermúdez

> *For many years, we have all been living in the realm of Prince Mangogul: under the spell of an immense curiosity about sex, bent on questioning it, with an insatiable desire to hear it speak and be spoken about.*
>
> Michel Foucault

A few months after *Las edades de Lulú* (*The Ages of Lulu*) won the coveted First Prize of the erotic collection "La sonrisa vertical" (The Vertical Smile), *Marie Claire* (Spain), one of the major European women's magazines, published a revealing interview (August 1989) with Almudena Grandes, the young author of the novel.[1] The interview's suggestive title, "Almudena Grandes: inventora de Pasiones y perversiones" (Almudena Grandes: Inventor of Passions and Perversions) is but the first emblem of the (con)fusing nature of the novel.[2] For couched in the choice of the words *passion* and *perversion* an implicit and important distinction is metonymically suggested, between "erotica" and "pornography," between what is supposedly normal in sexuality and what supposedly goes beyond the boundaries into deviance.[3] But the presentation of Grandes as a simultaneous creator of "passions" and "perversions" also (con)fuses the murky landscape of the imprecise boundaries between the erotic and the pornographic. This already complex and unresolved territory is further complicated by the article when Grandes's literary and personal biography is placed in a gendered discourse that establishes assumed differences between male and female erotic writers.[4] By situating, even unwantingly, *Las edades de Lulú* at the crossroads of all these issues, I believe the interview is quite revealing of the achievements and questions raised by the novel.

Against the regulatory backdrop that aims to separate what is properly erotic and what is not, what belongs to male and female erotic arenas, it is not surprising that the interview moves along formulating a number of speculations on the explicitness of the sexual behaviors represented in the novel. But what definitely draws the interview's attention is the perverse nature of these behaviors in Lulú, the young female narrator and protagonist of the novel. Such emphasis on perversion overshadows the qualities of sexual fantasy, role play, and performance developed by Grandes's novel, but brings to the spotlight the struggles between the private and the public spheres when dealing with issues of sex and sexuality.

Activated by the mechanism of treating sexuality as "the great secret," the term *pornography* is not even enunciated in the interview but suggested by the mentioning of sadomasochism and pedophilia (23), two of the sexual activities represented in *Las edades de Lulú*.[5] Both sexual practices are summoned by the interviewer in an effort to emphasize both the "rawness" of Grandes's fiction—in the context of her being a female writer—and her character's latent perversity. Interestingly, the more the interviewer tries to elicit from Grandes a condemnation and demonization of perversion, the more Grandes insists on emphasizing the fairy-tale nature and the fantasy scenario dramatized by *Las edades de Lulú*. In claiming, "Mucha gente... [m]e censura que cuente un cuento de hadas; es de suponer que los cuentos de hadas...deberían ser mucho más ligeritos" (Lots of people...censure me for telling a fairy tale; it is assumed that fairy tales...should be much lighter) (23), Grandes reserves the right to tell not only a fairy tale but a "heavy," excessive one, indeed. It is not surprising, then, that the implicit suggestion of perversity is laid bare immediately after Grandes defines the novel as a fairy tale.

That is when Reyes-Ortiz, the interviewer, fires back with, "La verdad es que, para un cuento de hadas, la narración de una escena tremenda de sadomasoquismo..." (The truth is, that for a fairy tale, narrating a dreadful sadomasochist scene...) (23), questioning Grandes's definition. The rhetorical strategy of the ellipsis dots interrupting the sentence negates the possibility of finding such a scene in a fairy tale. Hence, the absence inscribed by the use of the suspension points signals, for Reyes-Ortiz, the unnameable nature of the novel: deviant and abnormal. Since *Las edades de Lulú* has turned away from what is assumed as proper conduct in fairy tales, the interviewer's comments aim at placing the novel in the pornographic field organized simultaneously around "normal" and "perverse" sexualities and around "normal" and "perverse" literary ways of narrating them.[6] In what follows I wish to examine, within the realm of the fantasy scenario proposed by *Las edades de Lulú,* the transgressive nature of Grandes's enterprise and the possible ramifications on her implicit use of what I call the "pleasure principle." My point is that probing into the role played by perversion in *Las edades de Lulú* may allow us to question and reevaluate notions that assign a priori categories of "good" and "bad" in terms of sexual pleasures for women.[7]

First, by ascribing her story to a genre particularly associated with a children's world of fantasy and magic, and then by refusing to follow the expected pattern within the mode, Grandes critically revisits the fairy tale, calling attention to questions of narrative and genre. Thus, Grandes's comments serve both as a warning and as a challenge: the reader is warned that the novel cannot be read outside particular literary conventions that deal with fantasy, and then is challenged to question those conventions. In fleeing from the conventions of erotic literature into the realm of fairy tales, Grandes clearly posits fantasy as the basis for dealing with sex and sexuality and its representations. What are the "real" implications of such premises and which is the story of Lulú that allows for such proposals?

Inscribed by its author primarily as a fairy tale, the novel nonetheless seems to tell a tale common to all coming-of-age narratives: Lulú, the female narrator, relates her journey toward sexual self-knowledge in counterpoint to familial and Spanish social history. But while Grandes's novel follows the pattern of the bildungsroman, in its narration of a story of becoming, it simultaneously transgresses it with a "counternarrative" of sexual awakening and a questioning of the conventions of stories of becoming.[8] *Las edades de Lulú* is the story of a teenaged girl—María Luisa Ruiz-Poveda y García de la Casa, affectionately known as Lulú—entering the world of erotic cravings and sexual experimentation in her path toward womanhood. By naming it a fairy tale, Grandes wants us to inscribe this story of becoming within the realm of fantasy.

It is not without relevance to my reading that psychoanalysis has already established for us the distinctness of the sexual drive as one whose object is pleasure and its satisfaction.[9] Thus, sexuality is a separate drive that emerges from the biological—the drive to self-preservation from the nonsexual function of feeding—but that has as its object satisfaction and not survival.[10] This desire for pleasure is supported by fantasy as a veritable mise-en-scène. Hence, as Elizabeth Cowie puts it, sexuality "arises in the emergence of fantasy" (136). It is in this sense that sexuality and fantasy meet in Lulú's (fairy) tale. Moreover, Grandes's authorial exercise of assigning the novel to the realm of literary fantasy proves to be an oppositional maneuvering designed to liberate both the assumptions about women's erotic literature and women's sexual practices. How does Grandes achieve this?

The notion of "novel of formation" or "apprentice novel" associated with the bildungsroman is also dramatized in *Las edades de Lulú* by the role played by Pablo, Lulú's older brother's best friend, who later will become her husband and the father of her daughter, Inés. Pablo, twelve years her senior, plays the roles of father figure and sexual partner, becoming Lulú's ardent supporter in her exploration of perversions. Her fascination with the thin line separating normalcy from perversion drives her to embark on a series of sexual encounters, especially with homosexual men, where roles merge and overlap, and positions are constantly shifting. I will later have more to say about the wide range of questions raised by the novel in regard to power, pleasure, and gender in the bonding of heterosexual and homosexual pleasures; however, what I want to stress now is the nonlinear progression of time in the way the story is actually presented to us. Thus, the apparently simple summary of the plot is rendered (con)fusing in the novel by the temporal inversions and narrative elisions with which Lulú chooses to tell her story.

Taking us back and forth through time, the narrator constantly interrupts the narrative with a combination of flashbacks, fantasies, and prolepses that work to generate the (con)fusing nature of the novel. At moments, some of the facts given are merely circumstantial, to indicate that such an event has taken place later in the chronology of time. That is the case when Ely, a transvestite prostitute, appears early on in the narrative as a person close to Lulú's life (75–76), but it is only later (95–113) that we "discover" that both Pablo and Lulú had, early on in the actual sequence of events, a ménage à trois with him/her. The reader's first encounter with Ely is, therefore, in the time frame of the story, Lulú's last. This disjunction between story and plot tantalizingly prevents and permits the reader's acquisition of knowledge and functions as a seduction tool to entice and arouse the reader.

If one of the aims of an erotic novel is to arouse the reader's interest in more ways than one, the temporal authorial manipulation self-consciously underscores, in more ways than one, the dynamics of pleasure and seduction at play in the novel. It is in this connection that Foucault's epigraph reminds us how the insatiable desire for pleasure is intertwined with the "knowledge of pleasure: a pleasure that comes of knowing pleasure" (77).[11] Hence, the encounter of textual and fictional arousals, of textual and fictional desires in a novel of female development flauntingly exposing the "pleasure that comes of knowing pleasure," can be seen as an attempt to complicate the issue of female development in a number of overlapping ways.

The novel exposes both its self-conscious nature and the complex issues operating in sexuality from its first paragraph.[12] There the reader is invited to a pornographic video session by Lulú, seduced into watching her watch the film: "supongo que puede parecer extraño pero aquella imagen, aquella inocente imagen, resultó al cabo el factor más esclarecedor, el impacto más violento" (9) (I suppose it might seem strange but that image, that innocent image, turned out to be the most illuminating factor, to have the most violent impact [1]). One would do well to consider the massive weight that this metafictional introduction achieves within the total narrative structure. Though presented as part of the "natural" setting of the novel's world, it is a mise-en-abîme of the presence of the text in the reader's world and of the ways *Las edades de Lulú* seeks to disrupt the reader's conditioned response to reading in general and to the reading of this erotic novel in particular. Thus, while the metafictional turn displays both the artificial nature of the story and the artifice that produces it, the semantic reverberations of the four adjectives—"strange," "innocent," "illuminating," "violent"—elicited by the image reach a certain pornographic intensity by attaching to the viewer and the act of viewing a paradigmatic significance. At one level, this is achieved by the indication that what the reader is about to witness appears to be innocent—without knowledge—but will both shed light on the issues at hand and will infringe on the conventional. Thus, the true content of the narrative has as much to do with the fate of Lulú as a character as with the fate of this image as it undergoes several metamorphoses in the novel.

The choice of a pornographic film to function as a model for the novel appears to me to be one of Grandes's most remarkable achievements. Through the identification with a pornographic film, *Las edades de Lulú* blurs even more the already complex and un-resolved boundaries of the pornographic and the erotic. On one hand, it moves the text further into the realm of the pornographic, and thus away from the erotic aura that is associated with and more acceptable for women.[13] This transgression expands and lib-erates the geographies of both "women's literature" and "women's sexuality" from the enclosed stereotypical representations as-signed to them. On the other, by using a porn film as a model, Grandes can explore Lulú's taboo-breaking sexual fantasies in a cinematic representational manner that underscores the explicit and the perverse, the bonding between sex and violence in certain experiences of human sexuality. In both cases, Grandes's strate-gic use of visual fetishism and latent voyeurism, both within and outside the text, encourages the reader/viewer to examine his or her own implication in the fantasies aroused by the images of "that radiant intertwining of bodies" (1).

When the camera comes to caress the human bodies placed in front of it, we are invited to participate in Lulú's visual fetishism by looking at things in the way she instructs us:

Aquella era la primera vez en mi vida que veía un espectáculo semejante. Un hombre, un hombre grande y musculoso, un hombre hermoso, hincado a cuatro patas sobre una mesa...Indefenso, encogido como un perro abandonado, un animalillo suplicante, tembloroso, dispuesto a agradar a cualquier precio. Un perro hundido, que escondía el rostro, no una mujer. Había visto docenas de mujeres en la misma postura. Me había visto a mí misma, algunas veces. (9)[14]

The narrator's emphasis on underscoring the particularity of this image is stirred by the fact that the sexual roles generally associated with pornography — degrading, violent actions and representations of women — are transgressed in this sexual fantasy where, in the context of a sadomasochist scenario a man is going to be sodomized by another man.[15]

Within the setting dramatized in the novel, Lulú's description of the image questions the notion that pornography is, as described by Michael Kimmel, "about women as men want them to be, and about our own sexual selves as we would like them to be" (xi). By confronting the reader with one possible scenario that contests this assumption, *Las edades de Lulú* proposes not to subsume one gendered form of desire, or one sexual-preference form of pleasure to another. On the contrary, by representing a "perverse" form of pornographic setting with a heterosexual woman watching a gay pornographic video, the novel requires us to go to the heart of difficult and complex questions regarding sexual identity in the formation of gendered subjects. Lulú's perverse sexual fantasies, in which heterosexual and homosexual desires encounter each other in an ever oscillating manner, stress the importance of adopting, as Donna Haraway suggests in her discussion of cyborgs, "a slightly perverse shift of perspective [that] might better enable us to contest for meanings, as well as for other forms of power and pleasure" (154). Thus, by dramatizing sexual activities such as fetishism and voyeurism that seem built into the cinematic medium, *Las edades de Lulú* sets in motion the discovery of new forms of knowledge and pleasure.

And yet, Lulú's comments also underline the fact that the image, the pornographic image, is always part of a complex signifying system of the sexual working across the differences of sexual preferences or biological sex. By stressing that what we are all watching through her eyes is *un espectáculo*,[16] the display of a performance, Lulú makes visible the fact that we are observers implicated in an event we cannot fully experience. This ever contracting distance between the enactment and our viewing of it requires us to pay attention to, as Elizabeth Cowie puts it "the complex signifying process set in play by what is termed 'sexual imagery'" (135). From this perspective, the sexual arousal elicited by sexual imagery is first and foremost a matter of signification.

The pornographic image of the kneeling man waiting to be pleasured, already ready, comes to be a sign of the desire of the spectator while offering a fantasy scenario. Thus, the image of a kneeling male figure in the scene offers not only a surrogate with whom Lulú, as a woman, can and does identify, but also offers a mise-en-scène of "the desire to desire which pornography represents" (Cowie 137). The crucial point is not to assume that sexual arousal in the spectator is produced as a corresponding stimulus-response condition, but to see how the image is already a connotative system signifying the possibility of sexual satisfaction.[17]

Moreover, the desire for visual pleasure that comes with Lulú's positioning as a voyeur also allows her to adopt, as a woman, the positions normally enjoyed by men in the so called "girl-girl" numbers aimed at heterosexual male audiences.[18] Note, however, that there is no simple reversal making in this scene, because what fascinates Lulu is the undoing for her as a woman of the two distinct forms offered in the sexual fantasy of pornography: the doing or the being done. The undoing comes from the reversibility of the active and passive scenario that the gay sexual fantasy is offering her: the "big muscular" man—with its implicit suggestion of virility and masculinity—waiting to be done.[19] The suggestion of flexibility and reversibility in the roles played in the fantasy scenario emblematized by this very first pornographic image gets to be further enacted and explored in the ensuing sexual encounters awaiting the reader.

When the narration of the video session is done with, Lulú brings us to a domestic setting in the immediate present where the situation of the main characters, Lulú and Pablo, is explained. While Lulú is dealing with problems at work and with her daughter Inés's antisocial behavior in school (21–22), we are informed that Pablo is involved in a comfortable new relationship with a younger woman (21). All of this serves as the starting point from which Lulú's sexual journey both back to the past and to the future will develop. In its retrospective leap, the narrator details for us her first sexual encounter with Pablo (22–69), and reveals some of the dynamics at play in their relationship "intuía por primera vez que aquello . . . todo aquello, no era más que el prólogo de una eterna, ininterrumpida ceremonia de posesión" (I sensed for the first time . . . that it was all nothing but the prelude to an endless, uninterrupted ceremony of possession) (60; 45). The paradigmatic significance of this first time lies in the fact that the remembered images of this original sexual pleasure — "todavía soy capaz de recordarlo perfectamente" (I can still remember it all perfectly) (22; 11) — will inform and enhance the pleasures of the following experiences.

In its movement forward, the narration takes us to the moment when Lulú, after a night out with her friend Chelo, gets the video whose pornographic image greets us at the beginning of the novel: "la cinta estaba metida en su estuche, encima de la televisión, la vi nada más entrar" (The video was in its box, on top of the television; I saw it as soon as I came in) (82–83; 64). But what caught Lulú's attention and brings us back to my discussion of the metamorphoses of that first image is a hermeneutical exercise. In her description of the photographic image announcing the contents of the video, Lulú acknowledges the discovery of a new symbol: "Más o menos encima de su cabeza aparecía un símbolo que no había visto nunca, tres circulitos, los primeros con una flechita, el tercero con una crucecita también ascendente, entrelazados entre sí" (More or less above her head there was a symbol I'd never seen before, three linked circles, the first two with a little arrow, the third with a little cross, all pointing upwards) (83; 65). The iconography of these two symbols simultaneously representing male and female identities, and homosexual and heterosexual desires, gets to be tested in *Las edades de Lulú*.

Encoded in the triangular representation, the two symbols identifying male and female gender identities are merged and (con)-fused in the novel through the transgressive role of Lulú's quest for perverse triangular sexual encounters. Lulú's desire to see more, to know more about other and different sexual pleasures finds in the emblematic representation of the video's cover an iconography for "undoing the rigid hierarchies that underlie sexual difference" (Williams 1993, 234). Nowhere does this undoing, the transposition of positions, become more apparent than in the threesome encounter between Pablo, Lulú, and Ely, a transvestite with silicon breast implants. But it is important to remember, in the context of the development aspect of the bildungsroman, that it is Lulú who sets in motion the possibility of this encounter by acting on one of her perverse desires: "había sido uno de mis juegos favoritos tiempo atrás, cazar travestis" (At one time hunting transvestites had been one of my favorite games) (95; my translation). While Lulú's control over her sexual fantasies empowers her supporting her sexual agency, her desire for men passing as women can only be ascribed to a space of adventure and fantasy that recognizes endless possibilities of sexual pleasures. Hence, a comprehensive coverage of contemporary sexuality will cover a wide range of elements, as Susie Bright defends in a recent interview with Mark Ehrman: "It's fun to talk about how these elements combine, . . . to just keep stirring the mix and seeing what's going to bubble up next" (10).[20]

The fact that Ely is both a transvestite and, at least partially, a transsexual, deconstructing the gender binarism of the male/ female pole, is the actual transgression of this encounter. The combination of several sexual numbers such as Lulú's and Ely's "lesbian" breast touching and kissing (102–03), Ely's masturbation (109), Pablo's fellatio simultaneously by Ely and Lulú (109), and the "straight sex" number between Lulú and Pablo (110) appear to comply with the various sexual acts that constitute the conventions of the pornographic genre.[21] But this setting is (con)fused and questioned by the destabilizing role played by Ely whom in her/his body combines female breasts with a male penis while dressed in

> una minifalda azul eléctrico de plástico, imitando cuero,
> unas sandalias altísimas atadas con cordones y una blusa
> de gasa con dibujos blancos, morados y azules; al cuello,
> un foulard de la misma tela. (99)[22]

The challenge posed by Ely's somewhat transsexual body and his transvestism resides in the fact that it is a disruptive element that renders inoperable, as Marjorie Garber remarks, "easy notions of binarity, putting into question the categories of 'female' and 'male,' whether they are considered essential or constructed, biological or cultural" (10). Hence, Ely embodies the "third sex" that cannot be easily assimilated either to the poles of gender binarism or to a sexual dimorphism by her/his transvestism and her/his partially transsexual body. The permeability inscribed on Ely's body as an unidentifiable site becomes the "space of possibility" articulated by Garber (9–17).

It is in this anatomically female and biologically male body that Lulú will be able to explore similar erogenous zones of the female body and different ones of the male one:

> Volví a tocarle estaba empalmado, desde luego.
> Entonces le levanté la blusa y me metí una de sus tetas en la boca sin apartar la mano.
> Era monstruoso.
> Me colgué de su teta, la besaba, la chupaba, la mordía y movía la mano sobre él, le frotaba a través del plástico azul . . . (102)[23]

These provocative contradictions that intermingle pleasure and the power to inspire horror are explored by Lulú, who emerges as the more knowledgeable and the more powerful of the two as Ely admits: "Eres una mujer de carácter, ¿eh?" (You are a woman who knows what she wants, aren't you?) (102; 82). But in this simultaneous negation and affirmation of a lesbian and a heterosexual encounter, both Ely and Lulú get to discover a whole new range of possibilities allowed by the presence of what appears to be a multipurpose body. Thus, the "perverse dynamics" set in motion by Ely's body reconfigures all the sets of relationships involved in this triadic encounter putting in question the very notion of sexual identity and self-sufficiency.[24]

Lulú's sexual empowerment comes, then, not by her establishing an "integrated" self, as certain notions of the novel of development may suggest, but by constantly positioning herself at the crossroads of incoherent, clashing, and unstable notions of identity and sexual pleasure. Thus, Lulú's flexibility allows her to shift between the position of subject, object, and witness throughout the novel.[25] It is again in a take of this witness-voyeur stance that Lulú will further explore her perverse sexual desires through her fascination for watching homosexual men coupling. In this episode of the narration Lulú, who initially hires three homosexual men to perform sex for her—"veinte talegos. Es mi última oferta; total, sólo voy a mirar" (twenty thousand. That's my last offer. I mean, all I'm going to do is watch) (170; 143)—ends up participating in a ritual orgy involving the three men and herself.

Among the three homosexuals, Jimmy, Mario, and Pablito, Jimmy is obviously the most dominant one occupying also the "top" position, while Pablito is the most submissive, occupying the "bottom" one. The scenario of this threesome is further complicated by Lulú's assuming a "masculine" position as the paying voyeur. But, things are rarely what they seem, as Lulú's invitation to participate in the orgy is going to make clear:

> Jimmy me preguntó si no pensaba desnudarme, su voz parecía una invitación, lo hice, me desnudé completamente, . . . y me acerqué a él, me tumbé en la mesa, una mesa baja, boca arriba, siguiendo sus instrucciones, él seguía hablando,—tú nunca te has follado a una tía, ¿verdad?—, Pablito protestó, dijo que sí, que por supuesto que lo había hecho, pero mentía, hasta yo me di cuenta—pues ya va siendo hora, ya eres mayorcito para probar—. (176)[26]

After Jimmy forces Pablito to have sex with Lulú—by penetrating him and thus producing an erection in Pablito, so that he may enter Lulú—she ends up occupying the bottom position of this sexual chain. By both following Jimmy's instructions and placing herself on her back, Lulú relinquishes her control over Jimmy. Thus, she moves within the space of one sexual fantasy scenario from the controlling subject and witness position to the object one. But, as the shifting of positions makes clear, being sexually empowered, paradoxically, does not always mean being in control.

Context is, of course, crucial, and the key in this scenario is Lulú's attitude toward what it means to be voluntarily out of control. The paradox implicit in this sentiment is indeed a delicate one, and I am aware of its potential dangers, but it is also necessary, if women are to experience full sexual agency and pleasure, to beware of the arguments that limit sexuality to, as Linda Williams puts it, "the condemnation of unorthodoxies measured against an orthodox norm" (23). For as soon as these terms are questioned in the novel, expectations are forced to be released because they are (con)fused and merged at every turn.

We must attempt, then, to deflect the inflexibility of these terms, even, when the unorthodoxy appears to be in this case the fact that Lulú chooses to partake a very "orthodox" position in this scenario of the bottom female penetrated by the top male.[27]

This reverting to "normal" gender roles takes us to the novel's final, and perhaps controversial, scene. There Lulú, dressed in one of her and Pablo's favorite sexual outfits — "una camisa de recién nacido hecha a la medida de una niña grande" (a little newborn baby's blouse made to fit a big girl) — waits for Pablo to come back with the familiar aroma of freshly made *porras* (259–60). The traditional sexual model structure of the dominant male and the submissive female couple to which Lulú and Pablo seem to belong, is (con)fused and tested both through the perverse dynamics of sadomasochism and Lulú's constant sexual empowerment.[28] Thus, the end result is a constant reshaping of powers, pleasures, and pains that simultaneously reifies and dismisses Lulú and Pablo's sexual and marital relationship. Lulú's ability and freedom to move between the roles of subject, object, and witness at will, proves to be her perverse strategy to achieve sexual empowerment. And, as *Las edades de Lulú* points out, this "if-it-feels-good-do-it" attitude, the "pleasure principle" attitude, could be a viable option for women in achieving sexual agency. But this possibility is not without problems and complex turns, and we need constantly to rewrite and reevaluate them. In this sense, then, *Las edades de Lulú* proves to be the fairest fairy tale of them all.

Notes

1. Almudena Grandes (Madrid, 1960) has published two more novels since *Las edades de Lulú* (*The Ages of Lulu*) made her famous: *Te llamaré Viernes* (1991) (*I Will Call You Friday*), and *Malena es un nombre de tango* (1994) (*Malena Is a Tango's Name*).

2. The interview was conducted by Igor Reyes-Ortiz.

3. On the subjective nature of the distinction between "erotica" and "pornography," Ralph Ginzburg stated, in 1959, that "no truly satisfactory definition of erotica (and/or pornography or obscenity) has ever been devised. The concept is entirely too subjective." Almost thirty years later the topic remains as entangled as ever, and no amount of clarification seems to untie the knots of confusion. According to Elizabeth Cowie, when debating the issue of pornography there is a confusion arising from, among other things, "the attempt to distinguish between permissible sexual imagery and 'pornography,' where the permissible imagery is

variously claimed as 'erotic' or 'art' or 'socially redeeming' in contrast to 'pornography'" (133, quotation marks in the original). Moreover, David William Foster, while discussing Griselda Gambaro's *Lo impenetrable,* further develops these distinctions, arguing that "such an approach assumes that there is nothing socially redeeming about pornography as such, which is certainly a signpost of any cultural uneasiness about cultural texts stripped of the moral definitions of sex and the need to erect a secure ideological disjunction between bad pornography and healthy erotics if one is a liberal citizen and between bad pornography/eroticism and ennobling spirituality if one is conservative" (284–85). In the context of Spain's recent publishing boom on *literatura erótica,* Foster's point is well taken. Consider, if not, Fernando Valls's prescription for finding an appropriate language for erotic literature: "La peculiaridad de este lenguaje (se tiende a olvidar que *primero debe ser literatura y, luego, además, erótica*) debería estribar en su tendencia a la evocación, a la alusión velada" (the peculiarity of this language [it is usually forgotten that first it must be literature, and, then, also, erotic] should stress its tendency to evocation, to covert allusions) (30; emphasis mine).

4. The first question of the interview inscribes the whole discussion of the novel within a gendered discourse that places sexual explicitness and "rawness" in the domain of male erotic writers: "Me ha llamado lo cruda que puede ser su novela en algunos momentos, lo que no suele ser corriente en novelas de corte erótico escrita por mujeres" (The rawness of some of her novel's passages has caught my attention; such rawness is not common in erotic novels written by women) (21). Reyes-Ortiz's comment is but one of a series of statements that had led a well-recognized critic such as Francisco Umbral to dub *Las edades de Lulú* as the "historia de una varona" (21). This supposedly "masculine" attribute of both the author and the character springs from the fact that the perversion and violence of the novel are perceived as something so alien to women that only a *varona* could be involved in such enterprises. Of course, the adjective applies to both Lulú, the character involved in such sexual practices, and the author, Almudena Grandes, who writes about them. See Juan Cantavella for comments on the increasing number of female writers in a paradigmatically male-authored genre.

5. At least three times during the interview Igor Reyes-Ortiz requests that Grandes explain the unusual "rawness" of her novel. The first is after stating that the central topic of *Las edades de Lulú* is the protagonist's voyeuristic attachment to homosexual encounters (21). The implicit perversity, in this case, stems from the fact that Lulú, the voyeur, is a heterosexual woman who finds pleasure in watching homosexual men perform sexual acts. In the other two instances, masochism and pedophilia are alluded to (23).

6. The pornographic field comprises diverse and differing discourses and institutions — sexual medicine, religious discipline, the erotic/pornographic book trade, pedagogy, policing, legislation. See Hunter, Saunders, and Williamson (12–56). See Kendrick for a history of pornography.

7. I agree with Linda Williams that perversion is difficult to defend (235), but I also agree with her emphasis, drawn from other feminist thinkers, on our need to rehabilitate the term for feminist analysis (236–39).

8. Wilhelm Dilthey enunciated in 1906 what has come to be the most cited definition of the term. An English translation from the German is offered by G. B. Tennyson in his study of the genre: "[The *bildungsroman*] examines a regular

course of development in the life of the individual; each of its stages has its own value and each is at the same time the basis of a higher state. The dissonances and conflicts of life appear as necessary transit points of the individual on his way to maturity and harmony" (136). For an insightful reading of this genre in the context of women's literature see Susan Fraiman.

9. Drawing from Jean Laplanche's analysis, Cowie summarizes this process while explaining the distinct satisfactions and pleasures that the infant gets from sucking the breast: "The feeding still nourishes the child, but the experience of satisfaction in feeding has been *split off through the function of representation — the breast stands for a possible satisfaction — and thus moves into the field of fantasy,* and by this very fact starts existing as sexuality" (136; emphasis mine).

10. MacKinnon, on the contrary, considers sexuality as a socially determined construction: "Sexuality to feminism is, like work to marxism, socially constructed and at the same time constructing" (49).

11. Foucault distinguishes, in volume two of *The History of Sexuality,* between two ways of organizing the knowledge of sexuality that separate Western cultures from non-Western ones (91–92). In the former, knowledge is organized as an *ars erotica,* in the latter knowledge is configurated as a *scientia sexualis* by which modern sexuality is constructed according to a combination of power and knowledge.

12. That the video she is watching is, indeed, a pornographic video is established by Lulú early in the novel when she is describing the erotic activities of the three characters involved in the scene (two males and a female). The unusual urgency with which one of the males and the female start kissing, prompts this comment from the narrator: "Apenas un instante después comenzaron a besarse de una manera salvaje, urgente, insólita en una película pornográfica" (Almost immediately they started to kiss with a wild intensity which was unusual in a pornographic film) (12, 4). The novel has appeared in English, translated by Sonia Soto as *The Ages of Lulu* (1994); quotations in English are from this edition unless otherwise noted.

13. Here the interview is, once more, illuminating. Grandes sees a connection between erotic "women's literature" and "women's sexuality" as follows: "La literatura erótica escrita por mujeres es como una prolongación del mundo de las mujeres en general, tal y como lo ven los hombres, reflejada en una sexualidad mucho más blanda, mucho más tibia. Es lo del supuesto refinamiento sensitivo del mundo de las mujeres que se evoca a menudo y que yo no sé lo que es. (Erotic literature written by women is, in general, a prolongation of the world of women, as it is perceived by men, and it is reflected in a softer, more lukewarm, sexuality. It is the supposed refinement of women's worlds that is always mentioned and that I do not know what it is) (21).

14. I had never seen anything like this before. A man, big and muscular, a beautiful man, on all four legs on top of a table. . . . Defenseless, cringing like an abandoned dog, a pleading, trembling little animal, eager to please at all costs. A battered dog, hiding its face, not a woman. I had seen dozens of women in that same posture. Including myself, a few times. (64)

15. This notion has been the point of contention between the positions taken within the debate on the role played by violence in pornographic literature and film. Thus, we have on one hand the antipornography position that "pornography

is the theory, and rape the practice" as expressed by, among others, Morgan (139). On the other side of the spectrum, we have the position summarized by Williams, who would like to elicit a "consideration of what pornography is and what it has offered those viewers . . . who have been 'caught looking' at it" (xi). For more on the former position see Vance, Ellis, Segal, Cowie, Loach, and Williams (1993). For more on the latter, see Dworkin, Griffin, Lederer, and MacKinnon.

In the context of Spain the debate has not acquired the proportions and dramatic overtones of that in the United States and England. Interestingly enough, recent studies on pornography have appeared under the more general and prudent denomination of *erotismo* (Zavala). Zavala specifically argues that "la pornografía se concibe como una práctica sistemática de explotación y subordinación basada en las diferencias sexuales que afecta muy directamente a la mujer" (pornography is conceived as a systematic practice of exploitation and subordination based on sexual differences that directly affects women) (165).

16. The dictionary provides, both in English and Spanish, revealing definitions of the term where the notions of performance and "bad behavior" meet. In Spanish, *espectáculo* is defined as (1) "Función o diversión pública celebrada en un teatro, circo o en cualquier otro edificio o lugar en que se congrega la gente para presenciarla," (2) "Aquello que se ofrece a la vista o a la contemplación intelectual y es capaz de atraer la atención y mover el ánimo infundiéndole deleite," (3) "Acción que causa escándalo o gran extrañeza." In English, *spectacle* conveys three very similar meanings: (1) "Something that can be seen or viewed, specially something of a remarkable or impressive nature," (2) "A public performance or display, especially one on a large or lavish scale," (3) "A regrettable public display, as of bad behavior."

17. With respect to the processes involved in sexual fantasy and sexual images see Cowie (136–52).

18. Williams reminds us, nonetheless, that even though these numbers were originally constructed for heterosexual male viewers they could, and indeed have been "appropriated to different ends by different viewers, [and] performed with inspiration by atypically enthusiastic performers" (253).

19. Gay men's pornography, as Mandy Merck writes, "has proved as controversial as its heterosexual counterpart, if only because the two have so often been equated" (217). For reflections on this particular equation see Richard Dyer's essay. For her part, Williams considers that "part of the pleasure of gay male porn would seem to reside in its play of both similarity and difference from this 'norm'" (1993, 245).

20. I would like to thank Adán Griego for bringing to my attention this article, and for both encouraging and gently prodding comments.

21. At least the conventions of the pornographic genre in film. For more on this aspect see Ziplow's guide and Williams's discussion of the same (1989, 126–30).

22. He was wearing an electric blue plastic miniskirt [a leather imitation], extremely high-heeled sandals with thongs, and a crepe blouse with a pattern in white, purple, and blue, with a matching scarf around his neck. (78)

Ely is not, according to the conventions of transexualism, a de facto transsexual since he has not surgically removed his penis. But, I believe this double gender-bending inscribed within and by Ely's body works as a celebration of "bodies, pleasures, and knowledge, in their multiplicity and their possibilities of resistance" (Foucault 157). With respect to "transsexuals" and "transvestites" see, for example, Garber's reflections on these topics, which are probably the most compelling to date. See also Bullough and Bullough.

23. I touched him again. He definitely had a hard-on. Then I lifted his blouse and put one of his tits in my mouth without taking my hand away.

It was freakish.

I hung onto his tit, kissing, sucking, biting it, and rubbed him with my hand, on top of the blue plastic. . . . (81)

24. The term "perverse dynamics" belongs to Jonathan Dollimore (1–16). Williams precisely considers that this dynamic functions in all forms of sexual fantasy: both within heterosexual pornography and outside it, in the non-dominant, non-mainstream forms of gay, lesbian, sadomasochistic and bisexual moving-image pornographies (1193, 243).

25. That Lulú plays the role of witness both within the context of the story and in relationship to the reader is emblematized by the role she plays in the pornographic video episode.

26. Jimmy asked me if I was going to get undressed. His question sounded like an invitation—so I did. I got completely undressed, . . . I went up to him, then lay on the table, a low table, on my back, following his instructions. He went on talking: "You have never fucked a woman, have you?" Pablito protested, said he had, but he was lying, even I realized that. "Well, it's about time you tried, you're a big boy now" (148).

27. Obviously, the scenario in which the sexual encounter takes place is not an orthodox one. But this desire to relinquish power or participate in sadomasochistic sexual fantasies can be better understood under the light of the new trend in feminist thought called "do me" feminism as per Tad Friend 's now famous *Esquire* article. On the significance of this new trend for reading *Las edades de Lulú* I defer to Jeanne Railey, a student of mine in the Honors Project Program. For Railey, "sometimes the most perverse and transgressive fantasies, especially for a feminist, are the most 'normal' ones." I thank her for bringing to my attention Friend's article.

28. Lulú's position of vulnerability appears very clearly in the scene where Pablo sodomizes her in an act of rape (159–61). But, in another subversive turn of the novel that surprises our expectations, Lulú reflects on the relationship between pleasure and pain as follows:

> El recuerdo de la violencia, añadió una nota irresistible al placer
> que me poseía, desencadenando un final exquisitamente atroz . . .
> Hemos echo tablas, pensé, hemos intercambiado placeres
> individuales, me ha devuelto lo que antes me había arrebatado. Este
> pensamiento me reconfortó. Era un punto de vista, discutible, desde
> luego, pero no dejaba de ser un punto de vista. (161)

> (The memory of his violence added an irresistible note to the
> pleasure taking hold of me, setting off an exquisitely brutal climax. . . .
> We're quits, I thought. We've swapped individual pleasures, he's
> given me back what he earlier snatched away. I found the thought
> comforting. It was definitely a debatable point of view, but still a point
> of view. [134])

Lulú's comments precisely underscore the complex nature of sadomasochism and the contradicting points of view on the very same issue. For more on these controversial aspects of human sexuality see Studlar and Williams (1989), among others.

Works Cited

American Heritage Dictionary of the English Language. 3rd ed. Boston: Houghton Mifflin.

Bullough Vern L., and Bonnie Bullough. *Cross Dressing, Sex, and Gender.* Philadelphia: University of Pennsylvania Press, 1993.

Cantavella, Juan. "El sexo también está en los libros." *Leer* 28 (1990): 29–33.

Cowie, Elizabeth. "Pornography and fantasy: Psychoanalytic perspectives." In *Sex Exposed: Sexuality and the Pornography Debate.* Ed. Lynne Segal and Mary McIntosh. New Brunswick: Rutgers University Press, 1993, 132–52.

Dilthey, Wilhelm. *Das Erlebnis und die Dichtung: Lessing, Goether, Novales, Hölderlin.* 1906. 14th ed. Göttingen: Vandenhoeck und Ruprecht, 1965.

Dworkin, Andrea. *Pornography: Men Possessing Women.* New York: Putnam, 1979.

Dyer, Richard. "Gay Male Porn: Coming to Terms." *Jump Cut: A Review of Contemporary Media* 30 (1985): 27–29.

Ehrman, Mark. "Susie Bright Tells All," *Los Angeles Times Magazine,* July 24, 1994, 8–12.

Foster, David William. "Pornography and the Feminine Erotic: Griselda Gambaro's *Lo impenetrable.*" *Monographic Review/Revista Monográfica* 7 (1991): 284–96.

Foucault, Michel. *The History of Sexuality.* Vol. I. *An Introduction.* Trans. Robert Hurley. New York: Pantheon, 1978. Translation of *La volonté de savoir,* 1976.

Fraiman, Susan. *Unbecoming Women: British Women Writers and the Novel of Development.* New York: Columbia University Press, 1993.

Friend, Tad. "Yes." *Esquire,* February 1994, 48–56.

Garber, Marjorie. *Vested Interests: Cross-Dressing and Cultural Identity.* New York & London: Routledge, 1992.

Ginzburg, Ralph. *An Unhurried View of Erotica.* New York: Ace Books, 1958.

Grandes, Almudena. *Las edades de Lulú.* Barcelona: Tusquets, 1989.

———. *The Ages of Lulu.* Trans. Sonia Soto. New York: Grove, 1994.

Griffin, Susan. *Pornography and Silence: Culture's Revenge against Nature.* New York: Harper and Row, 1981.

Hunter, Ian, et al. *On Pornography: Literature, Sexuality, and Obscenity Law.* New York: St. Martin's Press, 1993.

Kendrick, Walter. *The Secret Museum: Pornography in Modern Culture.* NewYork: Viking, 1987.

Lederer, Laura, ed. *Take Back the Night.* New York: William Morrow, 1980.

Loach, Loretta. "Bad Girls: Women Who Use Pornography." In *Sex Exposed: Sexuality and the Pornography Debate.* Ed. Lynne Segal and Mary McIntosh. New Brunswick: Rutgers University Press, 1993, 266–74.

MacKinnon, Catharine A. *Feminism Unmodified: Discourses on Life and Law.* Cambridge: Harvard University Press, 1987.

Morgan, Robin. "Theory and Practice: Pornography and Rape." In *Take Back the Night.* Ed. Laura Lederer. New York: William Morrow, 1980, 139.

Railey, Jeanne. "Fantasy and Sexual Agency in *Las edades de Lulú*." Unpublished paper, July 1994.

Real Academia Española. *Diccionario de la Lengua Española*. 21 ed. Madrid: Espasa-Calpe, 1992.

Reyes-Ortiz, Igor. "Almudena Grandes: Inventora de Pasiones y Perversiones." *Marie Claire* 16.23 (1989): 21–23.

Segal, Lynne. "Sweet Sorrows, Painful Pleasures: Pornography and the Perils of Heterosexual Desire." In *Sex Exposed: Sexuality and the Pornography Debate.* Ed. Lynne Segal and Mary McIntosh. New Brunswick: Rutgers University Press, 1993, 65–91.

Studlar, Gaylyn. *In the Realm of Pleasure: Von Sternberg, Dietrich, and the Masochistic Aesthetic*. Urbana: University of Illinois Press, 1988.

Tennyson, G. B. "The *Bildungsroman* in Nineteenth-Century English Literature." In *Medieval Epic to the "Epic Theater" of Brecht*. Ed. Rosario P. Armato and John Spalek. Los Angeles: University of Southern California Press, 1968, 135–46.

Valls, Fernando. "La literatura erótica en España entre 1975 y 1990." *Insula* 530 (1991): 29–30.

Vance, Carole S. "Negotiating Sex and Gender in the Attorney General's Commission on Pornography." In *Sex Exposed: Sexuality and the Pornography Debate*. Ed. Lynne Segal and Mary McIntosh. New Brunswick: Rutgers University Press, 1993, 29–49.

Williams, Linda. *Hard Core: Power, Pleasure, and the "Frenzy of the Visible."* Berkeley: University of California Press, 1989, xi.

———. "Pornographies on/scene." In *Sex Exposed: Sexuality and the Pornography Debate*. Ed. Lynne Segal and Mary McIntosh. New Brunswick: Rutgers University Press, 1993, 233–65.

Zavala, Iris M. "Arqueología de la imaginación: erotismo, transgresión y pornografía." In *Discurso erótico y discurso transgresor en la cultura peninsular: siglos XI al XX*. Ed. Myriam Díaz-Diocaretz and Iris M. Zavala. Madrid: Ediciones Tuero, 1992, 155–81.

◆ **Chapter 8**

El Diario de José Toledo: A Queer Space in the World of Mexican Letters

Marina Pérez de Mendiola

Judging from the homophobic response in 1991 disclosed by Mexican state officials to a gay conference to be held in Guadalajara, Mexican gay and lesbian groups such as GOHL (Grupo Orgullo de Liberación Homosexual [Homosexual Liberation Pride Group]), Colectivo Sol (Sun Collective), and Patlatonalli still have a long way to go. This said, Mexico is also one of the first countries in Latin America to decriminalize homosexuality, and it boasts perhaps the longest history of gay and lesbian activism, as outlined by Matthews:

> In the midseventies, a gay men's discussion group emerged at the Autonomous Metropolitan University (UNAM). Its members went on to found the first gay militant group, the Homosexual Front for Revolutionary Action (FHAR). Other groups, such as the lesbian Oikabeth and cosexual Lambda emerged soon after. By the late seventies, Mexico City had its first gay pride day march. (58)[1]

Since the late seventies, Mexico City has been the site of many gay and lesbian pride marches. Numerous cultural and artistic events have also taken place in support of homosexual liberation. One of the most significant events was the creation of Semana

Cultural Gay (Gay Cultural Week) in June 1982, whose slogan was "We Are Everywhere." Semana Cultural Gay occurred every year, with the exception of 1983. Today it provides a space for cultural and artistic expression of Mexican gay and lesbian communities as well as for individuals and organizations — whether social, political, or professional. Moreover, this event brings together people who are eager to share their views, ideas, and concerns, or simply to cooperate and work with gays and lesbians as full members of society.[2] The Universidad Nacional Autónoma de México (National Autonomous University of Mexico) and the Círculo Cultural Gay (Gay Cultural Circle) organize these events, and the Museo Universitario del Chopo (Chopo University Museum) has hosted them since 1987. These organized events give the community not only a sense of continuity, but also a sense of affiliation with more institutionalized sectors of Mexican society.

Carlos Blas Galindo, a fervent defender of gay and lesbian artistic expression, reminds us that in Mexico "the first groups to engage in the battle for homosexual liberation were essentially made up of intellectuals, artists, and students" (16; my translation), who were later joined by more radical political and social groups. The field of literature in Mexico has been particularly propitious to the dissemination of the themes of homosexuality and to the inscription of gay and lesbian sensibilities in aesthetic terms.[3] *El diario de José Toledo* (José Toledo's Diary; 1964) by Miguel Barbachano Ponce (1930) is paradigmatic of the inscription of homosexuality in the aesthetic category of literature. The study of this novel opens at least two lines of investigation that I propose to examine here. The first deals with various textual strategies Barbachano Ponce deploys in order to debunk and erode the precognitive literary and social foundations on which more traditional literary texts are erected. The second issue deals with the narrativization of homosexuality in Mexico in the 1950s. I then examine the ontological and epistemic choices posed by the novel and the ideological and political implications this fictional discourse had within the specific sociohistorical context of its production.

Barbachano Ponce wrote his first novel in the midst of a literary euphoria. Indeed, the 1960s marked a healthy break from traditional Mexican literary production. Authors like José Agustín and Gustavo Sainz initiated an imaginative and defiant narrative, shaping a provocative new language inspired by their surrounding reality. These constantly transforming narrative techniques strove to translate contemporary social and political preoccupations and commitments. They also hoped to convey the diversity that shaped urban Mexican society and culture (cf. Poniatowska 167–206). *El diario de José Toledo,* which earned recognition as the first novel in Mexico to openly inscribe homosexuality in literature (Schneider 82), could not have come out, so to speak, at a better moment. Yet, however timely his statement was in 1964, Barbachano Ponce failed to find a publisher for his novel. Far from balking at defeat, he resolved to publish it at his own expense. Twenty-four years went by before the publishing house Premiá reprinted *Diario* in 1988. Today, to find *El diario de José Toledo* in a bookstore—even in Mexico City—remains an arduous undertaking. What explains the meager dissemination, past and present, of this publication and the leaden silence encompassing it?

The 1960s in Mexico proved to be liberating only for a few, and Barbachano Ponce did not benefit from the magnanimity of Mexican readers. In a recent conversation, the author acknowledged that the publication of this novel considerably hindered his career as a writer. This adversity was clearly a result of the censorship imposed by homophobia. He confronted his marginalization in the world of Mexican letters. Barbachano Ponce attributes the negative reception of his work to the closemindedness of the Mexican literary establishment of the time. Unwilling to accept marginalized authors whose writing challenged the social construction of gendered subjects, the literary establishment refused to grant legitimacy to the questions raised by these constructions. Undoubtedly, Barbachano Ponce was ahead of his time.

When reviewed, *El diario de José Toledo* received largely negative criticism. To this day, Federico Alvarez's article, "José Toledo contra Barbachano Ponce," represents the most virulent attack on the novel. First, Alvarez objects to Barbachano Ponce's "erroneous and aliterary" use of the diary-novel, admonishing him for not adhering to the rules defining the genre. His second point of contention, a question I will take up in the second part of this essay, has to do with José Toledo's fictional composition as a character. Alvarez condemns what he defines as José's feminoid characteristics and his *cursilería* (tackiness), which contributes, in his eyes, to the ridicule of (Mexican) homosexuality. I propose that this interpretation — like those provided by most of Barbachano Ponce's detractors — derives from a misreading of *El diario de José Toledo*.

Literary and Social Legitimacy: Supplement and Mimicry

I would first like to focus on the novel's literary quality, which Alvarez puts into question. Although the title of the novel suggests that it will read as a *diary-novel*, the reader does not find the common tropes nor the characteristics that traditionally constitute the genre.[4] Barbachano Ponce, as I intend to show, did not want to be bound by the rules of the genre. Rather, the word *diary* intimates the use of the genre as a literary device, fulfilling "the diary's potential as a literary strategy" (Abbott 18).

The novel is composed of two different kinds of narrations: the first person, narrative of José Toledo's diary, and a novel-like narration primarily in the third person, which alternates with the diary entries. Each of José's entries is entitled *El diario de José Toledo* and marked by an undated day of the week. In the diary, the first person "I" interplays with the second person "you," and the past tense alternates with the present tense. The second person narrative points to an addressee, Wenceslao, José's ex-lover. José relies on the present tense when referring to his letters to Wenceslao, but we find no epistolary exchange between the two characters, and José's letters are not transcribed in the diary. The messages in the letters are never revealed, and the reader can only intimate from the entries in José's diary the content of those missives. However, this aspect of the novel invests the diary with qualities typical of the epistolary novel, therefore indicating the desire to engage in communication and to go beyond the notion of privacy and isolation specific to the diary. The second text, the novel-like narration in the third person mentioned earlier, precisely performs the function of offsetting the lack of epistolary exchange, to add multivocality to the narration and develop themes that the diary only outlined. Moreover, I wish to argue that the third person narration also serves to give the novel in its entirety a certain literary legitimacy by producing a complex textual system. Let us pursue the notion of legitimacy.

At the end of the novel, the third person narrator states that the diary was found in a bus. Abbott, in his book on diary fiction, explains that "in the eighteenth century, the diary was employed to give the illusion of literary found object, something that people write but that is not supposed to be art" (18). I suggest that Barbachano Ponce chose to use the diary in half of his novel as a means to cross the boundaries between society and literature, between allegedly high and low literature (respectively, the novel-like narration and the "literary" found object that is not supposed to be art), thus creating a device to bring to the fore taboo issues such as gender identity and homosexual desire. To give to José's narration the illusion of being real, the author presents the idea that the diary was found. In the diary, the narration is centered exclusively around José's jealous and passionate love for Wenceslao, whereas the novel-like narration only alludes to homosexual love, resubmerging it into clandestinity and displacing it with accounts of heterosexual relationships. In the novel-like narration "the closet still operates as a shaping presence" (Sedgwick 68) at the center of which stands Wenceslao and his denial of homosexuality. This type of veiled inscription of social and literary taboos acquiesces to the aesthetics of mainstream literature. It complies with the customary idea in most literary arenas that secrecy and clandestinity are the leaven of any good narration dealing with difference. The second text is therefore encoded, and the reader faces long cryptic passages narrating Wenceslao's dreams. Yet, the semantic field in these passages reasserts oppression, persecution, inertia, and anxiety:

> Wenceslao, en sueños, caminaba por estrechas callejuelas sin salida, cuyos bordes de piedra eran lamidos por aguas verdes e infectas. El solo pensamiento de caer en ellas le produjo asco. Quiso huir de ahí... Se encontró otra vez deambulando por las angostas callejuelas. Al tratar de evadir el charco maloliente resbaló, cayendo en su seno viscoso. Lo que antes era un pecinal ahora era un mar de aguas glaucas y tranquilas. (32)[5]

The French literary magazine *Lire* recently devoted an issue to homosexuality and writing. Once again, most of the authors agreed that to "avow the unavowable" — that is, in this case, homosexuality — during the act of writing, disempowers the literary text.

The condition of writing, they add, is governed by secrecy, and the confession of homosexuality prevents the novel from becoming a so-called great book.[6] In the same vein, Alvarez denounces the diary's realism, which in his eyes detracts from the diary's literary quality: "Un diario tan real, tan increíblemente real, que resulta, en él, ilegible, aliterario" (xvi).[7] As if Barbachano Ponce anticipated this type of criticism, he created the novel-like narration, the literary component of the novel to be read not only as the legitimate text, but rather as a supplement, which Derrida defines in the following terms:

> The supplement adds itself, it is a surplus, a plenitude enriching another plenitude, the *fullest measure* of presence. It cumulates and accumulates presence.... Whether it adds or substitutes itself, the supplement is *exterior*, outside of the positivity to which it is super-added, alien to that which, in order to be replaced by it, must be other than it. Unlike the complement...the supplement is an exterior addition. (144–45)

In order for the diary to exist as a literary piece this exterior super addition is vital. Alvarez considers what I chose to call the supplement as "the best part of the novel." This is the site of Barbachano Ponce's transgressive practice that escaped most critics. This text, the novel-like narration as supplement, diverted the attention of those readers who were not open to literary and social transgression, and it subversively confirmed the interdict, the supposedly aliterary text of the diary. The supplement possesses multiple powers of subversion, Derrida explains, because it

> has not only the power of procuring an absent presence through its image; procuring it for us through the proxy [procuration] of the sign, it holds it at a distance and masters it. For this presence is at the same time *desired* and *feared*. The supplement transgresses and at the same time respects the interdict. (Derrida 155; my emphasis)

The novel-like narration trangresses by positing itself as the literary plenitude enriching an aliterary plenitude, which is the diary. But at the same time it "respects the interdict," since the diary could not have its place within the artistic realm without the second text providing it with the "fullest measure of presence."

Furthermore, whereas critics commonly assume that a nonfiction text could not exist as a literary artifact without the type of supplementation we read in this novel, Barbachano Ponce was eager to show that texts, like this diary, can effectively, and in an equally subversive fashion, supplement the literary one. Critics have too easily reduced the complexity of his composition by positing a mere Manichaean logic between two apparently incompatible texts. Nevertheless, the novel-like narration supplements the diary, which in turn supplements its supplement. Barbachano Ponce could in fact be denouncing the exclusiveness of the taxonomic discourses that prevailed in the literary discourse of the time. With José's coming out in the diary (the aliterary text), Barbachano Ponce challenges regimes of power and discourse, risking literary exclusion. Conversely, with such a character as Wenceslao, whose sexuality is socially and textually closeted, he affirms and maintains social and literary decorum. Thus, by collapsing the aesthetic with the real, Barbachano Ponce manages to debunk authoritative texts, structured by sexual politics and literary conventions, while remaining within the framework of the literary conventions his novel seeks to undermine.[8] We might surmise that Barbachano Ponce subversively mimics the recognizable text within the production of literary discourse in order to give immanence to literary and social difference, to the diary and to homosexual desire. It is precisely through the analysis of the concept of mimicry in this novel that one can reveal the inextricability of the link between the diary and the novel-like narration, between their form and content.

In a recent study on gay and lesbian literature in Latin America, Foster devotes a few pages to *El diario de José Toledo*. He argues that the clichés of sentimental love in this novel could be read as "part of a bourgeois concept of heterosexual love that one variety of homosexual identity unfortunately, if not pathetically, *mimics*" (58; my emphasis). The notion of mimicry raised by Foster in the context of sexual identity formation in fiction is an important issue that needs to be examined more closely. Although Foster does not provide specific examples, I would like to take up the question of what he might consider to be a putatively pathetic mimicry of heterosexual behaviors.

José's narration mainly exposes the events that refer to Wenceslao and the anguish caused by the breakup of their relationship.
José's consuming passion for Wenceslao permeates each line of
the text and is rendered by an oppressive semantic composition.
His emotional affliction shapes a text infused by pain and suffering. The constant repetition of words like "desperate, anguish,
suffer, ailing soul, cry, restless, agony" conveys José's continuous
mortification, which in a sense constitutes the thematic foundation of the diary. The reiterative quality of the beginning of each
entry also emphasizes the quotidien agonizing distress: "Como
de costumbre, me levanté temprano . . . estuve esperando que me
hablaras por teléfono . . . Lunes, otro día triste para mí" (13, 30, 13).[9]
This gives the narration a sense of circularity, with no exit, no future. However, this diary is not only based on self-observation
or self-pity. Rather, it ventures to explain, to open itself up. First,
this debunks the notion that a diary by definition is private. Still,
José is less concerned with crossing the threshold between the private and the public than with breaking away from the cultural
practice of secrecy as exemplified in the novel-like narration. As
Herdt puts it, secrecy,[10] in the Masonic sense of the term, suggests
complicity, maneuvering, and even conspiracy to overthrow hegemony. Yet, when secrecy is not lived within a group or shared,
we are in the realm of the secret self. The notion of secret self implies separation from the social group, which in turn allows for
the hegemony to maintain deviancies imprisoned in the strait-
jacket of social conventions. In order to avoid the neurosis provoked by the hiding of the self, José prefers to confess. Although
privacy is implied in the act of confessing, it allows him to transcend his secret self. He defies the culturally prescribed notion
of protection that in theory justifies the secret self. Rather than
seeing protective qualities in the act of self-secrecy, José perceives
it as a strategy to restrain and to control any citizen who may
wish to open the secret self to the outside. Thus, by identifying
his object of love as male, José reveals his homosexual desire,
and his intention to go beyond the secret self. However, the act
of confession endangers the self, which compels José to resort to
problematic strategies like the universalization of experience and,
consequently, mimicry.[11]

The insistence, throughout the diary, on an impossible love and painful relationship, works to give his experience a sense of universality. It is made clear, throughout the narration, that society denounces homosexual love, alienating and stigmatizing those who engage in it, particularly if acting upon their desire.[12] José always refers to his love for Wenceslao in almost platonic terms, remaining chaste and controlled. This tendency to minimize the sexual encounter and to aestheticize sexuality accounts for José's hope for social inclusion through the universally shared experience of pain and love. These are concepts that transcend the notions of gender, class, and race. With this idea of commonality José wishes to neutralize indignation, striving for acceptance. Several references in the text point to his concern to cohere, yielding to the very society that placed him in a state of nonidentity: "Quedé dormido besando la esclava y la medallita que *mi marido* me regaló el día que decidimos unirnos por toda la vida..." (52; my emphasis).[13] When referring to Wenceslao as his husband, José clearly expresses what I choose to call a coerced need to remain within the institutionalized heterosexist gender, sexual, and economic framework. Clearly, José is at the threshold of the closet, not quite in, and not quite out either. At the same time, he invites the reader to cross the same boundaries, to enter the intimacy of the diary, to participate in the act of coming out. It is a cry for approval.

Catholicism and faith constitute another cultural paradigm on which José draws in order to undercut—as Johnson puts it in her article on Hurston—"the absoluteness of the opposition" between gay and straight people (322). Throughout his narration, José confides in God, and especially in the Virgin Mary—the mother of all Mexicans—praying for assistance, and emphasizing that all Christians are worthy of mercy and forgiveness. Later, however, José feels abandoned and enters a phase of guilt and self-incrimination, characteristic of Christian morality:

> Ya la Virgen no me escucha ni me ayuda, creo que me ha olvidado para siempre, quizá por quererte demasiado. (43)

> Ruego a Dios y a la Virgen que te traigan con bien a mi lado...lo pido aunque estoy maldito por el cariño que siento por ti, pero no lo puedo remediar, quizá a la hora de mi muerte pague la culpa de tener un amor que no corresponde a una persona normal. (86)[14]

Moreover, as mentioned earlier, José's narration transcends introspection by addressing itself to Wenceslao. But the protagonist also alludes to a multiplicity of characters who are part of his daily life: his colleagues from work, his family, his friends. The second narration provides a space for the literary and social development of these characters. Each section of text following a diary entry has a title with the names of Wenceslao and the characters present in the particular segment. Interestingly enough, all the straight characters are also wracked by despair because of personal problems. Socorro, José's sister, is expecting a child outside of marriage, and she has to confront her father's anger and society's reprobation; Carrin's wife is having an affair; both Wenceslao's and José's mothers think that they have failed in their marriages and as individuals.

One could indeed, as Foster suggests, read José's behavior, and diagnose it as fitting the economy of "compulsory heterosexuality," to use Wittig's term coined in her work on lesbian sexuality and its representations. However, it is important to emphasize that during the late 1950s, social and literary inscription of homosexuality in Mexico was already a subversive challenge to these institutions. To inscribe homosexuality as a site of difference aiming at different representations of love and pain was most probably viewed by certain authors as too radical. Furthermore, Herdt also reminds us in his work on secrecy that they still had to create a language to express feelings and attitudes that were "unclassifiable." This could be said of Barbachano Ponce's novel. Yet, couldn't Barbachano Ponce have resorted to the notion of commonality, as critics like Johnson suggested in another context, to "disguise, to dissimilate, to resemble rather than contrast," as the idea of "sameness allows for the social and literary inscription of unsameness" (323)? Shouldn't we then reconsider the notion of mimicry?

The fields of psychoanalysis and colonial studies provide us with interesting and innovative ways to conceive the concept of mimicry when dealing with the colonial subject and, by extension, with the problem of identity formation of sexual, cultural, and social minorities. Bhabha's clarification of Lacan's definition of mimicry is particularly relevant to this study. Bhabha writes that "mimicry is like camouflage, not a harmonization or repression of difference but a form of resemblance that differs/defends presence by displacing it in part, metonymically" (131).[15] Doesn't José's diary, and his expression of love and pain, constitute a way of defending its literary and social presence? Bhabha goes on to say that "mimicry is the desire for a reformed, *recognizable other,* as a subject of a difference that is *almost the same, but not quite....* [Yet] the menace of mimicry is its *double* vision which in disclosing the ambivalence [of heterosexual discourse, in the case of our study] also disrupts its authority" (126–29). This elucidation of mimicry allows us to recontextualize and to reassess Barbachano Ponce's work, keeping in mind the challenging question of mimeticism and representation. Mimicry might be construed as representing immanence, negative difference, or normativeness. But it should also be rethought, as Bhabha does, in terms of a device, a strategy that allows us to subvert, to disturb from within textually and socially based representations, and to undermine sexual difference.

José Toledo; or, The Emasculation of the Mexican Gay Male

Barbachano Ponce's inscription of homosexuality opens another complex line of issues. The most polemical one springs from Alvarez's critique that views José's sensibility as a "trope of the female soul in a man's body" (Silverman 339). Before I begin to examine the social implications of this type of critique, I would like to provide essential cultural and historical markers in order for us to understand why the image of strong masculinity within homosexuality has been mainstreamed in Mexican literary narrativization and in its fictional construction of gay characters.

As Monsiváis argues in a recent article on the consequences of the so-called sexual revolution in Mexico, the feminist movements of the 1970s opened the road for dramatic changes in sexual behaviors (174). This led to an increasing participation of women in the social, economic, and political realms, as well as in the legal field, revindicating equality with men. Monsiváis also attributes those changes to the process of secularization, or, as he puts it, the *descatolización* (de-Catholicization) of Mexico (169). In the late 1950s and early 1960s, sexism and moral judgment strongly prevailed. Although since 1917, the Church continually lost political power, the effect of Catholicism on sexuality, and particularly on gay sexuality, still defined, to a great extent, sexual identity formations.

In his review of Cantarella's book on bisexuality in the ancient world, Griffin reminds us that "when Christianity came into power [in Rome], Saint Paul inherited from the Old Testament a complete condemnation of homosexual acts (especially in strong contrast with Greek ideas) of the active partner, who caused defilement and who sowed on stony ground the seed which should have engendered children for the people of Israel" (30). Further, Griffin explains that by the end of the fourth century, "passive homosexuals, rather than active ones, took the brunt of the anger of Christian emperors, because the church wanted to condemn all homosexuals, but compromised in the face of the opposition of traditional pagan society by punishing only the perennial unpopular group [the passive homosexuals]" (30).

In Mexico, as in many other countries dominated by centuries of practicing Catholicism, the hegemony of male order and phallic masculinity, as exemplified by the patriarchal family, remained unchallenged. In her book *Plotting Women,* Franco includes a revealing passage by Ignacio Ramírez, who in 1886 wrote that "all nations owe their fall and ignominity to a woman" (xviii). Indeed, Ramírez could have provided many accounts of this type of historicization of woman. The Christian myth around Eve, who denied humanity the right to a world without pain and suffering, is only one of them. In Mexico, Doña Marina, or the Malinche, is *the* historical person to "fit the bill of the female treachery" as Franco puts it (xviii). Franco adds that Octavio Paz, in his *El laberinto de la soledad* (*Labyrinth of Solitude*; 1950),

> located the "Mexican disease" precisely in this ambiguous subjectivity of the sons of the Malinche who were shamed by her rape (conquest) and thus forced to reject the feminine in themselves as the devalued, the passive, the mauled and battered, as la chingada, the violated, the one that has been screwed over, fucked, and yet is herself the betrayer. (xix)

Samuel Ramos went even further in his *El perfil del hombre y de la cultura en México* (*A Profile of Man and Mexican Culture*; 1934), where he posited:

La obsesión fálica del "pelado" no es comparable a los cultos fálicos, en cuyo fondo yace la idea de la fecundidad y la vida eterna. El falo sugiere al "pelado" la idea del poder. De aquí ha derivado un concepto muy empobrecido del hombre. Como él es, en efecto, un ser sin contenido sustancial, trata de llenar su vacío con el único valor que está a su alcance: el del macho. Este concepto popular del hombre se ha convertido en un prejuicio funesto para todo mexicano. Cuando éste se compara con el hombre civilizado extranjero y resalta su nulidad, se consuela del siguiente modo: "Un europeo — dice — tiene la ciencia, el arte, la técnica, etcétera, aquí no tenemos nada de eso, pero . . . somos muy hombres." (Quoted by Monsiváis, *Escenas de pudor* 105)[16]

Therefore in order to *be* Mexican you have *to be a man*; " 'tener muchos güevos' es el único idioma de la grandeza," adds Monsiváis (104; having balls is the only language for greatness). "To be a man" was considered to be the highest social honor, the epitome of successful social conduct, of social order. Signs of femininity ("fragility, sensibility, refinement") would irremediably void masculinity, for the macho can only be so by reaffirming women's inferiority. "To be a man" even became the essence of Mexicanness, thereby implicitly denying women the right to Mexican national identity. This history might explain the logic behind Alvarez's thinking. Alvarez, who, although responsive to the systematic closeting of gay issues in literature, could write the following about José's representation: "Choosing a ridiculous homosexual, banal, lacking sensibility, spiritual richness, imagination, ingenuity (not to mention talent) . . . is to imply that all homosexuals are the same. . . . [All these characteristics] little by little shape his *feminoid psychology*" (2–3; my emphasis).

Yet, this perception — a feminine, therefore tarnished, image of homosexuality — is rather unsettling if one examines what it implies about the social construction of homosexuality. Again, there is no doubt that heterosexual males — even females — could contain José in the cultural stereotype that tends to negatively associate femininity with homosexuality. Nevertheless, we could also present this novel as an effort to denounce rugged machismo, and to engage in a reconceptualization of the semantically overcharged notion of virility in Mexico.[17] After all, Paz himself wrote that "la frase 'soy tu padre' no tiene ningún sabor paternal, ni se dice para proteger, resguardar o conducir, sino para imponer una superioridad, esto es, para humillar" (73).[18] In countries like Mexico, males tend to consider sexuality between men as an extension of male bonding. Homosexuality should not in any way undermine manliness (*hombría*), and as long as it is not associated with passivity, inertia, and overture, but rather with activity, aggressivness, and closure, homosexuality cannot be dismissed, much less ridiculed (Pérez de Mendiola 9). It is not so much the idea of same-sex desire that Mexican culture questions. It is the idea that men could actually degrade themselves by acknowledging femininity within their homosexuality, forcing them to cross the boundaries between genders and collapse gender divisions. Alvarez's critique of José's deviant masculinity suggests that Barbachano Ponce might have written a homophobic novel, since he could not transcend the cultural stereotype based on this trope of inversion (woman's soul enclosed in a man's body), a true reflection of traditional homophobic Mexican attitudes. For Alvarez, José's femininity takes away from himself, and by extension from the homosexual community at large, the most legitimate part of themselves, their masculinity. By doing so, the feminine prohibits any acting out of masculine roles, the essence of manliness/Mexicanness.

It seems to me that Barbachano Ponce's representation of José could be read differently. We could see this composition as a way to debunk another deeply entrenched cultural stereotype in Mexico: the one that insidiously posits as a norm that male same-sex desire can only be conceived within the parameters of masculinity, and that impedes, if not violently condemns, homosexuals who acknowledge and wish to act out their femininity. According to this perspective, we understand this novel as a process of unlearning assumptions, "as a subversive alignment with femininity" (Silverman 343). It also presents a way to eschew conventional masculinity by offering other paradigms of sexual identity. Furthermore, Silverman cogently suggests that "we must entertain the possibility that a gay man might deploy signifiers of femininity not only because to do so is to generate a counterdiscourse, but because an identification with 'woman' constitutes the very basis of his identity, and/or the position from which he

desires" (344). While Barbachano Ponce's inscription of homosexual desire could be construed as a sign of homophobia, Alvarez's critique can in turn be interpreted as emerging from a
profound misogynistic position.

Despite the book's apparent straightforwardness and the seemingly facile reaffirmation of a prejudicial cultural stereotype, Barbachano Ponce questions the traditional stability of these norms
pointing to the unreconciled ambivalence in Mexican culture between femininity and masculinity, heterosexuality and homosexuality. This novel, and the diary sections in particular, function
as the thetic that Kristeva defines as

> that crucial space on the basis of which the human being
> constitutes himself as signifying and/or social. . . . It is the
> very place textual experience aims toward. In this sense,
> textual experience represents one of the most daring
> explorations the subject can allow himself, one that delves
> into the constitutive process. But at the same time and as a
> result, textual experience reaches the very foundation of
> the social . . . that which is exploited by sociality but which
> elaborates and can go beyond it, while distorting and
> transforming it. (67)

José loses his diary on the 27th of October, 1958. One month later
at the age of twenty, on November 20, he commits defenestra-
tion. Many things could explain such an act: the loss of the diary
that provided him emotional release, the possibility that everybody might actually learn the contents of the diary; the hopeless-
ness of ever being able to share his love with Wenceslao; and,
ultimately, the social negation of the position from which he desires. The act of suicide clearly speaks of José's desperation. However, death does not only chastise José's act of transgression. We
know that his death predates the second narration, the one the
author acknowledges as his. The publication of the book as two
supplements supplementing each other and the challenging inscription of homosexuality as nonphallic masculinity made Barbachano Ponce, in the eyes of the literary community and of society, doubly complicitous with José. This induces another kind
of suicide, the professional suicide of Barbachano Ponce, who,
after publishing his novel at his own expense, had to withdraw

and was excluded from the literary scene for more than twenty years. This certainly delayed the coming out of gay and lesbian characters as well as their "coming in" to the history of Mexican literature.

Notes

1. I am grateful to Panivong Norindr and Robin Pickering-Iazzi for their valuable comments on earlier versions of this article. The first march of a gay and lesbian group took place on July 26, 1978, in Mexico City during the commemoration of the 1968 student movement.

2. For a history of Semana Cultural Gay, see Galindo, "Cultura artística y homosexualidad." Galindo is a cultural critic specializing in visual arts, and he was one of the first to denounce the censorship surrounding the Semana Cultural Gay in 1989; see his "Censura en el Museo del Chopa" and "Reseña de una censura negada."

3. *Latin American Writers on Gay and Lesbian Themes,* edited by David William Foster (Greenwood Press, 1994), offers a good number of entries on Mexican literature.

4. For an analysis of the genre and its conventions see Martens, *The Diary Novel;* Abbott, *Diary Fiction;* and Field, *Form and Function in the Diary Novel.*

5. Wenceslao strolled along narrow side streets without exit, streets whose stone edges were grazed by green and tainted water. The mere thought of falling in it disgusted him. He wanted to flee from there. . . . Yet he found himself wandering again along narrow alleys. While trying to avoid the stinking puddle, he slipped, falling into its slimy center. What once was a quagmire became an ocean of glaucous and stagnant water.

6. See Assouline, "L'Homosexualité est-elle un atout littéraire?" and his "Entretien avec Roger Stéphane."

7. A diary so real, so incredibly real, that it becomes unreadable, aliterary.

8. At the same time, the concept of substitution, intrinsic to the Derridean definition of supplementarity, also leads us to read the second text as a product of sublimation (I use the definition of sublimation provided by Laplanche and Pontalis 431–33). This narration can be perceived as part of the artistic creation that Mexican society at that time held in "high esteem," while at the same time providing a space where the artist could sublimate what he and his readers most repressed: literary, social, and sexual marginality.

9. As usual, I got up early, waiting, as every morning, for your phone call. Monday, another sad day for me. . . .

10. I am indebted to Gilbert Herdt for his enticing analysis of the complex relationship between public, private, and secret that he recently presented at the Center for Twentieth Century Studies at Milwaukee in a paper entitled "Public, Private, and Secret: Secrecy and Individual Rights in Society."

11. The semantically charged verb "to confess" requires on my part an explanation about how I use it. The fact that I link the notion of privacy with the act of confessing is undoubtedly due to my Catholic upbringing. What comes first to

mind is the presence of a priest receiving a confession, a priest in whom one confides and who is bound by "professional secrecy." However, to use this verb in the context of this work has its dangers. In most dictionaries, to confess is "to tell or make known (as something wrong or damaging to oneself), to admit; to acknowledge (sin to God), to disclose one's faults" (*Webster's*). The notion of wrongdoing and of sin, usually implied in the act of confessing, opens the door to a facile equation between José's confession and an admission of guilt. Yet, when referring to José's confession, I see a man expressing himself willfully about his acts, ideas, and feelings. He is not confessing blamable acts, "murmuring low into priestly ears" (to use Gide's formulation). He is not admitting something he is ashamed of. He just wishes to come out. Yet, I am aware of the fact that his coming out will always be construed as an evidence of guilt by those who already consider his "secret" a sin.

12. In an article on José Joaquín Blanco's *Las púberes canéforas* (The Pubescent Maidens; 1983), I note that in this novel homosexual intercourse does not define the characters' sexual identity if the person engages in sexual activity in exchange for monetary or other types of material gain. In *El diario de José Toledo*, this is equally true. Wenceslao's parents are aware of their son's relationship with José. Although they opposed it, they tolerate it because of the financial help José gives to Wenceslao.

13. I fell asleep kissing the bracelet and the medal my husband gave me the day we decided to unite forever.

14. The Virgin Mary does not listen to me any longer, nor does she help me; I think she has forgotten me forever.... I plead God and the Virgin for your return.... I plead although my love for you has damned me. But I cannot remedy it, and perhaps, when death comes, I will have to pay for I am guilty of a love that does not correspond to the love of a normal person.

15. Bhabha's article begins with an epigraph gleaned from Lacan's *Four Fundamental Concepts of Psycho-Analysis*: "Mimicry reveals something in so far as it is distinct from what might be called an itself that is behind. The effect of mimicry is camouflage.... It is not a question of harmonizing with the background, but against a mottled background, of becoming mottled — exactly like the technique of camouflage practiced in human warfare" (99).

16. The phallic obsession of the *pelado* does not bear comparison with phallic cults, which are based on the idea of fecundity and eternal life. The phallus suggests to the *pelado* the idea of power. This gave rise to a very impoverished definition of manhood. Since the *pelado* is a shallow human being, he strives to fill his void with the only valor within his reach: the bravery of the macho. This popular definition of man has become a fatal prejudice for every Mexican. When compared with the foreign and civilized man, which reveals his "nonexistence" or insignificance, the Mexican consoles himself in the following way: "A European — he says — has science, art, technology, and so on; we have nothing of that sort here, but ... we are real men."

17. As I mention elsewhere, as early as the fifties, many of Barbachano Ponce's plays and their themes questioned the social configuration of gender relations, the hegemony of heterosexual epistemology. He was also a precursor of bringing together two tropes of difference, race and homosexuality, in contemporary Mexican letters.

18. The sentence "I am your father" does not have a paternal flavor, nor is it uttered to protect, to shield or drive; rather, it wishes to impose a superiority in order to humiliate.

Works Cited

Abbott, Porter H. *Diary Fiction: Writing as Action.* Ithaca: Cornell University Press, 1984.

Alvarez, Federico. "José Toledo contra Miguel Barbachano Ponce." *La cultura en México, Siempre* 136 (septiembre 23, 1964): xvi–xvii.

Assouline, Pierre. "L'Homosexualité est-elle un atout littéraire?" *Lire* 206 (novembre 1992): 18–23.

———. "Entretien avec Roger Stéphane." *Lire* 206 (novembre 1992): 18–23.

Barbachano Ponce, Miguel. *El diario de José Toledo.* Mexico: Premiá, 1988.

Bhabha, Homi. "Of Mimicry and Man: the Ambivalence of Colonial Discourse." *October* 28 (spring 1984): 125–33.

Derrida, Jacques. *Of Grammatology.* Trans. Gayatri Chakravorty Spivak. Baltimore: The Johns Hopkins University Press, 1976.

Field, Trevor. *Form and Function in the Diary Novel.* London: Macmillan, 1989.

Foster, David William. *Gay and Lesbian Themes in Latin American Writing.* Austin: University of Texas Press, 1991.

Galindo, Carlos Blas. "Censura en el Museo del Chopa." *El financiero,* 14 de junio de 1989, 79.

———. "Cultura artística y homosexualidad." *Ex profeso: Recuento de afinidades.* Mexico: Círculo Gay, 1990, 16–21.

———. "Reseña de una censura negada." *El financiero,* 20 de junio de 1987, 27.

Gates, Henry Louis, ed. *Race, Writing, and Difference.* Chicago: University of Chicago Press, 1985.

Griffin, Jasper. "The Love that Dared to Speak its Name." *The New York Review of Books,* October 22, 1992, 30–33.

Johnson, Barbara. "Threshold of Difference: Structures of Address in Zora Neale Hurston." In *Race, Writing, and Difference.* Ed. Henry Louis Gates. Chicago: University of Chicago Press, 1985, 317–29.

Kristeva, Julia. *Revolution in Poetic Language.* Trans. Margaret Walk. New York: Columbia University Press, 1984.

Lacan, Jacques. *The Four Fundamental Concepts of Psycho-Analysis.* Trans. Alan Sheridan. New York: Norton, 1981.

Laplanche Jean, Pontalis J. B. *The Language of Psycho-Analysis.* Trans. Donald Nicholson-Smith. New York: Norton, 1973.

Martens, Lorna. *The Diary Novel.* New York: Cambridge University Press, 1985.

Matthews, Tede. "Bienvenidos a Jotolandia." *Out Look: National Lesbian and Gay Quarterly* 15 (winter 1992): 56–61.

Monsiváis, Carlos. *Escenas de pudor y liviandad.* Mexico: Grijalbo, 1988.

———. "Paisaje de batalla entre condones." In *El nuevo arte de amar.* Mexico: Cal y Arena, 1990, 167–77.

Pérez de Mendiola, Marina. *"Las púberes canéforas* de José Joaquín Blanco y la inscripción de la identidad sexual." *Inti: revista de literatura hispánica* 39 (spring 1994): 135–53.

Poniatowska, Elena. *¡Ay vida no me mereces!* Mexico: Joaquín Mortiz, 1991.

Schneider, Luis Mario. "El tema homosexual en la nueva narrativa mexicana." *Casa del tiempo* 49–50 (1985): 82–86.

Sedgwick, Eve. *Epistemology of the Closet.* Berkeley: University of California Press, 1990.

Silverman, Kaja. *Male Subjectivity at the Margins.* New York: Routledge, 1992.

Chapter 9

Camilo's Closet: Sexual Camouflage in Denevi's *Rosaura a las diez*

Herbert J. Brant

Marco Denevi is one of Argentina's most influential and important prose writers. One of the most distinctive features of his writing is the creation of a situation in which a presumed truth has been concealed with a mask. Consequently, in Denevi's work there always seems to be an uneasy tension, a nagging suspicion that something is definitely not what it appears to be. As the reader proceeds through the narration, the numerous false facades that hide the unexpected and sometimes shocking truth lying underneath are slowly chipped away. Denevi's numerous *informes* (reports), *vindicaciones* (vindications), and *versiones* (versions) of people, historical events, literary characters, and Western beliefs consistently reveal Denevi's conviction that truth is covered by a superficial veneer, suggesting that layer after layer of built-up illusion and falsification have completely obscured reality. Denevi's mission, it seems, is the work of stripping away all the falseness in order to get down to the glaring truth, however pleasant or unpleasant that might be. Consequently, Denevi's writing shows a marked tendency for the ironic surprise ending: the narration leads the reader on, very carefully setting up a specific set of expectations, only to violate them suddenly in the end by revealing unexpected pieces of information. This surprising alteration of the appearances that earlier had been taken for granted provides the reader with a flash of revelation that forces a reappraisal of every detail that had come before. One could say, then, that Denevi's work is the "outing" of a truth that, for whatever reason, had been closeted, so to speak, by a series of falsifications.

A related aspect of Denevi's fiction is the painstakingly detailed creation of a character's personal identity that later is exposed to be something completely different. This feature is manifested frequently in characters who pretend to be something or someone they are not: Leonides Arrufat in *Ceremonia secreta* (*Secret Ceremony*; 1961) allows herself to play the part of a disturbed young girl's dead mother, and Adalberto Pascumo in *Un pequeño café* (A Small Café; 1966) assumes the role of an office executive when he is, in fact, merely a file clerk.

But it is in Denevi's best-known novel, *Rosaura a las diez* (*Rosa at Ten o'Clock*; 1955), that the masking of characters is most complex and satisfying. This complexity of character, along with other sophisticated narrative elements, makes the novel not only an elegant work of fiction, but also an enormously popular one. Evidence of its popularity are a rather successful adaptation of the novel to film and, perhaps more important, an American student edition of the text. The student edition of *Rosaura a las diez* makes it one of the most widely read Latin American novels. In spite of the novel's popularity, it seems that one particular feature of the main character's identity has gone unperceived and unnoticed by readers and critics. Because the narration deliberately creates a confusion regarding the identity and existence of Rosaura, the reader is made to focus attention on her. While the reader is busy piecing together all the clues surrounding Rosaura, the mystery of Camilo Canegato's identity as a closeted homosexual goes unexamined. The purpose of this study, then, is to investigate the results of an invisible, veiled, and oppressed sexuality that forms the central motivating factor in *Rosaura a las diez*.

Rosaura a las diez, like most detective fiction, is a novel that presents the reader with a false view of reality throughout the bulk of the work, only to expose the falseness and reveal the truth in the final few pages. The novel, therefore, proceeds on two levels. The first, the mystery level, as Lichtblau has indicated, is the story told in five parts, each with its own particular narrative point of view, thereby presenting the reader with an incomplete, partial, and lopsided impression of the story. The second level, underlying the first, is the truth, unknown to the reader until the end of the novel. The testimonies of the different narrator-characters that make up the first-level narrative come as the result of a police inquiry into the death of a woman named Rosaura. Each of the narrator-characters living at the boarding house La Madrileña adds a few more pieces to the puzzle that surrounds the identity of Rosaura. The different narrators tell the story of one of their fellow boarders, a quiet, self-effacing portrait painter and painting restorer named Camilo Canegato, who falls in love with the very mysterious and beautiful Rosaura. Camilo and Rosaura eventually get married, but on their wedding night Rosaura is found murdered, and Camilo, naturally, is the most likely suspect. The novel progresses with each of the narrative segments revealing information known only to certain characters and culminating in the resolution of the mystery surrounding the identity of Rosaura, her relationship to Camilo Canegato, and her murder.

When discussing this novel, most critics have concentrated on the way in which the text conceals and reveals the mysterious identity of Rosaura, the woman who is real, but at the same time, unreal. The final pages of the novel disclose the secret of Rosaura: she is a former prostitute whose real name is María Correa (aka Marta Córrega), and Camilo Canegato has used her as a prop to play the part of the imaginary lover he has told all his fellow boarders about. Because Camilo is such a painfully shy and lonely man, he invents a girlfriend: "Otros sueñan que son millonarios. Yo soñé que una mujer me amaba" (*Obras completas* 1.265).[1] The reader later discovers that the personality and life story of Rosaura are only a fiction elaborated in the mind of Camilo, and that to provide visual proof of her existence for the others, he has used a picture of the real María Correa, without her knowledge. María, it turns out, is the daughter of a woman who had done Camilo's laundry. For a little extra income, María's mother arranges with Camilo to use her as a prostitute, enticing him with her photograph. Camilo visits her regularly for a time, but when María suddenly disappears, he is told that she has died. Assuming that he will never see her again, Camilo decides to use her picture as the basis for a painted portrait. Unfortunately for Camilo, he does not know that María is, in fact, not dead; she has merely gone to prison. When she gets out, she again is forced to depend on prostitution for survival. Desperate to escape her abusive pimp, El Turco Estropeado (Slit Turk), María finally remembers the only person who might be able to provide her with a safe haven: that odd man her mother used to do laundry for, Camilo Canegato. She finds his address, and when she arrives at the boarding house, much to her surprise, everyone in the house acts as if they know her and are perfectly delighted to see her. They call her Rosaura and are ready to cater to her every need. When faced with the choice between returning to her pimp, and pretending to be a person named Rosaura inside a very protected environment, María agrees to keep Camilo's secret, playing along that she really is the tragic heiress Rosaura. Despite a mutual loathing from the days when Camilo used María as a prostitute, the momentum of their charade and the emotional investment of the boarders in their romance propel María and Camilo into a real wedding. Immediately after the marriage ceremony, María and Camilo unknowingly check into a hotel owned by El Turco, who, in an act of revenge, murders María.[2]

As it turns out, everything that the reader has learned about Rosaura's entire existence — her past, present, and future — all are the products of Camilo's mind. He invents her, he molds her and breathes life into her. But why? Why does Camilo need to create an *imaginary* woman to love, rather than going out and meeting real flesh-and-blood women? What is the particular value for him of a woman who (he thinks) has no material reality and who exists solely in his imagination, inaccessible to the scrutiny of others? It seems that mere loneliness[3] really cannot account for his strange need to fabricate a lover. There must be something peculiar, something "queer" about Camilo that forces him into an affair with a woman that doesn't exist. For me, the mystery of Rosaura's identity is best understood as the result of the societal exigencies on the main character, Camilo Canegato, to disguise his private homosexual orientation[4] with the grand display of a public (heterosexual) identity. In short, the enigma of *Rosaura a las diez* really revolves around how Camilo carefully builds a closet and the disastrous consequences that result from such a construction. The closet, as Eve Kosofsky Sedgwick has so brilliantly analyzed, becomes the centralizing location for the secrecy and obscurity surrounding a gay man's identity, the withholding and masking of information: "The *special* centrality of homophobic oppression in the twentieth century . . . has resulted from its inextricability from the question of knowledge and the processes of knowing in modern Western culture at large" (33–34). It is this process of concealing, revealing, and ultimately knowing that produces the mystery of Rosaura. Camilo Canegato is the central axis around which the entire narration turns. The reader first meets Camilo through the narration and perspective of Sra. Milagros Ramoneda de Perales, the owner of the modest but self-reputedly respectable boarding house where Camilo comes to live. Sra. Perales's first impression of him is somewhat favorable, but she notices something odd about Camilo:

> Calzaba unos tremendos zapatos, los zapatos más estrambóticos que he visto yo en mi vida, color ladrillo, con aplicaciones de gamuza negra, y unas suelas de goma . . . Así querrá él aumentarse la estatura, pero lo que conseguía era tomar ese aspecto ridículo del hombre calzado con tacos altos, como dicen que iban los duques y los marqueses en otros tiempos, cuando entre tanto lazo y tanta peluca y tanta media de seda y encajes y plumas, todos parecían mujeres, y, como yo digo, para saber quién era hombre, harían como hacían en mi pueblo con los chiquillos que por los carnavales se disfrazaban de mujer. (*OC* 1.43)[5]

In this passage, Sra. Perales suggests that Camilo's outward appearance is a mask—drag—calling into question his sexual orientation. The initial presentation of Camilo in the novel immediately throws doubt on the character's identity as a male, thus creating in the reader a nagging uncertainty about Camilo's sexuality.[6]

Sra. Perales goes on to describe Camilo as well behaved, quiet, but above all, exceptionally shy and timid. When he first moves into her house, he cannot look people in the eye and immediately blushes when spoken to. His shyness around women, however, is particularly intense. As Sra. Perales describes it, "Su timidez, especialmente con las mujeres, era casi una *enfermedad*. Recuerdo que tenía yo una pensionista, mujer de rompe y rasga, artista de teatro. La Chelo, le decían. ¡Ay, Jesús! El terror que infundía en Camilo la sola presencia de La Chelo es cosa de no creerlo" (*OC* 1.58; emphasis added).[7] Camilo's terror around women, especially those whose sexuality is prominent (as suggested by her profession and her nickname that emphasizes a shapely figure) implies that real women, women of flesh, repel him. This same repulsion is repeated in a conversation between Camilo and Sra. Perales:

> —Don Canegato, lo que usted necesita es casarse.
> —¿Casarme? ¿Casarme?—repetía, mirándome todo
> *azorado, como si yo le propusiese alguna inmoralidad.*
> —Sí señor, casarse, que es, si no me equivoco, lo que hacen
> los solteros. (*OC* 1.61; emphasis added)[8]

At first, because of Camilo's lack of contact with the opposite sex, it is supposed that he has no sexuality of any kind. As time passes, and Sra. Perales's three daughters develop into adolescent girls, Camilo, who has never shown any sexual interest in women, goes through a series of identity changes in the house: "Y él, que antes había sido como un hermano mayor, después fue como un tío soltero de todas ellas, o como el padrino de un lejano bautismo ya olvidado" (*OC* 1.63).[9] Camilo's presence as an adult male has never been viewed in sexual terms, and now that the girls are maturing, Camilo's role must be altered in order to adapt to changes in them. Camilo has now acquired the honorary title of "bachelor uncle," which, as is quite well known, a common euphemism for a middle-aged man who does not seem to possess any sexuality, at least not a putatively normal one, because he does not appear to conform to society's heterosexist standard.

Once Sra. Perales has brought Camilo's status out into the open as an unmarried adult male in a house full of young adolescent girls, letters suddenly start to arrive for him. They are written on perfumed pink paper with "una letra redondita, pequeñita, prolija. Vamos, una letra de mujer" (*OC* 1.65).[10] Considering Camilo's isolation from appropriately available women, and his almost pathological shyness, news of the letters spreads throughout the boarding house, with the boarders inventing a multiplicity of theories to explain Camilo's sudden contact with women. The writer of the letters, the person with the woman's handwriting, is, of course, Camilo himself writing under the delightfully suggestive name Rosaura. The letters will provide Camilo with cover, camouflage, the deceptive masquerade of a (hetero)sexual relationship. The strategy of using forgery for deceptive purposes is nothing new for Camilo. The reader discovers later, during Camilo's interrogation by the police, that his aptitude for outright fakery and deceit is very well developed. His profession as an oil painting restorer is complemented by his ability to *forge* the work of other painters, imitating their style: "Yo me especializo en la escuela inglesa. Tenía un cliente que era loco por Reynolds. Me entregó quince fotografías de otros tantos familiares, para que yo se las convirtiese en quince retratos al estilo de Reynolds. Quedó muy satisfecho y me pagó bien... Imitar, je, je, imitar no es difícil" (*OC* 1.251).[11] Like the letters, Camilo's painting is not dedicated to the expression of his own interior reality, but rather to the imitation of an exterior, *other* reality. So, too, his sexuality becomes the public imitation of an extrinsic model, on display like a painting, rather than the manifestation of his own innate desires.

In order for the forged letters to serve their special purpose, their contents must become public knowledge. So just in case Sra. Perales isn't sneaking into his room to read the letters — and indeed she is! — Camilo sends a letter to the boarding house without an addressee, without his own name, thereby making it the property of the house itself, or rather Sra. Perales, its owner, with the result that its message will become known to everyone in the house.

Once the affair has circulated among the boarders and they have discovered that Camilo's sexual activities fall into the societally approved, normal category, the painter creates what might seem to be the perfect reason — or excuse — to put an end to the affair and to put the charade to rest. Camilo invents the story of Rosaura's cruel and brutal father who promises her to another, more suitable man, thereby making it impossible for Rosaura and Camilo to marry, much less to see each other ever again. This use of an angry and threatening father figure seems to display unmistakably classic Freudian undertones. Part of Freud's oedipal theory posits that "fear of a father is set up because, in the very earliest years, he opposes a boy's sexual activities" (190). Closely related to the fear of Rosaura's father is Camilo's apparent feeling of persecution. Notable, too, is Freud's conclusion that *"paranoia persecutoria* is the form of the disease in which a person is defending himself against a homosexual impulse which has become too powerful" (424). In other words, Camilo's explanation for the tragic and sudden ending to his affair with Rosaura serves not only to release him from the pressures of the deceitful tale of romance, but also to reveal, consciously or unconsciously, his erotic attraction to men. At this point, with the insurmountable opposition of Rosaura's father, it seems that Camilo can finally breathe a sigh of relief from the pressure of having to keep up the appearances required by the fictional account that marks his entry into the world of "compulsory heterosexuality." He has fulfilled his obligations to the societal demands that he publicly conform to the one and only acceptable sexual behavior.

Unfortunately for Camilo, though, the charade does not come to an end as neatly as he had hoped and planned. Due to the fact that Camilo has actively encouraged a sense of ownership of the romance between him and Rosaura, the boarders, especially Sra. Perales, will not permit him simply to give her up. In order to goad him into action, Sra. Perales again calls Camilo's manliness and sexual orientation into question when she insists that he "fight like a *man*" for Rosaura instead of collapsing under the brutal demands of the father: "¿Y usted lo va a permitir? *¿Y usted es hombre?* ¿Pero qué clase de amor es el suyo, que se amilana a la primera dificultad?" (*OC* 1.145; emphasis added).[12] Sra. Perales's humiliation tactics, however, do not have time to take effect. Camilo's masquerade takes an unexpected turn: while everyone in the boarding house is having dinner, Rosaura (María) suddenly appears at the front door. With Rosaura's arrival, Camilo finds himself hopelessly trapped inside the fiction he has created to give himself a public heterosexual identity. He is forced to keep up the deceit all the way to the altar and the honeymoon bed, with tragic results.

One of the boarders, David Réguel, however, is not convinced in the slightest of any seriousness in the relationship between Camilo and Rosaura; he sees right through Camilo's pretense. Is there something special about David that provides him with such insight into and understanding of Camilo's situation? The first clue comes when Camilo insists that Sra. Perales not let David know about his supposed affair with Rosaura (*OC* 1.120). It is not clear exactly why Camilo should object to David's having that knowledge, since everything Camilo has done up to this point is calculated precisely to make his affair with Rosaura as widely known by the boarders in the house as he possibly can.

The most important clues to David's ability to perceive the deceit in Camilo's affair are contained in his testimony to the police. The title of this section of the novel is called "David canta su salmo" (David Sings His Psalm). The reference to the biblical psalmist might seem gratuitous at first glance, but for me such an allusion also makes a veiled reference to David's intimate relationship with Jonathan: "Then said Jonathan unto David, Whatsoever thy soul desireth, I will even do it for thee" (I Sam. 20:4); "And Jonathan caused David to swear again, because he loved him: for he loved him as he loved his own soul" (I Sam. 20:17); "I am distressed for thee, my brother Jonathan: very pleasant hast thou been unto me: thy love to me was wonderful, passing the love of women" (II Sam. 1:26). By means of the title of David's testimony and the information within it, Denevi has set up a very strong doubt in the mind of the reader with regard to David Réguel's sexuality and his relationship to Camilo Canegato. If the two men were indeed involved emotionally or physically, the presence of Rosaura and the attention paid to her would certainly place a heavy strain on their relationship.

The strain becomes clear on three separate occasions when Sra. Perales mentions that David is trying to make Camilo *jealous*. But of what or of whom? Is Camilo supposed to be jealous of Rosaura or of David? In the first instance, when everyone sees the portrait of Rosaura for the first time, Sra. Perales tells the reader that David insists that he has actually seen this person named Rosaura. Naturally, Camilo is terrified and Sra. Perales concludes that David is only saying that he knows her in order "clavarle una banderilla y darle celos y hacerlo sufrir" (*OC* 1.129).[13] Translated literally, however, Sra. Perales is asserting that David was saying that he knew Rosaura in order to "stab him [Camilo] with a banderilla" (the brightly colored spears used by matadors in the bullring). Her statement is odd considering that it has never been revealed why David would be angry enough to wound Camilo intentionally and maliciously — unless there were some reason that only the two of them knew. The symbolic implications of this phrase — the imagery of David wanting to penetrate Camilo with an unmistakably phallic instrument — only reinforces the notion that there is a sexual link between the two men.

Later on, when Rosaura moves into the boarding house, Sra. Perales observes David Réguel shamelessly fawning over Rosaura despite the fact that Rosaura is engaged to Camilo. Strangely enough, this unusual behavior does not seem to have any visible effect on Camilo: "En Camilo tampoco noté nada raro. Celoso, desde luego, y ya se imaginará usted de quién" (OC 1.175).[14] Sra. Perales's phrase is playfully ambiguous here, leaving the reader to wonder whether Camilo is jealous of Rosaura or of David. It does appear quite obvious, however, that David's highly exaggerated and theatrical performance could not possibly be considered a serious attempt at seducing Rosaura. The fact that David is making such a blatant public display indicates that he is less concerned with attracting Rosaura than he is with letting everyone see his interest in someone of the opposite sex, especially the person who is supposedly engaged to Camilo, while at the same time inflicting an emotional wound on Camilo.

The final instance when Sra. Perales declares that Camilo must have been jealous comes when Camilo and Rosaura have a loud screaming fight. David comes into the room to comfort Rosaura and he then proceeds to insult Camilo. Again, with her characteristic, deliberate imprecision, Sra. Perales tells her interlocutor and the reader: "saque usted de esto las deducciones y las consecuencias que más le gusten. Yo me reservo las mías. Y digan después que Camilo no tenía razón de estar celoso" (OC 1.177).[15] It seems likely that Sra. Perales, not understanding the nature of the relationship either between Camilo and Rosaura or between Camilo and David, makes the mistaken assumption that it must be Camilo who is jealous. On the contrary, what Sra. Perales describes demonstrates that the jealousy is emanating from David. Seeing the object of his desire, Camilo, continuing his relationship with Rosaura, David tries desperately, in more and more intrusive ways, to sabotage the seemingly inevitable wedding between Rosaura and Camilo.

With jealousy and a sense of betrayal as primary motives, David's statement to the police can be viewed from a perspective that casts doubt not only on the two men's sexuality and their relationship to each other, but also on the veracity of David's view of the incidents leading up to Rosaura's murder and his psychological analysis of Camilo. David makes it clear from the very beginning of his narration that he believes reality to have a false front and that he is able to discern the truth behind the disguise: "yo soy de aquellos que no ignoran que la realidad tiene dos caras, qué, dos caras, veinte caras, cien caras, y que la cara que más a menudo nos muestra es falsa y hay que saber buscarle la verdadera" (*OC* 1.190).[16] David views his goal, then, as the exposing — the outing — of Camilo Canegato's true nature for all the world to see: he is "un biombo, un biombo de simulación, de mimetismo, pero yo le quitaré para ustedes esa pantalla y ustedes lo verán tal cual es.... No es un hombre. Es la *maquette* de un hombre, la muestra gratis" (*OC* 1.190).[17] And David knows what he's talking about: like himself, Camilo is forced to live a life composed of deceptive appearances and false facades that hide his own authentic identity. As a homosexual trying to survive in a threatening and unsympathetic society, Camilo ceases to exist as a "real man" and is forced to convert himself into an artificial creature by the requirements of the closet and its "excruciating system of double binds" (Sedgwick 70).

Camilo Canegato's forced deception, the creation of a heterosexual partner, has very tragic consequences. First is the betrayal of Camilo's identity and dignity as a human being. Camilo is spiritually and emotionally murdered by a heterosexist system of oppression from which there is no escape. Camilo's chronic timidity and shyness, the result of an overwhelming sense of fear of other people, his inability to function on more than a mere subsistence level of existence, and his crushing self-effacement condemn him to a perpetual state of self-murder.

In *Rosaura a las diez*, Camilo Canegato lives a miserable, depressing, and hopeless life because the patriarchal, homophobic society in which he lives forces him to submit to a narrowly defined model of human sexual behavior. With such pressure to conform to a norm that does not permit any diversity or authenticity, he is compelled to conceal his own essential nature as a homosexual and, as a consequence, create a falsified self-identity. The dishonesty and deception take on a life of their own, multiplying, growing out of control, until the power of their falseness annihilates his own sense of self. Camilo's falsified self-identity represents the ultimate dangers and degradations of the closet. For Camilo, the closet is not a place of refuge and security that safeguards him from the inquisitive and punishing scrutiny of society's enforcers of sexual orthodoxy; it is, instead, a prison cell, a cage that neatly binds and restricts him for easy persecution. Because creating and accepting a closet is tantamount to creating and accepting one's own victimization by an oppressive and unjust force, the closet destroys, rather than protects. As Richard D. Mohr so eloquently asserts: "Life in the closet is morally debased — and morally debasing. It frequently requires lying, but it always requires much more. . . . The life as lie chiefly entails a devolution of the person as person, as moral agent. The whiteness of the individual lies might be forgiven as self-defense, but the dirtiness of the secret that the lies maintain cannot be. The dirt is the loss of self, of personhood, the loss of that which makes human life peculiarly worth protecting to begin with" (32).

Notes

1. "Other men dream about becoming millionaires. I dreamed that a woman loved me" (160). The Spanish text I am using is from the first volume of Denevi's *Obras completas*, abbreviated as *OC*. All quotations in English are from Donald A. Yates's translation, indicated by the abbreviation *Rosa*.

2. The murder of Rosaura/María is very troublesome. On one hand, the death of Rosaura as Camilo's fake heterosexual partner is the inevitable result of the exposing of his deception. I imagine that throughout history there have been countless such invented heterosexual companions who have come into existence solely to satisfy the societal coercion of gay men into what have been considered acceptable sexual relationships. And I imagine, too, that all of these characters have dissolved or disappeared once their falseness has been exposed. On the other hand, the death of the flesh-and-blood María Correa is horribly cruel and opens up a variety of issues that demand a detailed and in-depth feminist critique that is not possible here.

3. I must differ with Ricardo Enrique Monaco's view that Camilo's loneliness is of the general existential variety. Camilo himself makes it clear that what he most longs for is *male* camaraderie. His isolation from male affection is most acute when sitting in the bar Los Tres Amigos: "En aquel salón bullicioso y turbio, donde los hombres profesaban el rito secreto y potente de la amistad, en medio de aquellos grupos que fumaban y conversaban y se llamaban y reían y

jugaban, yo me sentía tan solo y tan triste . . . ¡Me hubiera gustado tanto que alguien apareciese en la puerta del bar, me saludase desde lejos, cruzara entre las mesas y viniera a sentarse frente a mí!" (*OC* 1.254; "In that noisy and bustling room, where men professed the secret and powerful ritual of friendship, in the midst of those groups of people who smoked and talked and called to one another and laughed and gambled, I felt completely alone and sad. . . . I wanted so much for someone to appear at the door of the bar and greet me, and then come through the maze of tables and sit down opposite me!" [*Rosa* 152]).

4. Some may reject my assertion of Camilo's homosexuality, citing his use of María Correa as a prostitute. Paying a prostitute for a sexual climax can hardly be considered firm proof of a heterosexual identity. At a time when gay sex was considered blasphemous, immoral, and sick, prostitutes were frequently the only sexual outlet for many gay men who could not or would not dare to engage in a sexual encounter with another man.

5. He was wearing a pair of huge shoes, the most outlandish shoes I've ever seen in my life, rust-colored, with chamois trim, and rubber soles so thick that it looked as if the little fellow had walked on wet cement and it had stuck to the bottom of his shoes. He wanted to increase his height this way, but all he managed to do was to take on the ridiculous appearance of a man wearing high heels, as they say dukes and marquises used to do in olden times, when, with all those bows and wigs and silk stockings, they all looked like women; in order to find out which was a man, they must have done what they did in my home town with the boys who dressed up as women during carnival time. (*Rosa* 8)

6. The fact that Camilo appears to possess a male as well as a female aspect to his appearance, a "conjunction of opposites," is reinforced by his surname, Canegato, which means "dog-and-cat."

7. "His shyness, especially with women, was almost *chronic*. I remember I used to have a boarder, a woman to be wary of, who was a stage performer. La Chelo, they called her. Lord! You wouldn't believe the terror that just her presence would inspire in Camilo" (*Rosa* 17; emphasis added). It is interesting to note that Yates's translation has "chronic" where the original Spanish has the word *enfermedad* (sickness). I believe that Denevi's original wording is intentionally indicating something more deep-seated in Camilo than mere timidity. Shyness was never considered an illness by the American Psychiatric Association (APA), but homosexuality was. Only in 1973 did the APA remove "ego-dystonic homosexuality" from its *Diagnostic and Statistical Manual of Mental Disorders*.

8. On other occasions, I would say, "Mr. Canegato, what you need is to get married."

"Get married? Married?" he would repeat, gazing at me in *horror as if I had suggested something immoral*.

"Yes, sir, get married — which, if I'm not mistaken, is what bachelors often do." (*Rosa* 20; emphasis added)

9. "And he, who once had been their older brother, now became a bachelor uncle to all of them, or maybe more like the godfather of a distant, now-forgotten baptism" (*Rosa* 21).

10. the small, round, fastidious script of a woman. (*Rosa* 22)

11. I'm a specialist in the English school. I used to have a client who was mad over Reynolds. He gave me fifteen photographs of family members and had me

convert them into fifteen portraits done in the Reynolds style. He was delighted and paid me handsomely.... Imitate—ha, ha—it's not hard to imitate. (*Rosa* 150)

12. Are you going to permit it? *And you call yourself a man*? What kind of love do you feel anyway if you run off terrified at the first scare? (*Rosa* 75; emphasis added)

13. "to irritate Camilo, to make him jealous and upset him" (*Rosa* 65).

14. I didn't notice anything especially odd about Camilo's behavior either. He was jealous, of course, and you can imagine of whom. (*Rosa* 95)

15. draw your own deductions and conclusions. And I'll draw mine. Just don't let anyone say that Camilo never had any justification for being jealous! (*Rosa* 97)

16. I am one of those people who is aware that reality has two faces. What am I saying, two faces? It has twenty, a hundred, and the one most often shown to us is false and one must learn how to look for the real one. (*Rosa* 107)

17. A protective screen has been surrounding Camilo Canegato, a screen of pretense, of mimetism, but I'll remove that screen for you and you will see him for what he is.... He's not a man. He's the *maquette* of a man, the free sample. (*Rosa* 107)

Works Cited

Denevi, Marcos. *Ceremonia secreta*. Garden City, N.Y.: Doubleday, 1961. *Secret Ceremony*. Trans. Harriet de Onís. New York: Time, 1961.

———. *Obras completas*. 6 vols. Buenos Aires: Ediciones Corregidor, 1980–84.

———. *Rosa at Ten o'Clock*. Trans. Donald A. Yates. New York: Holt, Rinehart and Winston, 1964.

Freud, Sigmund. *Introductory Lectures on Psychoanalysis*. Trans. and ed. James Strachey. New York: Norton, 1966.

Lichtblau, Myron I. "Narrative Perspective and Reader Response in Marco Denevi's *Rosaura a las diez*." *Symposium* 40.1 (1986): 59–70.

Mohr, Richard D. *Gay Ideas: Outing and Other Controversies*. Boston: Beacon Press, 1992.

Monaco, Ricardo Enrique. "Soledad e incomunicación en dos novelas de Marco Denevi." *Revista Universitaria de Letras* 2.2 (1980): 295–313.

Sedgwick, Eve Kosofsky. *Epistemology of the Closet*. Berkeley: University of California Press, 1990.

◆   **Chapter 10**

Monobodies, Antibodies, and the Body Politic: Sara Levi Calderón's *Dos mujeres*

Claudia Schaefer-Rodríguez

Es la modernización nuestra bandera.
> Carlos Salinas de Gortari, "El Plan Nacional de Desarrollo:
> 1989–1994"

Society is never a disembodied spectacle.
> John O'Neill, *Five Bodies* 22

Uf, para mí descubrir que me gustaba una mujer fue como para Cristóbal Colón descubrir las Américas. Nunca antes se me había ocurrido la posibilidad.
> Sara Levi Calderón, *Dos mujeres* 164

In the current cultural climate of demolished walls and toppled public monuments, it seems noteworthy, even a bit disconcerting, to find in place an internationally orchestrated and promoted art exhibition such as *Mexico: Splendors of Thirty Centuries,* which made the rounds of U.S. museums from New York to Los Angeles before it moved on to Monterrey, Mexico, in 1992. Through this officially sanctioned assemblage of diverse images clustered around the unifying concept of the alleged splendors of a "unitary will" (as Octavio Paz writes in the introductory essay for the exhibit catalog [4]) stretching from the Meso-American past to the 1990s, there is insinuated a narrative continuum, a totalizing story of unbroken Mexican cultural threads woven across time and space, whose *mythos* represents the basis and overt legitimation of modern Mexico. This manifest proclamation—and, one might add, exportation—of identity is particularly revealing at the present time since the breaching of national boundaries, already a given reality due to the porousness of geographical divisions where labor sources and mass media technoculture are concerned, is about to be sanctified by NAFTA, the free trade agreement negotiated by the United States, Mexico, and Canada. How this myth of national identity functions and, if indeed it continues to function, whether it is becoming, as Mexican anthropologist and cultural journalist Roger Bartra suggests, "dysfunctional" (12), are, at least in part, the subjects of this essay, whose main concerns are the complex relationships among individuals and communities.

In spite of what cultural critic Homi K. Bhabha accurately sees as the impossible unity of the nation as a permanent symbolic force, given the transitional nature of social reality and the imagined community's constant coming-into-being as a system of cultural signification, one nevertheless cannot deny the real and persistent attempts to create an "aura" (Brennan 58) of national community through the invention of an evolutionary narrative of historical continuity and progress that includes as well "the narcissism of self-generation" (Bhabha 1) or zero degree of national identity. The project of nationalist discourse, then, is to excise any and all images of conflict and instead celebrate the splendors of the formation of the one from the many, the composite one, thus "securing an identification between politics and culture ... [and establishing] a structural relation between the nature of culture and the peculiarities of the state" (Bartra 10). The naturalizing of this holistic conception of national unity — a tacit agreement as to the origins, heroes, genealogies, and collective project of which, as President Salinas affirms, "we [Mexicans] are *all* proud" (from the exhibition program) — is grounded in the relative homogenization and coherence of political culture, in Mexico a legitimizing process hardly coherent with the economic development typical of the late twentieth century.[1] In this context, therefore, we must consider — as Jürgen Habermas strongly argues in his social analysis — the national project of modernity along with the process of modernization without viewing the former (the cultural) as either a necessary cause of or precedent for the latter (the social) but rather viewing both as two pieces of the dynamic whole of everyday life. What Bartra defines as modernization — "the capitalist transformation of a society, based on industry, science, and secular institutions ... the *real state* of capitalist social and economic development" (15; emphasis added) — as opposed to modernity — "the imaginary [or imagined] country whose legitimating network traps civil society" (15) — is out of sync in Mexico except in the rhetoric of official culture. In other words, one might accurately conclude that Mexico's incomplete but institutionalized modernity (via the vehicle of the Partido Revolucionario Institucional [PRI; Institutional Revolutionary Party]) is a modernity of excess or, if you will, an excess of modernity that masks the misery behind the splendors. As Bartra writes, "The country is replete with modernity, but thirsty for modernization" (15), for which he proposes the necessity of "la desmodernidad" (11; demodernization), a term he relates in satirical fashion both to the existence of "un *desmadre* económico" (the mother of all economic disasters) and to the hope of (that universal buzzword) "postmodernity" defined as "the constant transgression of all borders..., [the possibility of being Mexican] without subjecting oneself to a state or territory: [the experience] of a deterritorialization and denationalization of the intellectuals" (15).

Is the original oppositionality of modernism, its "rebelling against all that is normative" (Habermas 5), to be wiped out as an aberration worthy of total rejection? Should there be substituted in its place an infinite plurality of shifting cultural artifacts and positions in which any concept of coherence, criteria for order, or legible surface for representation is deemed impossible? Can the process of modernization be welcomed and that of cultural development (modernity) lamented (or vice versa), as if they were totally separate and independent of each other and as if any discontent with societal changes could be projected onto the cultural manifestations of modernism alone? That is to say, is the individual decentered subject to be considered the only basis for representation, since any mention of a collective project raises immediate fears of some type of master narrative of nationalism? Or does the possibility exist for a new type of modernist project that might aim toward relinking modern culture with an everyday praxis of community without just nostalgically recovering the lost "narratives of mastery" (Owens 65)? We shall examine both the hopes and the realities of these projects in terms of the Mexican cultural context and those who are drawn, willingly or otherwise, into participation.

The conflation of *lo moderno* (modernity) and *lo extensivo* (quantity) is what Sefchovich cites as the axis of official political culture in contemporary Mexico (261). She argues that in recent times:

La cultura en México ha consistido, lo mismo que la economía, en acumulación, en dar más: más conferencias, más número de ejemplares en las ediciones de libros, más museos, conciertos, películas, casas de cultura, premios, festivales, homenajes y conmemoraciones. Cultura en México quiere decir... un Estado promotor que cuando no organiza directamente, entonces, patrocina o apoya, o por lo menos permite todos los eventos y publicaciones que deseen hacer los intelectuales, y que incluyen todas las posibilidades del quehacer de la mente y de las manos, siempre y cuando no se exceda el único límite que son las críticas dirigidas contra él y contra los mitos que nos alimentan. Hoy como nunca en nuestra historia y como en pocos países del mundo la oferta de posibilidades culturales en México excede cualquier fantasía, sueño o deseo. Quizá por esta tradición histórica que le da tanto peso a la imitación, quizá por nuestro viejo deseo de ser aceptados por el mundo como país civilizado, o quizá por nuestros persistentes afanes de modernidad ... (Sefchovich 262)[2]

These splendors of modernity are signaled by the ability to offer consumers what they, as a nation, as Mexicans, want: an endless accumulation of products paralleled by an equally vast series of symbolic goods of diverse and even contradictory nature (the state no longer even needs to feel directly threatened since cultural and economic privatization have shifted the scenario to individuals and denationalized companies and enterprises who front for it), wrested from their original contexts and assembled into a collection that can be "brokered" (cf. Hollander 47) as the images establishing Mexico's place in the New World Order just as works of art are traded at auction. Rather than decentering Mexican culture (after Bartra), this self-promotion identifies it as a strategic clearinghouse for things flowing north as well as south over its borders. In this sense, the image of modern Mexico is one of middleman par excellence.

The discourse of this so-called transition to democracy and modernity is being overseen by a trinity of "presiding 'angels'" (Goldman 23): president and U.S.-educated economist Carlos Salinas de Gortari, Nobel Prize winner Octavio Paz, and Emilio Azcárraga, Jr., the majority shareholder of the international media conglomerate Televisa. Together they have carefully edited and packaged an image of Mexico as a unique "work of art" (from a paid advertisement in the *New York Times,* fall 1990) worthy of a place in any discriminating connoisseur's collection. In what can only be termed a masquerade of modernity, there is relentless emphasis placed on the state's guarantee of personal integrity and individual rights as the cornerstone of this new nation, the "eje de un trato [social] civilizado y *moderno*" (González Rodríguez xi; emphasis added; core of a civilized *modern* [social] order) and the overt celebration of "what is truly modern in modernity, the tolerance for radical change, novelty, the unusual [while still finding oneself in actuality] vilified, or worse, ignored, (or worse still, embraced, lionized) by the public representatives of bourgeois modernity" (Pippin 41). The key concept here is the public spectacle (masquerade) of embracing critique and democratic pluralism while simultaneously passing strict new legislation on the broad category of "delitos sexuales" (sexual crimes) and pornography (defined in general terms as "la fabricación, reproducción o publicación de libros, imágenes u objetos obscenos" [the production, reproduction, or publication of obscene books, images, or objects], whatever this might or might not encompass; González Rodríguez x), censoring what is categorized as the "sucio, feo, intolerable" (González Rodríguez x; dirty, ugly, intolerable), and disarming alternative ideas and projects by means of an appearance of tolerance and even benign promotion. Once again, this suggests Sefchovich's assessment of "dar más" (greater quantity), the philosophy that more is better, since a multiplicity of discourses can coexist in a harmless narrative soup in a liberal act of public generosity toward "all Mexicans" (to paraphrase Salinas's pronouncement). This is the willing sacrifice to "[el] costo de las modernizaciones" (González Rodríguez xi; the price to be paid for modernization) in order to maintain the physical and moral health of the national agenda.

Institutional apologist and intellectual Octavio Paz calls this celebration of integrated splendors "[el] velorio ideológico" (Fazio 183; the ideological wake) for the dead narrative of socialism and a defense of the discourse of neoliberalism put forth by Salinas's government in its declared national project of "libertad y desarrollo" (freedom and development). Against what he sees as the diabolical forces of antipluralism, Paz writes, "La gran interrogante de nuestro siglo es cómo construir la libertad. Todos sabemos que para que haya libertad es necesario el mercado..., el mercado... es una conquista de la modernidad" (Fazio 184; Our century's greatest question is how to build [real] freedom. We all know that in order to have freedom, a [free] market is absolutely essential..., the marketplace is a conquest of modernity). His careful and deliberate choice of words is not to be overlooked. To throw out the term *conquest* these days is to construct yet another bridge across the cultural continuum and therefore avert the possible opening or admission of an abyss, in either of the conquests (by the Europeans or by free trade). This is a symbolic reference to the past in order to justify the present as another natural part of the Mexican spirit, a present in which it is taken for granted that we all know of the natural fluidity between tradition and modernity, that one sole will persists, that there is a single way of being Mexican, and it consists of conquering and discovering "el rostro oculto de la nación" (Paz 54; the hidden face of the nation) ebbing and flowing through history and in need of constant liberation, in this case by means of an alliance with those in favor of NAFTA. In his speech announcing the "Plan Nacional de Desarrollo 1989–1994" (National Development Plan 1989–1994), Salinas confirms this vision in his opening exhortation to the nation by stating: "Cambio e identidad son así las bases que guían cada parte del Plan. Debemos cambiar para poder mantener la esencia de la Nación. De nada servirá el cambio si perdemos a la Nación que somos y heredamos, si abandonamos una historia de anhelos y luchas en común" (Salinas n.p.; Change and identity are thus the bases that guide each part of the Plan. We must change in order to maintain the essence of the Nation. Change will be useless if we lose ourselves and the Nation we have inherited, if we abandon a common history of desires and struggles). The historically pejorative term *malinchismo*[3] is given a strange and paradoxical twist in the process, depending on who uses it: for Salinas and Paz, to open up the country is a positive act that harmonizes with the historical development of the nation; for steadfast nationalists of the country's highland areas it still might (and in fact does) conjure up the selling out of Mexico to foreigners. The privatization of the media such as Televisa (the centerpiece of the country's culture industry in Adornian terms) is the perfect vehicle for this expression and promotion of the so-called liberated variety of the modern free market. As Paz himself writes: "Perseguimos a la modernidad en sus incesantes metamorfosis y nunca logramos asirla. Se escapa siempre: cada encuentro es una fuga" (68; We pursue modernity in its never-ending transformations, and we can never quite grasp hold of it. It always slips away: each encounter is another escape). Isn't there just a shadow of the incessantly postponed gratification of the capitalist market economy — more needs, needs in common, new products, constantly unfulfilled desires — lurking in this description of the modern?

Within the Mexican political economy of modernization, the legitimated existence of plural society, balanced in some fashion between a liberal spirit of acceptance and tolerance and "un ejercicio moderno de la autoridad, porque, sin menoscabo de la participación y el acuerdo, no renuncia [el estado] a sus responsabilidades de hacer prevalecer el interés general" (Salinas n.p.; a modern exercise of authority, because, without diminishing participatory politics and reaching an accord [the State] does not waive its responsibilities to have its general interests prevail), is communicated through the images of an erotic economy as well. The lived physical bodies that constitute the larger body politic, what philosopher John O'Neill vividly calls "the very flesh of society" (*Five Bodies* 22–23), are the terrain in which all social behavior is grounded and all political life is rooted. The circulation of these images is based, according to O'Neill's schema, on a three-level interrelated model of the body politic that is composed of the bio-body (the domain of the family, the discourse of well-being and health), the productive body (the discourse of self-control, production, work, and surplus), and the libidinal body (the realm of the personal, happiness, creativity, contentment, desire). While Salinas constantly makes reference to "un horizonte de progreso personal y familiar" (a horizon of progress for the individual and the family) in his public addresses, suggesting not just an administrative power over lived bodies, but also the sustained production of other (similar) bodies restrained within the parameters required by the agenda of modernization, there is a concurrent discourse of "civic privatism" and "public depoliticization" (O'Neill, *Five Bodies* 77: see also Habermas on the powers of the administrative state). Fostered by the state, on one hand this encourages the pursuit of consumption and leisure, and, on the other, it promotes a "therapeutic" (O'Neill, *Five Bodies* 138–39) model of society whose health and well-being are guaranteed by a celebration of the splendors of youth, fitness, beauty, affluence, and heterosexuality. These are the very qualities needed for the smooth functioning of the process of modernizing, the perfect prescription for a healthy body politic.

In other words, plurality is fine if on the surface everyone looks and buys the same, i.e., as "identical consumers of identical goods" (Van Den Abbeele xii); and it is also true that "consumers can be taught to disvalue their biological bodies entirely, except as those bodies are reappraised in the willing consumption of industrially mediated experience" (O'Neill, *Five Bodies* 101), a proposition justified once again by its linkage to benefits for the underlying identity of the nation. Moreover, the therapeutic authorities of advertising, the culture industry, and the media, including film, television, and videos, intervene in the life of those outside the agency of the family to cure (no longer discipline or punish, since, after all, this is the allegedly modern post-1968 state) any individual who refuses to render service to the forces of production alone, to become a "monobody" (O'Neill, "Aids" 81) bound into the workplace as the widely touted locus of free exchange and of theoretically equal subjects under the social contract. The regulated body, the one whose health depends on self-control and desires channeled into the streamlined production and consumption of an egalitarian, classless, and participatory "modern" Mexico, is the product of the studied indifference and tolerance so glorified by and assimilated into the official culture of the metropolis. For if it is true, as Carlos Monsiváis asserts, that the population explosion of the cities has led to the cultivation of a "deliberate ignorance" (72) of others and an avowed disinterest in the censorship of any behavior, it is equally true that the media promotion of an international culture of infinite options has paved the way for what Sefchovich has already called the aspirations of *lo extensivo,* or the goal of accumulation as the principal and incontrovertible sign of societal modernization and the clearest form of the already mentioned civic privatism and public depoliticization. Owing to the sheer quantity of citizens, this signals the transition to a culture of ceremoniously looking the other way when it comes to dissidence. It must be noted that Monsiváis equates modernity with Americanization (71) and that he calls the consumption of the flood of media images an act of "cultural voyeurism" (73) that stimulates a desire for imitation, a process that is then subsequently funneled into the discourse on national identity, and so a circular cultural movement.

Inoculating the body politic against alternative political and cultural agendas, the official discourse of modernization allows the free circulation of a novel like *Dos mujeres* (1990) by Sara Levi Calderón (1942) for instance, although its contents could conceivably represent a serious challenge to the unitary concept of community based on ethnic origin (one of the protagonists is Jewish), class (one character is wealthy and one is a struggling artist, giving rise to the breakdown of the image of social homogenization), and sexual preference (both of the main characters are lesbians). As the book cover of the Spanish edition puts it, this is "una historia fuera de lo común, un amor que enfrenta un antagonismo con la sociedad y se expresa de una y mil formas. Una novela erótica que profundiza en la relación de dos mujeres que se aman sobre todas las cosas" (an uncommon story of a love that confronts social antagonism and expresses itself in a thousand and one ways. An erotic novel that delves into the relationship between two women who above and beyond everything else are in love with each other). The fact that it is a love story, complete with happy ending, masks much of the possible challenge to society, however. In any case, variety seems to be everything here since market exposure to these members of the political and cultural community is used in this context to stave off any real threats to so-called orderly conduct, the peace and prosperity that Salinas proclaims all Mexicans enjoy, by means of a liberal discourse of moral immunization. If the human body is potentially both the flesh of society *and* the text of protest, then social consensus is actually maintained and not ruptured by the process of allowing a small dose — a novel here and there, the Semana Cultural Gay (Gay Culture Week) at the Universidad Nacional Autónoma de México (Autonomous National University of Mexico), roundtables, films, plays, and a certain number of periodicals — into circulation in the body politic to build up a capacity of resistance and to counteract subsequent (pathogenic) attack by collective organisms. We must note that the operative word here is *collective*, since the organization of alternatives to the (official version of the) nation joins individuals in movements with agendas of radical change. Identity politics, on the other hand, can be judged as the manageable isolation of alleged invaders in an otherwise harmoniously functioning collectivity of social organs.

But while Monsiváis, for example, cites October 2, 1978, as the precise date for the beginning of the process of so-called tolerance toward homosexuals in Mexico, the basis of that ostensibly democratic public acceptance has been greatly eroded. On that tenth anniversary of the Tlatelolco massacre, a large contingent of gay men and women joined the commemorative march through the streets of Mexico City, showing open solidarity and shared militancy with sectors of the political left. Starting in the late 1970s, a drive by President López Portillo to foster a visible climate of democracy actively sought the participation of more political groups in the electoral process (a move that appeared to encourage variety, but in reality solidified the official institutions of the PRI). But even this was cut short by the retrenchment of Mexican social classes after the oil boom fizzled in 1982, producing a crisis within the gay and lesbian movements, which had aligned themselves with the human rights and class issues of the left. This process of retrenchment describes the abyss between social and economic classes growing ever wider in the contemporary *nuevo porfiriato* (second coming of Porfirio Díaz's dictatorship), as it currently is sometimes referred to, with the concept of tolerance subsequently being identified with more educated and affluent circles—those in control of the media, the economy, and investment in the arts—or, as Juan Carlos Bautista observes, "La tolerencia [es] para quien pudiera pagarla" (60; Tolerance [belongs] to those with economic means). These indeed appear to be parts of the splendorous vision those who would modernize have of certain individual rights in Mexican society, accompanied by the (liberal democratic) hope that the same vision might some day trickle down to those in more misery and less splendor. Bautista goes so far as to lament the loss of oppositionality, not as a glorification of the permanently peripheral but in terms of "la pérdida de los beneficios de la marginalidad a cambio de las dudosas ventajas de la tolerancia del consumo" (60; the loss of the benefits of marginality in exchange for the doubtful advantages of the tolerance of consumer society). An identity based on consumption and the values of the market puts an end to solidarity and community while it accentuates class difference in their place, the economic differences created between those with first access to modernization and those still "thirsty" for it (as Bartra has written [15]).

While two recent bestsellers, Angeles Mastretta's *Arráncame la vida* (*Mexican Bolero*; 1985) and Laura Esquivel's *Como agua para chocolate* (*Like Water for Chocolate*; 1989), celebrate the heterosexual female subject coming of age in a unitary counterpoint with national music (the bolero) and typical national recipes (the latter novel's subtitle is "Novela de entregas mensuales con recetas, amores y remedios caseros" [A novel in monthly installments with recipes, romances, and remedies]), respectively,[4] the sexual economy of *Dos mujeres* is decidedly dual and it problematizes the representation of the unified body/body politic by means of the *retrato hablado* (263; word portrait)[5] and the examination of the still portraits produced by "la máquina de congelar momentos" (193; the instrument that freezes moments), in which two complex social identities and a novel-within-a-novel are simultaneously constructed. Moreover, not only is there a physical and emotional relationship between two women—Genovesa the artist and Valeria the writer—but each is presented as two women in one: "La que me permitía gozar plenamente de la vida y la otra que me lo impedía" (30; The one who lets me fully enjoy life and the other one who forbids me to). These double narratives address all three levels of the body politic as well as the tension of their intersections—the biological body (the family), the productive body (work and production/reproduction), and the libidinal body—in the social articulation of the subjects. What is most problematic, however, and the element that might potentially tie this narrative to a new discourse of a practicable modernism, is the discourse of agency of these subjects as a collectivity and the question of around just which concepts of resistance, if any, an alternative community might cohere.[6] In other words, is *Dos mujeres* proposing a discourse of alterity, or does it represent a more comfortable integration?

Instead of a public exhibition framed in the space of an art gallery or museum, *Dos mujeres* offers splendors of a different sort, ones kept in an album—"mi herencia visual" (15; my visual legacy) as Valeria calls it—which reveals and solidifies the topographies of these women's desires and their "lived bodies." It matters little whether or not there is actually film in the camera; their lived experiences are captured in and on their very flesh, and as subjects frequently held economic and cultural hostage by familial and corporate institutions with overt pretensions of modernization, they politicize the realm of the everyday out of tolerance into critique, at least on an individual level. Freezing moments and identities in time, the camera documenting their experiences (the eye of the narrating I) forces the spectator to respond to the objects and individuals of this world in a conscious way rather than through mandated acceptance or tolerance. It is a one-on-one encounter. For the two women, "La cara escondida de Nueva York" (95; New York's [hidden] cruel face) composed of Avenue A, heroin addicts, and ghetto life, is registered just as much as the details of Genovesa's face and body are fixed in the eye and lingered over in the mind's eye of Valeria. However, just as Roland Barthes's volume *Camera Lucida* traps Valeria's gaze in Genovesa's studio, and as reality lives beyond the aesthetically captured moment—"el beso que nos dimos duró más que el click" (87; the kiss lasted longer than the click)—in Barthes's words, "the Photograph always leads the corpus I need back to the body I see" (4), a journey back to the encounter with a specific reality and corporality, not to a mere shadow of a lived desire, but back to the object of desire itself. Instead of a displacement "fueled by the inaccessibility of the object and dissatisfaction with the real" (Hutcheon 144), a desire endlessly anticipatory and deferred into the future, Valeria's desire is constantly actualized in the present in multiple spaces and forms. "Mi deseo por ella era tan evidente que decidí no luchar contra él" (36; I felt such strong desire for her that I decided not to fight against it), she decides as she looks for the words to express what she feels, finding them—of all places—in a work of literature as she confesses "Tuve deseos de leerle el archileído capítulo siete de *Rayuela*" (57; I wanted to read her the thousand-times-read chapter seven in [Julio Cortázar's] *Hopscotch*) since she identifies something of Cortázar's *flâneuse* character of La Maga in Genovesa. The mere evocation of that brief first person narration of the ardent encounter between the mouths and fingertips of two lovers is enough to arouse Valeria's passion even more, creating a corresponding effect in Genovesa and precipitating their own physical encounter.

The center of contact between Valeria and Genovesa is the visual perception of the other, each acting as a mirror for the other's actions and relentlessly observing the other to possess her — and, through this procedure, to possess herself — by means of this reciprocal gaze. Valeria concludes that to part the veil covering Genovesa's innermost secrets she must begin with her eyes: "Pronto supe que la entrega de su cuerpo era lenta. Había que acariciarla con la mirada" (60; She gave herself slowly. You had to caress her with your eyes). It is through this look that Valeria identifies her own desire that, in turn, becomes Genovesa's own in a process of identification and appropriation: "Tenemos la mirada idéntica" (76; Our eyes look exactly the same), Genovesa confesses in alarm during one of their first encounters after a series of failed attempts at intimacy. Her first reaction is to cover them up, but she subsequently accepts the feelings brought on by this "contagious" desire (65). Ubiquitous mirrors add to this series of narcissistic images, reflecting back the bodies of the two women so that they might identify themselves as the real subjects of this passion: the mirror becomes a medium, an "accomplice" (71) that fixes and multiplies the presence of Genovesa and Valeria, much as the eye of the camera does. Yet both the mechanical and technical means of reproducing the image, in Barthes's words once again, reinforce the need to revert to the material body from which the representation is drawn. (And it is in this very "materiality" where many of the paradoxes occur, as we shall see shortly.)

These erotic moments, far from the sedate portraits and posed self-portraits of the formal art exhibit, are declarations of pleasure unhinged, in a sense, from the framework of fixed representations of gender that circulate in an essentially patriarchal capitalist economy. They embody, in fact, what Barthes refers to as the "ecstasy" of the photograph, a confrontation with "the wakening of intractable reality," rather than a subjection to "the civilized code of perfect illusions" (119) of reality-turned-art. Backing off somewhat from consumer society–constructed norms of desire, and perhaps even its pandering to the libidinal body, one brought into compliance by "titillating and ravishing its sensibilities while at the same time it standardizes and packages libidinal responses to its products" (O'Neill, *Five Bodies* 81) based on competition, profit, production, consumption, plurality, and so on, *Dos mujeres* is not beyond culture and politics, but within their very spaces. It proposes to carve out possible alternative territories — like the "sitio candente" (36; white-hot spot) and "punto de fuga donde convergían todos los ángulos" (37; vanishing point where all angles meet) — inside and outside Mexico and within the everyday, in spite of the family's seemingly generous offer of an all-expenses-paid exile to New York or California or Paris, from whose distance all liberal acceptance (tolerance) flows. Despite these attempts at erasure, however, Valeria and Genovesa are drawn back from self-exile at least temporarily into "the belly of the beast," as it were, when a Mexican publishing company offers Valeria a contract for her autobiographical novel, endowing it with symbolic capital absent from their "lived bodies." The artifact — *Dos mujeres* — assumes a material life that offers no real space for its protagonists to inhabit. Thus, exile becomes their "vanishing point," a fact startlingly akin to Bartra's proposal of "deterritorialization" and "denationalization" (15) discussed earlier.

Levi Calderón's text is suffused with a strong sense of the media and its gendered images, as indicated by the characters' encounters with chic young inhabitants of the Zona Rosa tourist area of Mexico City who, like minor cosmopolitan deities cloaked in designer splendor, wander "amidst the debris of urban crime and desolation" (O'Neill, "Aids" 81), shouting insults and obscenities at Genovesa and Valeria, who stroll embracing each other once they have declared themselves outside the masquerade of complicit participation in the images of a homogeneous (national) identity. From the very outset there is a sense of the need for acting and representation, for a simulacrum of life projected from behind a "disfraz de cada día" (42; everyday disguise), beginning with the Cavafis epigraph from "El Rey Demetrio" (The King Demetrius), who, abandoned by the Macedonians in favor of another king, removes his visible symbols of power and takes on another identity (as a commoner), and running through Valeria's accounts of her coming-of-age fifteenth birthday party, her wedding (whose paralyzed gestures she recounts in the third person), and her violent confrontational dealings with her family. Seeking a liberation from this immersion in the common "we" promoted through cinematic and other mass media images of young, docile, heterosexual women—divorcées, even with two children, are no longer a putatively modern problem, as long as they remarry "antes de cumplir los cuarenta años o después ya no les gustaría[n] a los hombres" (32; before turning forty because men wouldn't like [them] after that)—Valeria is seduced by the appearance of freedom of struggling young artist Genovesa. Fourteen years her junior, in denial of her own feelings for another woman and yet living the capitalist fantasy of the free market in which "amar a una mujer era una etapa por la que tenía que pasar" (90; loving a woman was only a stage she had to go through) in order to be liberated, Genovesa is the catalytic figure onto which Valeria projects her fantasies and through which she attempts to construct her own identity as an independent woman.

At first, the very fantasy images culled from Hollywood films that she has constantly and consciously criticized in her mother's upwardly mobile integrationist discourse are those she herself relies on for her own love story (the novel of her life; the texture of her life story as well). Populated with internalized ideals of feminine beauty and eternal youth presented as natural objects of desire, such as Mexico's legendary love balladeer Agustín Lara's vision of the equally legendary Mexican actress "María Félix bajo palmeras borrachas de sol" (84; María Félix under palm trees intoxicated by the sun), they seem to be strangely compatible with her passion for Genovesa, even though she comments that her new twist on the classic love story does appear to break the stereotype of the implied actors for each role; "que fuera [mi gran historia de amor] una mujer no era cualquier cosa" (61; [that my great love] starred a woman was no minor thing), she tells the reader. Although this sense of a paradigmatic love story just waiting for the right individual to come along and play the role of object of Valeria's grand passion eventually is overridden by the demand to construct an identity inside the domain of social reality and not from a distant utopian space moving to the rhythms of Patti Smith's album *Horses*, it is a process fraught with constant challenges by the biological and productive aspects of the body politic.

"Yo me dejé llevar por ella" (10; I let myself be led by her), Valeria concludes in retrospect, as if Genovesa were the personification, the embodiment, of the other woman within herself that needs to be set free. Naively seen as a complete rupture with the past ("lo anterior moría y el presente nacía golpeando" [42; the present moment was born with a bang and all that existed before died irrevocably away]) and with the "formaciones graníticas" (60; hard edges) and "valores introyectados" (78; internalized fears) that constantly threaten to impede their passion (and frequently do so, as in their decision to separate at the end of the first part of the text), this process cannot so easily abolish into oblivion these social and cultural traces by mere wishful thinking. We must keep in mind O'Neill's discussion of the therapeutic strategy of the state in national discourse, with its proposal to cure transgression against and within the integrity of the collective organism by cataloging and predicting antisocial conduct (see O'Neill, *Five Bodies* 139). Alterity and resistance are thereby defused through their incorporation into a false space within the liberal community (the book is there, the two women are not), institutionalizing and celebrating a commitment by the individual to his or her own material desires and self-worth alone, and multiplying the agencies of the avowedly benign face of the state that affords treatment and therapy to protect and serve the "distraught family" (O'Neill, *Five Bodies* 145). From the discipline-and-punish model of Valeria's mother, father, brother, and sons, all of whom believe she can be beaten into correction, she passes to her husband Luis's curative care. After finding her in the shower with Sandra, another "liberated woman" and the wife of a close friend, Luis concludes that she has just not learned the right lessons — "no había aprendido a ser mujer" (153; the essential thing was that I hadn't learned to be a woman) — and he generously assures Valeria that he will correct her aberrant course, as befits his position of power in the family and in society. She recounts their discussion in terms of his condescending attitude and assumption of control: "Me comunicó acariciándome la cabeza que lo que yo tenía era una enfermedad y agregó que las enfermedades se curan. El iba a ayudarme" (166; Patting my head, he announced that what I had was an illness and illnesses can be cured. He was going to help me). Instead of awaiting his treatment, she leaves home and goes to acting classes and puts to her own use a bit of the antibody theory itself — she decides that by studying the art of the theater she can confront and counteract her own masquerade. By going through the violent public spectacle of breaking through the metaphorical "membrana violeta como un molusco que se ceñía a mi cuerpo" (167; violent membrane, like a mollusk, [that] enveloped my body) since childhood, Valeria rejects the chic *Metropolitan* magazine version of heterosexual femininity surrounding and engulfing her. But she finds it much more difficult to abandon the class privileges accorded a woman of her social and economic background; as the daughter of a wealthy Jewish immigrant, poverty becomes the hardest punishment for her to accept. Her liberty concerning sexual desires is so postulated on material comfort that without her family as the source of financial support, even in rebellion, she is lost. When her American Express card is rejected and she is stranded penniless on the California coast, after careful consideration she arrives at the conclusion that "Ya me chingaron. Até cabos: ya me desheredaron" (215; [They've screwed me.] I put one and one together. They've just taken my inheritance away). Once left without her class identity embodied in the visible signs of economic privilege, Valeria begins to "detest" (217) the freedom she has been defending all along, since it no longer has the correlative freedom of movement — the control over places to travel, the possibility of escape, access to anywhere at any time — she has always had at her command. She decides on self-exile — from her mother, from her sons, and at least for a while from Genovesa, who has left her for a man whose promises of hearth, home, and children are irresistible (although maybe only as another so-called phase of experimentation) in order to write the very same coming-out autobiographical novel we are reading.

The introjection of such an essentializing notion of liberty, a concept presented here as intrinsically valuable in some absolute and abstract form, and perhaps at best only marginally instrumental in the construction of alternative identity, is quite problematical in that it seems to posit a defense not of contestation and radical change, but of splintering and breaking off. To paraphrase Bautista's remark on the accessibility of tolerance for the well-to-do, this freedom might be rendered by the expression "each woman for herself." And this allows for much the same free circulation of privileged individual subjects around and around the social bloodstream as it does of national treasures back and forth across airwaves, movie screens, and museum halls, with cultural objects and images collected, organized, and exhibited by some free market *bricoleur* (one who scrounges up bits and pieces of former constructs and masterfully recombines them to produce new creations) whose activity is based on the process of modernization, as well as used to confirm (in a perfectly circular argument) the existence of that very process. By circularity I refer to the use of a self-fulfilling notion that the exhibitionism permitted to plurality and modernity in the social body's cultural products both validates what is contained in official discourse and convinces the recipient (reader, observer, cultural voyeur) that this will lead to its stated goals as well. We must ask ourselves, therefore, whether the deliberate ignorance of the inhabitants of the modern metropolis observed by Monsiváis puts forth self-sufficient subjectivity to replace the abandonment of any critical attempt to identify, on one hand, communities of human experience and, on the other, those who even, or maybe I should say especially in the accelerated homogenization of late-twentieth-century capitalism, use the production of a continuous supply of cultural goods that seem to offer an unbroken horizon (Rowe and Schelling 1) to control the social agenda in new and more insidious ways behind the masquerade of democracy and acceptance, when, in fact, they count on societal disorganization and a fear and loathing of narratives of mastery, as well as the reality of unequal access to real freedoms, as a strategy to demonize collective opposition. In the simplest terms, we might ask whether Levi Calderón's narrator is permitted to speak of her desire for another woman because, after all, this is the story of only two women who occupy a space of permitted — somehow legalized — opposition and who have the right to a certain amount of indulgence or tolerance since, in Valeria's words, "las mujeres de mi clase social podemos hacer de todo, siempre y cuando no sea en serio" (206; women in my social position were allowed to do anything as long as we didn't take it seriously).

In the schema of modernization, then, this text must be negotiated by the critical reader not only as a highly visible sign of Mexican "progress" in the arena of social tolerance, but as a marker of more complex societal relations as well. Whether it is a signal of something to be "taken seriously" (as Valeria remarks) as far as the lived experiences of gay women in Mexico are concerned, and whether it mirrors the freedom of the marketplace or the "stages" a nation needs to go through to belong, or whether it is a forerunner of a real alternity, are issues intimately bound into the story of these two women, a story with a deceptively simple title.

Notes

1. Bartra points out that the myth of national identity is "popular" and "anti-capitalist," two reasons leading to its loss of function for its contradiction of the economic policies of capitalism (cf. 12). It is possible, however, to consider the popular as another locus of imposition from above (as a populist strategy used to gain or maintain power).

2. Culture in Mexico has consisted of accumulation, the same as in the economy; it has meant producing more: more conferences, more publication runs of books, more museums, concerts, films, cultural centers, prizes, festivals, homages, and tributes. Culture in Mexico means ... a promotional State that even when it does not directly organize, then it either sponsors or supports, or at the very least permits all of the events and publications that intellectuals might wish to have, including all of the mental and physical possibilities imaginable, as long as one boundary is not overstepped — there cannot be any criticism directed against the State itself or against any of the myths that nourish it (us). Today as never before in our history and as in few other countries in the world, the supply of cultural possibilities in Mexico exceeds any fantasy, dream, or human desire. Perhaps this comes from our historical tradition that has given so much importance to imitation, perhaps it comes from our long-standing desire to be accepted by the rest of the world as a civilized country, or perhaps we owe it all to our anxious pursuit of modernity.

3. Taken from the mythicohistorical figure of La Malinche, *malinchismo* refers to behavior and attitudes considered treasonous to the Mexican homeland (*patria*) and its national agenda, acts of one whom Cypess describes as "the individual who sells out to the foreigner, who devalues national identity in favor of imported benefits" (7).

4. Carlos Monsiváis sees a political culture of both the left and the right coming together over these cultural artifacts that triumph on the list of current best-sellers. He writes: "Ahora, la ultraderecha se concentra en combatir el aborto y el condón, y la ultraizquierda se aferra a su probado rechazo a la lectura. Y lo reconozcan o no, y mucho más de lo que se admite, se va unificando la cultura pública de la derecha y de la izquierda: las mismas películas, los mismos libros de moda (García Márquez, Paz, Kundera, Yourcenar, el *Thriller*, Asimov, Mastretta, John Le Carré), la misma música: Bach, Mozart, Madonna, el bolero. Fuera de las lecturas indispensables, de religión en un caso, de mantenimiento esforzado de los rescoldos utópicos en otro, la izquierda y la derecha obedecen a los dictados de la internacionalización cultural a la medida de las posibilidades" (Aranda

Luna 44; Right now, the far right concentrates on fighting abortion and the use of condoms, and the far left persists in its proven refusal to read. And whether they accept it or not, and much more than anyone admits, the public culture of the right and of the left is becoming more and more one and the same: the same movies, the same fashionable books [by García Márquez, Paz, Kundera, Yourcenar, thrillers, Asimov, Mastretta, John Le Carré], the same music: Bach, Mozart, Madonna, romantic ballads. Outside the indispensable readings, on religion in one instance, the forced upholding of the dying embers of utopia in the other, the left and the right obey all the dictates of cultural internationalization insofar as possible). One merely has to look at all the international press coverage in celebration of the recent Mexican film *Danzón* directed by María Novaro (Ballroom Dancing; 1992) to find another example of an integrationist search for sexual liberation.

5. The phrase brings to mind Gertrude Stein's use of the concept of word portraits to bridge between the visual and linguistic representations of identity.

6. Rosamaría Roffiel's 1989 novel *Amora* (the title is a feminized version of the Spanish word for love) reflects several notions of community in concrete terms. These include the Grupo de Ayuda a Personas Violadas (GRAPAV; Support Group for Rape Victims) and the Movimiento de la Liberación de la Mujer (Women's Liberation Movement), as well as the fem cooperative and even other, less formalized structures of cooperation and self-help among women.

Works Cited

Aranda Luna, Javier. "Entrevista con Carlos Monsiváis." *Vuelta* 174 (mayo de 1991): 43–46.

Barthes, Roland. *Camera Lucida: Reflections on Photography.* Trans. Richard Howard. New York: Hill and Wang, 1981.

Bartra, Roger. "Mexican *Oficio*: the Miseries and Splendors of Culture." Trans. Coco Fusco. *Third Text* 14 (spring 1991): 7–15.

Bautista, Juan Carlos. "¿El fin de la democracia gay?" *Nexos* 139 (julio de 1989): 60–61.

Bhabha, Homi K. "Introduction: Narrating the Nation." In *Nation and Narration*. Ed. Homi K. Bhabha. London: Routledge, 1990, 1–7.

Brennan, Timothy. "The National Longing for Form." In *Nation and Narration*. Ed. Homi K. Bhabha. London: Routledge, 1990, 44–70.

Cypess, Sandra Messinger. *La Malinche in Mexican Literature: From History to Myth.* Austin: University of Texas Press, 1991.

Esquivel, Laura. *Como agua para chocolate.* Mexico: Planeta, 1989. *Like Water for Chocolate (A Novel in Monthly Installments with Recipes, Romances, and Home Remedies).* Trans. Carol Christensen and Thomas Christensen. New York: Doubleday, 1992.

Fazio, Carlos. "El tío Octavio y el escribidor." *Nuevo texto crítico* 6 (1990): 183–89.

Goldman, Shifra M. "Metropolitan Splendors: the Buying and Selling of Mexico." *Third Text* 14 (spring 1991): 17–25.

González Rodríguez, Sergio. "Pornografía y censura." *Nexos* 152 (septiembre 1990): ix–xi.

Habermas, Jürgen. "Modernity—an Incomplete Project." *The Anti-Aesthetic: Essays on Postmodern Culture.* Ed. Hal Foster. Seattle: Bay Press, 1983, 3–15.

Hollander, Kurt. "Report from Mexico I: Art of the '80's in Monterrey." *Art in America*, October 1991, 46–53.

Hutcheon, Linda. *The Politics of Postmodernism*. London: Routledge, 1989.

Levi Calderón, Sara. *Dos mujeres*. Mexico: Diana, 1990. *The Two Mujeres*. Trans. Gina Kaufer. San Francisco: Aunt Lute Books, 1991.

Mastretta, Angeles. *Arráncame la vida*. Mexico: Océano, 1985. *Mexican Bolero*. Trans. Ann Wright. London: Viking, 1989.

Monsiváis, Carlos. "Paisaje de batalla entre condones." *Nexos* 139 (julio de 1989): 71–74.

O'Neill, John. "Aids as a Globalizing Panic." *Public 3: Carnal Knowledge Issue*. Toronto: Public Access Collective, 1989, 77–85.

———. *Five Bodies: The Human Shape of Modern Society*. Ithaca: Cornell University Press, 1985.

Owens, Craig. "The Discourse of Others: Feminists and Postmodernism." *The Anti-Aesthetic: Essays on Postmodern Culture*. Ed. Hal Foster. Seattle: Bay Press, 1983, 3–15.

Paz, Octavio. *In Search of the Present*. 1990 Nobel Lecture. San Diego/New York: Harvest/Harcourt Brace Jovanovich, 1990.

———. "Will for Form." Introduction to *Mexico: Splendors of Thirty Centuries*. New York: The Metropolitan Museum of Art, 1990, 3–38.

Pippin, Robert B. *Modernism as a Philosophical Problem*. Cambridge: Basil Blackwell, 1991.

Roffiel, Rosamaría. *Amora*. Mexico: Planeta, 1989.

Rowe, William, and Vivian Schelling. *Memory and Modernity: Popular Culture in Latin America*. London: Verso, 1991.

Salinas de Gortari, Carlos. "El Plan Nacional de Desarrollo 1989–1994 (31 de mayo de 1989)." *Nexos* 139 (julio de 1989), n.p.

Sefchovich, Sara. *México: país de ideas, país de novelas (Una sociología de la literatura mexicana)*. Mexico: Grijalbo, 1987.

Van Den Abbeele, Georges. Introduction to *Community at Loose Ends*. Ed. The Miami Theory Collective. Minneapolis: University of Minnesota Press, 1991.

Chapter 11

Not so Lonely: A Butch-Femme Reading of Cristina Peri-Rossi's *Solitario de amor*

Mary S. Gossy

When I first heard that Cristina Peri-Rossi had published an erotic novel I looked forward to *Solitario de amor*'s being an addition to the fairly small population of "out" lesbian novels published in Spanish. I opened the book at random in a bookstore in Madrid in 1988 and found the following passage:

> I do not love her body, I am loving her imperceptibly palpating membranous liver, the white sclera of her eyes, the bleeding endometrium, the perforated lobe, the stria of the fingernails, the small and turbulent intestinal appendix, the tonsils as red as berries, the hidden mastoids, the crunching jaw, the inflammable meninges, the vaulted palate, the roots of the teeth, the brown place on the shoulder, the carotid as tense as a cord, the lungs poisoned by smoke, the little clitoris set in the vulva like a lighthouse.[1]

The reference and homage to Monique Wittig's 1973 *The Lesbian Body* was fully apparent. A little taste of Wittig's book may be useful for comparison:

> M/y most delectable one I set about eating you, m/y tongue moistens the helix of your ear delicately gliding around, m/y tongue inserts itself in the auricle, it touches

the antihelix, m/y teeth seek the lobe, they begin to gnaw
at it, m/y tongue gets into your ear canal. (24)

The similarity that I want to highlight is the repetitive, scientific, anatomically correct terminology that the narrator uses to describe the activity of loving the body of the beloved. Wittig's text is almost nothing but a series of these erotic incantations, and it appeared that Peri-Rossi's text was echoing Wittig's stylistics because it, too, was a lesbian novel: that is, a novel in which a lesbian writer represents lesbian desire. In the case of such "lesbian novels," theoretical doubts about the relationship between a real and an implied author, between the human writer and the author function, disappear. To know or to believe that the historical author is a lesbian has specific aesthetic and political effects on the lesbian reader's interpretation and reception of a lesbian text. These effects are produced by the desire of an embodied lesbian to identify and make contact with the *body* of a lesbian author as it is (or may be) materialized in her writing. I know that it is true that some straight women have sex with lesbians; and as much recent research shows, some women who identify as lesbians sleep with men, sometimes, for various reasons. But lesbian desire is also mobilized by and for another woman whom the reader knows (because she or someone else who knows has said so) is a lesbian. Lesbian desire depends upon the presence of another lesbian, who has been narrated as lesbian. In terms of the reception of a lesbian novel, this other lesbian is the historical author who has come out, or been outed, as a lesbian.

The cursory browsing in the Madrid bookstore, combined with what I then knew of Cristina Peri-Rossi's work and life, led me to expect that *Solitario de amor* would be an explicitly lesbian novel. I bought the book without reading any more of it; like so many book purchases, this one was like a blind date; I had the distant recommendations of friends, and I was hoping for the best. But our perverse, nonlinear acquaintance in the bookstore proved to be insufficient. When I finally sat down to read it from beginning to end, on the second page I encountered the sentence, "So that I am condemned to live it in solitude" — "De modo que estoy condenado a vivirlo en soledad"(8). Was that "-o" at the end of *condenado* a misprint? No, two pages later, the "I" of the narrator describes itself as "shipwrecked," *náufrago,* and a "lost traveller," a *viajero perdido.* What kind of lesbian novel has a narrator that takes the masculine pronoun, anyway?

The historical author said, in a 1988 interview, "I feel completely identified with the protagonist, in spite of the fact that it is a man. I think that in this case it is irrelevant. Whether the protagonist is a woman or a man changes nothing."[2]

There are few things that are certain, but one of them is that in literature and in life, whether one is a man or a woman makes a difference; and that difference does change things. At first the presence of a narrator who insistently describes himself by saying "I am a man who...," "Soy un hombre que..." seemed to make *Solitario de amor* unavailable as a text for lesbian desire.

In the psychic space of desiring reading, it is precisely the uncertainty of the mark of sexual difference that opens the text to different readings. Like a four-year old doing her first sexual researches in an attempt to formulate sexual difference, I wanted to see exactly to what extent whether the protagonist was a man or a woman changed anything, so I began to look for the narrator's phallus — to see if he had one and, if so, what it was like. The characteristics of this phallus would help to show the extent to which the text might be read as a lesbian novel.

The narrator describes his lover Aída's genitals in insistent anatomical detail or simply as her "sex," *sexo.* He also uses the term *sexo* for his own sexual organ; the other term that comes up is "member," *miembro.* But nowhere in the book is this organ called "penis," *pene*; there are no "testicles," *testículos,* or any other less scientific but equally specific terms. There is no mention of an erection or of any of the other physiological attributes of a penis. Nevertheless, penetration is one of the sexual acts of the two lovers. The narrator introduces his *sexo* into Aída, who does not similarly penetrate him. The narrator says that his "sexo" is a "weak vine," *débil liana* that connects him to Aída; but in their act of lovemaking, while "the end of my member touches the head of your uterus," the narrator says that simultaneously, "we shake each other,... we snort, mucous membrane against mucous membrane."[3] Whatever the narrator's *sexo* is, it does not exclude the possibility of a meeting of genital mucous membranes, which is something that is possible when two women's bodies come together.

The other way that the narrator describes his genital contact with Aída is that she is the "lock," *la cerradura,* and he is the "key," *la llave.* The key in the lock is a symbol for heterosexual intercourse that predates Freud's use of it in dream symbols, but what is interesting about it here is that the key is a *symbol* for the penis, but not the penis itself. In the descriptions that he offers, the narrator's *sexo,* too, participates in the penis's symbolic economy, but is nowhere named "penis." Something that depends upon the penis for its meaning, but is not the penis itself, is the phallus.

It is not possible to say accurately that there is a penis represented in *Solitario de amor.* At no time, despite the frequency of the use of anatomical terms for the female genitalia in the book, is a penis mentioned by name. There is, however, a *miembro,* a *sexo* through whose erotic activity the narrator identifies himself as grammatically masculine. This brings us back to the body of the historical lesbian author, who has already told her readers that she feels "completamente identificada con el personaje protagonista, a pesar de que es un hombre." When a woman, fully cognizant of the fact that she is a woman, publicly identifies completely with the masculine, while fully cognizant that she is not a man, she produces a definition of herself as butch. Within this identification with and putting on of gender, it is important to remember that the masculine cannot exist in a vacuum. Its definition and continuity require a feminine counterpart, or as Sue-Ellen Case's now classic definition of the butch-femme relationship states, "You can't have one without the other." Case refers to the hyphen that customarily marks the term *butch-femme* as a "lesbian bar" that brings the two together. If a butch is defined in relationship to a femme, then her butchness, that which makes her masculine in reference to the femme's femininity, and keeps the two terms connected, may be graphically represented as that hyphen. Another name for this masculine term that the butch uses to connect with the femme, a term that is distantly founded upon the penis, but which displaces and exceeds it, is *phallus.* A woman who puts on the phallus in erotic reference to another woman is butch. When a lesbian reader reads that a woman wrote an erotic novel about a relationship between a "he," *él,* and a "she," *ella,* and that that woman, who is thus erotically obsessed with *ella*, "*feels* completely identified" with *él*, then the reader must conclude that what has come before her is a lesbian novel. This reception of *Solitario de amor* as a butch-femme novel of lesbian desire has several terms. One is the infantile, Freudian definition of gender difference; because there is no specifically embodied penis in *Solitario de amor,* the narrator may be read as masculine, but not male, that is, as butch. Another consists of the rumors, literary biography, and statements about herself that the historical author has made. People have said that she is a lesbian, she herself identifies completely with a masculine protagonist who is erotically obsessed with a woman, and she also says that *Solitario de amor* is "my most autobiographical book."[4] If it were not for my knowledge of the author's embodied sexuality, I might still be able to show on textual grounds that *Solitario de amor* has many elements that suggest that it is a story of lesbian desire, or at the very least something other than a heterosexual romance. But the knowledge that the author is a man or a woman, straight or gay, *does* change things for the lesbian reader, as it does in other contexts for other readers who find themselves oppressed and excluded from dominant discourses of race, class, or sex. There is interpretive significance in the relationship of the author's body to the reader's desire. The embodied identity of the author *is* a matter of desire for readers — and even for readers who fight over canonical questions of authorship, for the most philological of reasons. The scholarly quibbles of savants over the attribution of texts are a way not only to identify with the (supposed) author, but also to interact passionately — that is, frequently, homoerotically, but in a socially approved, scholarly way — with other critics. The reader's investment in interpreting the author's identity is — from Homer to Cervantes, and Shakespeare to Peri-Rossi — an erotic one. This relationship may not make for dispassionate readings (if dispassionate readings are possible at all), but it certainly can be a source of pleasure.

The pleasure of a femme reader before Cristina Peri-Rossi's butch text is at least partially conditioned by the text's representation of the lesbian phallus. Judith Butler says that this lesbian phallus "is and is not a masculinist figure of power; the signifier is significantly split, for it both recalls and displaces the masculinism by which it is impelled" (Butler 162). This significant split is evident in the statement "I feel completely identified with the protagonist, *in spite of the fact* that it is a man." The phrase *a pesar de que*, "in spite of," here invokes causation as much as it does obstacle. "In spite of" here means *"because* he is" and *"because* I am not" a man. The splitting of the meaning of the lesbian phallus continues in the word "identified," *identificada*. According to Wittig, the trace of the phallus in grammar is in the personal pronoun and the masculine and feminine endings that proceed from it.[5] The persistent "-a" at the end of *identificada* shows the limits that language puts upon a woman who wants to identify, or feels identified, with the man. But that "-a" is also the *precondition* of a butch identity. If, as Butler and Charles Bernheimer have it, "the phallus would be nothing without the penis" (Butler 157; cf. also Bernheimer), then the butch would be nothing without her *femme*-ininity. That is, if it were not for the lesbian (female-on-female) desire that she has for or in reference to a femme, the butch's masculinity could not exist. Butch-femme depends somewhere upon a female body for its definition. The "-a" in *identificada* in this context marks how the lesbian phallus is a split signifier or, similarly, where the terms "lesbian" and "phallus" may be brought together.

This "-a" persists in two points that are crucial to a butch-femme reading of *Solitario de amor*. As I mention above, the narrator refers to his "sex," *sexo*, as a "a weak vine," *una débil liana*, that connects him and Aída. (Peri-Rossi's cultural references in this text run from *La celestina* to Verdi to Lacan. Is it possible that she saw John Sayles's 1980 movie about a lesbian's coming out, *Lianna*?) This *sexo* is also *una llave*. Out of all the possible metaphoric representations of a phallus, why use two that are so clearly (if arbitrarily) grammatically marked as feminine? In both cases, the narrator's phallus carries a heavy layer of *structural* femininity. The question of *la llave* is of particular importance, because keys figure in the book's climax and end. The narrator always meets Aída for sex at her place. The relationship goes on for a long time, but the reader discovers at the end, when she is mad at him and will not admit him anymore into her life, refusing to answer the telephone or the door, that the narrator has no keys to Aída's house. He cannot let himself in. Earlier in the novel the narrator has said "I am a key," *Soy una llave,* and "Aída is a house,"

Aída es una casa—but when trouble comes into their relationship, it is a lack of a material, not a symbolic, key that separates the narrator from his beloved. In the text it is not stated why Aída breaks off contact. All that she says, through the locked door, is "I don't want to see you."[6] If *Solitario de amor* is a tragedy, it is because it is the story of how both characters, butch and femme, who can only exist together, lose their power to be in discourse when one refuses to tell her story along with the other. The negation of their relationship because of the lack of a material key— a *male* phallus, perhaps?—eradicates both of them from discourse. I wonder, and only wonder, if *Solitario de amor* could be the sad story of a butch in love with a heterosexual woman.

Perhaps you, dear reader, have had just about as much of the recurrence of the phallus in these books, and in this essay, as you can take, and see it as yet another form of evasion. But the phallus is under analysis because it is part of what makes a butch-femme reading possible, even starting with the book's epigraphs. The first epigraph quotes a fragment from Paul Valéry, "the strange gestures that lovers make to kill Love."[7] The idea of gestures and expressions, symbols represented by the body but not part of it, seems to concur with ideas of gender as performance, and phallus as something coming from, but not part of, the body. The other epigraph is also compelling. It is from Lacan, and says, "To love is to give that which one does not have to someone who does not exist."[8] True, on an abstract level, this may be a description of the fantastical nature of love relations between any two people. But on a paradoxically embodied level, it is an accurate description of a butch-femme relationship, in which the butch gives the phallus that she (by definition) does not have to the woman that the lesbian femme (by definition) is not. The epigraph from Lacan is, in this context, a negative definition of the butch-femme relationship.

On a more positive note, in the middle of the longest sex scene in the book, the narrator says, "Now the down of your pubis is my moustache."[9] An unambiguously "male" narrator would have a moustache, or the possibility of one, without this moment of oral-genital contact. But if we can set the phallus aside for the moment, perhaps we can finally remember what is even more crucial than the phallus to lesbian experience: Peri-Rossi's text shows that in the case of a butch-femme relationship, the lesbian *vulva* makes the man.

Notes

1. "No amo su cuerpo, estoy amando su hígado membranoso de imperceptible pálpito, la blanca esclerótica de sus ojos, el endometrio sangrante, el lóbulo agujereado, las estrías de las uñas, el pequeño y turbulento apéndice intestinal, las amígdalas rojas como guindas, el oculto mastoides, la mandíbula crujiente, las meninges inflamables, el paladar abovedado, las raíces de los dientes, el lugar marrón del hombro, la carótida tensa como una cuerda, los pulmones envenenados por el humo, el pequeño clítoris engarzado en la vulva como un faro" (15–16). Cristina Peri-Rossi, *Solitario de amor*; references in my text are to this edition, and translations are my own.

2. "Me siento completamente identificada con el personaje protagonista, a pesar de que es un hombre. Creo que en este caso es irrelevante. Que el protagonista sea una mujer o sea un hombre no cambia nada" (43). Susana Camps, interview with Cristina Peri-Rossi.

3. "El extremo de mi miembro toca la cabeza de tu útero"; "nos sacudimos,... resoplamos, mucosa contra mucosa."

4. "Mi libro más autobiográfico."

5. Monique Wittig, "The Mark of Gender," in *The Straight Mind and Other Essays* (Boston: Beacon Press, 1992), 76–89.

6. "No quiero verte" (172).

7. "los gestos extraños que para matar al Amor hacen los amantes."

8. "Amar es dar lo que no se tiene a quien no es."

9. "Ahora el vello de tu pubis es mi bigote."

Works Cited

Bernheimer, Charles. "Penile Reference in Phallic Theory." *différences* 4.1 (spring 1992): 116–32.

Butler, Judith. "The Lesbian Phallus and the Morphological Imaginary." *différences* 4.1 (spring 1992): 133–71.

Camps, Susana. "La pasión desde la pasión." *Quimera* 81 (1988): 40–49.

Peri-Rossi, Cristina. *Solitario de amor*. Barcelona: Seix Barral, 1988.

Wittig, Monique. *The Lesbian Body*. Trans. David Le Vay. Boston: Beacon Press, 1986. First English edition, 1975. Orig. Paris: Editions de Minuit, 1973.

◆ **Chapter 12**
The Case for Feminine Pornography in Latin America
David William Foster

Estás confusa porque te relato tudo isto?
Hilst, *Cartas de um sedutor* 59[1]

Porque cada um de nós . . . tem que achar o seu próprio porco. (Atenção, não confundir com corpo.) Porco, gente, porco, o corpo às avessas.
Hilst, *Contos d'escárnio* 77[2]

Sabia que não era para a gente se perguntar muito, que a vida é viável enquanto se fica na superfície, nos matizes, nas aquarelas.
Hilst, *Contos d'escárnio* 83[3]

There are few topics in contemporary cultural production that are more controversial, that more divide individuals into entrenched positions, than pornography. While pornography may be a central fact of human artistic expression, as archaeology and historical studies have amply demonstrated (cf. *The Invention of Pornography* for its relationship to modern culture in general), there is yet no adequate resolution as to how to interpret its role in a global conception of cultural production. For some, typically today such implausible bedfellows as religious fundamentalists (Attorney General's Commission on Pornography — the so-called *Meese Report*) and politically correct, interventionist feminists (paradigmatically, Dworkin and Dworkin, separately and as coauthors), pornography is to be both condemned and, in some effective legal way, banned: the former see it as the work of the anti-Christ, while for the latter, as the famous formulation goes, "rape is the practice; pornography the theory."

Others, most notably Kendrick, see pornography as part of a continuum of human artistic expression, where it functions as a form of cultural resistance, a Bakhtinian polyphony, a defiant countercultural manifestation. Marcuse was able to see in the erotic and its cultural expressions a liberating corrective to the destructive demands of civilization, while Soble develops an explicitly Marxist defense of pornography as a liberating discourse. In all of these formulations, the relationship between the erotic and pornography remains either underdistinguished or undertheorized (significant exceptions are the papers in *For Adult Users Only*). I do not recall who it was that said that the erotic is for the well-to-do, invoking perhaps the image of Anaïs Nin, writing elegant, pay-by-the-word texts for a wealthy client, or the exquisite silk-screen creations of classical Chinese and Japanese culture.

The possibility of a pornographic discourse (and allow me to propose for the purposes of this discussion that we understand pornography to be a narrative production that is explicitly sexual, with a privileging of the genital or that which is considered synecdochally genital) continues to be especially energetically debated within feminism. Thus, while there are those like Andrea Dworkin and Catharine MacKinnon who see it as a repugnant reduplication of patriarchal power, contrary opinions are offered by others such as Pat Califia, Sara Dunn, Kate Ellis et al., Lisa Henderson, Nancy Friday, Lisa Henderson (writing in part on Califia), and the essays in *Pornography and Feminism* who see in a specifically feminist pornography both a site for the examination of the dynamics of patriarchal violence and the possibility for constructing an erotics that reimages relations of sexual power.

The production by Latin American women writers continues to be scant, there being more of an emphasis on an erotic imagination that reterritorializes the body in order to escape the genital privileging of patriarchal sexuality:

> No partimos de la premisa de que la sexualidad constituye una categoría metodológica exclusiva, o que es la base única para examinar la identidad personal. Sin embargo, dado que la opresión y la represión sexual se encuentran entre las múltiples manifestaciones de la desigualdad entre los sexos, ¿cómo logramos que la cultura dominante sea más representativa de los intereses de la mujer? Para transformar las definiciones y categorías culturales opresivas debemos recurrir a la experiencia femenina, y tratar de comprender sus códigos, sus discursos y sus sistemas de signos; es decir, emprender el tipo de estudio que el análisis de la imaginación sexual en la creación

literaria femenina haría posible. ("Introducción," *El placer de la palabra* xviii; cf. quote from Luisa Valenzuela xix)[4]

Nevertheless, novelists like Cristina Peri-Rossi (1941), Alicia Steimberg (1933), Diana Raznovich (1945), and María Luisa Mendoza (1938; cf. Foster, "Algunos espejismos eróticos") have authored texts that constitute experiments in an inventory of feminine pornography; indeed, Brazil's Cassandra Rios (dates unknown; cf. Foster, *Gay and Lesbian* 120–24) and Adelaide Carrera (dates unknown) have even authored assertively mass-consumer soft porn, complete with appropriately lurid covers. The fact that this production comes from a large-market society like Brazil has undoubtedly to do with the greater incorporation in that country of a project of modernity that incorporates explicit space for cultural products that in a loose way can be called pornographic. Mexico and Argentina are other clear examples of modernized Latin American societies, and Claudia Schaefer-Rodríguez (this volume) has examined how the emergence in the former of the beginnings of a lesbian narrative has unquestionably to do with neoliberal market forces. Argentina is somewhat of a counterexample: modernity may have long been a byword of Argentine society, but there is still much of the cultural production that is of interest to this discussion that either remains quite clandestine (like so much production even during neoliberal periods of the military dictatorship); is excoriated on multiple fronts, some being really smokescreens for censorship (as, for example, when Enrique Medina's fiction is dismissed as bad writing, since it can no longer be banned legally); or is, quite simply, published abroad, as is the case of the texts examined in this essay by Alicia Steimberg and Diana Raznovich (the fact that they were published in Spain speaks to the newfound modernity of that Hispanic society).

Perhaps most prominent is the case of a self-acknowledged feminine pornographer, Brazil's Hilda Hilst (1930), who has declared her intent to devote her creative efforts to composing pornographic narratives. Perhaps the best way to describe Hilst's writing is as fugue-like. There is probably no available and reliable metric of discursive cohesion, although one generally associates with academic/formal writing in all languages some goal of achieving such a principle, which is based on the degree to which it is immediately apparent how components of a text interlock with each other, a feature of at least writing that is the basis of the use of the word *text* in its etymological meaning. If one of the characteristics of colloquiality is a relaxation of the academic/formal principles of textual cohesion, a relaxation that is usually quickly apparent in the attempts to transcribe colloquiality or to make it the basis of a textual production on the level of narrative exposition beyond the level of quoted direct speech (e.g., Cuba's Guillermo Cabrera Infante in *Tres tristes tigres* [1967]), colloquiality is especially notable in a language like Portuguese, which shares with French a rigidly codified learned standard.

Hilst is known as perhaps one of the most brilliant craftspersons of contemporary Brazilian prose. Without substantively altering the principles of textual production based on complex fugue-like patterns of semantic and narrative configuration, such that her texts often remain stunningly impenetrable after the most assiduous of (re)readings, Hilst has produced a number of works in which the multiple facets of sexual experience are sketched via an expository style that careens vertiginously from one image to another. There is no way to explain away this writing as perceptive erotic analysis, in the way in which it has been claimed that the pornographic redeems itself as the erotic by virtue of the latter's emphasis on inscribing the former in a structure of sufficient psychosociological introspection.

If the pornographic involves the representation of sexual activity that appears either to be unmotivated by anything other than "animal lust" or, in a presumable perversion of the lust that might be seen as a beneficent feature of the noble savage, as motivated by what we have come to consider the distinctive features of rape (violence in which the instruments of sex, paradigmatically the penis, are the weapons of assault), then it is questionable whether one can comfortably seek to distinguish Hilst's writings as erotic. Indeed, a text like *Cartas de um sedutor* (1991), written by a woman presumably familiar with the general debate in Western society over sexual violence and in particular with the considerations in Brazil since the return to democracy in 1985, when that country became one of the first in the world to establish police stations specifically serving the needs of female assault victims, derives much of its impact from the way in which it appears to conform to the hoariest notions of pornography in the form of narrative accounts of sexual exploits by men undertaken on the bodies of women. While there is some reference to homosexual acts in the text, they are not the woman-woman activity characteristic of male pornography (Benson), but rather male-male sex, which presumably because of the psychological dynamics of rape pornography, is virtually never to be found in traditional scripts.

There are two features of Hilst's text that relate it to conventional forms of male pornography. The first concerns the primacy of the voice of the male narrator. As the letter of a seducer, *Cartas* originates with a male speaker who sounds very much like the narrator of Henry Miller's paradigmatic reveries of phallic hegemony. This does not mean, to be sure, that the text is an unrelieved *jouissant* record of the satyr triumphant. Precisely because the narrator recounts his failures and limitations, his self-doubts and occasional remorse, does his story become all the more satisfying when he is able to overcome the obstacles to male supremacy and realize through acts on the female body (or the male body in homosexual versions of the same script) the full measure of his potency.

The narrative voice of this satyr triumphant expands to occupy every structural dimension of the text, such that there can be no room for any other voice to be heard, nothing that contradicts the imposing speaker: pornographic discourse is the paradigm of the monologic text as Bakhtin conceives of it. While there may be some some stray instances of dialogue, they basically serve to sustain the master's voice and in no way represent an opening toward a dialogism that might be one of the other ways in which a theorizing over the difference between pornography and the erotic might take place. Essentially made up of the text of Karl directed toward his sister, Cordélia, along with other narrative segments that appear to be either extrapolations of his letters or parallel narratives of Karl's, *Cartas* underscores the lopsided preeminence of the discourse of male sexuality by providing the reader only with Karl's letters and never with Cordélia's response to them, either in the form of written replies directed to Karl or as interior monologues, diary entries, or some other form of her reaction to them. Therefore, Karl speaks for himself and he speaks for Cordélia by either explicitly or implicitly replying for her, if no more than merely by pursuing an epistolary production on the assumption that yet another letter is called for and, indeed, welcome from his interlocutor's point of view.

Within this framework, Hilst's narrator strives for a maximum degree of sexual transgression, so much so that one could open a brief for his letters as so many delirious masturbatory fantasies, wishful thinking with little correspondence to actual life. Thus, Karl reminds Cordélia of their shared sexual couplings, while compounding the taboo of incest by bringing mother and father into the erotic *ars combinatoria* and by compounding its possibilities by adding a homosexual liaison for the father with a fifth party.

Karl's recounting of these exploits, reinforced by the privileged second person form characteristic of intimate letters, makes use of the *tu* form in two special senses. The first is the presence of direct address in pornographic narratives whereby the male voice describes to and prescribes for the woman the role she plays in the sexual drama; as might be expected, the indicative mode of exposition is frequently exchanged for the imperative and sub-junctive/jussive modes that mandate—directly and indirectly, respectively—the action of the woman.

The second use of *tu* in Hilst's text has to do with the special status of this pronoun in Brazilian Portuguese. Without going into the details of the extremely complex pattern of the second person in Brazilian Portuguese, a pattern that is quite a bit more complex than the corresponding system in Latin American Spanish (itself no simple matter to begin with), suffice it to say that the *tu* in *Cartas* is much more than a trace of intimate familiarity between the narrator and his interlocutor. The *tu* form in Brazilian Por-tuguese has basically fallen into disuse, except in some regional dialects: *você* is the familiar form, and it is universally used, ex-cept in very restrictively defined formal contexts, in which *o/a senhor/a* is the equivalent of the Spanish *usted* (both *você* and *o/a senhor/a* use third person verb forms; note that in biblical/litur-gical texts, *vos*, the second person plural form, is the pronoun of divine address, unlike Spanish, which uses the singular *tú*). Except in traditional lyric poetry, the Portuguese *tu* in its Peninsular uses is virtually unknown in Brazil. Thus, when Karl addresses his sister in the *tu* form it creates a lyrical connotation that, depending on how one wishes to view it, either accentuates the sexual exchanges or rudely clashes with them. What complicates the assessment here is the fact, however, that Karl's use of the *tu* is fundamentally divided. On occasion he resorts to the "poetic conjugation," the use of the pronoun with its correspondingly historical forms: *tu és* and its related conjugations. On other occasions, *tu* simply alternates with *você* and is used with the third person verb forms of the latter: *tu é*. This usage is distinctively colloquial, if not essentially untutored, and thus his address moves between the conventionally lyrical and what one might call a hard-edged colloquial intimacy (hard-edged because it enjoys none of the attenuating factors of a presumably conscious effort at verbal refinement). This hard-edged colloquiality is carried out metonymically by the fact that it would be hard to find another text of Brazilian literature that so resolutely engages in inventorying every possible lexical item for the vagina, the penis, the nipple, and the anus, with an impressive array of other erogenous zones, including the nostril and the ear, covered along the way.

The conjugation of traditional pornographic discourse features and a colloquiality pursued in terms of expository style, verbal forms, and sexual slang provides the specific texture of *Cartas de um sedutor*. Although one associates with parody a fairly transparent reinscription of the base text, toward rendering the recognition of parody at work unmistakable, an initial reading of Hilst's text leaves little room for viewing it in any way other than as parodic. Certainly, the sustained exploitation of the female body makes it difficult to view *Cartas* as in any way a defense of female sexuality. Even in the case of the woman Karl features, grossly nicknamed Cuzinho (little asshole; one wonders if there is not a trope intended here of *cuzinha*, kitchen, the special realm of the subjugated woman), who is obsessed with her desire to practice anilingus, the woman is less an agent of her own erotic fulfillment than she is one of Karl's pornographic fantasies developed in all of the extrapolations that characterize his narrative production.

In a sense, the fugue-like nature of Hilst's text (another characteristic might be surrealist delirium, this feature reminiscent of William S. Burroughs's writing) is what closes out the possibility of any counternarrative, of any dialogic interaction, in the way in which the pornographic is a textual coordinate of a sexual violence that also excludes any resistance, any alternative, any antiphonic response. If Hilst is producing anything other than pornography understood in this way, it is a sexual discourse that, because of its univocal imperiousness, excludes any alternative to it, whether in the form of human experience other than the erotic, a program of human passion other than the one it provides, or an articulation of a point of view regarding sexual history other than the one Karl and his equally hegemonic masculine surrogates provide. Karl writes his sister on one occasion prompting, provoking, forcing her memory:

> Palomita, lembras-te que mergulhavas o meu pau na tua xícara de chocolate e em seguida me lambias o ganso? Ahh! tua formosa língua! Evoco todos os ruídos, todos os tons da paisagem daquelas tardes ... cigarras, os anus pretos (aves cuculiformes da família dos cuculídeos ... meus Deus!) e os cheiros ... o jasmim-manga, os limoeiros ... e teus movementos suaves, alongados, meus movimentos frenéticos ... Ahhh! Marcel, se te lembras, sentiu todo un universo com as dele madeleines ... (65)[5]

Certainly, Hilst's expository form provides only glimmers of satisfaction for the reader accustomed to the dogged if always shocking transparency of conventional pornography, and certainly there might be room to correct the assessment provided here of what this text is about by insisting that fugue and erotic *ars combinatoria* function to enunciate a liberated sexuality where semantics and narrative action are demonstrated to be releasable from closed paradigms of the safe and the conventional. But, in either case, Hilst's text represents the intersection of the superficially pornographic and a form of narrative exposition that is exceptionally unique among the texts being considered here.

Hilst's *Contos d'escárnio* (1990), published explicitly as belonging to the author's commitment to writing pornographic literature (back jacket flap), centers on two oxymorons. The first is the rather obvious one of how a configuration such as that of the "feminine pornographic" is possible, unless it signals the female author's affiliations with a masculinist criterion of the sexual abuse and exploitation of woman (either as a woman's conscious alliance with hegemonic patriarchal structures or her unwitting collaboration with the instruments of her own degradation, the most obvious one of which being, precisely, her being made an unwitting accomplice), which would constitute a use of the adjective *feminine* as merely identifying the sexual identity of the author, but not her feminist ideology. To the extent that we have come to identify the pornographic not with the libidinous display of erotic activity (which in such an affirmation is implied to be unfettered by exploitative power and, quite the contrary, to be an evasion of it, as seen in the forces that would suppress the pornographic) but instead with a return to the root meaning of the term — writing about prostitutes — with the concomitant assertion that prostitutes are paradigms of the violent exploitation of the female body, the pornographic is the absolute icon of violence against women: Dworkin's image of intercourse as unremittingly the display text of masculinist expropriation of the feminine Other. If the erotic is anything other than pornography for the well-to-do, it is only something else if it can free itself from the semantic anchoring in prostitution to which an understanding of the pornographic has returned, which might be why a term like "feminine erotic" does not strike one as oxymoronic, but only tropic to the extent that it leaves open whether it has freed itself from the imperatives of the master masculine erotic.

Equally contradictory in appearance is the secondary term to be associated with Hilst's text, that of a "humorous pornographic," in the sense that violence, if it is understood really as violence without any mediating discursive strategies (e.g., violence in, say, a Bugs Bunny comic book, is putatively mediated by its framing as simple fun, involving nonhumans, in which no matter how much mayhem the characters are subjected to, they always reappear intact in the next frame or strip; alternative readings may strip away these mediating conventions, but they are first there as a not-to-be-challenged given that makes violence humorous), cannot be taken to be funny, and all the more so if the text inscribes the reader into the position of the victim of violence, which would seem to be a routine strategy of most writing and unquestionably of any attempt to lead the reader to repudiate the social scenario being portrayed.

But it is exactly in its dimensions as a humorous text that *Contos* is able to resolve the contradiction of the idea of a feminine pornography. This Hilst does by undertaking to drain the sexual encounter of its dramatic tensions: sex is, after all is said (the text) and done (the act), no big deal. One might immediately object that sex is certainly a big deal for those obliged through physical and ideological coercion to engage in it, but Hilst's rejoinder could well be either that she is talking about sex when it is without coercion — when it is sex and not violence in which sexual organs and their extensions are the bludgeons — or that what is often read as sexual coercion, especially under the aegis of seduction, corruption, and entrapment, merits possible revisionary considerations. One might note that this is precisely the circumstance of feminine S-M: whether the idea is outrageously disingenuous — S-M viewed as reenacting masculinist violence — or whether the apparent abuse of S-M can be reinterpreted as consenting sexual theatrics, one of whose virtues may be a catharsis of oppression (cf. Califia's introduction to her erotic writing, as well as her *Sensuous Magic*). Hilst's text makes no claim that sexual coercion does not exist nor that there is a pornography properly speaking that is its abetting record, but rather that there is a domain of sexuality that can be scrutinized within the parameters of the operant terms of her title, *escárnio* and *grotesco* (grotesque). The former term is of venerable ancestry in Luso-Hispanic letters, referring to that mode of textual production that is designed to outrage. In modern terms, this means a discourse of transgression, defiance, resistance, or polyphony. It is the return of the repressed, the speech of the subaltern, and multivocalness in the face of the monologic. This is why in its origins in medieval literature, *escarnio* (cf. English *scarn = dung*; the former probably has the same Germanic roots attributed to the Spanish word) was one of the popular modes opposed to the monologic discourse of the Church; indeed, some of its practitioners, like Spain's fourteenth-century Juan Ruiz, author of *El libro de buen amor,* were clerics who engaged in a rewriting *a lo profano* of the master texts. Hilst's other key qualifier, *grotesco* is understood to be a modern attribute, one in which less an opposition than a shifted reading is involved: the grotesque discovers deeper and hidden levels of meaning that frighten rather than affront, repulse rather than outrage.

These dual attributes work in Hilst's narrative to underscore a strategy of trivialization, which is the basis on which she proposes to demonstrate the nontranscendence of erotic encounters. Crasso and Clódia (note the classical resonances of their names) engage in a multiplication of erotic encounters that are compounded by his efforts as a writer (the text is one example of the production of erotic experience) and her efforts as a painter; Clódia specializes, in the tradition of Georgia O'Keeffe, in vaginal abstractions. There sexual exercises are a freewheeling set of bodily conjunctions marked by indiscriminateness as regards subject and object, agent and patient, pursuer and pursued. The multipleness of their erotic field is reduplicated by the mosaic quality of Hilst's/Crasso's text, which also encourages the reader to view sexual acts as the accumulation of superficial detail from which the depth meaning of the Freudian tradition and the cultural tradition it has inspired are absent. Thus, sex is demystified as a personal sin, as a psychological complex, as a social tragedy, as existential liberation, and as the compulsive nucleus of the Western tradition of cultural production. Although *Contos* is about sex, it is about how writing need not be about sex as a metonym of all of human experience.

Toward the demythification of sex, Hilst engages in a series of metatextualities that, because they are mocked and trivialized, function to induce scorn for the cultural frame of mind that attributes to the genres they represent vast and profound interpretations of personal and collective life as sexual dramas. In one sequence, the devil appears, ostensibly to torment the narrator of another author's writings (fragments supposedly of interest for their oedipal constructions, Crasso has included) for his sexual transgressions and to preview for him the hell fires of damnation that will torment him for his sins:

> Senti náuseas de repente e uma dor profunda no peito.
> Ainda pude perguntar-lhe: há uma outra vida?
> Sim. Milhões de crianças como eu. Você será uma delas. É tedioso e até inaceitável mas é assim. (93)[6]

Elsewhere, there are two theatrical fragments that mock, respectively, the turgid sexual dramatics of Shakespeare (Zumzum Xeque Pir, 53–66) and the Freudian narreme of father-son competition

(67–69), and one that parodies what appears to be the exquisite scatologies of Sade (70–74), one assumes in his guise as a forefather of erotic liberation (and not, as Angela Carter would see him, as a critic of power through sexual domination).

Hilst's text is hardly one of sexual ludics, in which there is supposed to be an ulterior meaning for the erotic, whether as the enactment of political oppression or as an opportunity for the ultimate *jouissance*. Thus, male sexuality, as the central scene in the oedipal family romance and as the site of the subjugation of those whom it leaves unempowered (women as a global social construction), is trivialized by Hilst's text, not because the exercise of sex as power does not take place but because it can be shown as not always endowed with the transcendent signifier that the Judeo-Christian, the Freudian, and the feminist traditions in turn have unequivocally attributed to it. It is for this reason that Hilst has no feminine/feminist agenda to offer in the place of the meanings that have been drained from sex (by contrast, say, to Griselda Gambaro's experimentation with pornography in *Lo impenetrable* [1984]; cf. Foster, "Pornography"). At the end of the novel, the narrator informs Clódia that he has been first in Paris and then in New York, where he has found a publisher for his manuscript, leading one to wonder if there is not a mockery here of the two poles of feminist understandings of sexuality, those that have restored the etymological meaning of *pornography*. Much fucking takes place in Hilst's pornographic writing, but it is all surface narrative, devoid of the resonances *fuck* has acquired as a vulgarism that is dirty not because it is vulgar but because of the violence that its very utterance is said to enact (cf. MacKinnon).

Hilst's texts point, then, in two directions. On one hand they undermine the profound meanings attached to the sexual by most of the Judeo-Christian tradition (not to mention others), and in this sense they resound of the postmodernist repudiation of depth psychology and master narratives. On the other hand, they mock dominant feminist interpretations of sex, at least sex involving female participants, as necessarily exploitative and violent. It may be going too far to say that Hilst has turned to narrative pornography as a particular positioning from the margins of her subalternity as a Brazilian writer in what may seem from the Third World as the overheated debates of First World feminism: it has been often noted that First World feminism seems to be irrelevant to the Third World, where socioeconomic violence, assuredly a masculinist patriarchal system, leaves most of society disempowered, irrespectively men and women. Equally, Hilst's complex narratives have little to do with touristy images of Brazil as a happy-go-lucky sexual haven (Parker). Rather, her humorous pornography stakes a claim to the validity of the proliferation of surface meanings, whether on the page, the canvas, or the body: "Resolvi escrever este livro porque ao longo da minha vida tenho lido tanto lixo que resolvi escrever o meu" (10).[7] It is symptomatic of Hilst's intranscendent writing that we are left unable to decide whether the antecedent of "o meu" is "livro" or "lixo," two words which, after all, in the dominant tradition of Luso-Hispanic assonance, are a paired rhyme.

One of the venerable scenographic topoi of literature is the shipboard, and the shipboard romance undoubtedly has always ranked high as a significantly recurring narrative formula for a wide spectrum of fiction. Indeed, passenger ships have come to exist today primarily as Love Boats, and in the best tradition of expanding markets, now offer package cruises catering to varieties of sexual tastes. And, paradigmatically, the Caribbean cruise, with its stations-of-the-cross approach to the attractions of tropical islands whose diversity derives from the crisscross of cultural influences in the area, is an inevitable setting for the most delirious of these romances.

La última noche que pasé contigo (1991) by Mayra Montero (Cuba, 1952) in Tusquets's La Sonrisa Vertical prizewinning pornography series, is the story of a midlife sexual discovery and an erotic recovery. Fernando and Celia, having just married their only daughter, embark on a cruise through the islands as a redefinition of their relationship. During the cruise they meet Julieta, who is something of a sexual shifter: the conflicting stories she tells about herself and why she is alone on the cruise are correlatives of the crucial differences in her personal and erotic relations with Celia and Fernando as individuals and then as a couple. The reader discovers at the end of the novel that Julieta was the woman to whom Fernando's grandmother lost her lesbian lover. Fernando as a child carried letters between his grandmother and

Angela, and texts of those letters are interspersed in the novel, although they are signed with a masculine pseudonym. Furthermore, it turns out that Julieta's husband is a former lover of Celia's. This brief characterization of the sexual pairings in the novel seems like too much coincidence, but if one views Julieta as a shifter, as a convenient element for bringing to the fore relationships between others, there is less of a need to raise the question as to whether Montero's novel is a put-on, a challenge to the reader to admire the labyrinthine combinations, in the fashion of a daisy chain, of everyone appearing to have sexual relations with everyone else, not exactly in perfect structural balance, but as an index of the counterimage to the patriarchal matrimony Fernando initally strives to impose. Or to maintain in the face of the loss of the immediate presence of the daughter, the primary metonymic sign of that matrimony.

Carlos Esterrich has written very accurately of the lesbian grounding of Montero's novel, both the lesbian relationship to which Fernando was witness as a child and which provided him with a potent image of a hidden female sexuality, and the lesbianism in his own wife's involvement with Julieta. The point that I would like to underscore here is the way in which that lesbianism is a determining factor in Fernando's interactions with his own wife and with Julieta. Although there is a certain amount of miscellaneous eroticism in the novel, both on shipboard and in the form of flashbacks, mostly of Celia's affairs with other men, the grand sexual scenes of the novel are saved for two juxtaposed seductions of the two female protagonists by island men. Both men are black, and both provide transport services: Celia's seducer ferries passengers between the mainland and an island in his boat, and Julieta's is a taxi driver. In both cases, the narrator describes the seduction in considerable detail, and in both cases the men are paradigms of the stereotype of the generously endowed buck. In both cases, the sexual act is described in details that border on a rape fantasy — that is, the erotic encounter is based on the men violently taking the women, whose intense shock and pain become intense, unforgettable pleasure under the effects of the masculine assault. Montero writes here using the narrative arsenal of the numerous cases in fiction in which violent and anonymous sex is reputed to be a glorious sexual awakening for a woman, and in which the supposed pleasure for both the woman and the witness to her orgasm through the medium of literature is enhanced by the crucial transgressive nature of the primitivism of the agent (with black men routinely fulfilling this role).

But there is a crucial difference between Celia's experience and Julieta's. Celia goes off on her own, and even if she is only quasi-conscious of her actions (and it is important to note that the event is told in the first person, thereby forestalling the possibility of a narrator or another character misinterpreting her responses and feelings), she offers herself for sexual seduction. Afterward, in almost a parody of closing tags in popular fiction, she states: "tuve la corazonada de que aquélla era la tarde más importante de mi vida" (154),[8] and she returns from the encounter "[sangrando] como una virgencita" (154).[9] There is little room to doubt that Celia has codified her sexual experience with the *botero* in such a way that it will become an integral and positive part of her psychological identity:

> Me despedí besándole la boca, el implacable filete de esos labios, una lengua que no se me negaba más, unos dientes que se me quedaron clavados en la carne, para que me acordara de su sabor en esa noche, para que me acordara mañana por la noche, y para que me acordara ahora y en la hora de mi muerte, y por el resto de las noches que iba a vivir sin él. (154)[10]

"Ahora y en la hora de mi muerte": this accommodation of the topos of the Marian protectorship definitively empties the description of Celia's sexual adventure of any implication of rape and converts it into the erotic core of the novel.

As opposed to the lesbian subtext, especially evident in Fernando's experience with female sexuality, genital heterosexism is rather triumphantly vindicated. Such a vindication necessarily involves the liquidation of the lesbian subtext, and this is effected through Julieta's seduction. Like Celia's, it also takes place in Guadaloupe (and this setting is presented with appropriate allusions to Josephine and Victor Hugues, perhaps as primes of female sexuality and revolution, respectively, although it is not clear that their reference is anything but part of the circumstances of tourism). But in this case, it is difficult to conclude that anything other than rape has taken place. Riding together in a cab, Fernando engages in heavy foreplay with Julieta. The cab driver, realizing what is happening, pulls over and turns around to watch. Fernando silently offers Julieta's body to him, and the man descends from behind the wheel and takes Fernando's place in the backseat.

As he once watched, although obliquely, the lovemaking of his grandmother and the woman who would leave her for Julieta, Fernando contemplates the sexual encounter between the cab driver and Julieta. In this case, it is Fernando who does the narrating, and at the end of the chapter, Fernando continues the rape by forcing a reluctant Julieta to confess that she enjoyed the encounter he stage-managed. Significantly, the imposed confession of pleasure is dominated by the imperative also to confess to the level of pain she has endured. These are the closing words of the chapter: "¿le había dolido o no?, dijo que sí, más alto, perra, y ella gritó que sí, que sí, que sí..." (172).[11] Fernando here may be avenging himself through Julieta's multiple rape for what he intuits to have been Celia's pleasure with another man or what he suspects has been the understanding between the two women, lesbian defined or not, that has excluded him. But also, in retrospect, in the nature of the unsent letter that closes Manuel Puig's *La traición de Rita Hayworth* (1967), provided by the unsent letter in which her lover informs Fernando's grandmother that she is abandoning her for Julieta, Fernando's act of violence is motivated by the ghosts of the sexual apprenticeship provided him by his grandmother and whose controlling motifs are the boleros that permeate all of the narrative schemata of the novel, beginning with its title. It is not clear the extent to which Fernando realizes who Julieta is, nor even that he ever understands the role she played in his early life after Celia, in the last scene between them, provides him with some information about her he did not yet know. But Celia destroys in his face a letter Julieta had left for Fernando before deciding to leave the cruise and to remain permanently in Guadaloupe (with the cab driver?), which would be the final narreme in the rape fantasy, in contrast to the rupture of Celia's codification of her seduction. Thus if Fernando is somehow settling accounts with Julieta for her role in his grandmother's unhappiness, he is basically unaware of it, which adds the dimension of feminist irony to the effect that the patriarchal agent is by virtue of his structural role unable to grasp what is happening: "he just doesn't get it."

But of course there is a problem here, one that the irony in fact reveals and that cannot be disavowed in the face of the erotic fulfillment Celia experiences and the feminist meanings it may have. I am referring to the triumphant nature of Celia's genital heterosexism versus the rape of the lesbian. Leave aside the pathetic dimension of the final unhappiness of Fernando's grandmother, because only a reactionary sexual code would prevent her lover from acting on the fact that she falls in love with another woman and would deny Julieta the right to seduce the grandmother's lover. Bolero-drenched clichés of betrayal and abandonment certainly have no place in a narrative of sexual liberation, and, indeed, they can only serve to mark where this liberation is from—and it hardly goes without saying that, ideologically, bolero lyrics echo the masculinist (even if it is true that there is some measure of a closeted, denied gay sensibility in the sentimentality of the male singing voice: cf. Luis Rafael Sánchez's *La importancia de llamarse Daniel Santos* [1988]). What is crucial here is the fact that, while at the same time, and in virtually the same exotic, tropical setting, the heterosexual Celia (who calls Fernando's grandmother *la maricona*) has a momentous sexual adventure, the lesbian Julieta is being raped at the hands of two men, one quite possibly as a form of revenge. Perhaps it would be possible to argue that Montero depicts Julieta's rape as evidence of the control of the patriarchy, which is even more violent when confronted with lesbianism (cf. references to Fernando's grandfather and the priest who confesses his grandmother on her deathbed), and Celia's sexual satisfaction as proof of the way in which women can come to manage their own erotic life, but there is an irresolvable conflict here between heterosexualism and lesbianism (which is never shown in any light more positive than the eventually frustrated romanticism of the grandmother's affair), which is in turn overshadowed by the masculinist bolero, that I am unable to argue away.

There has never been any doubt as to exactly where Diana Raznovich (1945) has been going with her writing: in all three of the

major genres, the Argentine writer has addressed in highly imaginative ways topics relating to gender and sexual identity and
undertaken the enormous project of constructing an erotic discourse that has some sort of sociopolitical meaning to it. *Mater
erótica* consists of two narratives, the first about twice as long as
the second. In both cases, the fall of the Berlin Wall is the backdrop to an erotic experience. In the first case, it is between the
wife of a member of the East German high command and a friend
of her teenage son; in the second case, it is between a double
agent of both Germanys who, under a death threat, lives out a
sexual idyll with a sixteen-year-old woman. In both cases, the
stories are told in the first person by the older person, in both
cases an element of bisexuality is involved, in both cases there is
some element of gender role exchange, and in both cases there is
reference to the climate of sexual repression that functions in all
of Western society, with establishment socialism being as draconian as capitalist democracy.

However, there is more of a narrative of transgression in the
case of the older woman, and more of a narrative of sexual exploitation in the case of the second. What Raznovich seems to be
staging here is a juxtaposition between the radical differences in
perspectives. In the second narrative, it is a masculinist perspective—the cynical double agent who lives out the hours before
he is assassinated, availing himself effortlessly of the body of an
essentially powerless woman, all in the context of free and libertine Paris, the capital of "Love" in all of its heterosexist mythology.
In the first and longer narrative, in the context of the masculinist
repression of female sexuality in an establishment socialism that
is homologous to traditional Western and Christian values, a feminist discourse is forged in which the fleshquakes of an awak-
ened sexuality foreshadow the structural earthquakes the woman
produces in the society around her.

Raznovich makes use of many of the conventions of masculinist pornography, beginning with the fact that, as an Argentine,
she chooses to write in an urban Peninsular dialect that provides
her with a voice jarringly different from her other writings, which
is much like the stilted language of her generic models. Moreover,
the setting of both stories in societies that are not Spanish speaking reinforces the otherness of her texts, although the first one is

more marked than the second in this regard. From a feminist point of view, pornography (which is what Raznovich seems to be reiterating in the second, masculinist-based story) is a profound dystopia that overlaps in significant ways with the actual society of the male abuser, the female victim, and voyeuristic readers whose gender identities position them in various ways with respect to that dystopia and who may even remodel it as a fantastic utopia in order to lead one out of the sexual conflicts of the real world (both for those who abuse and those who have internalized abuse as an ideal to be sought). Raznovich's proposition, in the first and feminist narrative, begins by configuring a dystopia that the non-communist-bloc reader is asked to grasp as reduplicating capitalist society, and then to accept the possibility of creating a utopian space within it based on a series of transgressions that install woman as sexual agent, with an agency that replaces feminine lack with a force capable of invalidating masculinist male phallic power. The first person narrative underscores the greater presence of the woman who no longer speaks the stasis of the *stabat Mater* (cf. Kristeva), but articulates the agency of the *Mater erótica* who will reconfigure society in a liberating and nonphallic fashion.

Despite the elements of bisexuality in both narratives, Raznovich's texts are ultimately resolutely heterosexist and genitalist, which means that she focuses on female/male sexual politics rather than alternate sexualities. Nevertheless, within this frame of reference (which also reduplicates conventional pornography), there is enough erotic delirium to demonstrate that even within traditional male/female roles there is a promise for sexual liberation.

Masturbation has always gotten somewhat of a bum rap. There are the biblical injunctions against the needless waste of the seed, a male-biased law that is surely the reflex of a society obsessed with the need for maintaining a level of population multiplication that would sustain its tribal or ethnic identity, if not enhance its power through numbers. In modern times, when the numerical stability of the population begins to be less of an issue, health hygiene technologies view masturbation as a threat to the moral fabric of society because of the alleged weakening of the mind induced by the intensely self-centering act of onanism; again, the major threat appears to exist for males, despite the growing re-alizaton of universal sexual urges in women (and not just as a perversion in some women that leads them to licentiousness and prostitution). Finally, although there may now be a growing recog-nition of the validity (if for no other reason than because of its persistent practice) of masturbation as a natural sexual release, one major dimension of the contemporary sexual revolution has been to decry masturbation as a deviation from the sort of proliferat-ing sexual unions the final loss of constraining taboos is supposed to achieve: masturbation is a selfish act to the extent that it rejects communion with others, the barriers against which the sexual revolution is supposed to demolish. Masturbation is a negation of the free sexual marketplace. Nevertheless, in a post-AIDS society, masturbation may be the only real form of safe sex (not, pace the ideology that promulgates it, abstinence, unless nonrelease can be promoted as a form of frustrated, and therefore heightened plea-sure, eroticism). The need to substitute new erotic practices for those associated with high HIV-risk contamination has opened up the possibility of actually encouraging masturbation, whether soli-tary or mutual, reflexive or reciprocal.

Alicia Steimberg's *Amatista* enters the discourse on masturba-tion from the perspective of a feminine narrative voice — indeed, it is perhaps the first Hispanic novel in which masturbation is the central theme, there being few other texts in which it is pre-sent only as one narrative incident (e.g., the disquisition on male masturbatory techniques in Enrique Medina's *Strip-tease* [1976]). *Amatista* is a series of encounters between an unidentified woman, whose recounting of them constitutes the text of the novel, and a *doctor,* whom she initiates into an enhanced enjoyment of the sex-ual act. The text is specifically and insistently heterosexist because it is centered on the conceit of a woman of unspecified qualifica-tions serving as an erotic guide for a professionally titled man, per-haps even learned in letters and the culture of human society that his title implies. Here the woman assumes overtly a series of sex-ual privileges that are conventionally denied her: it is she who pos-sesses the superior knowledge about the dynamics of sex, despite the status of the man as a *doctor* (a title that in Spanish, it should be noted, is not synonymous with medicine but conserves its et-ymological meaning of [professionally, academically] learned); it is she who serves as the agent, the initiator, the controller of the sexual act; it is she who possesses specialized knowledge about techniques and utilities that enhance and sustain pleasure; and it is she who has the right to talk about sex, both as an element of the sex act — talk as a technique of sexual stimulation — and as a consequence of sex — the formal recollection of sex in the form of a report, a memoir, or a novel.

Actually, there are three dimensions of narrativized sex in Steimberg's novel, all attributed to the narrator-participant; all three are transgressive as far as conventional Western, and especially Hispanic, images of female sexuality are concerned. In the first place, the first person narrator attributes to herself the privilege of narrating her erotic education of the man, who is as ideally responsive as any teacher could hope for and who, in his compliance with her performance instructions, is as ideally obedient as any pornographer could hope for from a character. The fact that the student is a man and the teacher a woman inverts one pornographic norm, albeit not an exclusive one, while the fact that the woman's sexual knowledge stands in an inversely proportional relation to her pupil's ignorance about the enhancement of sexual pleasure contravenes the principle of masculine superiority in both the realm of knowledge and the realm of experience.

In order to fulfill her role as teacher, the narrator explains to her pupil practices that will increase erotic pleasure. Part of the controlling conceit of *Amatista* that begins with the identification of the man/pupil as *doctor* is in the use of a stylized primer designed for the elementary teaching of the alphabet, a reference to which opens the novel: "Era un alfabeto de letras traslúcidas y cambiantes, con arabescos, proyectado en una pantalla. Lo seguí letra a letra" (9).[12] The narrator recounts to the reader her sexual docency as she explains to her student what he is to do in order to profit from her knowledge, what techniques she will teach him, and of what strategies she will avail herself in order to maximize his pleasure. It is this role of the woman as the speaking agent of sex, complemented by the virtually absolute mutism of the man, for whom she in many cases speaks, either by telling him what to say or by directly attributing words to him, that is also transgressive with respect to the conventions of pornography. In a novel like John Cleland's *Fanny Hill,* the woman may be the narrator, but she is only circumstantially the sexual agent, since it is clear that she is enacting and recounting the sexual fantasies of the male discourse, which include the compliant receptivity of the woman. In *Amatista,* it is the man who is complying with a sexual script articulated by the woman, which she patiently expounds to him in an efficiently pedagogical manner.

Finally, the novel is transgressive in a third narrative dimension by virtue of the sexual anecdotes the teacher tells her student, veritable Boccaccian exempla of sexual performance. The narrative pivot of all of these anecdotes is Amatista, which the reader can rightly presume to be either legitimately autobiographical or a fantasy doubling of the narrator/pedagogue. As she explains to her student: "Escuche, doctor, que hasta un hombre de mundo como usted necesita a veces que le cuenten historias" (9).[13] These *historias* are all tales of idealized sexual accomplishment — idealized in the sense that climax is always triumphantly achieved and idealized in the sense that no antagonistic forces ever intervene to thwart triumphant climax: in short, these anecdotes are the very quintessence of the sort of erotic exploits one associates with classical pornography in the glorious beauty, the superb proportions, and the unfettered lugubricity of the performers the narrator evokes. That it is a woman recounting them to a man in the context of an erotic education underscores the feminist conceit of Steimberg's novel.

But there is another dimension to this conceit that has to do with the question of masturbation. Although the narrator's exempla are reminiscent of classical pornography (which she ironizes by metacommentary asides on the language she cannot avoid using in telling them, begging his pardon for words that are too technical, too graphic, or too colloquial), her own encounters with the *doctor* deviate significantly from the narrative schema underlying her anecdotes. Although compulsory heterosexuality is maintained throughout as part of the woman-teaches-man conceit, there are two significant departures that point toward the author's feminist consciousness. One involves the degenitalization of the sexual act. The Amatista anecdotes, as befits their nature as stock narrative formulas, are centered on genital contact, but the female pedagogue is concerned with the total eroticization of the body. And while there is not as complete a survey of corporeal geography as the demanding reader might want, the teacher's attentions to her student's body studiously concentrate on non-penile stimulation:

> Voy a usar una crema suavizante con aceite de pepitas de durazno y muy delicado perfume. Sólo sentirá un frío juguetón con el primer contacto y enseguida el masaje generará calor. Comenzaré por los huecos detrás de los dedos del pie izquierdo. No habrá centímetro de su piel por donde no pasen mis dedos. (23)[14]

A concomitant aspect of total eroticization is the enhancement of sexual release through delay and displacement. In order to overcome the brutish macho practice of the immediate exploitation of the feminine body and the subsequent casting aside of the woman—the practice of the wham bang, the three-minute fuck—the woman wishes to teach the man the virtues of prolonged sexual involvement, not just a courting ritual that is the prelude to sex, with or without sustained foreplay, but an arousal whose culmination is almost indefinitely postponed, such that coitus becomes almost a minimal stage in the entire erotic narrative, but for all that a much more intensely climactic one.

Yet another aspect of the man's sexual (re)education must hinge on the merits of displacement, whereby sexual utilization of the other's body is not a necessary imperative in the erotic narrative. This is where the recodification of masturbation comes in: masturbation not as an ingredient of foreplay or as a form of *faute de mieux* release (as transient homosexuality in all male environments is often touted to be), but masturbation as a sexually climactic experience for the individual, even when an appropriate sexual partner is present. The narrator encourages her pupil to engage in masturbation, and she explains its virtues to him, instructs him how to do it, and even commands him at certain points to jack off. Although masturbation does not emerge from *Amatista* as the master sexual act, the fact that the narrator uses it as an essential ingredient in her pedagogy is in sharp contrast to the conventional intergenital sex on which the Amatista anecdotes are based.

There is, however, another dimension of masturbation in Steimberg's novel that justifies the way in which I have fronted this sexual practice in my presentation of *Amatista*. I refer to the conventional wisdom that pornography is a form of voyeurism that is fundamentally an inducement to masturbation: the image of teenage boys engaged in the solitary vice behind locked bathroom doors, hunched over raunchy girlie magazines they smuggle past their parents' watchful vigilance. But surely all cultural productions prosper through some sort of voyeurism, in that it provides the reader/spectator with something like a sanitary, privileged access to the life, thoughts, and conduct of others. This is especially evident in reader access to the most innermost feelings and fantasies of characters in stream-of-consciousness formats: the scandal over the closing Molly Bloom episode in Joyce's *Ulysses* may have had as much to do with embarrassment over the intrusion of privacy promoted by the novel as it did with the content of Molly's ruminations. In any case, at best pornography foregrounds the voyeuristic dynamic of display texts in culture, and if it promotes masturbation, that may be a reflex of the equally solitary nature of both reading and onanism, especially since reading, like culture in general, presumably stimulates all sorts of psychosomatic responses, sexual arousal being only one of them.

The point with regard to Steimberg's novel is the way in which the interdependence of reading and masturbation are foregrounded in the way in which the inner texts of the pedagogue are part of the arousal of the man, which his female teacher channels in terms of masturbatory practices as a complement to enhanced sexual fulfillment, genital deterritorialization (even when a return to the penis is the end result of the lesson), and the deferral of climax in order to augment its intensity. If, however, there is anything specifically feminist in this program—and certainly the narrative centering on a woman and her espousal of sexual practices that exceed the strict limits of brief, territorialized, and unreflexive macho sex—it lies less with the highlighting of masturbation, which does in fact occur in some feminist, and particularly lesbian, formulations, than it does in the disruption of a masculine dominance that has traditionally denounced onanism as unmanly in the bypassing of reproductive sex, the exclusion of the Other

(i.e., the utilization of a woman's body), and in the reflexive indulgence in erotic fantasies, all of which are at issue in the edu-
cational program of the *doctor*'s teacher.

The texts that are examined in this study clearly do not belong to
the category of violent pornography that is the main point of concern in the Dworkin/MacKinnon tradition and in the theorizing
that underpins *For Adult Users Only,* whose subtitle is *The Dilemma
of Violent Pornography.* Clearly, what is debatable is what constitutes violence and whether any significant distinction can be
maintained between violent pornography and pornographic (i.e.,
genitally based) erotics on one hand and between real rape and
theatrical sex (Califia's "sensuous magic") on the other. Steimberg's novel comes as close as anything written in Spanish to
theatrical erotics as part of a program of cultural resistance to
compulsory heterosexuality and to normative "straight" definitions of sexual enactments, questions that underlie Raznovich's
and Montero's narratives but without attaining the same degree
of characterization *Amatista* manifests.

But it is undoubtedly in Hilst's texts, and especially in their
writerly nature, where one finds the most complex depictions of
erotic revisionism in Latin America. Undoubtedly this has to do
in large measure with a tradition of erotic culture in Brazil that
sustains Hilst's perspectives: it may be a culture fraught with heterosexism, racism, and sexism by contemporary feminist standards, but it does unquestionably provide the reader with semantic
horizons against which to undertake the understanding of Hilst's
figurations of sexuality—indeed, to undertake even to accept
them as legitimate public-access cultural products, something
which, I venture to say, would be more difficult in the Spanish-
speaking societies, including Argentina. It is evident that one must
be careful not to apply hegemonic English- and French-language
cultural priorities to an assessment of this writing, a danger that
is as present for feminism in general and lesbian/gay thematics
(cf. Foster, "Homoerotic Writing and Chicano Authors" and "Some
Proposals") as it is for the pornographic.

Yet it would certainly not be acceptable to frame this writing
in such a way that it would lose specificity as a definable corpus
of cultural production, which would be the case if it were sub-

sumed under a more general category of the feminine erotic. The fact that Montero, Steimberg, and Raznovich all published their novels outside their native countries (in Montero's case, this is true whether one views her native country as Cuba or as Puerto Rico) and the fact that there is a clear difference in the implied reader of the complex language of Hilst's texts and the cliché-ridden transparencies of Rios and Carrara's hyped bestsellers (Rios is wont to say, with little evidence, that she is the most banned writer in Brazil, a statement that directly contradicts the statistics of her sales) means that there is some problematical dimension about this writing. Whether or not it will come to constitute a significant bloc of Latin American feminist cultural production, and whether or not it will be overridden by the dominant emphasis on an erotics that supersedes genital sexuality, as in the case of the texts in *El placer de la palabra* or Denser's two collections for Brazil, will depend on the particular directions feminist writing continues to assume in Latin America.

Notes

1. Are you confused because I am telling all of this to you?

2. Because each one of us . . . has to find his own pig. (Careful not to confuse that with body.) Pig, everybody, pig, the body inside out.

3. I knew that it wouldn't be appropriate to ask too much, that life is viable as long as it stays on the superficies, in the nuances, in the watercolors.

4. We did not begin with the premise that sexuality constitutes an exclusive methodological category, or that it's the only basis on which to examine personal identity. Nonetheless, given the sexual oppression and repression that are found in the multiple manifestations of inequity between the sexes, how could we be able to make the dominant culture more representative of women's interests? In order to transform definitions and oppressive cultural categories we have to turn to women's experience, and to try to understand its codes, its language, and its system of signs; which is to say, undertake the kind of study that the analysis of sexual imagination in the women's literary creation would make possible.

5. Palomita, do you remember how you used to plunge my bread into your cup of chocolate and then would lick my prick? Ah! Your beautiful tongue! I'm able to evoke all of the sounds, all of the tones of the landscape of those afternoons . . . cicadas . . . the black anuses (the hooded birds from the family of the cuculiformes . . . my God!) and the fragrances . . . the jasmine-mango . . . the lemon trees . . . and your gentle movements, extending yourself, my frenzied movements . . . Ah! Marcel, if you remember, the entire universe felt like the madeleines.

6. I suddenly felt nausea and a profound pain in my chest. I still managed to ask him, "Is there another life?"

Yes, millions of children like myself. You will be one of them. It's tedious and even unacceptable but that's just the way it is.

7. I made up my mind to write this book because throughout my entire life I have been reading so much garbage that I decided to simply write my own.

8. I had the hunch that that would be the most important afternoon of my life.

9. bleeding like a little virgin.

10. I took leave kissing him on the mouth, the implacable meat of those lips, a tongue that would not be denied to me any longer, those teeth that remained stuck in my flesh, so that I would remember their flavor on that night, so that I would remember tomorrow night, and so that I remember now and in the hour of my death, and for the rest of the nights that I would live without him.

11. Had it hurt her or not? She said yes, louder, bitch, and she shouted that yes, yes, yes.

12. It was translucent and iridescent, with arabesques, projected onto a screen. I followed it letter by letter.

13. Listen, doctor, even a man of the world like yourself needs once in a while to be told a story.

14. I'm going to use this lotion made of cherry seeds and lightly scented. You will only feel the tickling cold with the first contact and soon the massage will generate heat. I will begin with the hollow area underneath your toes on the left foot. There will not be even a centimeter of your skin that my fingers will not touch.

Works Cited

Attorney General's Commission on Pornography. *Final Report [Meese Report]*. Washington, D.C.: Government Printing Office, 1986.

Benson, Peter. "Between Women: Lesbianism in Pornography." *Textual Practice* 7.3 (1993): 412–27.

Califia, Pat. *Macho Sluts: Erotic Fiction*. Boston: Alyson, 1988.

———. *Sensuous Magic*. New York: Masquerade Books, 1993.

Denser, Márcia, comp. *Muito prazer: Contos*. Rio de Janeiro: Editora Record, 1982.

———. *O prazer é todo meu: Contos eróticos femeninos*. 2a ed. Rio de Janeiro: Editora Record, 1985.

Dunn, Sara. "Voyages of the Valkuries: Recent Lesbian Pornographic Writing." *Feminist Review* 34 (1990): 161–70.

Dworkin, Andrea. *Pornography: Men Possessing Women*. New York: Perigee, 1981.

——— and Catharine A. MacKinnon. *Pornography and Civil Rights: A New Day for Women's Equality*. Minneapolis: Organizing Against Pornography, 1988.

Ellis, Kate, Barbara O'Dair, and Tallmer Abby. "Feminism and Pornography." *Feminist Review* 34 (1990): 15–18.

Esterrich, Carlos. "Mayra Montero." In *Latin American Writers on Gay and Lesbian Themes: A Bio-critical Sourcebook*. Ed. David William Foster. Westport, Conn.: Greenwood Press, 1994, 251–54.

For Adult Users Only: The Dilemma of Violent Pornography. Ed. Susan Gubar and Joan Hoff. Bloomington: Indiana University Press, 1989.

Foster, David William. "Algunos espejismos eróticos [*De Ausencia* de María Luisa Mendoza]." *Revista de la Universidad de México* 37 (1984): 36–38. Also as "Espejismos eróticos: 'De Ausencia,' de María Luisa Mendoza." *Revista iberoameri-*

cana 132–33 (1985): 657–63. Also in his *Alternative Voices in the Contemporary Latin American Narrative.* Columbia: University of Missouri Press, 1985, 131–36.

———. *Gay and Lesbian Themes in Latin American Writing.* Austin: University of Texas Press, 1991.

———. "Homoerotic Writing and Chicano Authors." Unpublished paper.

———. "Pornography and the Feminine Erotic: Griselda Gambaro's *Lo impenetrable.*" *Monographic Review/Revista monográfica* 7 (1991): 284–96.

———. "Some Proposals for the Study of Latin American Gay Culture." In *Cultural Diversity in Latin American Literature.* Albuquerque: University of New Mexico Press, 1993, 25–71.

Friday, Nancy. *Women on Top: How Real Life Has Changed Women's Sexual Fantasies.* New York: Simon and Schuster, 1991.

Gambaro, Griselda. *Lo impenetrable.* Buenos Aires: Torres Agüero, 1984.

Henderson, Lisa. "Lesbian Pornography; Cultural Transgression and Sexual Demystification." *Women and Language* 14.1 (1991): 3–12. Also *New Lesbian Criticism: Literary and Cultural Readings.* New York: Harvester Wheatsheaf, 1992, 173–91.

Hilst, Hilda. *Cartas de un sedutor.* São Paulo: Editoria Paulicéia, 1991.

———. *Contos d'escárnio: Textos grotescos.* São Paulo: Edições Siciliano, 1990.

The Invention of Pornography: Obscenity and the Origins of Modernity, 1500–1800. Ed. Lynn Hunt. New York: Zone Books, 1993.

Jaramillo Levi, Enrique, comp. *El cuento erótico en Mexico.* Mexico: Editorial Diana, 1975.

Kendrick, Walter. *The Secret Museum: Pornography in Modern Culture.* New York: Viking, 1987.

Kristeva, Julia. "Stabat Mater." In *The Kristeva Reader.* New York: Columbia University Press, 1986, 160–86.

MacKinnon, Catharine A. *Only Words.* Cambridge: Harvard University Press, 1993.

Marcuse, Herbert. *Eros and Civilization.* New York: Vintage, 1962.

———. "On Hedonism." In *Negations.* Boston: Beacon Press, 1968, 159–200.

Mendoza, María Luisa. *De Ausencia.* Mexico: Editorial Joaquín Mortiz, 1974.

Montero, Mayra. *La última noche que pasé contigo.* Barcelona: Tusquets, 1991.

Montero, Rosa. "El misterio del deseo: así son y así viven las lesbianas en España." *El país semanal* 141 (31 de octubre, 1993): 16–27.

Parker, Richard G. *Bodies, Pleasures, and Passions; Sexual Culture in Contemporary Brazil.* Boston: Beacon Press, 1990.

Peri-Rossi, Cristina. *Fantasías eróticas.* Madrid: Edición Temas de Hoy, 1991.

El placer de la palabra: Literatura erótica femenina de América Latina: antología crítica. Mexico: Planeta, 1991.

Pornography and Feminism: The Case against Censorship. Ed. Gillian Rodgerson and Elizabeth Wilson. London: Lawrence and Wishart, 1991.

Raznovich, Diana. *Mater erótica.* Barcelona: RobinBook, 1992.

Soble, Alan. *Pornography: Marxism, Feminism, and the Future of Sexuality.* New Haven: Yale University Press, 1986.

Steimberg, Alicia. *Amatista.* Barcelona: Tusquets, 1989. 2d ed., 1990.

Chapter 13

The Pornographic Subject of
Los borbones en pelota

Lou Charnon-Deutsch

In 1991, Ediciones El Museo Universal published an album of 89 watercolors, originally titled *Los borbones en pelota*, under the title *Sem*. The watercolors, signed "Sem" or "Semen" are thought to have been painted by Valeriano and Gustavo Bécquer, sometime during the period of 1868–69. The two dimensions of the Bécquer watercolors, the sexual and the political, intersect in important ways that have been touched on only briefly by commentators Lee Fontanella, Robert Pageard, and María Dolores Cabra Loredo, whose studies are included in the *Sem* volume. In the introduction to the *Sem* collection, an unnamed editor speculates that with this publication famed poet Gustavo Adolfo Bécquer (1836–70) will be rescued from four generations of purgatory and located not in the paradise expected for the author of the sublime *Rimas y leyendas*, but in hell. It is not that Gustavo and his brother Valeriano Domínguez Bécquer (1833–70) will *go* to hell for what they have created, but that their lives will at last be seen as a living hell (7), a chaos of sentiment and sex that has remained partially veiled to us until some unnamed party sold the *Sem* watercolors to the Biblioteca Nacional in 1986. Now the editor, together with commentators Fontanella, Pageard, and Cabra, can truly *unveil* the Bécquer brothers, "bringing to light"[1] a corrected version that will act as a "mirror to our world" (10).[2]

I have paraphrased the editor's remarks in order to demonstrate the extent to which Queen Isabel II, featured in so many of the watercolors, is still used to reveal not just the seamier side of her sexual deportment, but a fuller, more accurate vision of the artists who imagined her sexual excess. For modern-day viewers, the queen's body not only bears evidence of the terrible nothing behind the lifted veil, it provides a mirror that permits us both to see these men in a different light, and to view Isabeline society for what it *really* was. How at odds the fleshy and grotesque body of the queen seems with the ethereal specter of Becquerian rhymes and legends.[3] Yet the use value of both is not significantly different. Ironically, our modern use of the queen's body as "espejo" of the poet's disordered lives and times tallies well with the narcissistic love object that peoples Bécquer's works, the woman who the narrator of "El rayo de luna" says, "thinks like I think, likes what I like, hates what I hate, a kindred spirit, the complement to my being" (169).[4] If Bécquer imagined the essence of poetry as a veiled, ethereal woman, we imagine the essence of Bécquer as a soul tortured by the vulgarity and excesses of Isabel's reign, personified in the queen's wanton sexual activities.

Poverty, venereal diseases, dissipation, broken marriages, burdensome family responsibilities, and changing political and professional alliances all contributed to the untidy existence of the Bécquer brothers, but they do not explain why they may have chosen the queen and her entourage as their target for the caricatures they produced and possibly circulated among their friends, especially since they were under the protection of the court before it disbanded.[5] Nor do they explain the emphatically obscene content of so many of the sketches. To understand the anecdotal and figural content of the *Sem* watercolors it is necessary to explore a number of conventions and discourses that extend beyond the artists' personal trajectories: the influence of traditional French caricature; classical iconography; nineteenth-century Spanish anticlericalism and political cynicism; the conventional use of women's bodies to express what is on a man's mind; the importance of speaking for the/a queen; and the vagaries of Isabel II's personal life and how that life was characterized by the novelists and artists of the day.

Some of these topics are taken up in the commentaries accompanying the edition. For example, Pageard compares the Spanish watercolors with the French and Italian erotic caricature tradition, and Fontanella fills in with important information about the Bécquers' professional lives and historical and political contexts, including details about the queen's personal life. Fontanella also attempts a brief psychological interpretation of the caricaturist's art that he feels is necessary in order to "legitimate" the *Sem* watercolors. Hoping to deemphasize the obviously lewd content of the watercolors, he insists that the Bécquers' intention was primarily political; as jocose *costumbristas* they intended merely to reveal the "mysteries of the Palace":[6] "I repeat that these images can not be considered pornographic as far as their primary intention is concerned, although some of them are certainly obscene" (27).[7] Just as we often justify the pornographic content of art by appealing to its aesthetic value (Stoller, Freedberg), Fontanella justifies the obscenity of the watercolors by citing their political content and the personal turmoil of their creators. Such arguments are attractive for men, as Susanne Kappeler points out, because they "divert the opposition to their fantasies into indulgent understanding of their psychological difficulties" (38). Not wishing in any way to diminish their political content, I want to see if it is possible to reverse Fontanella's order of priorities and study these watercolors primarily for their pornographic content that derives from a shared complex of values.

It should not come as a surprise that a caricaturist uses the queen's body to propagate political views any more than that a painter or sculptor uses a beautiful female nude model to ponder death or exalt physical beauty. Conventional as this may be, of course, there is nothing "natural" about it. It's just that the use of the female body as facilitator of political and aesthetic communication has been so widespread for so long that it has come to seem natural (Kappeler). Artists will use whatever material is the most prized or exchangeable, including a queen, especially in Spain, where rumors abounded about Isabel's sexual adventures. Nor are the graphic arts the only to play with queenly representation. Showing the *queen* — the beautiful, modest, and virtuous

Christian woman—for what she really was would become an important literary device for the restoration novelists of the generation succeeding the Bécquers. Leopoldo Alas's Ana Ozores, *La Regenta,* is the classic example. Novelist Benito Pérez Galdós's 1906 description of the recently deceased Isabel II could easily describe his heroines Isidora Rufete (*La desheredada*), Fortunata (*Fortunata y Jacinta*), or any of a dozen of his other fallen angels:

> Her reign will be judged severely: in it we will see the origin and embryo of a good deal of our political vices; yet no one would deny the immense gentleness of this ingenious soul, indolent, as easily given to piety, forgiveness, charity as incapable of any sustained or vigorous resolve. Doña Isabel lives in a perpetual infancy; her greatest misfortune was to have been born a queen and to bear in her hands the moral direction of a people, a weighty obligation for such delicate hands. (*Memoranda* 1906, quoted in *Sem* 20).[8]

Other novelists have followed in Galdós's footsteps in reducing the queen-woman to the bodily by demasking her sexual or material excesses. Among turn-of-the-century examples, Valle Inclán's *La corte de los milagros* is notable for its descriptions of Isabel II as a great duck who waddles her way through official ceremonies, "luxious"[9] like a great "concubine"[10] or some "eight-cent paper doll" (353),[11] always with an eye for the young officers and *palaciegos* who pay her court. More recently, Ricardo de la Cierva has continued the tradition with a three-volume historical novel about the life and loves of Isabel II, "a bitch in heat looking for a partner to dominate her,"[12] as her husband Francisco calls her (250). The Bécquer brothers demonstrated that already in the 1860s the queen was a singularly useful medium for the intertwining of political and sexual verities. Their watercolors demonstrate both visual control of what Gustavo's poetry tried to prove was unrepresentable (the woman's body), and a savvy attitude regarding the shortcomings of Isabeline politics and morality. Theirs was an economic form of satire, collapsing political and sexual immorality of court and government into one grotesquely large and naked figure. It was also, I want to argue, a handy pretext for producing and enjoying pornography.

In order to make what would be for the editors of *Sem* an unpleasant reversal such as this, it is necessary first to discuss the various meanings of the term *pornography* as they could be applied to the *Sem* collection. The feminist debate centering on definitions of pornography grows increasingly complex as differing positions arise in response to rapid social change. Traditionally, the emphasis has been on *obscenity*, "the immoral or 'dirty' quality of the sex portrayed" (Kappeler 1). While some feminists today are concentrating on violence in their definitions of pornography, Ellen Willis, among others, adheres to the standard definition of pornography as an "image or description intended or used to arouse sexual desire" (462). Aware of the predominantly sexist bias of pornography, she still insists that we consider not only its use value, but its potentially radical impulse that rejects sexual repression and hypocrisy (464). Helen Longino sums up another of the most common arguments by defining *erotica* as the explicit depiction of sexual behavior and *pornography* as material that represents and indirectly endorses degrading and abusive sexual behavior (171). This definition links representation of sexual deeds with the possible harmful effects they produce in real-life sexual relations between men and women. Susan Griffin argues that pornography "is an expression not of human erotic feeling and desire, ... but of a fear of bodily knowledge, and a desire to silence eros" (11). In *The Pornography of Representation*, Susanne Kappeler focuses on pornography as a form of representation and therefore subject to a broader cultural critique that would incorporate varying discourses — economic, political, and artistic (1–4).[13] She locates the structures of power and domination that pornography emphasizes in many other forms of representation as well. Finally, more radical feminists such as Andrea Dworkin, whose campaigns against its publication are legendary, define pornography as the "depiction of women as vile whores ... women who exist to serve men sexually" (200).

The *Sem* watercolors contain elements that fit into all of these definitions of pornography. They clearly challenge the sexual hypocrisy of Spanish society, exhibiting the queen's sexual activities (inaccurately, it is important to mention) that were hypocritically masked by her fanatical devotion to religious figures Sor Patrocinio and Father Claret. The behavior depicted in the watercolors is not overtly violent, but it is often degrading, for example, in number 99, which shows the queen having sexual intercourse with a donkey as a row of other donkeys in their stalls ostensibly wait their turn. There is little use of conventional expressions of erotic desire in the *Sem* collection, but clear evidence of a fear of bodily knowledge, for example, in the exaggeratedly large or contorted sexual organs (numbers 10, 17, 74, 83, 84, 88, 97). The economic, political, and artistic dimensions of this pornography that Kappeler urges us to examine more critically are clearly tied even to the most obscene representations, and structured into them is a relation of artist to spectator that is classically pornographic. Finally, the queen in these sketches is, besides a metonym for the crown and Spanish politics in general, a "vile whore" willing to have intercourse indiscriminately with priests, nuns, soldiers, consorts, politicians, and even animals.

Several objections to the classification of the *Sem* watercolors as pornography could be raised. One, already mentioned, is that they were intended as political rather than pornographic representations. For psychiatrist Robert Stoller, "The less an artist has pornographic intent, the fewer the people who will find the work pornographic" (67). Of course, intention is notoriously difficult to ascertain, and there are no written accounts about either the intended meanings or use of the portfolio. At any rate, I am not claiming to know what the primary intention of these obscene representations was, only clarifying that their pornographic content (or that of any representation for that matter) does not depend only on the purpose for which they were primarily intended or the assigned meanings that later accrued to them in the hands of those who, for all their desire to *reveal* the real Bécquers, still want to protect them from accusations of being pornographers.

This leads to a second and more consequential objection: if, as is possible, the watercolors were for the private use only of the artists, can they be considered pornography? In the question of pornography the issue of audience is usually paramount. Implied in every representation is an author/artist and a reader/perceiver in a relation of production and exchange (Kappeler 3–4). These two subjects are not pictured in the frame, but are the framers, the subjects who use a graphic image to represent (something to) themselves. Is a representation pornographic if these two agents are one and the same? It is not known who, if anyone, saw the *Sem* sketches prior to the death of the Bécquer brothers. Fontanella offers the interesting conjecture that they were a compensatory gift to the editors of the periodical *Gil Blas* who had previously published less obscene political cartoons by Valeriano Bécquer under the pseudonym Sem (40). Thus, Fontanella seems particularly anxious to establish a male spectatorship for the *Sem* portfolio outside the Bécquers' private library. The reason for this could be that the sketches are so elaborate, so cynical and politically motivated, that it is difficult (disappointing?) to imagine that they did not circulate in some fashion, however reduced, among the Bécquers's friends or business associates. But by imagining a group of male spectators in the offices of *Gil Blas,* that is, by creating a new representation of the scene of looking, do we not add to the present-day perception of them as pornography? To what extent have Fontanella and the other editors of *Sem* corrected an earlier circulation lapse by providing modern-day readers wide access to the images in a now porn-happy Spanish society? Or should we argue that while the images might have seemed pornographic to a nineteenth-century reader they are only sociopolitical documents in the present era of relaxed censorship?

These and other questions are some of the issues that confront a researcher trying to ascertain the pornographic content of a work. Had one of these images been published in the irreverent *Gil Blas* the year it was painted, it would certainly have been judged pornographic, but to say that the images are not pornographic because their distribution was limited is to locate the definition of pornography not "in the representation itself, but in its distribution" (Kappeler 27). In agreement with Kappeler, I would argue that the pornographic content does not depend on their distribution but that even if it did, the distribution of the watercolors is now a fait accompli, and even if the sketches never circulated during the time of their execution, we know that two men, Valeriano and Gustavo Bécquer, painted them and then looked at them and saw what they wanted to see.

This looking and painting are preeminently masculine activities, as John Berger, David Freedberg, and many feminist art critics have recently argued (Kappeler 32). While graphically absent from most of the images, the male artist is prominently featured on the cover of the portfolio and helps to frame the activity of pornographic production. The title *Los borbones en pelota* is superimposed on the upper portion of the scene. The queen is lying across her royal bed, scepter in hand and crown at her feet. Her skirts are lifted and she displays her pudendum to "a line of palace suitors who legendarily attended to the regal desires of the queen monarch" (*Sem* 212).[14] Although the person who draws the veil revealing this terrible sight to the line of represented viewers is a woman, it is, in fact, an artist who will determine the reception of the revelation through his creative act of capturing the scene on canvas and later passing it on. Thus, the objectification of the queen through representation helps to ensure the subjectivity of the male as artist. In turn the artist insinuates at least two other absent parties, the actual artist of the watercolor (whether or not one of the Bécquer brothers), and a viewer who stands outside the frame and shares the actual artist's perspective on things. The sight behind the drawn curtain is a gift to *him*, a revelation in which truth about the woman is the object of exchange between artist and viewer. As such, the queen here is doubly objectified, first by the figure representing the painter, then by historical viewers of the scene of painting who can only interpret this as a scene of objectification. If the cover is unusual for its representation of the artist in the creative act, a surrogate viewer for the implied viewer is depicted in many of the most pornographic scenes of the *Sem* collection: he stands in the background, sometimes with a shocked or surprised look on his face, or he looks on with the keen pleasure of the voyeur who happily masturbates as the queen frolics with her lovers (see, for example, 97). Thus, all the information needed about the production and the *ideal* consumption of the watercolors is either inferred, as in the cover, or documented scenically in the subsequent watercolors.

In most definitions of pornography, a victim or victims are identified: a woman, a group or class of women, Woman. Who were the victims of the *Sem* watercolors? Can the queen be thought of as the victim if no one saw the watercolors but the artists? If so, are the men (such as the queen's consort, Francisco de Asís) also victims since they are just as obscenely represented and debased? Or, should we look elsewhere if we want to understand the exploitative nature of this pornography? Clearly, Isabel is depicted as the center of attention, a wanton, carnivalesque pleasure seeker, indifferent to the sex of her partners; their religious, social, or political position; and the place where she and her entourage perform their sexual acts. She is a mountain of collapsed flesh with a complacent, or sometimes even absent, expression on her face, an animal in heat whom men line up to service. A sexual object seen from more than a dozen angles, she has been stripped of any meaningful subjectivity outside of her political or sexual meaning for her viewers. Although the queen is the primary target in the largest number of the watercolors (she figures in nearly fifty of them), her husband Francisco de Asís appears in thirty of them, often pictured with a colossal pair of antlers marking him as Spain's most notorious cuckold. In fact, Francisco de Asís is *represented* as the principal victim of the watercolors: standing erect (23), kneeling (40), or blindfolded (53), he is forced to hold a candle over the bedside of his wife and her lover Carlos Marfori or to play the viola during their lovemaking (66); desperate at his wife's nude frolicking with Father Claret, Napoleón, and Marfori, he prepares to castrate himself with a long stiletto knife (74); pulled by a rope around his neck that is held by Claret, he trudges down a hill, bearing the queen's intimate friend, Sor Patrocinio, on his shoulders. In one hand Sor Patrocinio brandishes a whip high in the air while with the other she grasps Asís's antlers (99); in a kneeling position Asís holds Claret and the queen on his back while the queen fondles Claret's penis against Asís's buttocks (15); a shepherdess queen leads Asís along by a cord, dressed as a goat, while behind her Marfori lifts her skirts (17).

Of course, the fact that a man is consistently exploited does not make the *Sem* watercolors any less pornographic. The *Sem* scenarios are pornographic in part because they suggest that copulation is a grotesque, animalistic act. That nudity and sex are bestial is implied in the animal-like poses of the scenario, or the repeated animal motifs in the margins of the scenarios: Isabel galloping like a horse in the circus (5) or being mounted by a donkey (99); small dogs watching the queen's lovemaking from the sidelines (10, 15) or even mimicking the queen's activities (21); rats fleeing from the scene when Marfori and Isabel tumble from the throne (16); Francisco dressed as a goat (17); gargoyle figures next to the masturbating daughter of the queen (26); Pan feeding grapes to a nude Isabel as she is being paraded about by three men (47); Isabel riding a horse as Asís looks on, penis erect (57); Isabel clutching her sable fur as she is shown off as the fat lady in the circus (58); a small dog looking on as Margarita de Parma or Princess Maria Victoria de la Cisterna powders her genital area (76); Francisco de Asís making love to Sor Patrocinio as an unidentified black beast crouches under a tree.

The watercolors are also pornographic because in them the sexual relations between men and women are shown to be exploitative. The queen exploits her position to satisfy her sexual whims; politicians enhance their power and influence by exploiting the queen's sexual insatiability; instead of respecting her marriage vows, the queen takes every opportunity to crown her husband with the ignominious *cornudo*; Francisco buys the sexual favors of young novitiates. Instead of guarding the moral order, religious figures gleefully join in the sexual free-for-all. But it is a mistake to define the victims of pornography only as the depicted victims of the pornographic scenario. In other words, the scenario does not give full information about social or sexual victimization because it does not take full account of the author/artist and reader/ spectator structure and the effects of their exchange. Implicit in the *Sem* watercolors is a spectator who delights in the depiction of sexual degradation and extravagance. In fact, the variety of the sexual positions and activities lends the portfolio the quality of chapbook; no sexual composition is exactly the same as any other. The types of sexual activities depicted or implied run the gamut from masturbation (26) to sodomy (18) and fellatio (18); from group intercourse (10, 11, 15, 18, 21, 49) to bondage (9, 14, 17); homosexuality (21, 82) to bestiality (99) and castration or self-mutilation (74, 82, 93). Exhibitionism (58) and voyeurism (17, 18, 97) are often part of the performance. With their complex acrobatics, many of the scenarios seem clearly intended to astound the viewer. The viewer of the scene is, like the porn movie viewer, given the best advantage to see the sexual act of coitus. In fact, in some of the watercolors the positions of the sexual participants seem impossible to maintain, posed as they are to offer the spectator the fullest possible view of their genitals (32, 41, 59, 99). The props are as varied as the positions and types of intercourse: lovers embrace on the throne, on the floor, in royal or humble beds, in chairs large and small, on divans and cushions, on the ground beneath a tree or on a riverbank.

In addition to the variety of sexual acts, painstakingly displayed from a multitude of angles, the watercolors focus on male and female genitalia. Again, as in modern pornographic movies, the male penis is prominently displayed. Erect and usually oversized male organs are featured in more than one-fourth of the sketches. In eleven of them, more than one man is depicted with an erection, and in several of them, an entire row of men stand with penises erect. For example, in 5, Carlos Marfori parades the queen around a circular arena, putting her through her dance steps with a whip in hand. The pair have just entered the circus arena by passing through a chorus of half a dozen male figures, standing at attention with their penises erect. In 97, the queen sits on top of Carlos Marfori while her husband tries to enter her from behind. Behind Francisco, a line of nude soldiers masturbate as they look on. Female nudity (the queen's body in the majority of cases) is featured in thirty-nine of the sketches. The queen's breasts, buttocks, and pudenda are often exaggeratedly large. For example, in 10c the queen's pudenda are smothered in a mass of hair as large as the distance between her shoulders. The queen's midsection verges on the obese in many of the watercolors, but in some of them it is excessively large, for example, in 31, in which the queen's huge torso appears too large to be supported by such dainty ankles and feet, or in 58, in which the queen is depicted as the fat lady in the circus with the inscription "Come one, come all, see the celebrated fat lady who weighs five hundred kilos without her crown or scepter" (318).[15] The queen's head, as is customary in caricatures, is unusually large in proportion to her body, but her features are often ill defined except for her nose, which is bulbous and sagging like her breasts. Her eyes, if they can be distinguished, are unstriking, vacant, or puffy.

Besides illustrating the political vagaries of the throne, in several of the watercolors the queen's body mimics famous nudes in a grotesque parody of high art. For example in 37, "La Venus del . . . género humano"[16] she strikes the pose of the reclining nude of Titian's "Venus and Cupid with Prince Philip as Organist" and "Venus and Cupid with a Lute Player." The majestic landscapes and classical drapery framing Titian's nudes are replaced with the fringes and laces of Isabel's bedchamber with its rumpled

sheets and pillowcases. Titian's organist/lute player has been replaced with an image of one of the queen's political supporters,
either Luis González Bravo or Francisco Serrano. While Isabel's
body appears to be a close study of the Titian nudes (especially
that of "Venus and Cupid with a Lute Player"), her face has the
same complacency and dullness that characterize all of the *Sem*
paintings (10b, 17b, 21, 23, 34, 36, 45, 47, 53, etc.). The play on in-
congruencies is significant: the queen of Spain strikes an uncon-
vincing pose as the beauty queen, her head is ill suited for such a
voluptuous body. On the other hand, the sanctuary of art has
been violated by the vulgar queen; the beauty queen's bodily perfection is marred by reference to this homely face with a double
chin, when what belongs atop it is the blond Venus of the "Lute
Player" with her striking gaze and sensuous, parted lips. Like
many others, then, number 37 is a report on women's shortcomings; beauty and baseness are forever ruining the imagined perfection by showing up together, as Spain's novelists would constantly demonstrate in the decades to come.

Not surprisingly, given the Bécquers' penchant for the per-
forming arts, many of the watercolors depict nude, seminude, or
costumed figures in acts of performance: as marionettes (4); as
Parisian carnival revelers (17, 22); as *majos* (24, 45); as circus or
street performers (34, 36, 56, 57, 58, 62); or as cancan, bolero,
quadrille, or redondel dancers (5, 42, 69 70, 74, 102). The masquerade and lewd poses and costumes add to the general impression of a carnival-like atmosphere that runs through the entire
portfolio. Like the carnivalesque elements Bakhtin studied in Rabelais's work, this carnival atmosphere is a challenge to the existing order, hostile to the authority of the queen and the clergy,
making its points through the use of *grotesque realism* with its images of "the body as multiple, bulging, over- or under-sized, protuberant and incomplete" (Stallybrass 9).[17] But if, as Peter Stallybrass and Allon White argue, the political dimensions of carnival
are far more complex than Bakhtin imagined, tied especially to
moments of great social revolts and conflicts (15), it cannot be
said that the carnivalesque in these images challenges in any revolutionary way the sexual conventions of bourgeois society even
though we know they were painted in a moment of great politi-

cal turmoil. For all their irreverence and their mixing of high and low, the watercolors embrace rather than challenge prevailing gender codes and stereotypes.[18]

We can explain this conservatism by recalling that pornography always depicts or implies games of power or domination. In fact, as Kappeler and others have been arguing, representation in general cannot be divorced from the hegemonic discourses it inculcates in the viewer. The representation of pornography often asserts, even if implicitly, a gender ideology that figuratively puts women in their place. The *Sem* watercolors do this with the queen, even while it appears that it is the queen who is happily putting men in their place (in her bed). When we focus on the fact that this heap of flesh with an ugly face, this "hembra en celo en busca de macho dominante" (Cierva 250),[19] is the queen of Spain, we can begin to understand how women are the victims of the *Sem* watercolors even as the women represented in them appear so content to be sexual objects. The images of the wayward queen expose a terrible gender mistake: the person occupying the throne is of the *wrong* sex. In nearly every image Isabel demonstrates that she doesn't belong on the throne. She casts down her crown as she enjoys sex with Marfori (portada, 55), she has sex while seated on the throne (10, 17), she falls out of her throne during sex (16), she has sex or poses nude with the crown on her head (37, 21, 23, 59), and she wraps ceremonial ribbons about her nude body during sex (10). In 22 the queen dances the cancan in the Paris Carnival (a reference to her exile in France). Her velvet, ermine-lined train flies about her as she kicks up her heels. Her husband, Francisco, sits on the sidelines masquerading as a king, with the crown for once on *his* head and the scepter in *his* hands, the queen's fool. Here as above in the Titian parody, there is a double play of masquerade: Isabel is masquerading as queen when she is *really* a dance hall prostitute, or she is masquerading as a dance hall girl when she is *really* the queen.

The repeated juxtaposition of queen and dance hall or circus performer emphasizes the sexual travesty of the queen's inappropriate position(s). In number 48 the queen stands with her back to a large assemblage dressed in a dance hall costume rimmed with gold tassels. To her right stand the "leales,"[20] among them Francisco in the garb of a white knight. To her left stand the "le-los,"[21] Father Claret and Sor Patrocinio. On her head rests a rather reduced gold crown. In one hand the queen holds a whip and in the other a pirate's flag. The queen, it seems clear, is a pirate who has stolen the throne and now keeps her loyalists captive. Her husband Francisco stands in the background as an embarrassing reminder of this sexual usurpation. On the wall above the vaulted room another flag depicts the pirate queen's insignia: beneath a skull and crossbones a kneeling man has his head cut off; beneath a second skull a man's body hangs limply from a gallows, shadowy references to the violence of the Carlist wars. In the background a row of figures dangle from ropes on a communal gallows; again references to both the symbolic and the physical violence of Isabel's reign.

In this as in other sketches, Francisco embodies the queen's hapless victims; his head is intact, but his sex is not. He cannot be the king because he is married to the queen. Isabel keeps her husband as a pet instead of the opposite arrangement sanctioned by Spanish society. Isabel's power is symbolized both by her sexual proclivity and her usurpation of the phallus. She wields her power by literally having the phallus at her disposal whenever she calls for it; it is even figured on her staff in 93. She is the desirable but terrible phallic mother whose castration threats are graphically represented. Francisco, on the other hand, comes perilously close to losing his penis; his political and sexual powerlessness are symbolized not only by his act of self-mutilation in 74, but by the fact that all the erect penises he sees penetrating or masturbating near the queen are not his. A metaphor for the hapless male who leaves his manhood at the steps of the throne, Francisco naturally evokes the sympathy of the viewer as clearly he did the writer of the inscription of number 71:

> Your noble face has been tarnished
> by a cloud of dishonor,
> Quickly wipe away this blemish,
> Cut your horns, Señor;
> The entire world is pointing at you,
> Europe dubs you a cuckold,
> and "Cuckold" echos
> throughout the land. (340)[22]

According to Stallybrass and White, "The grotesque is formed through a process of hybridization or inmixing of binary opposites, particularly of high and low, such that there is a heterodox merging of elements usually perceived as incompatible, and this latter version of the grotesque unsettles any fixed binaryism" (44). However, the transgressive element of the grotesque does not automatically imply political progressiveness: "Often it is a powerful ritual or symbolic practice whereby the dominant squanders its symbolic capital so as to get in touch with the fields of desire which it denied itself as the price paid for its political power" (201). This discussion of the grotesque and of the inmixing of binary opposites, however, does not refer to the relations between man and woman (here queen and consort), but to the relations between dominant bourgeois classes and the "stratifications of bodies and cultures" that bourgeois society produced in its process of differentiation from the "low Other" (202). However, we could argue that there are certain similarities between this concept of the grotesque and the grotesque effects of the *Sem* watercolors. Like the grotesque manifestations studied by Stallybrass and White, the *Sem* watercolors do not fundamentally challenge categories. They do not, for example, make the viewer suspect that there is anything wrong with the basic sexual categories of man and woman, only that something has gone terribly wrong and turned the sexual hierarchy of the binaryism topsy-turvy.

To pursue this notion that the *Sem* watercolors fixate on inappropriate gender roles (thereby promoting conventional sexual arrangements), it is useful to compare the Bécquer sketches with pornographic representations of Isabel's Italian counterpart, Austrian-born Queen María Sophia and her Bourbon husband, King Francis II of Naples. Although most of the pornographic photomontages depicting the Neapolitan royalty that were used as *cartes de visite* have been lost, their description is contained in a pamphlet that was extracted in a recent article by Kathleen Collins.[23] In one of the images, reports Collins, a nude María Sophia is "bathing in a round bathtub 'in which there were objects of unmistakable form floating'" (297). In one the pope enters her chamber while the queen sleeps; in others, the queen is having intercourse with an officer of the Zouaves. Collins reproduces two other *cartes de visite,* one of María Sophia and her husband riding a giant phallus through the air, the second of just Francisco riding sidesaddle on a winged phallus. These photomontages make it clear that María Sophia, like her Bourbon counterpart Isabel II, rides on the sign of the phallus: they float about her in the bathtub and carry her off into the sky. The phallus/penis as a sign has political as well as sexual significance in all of these pornographic sketches. Who has it and who doesn't have it, who uses it and on whom, who gets it and where—and, what is it? are all questions that pertain.

Postmodernist psychoanalytic theorists take great pains to separate the notion of the phallus from that of its physical counterpart, the penis. Feminist theorists, however, have often insisted upon the inseparability of the two, noting that whether one possesses the phallus or not cannot be separated except in fantasy from the facts of biological sex. Power, symbolized by the phallus, resides in those whose anatomy signals them as men because of their penis. But a fear that this is not really so, or that things could be different, informs much popular art and most pornographic representation. Underlying the satirical vision of Isabel's desecration of the throne is a fear that the penis does not mark the power of the throne, that the phallus is a free-floating signifier, as Lacan would have it. The penis, detached from its rightful owners, has become associated with the queen. This can be seen in the two watercolors in which a detached penis is prominently featured. In number 82 the queen lies on a divan, her face given over to her complete contentment. Sor Patrocinio lies between her legs with her arms stretched about the queen's neck. A huge, pendulous breast (replacing the penis of so many of the watercolors) protrudes from the nun's garment and rests against the queen's midsection. On the floor beside the divan, where the two women smile into each others' faces, lie a penis and scrotum, much smaller than the giant, erect penises of the previous watercolors. The inscription "Who wants fat/candle grease?"[24] is not glossed by commentator Cabra Loredo, although it could give rise to multiple interpretations. What is especially "fat" in this image are the body parts of the queen and her favorite: the queen's cheek and chin, her thighs and arms, Sor Patrocinio's breast and stomach and thighs. "Fat" (*sebo*), then, could refer to the collective female sebum or *fat* of the two entwined bodies. In fact, the farther we move away from the image the more the women's bodies resemble a pile of tallow or suet. On the other hand, the detached penis could be the tallow that could (if the person to whom the question is directed wanted it to) shed light on this scene. There is a direct relation between what is happening on the couch and the severed organ on the floor. Perhaps the penis has been spent, its *suet* used to increase/grease the pleasurable contact between the two women. There are no clues to the correct interpretation of the *sebo*. It is evident, however, that the penis discarded on the floor at the queen's side has shed the potency of previous images. It belongs to no one and has no obvious use except perhaps as a warning. Although viewers might regard it with disgust or fear, the women are oblivious to it; they have found their pleasure elsewhere.

Number 93, an equally enigmatic watercolor, can serve as a conclusion to this discussion of the detachable penis. It shows a pensive (or satiated?) queen seated with her legs spread apart on a nondescript object in what looks like a grove of bamboo or some other dense wooded area. She is in a typical harem pose, but her dress resembles the circus costumes in 34, 48, and 57; she wears a gauze chemise with gold trim and a gold necklace, bracelets and straps wound about her slippers and ankles. Between her legs the queen holds a staff crowned with a severed, erect penis with wings outstretched. The penis is emitting drops of semen. The inscription reads, "Don't be lewd and cover up, cover up that thing" (370).[25] It isn't clear if the exhortation is for the queen to cover her own sex or to cover the offending penis-staff. But what is clear is that the penis, instead of being where it *belongs* (see numbers 6, 15, 17, 41, 55, 59, 66, 85, 86, 88, 95, 97, 99), has become a symbol for the queen's terrible power. Though its wings are outspread, it is firmly attached to the staff that the queen holds between her legs as if it were her very own phallus. The queen's rule is a sexual travesty, the penis of the man with whom she may have just copulated (González Bravo? Carlos Marfori?) has been displaced and landed atop her staff, where it becomes an overdetermined symbol that encompasses both psychological fears and complex historical relations between the queen and her subjects. It bears witness both to the awful power she wields over men (whence my term *travesty*), and to the power of the penis in shaping the perception of the Spanish monarchy. Truly, as Pérez Galdós argued about Isabel's moral responsibilities, this staff represents a "heavy obligation for such tender hands."[26]

Notes

1. "damos a luz" 10.

2. "espejo de nuestro mundo" 10.

3. The attribution of the watercolors to the Bécquer brothers will no doubt present certain problems for art critics, chief among them that there are stylistic inconsistencies between forms and figures of Valeriano Bécquer's published work and the *Sem* watercolors. For comparison, see María Dolores Cabra Loredo's edition of the Bécquer brothers' work for *La Ilustración de Madrid*. Also see the issues of the periodical *Gil Blas* and Rafael Montesinos's *Bécquer: Biografía e imagen*.

4. "piensa como yo pienso, que gusta de lo que yo gusto, que odia lo que yo odio, que es un espíritu hermano de mi espíritu, que es el complemento de mi ser."

5. As Pageard points out, when attempting to explain the choice of subject it is important to take into account that even the patrons of the Bécquer brothers like Narváez and González Bravo became targets of their satire.

6. "misterios de Palacio."

7. "Repito que estas imágenes vienen a ser no pornográficas en cuanto a su intención primaria, aunque algunas sí son obscenas."

8. "Se juzgará su reinado con crítica severa: en él se verá el origen y embrión de no pocos vicios de nuestra política; pero nadie niega ni desconoce la inmensa ternura de aquella alma ingenua, indolente, fácil a piedad, al perdón, a la caridad, como incapaz de toda resolución tenaz y vigorosa. Doña Isabel vivió en perpetua infancia y el mayor infortunio fue haber nacido Reina y llevar en sus manos la dirección moral de un pueblo, pesada obligación para tan tiernas manos."

9. "frondosa."

10. "manflota."

11. "peponas de ocho cuartos."

12. "hembra en celo en busca de macho dominante,"

13. "Pornography — writes Kappeler — is not a special case of sexuality; it is a form of representation. Representation, therefore, not 'real-life sex,' should be the wider context in which we analyze the special case of representation: pornography" (2). However, she adds that there is a dialectical relation between "representational practices which construct sexuality, and actual practices, each informing the other" (2).

14. "pretendientes palaciegos que legendariamente acudía a los regios deseos de esta monarca."

15. "Entren todos y verán / la célebre niña gorda, que pesa quinientos quilos / sin el cetro ni corona."

16. "The Venus of ... the human race."

17. Stallybrass and White (glossing Bakhtin) describe the norms of the grotesque body as "impurity (both in the sense of dirt and mixed categories), heterogeneity, masking, protuberant distension, disproportion, exorbitancy, clamour, decentered or eccentric arrangements, a focus upon gaps, orifices and

symbolic filth (what Mary Douglas calls 'matter out of place'), physical needs and pleasures of the 'lower bodily stratum,' materiality and parody" (23).

18. This conclusion concurs with that reached by Barbara Weissberger in her work on a poem in the *Cancionero de obras de burlas* entitled "Carajicomedia": "The poem's marked anxiety about masculine sexual inadequacy is a response to female sovereignty, in itself an anomalous condition that inverts the entire medieval gender hierarchy" (7).

19. See note 11.

20. "loyal."

21. "stupid."

22. Vuestra noble faz empaña
El ñublo del deshonor,
Desfaced presto esa niebla,
Cortaos los cuernos, Señor;
Que el mundo entero os señala,
La Europa os llama cabrón,
Y "Cabrón" repite el eco
En todo el pueblo español.

23. "Photography and Politics in Rome: The Edict of 1861 and the Scandalous Montages of 1861–1862." Quoting portions of the article, Fontanella (45) comments on the similarities of María Sophia's and Isabel's situations.

24. "¿quién quiere sebo?"

25. "No seas lividinosa / y tapa, tapa, la cosa."

26. "pesada obligación para tan tiernas manos."

Works Cited

Bécquer, Gustavo Adolfo. *Obras completas*. Intro. Joaquín y Serafín Alvarez Quintero. Madrid: Aguilar, 1973.

———, and Valeriano Bécquer. *Sem: Los borbones en pelota*. Ed. Robert Pageard, Lee Fontanella, and María Dolores Cabra Loredo. Madrid: Ediciones El Museo Universal, 1991.

Berger, John. *Ways of Seeing*. London: British Broadcasting Corporation and Penguin Books 1985 rpr. (first ed. 1973).

Cabra Loredo, María Dolores, ed. *Textos de Gustavo Adolfo Bécquer acompañados de dibujos de Valeriano Bécquer publicados durante los años 1870 y 1871 en La Ilustración de Madrid*. Madrid: Ediciones El Museo Universal, 1983.

Cierva, Ricardo de la. *El triángulo*. Vol. I. *Alumna de la libertad. Adolescencia y perversidad de Isabel II: los cuatro primeros amantes*. Madrid: Planeta, 1988.

Collins, Kathleen. "Photography and Politics in Rome: The Edict of 1861 and the Scandalous Montages of 1861–1862." *History of Photography* 9 (1985): 295–303.

Dworkin, Andrea. *Pornography: Men Possessing Women*. New York: Pedigree Books, 1981.

Freedberg, David. *The Power of Images: Studies in the History and Theory of Response*. Chicago: University of Chicago Press, 1989.

Griffin, Susan. *Pornography and Silence: Culture's Revenge against Nature*. New York: Harper and Row, 1981.

Kappeler, Susanne. *The Pornography of Representation*. Minneapolis: University of Minnesota Press, 1986.

Longino, Helen. "Pornography, Oppression and Freedom: A Closer Look." In *Women and Values: Readings in Recent Feminist Philosophy*. Ed. Marilyn Pearsall. Belmont, Calif.: Wadsworth, 1986, 167–76.

Montesinos, Rafael. *Bécquer: Biografía e imagen*. Barcelona: Editorial RM, 1977.

Stallybrass, Peter, and Allon White. *The Politics and Poetics of Transgression*. Ithaca: Cornell University Press, 1986.

Stoller, Robert J. *Observing the Erotic Imagination*. New Haven: Yale University Press, 1985.

Valle-Inclán, Ramón del. *El Ruedo Ibérico: Primera Serie*. Vol. I. *La Corte de los milagros. Opera omnia*, Vol XXVII. n.p., n.d.

Weissberger, Barbara. "Male Sexual Anxieties in *Carajicomedia*: A Response to Female Sovereignty." In *Poetry at Court in Trastamaran Spain: From the Cancionero de Baena to the Cancionero General*. Medieval and Renaissance Texts and Studies Series. State University of New York Press. Forthcoming.

Willis, Ellen. "Feminism, Moralism, and Pornography." In *Powers of Desire: The Politics of Sexuality*. Ed. Ann Snitow, Christine Stansell, and Sharon Thompson. New York: Monthly Review Press, 1983, 460–67.

Chapter 14

Codifying Homosexuality as Grotesque: The Writings of Virgilio Piñera

Ana García Chichester

More than a decade after his death in 1979, Virgilio Piñera's literature is still relatively unknown compared to that of many of his contemporaries. His contribution to Latin American theater and to Cuban narrative is undeniably important. Similarly, he exercised great influence on a younger generation of writers with whom he came in contact during his years at the helm of *Ciclón* (Cyclone; 1955–59), such as playwrights José Triana (1935) and Antón Arrufat (1935), and novelists such as Severo Sarduy (1937–93) and Reinaldo Arenas (1943–92) (González Echevarría 23). And yet, Piñera's work remains elusive; perhaps more than any other Cuban writer, as Julio Matas recognizes, he reminds us of other writers in contemporary world literature who have been spurned and ostracized, singularly among them Alfred Jarry and Witold Gombrowicz, whose works, like Piñera's, must be considered in terms of their marginalism (22).

Piñera was born in 1912 in the colonial city of Cárdenas. From 1924 to 1937 the family resided in Camagüey, where he finished his secondary studies. He moved to the capital to study at the University of Havana; however, he failed to finish his degree, despite having written an insightful doctoral thesis on the poet

Gertrudis Gómez de Avellaneda (1814–73), which he never defended, guided by a characteristic spirit of rebelliousness and contradiction. The Cuban capital Piñera encountered on his arrival was, without a doubt, an exciting and stimulating city for a young intellectual from the provinces. Two years older, José Lezama Lima (1910–76) was already publishing *Verbum* (June–November 1937), followed later by *Espuela de Plata* (Silver Spur; 1939–41). Both publications must have influenced Piñera's early development in view of the fact that his first literary efforts were in poetry, the main focus of these journals, as Alessandra Riccio points out (343–89). Of much greater impact was his association with Lezama and the group of poets connected to the magazine *Orígenes* (Origins; 1944–56), to which he contributed for many years, though sporadically. By the latter part of the 1940s, Piñera had almost completely abandoned poetry in favor of drama and narrative, genres better suited to the satirical aspects of his work. His collaboration in *Orígenes* was, in fact, rather problematic because his literary philosophy differed to such an extreme from the neobaroque commitments of Lezama and the group of poets associated with the magazine. Still, there is a baroque sensibility in Piñera's work that can be traced to his early association with Lezama, particularly in his short stories.[1]

Disenchanted with the lack of opportunities for writers in Cuba, Piñera accepted a post in Buenos Aires in 1946. During the next twelve years, with the exception of a couple of brief visits to Cuba, he lived in this self-imposed exile. It proved to be a period of intense production. In addition to several short stories and essays that appeared in the Argentine magazine *Sur* (1931–70), he published two notable works of fiction during this time: his most perplexing and complex novel, *La carne de René* (René's Flesh; 1953), and his masterful collection of stories, *Cuentos fríos* (*Cold Tales*; 1956). He returned to Cuba in 1958 to coedit José Rodríguez Feo's aggressive new journal *Ciclón,* following Rodríguez Feo's violent departure from *Orígenes.*

His dramatic oeuvre, for which he is deservedly recognized as one of the earliest exponents of the Theatre of the Absurd as well as its first practitioner in Latin America, opens with *Electra Garrigó* (1941), which Raquel Carrió Mendía has called the first drama of the Cuban theater and a profound meditation on Cuban identity

(872–73). His dramas also include *Falsa alarma* (False Alarm; 1948), *Jesús* (1948), *Los siervos* (The Serfs; 1955), *La boda* (The Wedding; 1957), *Aire frío* (Cold Air; 1958) — a continuation of his analysis on the family nucleus begun with *Electra* — *El flaco y el gordo* (The Skinny Man and the Fat Man; 1959), *El filántropo* (The Philanthropist; 1960), and *Dos viejos pánicos* (Two Old Fears; 1968), which earned the 1968 Casa de las Américas (House of the Americas) prize from Cuba's national arts and humanities agency. Among his short dramas are *La sorpresa* (The Surprise; 1960), *Siempre se olvida algo* (Something Is Always Forgotten; 1963), *Estudio en blanco y negro* (Study in Black and White; 1965), *El no* (No; 1965), *La niñita querida* (The Darling Girl; 1966), the posthumously published short play *Una caja de zapatos vacía* (An Empty Shoe Box; 1986) and a collection of unfinished plays collected as *Teatro inconcluso* (Incomplete Theater; 1990). Yet to be published are the dramas *Handle with Care* (1969), *Ejercicio de estilo* (An Exercise in Style; 1969), *Un arropamiento sartorial en la caverna platónica* (A Sartorial Bundling in a Platonic Cavern; 1971), *Las escapatorias de Laura y Oscar* (The Flights of Laura and Oscar; 1973), and *El Trac* (1974).

Inexplicably ignored by earlier literary criticism, Piñera's narrative has undergone greater critical scrutiny in recent years (Chichester 132–47). Absurd techniques borrowed from the theater and the prevalence of grotesque images characterize his short stories, arguably his most important work. The collections are *El conflicto* (The Conflict; 1942), *Poesía y prosa* (Poetry and Prose; 1944 — which includes stories that explore the author's early interest in Sartre's existentialist philosophy), and *Cuentos fríos* (*Cold Tales*; 1956 — which contains his best one-page "ministories"). They are followed by *Cuentos* (Tales; 1964), which collects all of the stories previously published with the exception of "El muñeco" (The Dummy), which is only included in *Cuentos fríos* (therein Piñera ridicules the president of a republic, and although the story was written in Argentina in the first part of the decade of the 1950s and is directed at the Peronist regime, it was left out of the Cuban-published *Cuentos* because of the politically sensitive nature of its subject). Most of Piñera's better known short fiction is found in the volume *El que vino a salvarme* (The One Who Came to Save Me; 1970), which also contains a few stories from the 1960s and 1970s. Posthumous and previously unpublished short fiction has been collected in the volumes *Un fogonazo* (A Muzzle Flash; 1987) and *Muecas para escribientes* (Grimaces for Writers; 1988).

Although infrequently mentioned as a novelist, Piñera also cultivated this genre. In his three novels he explores the absurd and fantastic nature of everyday reality. Rodríguez Feo defends the portrayal of fantastic elements in *La carne de René* by emphasizing that "el mundo alucinante allí descrito observa cierta relación con el mundo de nuestros actos cotidianos" ("Una alegoría" 165; the hallucinating world described in it bears a certain relationship with the world of our everyday acts), and thus insisting that Piñera's literature was within the realist tradition, a well-intended attempt to explain his work to an unreceptive and conventional reading public. Examples of characters who possess mysterious phobias and unnatural flaws are common in Piñera's work. In *Pequeñas maniobras* (Small Maneuverings; 1962), the novel's central figure, Sebastian, is a picaresque homosexual, paralyzed by an unexplained and irrational fear. In reference to the central character in this novel, Ernesto Méndez y Soto points out: "Las alusiones a la inversión del personaje aparecen a lo largo de la novela. Desde las primeras páginas, Piñera deja señales que, acumuladas y analizadas cuidadosamente, revelan la proclive naturaleza de Sebastián" (450; The allusions to the character's sexual inversion appear throughout the novel. From the first pages, Piñera includes signs that, collectively and carefully analyzed, reveal Sebastian's nature). His last novel, *Presiones y diamantes* (Pressures and Diamonds; 1967), like the play *Dos viejos pánicos,* is a scathing though veiled attack on the Cuban revolution. In it a very precious and much desired diamond called Delphi (an anagram of Fidel), turns out to be a fake, a trick that resulted in the removal of the book from circulation in Cuba (Arenas 21). Piñera's poetry includes *Las furias* (Furies; 1941), a volume that contains some of the most somber verses ever written in Cuba, according to Cintio Vitier (478). With the publication of *La isla en peso* (The Island in Balance; 1943) Piñera finds his own voice; included in this collection is his poem "Vida de Flora" (Flora's Life), in which Flora's comically enormous feet become an image of bitterness and despair:

Flora, tus medias rojas cuelgan como lenguas de
  ahorcados.
¿En qué pies poner estas huérfanas? ¿Adónde tus
  últimos zapatos?
Oye, Flora: tus pies no caben en el río que te ha de
  conducir a la nada;
al país en que no hay grandes pies ni pequeñas
  manos ni ahorcados. (Vitier 482)[2]

La vida entera (An Entire Life; 1969) and the volume *Una broma colosal* (A Colossal Joke; 1988) complete his poetic output. Published after his death, the latter contains many nonsensical poems, some in French, as well as "El hechizado" (The Enchanted), a poem dedicated "A Lezama, en su muerte" (To Lezama, on his death). In many of these verses the torment Piñera endured toward the end of his life because of the Cuban government's persecution of homosexuals cries out: "Heme aquí apocado, con correas en los puños /...el hueso tibia cruge tanto como la palabra libertad" (*Una broma* 109; Here I am, belittled, straps around my wrists /...my shinbone cracking much like the word freedom).

From its very beginning Piñera's work ran against the current of Cuban literature, which had a strong realist tradition. With *Electra Garrigó, El conflicto,* and *Poesía y prosa,* Piñera emerged as a member of a tiny minority of Cuban writers who were committed to vanguard tenets.[3] A despairing vision of the individual's existence coupled with absurd techniques in both theater and narrative, depersonalized characters, shockingly grotesque themes and imagery, black humor, the predominance of trivial and irrational elements, the inversion of the "normal" or "natural" order of things, and the use of objective language epitomize Piñera's literature. If, in fact, while reading one of Piñera's texts the reader feels tempted to walk away, it is because she is reacting to the author's brutal treatment of reality and to his representation of the world as absurd and irrational, a place almost literally upside down, too sinister to bear further study. Indeed, Piñera's intent is to challenge us, to uproot our preconceived notions as readers of literature and to demolish our traditional expectations only to replace them with duplicity, uncertainty, and ambiguity. The mocking of all things, including the most taboo and sacred subjects — a manifestation of absurd and grotesque humor — is present in Piñera's theater and in his short stories, serving as a form of skepticism associated by Jorge Mañach with the characteristics of *choteo*, a particularly irreverent and rebellious attitude of the popular sectors of the Cuban population against all authority and matters of seriousness.[4]

At a time when the subject of sexuality in literature was a taboo, it should not be surprising that its treatment in Piñera's writing is mostly symbolic, clandestinely embedded in carefully constructed images. To be sure, man's sometimes agonizing dependence on his body and its needs is always present in Piñera's work. What strikes Piñera's readers, however, apart from the absurd and grotesque nature of his vision, are the disquieting metaphors that reveal a subversive order struggling to surface. It is in this new order that calls for the reader's acceptance of an abnormal, irrational, grotesque, and absurd perspective that we find the revelation of the homophobic and homosexual dimension in his work. Oftentimes revealed by the presence of fantastic elements and transfigured as a result of a process of internalized abstraction (from literal to figurative), the homosexual dimension is always linked to the energy and the imagination of the artistic spirit.

In one of his early and rarely studied short stories from *Poesía y prosa* entitled "Proyecto para un sueño" (Design for a Dream), we find themes and techniques echoed throughout Piñera's narrative. Constructed around the image of the double, this story follows the difficult and at times precarious efforts of a narrator in pursuit of an indifferent friend, his double image. His desire is to "interest him in something, to earn his gratitude, so he would buy me coffee and a roll" (*Cold Tales* 23). In their rapid travels through streets blurred by a constant rainfall, the doubles enter a space composed of multiple galleries, each with its own architectural peculiarities. Piñera describes in detail one of these spaces, equipped with a trapdoor, where men who have become their favorite animals inhabit numerous cages. The reference to black slavery is clear, as is the image of a black and yellow marble floor, which in turn is mirrored by trapped tigers (the favored species), who occupy three hundred thousand cages.[5]

The black and yellow color code (which appears in other stories) is a representation of what Piñera considers important elements in Cuban identity: namely the black African slave and the
Chinese immigrant, whose presence in Cuba has come to symbolize the superstitious and the erotic, respectively. The color code
in the story — black personifying a group rejected and ostracized,
yellow applied to the Chinaman and its erotic function, and white
in the symbolic *leche* (milk) and its association with semen — form
an ethnic unit. Quite obviously, in this story the author offers a
reflection of ignored sectors of Cuban society. These associations
are familiar to readers of contemporary Cuban literature, in particular of Sarduy's novel *De donde son los cantantes* (*From Cuba
with a Song*; 1967), which reflects on the subject of Cuban cultural
identity. The black motif is further developed in the story as the
appearance of the men-tigers is followed by a parade of native
seeds and herbs, reminiscent of those used by witches and sorcerers (*brujos*) in preparing potions (Ortiz 76–77) and an orchestra of six black men playing a "popular dance tune" (a *son* as it
appears in the original Spanish). Next, the doubles visit an unorthodox "church" where "there was no altar and in the center
of the nave was a kind of alabaster channel through which ran
steaming, black coffee.... Walking around the channel, one would
dip the cup into the coffee and drink without losing the rhythm
of the circle" (28). Thus, surrounded by motifs that suggest the
influence of African elements in Cuban popular culture, the occult world of witchcraft or *santería* enters the narration in the form
of a religious ceremony of a suspiciously illicit type.

The last paragraph of this brief story narrates events that belong, in fact, to the realm of the surreal. Upon leaving the church,
his friend slips and falls in the mud produced by the torrential
rain and tries to drag the narrator with him, but he struggles to
get away and screams for help, evidently appalled by the nature
of this "mud." Taken before a female figure of the "highest authority," the aggressor — now perceived as a pervert — is expelled, and
the narrator is ordered to wear a disguise and greet "friends"
(meaning friends of a more conventional type). The narrator acquiesces but covers his face in shame, presumably in order to
avoid seeing his double's image mirrored in his own. As he departs, he is approached by the aggressor (already back from his

exile) and by a Chinaman, and they try unsuccessfully once again to subject him to the appalling act: "He flung himself on top of me while the Chinaman was getting ready to stab me, but responding to my shouts, the police came to my rescue, and we were once again brought before the highest authority, where this time he was condemned to eternal exile" (28–29).

This erotic ending signals the triumph of "authority" and conventionality over the surreal and fantastic dimension of this world. The narrator's rejection of the so-called seductive mud, as well as the sexual adventure implied in the "stabbing," is significant in that it points to a perception of the homosexual experience as a fearful and condemnable act. And yet Piñera's ambivalence toward this subject is apparent in the narrator's regret of his failed mission: "As they were taking him away, I remembered with total clarity, with magnificent distinctness, that my task was to follow him without rest so that he might buy me coffee and a roll" (29). However, through the transformation of the commonplace into fantasy, the text alters the narrator's original wish to consume *café con leche* (*café au lait*) into an erotic same-sex desire, which, although rejected, is still latently present. The nostalgic tone of the last comment leads the reader to the beginning of the story, that is, to the narrator's search of a "friend" who would satisfy his desire, a quest now renewed as the cyclical ending of the story would imply. Therefore, the narrator's own homosexual inclination would seem to triumph over his homophobia, and the text closes by coming full circle to its initial image.

In addition to "Design for a Dream," the technique of the double and its usual association with a split psyche (Ibieta 975–91) which, I believe, is a reference to a divided homosexual personality, appear in other short stories, most notably in "La caída" (The Fall) and "El que vino a salvarme" (The One Who Came to Save Me), both from the collection *El que vino a salvarme*, as well as in the novel *La carne de René*. In "The Fall," the doubles have climbed to the top of a cliff. Playing with the concept of inversion, the author focuses his story on the grotesquely violent nature of the descent. An example of Piñera's penchant for double meanings, the story narrates how the doubles begin to fall from a *pichacho* (not a *picacho*, which would imply a smallish cliff, but a deprecatory colloquial euphemism for the male sexual organ).

In their descent, they are rapidly dismembered, unable to protect their bodies from the violence of the fall. However, as the end approaches and what is left of each body (one saves his eyes, the other his graying beard) touches the ground, the impact comes about as a peaceful and sacred moment, finally revealing to the reader the sexual implications of this purposeful fall.

In the play *La boda* and in stories from *Cuentos fríos* like "Las partes" (The Parts), "El cambio" (The Switch), "La transformación" (The Transformation), and "Cosas de cojos" (Affairs of Amputees), the subject revolves around the appearance of something bizarre, be it a defect that transforms seemingly common beings into aberrations or a mistake that turns an ordinary situation into a representation of the extraordinary and grotesque nature of things. In each case, Piñera's dismantling of the old order in favor of the new demands the reader's acceptance of the irrational and fantastic as also "normal." In a story like "Affairs of Amputees," the natural and "logical" mate for a male amputee is another male amputee missing the opposite foot with whom he could share a pair of shoes. The affiliation of a male amputee with a female, from this point of view, would seem incongruous. In Piñera's work, then, the existence of the odd and the bizarre within the conventional is always vital, and by stressing its importance the author turns the extraordinary into an essential component of a whole entity. Seen in ethnic terms (going back to "Proyecto para un sueño") this would mean the acceptance of the African and Asian influences on Cuban culture as equal in importance to the white European legacy. In more general terms, it would signify the embracing of sectors of society that have been previously ignored and excluded, indeed rendered invisible by the dominant class, like homosexuals. Among other taboos connected to the homosexual perspective in Piñera's work is that of anthropophagy, a subject that becomes the focus in another short story from *Cuentos fríos* entitled "La carne" (Meat) (in which self-consumption is the solution to the unavailability of meat), as well as in the drama *El gordo y el flaco* (after *el flaco* eats his fat hospital companion, thus becoming *el gordo*, a new cycle begins at the end of the play with the arrival of another *flaco* as his roommate). In both of these works, a semantic game is played between the two meanings of *carne* (as both meat and flesh). This ambiguity is explored more in depth in the novel *La carne de René,* in which Piñera offers us what is undoubtedly his most personal testimony regarding homosexual panic.

The description of a butcher shop where clients have euphorically converged to delight in the sight of meat opens the novel: "Los más próximos al mostrador meten de los garfios y aspiran con fruición el olor de la sangre coagulada. Es, por así decirlo, un día de fiesta nacional" (14; The ones closest to the counter fix their eyes on the huge beef quarters hanging from the grapples and breathe in with pleasure the smell of coagulated blood. It is, in a way, a national holiday). The representation of dismembered meat at the outset of the novel brings to mind the disfigured images of Billy's ending in Herman Melville's *Billy Budd* and of Dorian's in Oscar Wilde's *The Portrait of Dorian Gray.*[6] One could say that Piñera intends for his text to begin where these two classics of literature ended: that is, with the image of the human body as nothing more than a "piece of meat," disfigured by its commercial value. This would explain René's aversion to *carne* (avoiding contact with flesh and meat), which is viewed by people around him as a peculiar and mysterious phobia and makes him the subject of suspicion and speculation. The connection between René and homosexuality is obtrusively present early in the text, as Dalia Pérez describes him as "la encarnación viviente de un semidiós griego" (15; a living incarnation of a Greek demigod).

Complicating the narrative is the subversive homosocial world of La Causa (The Cause), to which René's father is its committed leader. Joining La Causa demands the recognition of the flesh as an instrument of torture and the willingness to self-inflict bodily wounds. The discovery of a painting depicting Saint Sebastian (René's double image) in his father's study alerts René to his expected role:

> La pintura presentaba a un hermoso joven, tal como lo había sido Sebastián, en actitud reposada, con la mirada perdida y una sonrisa enigmática. Hasta ahí el cuadro no ofrecía nada de particular, pero en lo que este óleo se apartaba del modelo tradicional era en lo referente a las flechas. Este San Sebastián sacaba flechas de un carcaj y se las iba clavando en el cuerpo. (32)[7]

The iconographic association of Saint Sebastian's image with homosexuality stems from his traditional portrayal as a beautiful youth, undraped, and appearing in a state of transport despite his tormented body. Characteristic of Piñera's preferential use of distortion, this Saint Sebastian derives his pleasure not from wounds sustained in battle but from the arrows — symbols of pestilence — he chooses to drive into his flesh.[8] The image of Sebastian (also the name of the main character in *Pequeñas maniobras*) synthesizes the conflict René must resolve: to suffer in silence the purposeful and systematic torturing of his body for the service of La Causa (pain) or for the service of women (pleasure). Either choice would mean relinquishing all claims to his body as a sacred and private domain. Torn between these alternatives, René is introduced to a clandestine world led by the comic yet monstrous Bola de Carne (Meatball), a grotesque caricature of a penis: "No tenía brazos ni piernas; . . . El tórax y el abdomen se juntaban formando una especie de bola, aumentada . . . por la cabeza, tan sumida en el pecho que parecía formar parte de éste" (213; He had no arms or legs; . . . His thorax and abdomen formed as they joined a kind of ball, enlarged . . . by his head, which had sunk so much into his chest as to appear to be a part of it).

Grotesque techniques are used in the description of the penis by male authors such as Alberto Moravia in *Io e lui* (The Two of Us; 1972). The grotesque tends to underscore the humorous condition of penile changes, which does not particularly negate the perception of this organ as powerful and mighty. As Peter Schwenger points out, comic and terrible at the same time, the grotesque is the style most appropriate to this subject because

> for all its comic element, [the grotesque] implies an underlying terror arising from the sense that things are out of control. There is a force behind the grotesque that is inhuman, both stupid and vital at the same time. It is a force strongly bound up with the physical; it is a force that goes to extremes. By virtue of is excesses, it deforms proportion and classical contours. In this respect, it is allied with caricature. (108)

The grotesque in Piñera's literature is linked to what Mikhail Bakhtin considers the origins of this type of humor. That is to say, it is a humor bound to cosmic, social, and corporeal images, to the deformation and mutilation of the body, and to physiological matters generally prohibited (Torres 82–83). In the privacy of his apartment and for the benefit of all present, Bola stages a tragicomic sexual performance with a young boy (Príncipe):

> Las luces se apagaron y cuatro potentes reflectores lanzaron sus chorros luminosos sobre el colchón. Ahora Bola había cesado en sus gritos y risotadas y su cuerpo rodaba silencioso como lo hace un astro en el espacio. También la música había cesado, así como las voces del Príncipe. Sólo se percibía el roce de la carne en el terciopelo del colchón... Entonces se oyó un llanto como de recién nacido; eran verdaderos vagidos lanzados por Bola, un llanto tan puro, tan desamparado que René se sintió conmovido. Dos criados, envolviendo a Bola en una sábana, se lo llevaron. (216–17)[9]

Meatball's is the painful existence of the closet, where conventional morality has no meaning. As we witness René's fascination for this world, his search for identity brings us back to the image of Saint Sebastian. René's eventual triumph over his homophobia must be seen as the inversion of the expected process of perversion and decadence initially identified with the saint. Unlike Wilde's final purulent portrait of Dorian Gray, the transformation of this Saint Sebastian is the reverse of Dorian's. Piñera's homosexual icon conversely progresses from pestilence to a state of grace. René's final acceptance of his true nature is thus seen as a liberation from the source of his distaste for *carne* and is, furthermore, a personal triumph over the paternal tyranny that would have forced him in the direction of La Causa and the denial of pleasure.

Undoubtedly, at the root of Piñera's distorted vision of the world as a weird and monstrous place lies not merely the existential feeling of displacement characteristic of his generation, but also a unique personal vision shaped by the homosexual perspective. As in *La carne de René*, in the short story first published in *El que vino a salvarme* called "El caramelo" (The Drageé) and dated 1964—after Piñera's brief incarceration—the monstrous figure of a boy-pig is a projected image of human evil and hatred directed at the narrator, the innocent victim of a society where fear rules over reason and truth. Another grotesquely disfigured character appears in slightly altered form in the deformed Pedrito (*Presiones y dia-*

mantes). In both cases, the fantastic invades the everyday reality of the narrative. However, as many stories reach their conclusions we find that the narrative has been overtaken by the author's black humor and use of nonsensical images, or by what has been referred to as a process of "disparatización de lo cotidiano" (absurd rendering of everyday things).[10] This contributes to an existentialist perception of life as a useless and absurd exercise. While most of Piñera's work (his short stories and his theater in particular) present everyday situations as a series of *disparates* (nonsense), his philosophy regarding the human condition is much more despairing than his customary use of *choteo* would have us believe.

In his masterful story "The One Who Came to Save Me," the story's narrator-character, now in his old age, is afraid of not knowing the precise moment in which he is to die. The real source of his fear, he tells the reader, is an experience he harbors as a deep and terrible secret that has haunted him throughout his life as an unspeakable and horrifying thing. To be precise, he witnessed in his youth a man's execution in the bathroom of a movie theater: "How did I see? I was in a stall taking a shit, and they couldn't see me; they were at the urinals . . . and all of a sudden I heard: 'But you're not going to kill me. . . . ' I looked through the grating and saw a knife slitting a throat, torrents of blood; I heard a scream, and feet running away at full speed" (*Cold Tales* 275).

What had originated as an ordinary fear, as time passes, becomes a progressively all-consuming obsession, a sickly and decadent curiosity. His only moment of happiness regarding this fixation had taken place aboard an airplane that had nearly crashed amidst a storm. This becomes for him an event of transcendental importance since his anguish "for once . . . had been transformed at forty thousand feet into a state of grace comparable to that of the most illustrious saints of the Church" (278). The knowledge of that fixed moment that now acquires religious connotations is thus compared to a sacred revelation.

The narrator's body, not unlike the fear that consumes him, represents an anomaly. The state of his aging body, paralyzed both physically (since the entire story is recounted from his deathbed) and emotionally (due to his obsessive concern), is grotesquely described:

I've become a worn-out exhibit from a museum of teratology and at the same time, the very picture of malnutrition. I'm sure it's not blood but pus that runs through my veins; my scabs — festering, purplish — and my bones seems [sic] to have conferred a very different anatomy on my body. My hip bones, like a river, have overflown their banks; my collarbone (as I lose my flesh) is like an anchor hanging over the side of a ship; the occipital bone makes my head look like a coconut bashed in with a sledgehammer. (278)

The body's grotesque aspect, made degenerate by the process of aging, becomes something more repugnant because of the emphasis on its monstrous and abnormal nature. The comparing of his hips with flooding waters, and of his bones to an anchor or a harpoon no longer grasping its point of contact but rather hanging loose and allowing the body to float adrift, confronts the reader with an image not unlike that of the airplane near the point of disintegration. Ship or airplane, the body as an uncontrollable vehicle is the image conveyed by the text. However, despite his corporeal disintegration, the narrator's mind continues pursuing the idea of capturing death on its path. The narrator begins a dialogue with the photograph of his deceased father. This is an exchange that must be seen as a moment of transition from the real (we could say corporeal) to the surreal nature of the narrative. The abrupt interruption of the fantastic element, familiar to Piñera's readers, takes place as the image of a young man is briefly revealed to the prostrated narrator through a reflection in the closet mirror. Closing his eyes and repeating to himself the words "now, now" the narrator beckons the return of the stranger:

Now he wielded a knife and was slowly bending over as I watched him intently. Then I understood that this stranger was the one who was coming to save me. I knew several seconds beforehand the exact moment of my death. When the knife sank into my jugular vein, I looked at my savior and said to him, through torrents of blood: "Thank you for coming." (280)

It is through the introduction of the inverted mirror image of the young savior and the description of the coup de grâce, which takes place intently (*fijamente*), that the text reveals to the reader its subversively erotic undercurrents. The cutting prong the young man brandishes, like many other images of sharp metal instruments frequently appearing in Piñera's stories, is a phallic image. This story, dedicated to the arrival of the young saving figure, should be read as the progressive revelation of a latent homosexual desire. The use of grotesque imagery to describe the condition of the narrator's mind and body thus functions as the representation of a desire that, because it has been repressed throughout an individual's existence, becomes the degrading illness that will eventually consume him.

The image of "torrents" of blood that concludes the story brings us back to the grotesque depiction of the decapitation in the movie theater bathroom, where the narrator describes himself as a voyeur and therefore as a participant in the supposed crime, a metaphor for the homosexual act. Beginning with this experience that is the origin of his irrational fear about not knowing the moment of death — that is, the moment of revelation — and the subsequent deformation of his body into a decrepit, abnormal, and monstrous image, the grotesque offers a perspective of everyday reality as repugnant and fearful deformation. The narrator's own homophobia has caused his paralysis and purulence. The saving presence of the young man, considered under these terms, would restore his mind and body to a former peaceful condition. The act that takes place at the end of the story and the revelation thereto implied, which frees him from his fear, become the link that takes him from his present decrepitude to his desired state of freedom.

With "The One Who Came to Save Me," Piñera's thoughts on homosexuality and homophobia come full circle since the writing of "Design for a Dream," in which the metaphorical "stabbing" is viewed in fearful terms. Written twenty-three years later during very difficult times for homosexuals, this story must be read as a meditation on fear and its capacities for self-destruction (also the theme in *Dos viejos pánicos*). It is clear that at the moment of receiving his "death" the narrator embraces the experience as the culmination of a long-awaited and desired search for truth, certainly not the truth about the moment of death's arrival, as the literal reading of the text would have us believe, but its inverted mirror image. The end of the story celebrates a genesis, that is to say, the momentous arrival of freedom from a lifelong and all-consuming and deforming homophobia.

Piñera's grotesque descriptions of homosexuals (Meatball, for example) often seem to condemn the nature of homosexuality. Nevertheless, the split personality of the closeted homosexual ("The One Who Came to Save Me," *La carne de René*) and the divided psyche of the double ("Design for a Dream") reveal his perception of homosexuality as a long and painful struggle for self-acceptance and individual expression. As exemplified by the works mentioned, Piñera equated aspects of everyday reality with abnormal, irrational, and grotesque elements. In many of his stories and in his novels, perhaps more than in his theater or poetry, the convergence of these elements leads to and makes possible the eruption of the fantastic order. The grotesque distorts, inverts, degrades; the fantastic exalts, liberates, and creates. Subversively contained in absurd and grotesque aspects of reality, the fantastic dimension struggles to the surface. The homosexual world in Piñera's literature, in a similar manner, is latently, surreptitiously present. This would mean, quite evidently, that homosexuality is bound to the creative process represented by both the grotesque and the fantastic. The absurd and the grotesque function as the catalysts to the appearance of the creative spirit personified by the homosexual and represented by the fantastic. Inversion and distortion (doubled and mirrored images) are the representation of the writing process, a disfigured rendition of our physical reality transfigured and made magical by the genius of the artist. What this means, then, is that the ambiguity we may detect in Piñera's work regarding his view on homosexuality is an expression of what this distortion represents, which is the essence of literature.

Piñera's enthusiasm for the revolution was dashed as early as 1961, when he was briefly incarcerated as a homosexual during the well-known *noche de las tres pes* (night of the three P's) in which prostitutes, pimps, and pederasts were seized and arrested.[11] This experience resulted in many years of living in fear and silence. After the condemnation of all his work because of his sexual preference and the subversive nature of his short novel *Presiones y diamantes*, he died in Havana in 1979 in virtual obscurity. The fear and despair expressed in Piñera's late work is unmistakable. Sex-

310 ◆ ANA GARCÍA CHICHESTER

uality, art, and death are perceived as the only forms of liberation, the ultimate escape from a panic that splits one's personality. A very personal comment by the author on this subject, regarding his play *Dos viejos pánicos,* summarizes his view:

> El que tiene miedo de sí mismo produce y consume su propio miedo, es decir, se incomunica, se aparta de la sociedad. Al apartarse paraliza automáticamente toda posibilidad de acción. Metido en un callejón sin salida, sólo le queda el juego estéril con su miedo. Es una personalidad dividida: una parte lo trasmite y otra lo recibe. (Zalacaín 69)[12]

Living far removed from society and from actively participating in his country's intellectual life was Piñera's only choice during his last years. Even without hope of having his work published, he continued writing undauntedly. Most of his work from this period reveals man's condition as an unsuspecting victim, condemned to a cavernous existence and kept alive by a powerful and consuming darkness. Indeed, at the end, Piñera returned to his existentialist beginnings. As expressed in the late poem "Un chistoso túmulo" (A Funny Barrow), written four years before his death, he saw life as a long preparation to nothingness, a path to the emptiness of not being:

> La cosa que soy ahora, esa cosa que la suerte
> me mandó ser, esta inerte transfiguración,
> ¿fue en verdad un ser humano o fue mixtificación?
> ¿qué fue este engendro que fui dentro de mi piel de
>   hombre?
> Pero déjenme así, por favor, no me nombren, no me
>   nombren
> Ahora no soy, no respiro, no vivo: tal es mi suerte,
> y créanlo o no, esta es la muerte, la muerte. (*Una broma
>   colosal* 55)[13]

Notes

1. Indeed, it cannot be said that Piñera and Lezama's relationship was that of spiritual *parentesco* (familial unity), as Lezama describes his ties with the founding members of *Orígenes* (Fossey 47). It is well known that Piñera and Lezama

differed in their literary philosophies; Piñera advocated the use of a simpler and more "objective" language and often ridiculed the ornately "baroque" style of Lezama and the group of poets associated with the magazine. Because Piñera soon stopped writing poetry, he did not concur with the journal's "intellectual formulation" that had its origins in "the meditation of poetry as a source and method of knowledge" (Santí 535; my translation). Rogelio Llopis points out that Piñera's reaction against *Orígenes* and its poetics was only partial: "His reaction against *Orígenes* has had a lesser impact than Carpentier's against criollismo" (150; my translation), and believes that his longer and more important short fiction "denota a las claras [sus] antecedentes origenistas" (151; clearly reveals his origenista roots). See also Dolores Koch's analysis of Piñera's use of techniques associated with the neobaroque style in his short story "Alegato contra la bañadera desempotrada" (Argument against a Free-Standing Bathtub) (83–86).

2. (Flora, your red stockings droop like the tongues of the hanged. / What feet will these orphans cover? Where to put your last shoes? / Listen, Flora: there's no room for your feet in the river guiding you to nothingness; / to the country where there are no great feet or small hands or people hanged.)

3. Lezama, whose *Enemigo rumor* (Enemy Murmur; Lezama's first collection of poetry) had appeared in 1937, and Nicolás Guillén (1902–89), with his new techniques in Afro-Cuban poetry, were part of this group. In narrative Lydia Cabrera (1900) published her influential *Cuentos negros de Cuba* (Black Stories from Cuba; a transcription of African and Afro-Cuban oral traditions and tales) in Spanish in 1940, and "Viaje a la semilla" (Journey Back to the Source) by Alejo Carpentier (1904–80) in 1944, also explored new directions. Examples of fantastic narrative appeared in the work of Arístides Fernández (1904–34) and of writers like Félix Pita Rodríguez (1909). However, these occasional examples were not enough to speak of a new narrative in Cuba before the 1940s (Arrufat 148).

4. For Piñera *choteo* is an intrinsic part of Cuban character and language. Thus, the familiar and specific language of the popular sectors of Cuban society, according to Carmen Torres, "se presenta como un vehículo que hace posible no sólo la degradación de falsos valores burgueses e individuales, sino la exaltación y afirmación de los valores de un cuerpo colectivo" (122; is presented as a vehicle that makes possible not only the degradation of false bourgeois and individual values, but also the exaltation and affirmation of the values of a collective body). *Choteo* in Piñera's work, so perceived, would be an affirmation of his preoccupation with the forgotten lower classes and with his desire to recognize their contribution to the whole of Cuban identity.

5. Here a story retold by Lydia Cabrera in *Cuentos negros de Cuba* comes to mind. It features a magical tiger (*ñáñigo*) very fond of playing an instrument of an uncertain type (*cocorícamo*) that allows him to levitate. It produces pleasure and pain, a "pleasure so intense, [an] unabating pleasurable pain, that he lost all judgment" (59; my translation). The image of the *cocorícamo* as a phallic symbol is obvious, as is the storyteller's intention that it be seen as magical and powerful. Cabrera's story differs greatly from Piñera's in intent, but the coincidence of the tiger image is curious because Piñera's use of color codes to represent African and Asian influences on Cuban culture and the association of each with magical and sexual powers are combined in this animal image.

6. On these two texts Eve Kosofsky Sedgwick comments: "The exquisite portrait [of Billy at the gallows and the old man Dorian, lying dead], the magnetic corpse swaying aloft: iconic as they are of a certain sexual visibility, their awful eminence also signalizes that the line between any male beauty that's articulated as such and any steaming offal strung up for purchase at the butcher's shop is, in the modern dispensation so much marked by this pair of texts, a brutally thin one" (131).

7. The painting represented a beautiful young man, as Sebastian had been, in a reclining pose, gazing far away and smiling in an enigmatic manner. Up to this point the painting did not offer anything of note, but in regard to the arrows this oil departed from traditional examples. This Saint Sebastian was pulling arrows from a quiver and driving them into his body.

8. In *Death in Venice* (1912), Thomas Mann uses the figure of Saint Sebastian to express the contrast in Aschenbach's character between his upright and rigid German side and a Mediterranean yearning for freedom. Jeffrey Meyers concludes that "Mann exploits the homosexual connotations in the iconography of St Sebastian, a beautiful, well-formed but helpless youth who is either dreamily indifferent to or masochistically ecstatic about the arrows ... that penetrate his thinly-clad body [and] he uses the image of the passive martyr ... to suggest the ambiguous relation of art and morality, of creative genius and self-destruction" (44). Much the same can be said of Piñera's metaphorical use of the saint's image. The association of Saint Sebastian with pestilence derives from the arrows piercing his body. Since the end of the seventeenth century, Saint Sebastian has been portrayed as the patron saint against plague and pestilence (Jameson 412–14).

9. The lights went off and four bright potent reflectors released their luminous streams onto the mattress. Now Meatball had ceased his cries and bursts of laughter, and his body was rolling silently much like a star in space. The music had also ceased, as well as Prince's shouts. Only the rubbing of flesh against the velvet of the mattress could be perceived.... Then a cry like that of a newborn was heard; it was Meatball wailing, and his cry was so pure, so lonely, that René felt moved. Two servants, bundling Meatball in a bedsheet, took him away.

10. Antonio Fernández Ferrer refers to this tendency in Piñera's work, explaining that (as evident in the short story "Affairs of Amputees"), it is characterized by the inclusion of "observaciones 'filosóficas' y detalles siniestros, doblemente efectivos y crueles por su incisiva brevedad; las contraposiciones entre la multitud y la individualidad; las hipérboles, la potenciación extremada del disparate...; los modos cínicos de enunciación, tales como la pregunta retórica o la generalización definitoria" (428; philosophical observations and sinister details, doubly effective and cruel due to their incisive brevity; the contrasts between mass and individuality; the hyperboles, the extreme power of the nonsensical phrases...; the cynical modes of enunciation, such as the rhetorical question or the generalized definition).

11. For accounts of this period in Piñera's life see Guillermo Cabrera Infante's "Vidas para leerlas" (Lives to be Read) about Piñera and Lezama. Cabrera Infante recalls Piñera's incarceration for alleged moral misconduct (10–11). Carlos Franqui has also eloquently narrated Piñera's confrontation with Castro during his conversations with artists, writers, and intellectuals at the Biblioteca Nacional in Havana in 1961 (263–64) as well as his subsequent arrest that year: "Colaborador

de *Revolución*, uno de los mejores escritores del país, integrado a la Revolución, polemista punzante, odiado de la burguesía, [fue] llevado al Príncipe, desvestido y vestido con las rayas y la P, como en uno de los cuentos del absurdo, que escribía Piñera" (282; A contributor to *Revolución* [Revolutionary Cuba's early official newspaper], one of the best writers in the country, committed to the Revolution, a biting polemist, hated by the bourgeoisie, [he was] carried away to the Príncipe [prison], undressed and dressed with stripes and a P, just like in one of the short stories of the absurd Piñera used to write).

12. He who is afraid of himself produces and consumes his own fear, that is to say, he retreats and isolates himself from society. In retreating, he automatically paralyzes all possibility of action. Without a way out of a dead-end road, all he has left is playing a sterile game with his fear. Fear divides his personality: one half transmits it and the other receives it.

Dos viejos pánicos explores the theme of fear in Tabo and Tota, two old souls who create their own double images, which allows them to temporarily transfer their fears, as they play at "killing" each other:

> TABO. Eso es, Tota, estamos muertos. (Ladeando la cabeza del lado de
> Tota. Pausa.) Es como tú dices. No tengo miedo.
> TOTA. ¿Ni siquiera al espejo?
> TABO. No, Tota, ahora ya no soy ni viejo ni joven, ahora soy un
> muerto. (Pausa.) ¿Y dónde estarán ahora Tabo y Tota?
> TOTA. (Con el brazo extendido a todo lo largo apuntando al fondo del
> escenario.) ¡Míralos, míralos! Tienen miedo. (33)

> TABO. That is it, Tota, we're dead. (Tilting his head toward Tota.
> Pause.) It is just as you say. I'm not afraid.
> TOTA. Not even of the mirror?
> TABO. No, Tota, now I'm not old or young, now I'm a dead body.
> (Pause.) And I wonder where Tabo and Tota are now?
> TOTA. (Her arm completely extended and pointing to the back of the
> stage.) Look at them, look at them! They're afraid.

13. The object that I am now, that object which fate / forced me to be, this lifeless transfiguration, / was it truly a human being or was it a fake? / who was this freak I carried within my male flesh? / But please, leave me this way, do not name me, do not name me / Now I am no longer, I do not breathe, I do not live: that is my fate, / and believe it or not, this is death, death.

Works Cited

Piñera's Works

Una broma colosal. Intro. Antón Arrufat. Havana: Unión, 1988.

La carne de René. Madrid: Alfaguara, 1985.

Cold Tales. Trans. Mark Schafer. Intro. Guillermo Cabrera Infante. Hygiene, Colo.: Eridanos Press, 1988.

El conflicto. Havana: Espuela de Plata, 1942.

Cuentos. Madrid: Alfaguara, 1990.

Cuentos fríos. Buenos Aires: Losada, 1956.

Dos viejos pánicos. Havana: Casa de las Américas, 1968.

El que vino a salvarme. Intro. José Bianco. Buenos Aires: Sudamericana, 1970.

Un fogonazo. Havana: Letras Cubanas, 1987.

Las furias. Havana: Espuela de Plata, 1941.

La isla en peso. Havana: Espuela de Plata, 1942.

Muecas para escribientes. Havana: Letras Cubanas, 1987.

Pequeñas maniobras. Havana: Ediciones R., 1963.

Poesía y prosa. Havana: Orígenes, 1944.

Presiones y diamantes. Havana: Ediciones Unión, 1967.

René's Flesh. Trans. Mark Schafer. Intro. Antón Arrufat. New York: Marsilio, 1992.

Teatro completo. Havana: Ediciones R., 1960.

Teatro de la crueldad. Havana: Instituto del Libro, 1967.

Teatro del absurdo. Havana: Instituto del Libro, 1967.

El teatro y su doble. Havana: Instituto del Libro, 1969.

Criticism

Aguilú, Raquel. *Los textos dramáticos de Virgilio Piñera y el teatro del absurdo.* Madrid: Pliegos, 1988.

Arenas, Reinaldo. "La isla en peso con todas sus cucarachas." *Mariel* 1.2 (1983): 21.

Arrufat, Antón. "Virgilio Piñera o los riesgos de la imaginación." *Unión* 2 (1987): 145–50.

Cabrera, Lydia. *Cuentos negros de Cuba.* 2a ed. Madrid: Ramos, 1972.

Cabrera Infante, Guillermo. "Vidas para leerlas." *Vuelta* 4.41 (1980): 5–16.

Carrió Mendía, Raquel. "Estudio en blanco y negro: teatro de Virgilio Piñera." *Revista iberoamericana* 152–153 (1990): 871–80.

Chichester, Ana Garcia. "Superando el caos: estado actual de la crítica sobre la narrativa de Virgilio Piñera." *Revista interamericana de bibliografía* 42.1 (1992): 132–47.

Fernández Ferrer, Antonio. "El <<disparate claro>> en Cortázar y Piñera." *Revista iberoamericana* 159 (1992): 423–36.

Fossey, J. M. "Antes de morir Lezama Lima." *Indice* 401–402 (1976): 45–49.

Franqui, Carlos. *Retrato de familia con Fidel.* Barcelona: Seix Barral, 1981.

González Echevarría, Roberto. *La ruta de Severo Sarduy.* Hanover, N.H.: Ediciones del Norte, 1987.

Ibieta, Gabriella. "Funciones del doble en la narrativa de Virgilio Piñera." *Revista iberoamericana* 152–153 (1990): 975–91.

Jameson, Anna. *Sacred and Legendary Art,* Vol. 2. London: Longman, Brown, Green, and Longmans, 1848.

Koch, Dolores M. "Virgilio Piñera, cuentista." *Linden Lane Magazine* 4 (1982): 14–15.

———. "Virgilio Piñera y el neo-barroco." *Hispamérica* 37 (1984): 81–86.

Llopis, Rogelio. "Recuento fantástico." *Casa de las Américas* 42 (1967): 148–55.

Matas, Julio. "Infiernos fríos de Virgilio Piñera." *Linden Lane Magazine* 4 (1982): 22–25.

Méndez y Soto, Ernesto. "Piñera y el tema del absurdo." *Cuadernos hispanoamericanos* 299 (1975): 448–53.

Meyers, Jeffrey. *Homosexuality and Literature 1890–1930.* Montreal: McGill-Queen's, 1977.

Ortiz, Fernando. *Los negros brujos: Apuntes para un estudio de etnología criminal.* Intro. Alberto N. Pamies. Miami: Universal, 1973.

Riccio, Alessandra. "La revista *Orígenes* y otras revistas lezamianas." *Naples, Intituto Orientali Annali, Sezione Romanza* 25.1 (1983): 343–89.

Rodríguez Feó, José. "Una alegoría de la carne." In *Notas críticas*. Havana: Primera Serie, 1962, 165–67.

Santí, Enrico Mario. "Lezama, Vitier y la crítica de la razón reminiscente." *Revista iberoamericana* 92–93 (1975): 535–46.

Schwenger, Peter. "The Masculine Mode." In *Speaking of Gender*. Ed. Elaine Showalter. New York: Routledge, 1989, 101–12.

Sedgwick, Eve Kosofsky. *Epistemology of the Closet*. Berkeley: University of California Press, 1990.

Torres, Carmen L. *La cuentística de Virgilio Piñera: Estrategias humorísticas*. Madrid: Pliegos, 1989.

Vitier, Cintio. *Lo cubano en la poesía*. Havana: Instituto del Libro, 1970, 479–84.

Zalacaín, Daniel. *Teatro absurdista hispanoamericano*. Valencia: Albatros Hispanófila, 1985, 61–71.

◆ Chapter 15

Eroticism and Homoeroticism in *Martín Fierro*

Gustavo Geirola

(translated by Melissa A. Lockhart)

> *Hombre con hombre hombre con hombres hombres hombres.*
> Osvaldo Lamborghini, *El fiord*[1]

José Hernández (1824–86), with his *Martín Fierro* (1872 and 1879), is undoubtedly the emblematic author of Argentine identity. Critics and cultural essayists have been unable to resist constructing around him a series of supposedly national and spiritual values concerning what it means to be Argentine. At the same time, they have established the canonical character of a genre known as the gauchesque.[2] The theme of the gaucho has passed through various stages of transformation, even though not all works of the era are considered to be part of the gauchesque genre: from Hilario Ascasubi (1807–75) to Bartolomé Hidalgo (1788–1822) and the *cielitos* (a form of lyrical poetry) and *diálogos* (a form of dramatic poetry) written during the struggle for independence, to *Martín Fierro,* including *El matadero* (The Slaughterhouse; ca. 1839) by Esteban Echeverría (1805–51) and *Facundo* (1868) by Domingo Faustino Sarmiento (1811–88), to the serial text by Eduardo Gutiérrez (1851–89), *Juan Moreira* (1879–80), and even including the modernist elaborations that, beginning with the nationalist mythologization of *La guerra gaucha* (1905) by Leopoldo Lugones (1871–1938), that culminate in *Don Segundo Sombra* (1926) by Ricardo Güiraldes (1886–1927) and the gauchesque duels in the stories of

Jorge Luis Borges (1899–1986). The aforementioned is not intended to characterize anything like a homogeneity of texts. Quite to the contrary: each work has its own rhythm in a continuous process of transformation. Moreover, in Hernández's own work one can discern not only the political emblematization of the gaucho, transformed into a symbol of national affirmation and machismo, but also the socioeconomic controversies that divide the ideologies of the diverse binary equations of Argentine historical development: countryside/city, barbarism/civilization, the interior/Buenos Aires, native/immigrant. The two parts into which *Martín Fierro* is divided, "The Flight of Martín Fierro," published in 1872, and "The Return of Martín Fierro," published in 1879[3] permit the visualization of these dichotomies within the same text (Viñas).

As for its being an epic poem, critics have attempted to find in the text all the indices of Hernandian literary culture and its Greco-Latin roots (Lugones, Unamuno), while at the same time pointing out those aspects derived from the author's own experience and knowledge of a sector of the population persecuted by the forces of order and exploited by the emerging oligarchy. However, the view of the gaucho in the first part, with his rebellion, his social criticism of hegemonic institutions and agents, and his idealization of the Indian, is converted in the second part into resignation and compliance with an established order at odds with the indigenous Utopia. Despite the polemic that many of these aspects have sparked both inside and outside academic circles, and the literary, even pamphletary utilization of the gaucho theme, as well as various aspects of the poem taken up in films, comic books, and other manifestations of mass popular Culture, there is neither a global nor a partial ideological study of Hernández's text based on noncanonical premises or original propositions concerning Argentine culture.[4]

Homosocial phenomena might well be mentioned here, including the inherent problematics associated with them (the case of the tango, for example), especially when they conceal a homoerotic dimension that, in a certain sense, could function as a semantic matrix capable of inspiring a series of readings whose strength would imply a new horizon of cultural considerations (Sedgwick). Borges establishes a subtle complicity between characters and the culture from which they emerge or that they represent emblematically:

> Martín Fierro, el individuo Martín Fierro, [es el] que
> conocemos íntimamente como acaso no nos conozcamos a
> nosotros mismos. (30)

> No acabamos de saber quién es Hamlet o quién es Martín
> Fierro, pero tampoco nos ha sido otorgado saber quiénes
> somos o *quién es la persona que más queremos*. (75, emphasis
> added)[5]

Indeed, Borges—who rejects the epic qualities of the poem
(35)—with his habitual paradoxical style emphasizes in his study
what in psychoanalytic terms is called "identification" (Masotta),[6]
leaving the door open to all kinds of conjectures about identity.
Yet, he nevertheless follows Lugones when the latter states that the
gaucho ignores the passionate complications of love's labors (54).
Similarly, he categorically sustains with a certain humorous can-
dor that *Martín Fierro*—in contrast to the other naturalist works—
dispenses with the "scandal of sex," because "the erotic life of the
gauchos was rudimentary" (68).

In his *Muerte y transfiguración de Martín Fierro* (Death and Transfiguration of Martín Fierro; 1948) Ezequiel Martínez Estrada writes
"an interpretation of Argentine life" commencing with Hernández's work, and he also affirms, like Borges, that "*Martín Fierro* is
a certain image of the world we inhabit but do not know" (2.382);
this postulation of the text as cryptic leads back to the fundamental nucleus in which Argentine being and identity come into play.
This unknowable background, this abject object, does not seem
to postulate itself in erotic terms for the author:

> El tema erótico está abolido, y aunque por ello mismo el
> Poema acuse en tono de limpieza moral y de severa
> censura a lo sexual, las figuras pierden su cohesión
> natural al privárselas de ese sentimiento natural de
> adhesión. (2.378)[7]

Martínez Estrada's insistence on the cancellation of all eroticism in the poem finds support in various scientific and pseudoscientific sources, such as sociology and Freudian psychoanalysis
or even the chronicles of the Spanish explorers. However, since
Martínez Estrada's central theme is the dissolution of the family
and an eroticism understood always as heterosexual, there is no
alternative but to favor certain values attributable to a sensitivity

that immediately creates problems when one contemplates the episode of Cruz's death:

> La congoja desesperante que nos refiere el Protagonista al perder a su compañero Cruz es acaso la única nota de emoción verdadera de toda la Obra, aunque la insistencia en lo patético roce, con su hipérbole, lo declamatorio. En el examen de la psicología de Martín Fierro se señala el episodio de la muerte de Cruz, desde el contagio hasta la sepultura, como de un *pathos* nuevo en la economía del Poema, y es enorme la diferencia de este pasaje con el informe aderezado de frases protocolares, de la muerte de su mujer en el hospital. (2.157–58)[8]

For Martínez Estrada, the Cruz episode is something that seems to lessen the value of the comfortable logic of the poem. It is a strange and unassimilable element that does away with the putatively symbolic figure of the protagonist and impedes the primary intention of the work to in some way provide the personal individualization of the gaucho (whether in the opinion of the public or of the critics, or in the very fascination that the character generated):

> Lo que da unidad al carácter de Martín Fierro es su angustia y su experiencia, porque los hechos corresponden más a la historia del país que a su biografía. Lo biográfico auténtico está en Cruz . . . La inesperada desviación, el desglose, lo encamina por otros derroteros — los del drama — , lo conduce a lo imposible. (2.349)[9]

One has the immediate temptation to think of "the impossible" in Lacanian terms (the real is the impossible), at least to begin to cut through the enigma that Martínez Estrada names "Otra fuerza" (2.349).[10]

Aside from the fact that, as David William Foster points out concerning gay literature, there are always "various contemporary hypotheses concerning sexuality" at work here (Foster 2), the denial of eroticism in the poem seems to be imputable to a certain critical resistance to, or to a certain negation of, Argentine culture. It's as if the national sentiment, or that which represents it, eponymous heroes or literary emblems, could not express eroticism except as a social disgrace or an abstract idealization (Bergman). This negation is even more pronounced when the recogni-

tion of eroticism is tied to its perverse or allegedly deviant forms
that, if at one moment can call into question the hypocrisy of any
pretension of decency, on another level—one more interesting and
dangerous—refers to a theoretical position of ethicopolitical implications ("libidinal politics," in the words of Silverman) and,
therefore, bespeaks the conjunction of power and desire with their
microphysical avatars (Foucault).

Ludmer has pointed out in her study on the gauchesque genre
a frequent process involved in admitting the presence of difference and foreignness, specifically immigration, in the perception
of the gaucho protagonist.[11] The Italian or the Spaniard (almost
always "Neapolitan" or "Galician" in Argentine culture) is presented by means of a process of "feminization": a coward, incapable of fighting with a knife, never taking on a heroic deed; tied
to his work and domestic duties, the immigrant is always on the
side of the strong and collaborates with the forces of oppression:

> Allí un gringo con un órgano
> y una mona que bailaba,
> haciéndonos rair estaba
> cuando le tocó el arreo.
> ¡Tan grande el gringo y tan feo
> lo viera cómo lloraba!
>
> Hasta un inglés sanjiador
> que decía en la última guerra
> que él era de Inca-la-perra
> y que no quería servir,
> también tuvo que juir
> a guarecerse en la sierra.
> (1.319–30)[12]

The entire fifth canto of the first part is dedicated to the denigration of the immigrant. Ludmer studies the linguistic, sexual,
and therefore cultural references in the following stanza:

> Era un gringo tan bozal,
> que nada se le entendía.
> ¡Quién sabe de ánde sería!

> Tal vez no juera cristiano,
> pues lo único que decía
> es que era *pa-po-litano*.
> (1.847–52)[13]

These words (Inca-la-perra[14] and papolitano) refer to a specifi-cally sexual semantic field (el perro hinca [fornica] la perra, papo designa la vulva [the dog rams into/fornicates the bitch; *papo* is used in vulgar terms to designate the vagina]). "These are the oral and written translation of foreign words into the voice of the Ar-gentine gaucho," and Ludmer adds that they are not terms "hurled as a challenge" (47). Since a challenge is only directed toward an equal, a man (even when, as we shall see, he requires women as intermediaries), the parameters of "feminization" are the result of an inversion of the abilities of the gaucho: in the face of his discretion and bravery, the foreigner is defined by treachery and cowardice; "la gringada [no sabe] atracar a un pingo" (1.892),[15] "no saben ni ensillar; / no sirven ni para carniar" (1.896–97);[16] neither do they have the courage to go near the cattle, even when they were thrown to the ground; finally, there are "delicaos / parecen hijos de rico" (1.905–6).[17] The gringos suffer the cold and the heat, they lack know-how when it comes to survival in the country, they are tightfisted and lack solidarity among themselves; all in all, "son güenos / pa vivir entre maricas" (1.915–16).[18] What seem to be outlined here are the elements that will operate in the trans-formation of Sarmiento's civilization-versus-barbarism equation and its immediate aggressive elaboration as a homophobic affront. The masculine assumes a rural dimension and "feminization" ends up as a product of submission of subjects to urban culture and, as a consequence, to the law of the State and the constitution of the nation. This is a generalized feminization that the poem only homologizes to what produces death, as the Absolute Master.

What is bothersome about the foreigner (brought in to pro-mote the ideal of progress) is not so much his difference, or even his condition as an invading subaltern (as will be developed later on in the theater of Florencio Sánchez [1875–1910]), but the ab-solute and dangerous proximity of the Other that must be dis-missed as less than a man; the same impossibility of constituting a family, alleged by Martínez Estrada — that is, the absolute inability of the gaucho to maintain lasting ties with a woman—becomes homologous with the intolerable obligation to live together with the immigrant:

> Yo no sé por qué el gobierno
> nos manda aquí a la frontera
> gringada que ni siquiera
> se sabe atracar a un pingo.
> ¡Si crerá al mandar un gringo
> que nos manda alguna fiera!
> (1.889–894)[19]

The fundamental paradox of the poem, in this sense, is given by the fact that the choice of the homoerotic object, as an instance of narcissism, has as its source the aggressiveness derived by this same specular construct: sexual discrimination, machismo, racism, and xenophobia have as a given and a cause not the difference of the Other, but his sameness, his similarity. This explains why the identification with the Other comes about as an analogy and an excess: the stories of Fierro and Cruz on one hand, the challenges of the Blacks and Indios on the other. If, in the first case, as a first person construct, Cruz and Fierro allow for a "love story," it is because, the challenge having been initiated, they both renounce the intervention of the State—that is to say, of the universality of the law. Self-exile in the open frontier becomes a requirement of the story to safeguard narcissism, or vice versa; in any event, the frontier here marks a limit of appropriations and a horizon that is idealized as "illegal." In the second aspect, the challenge that leads to the fight, always mediated by women, articulated by the look, seduced by the statuary image of the other, permits aggression to be unleashed toward what is also similar: what lies beyond the law that would display the illusionary emblem of the lack of castration.

The same happens later on when the semantization of the prison acquires hellish attributes ("es un infierno temido" [2.1872]),[20] due to the fact that the gaucho finds himself feminized by the presence of an authority to which he must submit. The masculine dimension is defined by freedom and brute force, and, in this environment, as we have said, only Death, as Absolute Master, may "feminize" the gaucho. If "yo soy toro en mi rodeo" (1.62),[21] it is because "para mí el campo son flores / dende que libre me veo" (1.991–92),[22] which contrasts with the words of Fierro's older son, for whom "en esa cárcel no hay toros / allí todos son corderos" (2.1851).[23] The masculine forms a paradigm with the animal force of progenitor, the wide open spaces, and freedom, while the feminine is configured as animal-offspring, closed space, and submission.

The immigrant is only one of many ways to configure the Other. There are also the racial (the Black man), the political (the Indian), the sexual (woman), and the class (the authority and the urban riffraff) dimensions. Many times these dimensions intersect, allowing for meanings of diverse consistency. The gaucho alone allows for a level of similarity in the code of his relationship with the Other: the other gaucho. It is in this context that the topic of friendship appears, a topic pointed out by critics (and glimpsed in Homer's *The Iliad*) that has yet to be pursued to its ultimate consequences.[24] To recognize the Other on the condition of equality is to imply not only a narcissistic dimension in the order of identification, but also to present the possibility of the choice of an erotic object under a discriminatory restriction.

Eroticism is not necessarily reduced to the level of the characters, but rather, when closely examined, is what motivates and serves as the origin of the story. "Al comienzo era el Amor"[25] could be an imaginary beginning for Hernández's story. Indeed, the poem presents the idealization of the past, when the gaucho was able to live harmoniously connected to the land, his wife, and his children, without the need for legal regulation:

> Yo he conocido esta tierra
> en que el paisano vivía
> y su ranchito tenía
> y sus hijos y mujer...
> era una delicia el ver
> cómo pasaba sus días
> (1.133–38)[26]

This "infantile" paradise is broken with the presence of the Other, the representative of order, who installs a limitation in the formerly infinite and expansive space of Love:

> Tuve en mi pago en un tiempo
> hijos, hacienda y mujer
> pero empecé a padecer,
> me echaron a la frontera
> ¡y qué iba a hallar al volver!
> tan sólo hallé la tapera. (1.289–94)[27]

We must review the entire text in order to gain access to this new infinity now subordinate to the universality of the Law and protected in the order of alliance. Martín Fierro's advice is, without a doubt, proof that the Superego has been attained and with it, undoubtedly, a new protection for narcissism:[28]

> Después, a los cuatro vientos
> los cuatro se dirijieron;
> una promesa se hicieron
> que todos debían cumplir;
> mas no la puedo decir,
> pues secreto prometieron. (2.4781–86)[29]

Family order (home, children, and wife) constitutes a totality on the level of property: it is the gaucho's capital, and, as a result, it may be lost and recuperated, and it is characterized by an order of substitution and supplementation. The rejection of family order and, as Martínez Estrada makes clear, specifically paternity, is maintained to the benefit of the universality of the Law. The presence of Fierro's children in the second part is not a whimsical addition to the poem. It is not necessary that there be so many children: two would suffice. What is at issue here is the process whereby, once Cruz is dead and the "law of the jungle" has been accepted (the destroyed body of the captive woman's small son and the body of the Indian finally strung up — the fragmented body here breaks with the idealization of the desert as beyond the law), the return implies the first stage in the internalization of paternity. For this reason, to return is to assume the particularity of paternity and the universality of the Law, and for this it is sufficient for his two children to be recognized. However, the repudiation of legal bonds is made very clear in the poem: the alliance between Fierro, his children, and Cruz's son is, in some way, private and clandestine, a pact of silence about the horrors of the past and the hiding of identity. It is the "national" solution that the poem tends to offer. The famous advice of Martín Fierro to his own children and to Cruz's son constitutes a set of elementary rules to live by for this fraternity of the marginalized. They take on the form of "words of wisdom" gained by way of brutal historical experience in order to give way to a petit bourgeois masculine moral order, one that guarantees the union between men who have been feminized by the Law and protected from assuming castration by virtue of macho, racist, and xenophobic illusions. The entire theologic order of honor, of love between brothers, of submission, pacifism, and renunciation, must undoubtedly have subsequent developments in the allegedly contestatory ideologies of subaltern sectors.

And the crises of these homosocial pacts must have their cause in an operant that is always articulated as this fundamental Otherness that we conveniently designate as "woman." It is the ubiquity of Woman that threatens the universality of the Law: if in the poem women are exchanged by men as the necessary catalysts to erotic masculine challenges, if they slip through the requirements of the Law, then, as one stanza seems to insinuate (2.4757–62; 183), it is that women are allowed to see the dimension of Woman as an absolute danger.

It is beyond the scope of this paper to underline the subaltern character of women or to count up their ephemeral presence in the poem, which is exactly what Martínez Estrada does. What is of interest here is, on the contrary, to see the undeniable inscription of Woman, as a mark of her indisputable difference in the written transformation operant in the poem. In any event, like the immigrant, the woman occupies a place as intermediary in order to permit all types of possible relations (love/hate) between men. Each time that a woman appears in the text, it is to permit the circulation of men, diverting the sexual by way of eroticism (much different when compared to what will occur later in the text *El fiord* [The Fiord; 1964] by Osvaldo Lamborghini [1940–85], where

eroticism is absolutely canceled out, with homoeroticism channeled directly into homosexuality or omnisexuality)[30]: the Black
woman (part 1, canto 7) is responsible for the duel with the Black
man, who challenges the racial difference and feminizes the Other,
transforming his animal-like nature (on the instinctive level) of
the bull (1.1193; 34) into a "tigra parida" (1.1222).[31] In the episode
of the braggart (part 1, canto 8) the fight has its origin in the ag-
gravation deriving from the reference "cuñao/hermana" (1.1289–
94),[32] who notices the circulation of the women and "la elastici-
dad del parentesco" (Martínez Estrada [2.357]).[33]

The captive permits the transition from the death of Cruz to
revenge against the Indian: this is the most interesting episode
for purposes of the discussion of homoeroticism that we are undertaking here. The kinesics of this duel may be read in an order
of fascination ("me miraba y lo miraba" [2.1156]),[34] masculine love
presented as an alternative of life or death, passive/active, up/
down, inserter/inserted. These moral games with the Other cannot
end in any way other than lethal, because the duel permits identification, and, at the same time, as we have already mentioned,
in every aggression, the racial component is lost. Only the relationship Martín Fierro–Cruz can conclude the duel with a resolution
sublimated in friendship (a subtle game of mirrors),[35] capable of
permitting a union, flight, and the constitution of the homoerotic
family "nest" beyond the frontier, beyond the law. It is the evoca-
tive restoration of the "golden age" of ancient happiness:

> Allá habrá seguridá
> ya que aquí no la tenemos,
> menos males pasaremos
> y ha de haber grande alegría
> el día que nos descolguemos
> en alguna toldería
>
> Fabricaremos un toldo,
> como lo hacen tantos otros,
> con sus cueros de potro,
> que sea sala y sea cocina.
> ¡Tal vez no falte una china
> que se apiade de nosotros! (1.2233–44)[36]

Later in the second part:

> Fuimos a esconder allí
> nuestra pobre situación,
> aliviando con la unión
> aquel duro cautiverio;
> tristes como un cementario
> al toque de la oración. (2.415–20)[37]

Martínez Estrada, even when underscoring the misogyny of Cruz (1.77; 5), would seem to overlook what his own arguments demonstrate. The sexual is not only given, as Ludmer would attest, by the specific reference of certain terms, but also from what is established syntagmatically in the semantic field without the necessity of direct allusion. In referring to women, Martínez Estrada points out that "más bien que como personas dramáticas actúan como instrumentos de las fuerzas del destino, y sólo se hacen sensibles porque faltan."[38] And he adds: "Una de las formas cariñosas de nombrarlas, 'pilcha,' las equipara a una prenda de vestir o del apero, y más a la *cobija* de dormir, con lo que la metonimia cobra cabal sentido" (2.371, emphasis added).[39]

A few pages earlier, Martínez Estrada cites the stanza in which, if one accepts as valid the reference to the *cubijas* to designate woman, then the relationship Fierro–Cruz is presented not only as a family life, but also as an exchange of the husband/wife roles:

> Guarecidos en el toldo
> charlábamos mano a mano;
> éramos dos veteranos
> mansos pa las sabandijas,
> *arrumbaos como cubijas*
> cuando calienta el verano. (2.433–38)[40]

The amorous masculine utopia can be realized and sustained only in the space of barbarism, because the look of the Indian is from the beginning devalued and because the desert—in the first part—forms an illegal utopic space. However, in the presence of civilized men, love between men requires forms of machismo and challenge (part 1, canto 8).

The story involving Cruz is a sentimental novel permitted by a double operation: the possibility of living together (2.408 [75]) in the domain of barbarism on the frontier to which they have escaped in their flight from civilization, where the possibility to live feminine emotivity is now liberated via the "feminization" of the Christian in the face of the savage: in this way the theme of "male crocodile tears" (Sedgwick 145–46), taken up in the first part in a reserved manner, continues marking with frequency this process as losses are accumulated (hut, children, and wife; later a friend) and logically in the manner in which he goes far away with Cruz toward the domain of the Indians. The masculinization of the woman, especially of the Indian woman, is structured symmetrically but inversely to the feminization of the gaucho (part two, canto 8). It is due to these transformations that language continues to exhibit the subalternization of the subject with the admission of prayer, with the use of diminutives, and the reversal of sexual roles. Cruz dies in Fierro's arms, entrusting a son to him; Martín Fierro prays to Jesus, then he collapses and cries on the tomb. It is for this reason that the friend (as a widow/er) can form part of his possessions ("mis pesamientos fijos / en mi mujer y mis hijos, / y en mi pago y en mi amigo" (2.964–66).[41] "Privado de tantos bienes" (2.967),[42] the gaucho does not know what to do with his life; immediately, the groans of the captive woman open up the field for a new amorous challenge, but Fierro's final destiny will be, as we have seen, return and submission to official culture (which Martínez Estrada designates by using the suspicious word "resurrection" [2.66]), the denunciation of paternity (separation of Martín Fierro from his sons and Cruz's, in the form of a cross, to the four winds), the pact concerning a secret, the attack on the ideology of the weak, and the repudiation of identity by the changing of names.

Literary criticism can, if it so chooses, attribute these matrices to the humanity of the hero or to the connection that the poem has with certain romantic parameters. However, from the rape of the young Unitarian by the robust slaughterhouse captain Matasiete in *El matadero* down to Borges's stories and the feminization of the dissident by torture as a barbarous script of recent military dictatorships, the sociopolitical evaluation and the cultural derivatives of these homoerotic matrices demand a more detailed development, at least if one is going to continue to hold *Martín Fierro* up as the paradigm by which, in homage to the birth of Hernández (November 10), Argentina celebrates a day of national tradition.

Notes

1. Man with man man with men men men.

2. Josefina Ludmer's book, *El género gauchesco: Un tratado sobre la patria* covers all the vicissitudes of the genre's gestation and transformation.

3. It should be noted that the translation of the poem by Henry Alfred Holmes is in prose form as opposed to verse and that the excerpts from the translation will be followed by the page number.

4. The anthology prepared by Francisco Herrera seems to examine these aspects relating to eroticism in national culture. Thus, in the prologue, speaking of *El matadero,* he asks: "¿Dónde encontrar una confluencia del lado oscuro del erotismo, la castración no metafórica, lo prohibido, la transgresión, la ordalía, la violación y la muerte como en el relato de Echeverría?" (Where does one find a confluence of the dark side of eroticism, nonmetaphorical castration, the prohibited, the trial by fire, rape, and death such as we find in Echeverría's story? [9]). This promising inquiry quickly dissolves when the author states that his anthology will only include texts that reflect the impact of the last postwar period and the "distention" produced by the "revolution of the sixties" (11). If it is hoped that the subject will be dealt with in a new volume, the hope of a rereading of the classics is frustrated when Herrera affirms that "nuestra literatura decimonónica carece de irrupciones eróticas dignas de mención, y no es muy diferente de lo que ocurre en las primeras décadas de este siglo. *Nada en la extensa saga de lo gauchesco,* ni en el naturalismo expurgado de Martel o Cambaceres, ni en la picaresca costumbrista de Fray Mocho o Payró, ni en el prolongado canto de cisne del modernismo" (nineteenth-century literature is lacking erotic examples worthy of mention, not unlike what we find in the first decades of this century. *Nothing in the extensive saga of the gauchesque,* nor in the sanitized naturalism of Martel or Cambaceres, nor in the local-color picaresque of Fray Mocho or Payró, nor in the prolonged swansong of Modernism (11, emphasis added). If one thinks of Cambaceres's *Sin rumbo* (1885) or *Los invertidos* (1914) by José González Castillo (Foster 23–32), the least that one can note is Herrera's injustice toward an area of texts, especially if he is basing himself on Bataille or Lacan, as he claims to be.

5. Martín Fierro, the individual Martín Fierro [is someone] we know more intimately than perhaps we know ourselves. We never find out who Hamlet is or who Martín Fierro is, but neither has it been granted to us to know who we are or *who is the person that we most love.*

6. The Freudian-Lacanian bibliography concerning this topic is very extensive. If we refer to Masotta it is because, among other things, he makes identification a key concept in his text.

7. The erotic theme is abolished, and even though the poem rings of moral cleanliness and the severe censure of sex, the characters lose their natural cohesion upon depriving them of that natural feeling of adhesion.

8. The despairing grief that the protagonist relates to us upon losing his companion Cruz is perhaps the only mention of true emotion in the entire work, even if the hyperbolic insistence on the pathetic comes close to being declamatory. In the examination of the psychology of Martín Fierro the episode of Cruz's death is singled out as a new *pathos* in the economy of the poem. And the difference is enormous between this passage and the account of the death of Fierro's wife in the hospital, embellished as it is with protocolar phrases.

9. What gives unity to the character of Martín Fierro is his anguish and his experience, because the facts correspond more to the history of the country than to his biography. The authentic biography is in Cruz. . . . The unexpected deviation, the missing parts, guide him down other paths — those of drama — lead him to the impossible.

10. another force.

11. Ludmer: "Desde abajo, desde el ascenso incesante de voces no escritas que el género incorpora en su historia, se llega a la orilla más baja del género: para definir al gaucho como hombre argentino hay que cambiar el sexo, el género, del extranjero" (49; From below, from the incessant ascent of voices not written that the genre incorporates in its history, one arrives at the lowest shore of the genre, to define the gaucho as an Argentine man one must change the sex, the gender, of the foreigner).

12. There was a hurdy-gurdy Italian there. He had a monkey that danced, and was making us laugh indeed, when they took him. Big and ugly that Italian was, and how he did blubber! Even a ditch-digging Englishman, who used to say during the late war that he was from "Hinglan" and wouldn't serve, he, too, had to run to the hills for his life (11).

13. He was a *gringo*, so stupid nobody could make out what he said. Who knows where he had come from! Maybe he was not even a Christian, for all he could say was, he was a "Pa-po-litano!" (24).

14. *Inca-la-perra* is a play on words for the Spanish *Inglaterra* (England). In his translation of the poem Holmes uses "Hinglan" for England.

15. these gringos who can't so much as mount a horse (25).

16. they can't even saddle a horse, they can't even cut up a beef (25–26).

17. And indeed, when it comes to being fussy, they're as fussy as a rich man's son (26).

18. Blest if they're not just good for living among milksops (26).

19. I don't see why the government sends here to our frontier these gringos who can't so much as mount a horse. They must think they're sending something perfectly terrible among us, when they send a gringo! (25).

20. it is a dreadful hell (111).

21. I'm a bull in my own roundup (4).

22. For me the whole plain is covered with flowers, as soon as I'm free (28).

23. no bulls in that prison, they're all lambs (111).

24. With respect to this, Martínez Estrada refers to this dimension as "un problema de difícil diagnóstico" (a problem not easy to diagnose), and, he adds, "descontada la hipérbole con que el Autor magnifica ese estado de tristeza, no habitual en su modo de describir ninguna pasión, el problema de cómo circunstancias naturales y bien conocidas pudieron ligar a dos seres desdichados en tan fuerte lazo queda como incógnita" (1.85; discounting the hyperbole with which the author

magnifies this state of sadness, not very habitual in his way of describing any passion, the problem of how natural and well-known circumstances can connect two forsaken souls in such a strong bond remains unknown).

25. in the beginning was love.

26. I knew this country when the gaucho lived in it, and had his home, his wife, and his children. It was a delight to see how he spent his days! (6).

27. In my home district I once had sons, herds, a wife. Then came misfortune and they sent me to the frontier. . . . And what should I see, when I returned, but the ruins of my home — naught beside! (10).

28. If we accept Martínez Estrada's version of Cruz as a traitor and as the destroyer of Martín Fierro (1.75–82), then we can come to the conclusion, via Lacan's *Seminario XX,* that the "secret" of verse 4786 allows for a specific interpretation: the other aspect of the Superego, to the extent that it is obscene — that is to say, linked to pleasure, and by way of this, to the "pact" — turns out to be what favors more the emergence of terrorism than it does transgression.

29. Then to the four winds scattered those four, giving each other a promise all were bound to keep — but I can't tell it, for they made it a secret. (185).

30. I am indicating with this word what in psychoanalysis would be directly "pulsional," since pulsion has no object.

31. tigress with cubs (35).

32. brother in law/sister (36).

33. the elasticity of blood bonds.

34. We stood thus, he eyeing me and I looking at him (93).

35. Cruz, replaced by the Commander and incapable of avenging the affront (I, vs. 1777–800), *crosses* his castration with Fierro's bravery before the group of military men. The ideal of I and the I ideal, as much from Fierro as from Cruz, weave a network that sustains all of the "enigma" of the character, of the double and of the encounter. Martínez Estrada says it without hesitation: "Las vidas de Martín Fierro y de Cruz son complementarias: fundiéndolas se obtiene una sola biografía" (The lives of Martín Fierro and Cruz are complementary; in melding them together one obtains only one biography" (I, 82)

36. There'll be safety there, and none here! We shall have less to bear, and great happiness in prospect when we come upon some Indian village. We will make a tent, as do so many others, from horses' hides: parlor and kitchen all in one. Perhaps some Indian woman will be kind to us! (59).

37. There we concealed our poverty, lightening with our restored friendship the pains of captivity, but — after all — as mournful as a graveyard at vespers (75).

38. as dramatic characters they act as instruments of the forces of destiny, and they only become sensitive because they are lacking.

39. One of the endearing ways of referring to them, as *pilcha,* equates them with an article of clothing or some sort of tool, and more so with a blanket, with which the metonym gains exact meaning.

40. Tucked inside our little tent, we would chat away side by side. We were two veterans, well used to the vermin and sprawling *idle as blankets* abandoned in summer's heat (76, emphasis added).

41. with thoughts fixed on my wife and sons, my home and my friend. (89)

42. Reft of so many helps (89; "helps" is a mistranslation of *bienes* = goods, wealth).

Works Cited

Bergman, David. *Gaiety Transfigured: Gay Self-Representation in American Literature.* Madison: University of Wisconsin Press, 1991.

Borges, Jorge Luis. *El "Martín Fierro."* Buenos Aires: Columba, 1953.

Foster, David William. *Gay and Lesbian Themes in Latin American Writing.* Austin: University of Texas Press, 1991.

Foucault, Michel. *Microfísica del poder.* Madrid: La piqueta, 1979.

Hernández, José. *Martín Fierro.* Mexico: Editorial Kapelusz Mexicana, 1978.

———. *Martín Fierro: The Argentine Gaucho Epic.* Trans. and Intro. Henry Alfred Holmes. New York: Hispanic Institute in the United States, 1948.

Herrera, Francisco. Prologue. *Antología del erotismo en la literatura argentina.* Ed. Francisco Herrera. Buenos Aires: Editorial Fraterna, 1990.

Lacan, Jacques. *El Seminario XX: Aun.* Barcelona: Paidós, 1985.

Lamborghini, Osvaldo. *El fiord.* Buenos Aires: Ediciones Chinatown, 1969.

Ludmer, Josefina. *El género gauchesco: Un tratado sobre la patria.* Buenos Aires: Sudamericana, 1988.

Lugones, Leopoldo. *El payador.* Buenos Aires: Otero y Cía., 1916.

Martínez Estrada, Ezequiel. *Muerte y transfiguración de Martín Fierro.* Mexico: Fondo de Cultura Económica, 1948.

Masotta, Oscar. *Lecturas de psicoanálisis: Freud, Lacan.* Buenos Aires: Paidós, 1992.

Sedgwick, Eve Kosofsky. *Epistemology of the Closet.* Berkeley: University of California Press, 1990.

Silverman, Kaja. *Male Subjectivity at the Margins.* New York: Routledge, 1992.

Unamuno, Miguel de. *"El gaucho Martín Fierro*: Poema popular gauchesco de don José Hernández." *Revista española* 1.1 (1894): 5–22. Also *Obras completas.* Madrid: Afrodisio Aguado, 1958, 8.47–63.

Viñas, David. "José Hernández, del indio al trabajo y a la conversión (1872–1879)." In *Indios, ejército y frontera.* Mexico: Siglo XXI, 1982, 159–64.

Chapter 16

Intricacies of Brazilian Gayness: A Cross-Cultural and Cross-Temporal Approach

Dário Borim Jr.

Some of the changes Brazilian society undertakes in the late 1960s and 1970s exemplify an authoritarian aspect of its sociopolitical values and dynamics. This aspect has much to do with the division of people into two mutually exclusive categories, the domains of masculinity and femininity, which I would like to discuss by focusing on homosexuality. While reviewing pieces of colonial literature and cultural anthropology, I propose to retrace ties between the past and the present of Brazil.

When the military tightened the individual's freedom of expression to a minimum in 1968,[1] the human body became not only the center of social and political tensions (in the sense that it was directly the object of imprisonment, torture, and death), but also a symbolic form of protest and a means of personal liberalization. Escaping the evils of militarization from both the Right and the Left, men and women then take a "nonpartisan solidarity,"[2] which is almost always associated with the use of drugs and with (homo)-sexuality, according to João Silvério Trevisan (166). Such circumstances mark the start of what is called the gay boom in Brazil. Despite their desire to salvage the "nation" as a whole from oppression, some factions of the Left, however, would not only despise the Gay Movement but also ban gay individuals from their artistic and political enterprises. The Teatro de Arena (Arena Theater), for instance, one of the most important centers for the theater based on socialist ideology in the 1960s, declined to cast gays (Trevisan 162). One of the Arena mentors is Augusto Boal (1931), who now lives in Paris, where he works with his controversial Theater of the Oppressed. Gianfranceso Guarnieri (1934), one of the best-known actors of Brazil and Boal's coauthor in many classic plays like *Eles não usam black-tie* (They Don't Wear Black-Tie, 1958), *Zumbi* (1965), and *Tiradentes* (1967), declared in 1981 that "performance on stage had to be that of men — corporeal expression and speech had to be clear. We ended up banning those we considered homosexuals" ("Guarnieri" 9).

Playwright and actor Guarnieri does not fully spell out the terms by which he and other messianic artists would determine who was and who was not "homosexual." Projecting his cryptic comments onto the large and confusing scenario of Brazilian sexual symbolism, I'm tempted to say that what he refers to is the *viado*, a queerlike stereotypical figure whose Portuguese name alludes directly to *veado* (deer). What seems to be an "anomalous effeminacy of what should rightfully be male virility and activity," says Richard G. Parker, is linked to the popular perception of "the most frail and delicate" of all animals (45).

Obviously, to some, but not quite to others, the *viado* is not a legitimate representative of all gay men, since very many of the gay men show no signs of fragility or effeminacy. Some actually hate women and all the physical and psychological traits associated with them, according to Trevisan. Others live an exclusively homosexual life and yet do not accept the gay community; they may even detest any claims of loyalty to a group of peers. Trevisan also elaborates on the category the Brazilian media calls the "promiscuous heterosexual" for whom whatever sexual object comes along is fine, as long as his supposed macho condition in society is not jeopardized — that is to say, as long as other people think of him as paradigmatically macho. Peter Fry and Edward MacRae accurately explain that, according to Brazilian popular ideology, the young man who plays the active role with a fag is called "man" or "macho man" (43).

Origins and Developments of Gayness

One plausible way to explore Brazilian gayness[3] is the study of social and sexual behavior among Amerindians, which has been reviewed by scholars during the quincentennial of the 1492 encounter. One of these scholars, José Piedra, is mostly concerned with sexuality in the region where Amerindians and European travelers first met. He argues that those who would be willing to deal at all with the colonial search for the history of the Caribbean libido would be compelled to declare that the early chroniclers preferred not to think of themselves as having gender or sex worth debating, much less debatable gender and sex. The likely exception would have been made by the chroniclers in order to praise themselves for having the right gender and sex or "to chastise others for having the wrong gender qualities and too much of the wrong sex. Even such a reticence has important repercussions in our present-day libidinous clichés" (232).

Particularly interested in Brazil, anthropologists Fry and MacRae opt to examine gayness through the differentiation between biological and social aspects of human sexuality. Their discoveries corroborate the notion that the people called homosexuals suffer from no differential condition, but are led, to a great extent, by societal pressures to assume rather unorthodox roles that are nothing but variations from those social roles normally attributed to men and women. Inclining toward an almost thorough relativization of gayness, Fry and MacRae argue that there are just as many forms of representing and practicing homosexuality as there are societies, historical eras, and distinct groups within each society (7–16).

Notwithstanding their awareness of the pitfalls of oversimplification, Fry and MacRae set out to probe consistencies and disparities of homosexuality in "popular Brazil"[4] by comparing its purported manifestations to certain Amerindian groups. They initially say that, unlike the modern, industrialized societies in general, certain small Amerindian tribes used to have a considerably homogeneous way of regarding social roles and homosexuality. Basing their opinions on material researched by anthropologist Pierre Clastres, Fry and MacRae produce an interesting discussion on the Guayaki Indians from Paraguay. One anecdote is truly elucidating. Two of their males do not fit in the social models prescribed by very old prohibitions: men could not make baskets and women could not hunt. Yet, since Chachu and Krembégi could not handle any hunting, both take to making baskets and following women around.

Chachu is looked down on by the other members of his society for crossing the social barrier of his sex role. The men hold him in disdain, the women in mockery, and children in lesser respect (35). Krembégi, in turn, could recuperate some of his social prestige by crossing not only the social barrier, but also the sexual one. Krembégi lets his hair grow and learns how to manufacture ornaments like the women of his tribe. Because he prefers to assume the so-called passive role in sex, the hunters go after him and he becomes a *kyrypy-meno*, the lower status of an "anus-for-love-making" (34).

Krembégi's passive homosexuality is well known, but the hunters' active masculinity is in no way jeopardized in the eyes of the tribe, a phenomenon that resembles today's cover-up of active homosexuals in Brazil. Among the Indians of Paraguay and in many social spheres of Brazil, "a strong distinction between masculinity and femininity is accompanied by another equally strong division between sexual 'activity' and 'passivity'" (35). Among men, sexual relations are permitted whether homosexual or heterosexual, as long as the individual is top. For the Guayaki, as well as many contemporary Brazilians, passive homosexuality must be avoided by "real" men. The Guayaki had very little privacy — living in a small community as they did — and it was, therefore, nearly impossible to practice such sex without it becoming public news (Fry and MacRae 36). The average pressure Brazilian gay individuals may feel is probably less overwhelming, but it certainly remains strong enough to cause a good portion of them never to reveal or even assume their most natural or urgent sexual orientation.

Interesting lines of analogy can be drawn between sexual and gender patterns in Brazil and the Caribbean as well. Piedra's work, for instance, explores the undebatable continuum of "hypergendered and oversexed Caribbean images for sale" from colonial to postcolonial times (232), which resemble the erotic features of Portuguese America not only in the early 1500s (regarded as such by

European travelers), but also in today's world-famous Carnival extravaganzas (advertised as easy, fantastic sex for all). Despite the censorship imposed by Bartolomé de Las Casas (1474–1566), Piedra has found enough outstanding gender and libidinal markers in the earliest writings by Christopher Columbus (1451–1506), especially the "secret love life of cannibals and Amazons" (238).

According to Columbus and some of his contemporary Europeans, the "libidinally dangerous natives" of the West Indies live off of the mainstream archipelago. They inhabit two mysteriously fascinating islands, one supposedly occupied by cannibals, the other by Amazons. Both islands are construed and/or depicted as "libidinal stages for freak shows geared toward a writing/reading/paying Spanish public that would not necessarily mix with the actors and actresses" (Piedra 238). Illiterate and "primitive," these islanders, much like the Brazilian Indians, lack "textual challenges that are present, for instance, in the mightier writing peoples of Mesoamerica and the equally feisty peoples of Andean America" (245). Exotic, therefore erotic, Caribbean nakedness in body and soul instead provides the adventurers with some compensation that causes the Europeans' imagination (at home and abroad) to run wild.

Piedra's conclusions assert that, at least in the Caribbean seen by the Europeans, cannibal males would eat mostly other males with some sort of erotic pleasure. Amazons, as lesbianesque warriors, in turn, would "fight for the sake of love of their own kind," and, when they mate with men, they do it "for the exclusive purpose of giving birth to females." Quoting chronicler Perez de Oliva (1494–1533), the Amazons' male offspring are "disposed of, sometimes eaten" (246). Both images of sexual and gender distortions "are fraught with homoerotic and homosexual potential" (252). According to Columbus and others, cannibals are condemned by God to live on men-only islands, whereas Ramón D. Pané (?–1571) and another group of travelers insist that men and women become homosexuals "after being expelled from Paradise-like islands to others" from which they have to "reinvent their respective genders and 'marital,' or at least procreative, relationship" (Piedra 253).

Piedra indeed constructs convincing theories in regard to the Renaissance Spaniards' attitude toward the cannibals and the Amazons. On one hand, "cannibalistic behavior is certainly a distorted picture of gay sexual practices or of the search and experience of the Third Sex" (253). Both pictures, he adds, correspond to Spanish images of incompleteness to be fulfilled in the New World. The idea of "cannibalistic transubstantiation complements these men's lack of pleasure in procreation." Furthermore, the notion of the native's "androgyny and hermaphroditism justifies and enhances the bodily possession of the Other as an avenue for the colonizer's self-empowerment" (253). On the other hand, the Spanish Renaissance concept of lesbianism is that of empowered *marimachos* ("macho or butch Marias," as Piedra explains the term). In other words, they "are portrayed as lovely images of aggressive womanhood" (254). To Piedra, this is a "male fantasy that backfires." He sustains that they "not only reject men, except as entrapped baby-makers, but be they 'butch' or 'fem' they also remain perfectly acceptable females in their own right—or at least on their own island" (254).

"If the sexual activities of these cannibals can only be deduced, their gender typification is far more obvious," Piedra contends.[5] He tells how Columbus and others describe these men with very long hair (like women wore their hair in Castile), and, according to Columbus, "other features showing that they subject themselves to pain for the sake of what they take to be beauty" (253). Traits like these, charges Piedra, "remain to this day symptoms of feminine leanings and, in a male, [are] traditional stigmas of gay behavior." Women also are given a special place within the male-centered rationalization on sodomy, the "way by which it is justifiable to make love to anyone, as a token of war—as long as the token is a woman or womanlike" (252). The Amazon, therefore, is the woman "who has taken up archery in order to symbolically become a man by piercing the body and/or the heart of males." That way the Amerindian women too "get to make holes and justify their lovemaking as a manly act of empowerment" (252).

Among the natives of North America, the changes in sexual and social orientation of the berdaches, the generic term applied to Indian men who "transformed" themselves into women, bears some resemblance to those among the Guayaki, with one difference: supernatural powers. Generally speaking, the berdaches "were well accepted and, in many cases, attributed exceptional powers of healing and prophecy" (Fry and MacRae 37). The opposite transformations occur, too. The authors mention the case of a woman of the Kutenay group born in the late eighteenth century. She married a male Canadian colonizer but later returned to her tribe alone dressing and acting like a male: playing cards, hunting, and fighting. Ququnok Patke, her name, not only claimed special powers, such as prophecy, but also performed the important role of negotiating peace between tribes in strife, such as the Blackfeet and the Flatheads.[6]

There are no berdaches left in the United States anymore, Fry and MacRae point out. Their end was brutal under the civilizing endeavor that conquered them in the name of Christ and progress. "The berdaches were persecuted and ridiculed by the white colonizers, and members of the Bureau of Indian Affairs forced them to dress according to their biological sex." Native Americans themselves started to see a source of humiliation and shame in the institution of the berdache. Fry and MacRae inform us that there was at least one case of suicide, in which the berdache's family insisted that s/he hunted with the men of the tribe. The berdaches and the sexual values of the society they belonged to, conclude the authors, "were victimized by a sexual ideology that classified homosexuality as crime, sin, and disease" (59).

The chief similarity connecting societies like the Guayaki, other Amerindians, and "popular Brazil" lies in the fact that people are not classified into homosexual or heterosexual categories simply according to their supposed sexual behavior. The prevailing scheme is that of social and sexual identities resulting from the combination of biological sex and gender roles (Fry and MacRae 39–43). In this respect, a Brazilian boy is called *bicha*, or "queer," not necessarily because he is thought of as one engaged in homosexuality, but because, "vis-à-vis other markers of masculinity/femininity like voice timber, make-up, clothing, toys, and sports preferences he supposedly appears to be effeminate. It is assumed, nevertheless, that if that boy gets sexually involved with men, he is 'femininely passive,' and the other men are 'top machos'" (43).

In other words, what Fry and MacRae suggest is that the popular conceptualization of sexuality in Brazil stresses the domains of "masculinity" and "femininity," "activity" and "passivity," or the notion of who is top and who is bottom, rather than the split between homosexuality and heterosexuality, aspects that "play a sneaking role in that pattern" (49–50). If that pattern were more concerned with homosexuality in and of itself, "then the man who 'had an affair' with a queer certainly would have to be called 'homosexual' or something of that sort" (50).

"Popular Brazil," as the two authors contend, is very old and, indeed, borrows prejudices from a very old Europe. In that regard, René Jara and Nicholas Spadaccini remind us that the "projection onto Amerindian reality of the images that the Europeans had of their own Other was a favorite discursive strategy" (10). The critics highlight the significance of the dichotomy nobility versus savagery — the us and them of medieval European imaginary — at a time when the Spaniards had finally conquered Granada from the Moors after half a millennium and glorified blood purity against the so-called inferiority of the northern Africans. It was definitely a time of changes, since, as Roy Nash recalls, "the first contact of the Portuguese and Spanish with a darker-skinned people was the contact of the conquered with their brown-skinned conquerors" (37).[7]

Jara and Spadaccini also show how, apart from the notion of religious conversion hiding the State policy of expansionism, "the very concept of Western civilization might be at stake if male domination, heterosexuality, hierarchies of gender and power, and notions of property and land tenure came tumbling down" (17–18). After observing similar phenomena in Fernández de Oviedo (1478–1557), Amerigo Vespucci (1451–1513), De Bry (1528–98) and other pioneering European travelers to the Americas, Jara and Spadaccini charge that "a strategy of moral and physical remaking of the Amerindians is undertaken." According to that logic, the Amerindian males are the opposite of the Europeans, inasmuch as the American males are effeminate (lacking body hair) and inclined to Socratic love (18).

Perhaps an even sharper analysis of how the Europeans understand the Amerindians relates to how and what the Americans worship and eat and how they have sex. In this regard, James B. Scott, Etienne Grisel, and Roberto Reis make an outstanding point, which Jara and Spadaccini explain:

> The central feature of the natives' inferiority... was their inability to discriminate, as seen in their culinary, religious, and sexual habits. Thus, in this discourse, the consumption

of human flesh and of lower species of animals and plants signaled the natives' failure to distinguish between the edible and the inedible. Devil worship was also a result of the same characteristic: the Indians could not distinguish between genuine faith and a set of false beliefs crafted by satanic cunning. . . . Sexual deviations were explained by the generalized selection of the wrong mates indulging in bestiality, lesbianism, sodomy, incest, and other unnatural practices. The central Indian offenses—sodomy, idolatry, and cannibalism—were thus explained. (20–21)

Reis reminds us, though, that today we have very distinct interpretations of these and other aspects of Brazilian Indian cultures. For one thing, he utilizes Florestan Fernandes's insight into the rituals concerning anthropophagy: "They were sacralizations of the spirit of bravery and of the desire to preserve the cultural patrimony that was threatened by enemy tribes" (466–67). Yet, this is obviously not the notion that the first Europeans in America share with their readers and sermon listeners. The common cannibalistic feasts,[8] which soon become a cliché image in the writings and pictures by foreigners on the Americas, "are in metonymic relation with sexual disorder," add Jara and Spadaccini (21).

The connection between such views of abnormal eating, drinking, and copulating and the prevailing modes of thinking during the late Middle Ages and early Renaissance is obvious. French Calvinist Friar Jean de Léry (1534–1611), living in Brazil between 1556 and 1558, confirms the connection between "barbecued human flesh" (a typical case of Léry's dramatic choice in lexicon) and "the three failures of temperance" (Jara and Spadaccini 21). The French Calvinist tells us that "it is mainly when feathered and adorned that they [the Tupinambás] kill and eat a prisoner of war in bacchanals pagan style, of which they are inebriated ministers" (Léry 132).

The European way of practicing bigotry is suggested not only by the first chroniclers from abroad, but also by an array of documents relating to the Roman Catholic Inquisition in Brazil. Unlike Léry, who apparently watches and registers his impressions in private writings to be published a few decades later, other Europeans in America set out to punish individuals accused of sins like sodomy. Fry and MacRae show how the allegedly deviant could easily end up in the bonfires either as a result of another person's denunciation or his/her own confession.

The records of the Holy Office available today in Bahia testify to a demystifying theory: the "active" individual — the top, or the "agent," as the Holy Office put it in the sixteenth and seventeenth centuries — isn't necessarily a superior in social status or an oppressor in interpersonal dynamics in relation to the so-called passive — the bottom, or "patient," for the Holy Office. On one hand, Patrícia Aufterheide suggests that the active partners in general have higher social status than the passive. The point is illustrated by the case regarding Fernão Roiz de Souza. He is said to have been a white son of an (ex)aristocratic family who, at the age of eleven, works as a servant at the governor's mansion. He has to submit himself to a passive role at gunpoint. "As he grows older, he turns himself into an 'active,' always searching for partners from lower social strata like mulattos and women" (Fry and MacRae 51).

Gay activist Luis Mott, who manages to identify 135 sodomites among the Holy Office victims, observes various other cases that follow suit. Nevertheless, he also comes across a significant number of files in which the more advantaged of two partners is the sexually passive one. In regard to sodomy relations between blacks and whites, Mott informs us that there is

> a whole continuum of interactions, sometimes the white individual exerting his power and prepotency typical of upper casts, sometimes the person of color finding out numberless subterfuges by which s/he would become the power holder at least during this dualistic microuniverse established by homoeroticism. (Fry and MacRae 51)

What the documents suggest, therefore, is that the dichotomy top/bottom, or active/passive does not necessarily repeat the social hierarchy between the two partners.

If the image of the homosexual male in the Americas appears to be blurred in sin and myth, a distortion mostly concocted by the century-old prejudices of the European colonizers, there seems to be, likewise, a great deal of mythology and other misconceptions that categorize the Brazilian "female homosexual." The European counterparts to the lesbians of the Americas are none other than pagan witches, a concept rigidly formed by farmers against the evil peasant revolts in late medieval times. It is interesting to keep in mind that, on one hand, "European witches of the sixteenth and seventeenth centuries wore no clothing" (Jara and Spadaccini 21–22). On the other hand, it is not rare to find paintings in which the joys of eating are associated with American female lesbianism and masturbation (Jara and Spadaccini 21).

As the berdaches' case suggests, lesbianism has actually been related to supernatural power for a great many years. Apart from sexual or social behavior per se, the very nakedness of the Amerindian women automatically became an obsession for the Europeans. Nearly always painted without clothes, their habit or the idea behind it was "associated with witchery and devil worship" (Jara and Spadaccini 21). Léry, for instance, is eager to explain why. At first he says that men, not women, teenagers, or children, often wear a certain large leaf tied to cotton strings to hide their genitals. Though it may look like a consequence of the little natural shame they still have, Léry supposes they wear such a thing "in order to hide some disease which attacks their organ at an advanced age" (112–13). What Léry has to say about women, in turn, deserves a more comprehensive picture:

> What marveled us most about those Brazilian women was the fact that, despite their way of neither painting their bodies, thighs and legs, like the men, nor covering themselves with feathers, we never managed to have them get dressed, even though we often gave them cotton dresses and shirts. . . . And so strong was their habit and so delighted were the Tupinambá women by their nakedness, that they obstinately resisted getting dressed, whether they lived in plain freedom on the Continent, with their parents and family, or remained war prisoners, which ones we had bought and kept in the fortress to work; even though we covered them by force, they would tear off their clothes as night fell and wander around nude on the island, for sheer pleasure. And if they were not obliged by the power of the whip, they would prefer to suffer the heat of the sun and bruise their bodies on the continuous job of moving earth and rocks, rather than tolerate the most simple object on their skin. (120)

What is implied here is the Tupinambá women's pathologic obsession with bare skin and water.[9] It seems as though in their minds—or, more likely, in Léry's mind—they need to cleanse their bodies and spirits from the dirty influences of Satan. Father Manuel da Nóbrega (1440–1500), indeed, refers to such women as naturally possessed by demons. After talking to their shaman, he says, they start to shake in such a way that they look "diabolical, which they certainly are, lying on the ground and foaming at the mouth" (64).

What Léry, Nobrega, and many other European chroniclers, especially friars and priests, seem to be doing is ensuring that they deny their awe and/or sexual interest in the Amerindian women while prescribing them a devilish and lesbianesque character. Unavoidably disturbed, the Europeans opt for various subterfuges, one of which is to say they impose clothes on them.[10] Another way of handling nudity and desire is adopted by men like Jesuit Father José de Anchieta (1534–97), who allegedly claims to be saving the Amerindians' souls by writing endless prayer-poems on the sand dunes.

The common approach to the nakedness, however, has to do with a response to the confirmation or transgression of European mainstream morality, particularly where it grants men some special rights over women's rights. Léry, for example, is surprised that Tupinambá men can live in polygamy (he says he sees one with eight wives). Léry's understanding is that the larger the number of women, the braver the men are considered (223). Even if there is one woman who is always the most beloved, the others neither revolt against it nor show "signs of jealousy," Léry points out. They all live in peace, busy with the household chores, weaving hammocks, cleaning the garden, and planting their seeds.

Up to that point, Léry's reasoning has kept a somewhat respectful tone of description. His next point reveals much higher bias, however. He invites the reader to ponder if European women would accommodate this matrimonial setting—were men permitted by God, the Christian God, of course, to have more than one wife. His greater concern with the men's well-being is clear, for he states that it would be better "to condemn man to the slave galleys rather than launching him into so much intrigue and jealousy" (224). Despite the metaphorical aspect of his language, Léry is alluding to a hypothetical polygamy among the good ladies of Europe (not the witches of the countryside) with images suggesting their evil nature. How could "our ladies live united if the simple precept of helping and salvaging their husbands, imposed by God on women, already turns them into the family demons within their own homes?" (224).

Léry's account, told with considerable misgivings, of sexual life among the Tupinambá also discusses adultery and sodomy. Such two great Christian taboos take the same grave role in the minds of Amerindians, according to the doubtful eyes of the French Calvinist, naturally. As for the former, Léry contends that a woman's adultery (not a man's) causes so much horror[11] to the Amerindian that the deceived man could "repudiate the faulty woman, dispense her ignominiously or even kill her, such that natural law prevailed" (224). As for the latter, the Calvinist charges that when the Tupinambá women disputed and insulted one another they used the word *tivira*, from coastal Tupy language, which means sodomite. "This makes me believe, though I cannot tell for sure, that among them there was this abominable vice," adds Léry (224).

Surprising as it may seem to the late-twentieth-century reader, Léry is one of the most resourceful and least bigoted authors among the early Europeans in America.[12] Notwithstanding the remarkably gross examples collected here, he is more disposed than others[13] to describe and interpret, rather than judge and condemn. Though this exception may have been taken overboard, in the sense that Léry tends to ignore power relations behind the sexual patterns and the meanings, he has actually been praised by Claude Lévi-Strauss "for instituting cultural relativism" (Reis 456). Reis adds that Léry "incorporates a certain polysemy and a level of ambiguity" that is absent in Pero Vaz de Caminha (1440–1500), Nóbrega, Pero de Magalhães Gandavo (1500–76), among others.

Whether his own appraisal has also been a little far-fetched or not, Reis, indeed, quotes Léry where the Calvinist most visibly employs a critical eye toward not only Brazil (the so-called French Antarctica), but also his homeland. Reflecting on the Christian fanaticism and its brutalities that had taken place in Lyon on August 24, 1572, Léry confesses, "I am a Frenchman, and I hate to say it." He then wonders, "Among other actions of horrendous memory, was it not more barbarian than the savages' deeds, when the slaughtered victims' body fat was auctioned and awarded to the highest bidder [the Governor of Lyon]?" (Léry 203). In Reis's quote Léry, therefore, accedes to acknowledging the ugliness of his own culture:

> Let us not completely abominate the cruelty of the anthropophagous savages. Among us there are more [sic] creatures just as abominable, if not more, and more repulsive than those who attack only enemy nations from whom they want revenge. It is not necessary to go to America, not even leave your country [France], to see such monstrous things. (Reis 456; Léry 204)

It seems likewise reasonable to look at Léry's case as an example of how people persecuted for their religious beliefs — like himself, who was nearly executed by Catholic militia in France and Switzerland — can still be very prejudiced and incapable of understanding adverse social behavior or unknown modes of spirituality. In other words, oppression does not necessarily make the oppressed likely to accept and gain insight from diversity.

The same biases behind the stigma presently reserved for the passive homosexual alone in Brazil (and other parts of the world) may have led Léry to save the Tupinambá males from the label "sodomite," which, as I have shown, he is ready to attach to the Tupinambá women. This is one way by which the European would portray sexual hierarchy in order to corroborate the social hierarchy they lived in back in Europe. The sexual division of labor, which may be a sensible, pragmatic mechanism operating in so many different kinds of societies (ancient or new, so-called primitive or so-called advanced), does not necessarily signal a hierarchy of the sexes. In fact, it is normally believed that the diverse occupations held by men and women among the Brazilian Indians[14] are meant to be complementary, rather than hierarchical.

Alternative Behavior and New Horizons

Notwithstanding the old European hierarchical structure, surviving in contemporary Brazil via a male-centered ideology, various forms of alternative practices have taken shape. Coexisting with

Christianity in Portuguese America, the ambiguous nature of Candomblé ministers is probably one of the most striking counterparts to that of North American berdaches. The links between homosexuality and mystic power are thus similarly present among the Amerindian women and the African-Brazilian *pai-de-santo/mãe-de-santo*,[15] a campy figure who assumes a male identity during one half of the year and a female one during the other half. Candomblé congregations have no prejudice against homosexuality, say Fry and MacRae, and "not rarely will a young man or a young woman with difficulties at home (because of constant jeerings such as 'fag' or 'dyke') find in those religious communities a place where they are accepted" (54).

In their effort to make out the elements that possibly bind homosexuality and exceptional/supernatural powers or the image of sodomy and sexual transgression to that of witchcraft, Fry and MacRae contend that, for some people, such powers are some kind of compensation for individuals who do not want or do not manage to follow the most conventional lifestyles attributed to/assumed by men and women. Ridicule or condemnation[16] are likely the results of such an approach (56).

Another line of interpretation linking homosexuality and abnormal powers suggested by Fry and MacRae has to do with the breaking of social conventions of masculinity and femininity, complexities of which I have already elaborated. Since these conventions are so deeply rooted in society, "to do away with them requires a great deal of courage and originality" (Fry and MacRae 57). A strong personality and acute talent, therefore, become some of the attributes of gayness.

Somewhat similar to the second hypothesis, Fry and MacRae's third line of interpretation emerges from two notions regarding ambiguity: first, that it is always a possible source of creativity; second, that it has much to do with exceptional powers. Fry and MacRae believe that, apart from specifically religious points, like knowledge of the secrets of the cult or the capacity to heal and tell fortunes, creativity is one of the most important features of a *pai-* or *mãe-de-santo*.

There is undoubtedly something profoundly ambiguous in a woman who transforms herself into a woman-man, and in a man who becomes a man-woman (Fry and MacRae argue 57). They cite the anecdote of a *pai-de-santo* from Belém who speaks of the theatricality involved in Candomblé. He says he would have loved to follow a theatrical career as a transvestite if he hadn't been called on by the spirits. The two authors then emphasize that "among the qualities most frequently attributed to the 'queer' identity are creativity, artistic sensitivity, and humor, as if they were *natural* features" (58). These characteristics are common among gays "exactly because there is an important relation among artistic creation, ambiguity, humor, and a critical view of society." Such a view is often manifested by queers through a caricaturing effeminate behavior known as "camp" (58). A queer is somebody ambiguous by definition, they charge, since s/he has one sex that is biological and another that is social. Since the social stigma places them out of the formal centers of social power, the authors add, "they occupy a structural space on the fringes of society, from where at least a critical look at things is possible" (58).

There are many writers, though, who are differently concerned with the intricacies of labels like queer, lesbian, and so forth. Brazilian poet Leila Míccolis, for instance, explores not only the ontological aspects of the term *lesbian*, but also builds a long bridge right into the contradictions of its usage in today's Brazil. First she travels to the early-sixth-century B.C. Lesbo Island. Sappho was then a remarkable intellectual, the tenth of Plato's muses, a political activist against a Greek tyrant, who sent her into exile. She is said to have married, borne a daughter, and become a widow before the age of twenty-six, when she founded a school for young women. Sappho's liberal attitudes supposedly did not limit the object of her desire to the same sex or the opposite sex alone, which "makes it difficult for some radical, one-way lesbian groups of today to accept her," says Maria Carneiro da Cunha (Daniel and Míccolis 74).

According to Míccolis, the case perfectly illustrates the difference between how sex was understood in ancient Europe, on one hand, and in guilt-ridden Christian times, on the other hand. Whereas the Greeks tended to focus attention on eroticism (the impulse of Eros), the Christian evaluates the moral standard of the individual being loved. The concern shifted from one person's desire to the object of that desire. She informs us that Napoleon's 1804 Civil Code was the first to discriminate against people who "committed" pederasty, and so did the first Brazilian Civil Code, in 1823. The term *homosexuality*, however, allegedly appeared for the first time in print when Dr. Carl Maria Benkert (1824–82), a Hungarian physician, wrote about homosexuals' rights in 1869. Even though he qualified pederasty as an illness, the German activist Magnus Hirschfeld (1868–1935) founded the first scientific organization for that same purpose in 1897 (Daniel and Míccolis 74–75).

Certain attributes of public ignorance and prejudice die hard. Approximately one hundred years after the first small signs of a movement for gay rights (with all its misconceptions), Míccolis was once asked in a formal interview, "What does it mean to be a Lesbian?" She replied, "It must be a very strange being, a martian type. I've never seen one." In her opinion, there is no such specific human category, "since people are people, and homosexual or heterosexual are the actions they perform, not the people themselves" (73).

Míccolis anticipates her readers' reaction to an apparent paradox: if she doesn't believe in homosexuality, how can she explain the reason for a gay movement? She says her answer is easy: though people deny this culturally invented division between homosexuals and heterosexuals, society believes in the categories and discriminates against the former. Homosexuals, therefore, have all the right to assemble and fight prejudices, even those originating from that biased division (75).

One of the most relevant points Míccolis makes about the gay movement concerns its purpose, which is not simply the eradication of discriminatory laws[17] or integration of the "poor things" into mainstream society. The main purpose is the transformation of all society toward the pursuit of more pleasure in all deeds and more respect for variety in terms of behavior, rather than labeling people sick, abnormal, sex maniacs, or sinful. "The fight is not for homosexuals' rights, but human freedom," she contends (77). Political change alone does not suffice,[18] and Cuba is a pertinent example of a society where gays continue to be persecuted and oppressed.[19]

Míccolis and Trevisan share the opinion that, in Brazil, it is not until the late 1970s that a significant number of leftists begin to realize that sex, as she puts it, isn't "simply something private—

done by two people between four walls—but also an instrument of manipulation used by the system." The leftists had considered sociopolitical struggle as the only top priority, and all other claims as "small" or even "demobilizing" to the main struggle (78).

Trevisan, founder of one of the first groups for gay activism (Somos [1979]) and one of the first gay newspapers in Brazil (*Lampião* [1978]), chronicles in detail the (under)development of gay consciousness. He writes that the starting point coincides with the return of many political exiles, who had gained courage to come out and do something about the gay cause. They are the "prodigal children," who once felt rejected by the political groups and now returned to their abodes. Sporadic accomplishments of the movement take place in the 1980s, especially after the Grupo Gay (Gay Group) in Bahia opens a national campaign in 1981 against the Ministry of Education for its adherence to Code 302 of the International Classification of Diseases that states that homosexuality is a "deviance and disturbance." Following long and intense debate on campuses and legislature houses, the Federal Council of Medicine accedes in 1985 by denominating homosexuality as "other psychosocial circumstances" (Trevisan 225).

The love-hate relationship between the Brazilian Gay Movement and the Left continues, however. It becomes a history of silent rejection, acceptance, co-option, institutionalization, and dilution (Trevisan 211–20). That is the case with Somos, whose members seek autonomy and independence from any political party, but eventually give in to the growing power of the rhetoric imposed by the Trotskyites, who apparently join the group not only to seduce new comrades into their socialist cause, but also to destroy the Gay Movement. In 1983, some Somos members feel the urge to engage in serious campaign vis-à-vis the first AIDS cases emerging in the country. In control of the bureaucracy regulating the group, members agree that AIDS is a disease of bourgeois gays and thus it is far removed from proletariat concerns (Trevisan 220).

Gayness in Brazil and in the United States

Despite the fact that many views expressed by Míccolis intersect with those of Trevisan, the latter reinforces the risk of what he calls "the old hypocrite invisibility," which does nothing but strengthen mechanisms of repression. One cannot deny a name for an individual who often experiences homosexual desire (whether it is gay, lesbian, or transsexual), "even if it is for a mere question of methodology" (20). He ultimately equates the predominant image of the Brazilian gay community with today's stereotypical, and yet substantially accurate, image of Brazil itself. If compared to their American counterparts, Brazilian gays, in particular, and the Brazilian nation, historically speaking, are devoid of a strong ideology that sustains the political activism of the former and the political makeup of the latter (241): the prevailing order is ambivalence, contradiction, and paradox.

The disparity between gay ideologies in the United States and Brazil perhaps follows the general terms of DaMatta's synthesis regarding mainstream society and social minorities. The United States's social identity emphasizes the Puritan tradition, he says, which is "founded on a logic of exclusion that considers undesirable anyone who is not a member of the parish." One is either a member of the community or one is outside of it, "and all members are equal in accordance with the constitutional laws that govern it." But since racial difference is mostly undisguisable, it produces a real dilemma to an egalitarian credo. Race relations thus "reintroduce hierarchy by way of a natural ('racial') code." In Brazil, however, whose "daily life is founded on inequality, the experience of different ethnicities does not spill out of the personal and quotidian sphere...." Although its legal system adopts elements of exclusion/inclusion and equality, "an ideological pact hides and disguises differences, thereby making the ideology complementary." DaMatta calls this ideology a fable that, for instance, treats the "three races" of Brazil (black, white and Indian) as complementary, as opposed to the ideology of the white element upon which the United States was founded (4).

As another side of social disparity, the prevailing image of Brazilian gayness tends to be that of people who stand out as playful, campy, colorful, parodical, deviant, and ultimately baroque in their intensity and juxtaposition of opposites (Trevisan 237); whereas, their American counterparts appear to be individuals more serious and outspoken about their rights to live a dignified and separate life as they wish. If the 1992 presidential election in the United States demonstrated an intense political mobilization by the gay community, the most common representation of Brazil by recent anthropological discourse, in turn, emphasizes the Brazilian bend toward carnivalization, a scenario where the gay community emerges in their ludicrous form of protest and participation in a society that normally discriminates against them (33).

Carnaval is, indeed, inseparable from oppression. "We might say that there is a luxurious carnival precisely because there is social misery and little political space for the exercise of citizenship," contends DaMatta (13). Yet, there are aspects to consider, as suggested by Joãozinho Trinta, a samba school stylist: "Intellectuals are the ones who like poverty; the poor prefer luxury." The statement reminds one of not only the spontaneity and authenticity of carnivalization, as a ritual of trading social places, but also the fact that things do not always "go together." On the contrary, they may follow "complementary and apparently contradictory paths" (DaMatta 14). The stylist is also saying that during Carnaval the "social world is not encompassed by the values of linear and practical reason that tie ideas in Calvinist fashion to words and behavior." During Carnaval, therefore, an enormous number of men feel compelled to wear women's gaudy outfits, and the underprivileged disguise themselves as wealthy and noble, in a fashion by which "the rich and the poor, dominators and oppressed, express a difficult and profound relationship" (DaMatta 14).

One may easily argue that such phenomena occur in every society, which is possibly true, but in the Brazilian case, the tendency to establish opposite ideals just to blend them, or make rules somewhere, just to break them elsewhere, is outstanding. Homosexuality versus heterosexuality presents the same paradox. Parker relates to it as a "configuration fraught with contradictions." The same societal notion that prevents a man who sleeps with a queer from having his moral standing jeopardized is also capable of fulfilling the male's role as macho while possessing a prostitute. "He confirms and even pronounces his own masculinity" (Parker 51). DaMatta elaborates on a slightly diverse interpretation of such contradictions when he says that we should be less taken with the fact that we might have double or multiple standards, but more concerned with concepts such as "mixture," "confusion," "combination," and others that "designate what should really be understood: interstices and simultaneity, or, simply, relations" (3).

DaMatta builds a metaphorical dichotomy by which he investigates the "logic that presides over this apparently prelogical untidiness" of juxtaposed opposites such as slavery and liberalism, homophobia and a sense of machismo exacerbated by homosexual performance, or shame for the woman and glory for the man involved in the same sexual action. The metaphor is the duality of street versus home. It can be illustrated by the interaction between liberalism and slavery in the mind of a politician. "Precisely because I am a liberal in Congress," pertinent to the metaphorical universe of the street, "I have the 'right' to be a slaveholder or a paternalist at home." Rather than being a simple case of personal inconsistency, the anthropologist suggests that it is a "deeply rooted manifestation of a system that does not operate in linear terms and is not, in fact, governed by a single set of rules" (7).

Despite the gap (in DaMatta's anthropological terms), Trevisan sees no differences between American and Brazilian gay communities alone. One of the similarities is consumerism and the systems that keep the ghettos alive. He mentions the capitalist circuit of gay entertainment: exclusive clubs, saunas, and shows. There is also the literature and various other art forms that often portray the gay person as an individual with unrestrained self-complaisance, almost like a missionary on a holy cause or an exorcist resigned to fads and fashions of they day. Heroes: this is how they come out in their effort to integrate themselves into the market rather than subvert any established order. The gay boom thus becomes a new formula for consumption made available by the capitalist system through movies whose sole appeal is voyeurism or the bashing of macho men (178–79). The author reminds us that it is a mistake to think that subversion is inherent in the homosexual act by itself, or that sexuality in and of itself may foster solidarity among the oppressed (223).

Conclusion

One may argue that the exclusion of uncloseted gay people from the Left responds to gender ideologies that have been constructed throughout many centuries, a point that actually lies beyond our

historical grasp. Such ideologies end up establishing the boundaries of imagined communities[20] of men and women, Aristotelian
categories that, ideally, should not allow any spaces in between.
As any ideologies do, these concepts strive to reach their goals,
mainly to keep the continental divide between men and women
alive, while basing themselves on mechanisms of legitimacy that
vary in content and function, from *orbus christianus*, the hallmark
of God's endorsement for the Europeans, to pragmatism and to-
kenism, the centuries-old tradition of Amerindians.

In spite of the relative uncertainty regarding the true repre-
sentativeness of the material I have collected thus far, I feel con-
fident that a substantial number of early Amerindians, ancient,
medieval, and Renaissance Europeans, as well as contemporary
Brazilians, have shared, for a very long time, a reasonably similar set of sexual and social notions that insist on condemning ambivalence and ambiguity between the feminine and masculine
polarities of social behavior, a behavior whose counterparts in
sexual terms are mostly passivity and activity, if not devilishness
and decency. In the midst of punishment and ostracism, though,
segments of every society have found their way through such
barriers, whether by means of transsexual/gender play, religion,
folkways, formal politics, or the celebration of exclusion and transgression. With the advent of guaranteed civil liberties in industrialized societies, new forms of ideology not only legalize and
restore respect for those deviations from old norms, but also become highly influential in political terms. Not surprisingly, such
emergent ideologies go on claiming the uniformity of sexual and
social conditions supposedly characterizing the gay community.
Nevertheless, the dangers of smothering individual differences
and truthful complexities of all human attributes remain.

Notes

1. Late that year the Executive assumed all legislative and judicial powers
to repress the circulation of any negative opinions regarding the ideals of the
bourgeois 1964 revolution. Punishment included incarceration, brainwash, torture, exile, or death without formal trial.

2. All translations from Portuguese originals are mine, except for quotes
cited from works (re)published in English.

3. The term *gayness* refers to the sociohistorical conditions in which people
think and/or act in response to their homosexual drives or in response to other

people's attitudes toward these drives, whether or not such drives are ever enacted as deeds.

4. The authors evoke a Brazil that is "a little traditional, but not too much, which in one way or another is present in each one of us" (41). They include a Brazil with enclaves where, for instance, there is a strong homogeneity in ideas concerning "masculinity" and "femininity." They allude to ideas prevailing in schools, prisons, rural communities, and poor outskirts of Brazilian big cities, where gender stereotypes resist the changes of time (41).

5. Piedra's research also establishes a very meaningful relationship between the masculinizing and femininizing powers of sodomy in today's Spain and the politics of naming, particularly in regard to cannibals and Amazons. Like the Brazilian "promiscuous heterosexual," the sodomizing *bugarrón* ("buggerer" or, etymologically, "hole maker," as Piedra puts it) is not a homosexual at all. He is empowered and masculinized by sodomy "at the expense of the *maricón,* which in Spanish does not literally translate into 'buggered,' or 'holed man,' but rather a womanized man, a 'Mary Ann' " (252).

6. Given the ethnocentrism that contaminates most historical and anthropological material about the berdaches, Fry and MacRae argue, it is difficult to know how the transgender/transsexual Indian men/women really were. Some authors put them on a pedestal and argue that they were respected, even venerated. Other authors, interested in promoting European morality, emphasize that they were ridiculed. "The fact is that there are many ways of laughing and we will never know if the Amerindians' way of laughing came out of pleasure or aggression" (38).

7. "And the darker man was the more cultured, more learned, more artistic. He lived in the castles and occupied the towns. He was the rich man, and the Portuguese became serfs upon his land." Under such conditions, he adds, it would be deemed an honor for the white Iberian "to marry or mate with the governing class, the brown man, instead of the reverse. . . . Alfonso VI, who united Castile, Leon, and Galicia in 1073, to cite but one of many instances of marriages between Christian and Arab nobles, chose a Moorish princess, the daughter of the Emir of Seville, to be the mother of his son Sancho" (Nash 37).

8. Nash writes, in 1926, that it is "very significant that General Cândido Rondon (1865–1958), who has had more contact with existing primitive tribes in Brazil than any other man living, states that he has never yet run into any sign of cannibalism in the course of his work in Mato Grosso, although he has been constantly on the watch" (24).

9. Léry goes further to say that the men "would still wear something occasionally, but the women wanted nothing on their bodies and I trust they never changed their minds. In reality, they alleged, in order to justify their nakedness, that they could not dispense their baths, and it was difficult to undress that often, since every time they came across a fountain or a river, they would wade into the water, dip their heads, and propel their bodies like thin sticks beneath the water's surface, not rarely over a dozen times a day. Their reasons were quite plausible, and any efforts to convince them otherwise were, by the way, useless" (120).

10. Anthropologist Berta Ribeiro points out that the "elimination of body ornaments and its coverings obliterated the Indian characteristics and undifferentiated them from the Europeans and, at least, it gave the priests the sensation that they had tamed the Indians" (Reis 467).

11. André Thévet (1502–90), a Catholic chronicler whom Léry is often willing to contradict and debase, has similar ideas about the Amerindian men's reactions. Thévet is quoted in a footnote by Jacques Gaffarel (1601–81), the nineteenth-century editor of Léry's story: "If a woman happens to sin and becomes pregnant, the child is buried alive right after birth and the mother is slaughtered or abandoned to the young men" (Léry 224).

12. Historical, ethnographical, and musical document, this is certainly one of very few firsthand texts on early Brazil. Léry's talent for description makes his writing come alive in detail, and the pictures drawn by others on the same mission add up to preservation of cultures so rapidly changed if not dissipated. The text also contains a long dialogue and one of the first if not the very first transcription of Ameridian music (two chants in Tupy).

13. Pero Vaz de Caminha, Father Manuel da Nobrega, and Pero de Magalhães Gandavo are but a few names I am considering here. Rather emblematic of the bias one finds in such texts, a passage on the Tupy, which Reis quotes from Gandavo, may illustrate my point: "The language of these savages is one all over the coast: it lacks three letters — scilicet, the letters F, L, and R are not present, something that can cause amazement because this way they have no Faith, no Law, and no King [*Rei*, in Portuguese], making them live with no Justice or order" (454–55; Gandavo 53–54).

14. I am aware of the pitfalls of oversimplification. The image I have in mind is that of the tribes encountered by the Europeans along the Brazilian coast, mostly belonging to the Tupy group, which allegedly shared similar language, social structure, and lifestyle, like the Tupiniquim, the Carijó, the Goitacaz, and the Tupinambá. In regard to major diversity, Júlio Cesar Melatti points out an outstanding difference between the Tupinambá and the Inca: "Members of very distinct societies like the Incas and the Tupinambás, who spoke completely different languages and had different habits, were included in the same category: Indians. While the former were road and city builders and lived in an empire that was administered by a group of bureaucrats and organized in hierarchical social segments, the latter lived in villages in straw huts, in a society without social divisions, in which the highest political unity was probably the village itself" (Reis 468; Melatti 19–20).

15. Mott cites evidence found in a book written by a Portuguese army officer in 1681 that there was among the *quimbandas*, gentiles of Angola, "much sodomy, having one with the other their filthiness and muck, dressing like women." They "are fine sorcerers, for them to do everything evil. And all the other gentiles respect them and are not offended at all." The roots of Brazilian Candomblé are thus highly suspected to have originated in the western African country, the birthplace of a significant number of Brazilian slaves (Fry and MacRae 56).

16. The first Christian chroniclers from Europe in America, among other things, fail to understand that mystic symbolism deserves respect as such no matter what religion you follow. The contradictions of the European preachers are too obvious exactly because of their incapacity to understand that other individuals might look at them with the same incredulity they applied to the Amerindians. The Christian God might be the true one (let us not disregard the possibility), but the presence of the holy body of Jesus Christ in the Host will sound preposterous to a pagan, especially when he or she is told over and over that no one

should eat human flesh. José Maria de Paiva cunningly points out the tremendous difficulties the Portuguese priests had while condemning cannibalism and offering communion (96). Far from accepting the notions of ritual and spirituality (which may have a bearing on the adoption of cannibalism after wars), the Europeans matched two phenomena considered devilish, therefore making them more shocking and convincing to a society claiming the divine mission to convert all gentiles of the world.

17. It is important to note that the Brazilian Constitution or Penal Code laws contain nothing that contravenes homosexuals' rights, and yet the police not only often raid gay places, but also humiliate them in public. The police appeal to indirect means to justify it, one of which is the imperative to guarantee public decency and crack down on loitering (Trevisan 30).

18. "Traditionally speaking," says Míccolis, "the Right (represented by the church, aristocracy, bourgeoisie, institutional powers) have always been the most antagonistic to sexual freedom; however, ever since the French Revolution, the Left has criticized the Right but also inherited their rigid sexual morality. Engels condemned the 'disgusting acts of pederasty' among the Greeks and the 'ugly unnatural vices of the Germanic' [in *The Origin of the Family, Private Property and the State*] (Daniel and Mícollis 78).

19. See, for instance, the interesting cases of repressed homosexuality among socialists in Brazil and Portugal (D'Aguiar), and in Cuba and Nicaragua (Randall, and "The Ambiente").

20. Nation, gender, and ethnicity are taken here as the artifacts of two forms of ideologies: a "fabrication," on one hand, but also, and most thoroughly, as a grouping of individuals who share concrete and symbolic experience. Unlike Benedict Anderson's concept of imagined community, which he calls "the nation" (15–16), my notion of imagined community applies whether or not the individuals imagine a horizontal comradeship.

Works Cited

Amerindian Images and the Legacy of Columbus. Ed. René Jara and Nicholas Spadaccini. Minneapolis: University of Minnesota Press, 1992.

Anderson, Benedict. *Imagined Communities: Reflections on the Origin and Spread of Nationalism*. London: Verso, 1986.

Clastres, Pierre. *A sociedade contra o Estado*. 2a ed. Rio de Janeiro: Francisco Alves, 1982.

DaMatta, Roberto. "For an Anthropology of the Brazilian Tradition or a Virtude Está no Meio." *Latin American Program, Working Papers* 182. Washington: The Wilson Center, 1990.

Fry, Peter, and Edward MacRae. *O que é homossexualidade*. São Paulo: Brasiliense, 1983.

Gandavo, Pero de Magalhães. *Tratado da tera do Brasil; história da Província de Santa Cruz*. Belo Horizonte: Itatiaia; São Paulo: EDUSP, 1980.

"Guarnieri." *Pasquim* 607 (12-I-1981): 8–9.

Jara, René, and Nicholas Spadaccini. "Introduction." *Amerindian Images and the Legacy of Columbus*, q.v., 1–95.

Léry, Jean de. *Viagem à terra do Brasil*. Belo Horizonte: Itatiaia, 1980.

Lévi-Strauss, Claude. "A eficácia simbólica." In *Antropologia estrutural*. Rio de Janeiro: Tempo Brasileiro, 1975, 215–36.

Nash, Roy. *The Conquest of Brazil*. New York: Harcourt, 1926.

Nóbrega, Padre Manuel da. *Cartas do Brasil e mais escritos*. Coimbra: Universidade de Coimbra, 1955.

Paiva, José Maria de. *Colonização e catequese, 1549–1600*. São Paulo: Autores Associados/Cortez, 1982.

Parker, Richard G. *Bodies, Pleasures and Passions: Sexual Culture in Contemporary Brazil*. Boston: Beacon, 1991.

Piedra, José. "Loving Columbus." In *Amerindian Images and the Legacy of Columbus*, q.v., 230–65.

Reis, Roberto. "Authoritarianism in Brazilian Colonial Discourse." In *Amerindian Images and the Legacy of Columbus*, q.v., 452–72.

Ribeiro, Berta. *O índio na história do Brasil*. São Paulo: Brasiliense, 1982.

Trevisan, João Silvério. *Devassos no paraíso: a homossexualidade no Brasil, da colônia à atualidade*. Rio de Janeiro: Max Limonad, 1986.

◆ **Chapter 17**

The Ecstasy of Disease:
Mysticism, Metaphor, and AIDS in
Las Virtudes del pájaro solitario

Brad Epps

> *We have been taught the tongue of birds and endowed with all good things. Surely this is a signal favour.*
>
> The Koran

> *I have no need for my identity—I long for death; what use is "I" to me?*
>
> Attar, *The Conference of the Birds*

What is at stake when the ravages of the flesh nourish the ecstasy of the letter? What happens when the metaphorical condensation of love and death, so essential to the mystico-poetic tradition, is realized, actualized, literalized? How do readers and writers situate themselves with respect to texts that communicate sickness, especially when the texts engage the discourse of divinity? Despite their seemingly timeless appeal, these and other questions acquire immediacy and urgency in the crisis of representation (Simon Watney) and the brutality of idealization (Leo Bersani) that mark the age of AIDS. Brutally critical indeed: for even as AIDS has become a troubling site for academic inquiry, there remains within Hispanism a still more troubling tendency to turn a blind eye to it. Hence, when Juan Goytisolo's *Las virtudes del pájaro solitario* (*The Virtues of the Solitary Bird*) appears in 1988, important critics such as Julio Ortega and Luce López-Baralt quickly respond with articles that, while attesting to the canonical status of Goytisolo himself, virtually erase the text's problematic representation of AIDS in favor of a reading of the influence and intertextual play of San Juan de la Cruz and the Sufis. With the notable exception of Paul Julian Smith's study on death and simulacra, subsequent readings appear largely to mystify an already "euphemystic" space, one in which the political reality of AIDS risks being lost in textually inscribed analogies to everything from Chernobyl to the Bubonic Plague. Following what seems to be one of the safer leads of the text, critical reception is here an uneasy exercise in aversion. It is, in this respect, symptomatic of a *general* aversion to the disease and its discourses, an aversion whose ultimate function, whether intentional or not, may well be to keep academic practice safe from the realities and metaphors of AIDS and homosexual existence. Averting aversion, I thus propose to examine how Goytisolo's text represents AIDS and how AIDS, in representation, is received: not just in terms that are either positive or negative, but in others that are ambivalent, risky, at times even mystifying as well.

In *Las virtudes,* the reader runs the risk of what I will call the writing's dangerous inversions. Dramatically disregarding the classical unities of time, place, and action, and all but annulling unified characterization, Goytisolo's writing upsets an established order of meaning. Yet, more than the established disorder of meaning that is postmodernism is implicated in these inversions. For chief among the dangers of Goytisolo's text is the fact that its revision of the mystico-literary tradition is inseparable from the vision of homosexual pleasure and pain. This vision is dangerous because even as it opens readers to homosexual desire and confronts them with the immorality of homophobia, it comes close to reifying this desire as dangerous in and of itself: as if it were impossible to see homosexuality without always seeing disease and death as well. At other times, and in a way that particularizes the Freudian death drive, it comes close to making danger the veritable spur of homosexual desire, to making danger, and death, desirable. Arguably, these dangers are more or less visible, more or less pressing, depending on the reader. Gay or bisexual readers, for example, may view the danger as an all-too-intimate implication of their own flesh (the text is a terribly self-reflective mirror), while heterosexual readers may view the danger, when and if they view it, not only as the possible transmission of such intimacy but also as estrangement or exclusion (the text, as mirror, is terribly opaque). There are, to be sure, any number of other views, but the ones I want to keep in sight orient, as it were, an entire sexual and textual economy where desire and danger hold sway, and where risk has become an all-too-certain sign of identity.

Currently, risk marks the homosexual subject as bound to AIDS, whether he actually "has" it or not. Inasmuch as the considerably less momentous enterprise of reading is concerned, these identities of and at risk fracture the already fractured writing of Goytisolo. At the same time, AIDS is itself also fractured by the sheer fact that it does not respect the supposedly sharp boundaries of identity, that it is not a "gay disease." As Sander Gilman reminds us, "We are all at risk—we will all be ill, will fail, will die" (4). And so too with Goytisolo's text: we are all at risk, all implicated in the suffering and pain, nostalgia, and dystopianly inspired utopia that it narrates. And yet, keeping in mind that the text dates from 1988, when risk categories were especially rigid (though they persist strongly even today), we are not all implicated in the same fashion, nor to the same degree, nor with the same insistence. We do not all confront, or consider, the same living, the same dying, the same death, in and out of the act of reading. This does not mean that some of us, more intimately implicated, read "better" than others: that would be small solace indeed. But it does mean that we must contend with the fissures that keep us apart, as well as with the ties that bind, that we must question the minoritized view, on both the right and the left, that risk is an exclusive property as well as the liberal view that risk is equally shared. As Goytisolo suggests, the risk of reading, like the risk of identity, is both confinement and communication.

I want to emphasize the importance of the relations between reading and writing that *Las virtudes* occasions, but for now I want to stay with the risky signs of identity that are inscribed most closely in the text. Fragmented and fluctuant, *Las virtudes* presents the contamination, identification, and persecution of a group of "rare birds." These "birds," ultimately united into one lone and virtuous entity beyond life and death, are the birds of Farid ud-Din Attar's twelfth-century Persian mystical poem *The Conference of the Birds* and of San Juan de la Cruz's lost sixteenth-century treatise *Las propiedades del pájaro solitario* (*The Properties of the Solitary Bird*). At the same time, they are the birds of a feather of so-called homosexual subculture. These two registers—one divine and the other queer—are here virtually coextensive. In linking homo-sexuality to mysticism, Goytisolo, far from taking liberties with historical material, is following the lead of scholars. Thus, if San Juan de la Cruz's poetry reveals both Islamic and secular traces, Goytisolo merely brings to the fore the homoeroticism that Sufi poetry and an extensive secular tradition already contain. This ar-chaeology of desire, retrieving a past value for present purposes, enables Goytisolo to give fuller, more timely flight to the metaphor of the bird. Mystical and gay, Goytisolo's birds are privy to an arcane knowledge that spans centuries and civilizations, bodies and tongues; they inhabit a space at once sensual and spiritual, art-ful and amorous; they sway between muscular images of rough, wrestling boys (44) and aqueous desires for poetic infinitude (59). Almost a third of the way into the narrative, Goytisolo "identi-fies" some of them: a distinguished older gentleman, a young pro-fessor of Arabic, the prior or archimandrite of a Greek monastery, a seminarian, an enigmatic Kirghiz, and so on.[1] From East and West, in bathhouses and libraries, these men, frequently addressed in the feminine, know the pleasures of the text and the pleasures of the flesh. They are also, I hasten to add, diseased and dying: dying of radiation, of the plague, of AIDS.

Of all of these forms of disease and dying (living is here a problem in its own right), AIDS is the one that most provocatively dovetails Goytisolo's concern—prevalent in his work at least since *Reivindicación del Conde don Julián* (1970)—with sexuality and power. As Michel de Certeau indicates, "a strange alliance" linked 'mystic' speech and 'impure' blood" (84–85). Goytisolo, under AIDS, reasserts this problematic alliance: not just because it allows for sophisticated literature, but also because AIDS is the condition that most directly challenges the author's utopian projects of vin-dication, emancipation, and the free exchange of bodies. As San-der Gilman states, "the gratuitous appearance of the disease dur-ing the late 1970s" effectively binds together two distinct social issues: the rise in sexually transmitted diseases and "the growth of the public awareness of the homosexual emancipation move-ment" after the 1969 Stonewall riot in New York City (247). By the time *Las virtudes* is published (1988), the coincidence of dis-ease and homosexual desire in AIDS is well established in Europe and North Africa (i.e., Goytisolo's cultural milieu) as well. Among its effects is the increasingly virulent stigmatization of a sexuality that is already marginalized and embattled. With calls for separate identity cards, restricted travel, mandatory testing, forced internment, regulatory tattoos (William F. Buckley), "sidatoria"[2] (Jean-Marie Le Pen), and the like, an entire politics of control is mobilized not so much around AIDS itself as around people with AIDS, or HIV, or supposedly at risk: in other words: hemophiliacs, drug users, prostitutes, people of color, homosexuals. This is, in short measure, the politics that Goytisolo mobilizes, and resists, in his text: a politics reminiscent of others, elsewhere and in the past, but quite specific in its currency. Thus, without endorsing a reading in which a range of maladies (the plague, radiation, insanity, an accidental fall) are funneled into one supermalady, I nonetheless contend that AIDS and its metaphors are "privileged" in *Las virtudes del pájaro solitario*, and that every rapturously mystical turn entails a rather somber return to the contemporary reality of the disease. This is not to say that AIDS is the ground, or reason, of the text, for AIDS itself is, as we shall see, continually shifting across complex discursive and bodily fields. It is to say, however, that the discourse of the body is historically specific and that to avoid the reality of AIDS, and its disturbing linkage to homosexuality, is to encounter not so much freedom and security as textual entrapment.

And yet, entrapment of one sort or another seems here to be inevitable. For if readers may become "trapped" in the text by avoiding *reference* to the political reality of AIDS in the text itself, characters, or some semblance thereof, become trapped by *not* avoiding it.[3] Of course, where AIDS is depicted as "un destino escrupulosamente fatal" (12; "an inexorably fateful destiny" 13) and a "devastación programada" (16; "programmed devastation" 18), they appear to have little if no option. However much they may reminisce about a happier, safer past, however many hygienic precautions they may take, however much makeup they may use to cover up the sarcoma on their faces, they cannot run from a disease that, in the logic of Goytisolo's narrative, seems forever to mark them: "Estábamos atrapadas, hijitas, no podíamos resollar ni movernos, la tan temida había pasado al ámbito de nuestras pesadillas a encarnar aquella alegoría de la calva sembrando la cizaña" (12; "We were trapped, my dears, we couldn't breathe or move, the one we had so greatly feared had passed from the ambit of our nightmares to embody that allegory of the bald woman sowing discord" 14). The one so feared is AIDS personified, or phantomized, as the purveyor of death, the grim reaper, the Apparition or "Aparecida," the "pajarraco" or "Espantapájaros" (the "ugly bird" or the "scarecrow"), as mortality incarnate.[4] Interestingly, the name of the disease is reserved for the mysterious figure of Ben Sida (Ben Aïds in the English translation), a scholar of Sufism identified by Manuel Ruiz Lagos and the author himself as Abu-l-Hasan Alí ben Ismail al-Mursí o al-Andalusí, the Blind Man from Murcia (214–15). As textual transmitter of Sufi wisdom and blind bearer of undying beauty, Ben Sida is most intriguing, but here I want to continue sounding out the significance of the horrific figure of death, at once unavoidable and unnameable. Never actually named as such, AIDS (*Sida* in Spanish) still is shadowed in and as the figure of death, repeatedly evoked in a flurry of abbreviations and double syllables: "la Dama de las dos sílabas" (22), "el maldito adefesio de las dos sílabas" (33), "la desgalichada de las dos sílabas" (70), "la zancuda de las dos sílabas" (99), "el adefesio de las dos sílabas sembrador de cizaña" (131; "the Lady with the one-syllable name" 24, "the accursed, grotesque, one-syllable figure" 32, "the unkempt one-syllable apparition" 63, "the one-syllable long-legged one" 94, "the grotesque figure of the sower of discord with the one-syllable name" 123). So frightening are these sounds, these letters, that open and direct utterance becomes unbearable: as if to speak or write "Sida" were to say yes to its deadly gift: Sí da.[5] As if *Sida* were as awesome as the most proper of names, not to say as awesome as YHWH.

That the divine is uttered in *Sida,* in AIDS, is perhaps what Ben Sida proves best. He is, after all, not only versed in mystic poetry and sacred script, but in the use of pharmakons where poisons are curative and cures poisonous. His pharmacological function is critical, but here I only want to signal its reversibility. A similar reversibility seems to hold for the discourse of AIDS as well. For if saying yes to the name, to the Thing, is lethal, saying no is, it seems, not exactly inspired with life. In other words, AIDS affirms its presence in and through and despite negation. In short, it does not need to be spelled out for its meaning to be felt: "El crudo temor asociado a sus siglas, ese sentimiento de fatalidad que nos abrumaba desde su anunciada visita y conducía a la resignación de las bestias camino del matadero" (16; "The crude fear associated with her acronym, that feeling of fatality that overwhelmed us from the moment of her announced visit and led to the resigned attitude of animals on their way to the slaughterhouse" 18). The circumlocutions, tactics of evasion, and strategies of avoidance, the varieties of metaphor that the text deploys, all return, again and again, to the fearful sense that certain words, certain things, cannot be avoided. The inexorability of this return of meaning and mortality is such that all hope for escape or cure becomes sheer folly: "Nadie pensaba entonces en remedios ni curas, la plaga se había abalanzado a nosotras como un halcón en fiera y vertiginosa calada" (16; "Nobody thought at the time of remedies or cures, the plague had attacked us like a falcon in a fierce and dizzying dive" 18). This last image is compelling, not because it naturalizes disease as a falcon, but because it mobilizes it in a peculiarly significant way. To use the terms of I. A. Richards, metaphorical movement, though perhaps more graphic when the vehicle is a bird (halcón), implicates the tenor (plaga) as well. For if metaphor effects a movement from the sensible to the intelligible, the proper or ordinary to the improper or extraordinary, a movement that has itself been meta-phorized (*meta* = beyond + *pherein* = to bear) as ascendant, here it does so in order to effect also a descent, a dizzyingly violent plunge back into the realm of the narrator. Of course, if we confine ourselves to the text, if we do not refer to a history or reality outside it, we in effect limit this dizzying violence, remain balanced and sure and safe. Against this, I would suggest that the more vibrant reading is one where metaphor not only flies away from the realm of history but swoops back into it as well. This is, at any rate, how I read Paul Ricoeur's reading of metaphor as alive, living, and ontologically inspired: "No discourse ever suspends our belonging to a world" (43). That the world to which Goytisolo's metaphors pertain is one of disease and death, that the metaphors themselves are quick with death, that AIDS is not gainsaid in the verbal rush but is persistently shadowed forth, far from disempowering the text, keeps it moving. As with metaphor, the only hope of a text's being truly alive is in acknowledging the full range of its turns, including, if not especially, its turns to history and death.

The fatal return of meaning, dragging every flight of fancy back to a rather ruinous reality may account for the profoundly pessimistic tone of Goytisolo's text, but it is also, as I will be arguing, what constitutes its saving grace. In saying this, I am striving to lay the grounds for a reading that ponders something miraculous in the ruins of history. I am here drawing from Walter Benjamin's claim, in his essay on allegory and dialectics, that "it is common practice in the literature of the baroque to pile up fragments ceaselessly, without any strict idea of a goal, and, in the unremitting expectation of a miracle, to take the repetition of the stereotype for a process of intensification" (178).[6] These "highly significant" fragments are what he fashions as ruins. Benjamin makes much of ruins, describing them as "the finest material in baroque creation," as a way of "representing transitory splendor," and as fundamental to an "exuberant subjection of antique elements in a structure which, without uniting them in a single whole, would, in destruction, still be superior to the harmonies of antiquity" (178–79). Benjamin's reading of allegory is highly allegorical itself; his dialectics does not aim toward organic totality; and his interest in the baroque is motivated, in part, by the connection he perceives between it and the "decadence" (55) of his own age. Baroque allegory also helps him to resist another sign of his age, the symbol, whose fusion and flash produce "a resplendent but ultimately non-committal knowledge of an absolute" (159). His work wavers, in fine, between the material and the messianic, the political and the theological. The picture he paints is often bleak, but it has the advantage of allowing us to keep an eye on history even as we seem to immerse ourselves in aesthetic contemplation.

Within such a splendidly desolate panorama, I cannot but place the neobaroque allegory of *Las virtudes*. For here too history is written in "characters of transience" (177) and "irresistible decay" (178); here too earlier elements, those of the historical baroque among them, are combined yet not united in a supreme, if not superior, destruction; here too fragments are piled up and stereotypes intensified; here too ruins are rampant. Ruin, in effect, *appears* from the very beginning of the text and generates only other ruins, ruins of others. It is the unnameable figure of AIDS that "asistía impasible al proceso de *ruina* que nos transmutaba en una masa blanda e informe, impregnada de humores" (13), and

"recorría alhama y piscina con aires de dueña, husmeaba el apocalipsis de la cámara oscura, se deleitaba en el espectáculo del
salón, se retiraba de *las ruinas* del edén con el mismo frío desdén
con que había penetrado" (17; "witnessed impassibly the process
of *ruin* that transmuted us into a soft, formless mass, impreg-
nated with humors" 15, and "traversed sauna and pool with the
air of being the owner of the place, nosed about the apocalypse
of the black chamber, took great delight at the spectacle of the
salon, withdrew from *the ruins* of eden with the same cold disdain with which she had made her way inside" 19). Ruin is, in
other words, both cause and effect, instrument and object, subject and site. It is also the narrator who calls himself, herself, "una
verdadera *ruina* humana" (156; "a real human *wreck*" 144). And
it is what is called in the calling, not just of the self, but of another: "Repetía en mis adentros los versos del sufí maestro de
Ben Sida, el corazón dice que eres mi *ruina*, sea mi alma tu re-
dención, ya lo sepas o no!" (157; "I repeated to myself the verses
of the Sufi master of Ben Aïds, my heart says that you are my
ruin, may my soul be your redemption whether you know it or
not!" 145). Internally repeated, ruin is in the same sweep othered,
not only in the sense that it moves between Ibn al-Farid, Ben Sida,
San Juan de la Cruz, Goytisolo, the narrator, the reader, and the
mysterious "you" apostrophized by, or in, the poet's heart, but
also in the sense that it calls for a response, for redemption.

The manifestations of ruin are legion, but they are not united
in a single whole; they are not totalized as the essence of ruin.
Significant fragments, they signify instead the ruin of essence, of
the concept of essence, but again not wholly. For in ruin, something, in essence, remains. Something essential remains. Something miraculous. For Benjamin, miracle is all but essential to ruin;
unremittingly expected, it is what makes the fragment so significant, so fine a material of artistic creation. Yet Benjamin's miracle
is not, for all its messianic turns, one of symbolic reintegration in
which the ruin, the fragment, is forgotten. Instead, the real miracle is that the ruin, the remnant, the remainder, is also always a
reminder. And what it reminds us is that history, and nature, are
themselves ruinous, so much so that they ceaselessly call for redemption. As in the verses of the mystic master of Ben Sida, as
in the fragmented whole of *Las virtudes* itself, "ultimately in the

death-signs...the direction of allegorical reflection is reversed; on the second part of its wide arc it returns, to redeem" (232). Within the fatal return of meaning, then, there is a return of redemption. Again, as with the miracle, redemption is not figured, in Benjamin, as a complete and closed resolution of differences, as life everlasting or the death of death. "Redemption," as Martin Jay puts it, "meant a recognition of the loss, a calling of the unspoken decay by its right name, and not the reversal of its direction. Unlike what Bloch would call *Spuren* (traces), the detritus to be redeemed were not prefigurations of a future plenitude. Redemption is thus a category of a more 'negative' than positive theology" (251). Jay's formulation of the methodology of Benjaminian redemption is felicitous, because it echoes and anticipates many of the issues that I recognize, and name, in Goytisolo.

Recognizing loss as historically real and calling the unspoken, unspeakable decay in *Las virtudes* by its name, I do not aim to redeem the text by reversing its direction. That this direction is as much, if not more, toward the divine as the secular does not, at any rate, make a simple reversal very feasible to begin with. And yet, in its movement from metaphors of death to metaphors of life—from the "pajarraco" ("ugly bird") of the opening pages to the "pájaro solitario" ("solitary bird") of the concluding pages, from a beastly bird that *descends* into and *destroys* a realm of homosexual pleasure to a beautiful bird that *ascends* toward and *recreates* a realm of pleasure radically otherwise—*Las virtudes* does seem to effect a redemption that is also a resurrection and a reunion.[7] A story of salvation comes after a terribly reiterative story of danger, delirium, death, and decay; salvation comes, that is, after the fall ("la incomprensible y aparatosa caída de la escalera" 47; "the incomprehensible and spectacular fall from the stairway" 45). But it comes, quite significantly, in and as a leap: "ave inquieta y ligera, di un ciego y oscuro salto y, por una extraña manera, mil vuelos pasé de un vuelo para reunirme con mis pares en el vasto recinto de aquella hermosa pajarera" (167; "a restless and light bird, I gave a blind leap in the dark and, in some strange manner, I made a thousand flights in one to join my peers in the vast enclosure of that most splendid aviary" 153).

Given the eschatological impulse of the narrative, Goytisolo's leap is resonant with meaning (perhaps even a mystical nonmeaning).[8] It recalls Kierkegaard's leap of faith, thick with the dreadful anguish of existential freedom, as well as Heidegger's principle of reason (*Satz vom Grund*), which, with its attentiveness to the "voice" of Being, is also a leap from the ground, a bound of or from reason, a principle of ground, and so on.[9] For both, the leap, or principle, is difficult and demanding, requiring a certain adventurousness or vigilance, risk or expectant exposure.[10] It also recalls, and in a much more intimate mode, the leaps, bounds, tumbles, falls, and flights of Christian and Sufi mystics. Blind and dark, Goytisolo's jump pays homage to the role of darkness and blindness in the attainment of illumination and insight. In so doing, it invokes, even as it seems to short-circuit, the tripartite trajectory of purgation, contemplation/illumination, and union common, albeit in different ways, to Christian and Islamic mysticism.[11] Short-circuits it because, while the idea of the path or way may imply a straight, unidirectional unfolding, it is actually so labyrinthine and abysmal that it cannot be traveled in a self-possessed rational manner. The leap is in many respects virtually irresistible: passively assumed though actively desired, it flashes forth in and as the loss of the self, perhaps even as a disturbingly symbolic gift (Goytisolo's "dádiva mortal" 164, "fatal gift" 150 bears mysticism and AIDS).[12]

Negotiating a void of meaning, it is not surprising that the leap twirls in paradox. It is also not surprising that the leap suggests a resolution of paradox, a landing of some sort, on the other side. Once there, once over the "vértigo de la sima" (47; "vertigo of the abyss" 45) and reunited with his peers in "the Assembly of the Birds," the metaphors of resurrection appear as transparent as the mystical bird itself: "Resucitaba a una vida serena y diáfana, investida de una apariencia nueva y más fresca" (167; "I was reborn to a serene and diaphanous life, endowed with a new and fresher appearance" 153); "liberadas de una envoltura ilusoria y estéril, salidas del capuz y cesta opresores a la dulzura y novedad del riad, habíamos renacido ligeras y esbeltas" (169; "freed from an illusory and sterile envelope, emerged from the oppressive hood and basket into the sweetness and newness of the garden, we had been reborn light and lithe" 155). Yet, as well-worn and certain as such a redemptive trajectory may appear, there is something obscure as well. The shift, or leap, from the singular to the plural, the imperfect to the pluperfect, breath to birth, from "re-sucitaba" to "habíamos renacido," leaves us with the somewhat contradictory impression that even after the leap things were continuing to change and that things had already been changed. It may also be that the shift leaves us with the impression that time and identity are themselves contradicted, unsaid, said otherwise: that is to say, a mystical impression of eternity. Another impression, one more anxiously historical, may be that it leaves us, the readers, behind.

These mystical and historical impressions, in the reader and in the text, are not necessarily antithetical. First, leaving the reader behind, unable or unwilling to follow, mysticism secures one of its most prominent, and problematic, features: the incommunicability of *experience*.[13] Second, left behind, the reader occupies a space that remains, as it were, a *mystery* to the text: a space *beyond* (the beyond of) the text. Whether this beyond is any freer, any less a trap, than the other is a question to which I will arrive in due course. What I want to emphasize here is a tension between historical reality and poetic mysticism that does not resolve itself into a neat binary division. History, that is, does not ruin textual redemption (by denying its imaginary gains) any more than the text redeems historical ruin (by denying its real losses). Now, if Goytisolo's text appears to achieve a mystical transcendence by which the ruin of history is redeemed, if it appears to follow a path that ends up being faithful to a certain theological tradition, it is only because we forget to see the danger in appearances, in apparitions, that is the text's inaugural lesson. There death appears grossly majestic, unmistakable in its universality if unnameable in its specificity. In the final section of the text, however, death appears to have disappeared. And yet, for all the signs of redemption and resurrection, death, or something deathlike, still appears. Its appearance is far less imposing, and in a way far more insidious, than before. The "Asamblea de los Pájaros" is not a mere textual (re)solution, but a source of questions as well. The narrator may answer his question, "Quién y cómo era yo?" (168; "Who was I and what did I look like?" 154), by recognizing himself in a little mirror, but a number of other questions are not so easily settled. Not only does he reflect on the identity of the other birds around him, but he also asks how they have come to be together: "era una transmigración?," "había sido invitada ex profeso a ella?, se trataba de una convocatoria general? o, peor aún, habría caído tontamente como las demás, atraída por el silbo de un cazador artero?" (167; "was it a transmigration?", "had I been invited intentionally?, was it a general convocation?, or, worse still, could I have fallen like the others, stupidly taken in by the whistle of a wily hunter?" 153). These are troubling questions, especially the latter one, but there is yet another. Examining his surroundings, the narrator asks, almost nonchalantly, what turns out to be the final question of the text: "En qué ramaje o espesura de la pajarera se encontraba Ella?" (169; "In what branches or thicket of the aviary was She?" 155).

If the questions themselves are symptoms of doubt and anxiety, their echoes are even more disturbing. The clearest echoes are with Goytisolo's presentation of the persecution of homosexuals in Castro's Cuba. Occurring early on in the narrative, this relatively self-contained unit recounts the capture, detention, and imprisonment of "gay birds." Such draconian measures, against what the Castro regime considered a singularly unproductive mode of bourgeois decadence, spell the end of sexual "tolerance." In keeping with the elusive, even evasive, character of the narrative, Cuba and Castro are never explicitly identified: perhaps for the very reason that identity and identification themselves are here the central issues. Historically speaking, Castro's concern with sexual propriety spawned some rather devastating policies. Loath to review the validity of masculine signs, and unwilling or unable to free himself from prerevolutionary sexual ideology, Castro essentially reduces homosexuality to a matter of public appearance. The way people walk, talk, gesture, sit, and stand; their hair, clothing, complexion, and makeup; the books they read, the places they frequent, the company they keep: such are the signs of sexuality, itself a sign of cultural worth, moral responsibility, economic productivity, and political *fidelity*. It is in this respect that dissimulation and deceit become the paradoxical signs of "revolutionary" homosexuals for whom the revolution is itself a control of signs, a control by which whatever the state considers "ambiguous" is rigorously reworked. The manly reworking of men is, after all, the stated purpose of the Unidades Militares de Ayuda a la Producción (UMAP). Erected in 1965, these forced labor camps were justified as centers of reeducation and reorientation. Their motto, eerily reminiscent of the Nazi "Work Will Set You Free" emblazoned on the gateway of Auschwitz, was "El trabajo los hará hombres" ("Work Will Make You Men").

Goytisolo's "birds," after being threatened with confinement on bread and water, are likewise reminded of the way to regeneration: "Sólo el trabajo puede regeneraros y devolveros la dignidad, hijas de puta" (30; "Only work can redeem you and restore your dignity you bitches" 29). Grouped in "production units" and constantly subjected to propaganda speeches, these persecuted birds have an unmistakably Cuban air about them. Goytisolo later drives this connection home: "Ese pájaro sutil, incoloro, asexuado, tiene algo que ver con los que el regidor de nuestra muy fiel isla de Cuba hizo prender y enjaular recientemente en La Habana?" (94; "Does this subtle, colorless, asexual bird have anything to do with the ones that the governor of our very faithful island of Cuba recently arrested and put in jail in Havana?" 88). Having identified the principal historical model for Goytisolo's concentration camp in this section (there are also allusions to Pinochet's Chile, the Soviet Gulag, and the doubly significant Vel d'Hiv: the Parisian Vélodrome d'Hiver, which was the site of the 1942 roundup of Jews and which, in a dismal play of chance, now evokes HIV), having identified the model, I return to the question of identification and identity. I will no doubt return to it again, but inasmuch as it turns up repeatedly in the figures of AIDS, homosexuality, and history, I find it difficult to avoid. That the *question* of identity *has* been avoided in most critical readings of the text does not mean that it is not there, but rather that it is there, and not there, for different readers in different ways. In light of the deployment of mystical and postmodern rhetoric in *Las virtudes,* identity and identification are in fact *fundamental* questions. For if identity enables a certain communion and communication, it also enables control, quarantine, and confinement; it founds joy and suffering alike.[14] Identity is, in other words, a risk; but it is not a risk that is easily eliminated. Evasiveness, fragmentation, dissemination, and ambiguity may be important rhetorical strategies against the threat of painful confinement, but they run the risk of washing away difference and of missing the pleasures of a more intimate communication.

Carlos Fuentes's reading of *Las virtudes* is here illustrative. After extolling the text for its displacements, enigmas, and creative freedom, for its "aporte en castellano a la revolución permanente de la narrativa castellana" (28; "contribution in Spanish to the permanent revolution in Spanish narrative"), and for its challenge to mediocrity and the status quo, Fuentes declares that one of its primary purposes is sexual, or, as he puts it, amorous. The difference is telling, because love appears to be, for him, a thing of traditionally transcendent beauty: "Amorosamente realiza [*Las virtudes*] el milagro de negar la discontinuidad de los cuerpos reuniéndolos a través de un texto (un poema, una novela). No es algo nuevo: don Quixote y Dulcinea, Romeo y Julieta, Cathy y Heathcliff sólo trascienden su superación [*sic*, seguramente 'separación'] en el texto literario, vencedor de la muerte, único triunfo posible del erotismo" (28; "It lovingly works a miracle on the discontinuity of bodies by reuniting them through a text [a poem, a novel]. It is nothing new: Don Quijote and Dulcinea, Romeo and Juliet, Cathy and Heathcliff only transcend their separation in the literary text, conqueror of death, the only possible triumph of eroticism"). Nothing new indeed: Fuentes's reading is miraculous for the way it lovingly rewrites the text's homosexual couplings, imagined or remembered, in the terms of heterosexual couples. Even as he advocates a universality whose guiding sign is difference (24), he reads *Las virtudes* as if the reality it represents were no different from the one already so well established, as if the only possible erotic triumph lay between a man and a woman. In spite of, or perhaps because of, his privileged relation to Goytisolo (he is a fellow novelist and friend), Fuentes provides what I will read as a cautionary tale: the revolutionary text, ostensibly exploding the boundaries of identity, may not so much fly into something different as fall into a recollection of the same.

Attending more to the general fury of "revolution" than to the specificity of the fragments, Fuentes at once normalizes and (dis)misses a language that remains, for all its dispersiveness, identifiably gay. The problem with (dis)missing this language is that it effectively ratifies the "death" sentence already pronounced in the text: "Estábamos condenadas a desaparecer como pájaros de una especie extinguida" (30; "We were doomed to disappear like birds of an extinct species" 28). A universal language may be an appealing concept, but only insofar as one does not ask what, or who, must be silenced, translated, or betrayed. At the same time, this appeal is understandable: for even as the text sets up a comforting lure of universality, it describes a decidedly less comfortable lure of, dare I say it, peculiarity:

> Habían recurrido a la captura con señuelo, el chisme astutamente propalado por algún infiltrado y repetido después por pájaros bobos y periquitos, de que iban a regularizar nuestra situación y otorgarnos la salida, el cebo de una nueva escuela de baile para personas de sensibilidad artística... incluso el extravagante rumor de una visita de la gran duquesa Anastasia, apresadas a centenares en el lugar en el que habíamos sido convocadas, felices e ilusionadas con sus viciosas mentiras. (29)

> They resorted to the old trick of the baited trap to catch us, the rumor cleverly started by some infiltrator and then repeated by boobies and little lovebirds, that they were going to regularize our situation and allow us to leave, the lure of a new school of the dance for persons of artistic sensibility... even the incredible story of a visit by the Grand Duchess Anastasia, we were taken prisoner by the hundreds in the place where we had been invited to assemble, happy as larks and completely taken in by their vicious lies. (28)

It seems that the question of capture and "convocation" posed in the final section of the book has a historical antecedent. Against such a memorable backdrop, the prospect of taking the enticing bait of art only to end up caught in the net of political power, cannot be ignored even in a realm of apparent redemption. Rupturing the diaphanous surface of salvation, this question of self-entrapment cannot be easily stilled. Instead, it reverberates throughout the more transcendent passages and suggests a number of unsettling, earthbound answers: the "Asamblea" is the effect of an opiate, a forcibly induced hallucination, an elaborately staged deception; it is the product of a delusion, an escapist fantasy, a fraud; it is an imaginary refuge for a beleaguered ego, a fable to hoodwink death, an artful resolution of real contradictions, a cross-cultural intertextual trick. The text turns on itself, even as it ends, to keep us returning to the ruins with which it begins.

But there are other (re)turns as well: some as prepossessing as revolutionaries and some as ghastly as revenants.[15] Among the many identities that Goytisolo deploys in his depiction of Castro's Cuba is that of the Duquesa Anastasia, or "la marquesa," a burlesque caricature of Castro himself. Already well known among the gay community in Cuba, this caricature became even more established as a result of the film *Improper Conduct* (1984).[16] Besides being a provocative piece of humor, the image of the leader of the Cuban revolution as a rich, noble woman, serves as a sardonic commentary on what many gays saw (and see) as the pompous hypocrisy of Castro. Surveying the camp from his — "her" — coach, the Grande Dame of Macho Marxism is here the object of gay derision: not because Castro is made over into a woman, but because he is at once assimilated into a queer economy and kept commandingly apart. Inverted in the eyes of so-called inverts, Castro becomes what he most represses: he is a She with a *capital* letter, a veritable sight to see. Goytisolo is emphatic on this point, for in a regime where appearance is of the essence (style makes or breaks the man), the appearance of the masters of power is itself a site of ideological contention. Hence the import of Castro's visit to the camp; for his is not simply an arrival, but, in every sense of the word, an appearance: "una aparición, os lo juro, cuya aureola de exotismo nos arrebataba al escenario ideal de los cisnes" (31; "an apparition, I swear to you, whose aura of exoticism tore us away from the ideal setting of the swans" 30). As awesome as such an appearance is, it is also quite awful. In the language of Goytisolo's birds, Castro is not only an exotic marquise, he is also a bearer of suffering and death.

Castro's appearance, or apparition, is itself a stylized return of an earlier one who also targets gays. And, like Castro, this other figure also visits and victimizes in the same measure. From "la cruel visita del pajarraco" (19; "the ugly bird's cruel visit" 20) to the "visita de la duquesa Anastasia" (29; "the visit of the Grand Duchess Anastasia" 28), from one grande dame ("la dama de las dos sílabas" 22; "the Lady with the one-syllable name" 24) to another; and, finally, from the destruction of one supposed gay paradise (the sauna) to another (Cuba), allegory pursues its ruinous course. It is a course in which chronology may be broken, but history, in its breaks and fragments, is preserved.[17] AIDS appears first, in the beginning of the text, shaping everything that comes after (narratively speaking) and before (historically speaking); so that even when chronology is set straight, so to speak, it carries within it the specter of disease: "Eso se llama, digo yo, pasar de guatemala a guatepeor, del dominio de una marquesa propietaria de vidas y haciendas a manos de aquella que no anuncia jamás la visita, el maldito adefesio de las dos sílabas que nos tiene aquí confinadas" (33; "I'd call that jumping from the frying pan into the fire, from the domain of a marquise owning lives and landed property into the hands of someone who never announces her visit, the accursed, grotesque, one-syllable figure who keeps us confined here" 32). Reinaldo Arenas takes a similarly fatal view of history, and ends his posthumously published autobiography, *Antes que anochezca* (*Before Night Falls*), by declaring Castro responsible for Arenas's infection with HIV that drives him to suicide. Although more inclined to disseminate responsibility than to concentrate it in one source, Goytisolo seems to share Arenas's sense of destiny. In line with the notion of a visitation of death, Goytisolo writes of "una llegada prevista en...tratados de astrología secretos sobre las plagas del final del milenio, lectura paciente de signos agoreros del desastre que se cernía y bruscamente cobraba su presa" (12; "an arrival foreseen in...treatises on astrology concerning the plagues at the end of the millennium, a patient reading of divinatory signs of the disaster that cornered and abruptly caught its prey" 14). I will have more to say about the metaphors of fatalism and radical resignation that abound in Goytisolo's text, especially insofar as they are the conditions of possibility for metaphors of redemption and transcendence. But here it is precisely the way in which figures of death persist in the very redemption they enable. Because, while the "pajarraco" visits Castro's world, it also visits *other* worlds toward which the narrator, or text, so ardently aspires.[18] Its presence there is evoked in its very absence, in a question that I have drawn attention to earlier: "En qué ramaje o espesura de la pajarera se encontraba Ella?" (169; "In what branches or thicket of the aviary was She?" 155). And while this question may reveal nothing more than the anxiety, or hope, that She might, or might not, be among the mystical Asamblea, it still reveals a great deal. Ella, She, the Grande Dame, is, of course, a returning figure, the one who first appears at the top of the stairs in the sauna: "Ella, con sus zapatones, capa de vuelo y sombrero negrísimo de anchas alas" (14; "She, with her big shoes, voluminous cape and stark black broad-brimmed" 16): the obscure bird of devastation.[19]

To suggest that the specter of death haunts the instance of redemption is not to suggest that redemption fails. Far from it. Rather, it is to affirm an allegorical movement by which ruin is redeemed only insofar as it is remembered as ruin, only insofar as it remains. "For it is to misunderstand the allegorical entirely," Benjamin writes, "if we make a distinction between the store of images, in which this about-turn into salvation and redemption takes place, and that grim store which signifies death and damnation" (232). By "distinction," Benjamin means both a nondialectical and a Hegelian contradiction, both total separation and holistic resolution. Benjamin's vision of a fragmented interaction is, to my eyes, strikingly akin to Goytisolo's, for whom redemption is far from fissureless. Such interaction accounts, however, not only for a ruinous drag in paradise, but for a redemptive impulse among the ruins. Thus, in the allegory of Castro's Cuba, the prisoners of the UMAP stage a production of *Swan Lake* expressly for the Marquesa. Or more precisely, they transform an exercise in state propaganda, Tchaikovsky's ballet. Like everything in Goytisolo, it is a highly significant choice, in terms of authorship (Tchaikovsky's homosexuality), genre (ballet's sensitivity and delicacy as further homosexual signs), theme (love and death), and reception (as both high art and camp). More significant still is the description of the dance itself, the way it rehearses, in retrospect, the fluttering of the birds at the end: "La agonía del cisne nos *enaltecía* y actuábamos sin coartada, sólo *aspirábamos* a *alcanzar* la *levedad* concisa de su *aleteo,* el equilibrio *etéreo* de las puntillas, esa *inefable* expresión de languidez en el instante cruel de su ocaso, las botas y uniformes se habían transmutado en tutús y gasas de bailarina" (31, emphasis mine; "The death throes of the swan *exalted us* and we acted without ulterior motives, *we aspired* only *to attain* the concise *lightness* of her *fluttering wings,* the *ethereal* equilibrium of steps en pointe, that *ineffable* expression of languor at the cruel instant of her decline, the boots and uniforms had been transmuted into the tutus and gauze skirts of ballerinas" 30). As with the whirling dervishes that Goytisolo celebrates for their attempt to transcend the earthly, the prisoners make something almost religious out of political ritual.[20] But it is the aesthetic, in its sweetest, most flowery sense, that is here preeminent. A gay aesthetic — sublime, light, ethereal, and ascendent — is performed *out* of agony, not only from agony, but beyond it. It is the flight of a moment, rising to a point of ineffable languor only to exhaust itself almost immediately and fall back into the realm of cruel decline. Military boots and uniforms follow quickly, as if to drive home the folly of flight, but are themselves transformed into the vaporous garments of the dancers. Although the dancers themselves are subsequently transformed into gawkish birds, the spectacle of grace inhabits, however fleetingly, the spectacle of suffering.

The gay prisoners' imaginary rendition of *Swan Lake* is, Goytisolo suggests, revolutionary art: art whose signs are reworked and reoriented, not in the service of the state and its macho-militaristic uniformity, but in the service of freedom itself. Once again, Reinaldo Arenas, in *Arturo la estrella más brillante* (1984) (*The Brightest Star*), anticipates Goytisolo by exploring the pleasures and perils of artistic imagination in the UMAP. But whereas Arenas presents freedom as a radically solitary act full of anger and disdain for the guards *and* the other prisoners, Goytisolo depicts freedom as a solitary movement toward reunion, not only with those who suffer but with the agents of suffering (at least in their more abstract or ambivalent manifestations: "the Physician" [149], Ben Sida, perhaps in the end "Ella" herself). Goytisolo's solitary bird is, after all, a creature of *collective* endeavor in more than one respect. As Luce López-Baralt shows, Goytisolo's bird draws from previous formulations found in the Bible and the Koran, as well as in Avicenna, Attar, Suhrawardi, Rumi, and San Juan de la Cruz. And it bears a close correspondence to the Sufi figure of the *Simurg*, the king of birds whose identity is not bereft of plurality: "Si-murg" means "thirty birds." Goytisolo alludes to the Simurg at the very end of his text: "En grupos de treinta, como en el conocido texto persa, nos preveníamos para el arduo e incitante viaje . . . hasta la cima solitaria en donde reina S., el pájaro etéreo, incoloro y extático que alegoriza el alma desasida del mundo" (169; "In groups of thirty, as in the well-known Persian text, we were readying ourselves for the arduous and exciting journey . . .

to the solitary summit where S. reigns, the ethereal, colorless and ecstatic bird that is an allegory for the soul that has forsaken the world" 155). Several things merit attention here: the informative, almost scholarly style of the description; the concept of worldly detachment as central to allegory; and finally the fact that the "end" is still being prepared even as the text itself is ending, in other words, that transcendence is, narratively speaking, never actually realized in the text itself. It is this sense of continuing preparation that reveals the concept of worldly detachment as itself always attached to the world. What it also reveals is that freedom is not an instance of the divine but an insistence of the human: a mode of study and desire.[21]

Part and parcel of this freedom is, as I have said, vulnerability, risk. The risk of essence, some would say, but the risk of identity too. In the age of AIDS, such freedom is particularly heavy with meaning. As both Arenas and Goytisolo indicate, the risky freedom of gay identity entails stereotype and singularity, remembrance and refiguration. Goytisolo goes further, perhaps because less marked by personal experience, and vindicates the signs of gay identity at the level of a community. Prone to utopianism, he is also prone to pessimism; he knows that identity may not only be signed, but also emblazoned, branded, and tattooed on subjugated bodies. He knows that identity may be falsified and feigned, simulated and staged, enforced and assumed: "Nuestra apariencia vistosa es nuestra condena y las autoridades exigen que nos disfracemos de pájaros, capturadas en nuestras madrigueras, en espera de las carretas y jaulas que nos deben transportar al estadio, discutimos, discutimos sin parar de la especie avícola que elegiremos como si se tratara de un baile de carnaval" (158; "Our flashy appearance is our undoing and the authorities are demanding that we disguise ourselves as birds, caught in our hideouts, to await the carts and cages that will transport us to the stadium, we talked, we talked endlessly about what species of bird we are going to choose as though what we are discussing was a costume for a masked ball" 145–46). The suspicion that something is not quite right in paradise carries over, along with the leap, into the scene of redemption. Here too a question of entrapment naggingly persists, but, as before, so does memory. The persistence of memory enables these gay birds, though captured themselves, to attempt to recapture their identity, their sense of community: "Nos manteníamos al acecho de signos reveladores de una existencia pasada y, a través de gorjeos cortos y uniformes ... cantos de líquida cadencia o una mezcla de notas dulces y broncas, nos comprendíamos e identificábamos" (168–69; "We remained on the lookout for telltale signs of a past existence and, through short and uniform warbles ... songs of liquid cadence or a mixture of sweet and rasping notes, we understood and identified each other" 154–55).[22] This mutual understanding and identification, couched in terms of revelation and anamnesis, is collective without demanding conformity: some songs are uniform, short, and staccato, some mellifluous, and others mixtures at once raspy and sweet. Likewise, their bodies, no less than their voices, are bound in difference. Like the mystical languages of the birds, this "gay" language is a "signal favor," a gift of identity and of difference.

"Mysticism is," in the words of Michel de Certeau, "the anti-Babel. It is the search for a common language, after language has been shattered" (88). Goytisolo's search takes place in a shattered language, or better yet, as the shattering of language. As a result, it is a most *uncommon* language, and yet as such it sustains and searches for a common language, different, flamboyant, and queer as it may be. In many regards, this is a classical utopian project, and, like most utopias, its no-place is fantasized and fractured by history. Before de Certeau proceeds to his astonishing analysis of the mystic "I" and the foundational acts of the will, he charts the social and historical terrain of Western mysticism. As with Islamic mysticism, it presents some powerfully suggestive bases for Goytisolo's own endeavor: expressions of sensuality, morose delectation, plans of reform, charges of heresy, fears of orthodox reprisal, censorship, persecution, imprisonment, exile, even death. De Certeau speaks of "social disinheritance," of "groups, haunted by the certainty of extinction, ... [that] vacillated between ecstasy and revolt — *mysticism and dissent*," of the mystics' present as "the restricted scene upon which the drama of their doom was enacted" (85). Goytisolo's own restricted scenes — the sauna, spa, theater, prison, clinic, asylum, library, monastic cell, necropolis, and the text itself — upon which the drama of doom, and of joy, is enacted, are themselves continually shifting. And so they too seem unrestricted, polyvocal, and resolutely *scriptible*. Here again, there is

a tension between closure and openness, identity and nonidentity, a cut and flow of information. In *Las virtudes*, this cut and
flow is itself figured as an open wound, a site and sign of inter-
communication, an emblem by which solitude and suffering have
social significance: "también en soledad de amor herido" (170;
"as well in the solitude of wounded love" 156; from San Juan's
Cántico). Even at its most solitary, the text engages social identities
and historical meanings. De Certeau points out that this communal aspect of mystic discourse is not limited to the divine, as
if the mystics were themselves unhuman. "More generally," he
writes, "their *solidarity* with the collective, historically based suffering—which was demanded by circumstances but also desired
and sought after as a test of truth—indicates the place of mystic
'agony,' a 'wound' inseparable from the social ill" (86). For me,
the social ills that are inseparable from the wounds of Goytisolo's
text include AIDS and homophobia, themselves caught in the risky
problem of identity and identification, of language common and
uncommon.

Goytisolo's text is indeed an alluring web, a "red" (net) as well
as a "redada" (raid or roundup). Cast over an array of metaphors,
it pulls them together and apart, and is itself so pulled. For the
reader, this pull may be at times so furious, at times so soft, that
the resulting confusion makes of this net only a tangle.[23] But this
too, in a text as reticular as this, is one of the risks that is celebrated even as it is "resolved." At one point, the tangled narrative
pauses for self-examination, as it were. It asks, quite rhetorically,
if it is possible to unravel and reweave it, "descifrar las oscuri-
dades del texto, hallar una clave unívoca, desentrañar su sentido
oculto mediante el recurso a la alegoría" (59; "to decipher the
obscurities of the text, find a univocal explanatory key, get to the
bottom of its occult sense through recourse to allegory" 55). It
continues, thread upon thread, to weave a case against weaving,
to signify the impossibility of signification, to argue for the benefits of the end of argument and argumentation: "¿No sería mejor
anegarse de una vez en la infinitud del poema, aceptar la impene-
trabilidad de sus misterios y opacidades, liberar tu propio lenguaje
de grillos racionales?" (59; "Wouldn't it be better to plunge once
and for all into the infinitude of the poem, accept the impenetra-
bility of its mysteries and opacities, free your own language from

the shackles of rationality?" 55). Taking advantage of the reversibility of personal pronouns, the text addresses the readers of *Las virtudes* and the hermeneutic scholars and students of San Juan de la Cruz in one breath, as if they were the same. Entwining mysticism and postmodernism, it challenges us to give ourselves over to it, to drown ourselves in a sort of verbal, verbose infinitude. Playing on our desire for freedom, it asks us to close our eyes (*mystic* and *mystery* come from the Greek *myein*, "to close the eyes")[24] to the stultifying logic of interpretation. To do so, however, is to betray, quite paradoxically, one of the text's articles of faith: for to follow, to the letter, the lead of this passage is to take its language at face value, as meaning just what it says, reasonable, transparent, and literal. It is to be trapped in a reading manual and to read, quite clearly, that nothing can ever be clarified.

Amid this play of figure and letter, a certain improper indirection is directed as the direction most proper. And yet, meaning is not set free by understanding the "pluralidad y simultaneidad de sentidos" (59; "plurality and simultaneity of meaning" 55) as an imperative, a law. Which is perhaps to say that Goytisolo's text is in fact forever before the law, saying certain things even as it says others, saying AIDS even as it says so much else. Of course, one thing is to refer AIDS and its connections — both real and perceived — to homosexuality, and another thing is to refer to it as an inevitable and universal property and condition of homosexuality. As Simon Watney notes, "The older metaphors of sickness and contagion have been all but replaced by a discourse of fatality, with AIDS widely regarded as a syndrome of voluntary, deserved collective self-annihilation — the long awaited and oft prophesied spectacle of the degenerates finally burning themselves out" (21). Others, as if literalizing Gianni Vattimo's concept of weak thought, speak of a revalorization of powerlessness that is not gentle passivity but "a more radical disintegration and humiliation of the self" (Bersani 217). Watney no doubt overestimates the novelty of fatalistic discourse, but he is right to call attention to how the disease is written *back* into history as a necessary outcome of everything from liberalization and promiscuity to a collective death drive.[25] Goytisolo employs similarly fateful tactics, writing of omens and predictions (12), a willful propagation of the disease (117), and a "casi extinto y ya imposible amor?" (159; an "almost extinct and now imposible love?" 147). At the same time, what is perhaps most ethically and politically challenging in *Las virtudes* is the faithful assertion that AIDS is the positive destiny of gay men, a destiny that, far from being resisted, should be embraced as the loving price of (un)earthly union and transcendence. "¡La plaga," Goytisolo writes, "era un don sagrado, el castigo una bendición! quien le infectara en el ameno huerto deseado, el cuello reclinado sobre los dulces brazos del Amado, ¿no estaba presente en él en su misma ausencia?, en su extremado rigor no había una terneza?" (163–64; "The plague was a sacred gift, the punishment a benediction! Was not the one who had infected him in the desired garden of delight, his neck resting in the gentle arms of the Beloved, present in him in his very absence? Was there not a tenderness in his extreme rigor?" 149–50). Leaving aside for the moment the distressingly romanticized suggestion that the virus is the sign of a loving commitment, Goytisolo's ecstatically mortal (in)version reiterates and alters the metaphoricity of mysticism: reiterates it, because the individual subject desires the self-loss that comes of divine union; and alters it, because self-loss is revealed to be already the fearful function of the here and now. It is in the alterity of reiteration, in fact, that Goytisolo's writing can be seen to lose itself *from* mysticism even as it would lose itself in it.[26] What I mean is that *Las virtudes*, much to its credit, maintains a tense dialectic, intrinsic to the history of metaphor, between ruin and redemption, between distance, loss, and mortality on one side, and union, encounter, and eternity on the other.[27]

As Susan Handelman argues, metaphor is itself figured differently from culture to culture. In the Greek (i.e., Platonic) view, metaphor tends to be resisted as an artificial departure from the essential and the proper, as an "aberrant attribution" or "semantic impertinence" (Ricoeur 31). Metaphor is here all show and no substance, a danger to everything true and natural and normal, a danger to life itself. After all, as the bearer of change, metaphor figures a transference from the originary to the contingent; in so doing it spirits the literal body away from itself, projecting it as *nothing but* a letter. In the Christian view, metaphor, while potentially dangerous (as in St. Paul: although even he speaks of "the spiritual body"), is also a sign of eternity (as in St. John).[28] In the word made flesh, the sign incarnate, metaphor heralds the apotheosis of the literal body. It signals, in short, a condensation or union in which distance and division are overcome. The death of the literal is here its transubstantiation, and receives its fullest, most fervent expression in the mystic's "muero porque no muero"; "I die because I do not die".[29] Now, if Goytisolo reiterates this deathly mystical desire in which the word is fused to the flesh as spirit, if he utters the metaphor of timeless condensation, he defers and distances it in what de Man calls the "painful knowledge" of "an authentically temporal destiny" (207, 206). It is, moreover, the painful knowledge of historical time, the persistence of memory, that betrays the blessedness of disease as a function of desire: here the desire to translate disease into ecstasy. Given the fact that Goytisolo's text accepts and extends the popular discursive collapse of homosexual pleasure into disease into death, it accordingly misses not only the move to denaturalize a fatally homophobic teleology but also the attempts, by Patton and others, to refigure AIDS itself as a "chronic, but manageable disorder" (142). And yet, for the very reason that the equation desire = disease = death is so prevalent, it is scarcely surprising that Goytisolo, still desiring to desire, refigures death, the final term in the equation, as something less fearful, less final.

That metaphor is a problem of life and death, both in and out of the literary text, seems unavoidable. Indeed, given the facts and figures of AIDS, the places and displacements of the body, the letter, and the spirit are now more problematic than ever. Such, at least, is the upshot of an impressive array of writing on AIDS by Susan Sontag, Simon Watney, Cindy Patton, Leo Bersani, Linda Singer, and Rosi Braidotti, to name but a few. Though different in their methods and goals, all of these writers seem to agree that the forces of figurality take the body as a privileged site of social inscription, and that, with the advent of AIDS, the inscription of the body has "acquired" an evermore carceral and even apocalyptic aspect. AIDS is figured as a plague, a pollution, a divine retribution, a shattering of subjectivity, and an invasion; it is collapsed into homosexuality, into Africa, into degeneracy and masochism, transgression and rebellion, into pleasure itself: what Paula Treichler, in a metaphorical flourish of her own, calls an "epidemic of signification." Militarized and marshalled, demon-ized and sacralized, medicalized, poetized and politicized, AIDS bears the full force of figurality, becomes itself a figure, figuring in turn not only bodies and beings, but entire systems, secular as well as sacred. It is with this in mind that Sontag, concerned with "the struggle for rhetorical ownership of the illness" (181) and convinced that "metaphors and myths...kill" (102), struggles "against interpretation" and for a deprivation of meaning and a dissolution of metaphor (102). And while considerably less persuaded by the therapeutic possibilities of metaphorical dissolution, it is in fact along surprisingly similar lines that Patton represents the representations of AIDS as "inadequate, even sinister" (2) and that Watney warns against mythifying the disease (131). AIDS, as metaphor, as a factor and function of representation, plays itself painfully off the "bare facts." And yet, as all three writers know, the "bare facts" are themselves always metaphorically conditioned. As Watney observes, "When the very word 'disease' is itself so potent a metaphor, we cannot expect...[AIDS] to be entirely metaphor-free" (11). Metaphor and its power cannot be eliminated, dissolved, or liberated; indeed, says Sontag, at most it can only ever be "exposed, criticized, belabored, used up" (182).

It is amid images of exposure, use, and depletion that I see the tripartite problem of metaphor, mysticism, and AIDS as what makes Las virtudes so compelling. As I have indicated, most commentaries and, in certain respects, Goytisolo's text itself resist any such politically interested assertion as if it were the first terrible stage of a marasmic reading in which the textual body is weakened and pleasure wasted. For where textual value has become excess, exuberance, plurality, and indeterminacy, where readerly pleasure has become multifocality and dispersion, to spot the significance of AIDS, with all of its personal and political baggage, is to reduce and impoverish the text, to do it death. Without discounting the values and pleasures of postmodernism, what I am suggesting is that the affirmation of heterogeneity and indeterminacy per se entails, as a number of feminists have noted, the negation of specificity, accountability, and difference itself. Of course, this latter negation may itself be read as a reduction and impoverishment of the text. Unlike Sontag's exposure and depletion of metaphor, this alternate practice, while putatively celebrating figurative language, keeps AIDS and its metaphors discreetly off stage, ob-scene. The rapturous textuality of a certain postmodern critique—let alone the staid textuality of philological critique—cannot quite seem to confront the problem of metaphor as socially substantive.

Goytisolo's text is rapturously dispersive, true enough, but it is not without a narrative thread. As the narrator says, "Si a primera vista me extravío, mi discurso, con sus sesgos y quebraduras, tiene un hilo conductor" (10–11; "If at first glance I lose my way, my discourse, for all its zigzags and sudden breaks, has a leading thread" 12). Now, while one of the guiding threads is to be found in the works of San Juan de la Cruz, another is found in the discourse of AIDS. The narrator, subsequently shifting between persons and places, makes this guiding declaration on the second page, amid a description of the destruction of a bathhouse and the death of most of those within. Goytisolo's language is profusely metaphorical, as I have said, but even an *initial* reading leaves little doubt as to the nature of this destruction. I have already touched on the significance of the figure of death and the problem of ruin and redemption, but I want to follow the narrative thread even more closely: as if the fragments flowed.[30] As young and old engage in the lustral rites of the body, a gaunt and lanky specter descends the faded glory of an Imperial staircase and, with one horrific sweep of the hand, proceeds to reap his horrific harvest.[31] The passage is devastating, and is replete with references to millenary plagues, the ruin of Pompeii and Herculaneum, the bombing of Hiroshima, and the Holocaust. The tone, accordingly, is somber and fatalistic, with the narrator explicitly referring to "el crudo temor asociado a sus siglas, ese sentimiento de fatalidad que nos abrumaba desde su anunciada visita y conducía a la resignación de bestias camino del matadero" (16; "the crude fear associated with her acronym, that feeling of fatality that overwhelmed us from the moment of her announced visit and led to the resigned attitude of animals on their way to the slaughterhouse" 18). This is, to put it mildly, a disturbing picture of the demise of what Goytisolo presents as gay liberation: what was once the "paraíso llameante y fugaz" of the sauna (10; "flaming and fleeting paradise" 12) has now given way to "el apocalipsis de la cámara oscura" (17; "the apocalypse of the black chamber" or dark room 19). Although Bersani might point out the perilous falsity of the vision "lost bathhouses as laboratories of ethical liberalism" (222), and although Patton and Watney might note the more insidious perils of fatalism, the fact is that many of those who do read and write on the text skirt the issue entirely. Putting "disease" in quotation marks, Ortega effectively figures the figures of AIDS as absence, silence, disappearance, and loss: not the loss that fuels the painful self-knowledge of allegory, but the loss of the problematic substance of metaphor itself.

Metaphor is, as we have seen, ecstatic and deadly, mad and mystical, deceptive and true: the stuff, as Derrida indicates, of ontotheology and metaphysics.[32] While engaging the fields of philosophical knowledge, the metaphors of AIDS engage more necessarily still what philosophy tends to set aside: that is to say, politics, history, economics, medicine, the media, and popular culture. That said, it is at the uncertain juncture of so many shifting metaphorical fields that Goytisolo's text is — and yet of course is not — to be taken. By this I mean that *Las virtudes,* motivating mystical exegesis, literary commentary, and political critique, paradoxically goes against interpretation to the very degree that it generates and disseminates *nothing but interpretation.* Far from heeding the admonitions of Sontag and Watney, Goytisolo's text inflates meaning, explodes metaphor, and mythifies AIDS in a narrative that, as Paul Julian Smith states, "ultimately refuses both focalization and totalization" (52). Without disputing the spirit of such an assessment, it is my contention that the refusal of focus and totality, no less than the resistance to interpretation, is itself symptomatic of a particular form of textuality. If on one hand it is the textuality of pluralist platitudes and indifferent heterogeneity, on the other hand it approximates what Derrida designates as negative a/theology. Between theism and atheism, a/theology is a practice of paradox and desire, an obscure and passionate practice in which the alluring presence of the center — be it of Book, Humanity, or God — is infinitely sought in absence. In fact, in a way that Sontag scarcely envisions, negative a/theology is nothing other than the exposure, criticism, labor, and unending depletion *and* repletion of metaphor. What is more, if a/theology differs in its performance of metaphorical detachment and dissolution, its objective, like Sontag's, like Goytisolo's, like so many writers', is something like liberation and consolation.

Even though a/theology seems more in tune with the repetition of "pure anteriority" and the painful knowledge that the self is sundered from the nonself that Paul de Man (207) associates with allegory, it is precisely its refusal to refuse the image of symbolic union, transcendence, and reconciliation that prevents a/theology from closing down or certifying itself in the death of God.[33] Instead, this openness to the possibility of God, to the absence of God that some ethical thinkers, like Cévinas, post as the very condition of belief, is what is so astonishing about *Las virtudes*. After all, Goytisolo's writing, especially since *Señas de identidad* (*Marks of Identity*), is infamous for its celebration of carnality and denigration of spirituality. Leaving aside charges of blasphemy and sacrilege, which would only enhance the author's reputation as a prosaic *poète maudit*, for Goytisolo to have maintained an absolutely faithful atheism, while drawing so heavily from San Juan and the Sufis, would have here given way to mere satire. And although satire is one of Goytisolo's strengths, it is typically reserved for the self-designated guardians of truth, the established authorities of interpretation. In *Las virtudes*, the guardians of truth are themselves members of a militarized medical force: doctors, policemen, and critics all in one. Cast in the terms of a/theology, these guardians are what might be called theological readers, those readers who, like Menéndez Pelayo and Dámaso Alonso before the work of San Juan, experience an awe so intense that they dare not come near it (López 55). In the present context, the respectful approach of the theological reader may be read as a fear of straying from the straight and narrow, a fear of losing the self in an encounter with something, or someone, different. Against the theological reader's reverent fixation on the canonized image of writing, Goytisolo proposes a provocative encounter with loss and disappearance, a vindication of all that is discounted as odd and insignificant, all that is queer.

It is consequently no accident that the broken characters of *Las virtudes* are engaged in unorthodox and anagogic interpretation nor that a considerable portion of their suffering centers around the forced suppression of their readings. Literary history here plays an important role inasmuch as both San Juan and At-tar were persecuted for their writings. Past suffering, however, is all too easily forgotten; for the truth is that both writers have been co-opted by the very same history that professes to preserve their persecution. In the Spanish tradition, San Juan occupies, as his name makes clear, a sacred space; so sacred that, far from fir-ing the wrath of the guardians of orthodoxy, he is extolled as the purveyor of truth itself. Goytisolo, confusing San Juan with a lit-erary scholar who is also, at least in part, a person with AIDS, re-vives the suffering of the past by repeating, necessarily with a difference, the spirit, if not the letter, of uncanonical writing. In other words, he reads against the orthodox reading of San Juan's writing by situating its ecstatic, agonistic sensuality in the realm of the love that dare not speak its name. San Juan is ever so elu-sively, ever so latently, gay and brilliant and dying.

Goytisolo's painful confusion of the past and the present is a gamble because, as Cindy Patton has remarked, "the love that dare not speak its name is now asked endlessly to repeat its name in public" (55), and to repeat it as invariably fatal. But it is also a gamble, because in bringing the past up to date, in re-presenting it in such mystical ways, the present itself seems to recede, to shimmer away in a timeless, universal void. AIDS, after all, buzzes in a figural relay with everything from the Inquisition to Cher-nobyl to various Latin American dictatorships, and seems perpet-ually on the verge of losing all historical and political specificity whatsoever. For Ortega, indeed, AIDS is already lost, transferred and condensed without a trace into a nuclear accident. In its rad-ical discontinuity and wild indeterminacy, Goytisolo's text risks succumbing to what Smith, through Baudrillard, calls the "ver-tigo of catastrophe" (53); it risks, in other words, washing out suffering and resistance altogether. Risk, of course, is a loaded term, one to which I have had frequent recourse, and brings me back to the problem of metaphor, a problem I have never really left behind. The risk of loss, of death, is one that Goytisolo seems willing to take. It is, moreover, a risk that Leo Bersani, rejecting redemption as a treacherous lure, sets up as "the risk of self-dis-missal, of *losing sight* of the self" (222) and that Attar, some eight centuries earlier, advocated as follows: "Destroy the body and adorn your sight / With kohl of insubstantial, darkest night. /

First lose yourself, then lose this loss and then / Withdraw from all that you have lost again" (205).

It is a heady, seductive risk, this self-loss, but it is, I hasten to add, a risk that those deemed too extraordinary for the "general public" are expected to experience as our ordinary reading, our natural script, our truth. "Yo soy de una gente que cuando aman, mueren" (152; "I come from a people who, when they love, die" 140), the narrator, or the tremulously scripted voice of the narrator, tells us: and in so telling, in referring this "I" to "a people," tells some of us more than others. The loss of all losses, death, according to Baudrillard, is now an aberration, an abnormality. And yet, for the so-called aberrant, abnormal subject, death has become all too normal, has been mystified as all too material. Torn between the mystical and the material, Benjamin pronounced the temporal subject's risk of loss and disappearance thus: "Every image of the past that is not recognized by the present as one of its own concerns threatens to disappear irretrievably" (*Illuminations* 255). But in the metaphorical fury of fragmented bodies, the question thus remains: What image? What recognition? What disappearance? Whose, how, why?

Notes

1. This list of characters occurs on page 50. A Kirghiz (kirghís) is a person of Turkic origin living in the region of the same name (Southeast Central Asian region of the former Soviet Union, bordering on Northwest China). Other notable characters include La Dueña or Doña de la Sauna; the ambivalently patriotic figures don Blas and Doña Urraca; Ben Sida; and the specter of death. A number of these figures are in flux. The Archimandrite is described in terms similar to those used to refer to "una dama angulosa de atuendo elegante y un cigarrillo filipino encendido en el extremo de su larga boquilla de ámbar" 50 ("an angular lady in elegant attire and a lighted Philippine cigarette at the end of her long amber holder" 48). And the narrator, assimilated at one point (124) to a distinguished older gentleman, is also closely identified with San Juan de la Cruz. Ruiz Lagos has done an exceptional job in further "identifying" these figures. Almost all, as he demonstrates, are connected to Goytisolo's personal history.

2. *Sida* is "AIDS" in both Spanish and French. The word *sidatoria* (sidatorium) is a play on the word *sanatoria* but also, of course, on *crematoria*.

3. A sense of entrapment runs throughout the text, but it is interesting to note how often confinement is described as comforting (in the sense that ignorance and estrangement may be comforting). And yet, these characters are confined, not in order to escape infection, but because they are already infected. The

reference to Boccaccio is supplemented by masked references to Edgar Allan Poe's "The Mask of the Red Death." There is, of course, an entire relay among texts of disease: on the one side, texts that highlight communicability such as Daniel Defoe's *Journal of the Plague Year,* Albert Camus's *La peste,* and Thomas Mann's *Death in Venice,* and on the other, texts that highlight confined and isolated, if communal, suffering such as Mann's *Magic Mountain* and Alexander Solzhenitsyn's *Cancer Ward.* A text that enjoys an especially privileged place in *Las virtudes* is Francisco Delicado's *La lozana andaluza* (1528). Delicado's work is referred to in the first section of the book, in a particularly dense page (15) with references to François Villon's "Le Testament," Thomas à Kempis, and the Bible. Among the more notable connections between *La lozana* and *Las virtudes* are the use of dialogue, heteroglossia, the themes of pleasure and sexual adventure, and the idea of divine retribution or moral punishment.

4. "Apparition," though technically correct, does not fully capture Goytisolo's somber pun: "Aparecida" ends with *cida,* the sound, in most of the Hispanic world, of *sida* (AIDS).

5. My wordplay in Spanish is motivated by a highly successful public awareness campaign in the fight against AIDS. The word for AIDS in Spanish, *sida* may also be read as *sí da:* "yes, it gives." This linguistic accident was used in a series of fliers, posters, and televised spots to inform the public about AIDS. Hence, a picture of cartoon characters having sex without a condom was accompanied by the caption "SI DA" (i.e., this gives it), while a picture of the same figures having sex with a condom was accompanied by "NO DA" (i.e., this does not give it).

6. It is in this connection that Benjamin makes one of his most frequently quoted declarations: "Allegories are, in the realm of thoughts, what ruins are in the realm of things" (178).

7. I. A. Richards, cognizant of the metaphoricity of language speaks, metaphorically enough, of a resurrection not only in and through metaphor, but of metaphor: "however stone dead . . . metaphors seem, we can easily wake them up" (101). And later: "This favorite old distinction between dead and living metaphors (itself a twofold metaphor) is, indeed, a device which is very often a hindrance to the play of sagacity and discernment" (102). With respect to *Las virtudes,* the distinction may be no less a hindrance. For the beginning of the text (with all its metaphors of death) is as ecstatic, as "high-flown," as vital, as the end.

8. Within the framework of Goytisolo's œuvre, where spiritual faith is frequently denigrated, this jump assumes nearly Herculean proportions. One could even say that *Las virtudes* in its entirety constitutes a jump from the nomadism of *Juan sin tierra* (1975) or the terrorism of *Paisajes después de la batalla* (1982). This latter text, with its apocalyptically political vision of modern urban reality, may indeed be read, in retrospect, as a curious pre-text to *Las virtudes:* after the battle, in a ruined landscape, a virtuous solitude.

9. Benjamin also speaks of a leap. Referring to "the allegory of resurrection," he describes a process by which allegory rescues subjectivity, limits melancholy, and brings the very *idea* of resurrection out of the exclusive realm of *faith* in the divine (i.e., the nonhistorical): "And this is the essence of melancholic immersion: that its ultimate objects, in which it believes it can most fully secure for itself that which is vile, turn into allegories, and that these allegories fill out and deny the void in which they are represented, just as, ultimately, the intention

does not faithfully rest in the contemplation of bones, but faithlessly leaps forward to the idea of resurrection" (233).

10. Kevin Hart provides a good comparative reading of Kierkegaard and Heidegger within the frame of mysticism (245–52).

11. As Schimmel puts it, "Mystics in every religious tradition have tended to describe the different steps on the way that leads toward God by the image of the Path. The Christian tripartite division of the *via purgativa*, the *via contemplativa*, and the *via illuminativa* is, to some extent, the same as the Islamic definition of *shari'a, tariqa*, and *haqiqa*" (98).

12. Attar sings this loss as so total as to include a loss of faith: "The Self and Faith must both be tossed away; / Blasphemers call such action blasphemy— / Tell them that love exceeds mere piety" (56).

13. The question of experience enjoys special prominence in the discourse of mysticism. It is at the center of Georges Bataille's work, *L'Experience intérieure*, and haunts, in one form or another, virtually all readings of San Juan de la Cruz. The concerns are typically situated around the (in)communicability and (il)legitimacy of mystical experience, itself taken as if it were the ultimate guarantee of the poetic texts. These concerns are not, however, exclusive to critical commentary; they are also, particularly in the work of Santa Teresa, motivated by the mystics themselves.

14. Rife with contradiction, it is little wonder that identification spills into the joy and suffering of dis-identification. Identity, no less than disidentity, constitutes, as I have indicated, a risk, a danger: a danger that Goytisolo inscribes as the presence and absence of joy and suffering, not merely in the realm of historical ruin, but in the realm of mystical redemption as well.

15. Smith rightly points out the significance of such an insistent return: "It is the spectre or phantasm, the repressed term which returns in all its random violence to threaten the subject with death" (39).

16. Ruiz Lagos refers to a letter from Goytisolo in which the author clarifies the significance of the marquesa (227, n. 144).

17. Jameson's reading of Benjamin's distinction between allegory and symbol is here germane: "The symbol is the instantaneous, the lyrical, the single moment in time; and this temporal limitation perhaps expresses the historical impossibility in the modern world for genuine reconciliation to endure in time, for it to be anything more than a lyrical, accidental present. Allegory is, on the contrary, the privileged mode of our own life in time, a clumsy deciphering of meaning from moment to moment, the painful attempt to restore a continuity to heterogeneous, disconnected instants" (*Marxism and Form* 72).

18. This is, to be sure, only one of the ways of mapping this narrative movement: even as it describes returns and remembrances, its direction seems to be toward the future; it thus flirts with a certain teleology, however tortuous and open-ended. Another way to see it, also not without a certain teleological push, is by focusing on a middle term. In this reading, then, a transvestite Castro mediates, in good dialectical fashion, between the tattered specter of the sauna and the ethereal bird of the Asamblea. A third way is to focus on the end and to reconsider what in this way alone is recognized as the past.

19. Given the ambiguity of the passage "Ella" ["She"] may also refer to the soul (i.e., "la amada," and perhaps even, within the transvestite economy of the

text, God. Such a conflation of Death and God need not, of course, be read in Hegelian terms alone (i.e., God, or Spirit, negates the negation that is death, kills it *and* lifts it up, redeems it). It may also be read (Goytisolo *is* skeptical of the divine, remember) as a more somber reminder of the limits of redemption, as a trace of the mortal in the immortal. "Death can become a token of freedom," Marcuse affirms, and then goes on to remind us that, "even the ultimate advent of freedom cannot redeem those who died in pain. It is the remembrance of them, and the accumulated guilt of mankind against its victims, that darken the prospect of a civilization without repression" (237).

20. See Goytisolo's essay, "Los derviches giróvagos," in *Aproximaciones a Gaudí* (27–45). Mawlana, or Rumi, is there the subject of a rather fanciful meditation on dance, death, and transcendence. The dervishes execute a dance that has little in common, spatially speaking, with Western ballet; their dance is, as the name indicates, more of a spin than a leap.

21. "Carried to the extreme," writes Susan Handelman, "or under pressure of historical or personal catastrophe, and the need to find meanings within Scripture to accord with contradictory contemporary experience, commentary and interpretation can edge over into heresy—under the guise of the extension of the canonical, or even as open rebellion" (101). Although Handelman is here referring to a Talmudic tradition, her general argument holds, I believe, for Goytisolo's own "heretical" and "rebellious" interpretations of cultural history.

22. By recapturing identity I do not mean repossessing a once full property, an absolute core of meaning. As Goytisolo indicates, gay identity is in many respects the *assumption* of identity, the play across the lines of what passes for law and nature (a division of the sexes, of the surface or appearance from the depth of substance: hence the importance of makeup and masquerade, transvestism and parody). It is not, therefore, *opposed* to simulation any more than it is *resolved* as simulation. Instead, it understands identity as at once a remembrance and a performance as cumulative and individuated.

23. The connections between gnosis and bewilderment come from Maulana Abdurrahman Jami, a Sufi mystic who wrote in the fifteenth century. "To ponder about the Essence of God is ignorance, and to point to Him is associationism [*shirk*], and real gnosis is bewilderment" (quoted in Schimmel 6).

24. Schimmel gives this etymology on the first page of her study. It is also interesting to note that Ricoeur finds a visuality of a different sort associated with metaphor. According to him, Aristotle describes metaphors as placing something (an image) before or under our eyes. This distinction is intriguing because it bears out a common assumption regarding mystical and metaphysical knowledge: where one privileges darkness and interiority, the other privileges light and exteriority.

25. Both Mark Taylor and Bersani follow, via Georges Bataille, this Freudian path. My concern here, I might add, is not so much with the rhetorical persuasiveness of their arguments as with the ethico-political advisability of actually taking them seriously.

26. Derrida, in *Limited Inc.*, traces the etymology of reiteration and iterability (iter) to the Sanskrit, and suggests a lost originary link between repetition and alterity (7), arguing that "all writing must . . . be capable of functioning in the radical absence of every empirically determined receiver" and sender, and that "this absence . . . is a rupture in presence, the 'death' or the possibility of the 'death' "

of all concerned (8). He also speaks, in terms highly resonant for my reading of Goytisolo, of a risk of and exposure to unfelicity in all linguistic acts (15).

27. Paul de Man characterizes the former as allegory and the latter as symbolism. He follows Benjamin part of the way in this distinction, but only part. De Man is not interested, that is, in the ways these divisions turn in on themselves and turn out to include history. As Doris Sommer points out, his is indeed "a *rhetoric* of temporality."

28. Handelman, in a provocative reading of Derrida, associates metaphor with Christianity and metonymy with Judaism. She also discusses absence as the motivating ground of the latter.

29. This line, from San Juan's "Coplas del alma que pena por ver a Dios," has become one of the most recognizable in the mystic tradition.

30. *Las virtudes* makes repeated reference to such AIDS-coded terms as prophylaxis, blood tests, and fluids, both bodily (blood, semen, saliva), and textual (communication as contagion, language as a virus, reading and writing as the incorporation of foreign material, and the consumption of the book—as legend has it with respect to San Juan de la Cruz himself).

31. The opening of the text is revealing: "Había aparecido, se nos había aparecido, en lo alto de la escalera un día como los demás, ni más ni menos que los demás" (9; "The apparition had materialized, had appeared to us, at the top of the staircase on a day like the others, no different from the others" 11). The quotidian aspect of the scene is repeated and a certain casual monotony thereby underscored, for good reason: it is in and against the sense of ordinary, common, *normal* activity that the appearance appears so catastrophic. Repetition also works to bring home the *personal* significance of the catastrophe: "había aparecido, se *nos* había aparecido." I will insist on this point, because I have a sense myself that it does not appear so ordinary to everyone. After all, the setting of this deadly appearance is a sauna (or bathhouse), where the decor *appears* to be as wildly eclectic as the sex: perhaps even more for those who have never been there than for those who have. It is just this appearance of the wild and the normal, the extraordinary and the ordinary, that I find significant.

32. Ricoeur gives a persuasive reading of Derrida and Heidegger's somewhat different view of the ties between metaphor and metaphysics and resists the understanding of metaphor as a bearing beyond of the sensible to the intelligible. Ricoeur's own reading is, for me, a bit too vitalistic, but it does allow for the possibility of "rematerializing" metaphor, of moving not only from the sensible, concrete, and mediated to the intelligible, abstract, and immediate, but back and across.

33. Caputo maintains that a/theology "stays on the slash,... writes in between theism and a-theism" (28). Hence, to argue that God is indeed, and certifiably, dead is "to make a reductionist decision against God, to reduce the ambiguity of a genuine a/theology and to turn *différance* against God" (28).

Works Cited

Arenas, Reinaldo. *Antes que anochezca (Autobiografía)*. Barcelona: Tusquets Editores, 1992.

———. *Arturo, la estrella más brillante*. Barcelona: Montesinos Editor, 1984.

Attar, Farid Ud-Din. *The Conference of the Birds.* Trans. and Intro. Afkham Darbandi and Dick Davis. London: Penguin, 1984.

Bataille, Georges. *L'Erotisme.* Paris: Editions de Minuit, 1957.

Benjamin, Walter. *Illuminations.* Trans. Harry Zohn. New York: Schocken Books, 1968.

———. *The Origin of German Tragic Drama.* Trans. John Osborne. London: Verso, 1977.

Bersani, Leo. "Is the Rectum a Grave?" *October* 43 (1987): 197–222.

Braidotti, Rosi. "Organs without Bodies." *Differences: A Journal of Feminist Cultural Studies* 1 (1989): 147–61.

Caputo, John D. "Mysticism and Transgression: Derrida and Meister Eckhart." In *Derrida and Deconstruction.* Ed. Hugh J. Silverman. New York: Routledge, 1989, 24–39.

de Certeau, Michel. "Mystic Speech." In *Heterologies: Discourse on the Other.* Trans. Brian Massumi. Minneapolis: University of Minnesota Press, 1986, 80–100.

Crisógono de Jesús. *The Life of St. John of the Cross.* Trans. Kathleen Pond. London: Longmans, Green and Co., 1958.

de Man, Paul. *Blindness and Insight: Essays in the Rhetoric of Contemporary Criticism.* Minneapolis: University of Minnesota Press, 1983.

Derrida, Jacques. *L'écriture et la différence.* Paris: Éditions du Seuil, 1967.

———. *Limited Inc.* Evanston, Illinois: Northwestern University Press, 1988.

———. "La Mythologie blanche." In *Marges de la philosophie.* Paris: Éditions de Minuit, 1972: 247–324.

Foucault, Michel. *La volonté de savoir: Histoire de la sexualité.* Vol. 1. Paris: Editions Gallimard, 1976.

Fuentes, Carlos. "El honor de la novela: A propósito de Juan Goytisolo." *La Nación* (Buenos Aires) August 6, 1989, Section 4a, 3.

———. "Juan Goytisolo y el honor de la novela." *Antípodas* 3 (1991): 23–28.

Gilman, Sander L. *Disease and Representation: Images of Illness from Madness to AIDS.* Ithaca: Cornell University Press, 1988.

Goytisolo, Juan. *Aproximaciones a Gaudí en Capadocia.* Madrid: Narrativa Mondadori, 1990.

———. *Las virtudes del pájaro solitario.* Barcelona: Seix Barral, 1988.

———. *The Virtues of the Solitary Bird.* Trans. Helen Lane. London: Serpent's Tail, 1991.

Handelman, Susan A. "Jacques Derrida and the Heretic Hermeneutic." In *Displacement: Derrida and After.* Ed. Mark Krupnick. Bloomington: Indiana University Press, 1987, 98–129.

———. *The Slayers of Moses: The Emergence of Rabbinic Interpretation in Modern Literary Theory.* Albany: State University of New York Press, 1982.

Hart, Kevin. *The Trespass of the Sign: Deconstruction, Theology and Philosophy.* Cambridge: Cambridge University Press, 1989.

Heidegger, Martin. *The Principle of Reason.* Trans. Reginald Lilly. Bloomington: Indiana University Press, 1991.

Jay, Martin. *Marxism and Totality: The Adventures of a Concept from Lukács to Habermas.* Berkeley: University of California Press, 1984.

López-Baralt, Luce. *Huellas del Islam en la literatura española: De Juan Ruiz a Juan Goytisolo.* Madrid: Ediciones Hiperión, 1985.

————. "Inesperado encuentro." *Quimera* 73 (1988): 55–60.

Marcuse, Herbert. *Eros and Civilization: A Philosophical Inquiry into Freud*. Boston: Beacon Press, 1966.

Márquez Villanueva, Francisco. "Ser y estar en *Las virtudes del pájaro solitario* (La paradoja del arte de Juan Goytisolo)." In *Escritos sobre Juan Goytisolo*. Vol. 2. Almería: Instituto de Estudios Almerienses, 1990, 149–60.

Martín Arancibia, José. "No ha de callar." *Quimera* 73 (1988): 61.

Martín Morán, José Manuel. "Los espejos del pájaro solitario." *Revista de Literatura* 52.104 (1990): 527–35.

Nieto, José C. *San Juan de la Cruz: Poeta del amor profano*. Madrid: Editorial Swan, 1988.

Ortega, Julio. "Cántico de Juan Goytisolo." *La Torre: Revista de la Universidad de Puerto Rico* 4.15 (1990): 361–67.

————. "La huella sufí y el misticismo." *Diario 16* (Madrid) September 30, 1989, v.

Patton, Cindy. *Inventing AIDS*. New York: Routledge, 1990.

Richards, I. A. *The Philosophy of Rhetoric*. Oxford: Oxford University Press, 1936.

Ricoeur, Paul. *La métaphore vive*. Paris: Editions du Seuil, 1975. *The Rule of Metaphor*. Trans. Robert Czerny. Toronto: University of Toronto Press, 1977.

Ruiz Lagos, Manuel. *Sur y modernidad: Estudios literarios sobre Juan Goytisolo: Las virtudes del pájaro solitario*. Sevilla: Editorial Don Quijote, 1992.

San Juan de la Cruz. *Poesía completa y comentarios en prosa*. Ed. Raquel Asún. Barcelona: Planeta, 1989.

Schimmel, Annemarie. *Mystical Dimensions of Islam*. Chapel Hill: University of North Carolina Press, 1975.

Smith, Paul Julian. "Juan Goytisolo and Jean Baudrillard: The Mirror of Production and the Death of Symbolic Exchange." *Revista de estudios hispánicos* 23.2 (1989): 37–61.

Sommer, Doris. *Foundational Fictions: The National Romance of Latin America*. Berkeley: University of California Press, 1991.

Sontag, Susan. *Illness as Metaphor and AIDS and Its Metaphors*. New York: Doubleday, 1990.

Thompson, Colin P. *The Poet and the Mystic: A Study of the Cántico Espiritual of San Juan de la Cruz*. Oxford: Oxford University Press, 1977.

Treichler, Paula A. "AIDS, Homophobia, and Biomedical Discourse: An Epidemic of Signification." In *AIDS: Cultural Analysis Cultural Activism*. Ed. Douglas Crimp. Cambridge: MIT Press, 1988, 31–70.

Watney, Simon. *Policing Desire: Pornography, AIDS and the Media*. Minneapolis: University of Minnesota Press, 1989.

Ynduráin, Francisco. "San Juan de la Cruz, entre alegoría y simbolismo." In *Relección de clásicos*. Madrid: El Soto, Editorial Prensa Española, 1969, 11–21.

Young, Allen. *Los Gays bajo la revolución cubana*. Trans. Máximo Etlis. Madrid: Editorial Playor, 1984.

◆ Afterword

Naomi Lindstrom

Bodies and Biases: Sexualities in Hispanic Cultures and Literatures, the newest volume in the Hispanic Issues series, chooses as its terrain a thematic area that spreads out across literature, culture, society, and experience itself. It is difficult to think of any aspect of human life that is not potentially sexualized and, hence, potentially raw material for the cultural representation of sexualities.

Accordingly, the first problem that *Bodies and Biases* leaves open for each author to resolve is the identification of a text or corpus of texts whose examination will reveal aspects of the culture's expression of sexuality. Of the volumes of Hispanic Issues published as of this writing, *Bodies and Biases* is the single one that allows its authors virtually complete freedom to select their text. Many Hispanic Issues volumes are focused on an era, such as the Counter-Reformation (Volume 7), the Conquest of the New World (Volume 4 and, in great part, Volume 9, which, even in its more modern entries is delimited by the theme of conquered native peoples), the moments when literary production became institutionalized in Spain (Volume 1) and when this process reached a crisis (Volume 3). Volume 2, *Autobiography in Early Modern Spain,* was additionally delimited by genre, and Volumes 5 and 6 by the focus on a particular aspect or subset of one author's oeuvre. Even *The Politics of Editing* (Volume 8), the volume with the strongest thematic focus to date, necessarily limits authors to discussing *texts* in the sense of literary writings of some established importance needing to be organized in book form. But sexualities manifest themselves in every era, in all genres, in the expression of all types of people, and in texts ranging well beyond the written.

With the question of "What text?" or even "What is (i.e., counts as) text?" thrown wide open, the authors have arrived at very unlike answers in the delimitation of and approach to the evidence they study and present. Nonetheless, there are significant areas that are really quite sparsely treated. It is very notable that, although a note of ribaldry echoes from time to time and Robert ter Horst cites some saucy conceits, not one of the contributors is principally concerned with the vast tradition of using double entendres to sexualize discourse that is ostensibly on nonsexual themes. Since linguistic games, ambiguities, hidden meanings, and veiled allusions have often been grist for the literary-critical mill, the phenomenon of half-hidden sexual references would have seemed a natural topic. The converse of this practice is the use of terms of sexual passion to speak allegorically of a different theme, such as the union of the human soul with God or the relations between a people and its divinity. Here again, issues elaborately hidden in language do not seem to attract much attention from the critics in this volume (ter Horst and James Parr being exceptions). Perhaps a coy, sly, or suggestive expression is today associated with prurient snickering, while bluntness seems hygienic to contemporary ears.

On the whole, the contributors exhibit the twentieth-century preference for sexual talk that speaks its own name. In their own discourse, as well as in the texts they study, there is a tendency to name things plainly. Lou Charnon-Deutsch exemplifies this attitude in her approach to the pornographic caricatures in which Gustavo Adolfo Bécquer and his brother Valeriano ridiculed Isabel II of Spain and her circle. This critic proposes that the caricatures, rather than attesting to something else, such as politics or the artists' frame of mind, are actually about their visible subject matter: foolish-looking bodies, especially repulsive women's flesh, grotesquely oversized and contorted sexual organs, and sexual activity that debases the participants.

While a vast amount of humor centers on sexual themes, the critics in this collection venture only limited references to the manifestation of sexuality through joking, and are seldom inclined to engage themselves and their readers in this form of amusement. For example, David William Foster argues that the Brazilian Hilda Hilst offers a "humorous pornographic" in her fiction of the early 1990s, but his essay does not cite examples that might provoke hilarity in readers. The critics generally refrain from venturing sly remarks in their own voices. Their reluctance to seize the occasion for a laugh gives a distinctively abstemious effect. Only ter Horst and Parr, perhaps because they have been socialized into Golden Age–baroque literary conventions that provide serious writers with accepted outlets for levity, seem to feel at ease showing an openly jocose face to their readers while arguing their scholarly cases. One might surmise that, in the current era, literary intellectuals discussing sexuality are inhibited by an anxiety that, if they display wit, they will appear not to be taking their topic seriously.

Several of the essays that touch upon realist writing include references to prostitution or, more generally, the concept of the fallen, sexually degraded woman. Prostitution has long been regarded as a social problem, and the discourse that has grown up around it is one of social control and social hygiene, two topics of keen interest to many of the authors here. The relations between sexuality and health also receive some attention, stimulated in part by AIDS and in part by the many new analyses of disease and how illness is spoken of; Susan Sontag's *Illness as Metaphor* and the work of Sander Gilman appear to have set off this line of thought and writing. A special focus of attention is the mass of treatises and reports, from medical school dissertations to proposals for regulatory measures, issued by variously credentialed experts on sexuality, the body, public health measures, and hygiene.

The difficult exercise of thinking about pornography is central to the essays of Charnon-Deutsch, David William Foster, and Silvia Bermúdez. In part, concern with this issue arises from the new availability of pornography in Portuguese and, even more, Spanish; the publishing industry in Spain has been a tireless supplier. The Tusquets publishing concern, which runs an annual contest for new pornographic novels, has turned up fresh material, while many Spanish publishers have brought to light long-suppressed erotica. Apart from the abundance of new or newly published material, critics turn to this subject out of fascination with the issues it presents. The three essays that have *pornography* or *pornographic* in their titles all take into account the issues that certain feminists, most notably Andrea Dworkin and Catharine A. MacKinnon, have raised. The critics in this volume do not join the quest for a definition of pornography, long sought after in legal circles. However, they are extremely concerned with determining whether pornography is inescapably disadvantageous to women and whether it can under any circumstances be considered liberating.

Every one of the contributors is to some degree a social critic, though, as will be noted, some of them have found more suitable vehicles for their social critique than others. Like many social critics, they are harshly negative toward the mass media and condemn the use of sexually charged images and words to shape opinion. Critics from countries where the media are the most powerfully organized manifest alarm over state-owned or state-licensed monopoly television networks such as Globo in Brazil and Mexico's Televisa. Salvador Oropesa goes the furthest in recognizing the influence of these near-monopolies: "My hypothesis . . . is that television has to be considered as the chronotype where the term Mexican is being redefined. And television in Mexico is synonymous with Televisa."

Bodies and Biases brings together both established and newer scholars who, in their careers as investigators, tend to pursue very unlike research questions. The diversity of their choice of texts reflects the literary, cultural, and social issues that attract them as scholars. Many of the critics represented here are acutely aware that literary representations of sexuality are inevitably shaped by the real-world institutions — above all the family — prevailing in a given society. For them, real-world social structures are not only a necessary point of reference, but as much the object of study as the literary works they examine. In some cases (especially the essays of Roberto Reis and Gustavo Geirola), the family as an institution becomes the text these researchers would like to understand. Accordingly, they make an interpretive effort to read the family, with or without the mediation of literary representations. What they are actually reading, when not reading literature, is primary documentation and social studies texts about the family. Dário Borim pieces together a sample of what gets said in Brazilian society about gender deviance. His exemplary text includes early accounts of Brazilian Indians, writing by present-day anthropologists, and what might be classified as stray remarks by diverse observers. At the other extreme are critics, such as Silvia Bermúdez, who scrutinize a literary work and tend to speak of textual issues. Examining a single novel, Bermúdez focuses upon disruptive changes the author has made in the generic conventions of the fairy tale, bildungsroman, and tale of erotic adventure, which may or may not redound in favor of women.

If the texts analyzed in the course of these essays could somehow be assembled into one collection — an impossible task, since many essays examine nonwritten evidence — the resulting volume would be completely unrecognizable as an anthology of erotic writing. In fact, it might be unidentifiable as a thematic collection of any type, so extremely diverse are the options that the critics represented here have taken in choosing the objects of their scrutiny.

The canonicity or extracanonicity of the texts examined and the critics' historical relation to them represent major decisions on the part of the authors of these essays. Some researchers formulate their questions about sexuality using the concepts and terminology of the late twentieth century, but ask them of literary texts composed in an earlier era. They put forward their inquiries in a way considered bold or daring, but pose them about works that command the most mainstream respect, and that often have been read without reference to sexual issues. (As Javier Aparicio Maydeu observes in his study of the Spanish baroque *comedia*, it is an ingrained convention of the subgenre that the signs of sexuality should not overtly call attention to their nature as such, a principle one finds at work in many other works written before the modern vogue for setting forth bald, artless statements on sexual themes.)

The present afterword considers the essays in *Bodies and Biases* in a progression that does not reduplicate the order in which they appear in the volume. It begins with studies of the most securely established canonical texts and proceeds through analyses of increasingly less consecrated literary writings. The last essays considered are those that range furthest beyond the bounds of the literary in the evidence the authors present to support their generalizations. Throughout this retrospective review, a question that receives particular attention is the authors' choice of texts, in either a literal or an extended sense, that can provide clues to a society's concepts of sexuality.

The foremost example of an original, out-on-the-edge critical exploration of consecrated literary standards is the admirably insightful and subtle lead essay, Robert ter Horst's "The Sexual Economy of Miguel de Cervantes." In the course of this knowing and often witty analysis, ter Horst exhibits the accumulated erudition of a longtime Golden Age specialist and indefatigable reader of Cervantes. Yet, he also proves to have an up-to-date vision of hierarchical patterns of domination. Whether subjugation is as blatant as it is in rape and enslavement, or whether it is exercised less crudely, ter Horst sees the phenomenon as thoroughly sexualized and gendered. Those on the losing side of power relations, whether conquered foes, subordinates, women, or men who have become ridiculous by giving their hearts away, are all "feminized and eroticized." The coercion entailed in the governance of society, the seizure and enslavement of foreigners, the relations of inequality between victors and vanquished, the mystic's surrender to God, men's advantage over women in society, and the capture and holding of a lover's heart all involve a common issue: Who is to be master (or occasionally mistress)?

Clearly, ter Horst has been reading and understanding feminism and late-twentieth-century writing about power hierarchies, domination, and subjugation. At the same time, he has been rereading Cervantes, with apposite side glances at Garcilaso and Góngora and their literary lovers turned into galley slaves. While it is to this critic's credit that he keeps current, the article makes a revelation more important to Cervantes studies: Cervantes was a writer who already knew many things that are being said today about power, the social hierarchy, sexual interchange, and gender roles. Ter Horst presents a Cervantes well ahead of his era, and indeed of our own, in his analysis: "One of Cervantes's greatest discoveries as a novelist, perhaps his greatest, is his revelation and exploitation of the sexual marketplace, surely a fundamental factor in all systems of value and exchange, but one so far left unexplored even in this age of economics."

Over the years, it has occurred to many readers that Cervantes was distinctively advanced for his time in his understanding of narratology and concepts of textuality and reading. The legendary Argentine avant-gardist Macedonio Fernández singled out Cervantes as the isolated exception in the world's otherwise uninterrupted history of bad novel writing. Others have wondered aloud whether, possessing such a narratologically sophisticated writer, Hispanists have any real need for Greimas, Genette, Todorov, and so on. In line with the notion of a Cervantes ahead of the literary thought of his day is ter Horst's Cervantes, able to articulate a vision of sexual life as an immense system—a market or economy—of dominators, principally dominant males, ruling over various classes of subjugated others, whether women or men who have somehow missed their chance at mastery and the imposition of their manhood. "Sexual egalitarians are everywhere an alien presence," and what is universally understood, and highly functional in society, is one person unambiguously having the upper hand. Here we have a Cervantes who could carry on an exchange with Foucault, once they had found a mutually intelligible way to discuss their shared concerns. A further level of complexity is added into this analysis through the double perspective ter Horst brings into play. On one hand, it is almost as if he as critic, we as readers, and Cervantes were all contemporaries, our common preoccupations successfully bridging the centuries. On the other hand, ter Horst shows a subtle self-consciousness over the fact that he and his readers really inhabit a time very different from that of Cervantes, and that much of the terminology in which he phrases the shared preoccupations would be utterly incomprehensible to Cervantes.

If ter Horst can be said to draw on the tradition of psychoanalytic thought, it is indisputably the type of analysis that examines an entire society and its arrangements. In contrast, James Parr's "The Body in Context: *Don Quixote* and *Don Juan*" is, on the spectrum, closer to the mode of probing psyches one by one. Parr is painstakingly careful not to make Don Quixote and Don Juan into patients to be diagnosed long-distance; he stresses his awareness that both are artificial constructs. His essay often uses the terms of Freudian thought, but a Freudianism that has been transformed by literary studies. References to Norman O. Brown and Herbert Marcuse (though the latter's social critique is not fully engaged) bring the line of psychoanalytic thought up to the late twentieth century. Parr's joint consideration of the abstemious Quixote and the profligate Don Juan, who nonetheless turn out to exhibit many common traits, is an ingenious way of framing his analysis. He is an able advocate for his case that Cervantes and Tirso de Molina (especially the former) possessed many insights that psychoanalysis would later articulate.

Executed with professional expertise and grounded in thorough knowledge, this essay is like many other literary analyses with a strong Freudian conceptual basis; that is, it will speak most clearly to readers who particularly appreciate Freudian literary analysis. Its references are scrupulously up-to-date; the author has carefully included allusions to the society surrounding his characters; the essay is written directly upon the theme announced in the volume's title. Still, "The Body in Context" does not strike up a dialogue with the other essays in the volume. It stands out and apart as the neo-Freudian piece, quickly identified as such not only by its terminology but also by its characteristic drive to interpret. (Example: "Our mock hero is quick to suppress the *ano* of his last name in favor of a slightly more savory suffix.... This could be construed as an attempt to put anality behind him, so to speak. The *quixote* is the piece of armor that protects the thigh, thus serving to shift the focus from the anal to the genital, since the thigh is more closely associated with the latter area, and it might also be taken to reflect castration anxiety....")

The problem is not with Parr's dexterity, which is unquestionable, in the realization of his study. With ter Horst, he is one of the seasoned, polished scholars whose mastery of the conventions of scholarly writing stands out in a volume that includes many newcomers. Instead, the issue is how Freudian literary criticism fits into the overall critical scene. The difficulty concerns, especially, the Freudian thought that tends to prevail in the United States, with its individualistic and atomistic view of psychoanalysis as rehabilitation for maladjusted persons. The impact of feminism is profound throughout most of the collection, but feminism has made only a relative dent in "The Body in Context" (chiefly manifested in the avoidance of terms and assertions that might be construed as sexist). It is difficult to merge feminism and Freudian thought unless the latter is revised and reworked almost to the point of being reinvented. Though the volume is as dedicated to social and cultural as to literary criticism, a social critique can only be glimpsed, with effort, in Parr's essay. Unless psychoanalytic criticism is transformed into something as far from Freudian orthodoxy as revisionary-Lacanian feminism or what Julia Kristeva means when she employs the word *psychoanalysis*, Freudianism remains an isolated special-interest group or caucus among literary critics. Parr's knowledgeable professionalism throws into relief the fact that the model itself, not this one well-framed and well-argued essay, is what needs to be integrated into the critical enterprise. Critics following this unrevisedly Freudian conceptual path have yet to reach out and establish commonalities with the main current tendencies of critical thought.

Javier Aparicio Maydeu's "The Sinful Scene: Transgression in Seventeenth-Century Spanish Drama (1625–1685)" looks, as well, to a subject matter, baroque theater in this case, that has long been the province of Hispanic scholars. "The Sinful Scene" is like "The Sexual Economy" in that a critic is looking, from a twentieth-century perspective, at the ways in which an earlier era treated sexual manifestations. Yet, ter Horst's essay conveys a sense that Cervantes was, in his view of sexuality in society, our contemporary, concerned with issues that absorb the attention of twentieth-century intellectuals. Aparicio Maydeu's treatment of theater in the baroque age emphasizes the gap between the twentieth century and the world of seventeenth-century theater. This researcher examines what would today be considered cross-dressing on stage. What he analyzes is not dramatic writing but theatrical practices, and his concern is as much with the public reaction to theater practices as with what was actually occurring on stage. His exemplary citations are often from outraged contemporary guardians of virtue. But as his quotations from the era's moralists show, the issues for them were not the ones that would occur to a twentieth-century mind, with gender high on its list of anxieties: gender-bending, role reversal, and blurring of sexual categories. Instead, seventeenth-century critics were concerned with modesty, and above all with keeping women's bodies covered, since actresses in men's clothing afforded spectators a good look at their legs. Aparicio Maydeu historically reconstructs the baroque-era outlook on theater and morality, when a censorious environment drove manifestations of sexuality out of the overt text and displaced them either between the lines or beyond utterances, to the actors' clothing, appearance, and movements.

Though the critical work here is one of historical recreation, much of the interest of the essay is generated by Aparicio Maydeu's undisguisably twentieth-century perspective and his distance from the views he describes. The article conveys a sense that the seventeenth century, with its women encased in complicated, enveloping garments and its (for us) rather literal-minded notions of how to protect public morals, was very other and alien, and an implicit theme seems to be "The past is a foreign country; they do things differently there." While Aparicio Maydeu's documentation of the outlook of the past is scrupulous, his essay is not very consciously articulate about the issues of perspective it raises. Perhaps this critic might have meditated aloud upon the divergency that makes one century's modesty problem another's gender crisis, and that makes this critic's own perspective so extremely unlike that of the seventeenth-century moralists he cites.

"Desire and Decorum in the Twentieth-Century Colombian Novel," by J. Eduardo Jaramillo Zuluaga, takes as its object of study not so much specific novels, with their unique characteristics, as an evolving system of conventions. The subject is the repertory of strategies Colombian authors have utilized to refer to sexuality. Jaramillo Zuluaga's survey really begins in 1867 with *María*, which offers an abundant sampling of stratagems for conveying the intensity of one adolescent's desire for another without having to sacrifice the notion, fundamental to the novel, of an innocent idyll. The most frequent solution is displacement by cutting away from María's body to scenes of nature, and the strategy of averting the reader's gaze becomes well established in Colombian narrative. Jaramillo Zuluaga examines such devices as phrases or words that trail away into ellipsis points, words reduced to a single letter, words given in foreign languages so as not to defile the mother tongue, and numerous varieties of saying without saying. Knowledgeable and thorough, Jaramillo Zuluaga's essay is most distinguished by the idea of exploring "principles of decorum that govern descriptions," an ever mutating logic or grammar of propriety that determines what may and may not be said or published in a given era.

Gustavo Geirola's "Eroticism and Homoeroticism in *Martín Fierro*" offers a new look at a text whose canonical status has always been fraught with contradictions. *Martín Fierro*'s consecration as a respected national classic has often struck observers as bizarre, suggesting that the search for symbols of national unity knows no logic. The first installment of the work has an antisocial theme to it; the hero drops out of society in disgust; the Argentine government and its policies are attacked and denigrated. These features have not prevented the poem from being enshrined as a national classic. Geirola takes as his point of departure a characteristic of the poem, the otherwise alienated Martín Fierro's close attachment to his male sidekick. While this observation may sound a little like Leslie Fiedler's celebrated conjectures about Tom Sawyer and Huckleberry Finn, Geirola goes beyond the identification of a homoerotic bond. He enlarges the text under examination to include not only *Martín Fierro* but the body of writing about the poem as a largely unwitting diagnosis of Argentine society. Geirola's own essay forms part of this tradition, since he sees in the poem the signs of a society that sends the sexes off into different spaces, leaving women too little room to maneuver. "Eroticism and Homoeroticism" is (with Reis's) one of the essays in the collection in which the author, to pursue the analysis fully, has been required to read the social structure of the family as a revelatory, sometimes embarrassing text.

The novel that Herbert J. Brant examines, in a between-the-lines reading, has managed to attract a wide readership and be praised for its ingenuity without ever approaching modern-classic status. Marco Denevi's *Rosaura a las diez* has been singled out among crime novels for the extreme intricacy of its story and narrative construction. As a showpiece of tricky plotting, constantly playing cat and mouse with the reader and relying on characters with falsely constructed identities, *Rosaura* is fair game for Brant's ferreting out of evidence that not only the protagonist but his obsessive rival are operating from within the closet. Brant's "Camilo's

Closet: Sexual Camouflage in Denevi's *Rosaura a las diez*" stands sharply apart from the diagnoses of "repressed homosexuality" on the part of authors of characters that were long a standard fallback of criticism. As his title correctly indicates, his emphasis is not on Camilo but on the closet this miserably unhappy character inhabits, "because the patriarchal, homophobic society in which he lives forces him to submit to a narrowly defined model of human sexual behavior." Consistent with this outlook, Brant focuses the reader's attention on passages in the text that reveal the attitudes of those who surround the protagonist and drive him to construct an elaborate play of forged identities.

Lou Charnon-Deutsch, in "The Pornographic Subject of 'Los Borbones en pelotas,'" treats a text that is over a century old (watercolors that the Bécquer brothers executed circa 1868–69) yet newly displayed to the public (published 1991). Charnon-Deutsch's essay taps into her erudition about the artists, their circle, and contemporary opinion and conventions. Yet, as a specialist, she reaches the same assessment of the watercolors as would a casual observer. In her judgment, they are pornographic satire with Isabel II of Spain as its chief target and her husband, lovers, and hangers-on as secondary figures of ridicule. This approach is in part a retort to Lee Fontanella's commentary on the caricatures. Fontanella is sympathetic to the Bécquers and had accumulated a good deal of information about them, as well as about the objects of their mockery. He uses his specialist's expertise to reconstruct the brothers' psychological motivations and to legitimate the watercolors as something beyond pornography. Charnon-Deutsch has developed scant sympathy for the Bécquers and does not examine their intentions for guidance in assessing their caricatures. She plainly characterizes their work as pornographic and lewd, and identifies their disparaging attitude toward a female ruler. One might add that Fontanella makes a more appreciative audience for the Bécquers's efforts to amuse than does Charnon-Deutsch, who perceives in the images a joyless vision.

Charnon-Deutsch is certainly correct in noting that the caricatures are in the misogynistic tradition of expressing greatest repugnance at distinctively female bodily features. She recognizes that the queen's husband is also humiliated in caricature; he sports a monstrous rack of antlers and subserviently assists at his wife's couplings. Still (perhaps underestimating a little the shame of well-publicized cuckoldry), Charnon-Deutsch argues that the satiric weaponry is turned primarily on a woman. Her analysis supports the idea, coinciding with the lay opinion of many women, that women are the ones most degraded by pornography. She refers to contemporary written remarks by Benito Pérez Galdós to strengthen the case that Isabel was not only faulted for a poor reign but also resented as a woman. Beyond revealing a bias against women, Charnon-Deutsch is concerned with identifying in the caricatures the signs of a pornographic view of sexuality. In this outlook, "copulation is a grotesque, animalistic act" and "the sexual relations between men and women are shown to be exploitative."

This essay makes a methodological point about the uses researchers make of their knowledge of bygone eras. It questions whether exceptional familiarity with a figure from the past allows a researcher to justify actions and expressions that would repel a nonspecialist. For Charnon-Deutsch, an informed understanding of the Bécquers and 1860s Spain does not render their watercolors less pornographic than they would appear to an ordinary viewer in the 1990s.

At a far extreme from the historical studies of ter Horst, James Parr, and Aparicio Maydeu is a determinedly extracanonical, living-in-the-present selection of texts. The three Golden Age specialists work with often slyly cryptic texts and theatrical practices whose conventions work both to cover up sexuality in its most literal and unambiguous manifestations and to reveal it to those who know where to look. More present-minded critics have preferred to examine the impossible-to-miss manifestations of sexuality in the work of current-day authors who are now winning notice for being bold and frank in the treatment of sexual themes. Of these newer writers, many appear in the role of the sexual transgressor, outsider, or misfit, given to confusing usual categories.

If one thinks exclusively of recently written literature, it certainly can seem as if socially anomalous figures are hurtling onto the scene at a great rate, displacing authors, narrators, and characters of blander and more uniform social identity. Yet in a longer historical perspective, we are actually losing some of the categories of marginality that literature could once draw upon to pro-

vide its ambiguous outsiders. The once solidly constructed social category of *bastards* is rapidly losing its firmness. Those formerly identified as such, and more recently characterized as *illegitimate children*, are now the *children of single mothers*, in a common
class with the offspring of widows and divorcees. (It has often
been proposed to close down the category of illegitimacy officially via model birth certificates that do not indicate the mother's
marital status.) The destigmatization of out-of-wedlock birth is
just one example of the way in which, while new variants of social identity are always being constructed, others are being phased
out. The categorization of identity seems to be perennially in trouble, with classifications often having to be abandoned either because they have become too ambiguous and contradictory or else
because they have begun to offend and disadvantage some of
those classified.

The choice of a text by a newly emerged author with the features of a cultural outsider is common to several essays. Ana
García Chichester's "Codifying Homosexuality as Grotesque: The
Writings of Virgilio Piñera" makes a point of the late Cuban playwright's anomalous, marginalized status and the discomfort he
seems to have occasioned critics. Brad Epps's "The Ecstasy of Disease: Mysticism, Metaphor, and AIDS in *Las virtudes del pájaro solitario*" takes as its literary text a work by the Spanish writer Juan
Goytisolo, famed for his fascination with the ignored or rejected
aspects of any culture. Perhaps it is a sign of the times that Epps
introduces *Las virtudes* as a "text," but does not present it by means
of a word designating its literary genre. Beyond its examination
of *Las virtudes*, Epps's essay analyzes the discourses surrounding
illness, especially AIDS, and homosexuality. Epps insists upon the
aspects of Goytisolo's *Las virtudes* that other critics seem most
eager to ignore when they "virtually erase the text's extremely
problematic representation of AIDS in favor of a more discreetly
scholarly reading of the influence and textual play of San Juan de
la Cruz and the Sufis." The writer under study is hardly extracanonical, since he has already begun making his way onto required reading lists and into general anthologies. Yet, the very idea
that Goytisolo is not an excessively disturbing writer has Epps
disturbed. Part of Epps's effort is directed against Goytisolo's too

smooth assimilation into the mainstream, at the cost of leaving features of his texts unexplored.

Silvia Bermúdez, in "Sexing the Bildungsroman: *Las edades de Lulú*, Pornography, and the Pleasure Principle," deals with a new Spanish author, Almudena Grandes, who won attention in 1989 with a pornographic novel. Bermúdez takes up several issues concerning Grandes and her work. She repeatedly characterizes the novel *Las edades de Lulú* (The Ages of Lulu) as a boundary-blurring entity that disrupts categories. In asserting the work's power to break across borderlines, the essay might have taken more fully into account the fragility of the violated lines of demarcation. The classification of literature by genre is perennially in question, and any imaginatively written text reveals deviations from its genre. Other borders, such as those between pornography and erotica and between perversion and healthy pleasure, can never be clearly traced.

Of the various questions the essay treats, one is especially germane to *Bodies and Biases* as a whole. This is the issue of whether women have anything to gain from pursuing as great a variety of sexual experiences as possible. The heroine of *Las edades de Lulú* looks for for the type of sexual liberation widely idealized in the 1960s and early 1970s, when Herbert Marcuse's name and the term *polymorphous perverse* were often spoken. Her quest leads her into some scenarios where she is cast in a passive, submissive, or stereotypically feminine role. Bermúdez ponders the inclusion of these scenes, especially one where the heroine appears in a domestic setting, wearing a baby-doll nightgown, complacently awaiting the return of her roving husband. In contrast to Charnon-Deutsch and Foster, who argue a firm case pro or con, Bermúdez ends her commentary with a guarded assertion that Lulú has achieved some autonomy; she indicates that hard thought is still needed. While this essay touches on some issues with a long history of debate, it refers no further back than Foucault. The resulting essay is not designed to provoke historical reflection, though it is admirably up-to-the-minute, with a number of 1990s citations.

David William Foster's "The Case for Feminine Pornography in Latin America" indicates, from its very title, a defense of certain women authors of pornographic fiction. Hilda Hilst of Brazil receives the most detailed treatment. Of the authors considered, Hilst has most clearly set out to reinvent pornography. Mayra Montero (Cuba) and Diana Raznovich and Alicia Steimberg, both of Argentina, come in for briefer consideration, while other women writers from Mexico and Brazil are named as possible further examples. Foster finds in writing by Hilst, Montero, Raznovich, and Steimberg a feminine pornography. It is feminine not only in authorship, but also in its promotion of concepts, beliefs, and images favorable to women.

Foster is well aware that pornography has long been perceived as demeaning to women, even by those who would not actually ban it, and that this notion now has some research opinion supporting it. He chooses to argue that this is not necessarily the case, and that a woman writing pornography can turn it to women's advantage. He points out that, while intellectual opposition to pornography is currently claiming wide attention, there is also a countertradition of considering all expressions of sexuality potentially liberating. His essay belongs to this second line of thought.

Foster understands Hilst's pornographic writing to be parodic. In his analysis, she creates a "feminine pornographic," altering some time-honored features of pornography to achieve a demystifying effect. Hilst's parody of pornography makes sex appear less significant, deflates masculine pretensions, and burlesques certain varieties of feminism. Her writing tends to "drain the sexual encounter of its dramatic tensions; sex is, after all is said (the text) and done (the act), no big deal." Foster advances these ideas using the standard tools of textual analysis: the rhetorical skill with which he constructs and energetically propounds his argument, and the support of references to two narrative works by Hilst.

The case he makes is ingenious and original, but its validity is difficult to judge. His argument involves the meanings that Hilst's readers assign to her writing. It would be useful to examine other readers' opinions, if indeed any are available, of the relation between Hilst's fiction and standard pornography. The only other assessment that appears in the essay is Hilst's, taken from the back jacket of her 1990 *Contos d'escárnio* (Bawdy Tales). This study, a deftly executed example of literary criticism as persuasive art, is also a reminder of the difficulty of gauging the effects of pornography. Evidence internal to Hilst's writing seems inconclusive. Yet, in all fairness, we do not know what type of evidence could satisfy our curiosity as to how pornography affects the outlook of its readers.

Mary S. Gossy's "Not So Lonely: A Butch-Femme Reading of Cristina Peri-Rossi's *Solitario de amor*" is an intimate, self-conscious critique in which the student of a phenomenon relates her response to it. Gossy details her high advance expectations for the 1988 erotic novel *Solitario de amor* (Solitary of Love) by the Uruguayan Cristina Peri-Rossi, long associated with lesbian subject matter. Her urge to identify with the anticipated lesbian narrative meets with frustration when the narrator-protagonist uses grammatically masculine forms in self-reference and says "I am a man." Through persistent reading, though, she discovers that the narrator describes and names his lover's female organs precisely, but never clearly identifies his own as a penis. Through this and other textual evidence, information about the real-life author, and the force of her "desiring reading," Gossy then understands the narrator to be not male but butch, with not a physiological penis but a symbolic phallus. The novel becomes what she had eagerly wanted it to be, the account of a lesbian sexual liaison, allowing for "the pleasure of a femme reader before Cristina Peri-Rossi's butch text."

This analysis stands out for the frankness with which it takes its own author's responses, urges, and needs as points of reference. Gossy goes on to suggest that her reading, motivated by sexual desire, is more the norm than the exception in literary commentary. For instance, she characterizes "readers who fight over canonical questions of authorship, for the most philological of reasons" by asserting that "the scholarly quibbles of savants over the attribution of texts are not only a way to identify with the (supposed) author, but also to interact passionately—that is, homoerotically, but in a socially approved, scholarly way—with other critics." In such passages, the critical writing seems to be fueled by another deep-seated human drive, the desire to shock.

There is little consensus among the volume's critics over the efficacy of publishing daring texts and making defiantly open statements as a means of changing the attitudes of a society. Marina Pérez de Mendiola in "José Toledo's Diary: A Queer Space in the World of Mexican Letters" presents the Mexican novelist Miguel Barbachano Ponce in the broader context of openly gay cultural life in Mexico. The metaphor in the title gives an accurate clue to the essay's generally sanguine view that a writer with a frankly gay text can overcome resistance (in this case, twenty years of the work's virtual rejection) to open up a new space where otherwise the *modo standard* would predominate and to move closer to a pluralistic culture.

In contrast, "Monobodies, Antibodies, and the Body Politic: Sara Levi Calderón's *Dos mujeres*," by Claudia Schaefer-Rodríguez, turns a doubting eye on the achievement represented by the publication and reading of a novel that seems to disrupt cultural and sexual homogeneity. Schaefer-Rodríguez can easily enough enumerate the features, primarily the protagonists' lesbianism, but also their deviant class and ethnic identity, that could make *Dos mujeres* unsettling to Mexico's self-image as a unitary, relatively uniform community. But she goes on to speculate that the novel is in effect inoculating and immunizing its readers against differences they will need to tolerate if society's cohesion is to be maintained, and that Mexican society can absorb just such a text in a pseudo-pluralistic spirit of "unity in diversity." "In other words," Schaefer-Rodríguez asks, "is *Dos mujeres* proposing a discourse of alterity, or does it just represent a more comfortable integration?"

The divergence of outlooks between Pérez de Mendiola and Schaefer-Rodríguez is at its most striking when they use the same evidence to argue their very unlike points. Pérez de Mendiola cites as an accomplishment Mexico's accommodation of gay cultural activity: "Mexico is also one of the first countries in Latin America to decriminalize homosexuality, and it boasts perhaps the longest history of gay and lesbian activism...." Of Semana Cultural Gay (Gay Culture Week), Pérez de Mendiola says, "Today it provides a space for cultural and artistic expression of Mexican gay and lesbian communities as well as for individuals and organizations.... This event brings together people who are eager to share their views, ideas, and concerns, or simply to cooperate and work with gays and lesbians as full members of society." Contrast this hopeful panorama of a newly accepted diversity with Schaefer-Rodríguez's somber picture: "Social consensus is actually maintained and not ruptured by the process of allowing a small dose—a novel here and there, the Semana Cultural Gay (Gay Culture Week) at the Universidad Nacional Autónoma de México (Autonomous National University of Mexico), roundtables, films, plays, and a certain number of periodicals—into circulation in the body politic to build up a capacity of resistance and to counteract subsequent (pathogenic) attack by collective organisms." Schaefer-Rodríguez also suggests that the highly publicized wave of acceptance of alternate sexualities may be largely an elite phenomenon, and not really that new, as witness the long-standing acceptance of gays and lesbians in high entrepreneurial roles in media and the arts. She quotes Juan Carlos Bautista's dictum "tolerance belongs to those with economic means." Worth stopping to note is the use Schaefer-Rodríguez makes of the ambiguous catchphrase *identity politics*. In the context of her essay, it carries the connotation of a self-absorbed, perhaps even narcissistic, personal struggle that has the unhappy potential to divert attention from a problem much harder to tackle: achieving a society-wide acceptance of sexual diversity.

Schaefer-Rodríguez and Roberto Reis together are the dubious, questioning forces in this volume. Neither one of them is convinced that significant liberalization, let alone a "sexual revolution," has occurred when a society allows certain aspects of sexuality to be more overtly discussed and expressed. They serve as a counterweight to those critics, like Pérez de Mendiola, Salvador Oropesa, David William Foster, and Mary S. Gossy, and to a lesser degree Silvia Bermúdez, who are impressed with the innovative force of the texts they examine. While both Schaefer-Rodríguez and Reis deal with writings and phenomena that many would perceive as groundbreakingly frank and open, these critics remind their readers how difficult it is to alter established beliefs and structures. Schaefer-Rodríguez's analysis of *Dos mujeres* also contains a warning that cultural radicalism is the type of rebellion most vulnerable to absorption and assimilation by the dominant society. Her reading is also, implicitly, a cautionary note to critics too struck with the rule-breaking novelty of the texts they are presenting. She casts into doubt the often-assumed notion that the act of analyzing daring, bold, or offbeat texts will automatically serve to open up or decenter literary studies, and that the resulting analysis will take on a subversive charge.

Oropesa, perhaps the critic who is harshest in his comments on the mass media, is also the one who harbors the greatest hope that literature can help undo the ideological patterning caused by commercial popular culture. The opening paragraphs of his "Popular Culture and Gender/Genre Construction in *Mexican Bolero* by Angeles Mastretta" present a picture of popular culture acritically supporting the Mexican state's efforts to shape the nation's self-perceptions.

Surveying this landscape of collusion and acquiescence, Oropesa identifies an alternate force: "It is in this context where a more truly democratic literature is working, rewriting the texts developed by television, especially pop and camp texts." Mastretta's much-discussed novel *Mexican Bolero* exemplifies, in Oropesa's analysis, a knowing use of melodramatic and best-seller conventions to deflate and discredit the values these commercial popular forms would normally support. For Oropesa, *Mexican Bolero* is in a sense a rewriting of Carlos Fuentes's celebrated novel *The Death of Artemio Cruz*, a reading list standard. But at the same time it is undisguisedly intertwined with much less prestigious types of culture: television serials, melodramatic movies, and sentimental song lyrics. He sees Mastretta's mimicry of these forms as, first of all, a form of outreach: "Mastretta is interested in a far broader audience." But beyond issues of readership, Oropesa perceives Mastretta as skilled in bringing about an awareness of the ideological skew of the popular culture she often imitates or parallels.

As the volume's subtitular reference to *Cultures and Literatures* indicates, *Bodies and Biases* does not give literature pride of place among cultural forms. Many of the authors have pursued the option of bringing other modes of expression into their analyses. The mass media and especially television, singled out for its ability to render a society's crudest notions of gender and sexuality embarrassingly evident, exercise a fascination. So do the words of guidance pronounced by professionally credentialed specialists in the diagnosis of society's ills.

Of the writers whose essays range beyond literature, Roberto Reis in "Representations of Family and Sexuality in Brazilian Cultural Discourse" most clearly exemplifies the effort to read a text composed by a nation's culture. Moving beyond even the least artful forms of mass culture, he pieces together a body of evidence that includes images of beach-going; an episode witnessed in a supermarket; a survey of sexual habits; apartment floor plans; women's, men's, and adolescents' magazines; advertising and political slogans; popular catchphrases; the Globo communications network; and the recommendations of "hygienist" doctors concerning public health and the safekeeping of the family as an institution. The structure of the Brazilian family and, even more than the family, the incessant scholarly and public debates surrounding it, are among Reis's main objects of study. He reviews the inescapable *Casa-Grande e Senzala* by Gilberto Freyre and the lengthy reaction against Freyre, which, in his analysis, has at one time or another rejected everything in Freyre except the key notion of patriarchy. Reis's reading of the texts that comprise *culture* extends to what many would regard more standardly as *social context* or simply *society* itself. He is the first to point out that he has woven considerable portions of the text he analyzes out of what would more usually be considered context, that is, other-than-text. "Through the images of the family and the woman, as well as the configurations of sexuality in literature and mass culture, Brazilian society allows itself to be read," he says, and identifies "the subject of this essay" as "a reading of society." The evidence Reis marshals to support his contentions includes some literary works, particularly those of José de Alencar, who has long interested this critic. He also is drawn to the narrative of the decline of the family structure in the 1935 novel *Totônio Pacheco* by João Alphonsus. One might hope to encounter someday a fuller development of Reis's critical response to this narrative. It is worth pointing out that literary allusions begin to appear relatively late in Reis's essay. The author makes it clear that, in his approach, literary evidence possesses no primacy or privilege over the other types of material analyzed.

The wide *text* Reis casts is directly justifiable, since his prime concern is to raise questions about Brazil itself and its claims to enjoy an exceptional modernity in sexual mores. His essay here continues along the doubting, skeptical line that runs through his 1992 *The Pearl Necklace: Toward an Archaeology of Brazilian Transition Discourse*. Reis still has much to say about what he calls the transition period in Brazilian society, which in *The Pearl Necklace* is defined as approximately 1850–1950. In this new essay, the time frame is expanded and the transformations set off by the abolition of slavery are portrayed as still working themselves out in the present moment. His thesis and conclusions remain the same from the book to the essay. Like Schaefer-Rodríguez, he sees the social system as flexible enough to accommodate and neutralize what would seem to be drastic changes in the expression of sexuality, whether through word, dress, or act, and yet maintain its fundamental structures intact. He perceives the hierarchical, patriarchal, and conservative patterns of Brazilian society as still entrenched, their foundations hardly shifted, much less shaken, by superficially liberalizing trends, no matter how much the latter may have seized the spotlight and filled the public's imagination with images of sparsely clad, undulating, decorum-free Brazilians.

Dário Borim's "Intricacies of Brazilian Gayness: A Cross-Cultural and Cross-Temporal Approach" is a joint consideration of very disparate types of evidence concerning the phenomenon set out in the study's title. Borim looks chiefly at two types of texts that describe a population marked as Other in its ways of defining gender and expressing sexuality. One is accounts written during the colonial period in Brazil, in which Europeans describe the practices of the native populations that they hope to see converted to Christianity and Western ways. Brazilian Indians often disturbed the Europeans' sense of what was properly feminine and masculine, provoking the observers to reveal their beliefs about gender and sexuality. The other is a sample of the discourse of twentieth-century social science, in which the anthropologists Peter Fry and Edward MacRae look at gay men in Brazilian society and the beliefs held about this population. "Intricacies of Brazilian Gayness" includes as well a good deal of anecdotal evidence and cited remarks that reveal less about gays and lesbians in Brazil than about the features irreflexively attributed to them by their gender-obsessed fellow citizens.

Coordinating these unlike bodies of writing are Borim's own observations and speculations. Less orienting are his conclusions, which, perhaps in accord with his fascination with inconsistencies, he seems reluctant to set forth in a programmatic manner. He brings striking parallelisms and continuities to the fore, but is also particularly eager to point out contradictions. Though he seems reluctant to set out one main point or tendency in his essay, he organizes his exposition around certain themes or notions.

Several ideas have caught Borim's attention. He is interested in the concept that talk and writing about homosexuality often have their real focus elsewhere. Observations about gayness may be perceived as a subset of what is said about being male and female in society. Indeed, Borim very accurately and helpfully identifies the focus of his own essay as "the division of people into two mutually exclusive categories, the domains of masculinity and femininity, which I would like to discuss by focusing on homosexuality." Like ter Horst, Borim is drawn to the belief that the central issue in society is who prevails over whom. Borim cites research opinion that suggests that the significant line of demarcation is not between gay and straight people, but between dominant people, with dominant males being the prime case, and those who miss out on being dominant.

A recognizably consistent cluster of attributes that popular thought assigns to lesbians and gay men has also caught Borim's scholarly eye. He points out the tendency, which exhibits some consistency across divergent time periods and geographical areas, to ascribe certain types of exceptionality to individuals who deviate from the norm in their gender and sexual identity. These attributes very often include a special creative intensity and, in the case of gay males, a penchant for mockery and mimicry as sources of humor. From this rather plausible-sounding starting point, the ascribed traits become more exotic. The ever excitable popular imagination endows gays with healing powers and a talent for divination and supernatural feats. At the most extreme, lesbians are conflated with witches, and sodomy becomes a diabolical heresy requiring the scrutiny of the Inquisition. While these associations would seem to be nothing but stereotyping, Borim notes that stereotypes have the potential to turn themselves into social reality. A link between gayness and the supernatural actually is created, at times, by the stigmatization of homosexuality. Borim finds groups that cultivate mystical and magical practices offering satisfactory roles to individuals whose ambiguous sexual identity is making them uncomfortable in the general society. The strongest point of Borim's essay is its ability to bring the reader to see significant common lines of thought running through very disparate types of writing and utterances.

Bodies and Biases claims attention, not just for the statements it contains about the set of topics characterized in the title, but also for the signs it gives of the directions critics pursue in researching these themes. New examinations of often-studied literary works continue to flourish alongside readings of extracanonical texts. Yet, if one were to judge by this volume's contents and contributors, well-established researchers are the most apt to be attracted to well-established texts (with the occasional exception, like the outstanding case of David William Foster), and newly emerging critics tend to turn away from the required-reading list. The ideal of being able to read social institutions as though they were texts is expressed in phrases such as Reis's "Brazilian society allows itself to be read." Still, there must be signs before reading can occur, and in actual practice critics read society, the family, and the construction of sexual and gender categories through the mediation of various types of documents and utterances: imaginative literature, essays, popular-culture forms, ethnographic accounts, treatises, regulatory and public policy statements, social science research, and, finally, anecdotes and overheard remarks. Though texts with a distinctively literary character receive less of a privileged place than they once did, every one of the authors here reads with the easily recognizable type of interpretive tenacity that is the mark of researchers trained as literary critics.

◆ Contributors

Javier Aparicio Maydeu is an associate professor of Spanish literature at the Universitat Pompeu Fabra in Barcelona. He has published on contemporary Spanish fiction and on literature of the Golden Age, with an emphasis on seventeenth-century theater. He is the editor of Calderón de la Barca's *El José de las mujeres,* and he has published in the *Boletín de la Biblioteca Menéndez Pelayo, Criticón, Nueva revista de filología hispánica,* and *Diálogos hispánicos.*

Silvia Bermúdez is assistant professor of Spanish at the University of California, Santa Barbara.

Dário Borim Jr. has contributed to international journals such as *Chasqui, Quadrant,* and *Brasil/Brazil.* He taught language and literature at the University of Minnesota between 1988 and 1994. He is completing his doctoral dissertation on contemporary autobiographies and the conflict of individual versus community. Currently he teaches Luso-Brazilian Studies at the University of California, Los Angeles.

Herbert J. Brant is assistant professor of Spanish at Indiana University/Purdue University at Indianapolis, where he teaches all levels of Spanish language and Latin American literature. He received his A.M. and Ph.D. from the University of Illinois at Urbana-Champaign and wrote his doctoral dissertation on the Argentine author Jorge Luis Borges. His most recent research is on lesbian and gay literature of Latin America.

Lou Charnon-Deutsch is associate professor and chair of Hispanic Languages at State University of New York at Stony Brook. Her publications include *Gender and Representation: Women in Spanish Realistic Fiction* (1990) and *Narratives of Desire: Nineteenth-Century Spanish Fiction by Women* (1994).

Brad Epps holds a Ph.D. in Hispanic Studies from Brown University and is currently assistant professor in Romance Languages at Harvard University. He has published numerous articles and reviews on contemporary Spanish narrative and film. His book *Significant Violence: Oppression and Resistance in the Narrative of Juan Goytisolo* is forthcoming from Oxford University Press. His areas of research include modern Hispanic narrative, film, and art; questions of gender and sexuality; critical theory; and minority politics.

David William Foster is regents' professor of Spanish and Women's Studies at Arizona State University, where he is director of Graduate Studies in Interdisciplinary Humanities. He has published extensively on Hispanic literature, with an emphasis on narrative and theater in Argentina and popular culture in Latin America in general. His research interests also include Jewish culture and queer theory in Latin America. *Gay and Lesbian Themes in Latin American Writing* was published in 1991 by the University of Texas Press.

Ana García Chichester teaches in the department of Modern Foreign Languages at Mary Washington College.

Gustavo Geirola graduated from the University of Buenos Aires in 1977 and held an appointment as a professor at the Universidad de Salta and the Universidad de Tucumán and as a visiting professor at the Catholic University of America. Presently he is completing his dissertation at Arizona State University. He has published in international journals and *La Gaceta* of Tucumán. His book *El tatuaje invisible: Ensayos sobre la escritura del horror en Hispanoamérica* is forthcoming in Buenos Aires.

Mary S. Gossy is assistant professor of Spanish at Rutgers University. Her publications include *The Untold Story: Women and Theory in Golden Age Texts* (1989) and *Freudian Slips: Woman, Writing, the Foreign Tongue* (1995).

J. Eduardo Jaramillo Zuluaga is assistant professor of Spanish at Denison University. His book *Desire and Decorum (Three Points of Heresy in Colombian Novels)* is forthcoming from Tercer Mundo of Bogotá; the article included here serves as the framework for that study. He is currently working on a second book, *One Hundred Years of Reading José Asunción Silva.*

Salvador A. Oropesa (Malaga, Spain) received his Ph.D. from Arizona State University (1990). He teaches Peninsular literature and Latin American culture at Kansas State University. He is the author of a book on the Chilean writer Ariel Dorfman, and has published articles on feminine writers such as Rosa Montero, Laura Esquivel, and Angeles Mastretta.

James A. Parr is professor of Spanish at the University of California, Riverside. He is the author of books and articles on *Don Quixote* and the Spanish *comedia,* and he is editor of the *Bulletin of the Comediantes.* His student edition of Tirso de Molina's *El burlador de Sevilla,* which establishes a definitive text, appeared in 1993 with Medieval and Renaissance Texts and Studies series of SUNY-Binghamton.

Marina Pérez de Mendiola is assistant professor of Latin American literature and culture at the University of Wisconsin, Milwaukee. She is the author of several articles on contemporary Mexican literature and is currently completing a book-length manuscript on the evolution of different discourses around sexuality and sexual identities in contemporary Mexican literature.

Roberto Reis (Rio de Janeiro) was professor of Brazilian Studies at the University of Minnesota until his untimely death in December 1994. He published fiction and literary criticism both in Brazil and abroad. His most recent publications were *Toward Sociocriticism* (1991), of which he was editor, and *The Pearl Necklace* (1992).

Claudia Schaefer-Rodríguez teaches Hispanic literature and culture at the University of Rochester. Her publications include *Textured Lives: Women, Art, and Representation in Modern Mexico* (University of Arizona Press, 1992) and numerous studies on twentieth-century Spain and Latin America. She is currently finishing a book about gay and lesbian writers in contemporary Mexico.

Robert ter Horst holds degrees from Princeton and Johns Hopkins universities and is the author of many articles as well as *Calderón: The Secular Plays* and the forthcoming *Fortunes of the Novel*. He teaches at the University of Rochester.

Index

Compiled by Dário Borim Jr.